D1707009

BLACK and RED

W.E.B. Du Bois and the Afro-American Response to the Cold War, 1944–1963

Gerald Horne

STATE UNIVERSITY OF NEW YORK PRESS

David G. Du Bois granted permission to quote from the W.E.B. Du Bois papers at the University of Massachusetts, Amherst. Permission for use of the illustrations was granted by the University Library, University of Massachusetts, Amherst.

PUBLISHED BY
STATE UNIVERSITY OF NEW YORK PRESS, ALBANY

PRINTED IN THE UNITED STATES OF AMERICA

FOR INFORMATION, ADDRESS STATE UNIVERSITY OF NEW YORK PRESS, STATE UNIVERSITY PLAZA, ALBANY, N.Y., 12246

LIBRARY OF CONGRESS CATALOGING IN PUBLICATION DATA

HORNE, GERALD.
BLACK AND RED.

(SUNY SERIES IN AFRO-AMERICAN SOCIETY)
BIBLIOGRAPHY: p.
INCLUDES INDEX.
1. DU BOIS, W. E. B. (WILLIAM EDWARD BURGHARDT), 1868-1963—VIEWS ON WORLD POLITICS. 2. AFRO-AMERICANS—POLITICS AND GOVERNMENT. 3. WORLD POLITICS—1945- . 4. UNITED STATES—FOREIGN RELATIONS—1945- . 5. AFRO-AMERICANS—BIOGRAPHY.
I. TITLE. II. SERIES.
E185.97.D73H67 1985 303.4'84'0924 85-26127

ISBN 0-88706-087-0
ISBN 0-88706-088-9 (pbk.)

10 9 8 7 6 5 4

To the memory of my mother and my father

Contents

Illustrations

Preface

This work began as a dissertation at Columbia University under the supervision of Professor John Garraty. What motivated me to tackle this question was a dissatisfaction with the extant biographies of Du Bois, particularly their interpretation of his last years. As the text indicates, these works fundamentally ignored this rich period, which I felt indicated a certain ideological bias, among other factors. This question of ideological bias also prompted my interest in studying the Cold War. In the United States today, one has to swear to a veritable anti-communist vow before being allowed to criticize the unconstitutional squelching of civil liberties or favorably assess the role of the left—particularly the Communist Party-USA. To go where others feared to tread was another factor. I was also interested in exploring why Afro-Americans tended to be more progressive, generally, than Euro-Americans. The recent race for the presidency by the Reverend Jesse Jackson, who adopted positions much to the left of the major contenders and tended to receive consistent Black support, reinforced this belief. The prevailing wisdom was that Blacks were so concerned with survival questions and, as a persecuted people, quite wary about being persecuted because of alignment with the left, that they would not dare to buck the extant consensus on the Cold War.

Then there was the related issue of the prominent Blacks, from Lena Horne to Coleman Young, who did not show disdain for the left, which also sparked my interest; I was also not oblivious to the question of prominent whites who showed a similar inclination. As one who was born during a time when Cold War repression was reaching its apex and came to maturity as civil rights and anti-war movements flourished, I have had an intensely personal interest in exploring this subject. And as one who has been a civil rights lawyer and continues to maintain an interest in this presently besieged field, an examination of one who could veritably be denoted as the "Father of Civil Rights" had to stoke enthusiasm.

In pursuing this multi-faceted project, it was inevitable that I would receive the encouragement and assistance of many; to list them all would strain already taxed space limitations. But to ignore some would border on winning the triple crown of academic arrogance—misfeasance, malfeasance, and nonfeasance. Thus, my editors, Robert Smith and John Howard, merit special mention for seeing this study through to completion. Would that their interest in Afro-American Studies be replicated across the nation and globe. Betty Hughley, Helen Toppins, and, particularly, Sybil Wong typed (not word-processed) the many permutations of the work with their only compensation being my heartfelt thanks and enduring friendship. Carlton Brown was helpful in making copies. The Revson Fellowship I received from the Center for Legal Education at City College of New York, headed by the estimable Professor Haywood Burns, was critical in helping to produce this book. The exceedingly able librarians of City College and Sarah Lawrence College also merit my thanks.

There are others who merit even more effusive thanks. My parents, who were of hearty Mississippi peasant stock, and their parents, who were of hearty Mississippi slave stock, are worthy representatives of a community that allowed a worker like myself to grow, flourish, and produce. Though I willingly take responsibility for all errors of fact and interpretation imbedded in this work, any value it holds is not solely attributable to myself.

Introduction

In 1944, when Dr. William Edward Burghardt Du Bois returned to the National Association for the Advancement of Colored People (NAACP) for the second time, it—like the Afro-American community generally—was avowedly anti-colonialist and anti-imperialist.[1] By the time of his ouster in 1948 these trends had been reversed and the Association was well on its way toward anticommunism and an internal witch hunt. There were a number of factors responsible for this new twist, not the least of which was pressure from leading anticommunist circles. Simultaneously, Du Bois' view of socialism and his attraction to the Soviet Union remained positive and compelling; this trend was not alien to the Black community, especially among Black labor leaders and intellectuals. The split between these two powerful, influential entities—the NAACP and one of its chief founders—mirrored a larger fissure in the Afro-American community that was no less significant than the fabled Du Bois-Booker T. Washington controversy.

The Cold War as history has spawned a veritable cottage industry. Though initially pointing the finger of accusation at the Soviet Union as primary cause of this conflict,[2] historians have increasingly critically assessed United States foreign policy.[3] It is evident that the United States' experience in Vietnam and the rising anticolonial tide, generally, cannot be discounted in explaining this historiographical process.[4] The historians have been cognizant of how domestic realities affected United States foreign policy but they have examined, astigmatically and myopically, how Blacks and the civil rights movement influenced United States international posture.[5] Some have recognized how the pressure of millions of Afro-Americans could influence United States policy toward Africa, but this perception has too often been distorted by Cold War visions.[6] This omission is unfortunate since the racist treatment of United States Blacks made it difficult for the United States to win the hearts and minds of people of color in Asia, Africa, and Latin America in the contest with the socialist camp. This has been repeatedly acknowledged by leading business and political officials. In the historic 1948 United States Supreme Court case, of *Shelly* vs. *Kraemer,* the secretary of state's legal advisor, Ernest Gross, in a brief filed on behalf of the plaintiffs, put it bluntly: "the United States has been embarassed in the conduct of foreign relations by acts of discrimination taking place in this country."[7]

Similarly, the phenomenon often subsumed under the rubric "McCarthyism" had a particularly sharp racist edge. Robert Griffith has noted Senator Joseph McCarthy's close ties to the Dixiecrats—especially Senator James Eastland;[8] indeed, the repressors of Blacks and Reds tended to march in lockstep. And of course being a Black Red was the commission of more than a chromatic sin. Donald Crosby sees the motive force behind McCarthyism emerging from elites among Catholics in the South and elsewhere.[9]

This study will show that there was a close identification between the antiBlack and the antiRed—and that Du Bois did not escape their attention. Unfortunately, historians have not plumbed this phenomenon or the leftist tilt of the Black community generally. One recent study has pointed out that Blacks harbored fewer Cold War attitudes than their white counterparts; proportionately fewer Blacks than whites supported the Marshall Plan, Truman Doctrine, aid to Greece and Turkey, and other aspects of the anticommunist upsurge; Blacks were much less concerned about the influence of Communist parties in Western Europe and less antagonistic toward the Soviet Union.[10] A substantial body of Black opinion that cut across class lines felt that less attention should be directed toward fighting so-called communist subversion. Black leftists, like Paul Robeson, Benjamin Davis, and Claudia Jones, absorbed the blows early and heavy; but they continued to influence other Black activists, artists like Sidney Poitier and Harry Belafonte; writers like Lorraine Hansberry, John Oliver Killens, and Alice Childress; labor leaders like Ewart Guinier and Ernest Thompson; politicians like Coleman Young and George Crockett; civil rights leaders like Jack O'Dell and Ella Baker; civil rights lawyers like Earl Dickerson and Louis Redding; and journalists like Louis Burnham and Charlotta Bass. The organizations where Black progressives, that is, those opposed to McCarthyism and its detritus, played significant roles—the Progressive party, Southern Conference Education Fund, Southern Conference for Human Welfare, Council on African Affairs, Committee for the Negro in the Arts, Southern Negro Youth Congress, Civil Rights Congress, National Negro Labor Council, Communist party, U.S.A., and so on—received the most crushing blows. Yet one of the best kept secrets of contemporary Afro-American history is that the Blacks and whites that emerged from these groups—Charles Gomillion, James Dombrowski, Anne and Carl Braden, and others—went on to play critical and pivotal roles in the civil rights movement. Indeed, this continuity between left, Progressive party, and pre-Cold War activists ("premature anti-anticommunists" and whites who were "premature antiracists") and civil rights movement activists has managed to escape the notice of most students.

The confluence of the streams of civil rights and socialism, national liberation and peace, flowed ineluctably into Du Bois. A comprehensive biography of him would include his activities as novelist, poet, playwright, historian, and sociologist; author of over forty volumes and several hundred articles and pamphlets; editor and founder of one of the most effective polemical magazines in the United States; founder and officer of one of the most influential civil rights organizations; and doyen of peace and father of Pan-Africanism. Ranking Du Bois as the twentieth century counterpart of Frederick Douglass is hardly farfetched. His principal biographers tend to agree—up to a point; and that point is the onset of the Cold War. They see a radical and a somewhat inconsistent turn in Du Bois' activities in the post-World War II era that was not compatible with his past behavior. In an unscientific manner, they turn a blind eye toward any possible turn in United States policy from the early "detente" of 1941 to 1945. This facet is not peculiar to Du Bois' biographers but is reflective of a historiographical trend; the blindness that arises in some historians when it comes to looking at the tremendous impact of Cold War repression and maneuvers by economic and political swells can only be compared with a vampire's revulsion at the sight of the cross.[11]

Francis Broderick speaks of how Du Bois "abandoned the struggle for Negro rights to concentrate on world movements for peace and socialism." Elliott Rudwick notes how "only the far left continued to claim this man whom one observer described as a 'Prophet in Limbo' " Their admonitions have inexorably seeped into the body politic's evaluation of Du Bois. Somewhat in this vein is Richard Kluger's recent remark in an otherwise arresting popular study that Du Bois "in his declining years had given up hope that the American capitalist system would ever treat the Black man as other than economic fodder." In any case, the principal biographers of Du Bois shroud more than they reveal about his latter years.[12]

Du Bois, on the other hand, felt that although "my life from youth until after the first world war and depression had some significance," his latter years had "especial meaning for my people and the modern world." Du Bois, the historian, felt compelled to remind the writer Arna Bontemps that "my career did not end with Booker T. Washington . . . I hope you will not either over stress that earlier part of my career and forget that latter part." Borrowing a line from Mark Twain, he drily observed, "there seems to be a considerable number of persons who think that I died when Washington did, which is an exaggeration." Foreshadowing today's senior citizens and their plaint about age discrimination he remarked that "it is an old American custom to write off as a liability, if not total loss, the age of men in public work after they have passed fifty and to regard them as practically dead at seventy."[13]

Those who posit Du Bois' alienation from the mainstream of Black concerns are off base in a number of ways. First of all, the alienation might not have been as pervasive as some commentators imagine. Henry Steele Commager's view in 1948—after the launching of the Cold War—that Du Bois "today perhaps best represents the aspiration of the American Negro" was not without foundation, even after the political climate had chilled. Harold Isaacs, who continues the Broderick-Rudwick trend by averring that Du Bois "had despaired twenty-five years before of winning through to integration in American life," was forced to admit that in the embattled 1960s Du Bois was mentioned by civil rights activists more than any other figure as a major influence on their political thinking and development. John Hope Franklin's statement that Du Bois "will be remembered by all of us who find in his own work a pattern of thinking and an approach to our problems that will move us closer to their solution" is worthy of mention. Dr. Martin Luther King, Jr., was assassinated a few weeks after he had observed, at an affair sponsored by the left-leaning Black journal *Freedomways*, "history cannot ignore W. E. B. Du Bois. . . . We cannot talk of Dr. Du Bois without recognizing that he was a communist in his later years. . . . It is time to cease muting the fact that Dr. Du Bois was a genius that chose to be a communist."[14]

Secondly it can be questioned whether there was any radical, inconsistent turn in Du Bois' political posture during the post-World War II era. Dr. King was sufficiently perspicacious to recognize that Du Bois was "a radical all of his life" not just at the turn of the century; the soon to be martyred leader of the civil rights movement knew that time changes and what "radical" means shifts from era to era; he acknowledged that, like other titans, he sat on the shoulders of those who passed before such as Du Bois. Dr. King knew that what he said in 1966 might have gotten him lynched in 1906. Du Bois' radicalism did not suddenly burst forth like Minerva from the head of Jove after V-J Day in 1945. Du Bois was a socialist, or what he might term a "socialist of the path," all of his adult life. As a student in Berlin in 1893, he came into contact with what was at the time the most advanced socialist movement in the world.[15] Along with other socialists, such as Mary White Ovington, William English Walling, and Charles Edward Russell, he founded the NAACP. Subsequently he joined the Socialist Party but resigned in 1912 after he backed Woodrow Wilson for president on the John Dewey-type "pragmatic" ground that the southern-born governor had a better chance of winning, and then aiding Blacks. Du Bois later bitterly regretted this exercise in political pragmatism.[16] During this period and after, he constantly implored the socialists to address the special problems of the Black community and to jettison their idea that these issues could only be raised and solved in a future socialist Shangri La. Du Bois felt that fighting the noxious effects of racism—the badges of slavery—paved the way for socialism and democracy. He was an early advocate of what has come to be known as "affirmative action."[17]

As any good socialist should, Du Bois denounced what he perceived to be the undemocratic nature of the United States economy—he favored public over private enterprise—and its remnants, a poverty-stricken reserve army of labor with profits going to a few.[18] Perhaps the fact that these socialist views have not been widely accepted in the United States helps to explain why they are rarely noted, for example, in his great conflict with Washington. Whether in scoring United States policy on Haiti, discussing Liberia and rubber, observing Cuban Blacks, or advising the British Labor Party, during his early years and after he sought an economic thread not as a determinist but as an ultimately significant factor.[19]

This issue is reflected in his view of political issues generally. As a nineteen-year-old undergraduate at Fisk, he subtly analyzed the latest Balkan crisis.[20] He saw racism as an economic phenomenon at root; domestically, he viewed its primary importance as a tool to divide Black and white workers and as a means of profit for capitalists who could pay minority labor lower wages, for example, by stigmatizing certain jobs as Negro work. Internationally, he found this domestic pattern replicated in imperialism in Africa and colonialism in general, which he saw as economic problems at heart. As early as 1906, he served as a harbinger of the Non-Aligned Movement, the Group of 77, and the third world when he linked the integral connection between "the color line" and the world system of colonialism.[21] During his initial tenure with the NAACP and afterwards, he insisted that emancipation at home and abroad must be in the first place economic; the right to vote, for example, was seen as a prerequisite to this economic emancipation, more than an end in itself.[22] Though often ignored, Du Bois went to some length to amend his legendary thesis that "the problem of the Twentieth Century is the problem of the color line" to being a problem of "what we call labor," while remaining steadfast in the belief that color was the basis for a special exploitation and a super profit.[23]

While editing the widely circulated *Crisis,* he insisted that overcoming racism was vital to world peace,[24] and he clung fiercely to this notion throughout his life. This position reflected Du Bois' predilection for seeing the interdependence of political issues; a failure to do such means antiracism "does not become a part of the general liberal movement, and this makes it possible for people to be liberal concerning Negros and reactionary on any other advanced projects, and vice versa . . . peace is today and always has been very largely a racial problem, and that, on the other hand, the race problem cannot be satisfactorily settled if this continues to be a war-like world."[25]

Du Bois' views on race, class, colonialism, and imperialism formed an essential component of his views on war and peace. Du

Bois' still influential essay, "The African Roots of War," is indispensable when acknowledging the European jousting over colonies in Africa and the Middle East as a major cause of World War I. Du Bois saw racism and colonialism as a crosscut saw that bled both Black and white; not only because it buckled trade unions and depressed all wage levels but also because disfranchisement inflated the value of votes cast in the South and similarly deflated ballots in the North. He felt that the enormous profits to be gained in the colonized world inevitably induced competition amongst Western nations for their subjugation of these peoples, resulting in war and slaughter of Asians, Africans, North Americans. As for what is known as "inter-imperialist contradictions," Du Bois saw race prejudice directed toward the Japanese as a factor leading to World War II.[26]

Du Bois was not one to cling to a point of view if he felt that changing times had undermined it. He was quite forceful in noting "a social statement must ever be stated in terms of current attitudes . . . I pride myself on ability to learn, on seeing what appears before my eyes."[27] For Du Bois these words were no mere catechism to be recited and forgotten; he altered over time some of the more significant theses he had rendered. His concept of a "Talented Tenth" leading the Black community was altered to the point where it resembled a Leninist vanguard. His major restatement of this notion was made shortly before his ouster from the NAACP, appropriately at a conclave of the Boulé, the group that had come to see itself as the living embodiment of the talented tenth. In a speech in Wilberforce, Ohio, where Du Bois had lived some years earlier, before Sigma Pi Phi Grand Boulé, he reminded his audience that "a man who was broadly educated in 1900 may be widely ignorant in 1948, unless he has made conscious, continuous and determined effort to keep abreast with the development of knowledge and of thought in the last half-century."[28]

Du Bois agonized over this address and wrote several drafts. With self-effacing candor he acknowledged that this idea of a talented tenth had been criticized. "It has been said that I had in mind the building of an aristocracy with neglect of the masses." He vehemently denied this contention though he freely admitted that he may have overestimated the altruism of middle-class Blacks. But Du Bois was one who subscribed to the view that one shouldn't yell at the thermometer if the room changes temperature.[29]

He did not hesitate to refine his position on war and national liberation. "Force is not going to insure progress and no people is going to gain freedom and justice through war. I do not therefore expect, as I intimated in 'Darkwater,' a greater war of races as prelude to Negro freedom." Instead he expected colonialism to "break down of its own weight." Anticipating the resurgent Black nationalism of the 1960s, he added, "in short then, I do not believe that a Pan African movement in Africa based on colored nationalism is going to be the final answer to the present African problems. I do believe, however, that is going to be the beginning and probably will involve a great deal of bloodshed and misery."[30]

The phenomenon of Du Bois constantly reexamining his thought was not peculiar to the Cold War era. He told the prominent Black journalist George Streator, shortly after leaving the NAACP for the first time in 1934, that "I am not at all impressed by charges of changing my mind and methods. I shall always be willing to change my mind under circumstances when I see reason to do so, but I shall always have what seemed to me adequate logic back of my changes, and in this logic there will be nothing selfish or self-seeking." Thus, his oft criticized support of World War I was retracted.[31]

Du Bois constantly shaped and refined his views, as should be evident. On the threshold of the Cold War in 1944 he stepped back and analyzed this tendency in an article written for a collection pieced together by his old colleague Professor Rayford Logan of Howard University (appropriately entitled *What the Negro Wants*). Here Du Bois elucidated the evolution of his thinking as he noted the shifts in his thought in 1911 spurred by the Races Congress in London, in the post-World War II era spurred by the Pan-African Congress, and in 1928 spurred by a visit to the Soviet Union.[32] But the key point is that despite or perhaps because of these refinements, the core of Du Bois' thought, his passion for socialism, peace, and equality, remained immutable throughout.

Though some have seen permutations in Du Bois' stance toward the Soviet Union and Leninist political parties, the fact is that his work and cooperation with both remained rather consistent throughout. From the onset of the Bolshevik Revolution he was an enthusiastic admirer of the first socialist state.[33] Du Bois was not unaware that his praise of the Soviet Union was not universally accepted in the United States. By the same token, he realized that criticism of the Soviet Union was definitely not as widespread in his Black constituency as in other sectors of the country.[34] Though the so-called purge trials of the 1930s caused massive defections from socialism by those in the United States, Du Bois felt that they were justifiable because the United States "has used every modern weapon to crush Russia"; plus he saw this external pressure as inevitably leading to tight internal controls. Beyond this, however, Du Bois was a friend of the Soviet Union because he saw it alone among the big powers as rendering concrete aid, military and otherwise, to the colonized and semicolonized world.[35]

Du Bois was also an ally of Moscow because he felt that most major initiatives on peace and disarmament came from their foreign ministry and that this created favorable conditions for social progress. "The moment that Europe begins to disarm, that moment the development of darker nations begins in earnest. . . . This is the reason that the only nation at the disarmament conference which comes with clean hands and a real desire for peace is Russia."[36] As time passed, Du Bois praised Moscow for what he discerned as its forthright attempts to eradicate poverty, racism, and illiteracy—efforts which he had been making all of his life.[37] Compounding the situation was Du Bois' feeling that the reporting of activities in the Soviet Union by the U.S. press was wildly biased, which he contrasted with what he observed as favorable coverage of Mussolini; this reinforced his belief that most of the anti-Soviet criticisms were grounded in a virulent ideological prejudice.[38]

Du Bois' interest in the Soviet Union was a reflection of his longstanding interest in foreign affairs. Unlike other U.S. publications of that era, a cursory perusal of *Crisis,* while it was under his editorship, reveals a Brobdingnagian interest in events abroad. Articles on the colonized world, Europe, Latin America, Asia, Oceania, and so on, are sprinkled throughout its pages. Thus, it should come as no surprise that a contributing reason for his first departure from the NAACP in 1934, and a principal reason for his sacking in 1948, was the Association's posture on international affairs.[39]

Hence, Du Bois unswervingly backed the war against fascism. This was not unaccompanied by a certain amount of backing and filling. Because of what he saw as British legerdemain during the war to end all wars, England's evolving role as a barrier to Hitler's hegemony was not suffuciently appreciated by the good doctor.[40] Concomitantly, Du Bois' sensitivity to anti-Asian racism tended to blind him to the horrors of Japenese militarism. "I believe in Japan.

It is not that I sympathize with China less but that I hate white Euorpean and American propaganda, theft and insult more. I believe in Asia for the Asiatics and despite the hell of war and fascism of capital, I see in Japan the best agent for this end."[41]

So stood Du Bois in the year that the second great war broke out. Through the fire and destruction of this searing conflict was illuminated the simple fact that the racism that suffused fascism was untenable, in that it chained Black and white. This had a truly revolutionary impact on the world, as a primary foundation for colonialism was shattered. And in the United States, the racist ideology that was displayed most prominently in the South was back on its heels, on the defensive.

Du Bois supported the double-V—victory over fascism abroad and racism at home; and freedom for the colonized world was seen as cracking the spine of racism as a phenomenon.

As a qualitatively new era in the world was dawning, in a vortex of exceedingly complex and shifting events, Du Bois stood—not as a hackneyed caricature of a red, nor as a faultless, idealistic Black, but as a fluid and intelligent militant activist with large hopes of changing the world.[42]

CHAPTER 1

Du Bois Up Close

"The day after I was born, Andrew Johnson was impeached." Shortly before the march on Washington of 1963, W.E.B. Du Bois died. Spanning the centuries, the life of Du Bois runs like a red thread throughout the course of Afro-American history.[1]

But like many well-known figures, the private Du Bois is not as familiar as his public persona. Du Bois' alleged elitism and arrogance have been stressed, as previously noted, by his biographers. It is unavoidably true that, like many other prolific writers who have turned out scores of volumes and toiled tirelessly, he was not prone to suffer errors gladly. He once excoriated his friend Louis Burnham for the alleged mutilation of the reprint of his speech on Vito Marcantonio; it was deemed "an inexcusable breach of courtesy which I shall never forget." The leftist writer Elizabeth Lawson once sharply reminded Du Bois that, "it would be very nice if next time I call you don't hang up on me in the middle of a sentence." His wife and close friends conceded that his "lack of a 'telephone' manner has been a source of distress to his friends; his clipped, New England diction usually gives an impression of frigid inattention which is misleading. Dr. Du Bois rarely called anybody by telephone, preferring to write short letters." Du Bois' hallmark was complexity. Herbert Aptheker and Du Bois' other close friends saw him as more altruistic, retiring, and shy, which was contrary to the popular wisdom (and which may point to the fact that, like other public figures, Du Bois was more open among close friends). Thus, it was not at all shocking that Du Bois would prevail on NAACP board chairman, Dr. Louis Wright, to examine the face paralysis of the elevator operator in the Association building. In discussing Du Bois' conflicts and appeal, his personality is not a material issue, especially when one views his peers. It will be seen that Walter White, Roy Wilkins, and Du Bois' other peers could not be mistaken for graduates of a Dale Carnegie course and correctly this issue has not been part of the discussion of their careers. Moreover, it is crucial to stress that any eruptions in Du Bois' temper involved concern over political issues more so than personal ones.[2]

Though Du Bois' personality may not be a material issue, Du Bois' health most certainly is. When World War II ended, Du Bois was already seventy-seven years old. Without falling victim to the virus of age discrimination, it is possible to surmise that his advancing years may have had an impact on his acuities. And certainly it is not unreasonable to assume that because of his age, others may have viewed him with more veneration. Du Bois, himself, admitted that this may have been a factor in his being invited back to the NAACP. While making the debatable point that "old people are often hard to get on with," he conceded that, "I had been invited back not to work or think but to do nothing and let my name be used by the NAACP. If I had done this, I would have been secure for life."[3]

It should not be forgotten that Du Bois was not just an unusual Black but an unusual senior citizen as well. On the eve of his 1944 return to the NAACP, Dr. Louis Wright pronounced him "in excellent physical condition." Probably the most credible witness on this issue would be Truman K. Gibson, Black president of the Supreme Liberty Life Insurance Company, and a man with a material interest in making accurate health assessments. After Du Bois applied for a life insurance policy, Gibson told him, "with your conservative, well regulated mode of living, you should be here for a good many years to come. I personally know how careful you have been with reference to your health and diet." Because of strict actuarial limitations, however, he refused the policy, but his words still provide the most accurate assessment of Du Bois' health.[4]

It was no accident that Du Bois lived to be ninety-five. He was attentive to his health but was not a passive patient. He lambasted his physicians at the Life Extension Examiners for their alleged penchant for treating illnesses rather than engaging in preventive care and, subsequently, left their care. According to Aptheker, "he ate carefully, slowly and never to excess; he smoked no more than three cigarettes a day; he took care to sleep eight hours. . . . [H]e exercised; he took vacations; and he regularly visited a dentist and physician." This dutiful regimen provided Du Bois with boundless energy as his whirlwind transcontinental speaking tours would attest.[5]

In sum, it can be said that the diminutive Du Bois—5′6½″ and 167 pounds—paid careful attention to his health; swimming was not alien to him. And his herculean traveling and work schedule during this period attests to a special vigor.

It was good that Du Bois' health was not worse, since given his decidedly unhealthy bank balance, his survival otherwise would have been questionable. As the Cold War freeze hardened, lucrative freelance journalism assignments and other sources of income began to dry up. His economic health, like his physical health, had an impact on the pace and direction of his political work.[6]

Because of his legendary status in the Afro-American community and among the left, Du Bois was frequently prevailed on when Cold War victims wished to raise bail money or legal fees by way of a cocktail party or rally; for that matter, those backing unpopular causes in an era of rigidly enforced conformity often found it necessary to knock on Du Bois' door.[7]

Du Bois, far from affluent, often remarked on a trend he saw developing among Blacks to opt for high-paying jobs irrespective of whether they brought satisfaction and were socially useful. His income tax return for 1953 was not atypical of his Cold War years. From lectures, writings, and royalties, he picked up $2,021; the NAACP and Atlanta University each provided him with a $1,200 pension; social security brought him $720. The only dissimilarity that year was the sizeable $7,140 gift he received as a result of the World Peace Council prize. A yearly income of $5,142 is hardly a queen's ransom. In fact, it caused Du Bois some distress—again, especially after his trial—as when he was unable to pay for dental work.[8]

Du Bois married Shirley Graham, the brilliant writer and artist, eight months after his first wife's death at a time when he was subjected to intense pressure as a result of being indicted. Shirley and W.E.B. enjoyed a close and loving relationship and it is easy to surmise that marrying her added years to his life. Du Bois got on well with her family, especially her son David. After their marriage, Du Bois moved from his tiny apartment with a spectacular view at 409 Edgecombe Avenue in Harlem; Shirley had found the apartment for him when he moved to New York in 1944. Eventually they bought a home in Brooklyn Heights at 31 Grace Court from Arthur Miller, the playwright. Here he spent his last years before uprooting himself and departing for Ghana. He appreciated the expanded space and had congenial ties with his neighbors—which was not preordained given Du Bois' political status during the Cold War. The expanded space allowed him to indulge his curious customs of saving the papers, books, pamphlets, and so on that helps to comprise his legacy.[9]

After the Subversive Activities Control Board shut down the Council on African Affairs in 1956, Du Bois moved his office from there (at 23 West 26th Street in Manhattan) to his Brooklyn home. His office was the headquarters from which a number of successful—even historic—campaigns were launched. And without wandering off onto the byways of psychohistory, it is no less true that the contours and contents of an office tell much about the person. Shirley Graham (she continued to use this name frequently after their marriage), a writer of some facility, waxed rhapsodic in portraying it:[10]

> spacious, high ceilinged room . . . rows and rows of books, carefully catalogued . . . dominating the room is the life-size painting of Frederick Douglass . . . other paintings a landscape by Hale Woodruff, Japanese prints, spears from Africa and a brooding Buddha from India.

The "rows and rows" of books Shirley noted, were part of the 2,500 bound volumes that comprised his library, strong on African and race problems and Reconstruction. As he told an inquiring Duke University librarian, his office included about four "four-drawer steel files of papers, including letters from 1880 to 1957."[11]

There was a forest-like accumulation of letters, books, magazines, and so on in Du Bois' office. He understood German and French and read voraciously which helps to explain his astigmatism and corrective spectacles. He particularly studied African problems and subscribed to a mountain of publications from the continent;

his role at the NAACP and at the Council on African Affairs required it but his interest went beyond employment requisites. His journal subscriptions included: *New Times and Ethiopian News, Colonial Review, Newsletter of the League of Coloured People, West Africa, Empire, East Africa, Colonial Parliamentary Bulletin, Ethiopian Observer* (all from England), the literary magazine *Makerere* of the storied Ugandan College, *East Africa and Rhodesia,* the International African Institute's magazine *Africa,* and publications from the Information Bureau of both Liberia and Nigeria. The Afro-American press received his rapt attention, particularly the *Pittsburgh Courier* where his friend P. L. Prattis was editor. He read the Caribbean press and had a subscription to *The Nation, New Republic, Consumer's Union, Los Angeles Tribune,* and *New Statesman.* He regularly read *The New York Times, Daily Worker, Guardian,* Paul Robeson's newspaper *Freedom,* and its descendant, *Freedomways.* He read all these and more, not just to glean facts and information—though clearly this was a priority—but for political reasons. Many of these journals—from *The New York Times* to Barbados' *Beacon* to the *Daily Worker*—Du Bois saw as representative of particular class and economic interests that were important in forging political attitudes. Furthermore, Du Bois recognized that there were few in his Black and left constituencies who would have the time or the inclination to pore through so much material. With his many articles and speaking tours, Du Bois was a veritable town crier in an era when the communications media were becoming more restricted and hostile to currently unpopular notions.[12]

Du Bois' reading of Dylan Thomas and Agatha Christie should not come as a surprise. He himself wrote poems, novels, and plays and was a patron of the arts—in fact a "patron" of the Harlem Opera Society. Shirley Graham also averred that "his favorite recording [was] the Ninth Symphony by Beethoven." He bought Tschaikovsky and Vivaldi records. As his *Souls of Black Folk* evidenced, he appreciated Negro spirituals. Like many others, he thought television a vast wasteland though Shirley Graham attests that he enjoyed "Perry Mason." Du Bois' familiarity with popular culture was not limited to television. Du Bois found time to attend the fifth game of the 1947 World Series between the Brooklyn Dodgers—which just months earlier had become the first professional major league baseball team to employ a Black player—and the New York Yankees; Shirley Graham had arranged the ticket purchase. Du Bois saw films and was filmed, not just on the television shows (not to mention radio programs) on which he was able to appear during the Cold War in New York, Chicago, and elsewhere, but also at Donald Ogden Stewart's home in Los Angeles, by independent Black filmmaker Carleton Moss, and abroad, for example, in Stockholm, Sweden.[13]

It should be apparent that Du Bois was a complex individual who could both appreciate the nuances of dialectical materialism and savor popular culture. Some might not consider it surprising that he was ambivalent on the question of religious belief. At times he expressed a vague belief in God. But when he was asked to join the comedian Jimmy Durante and others in contributing to a book on prayer, he became downright caustic. However, the most articulate, thoughtful exposition of his view of religion was expressed to Mr. and Mrs. Lawrence Hautz, affluent Bahais from Milwaukee who materially assisted Du Bois during his trial.[14]

> I do not believe in the existence and rulership of the one God of the Jews. I do not believe in the miraculous birth and the miracles of the Christ of the Christians; I do not believe in many of the tenets of Mohammedanism and Buddhism; and frankly I do not believe that the Guardian of the Bahai faith has any supernatural knowledge.

Dialectical materialsm, theism or not, Du Bois—along with the president of the United States—may have had the most recognizable U.S. name abroad.[15] He knew the well-known political figures of the post-World War II era—Nkrumah, Sukarno, Ben Bella, Cheddi Jagan, Mao Zedong, Khrushchev, and others. When Nehru sent him a personally inscribed copy of his biography of Gandhi, it was not deemed overly unusual. On the other hand, indicative of how well known Du Bois was is that mail addressed "Dr. Du Bois, New York" would reach his door. Du Bois' charismatic candlepower often had a rock star-like effect on the overwhelmed fans that met him.[16]

The recognized popularity of W.E.B. Du Bois was a cast-down gauntlet to the leaders of the United States; his eminence and presence allowed him entreé into many places and provided a bully pulpit for him from which to proselytize on a mass basis. When similar voices were stilled, gone or underground, Du Bois was more than a symbol, he was a bountiful resource and seat of opposition; if it can be said that certain well-known novelists can constitute a government then Du Bois the novelist, historian, sociologist, and political analyst was an utter Comecon. Nevertheless, it would be unwise to forget that Du Bois' popularity reflected existing trends nationally and internationally in a considerable Black and left constituancy. Those who prefer to see prophets in limbo have managed to miss this crucial point but it was not lost on the leaders of the United States and their intelligence agencies. Even after Du Bois had died, the Air Force Office of Investigation reporting nervously, perhaps illegally, on the founding of the successor to the Young Communist League—the W.E.B. Du Bois Clubs, U.S.A.—fretted about mortality not killing the Du Bois legacy. After stating confidently and erroneously that Du Bois "may have been a concealed member of the Party as early as 1944" (note when his membership was alleged to have begun), the AFOI official went on to add:[17]

> In selecting the name of W.E.B. Du Bois Clubs of America the Party could count on killing more than a few birds with one stone . . . hope to win recognition and support from both domestic and international civil rights proponents, African nationalists and more particularly the Negro youth of the United States.

Throughout that significant turn in United States domestic and international policy known as the Cold War, Du Bois killed "more than a few birds with one stone." The vultures of racism and anticommunism were stoned repeatedly by him to the cheers of millions. Du Bois, the impeccably manicured, dapper dresser who liked vests, high-laced black shoes and corrective Oxfords, the afficionado of opera and television, the man seen by some as heartless and others as shy, was without a doubt an imposing political monument during a time when two critical epochs merged and emerged—the Cold War and the civil rights movement.

CHAPTER 2

A Militant, Anti-Imperialist Afro-American Community

It has been noted that Du Bois as radical cannot be understood or intelligently assessed without examining the Afro-American community in the United States. Though scandalously ignored by a number of historians, the fact is the U.S. Blacks have been among the vanguard of anti-imperialism and militant political activity. Philip S. Foner and George Walker, in their seminal *Proceedings of the Black State Conventions, 1840–1865,* allude to the cheering the revolutions of 1848 in Europe received and the strict solidarity with the age of revolution, generally, during these crucial meetings. A comparison of the situations of Blacks and the Irish was frequently made; parallels were drawn between the freedom of slaves in the Americas (not just those in the United States) and the freedom of serfs in Eastern Europe. Willard Gatewood has shed light on the nascent anti-imperialism in the Black community as the Spanish-American and the Anglo-Boer Wars were launched.[1]

The National Association for the Advancement of Colored People carried on and escalated this trend, and this was attributable in no small part to its co-founder and essential Black operative, Du Bois. In 1910 the association devastatingly condemned the Czar's expulsion of the Jewish people from Kiev. At a two-day conference sponsored by the NAACP in Washington, D.C., in May 1917, the assembled delegates drafted resolutions attributing the cause of

World War I to racism and profit seeking. Spurred by Du Bois, the Association also maintained a constant interest in Africa.[2]

When Du Bois returned to the NAACP in 1944, this anti-imperialistic, militant trend was all abloom in the Afro-American community, goaded by the exigencies of World War II. The "Great Patriotic War," as it has been termed, was a decisive watershed for Blacks. Richard Dalfiume has commented that "the war had stimulated the race consciousness and the desire for change among Negroes. . . . The hyprocrisy and paradox involved in fighting a world war for the four freedoms and against aggression by an enemy preaching a master race ideology, while at the same time upholding racial segregation and white supremacy were too obvious." This theme became a repeated refrain; indicative of its resilience and repetitiveness is that it was reiterated even after the Cold War had set in. Not coincidentally, racist ideology suffered staggering blows that forced a retreat from "Blacks as inferior beings" to "Blacks as subversive beings"; the manifold protests led by Blacks during the 1941 to 1945 period undercut old racist ideology and inspired a newer variety.[3]

Particularly active were Black soldiers like Coleman Young, Percy Sutton, James Jackson, and many others who engaged in a wide range of protest, confrontation, and passive reaction against Jim Crow and antidemocratic practices. The unity needed for war cleared the path for concessions. The NAACP catalyzed and organized these forces; its mass campaign against the segregation of Blacks' blood plasma by the Red Cross was especially effective in winning adherents; its fiery rhetoric inspired a future generation of civil rights leaders.[4]

Walter White, the mulatto insurance industry functionary who led the Association, employed white hot and eloquent language in his forays against imperialism. White's globe-trotting and fact-finding tours on behalf of Black interests were numerous and important. As the war wound down and ended, White continued to carry the torch. His first public statement after returning from a tour of the Far East was that restoration of the colonial system would lead to a third world war. A few weeks before Winston Churchill's Missouri peroration, White warned that Blacks and colored people around the world "are determined once and for all to end white exploitation and imperialism." It was little wonder that British intelligence and British diplomats wrung their hands furiously about White and worried about his effect on the colonies, Afro-Americans, and, ultimately, the conduct of the war.[5]

The British Empire was understandably concerned about White and the NAACP was understandably concerned about British colonialism. The NAACP focused intently on Britain because of their role as primary colonial power and because of the easy availability of their documents in English. This was singularly true of British policies in the colonial jewel, India. There was a clear identification with the harijans, the "children of God," the so-called untouchables; and parallels were drawn between the Afro-Americans and "The 'Negroes' of India." In September 1942 a typically bitter tirade against British policy in India was made. This trend of lambasting the lion continued full blast for a while after the war (though it is noteworthy that the Indian file at the Association dwindled to virtual extinction after 1947).[6]

In 1946 the national office of the NAACP issued a sharp protest against the slaughter of Indonesian and Palestinian youths by British troops to Prime Minister Clement Atlee during the latter's visit to the United States. The following summer, George Padmore, the itinerant Pan-Africanist journalist, took a personal swipe at the "cynicism of the British ruling class" in *Crisis.* Previously, Padmore had excoriated "American Big Business" and the "Anglo American Plan for Control of Colonies." L. D. Reddick, soon to be an advisor to Martin Luther King, Jr., and a long time friend of Du Bois, used *Crisis* to blast the "reactionary views of the British Prime Minister," and wrote "Africa: Test of the Atlantic Charter."[7]

It would be an error to see the NAACP's militance as *sui generis.* The fact is that the Black community was charged with turmoil and political ferment from the beginning of the war to the setting in of the political ice age. Even George Schuyler, the godfather of Black conservatives, was moved to preach, "a planned economy is imperatively needed." This all-sided militance was distilled most clearly with the issuance of the "Declaration by Negro Voters," by Black leaders of national trade unions, sororities and fraternities, professional organizations, the left-led National Negro Congress, and the NAACP; it is worthy of quotation as indicative of the political temperament of Blacks at an historic juncture.[8]

> We are concerned that this war bring to an end imperialism and colonial exploitation. We believe that political and economic democracy must displace the present system of exploi-

tation in Africa, the West Indies, India and other colonial areas.

This political ferment is mirrored in the Afro-American press during the war. Their pages are littered with the political activity—strikes, boycotts, picketing, letter writing, etc.—that coursed from shore to shore.[9]

Black Communists played a role in this upsurge, just as they had been active during the Scottsboro trial, the invasion of Ethiopia, "don't buy where you can't work campaigns," and the like. The discrediting of anti-Sovietism during the war created favorable conditions for alliances between the NAACP and Black Reds. *Crisis* informed its audience about "Benjamin Davis, Jr., [who] has the distinction of being the first Negro Communist elected to the New York City Council," and accompanied the article with an attractive photo, titles, schools (Amherst and Harvard Law School), and so on. When Davis filed a bill to establish a committee on interracial and group unity in the mayor's office, Thurgood Marshall—functionally third in command at the NAACP behind White and Wilkins—told him "please let us know specifically what can be done by us to help." Writers known as being close to the party, such as Dalton Trumbo, wrote for the NAACP organ. "Sahara," the film written by the artist, union official, and Communist party leader John Howard Lawson, was lauded, and the role drawn for the Black actor Rex Ingram was praised. This approach continued in 1947, when Marshall sent a telegram to New York congressmen asking them to oppose the contempt citations by the House Un-American Activities Committee (HUAC) in the Hollywood Ten case.[10]

Along with Du Bois and others Black Communist Doxey Wilkerson wrote an article for Professor Rayford Logan's "What the Negro Wants." The importance of Wilkerson's contribution is that, although written by a Black Communist, his prescriptions were neither more nor less radical than those from the other contributors from other parts of the ideological spectrum.[11]

Indeed, the thrust of the NAACP War Time Conference resolution in 1944 could easily have been written by Wilkerson:

> In common with progressive workers in all lands and from all groups we seek the ending of imperialism both as a matter of justice to the victims of imperialist exploitation and in order

> to remove a cause for war. The NAACP has special stake in the abolition of imperialism because the members of the various colored races constitute most though not all of the victims of imperialist exploitation. . . . Accordingly we urge as an important and effective step in the direction of the abolition of imperialism a system of international collective security.

It was not Doxey Wilkerson who castigated Churchill "and his class who would perpetuate imperialism for the benefit of the few." It was not Ben Davis who favored "alliance with a steadily powerful Russia than further alliance on an Anglo-Saxon capitalist world." It was Walter White.[12]

The militance of the NAACP and the Afro-American community was quite fruitful. For the NAACP there was a dramatic, quantum leap in membership that solidified and heightened its preeminent role as the leading political organization among Blacks. The point was reached where the political direction of Blacks generally could not be intelligently assessed without examining the NAACP: the NAACP had become the significant barometer of Afro-American political sentiments. Richard Dalfiume has noted the magnitude of this development. He observed that, "from 355 branches and a membership of 50,556 in 1940, the NAACP grew to 1073 branches with a membership of slightly less than 450,000 in 1946."[13]

Interestingly, this kind of spurt in membership during the 1940 to 1946 period was not replicated during the rest of the Cold War era, when United States-Soviet tensions increased. It may not be coincidental that during most of this period, that is, World War II, a consistently friendly approach to Russia predominated. Purges, which had been seen at one time as totalitarianism were then viewed as a necessary measure in preparation for an inevitable Nazi onslaught. The conflict with Finland was viewed in the same light. Even attitudes toward the Nazi-Soviet Non-Aggression Pact, collective security, and communism itself were altered significantly.[14] It is also striking that tremendous and striking gains by Afro-Americans—the biggest advance since Reconstruction and hardly duplicated since—were made during the war years in employment, housing, and against Jim Crow. This is not altogether surprising. First of all, it could be argued that U.S. detente with the Soviet Union, which made anti-Sovietism unfashionable, undercut and destabilized the right-wing forces who were a primary obstacle to

Black progress. Second of all, racist practices were seen as being an impediment to the antifascist unity that was so desperately needed to repel the Axis behemoth—particularly given the none too latent appeal of the Japanese in the Afro-American community. Racist practices had to be eroded, otherwise the potential for a Black fifth column would be increased. "Lord don't let this war end too soon" was heard frequently among Blacks. George Schuyler, business manager of *Crisis,* stated candidly that "a long war will aid the Negro."[15] Similarly, as repeatedly expressed in *Crisis,* the NAACP view of the Soviet Union was consistently favorable.

In light of staunch NAACP opposition to Anglo-American foreign policies, it was not expected that the association would greet Winston Churchill's "Iron Curton" speech—what may have been the opening fusillade in the Cold War—with cat-calls and derision. Walter White dug deep into his rhetorical bag, then labelled the Fulton palaver "a sleazy method of serving notice on the world that the United States is backing the kind of imperialist program Churchill advocates . . . a sad revelation of the lack of foreign policy which our government has . . . [a] tirade against Russia." Marking the importance of the speech, the NAACP national office issued one of its infrequent statements. In portentous tones of ill foreboding, the March 5 address of the British prime minister, accompanied by the former Missouri haberdasher, was blasted since "it would virtually insure continuation of imperialism . . . Great Britain's policies toward colonial peoples which have been continued by the present labor government can cause only shudders of apprehension as far as Churchill's proposal of an Anglo-American coalition is concerned."[16]

During the war, and as the Cold War began to ossify, the government was faced with a militant, anti-imperialist, anticolonial Afro-American community led by the NAACP. This community appeared to be a major stumbling block to Anglo-American foreign policy; its ties to Black leftists, including Communists, also appeared to spell trouble for White House domestic policies as well.

Thus, when the elderly socialist of the path was unceremoniously ousted from his post at Atlanta University in 1944, few eyebrows were raised when the NAACP invited Du Bois to become a sort of minister of foreign affairs, while bearing the title "Director of Special Research."

CHAPTER 3

Color and Democracy

Du Bois hit the ground running and quickly plunged into a maelstrom of political activity. He perceived his role as chief of a "sort of foreign affairs department of the NAACP." The man who was proclaimed the father of Pan-Africanism insisted that the greatest single question facing humanity was the ending of colonialism. Never one to shrink from monumental tasks, Du Bois accepted the challenge and announced publicly, "this is the problem to which I propose to devote the remaining years of my life."[1]

Color and Democracy: Colonies and Peace was written by Du Bois early in his second tenure with the NAACP. Its importance in assessing Du Bois is underscored by the fact that Du Bois used this title on his stationery. It is well to observe that this militant tract was received with the respect due a tome from the civil rights movement's patriarch; Pearl Buck and Melville Herskovits were among the favorable reviewers. The United States Navy alone bought 2,400 copies.[2]

Months before Pearl Harbor, he mused to Rayford Logan, "suppose that in my capacity as permanent secretary of the Pan-African Congress, I announce through you a fifth Pan-African Congress to be held in Port-au-Prince as soon as it is practical after the close of the present war with the understanding that such congress should immediately appoint delegates to wait upon the peace conference or any organizations which is re-arranging the world to put before them the demands of the peoples of African descent?"[3]

Then, in the spring of 1944, before he repaired to the NAACP, he contacted Paul Robeson, Amy Jacques Garvey (wife of the late Marcus Garvey), Max Yergan, and Dr. Harold Moody (chair of the London Missionary Society), "asking each if they would join me as conveners of a fifth Pan-African Congress to meet in London as soon as practical at the end of the war. I do not insist upon 'Pan-African' but suggested it merely to indicate a certain continuity since the first world war." Trying to attract as broad a base of support as possible, the enclosure indicated "no political changes in the relation between colonies and mother countries will necessarily be contemplated."[4]

George Padmore was also an essential participant in this process. He and Du Bois communicated with each other across the Atlantic, providing each other with basic intelligence. It was Padmore who was in closer touch with the anticolonial leaders based in London and abroad; it was he who informed Du Bois about the virtual unanimity of the colonized in Africa—left, right, and center—in support of either secession from or dominion status within the Empire. The journalist noted the Marxist and non-Marxist composition of Pan-African Congress (PAC) supporters; he devastatingly hacked away at French colonial policy and attempted to sway Du Bois away from holding the confab in Paris.[5]

These individuals were all essential to the process but it should not be forgotten that Du Bois was an employee of the avowedly militant, anticolonialist NAACP when he finally put the PAC into full motion. One of the purposes of the PAC, and one of Du Bois' essential duties on the job, was to get an organized expression of anticolonial sentiment to present "to the Peace Conference or conferences after the close of the war in behalf of the peoples of Africa and other colored groups." At the NAACP board meeting he successfully lobbied for his program and eventually the board sent President Franklin D. Roosevelt a resolution expressing angry opposition "to the return of liberated territories to colonial powers and suggesting the appointment of qualified Negroes to peace and other conferences on postwar and domestic policies."[6]

But as the war began to wind down, it became apparent that certain leading officials were not overly enthusiastic about the PAC, though it was not always apparent why. Seemingly, a proper foundation had been laid by contacts with Robeson, Logan, Padmore, and other essential parties. Du Bois had thoroughly briefed Ralph Bunche, William Hastie, Arthur Spingarn, Louis Wright, and Channing Tobias. The outline and content of the proposed meeting was aired. Nonetheless, as the time for the PAC began to peek over the horizon, Du Bois, without zest, conceded, "confidentially I do not think that Mr. White is particularly enthusiastic about this meeting but I shall do what I can to carry it through." Hastie probably reflected White's thinking when he expressed to the executive secretary doubt about the PAC's chance for success and frowned on the disproportionate number of African exiles in Europe who would be participating.[7]

On August 15, 1945, days after Hiroshima-Nagasaki and during a time when the NAACP was customarily in the slumber of vacation, Du Bois frantically told White that "while we have been waiting," the PAC had been called. Seeing the boat steam off from the port, White then requested a hurried meeting of the relevant board committee to determine concrete policy with respect to the convening of the PAC. Primary sessions of the PAC did not actually convene until the fall and Du Bois was probably just trying to light a fire under the board; he was not totally unsuccessful.[8]

Du Bois was the primary North American organizer of the PAC and generated a flood of correspondence to potential delegates abroad. From the correspondence it can be seen that Du Bois attempted to solicit ammunition to repel the then widespread notion that in reality colonialism was the only barrier between the colonized and savagery. Du Bois reached out beyond colonized Africa so that the PAC was attended and affected by anticolonial leaders from the British Empire generally. And this is not all. Du Bois insisted to Padmore, "we must not neglect the interests and opinions of French, Belgium, Portugese and Spanish Africans as well as Africans of West Indian and American descent."[9]

The predominantly Black and brown delegates who attended the PAC were not invited randomly. Padmore reminded Du Bois that, "all our delegates must have mandates from organizations and they will therefore speak not for themselves but for masses of people, representatives, not of the middle class strata and professionals in the colonies, but of the workers' organizations, the cooperative societies, peasant associations, labour parties and national liberation organizations." This was the emphasis with which the congress was conceived and brought into being.[10]

This did not preclude communication with those not affiliated or opposed to the anticolonial movement. Du Bois approached Jean de la Roche of the French Press and Information Service. He also wrote directly to Rene Pleven, French minister of finance and national economy and was able to directly reach the ministry of colonies. This was an era when the left in France played a significant role in the government and there was sympathy toward anticolonialism. The PAC was not held in Paris, though Du Bois was favorable to the idea, because the committee members calling the congress were mostly British subjects who had a then typical attitude toward French colonial policy. Du Bois was in touch with Harold Laski, chair of the British Labor party, Senator Robert Wagner of New York, CIO officials, and others in pursuit of this goal.[11]

Du Bois had to wrestle not only with the NAACP and sovereign governments but with his fellow citizens as well. After Du Bois had buttonholed Reverend Harry Emerson Fosdick of New York City's affluent Riverside Church about material support of anticolonialism, the eminent man of the cloth testily replied, "I cannot get even the dimmest idea as to what you mean by a colony . . . all this means absolute nothing to me." His voice drenched with sarcasm, Du Bois quickly answered, "I am enclosing a list of the colonial possessions in the world in order that you may realize that seven hundred and fifty million people on this earth live in colonies which have rights which no white nation is bound to respect." Du Bois evidently thought that a suggestion of the racism of Dred Scott would aid the cleric in perceiving human rights deprivation abroad. The notion that ignorance is closer to the truth than prejudice probably skipped through Du Bois' mind. From the ignorance of Fosdick he faced the prejudice of the philanthropist A. Phelps Stokes who voiced keen objection to participation of "any politician" who was "radical" in the anticolonial meetings. Ralph Bunche desired more participation of colonial governments as opposed to anticolonial organizations. But in these halcyon days, not all those with ties to the United States ruling circles placed obstacles in the path. Senator Arthur Capper of Kansas was not alone among congressmen in endorsing the idea of the PAC and Du Bois' own labors: "you are rendering valuable service to the NAACP."[12]

As if the Pan-African Congress were not enough, Du Bois set out to organize an international colonial conference in Harlem, about a month before V-E Day. This conference was a spectacular success and may have been the most significant signpost on the road to anticolonial independence. Certainly it was the most significant meeting of its type held in North America before or since. Yet this conference was something of a dry run for the PAC in that many of the same issues and personalities were present.

The Harlem conference was held April 6, 1945, at the Schomburg Library. A veritable all-star lineup of anticolonial advocates participated. Julio Pinto Gandia of Puerto Rico, A. W. Wendell Malliet of Jamaica, Kumar Goshall and Bhola D. Panth of India, Msung Saw Tun of Burma, Kwame Nkrumah of Ghana and others were there. An impressive array of Afro-American leaders appeared: P. Bernard Young, Jr., member of the Committee of Negro Editors visiting West Africa, Lawrence Reddick, Rayford Logan, W. A. Hunton of the Council on African Affairs and, of course, the spark plug of this effort—Du Bois.

Many of their demands seemed naive and farfetched to some at the time, but ultimately most became part of the world's agenda. They are also worth reviewing as a reflection of anticolonial thinking. In their initial draft the first listed demand was independence for United States colonies or inclusion in the United States.

They called for restoration to Ethiopia of land seized by Italy and that the "rights of natives in Libya, Eritrea and Somaliland be safe guarded under an International Mandate Commission." "Restoration of Manchukuo and Formosa to a democratic China and the independence of Korea" was urged on Japan. "Independence for India and Burma" and "immediate steps toward dominion status for Nigeria and the Gold Coast" was the appeal to Britain. As for "other parts of British Africa," for example, the Rhodesias (Zimbabwe and Zambia) and Kenya, it was said that "no white minority be given privilege to rule . . . admit native Africans to equal status with other citizens in the British Empire."

This Harlem conclave is also worthy of examination as a precursor to the better known Pan-African Congress. Both demonstrated that, unlike certain Black nationalists might have it believed, these Pan-Africanists saw anticolonialism as more than an African problem. They felt it was strategically, tactically, and morally necessary to embrace colonized Asia. Nor was it a simple Black-white struggle. In the British West Indies they did not call for the ousting of whites but only called for the "exercise of political power by the native born people."

On the other hand, Kwame Nkrumah and others felt that the conference could have traveled farther down the path of anticolonialism. The Ghanian leader intoned, "I object to the use of the word *mandate* . . . its use . . . implies sell-out to the colonial powers" (emphasis is in original). However, though some may have seen their remedies as not radical enough, those who held the reins of colonial power saw the results of the Harlem conference as too radical, and they acted accordingly.[13]

When the long awaited Fifth Pan-African Congress opened, it was not in Paris, nor in Liberia where it had also been requested to be held, but in Manchester—and it almost did not come off there. The British government was not eager to facilitate the entry into their country of an anticolonial conference or its advocates. Du Bois told Padmore pessimistically about the immense difficulty in getting a visa from the United Kingdom. His maneuvers to get a visa reflect the balmy political times: "I appealed to the President and got an interview with the acting Secretary of State." Apparently Du Bois prevailed on the philanthropist A. Phelps Stokes to prevail on Lord Halifax, British ambassador to the United States, to use his good offices to obtain a visa for him. Thus Stokes termed Du Bois the "most distinguished living Negro" and warned darkly that if a visa were not granted "it might have some unfortunate repercussions." A visa was quickly granted and he hopped quickly to London.[14]

Present at the congress were nearly two hundred delegates from sixty different countries. They were especially representative of the working classes. The Gold Coast was represented by the head of the Railway Union, which recently had staged a successful strike; the West Indies were represented, especially Jamaica, Barbados, and Guyana. Modestly, in his report to the NAACP leadership, Du Bois played down his role. He was one of seven elected to chair sessions and was ultimately chosen permanent chairman of the entire body. Du Bois and Mrs. Garvey were two of the five members of resolutions committees.[15]

The session on imperialism in North and West Africa was chaired by Du Bois. Nkrumah was the rapporteur and Padmore introduced the chairman; on October 17 the decision to appoint chairmen for each session was rescinded and Padmore declared Du Bois permanent chairman, as a token of esteem and respect.[16]

Kwame Nkrumah set the tone by stresssing militant actions—strikes, boycotts, and organizing. He emphasized how this PAC differed from past ones by not being as dominated by intellectuals but more so by workers.[17]

At the final session Du Bois was elected international president and given a silver cigarette box and a pledge of solidarity with the NAACP. The resolutions were militant in tone, like those of the Harlem conference, but not as international in scope. Yet this meeting, which was an essential catalyst of the postwar anticolonial upsurge, was snubbed by the white press. As a consequence, when anticolonial revolts broke out, it was a short step to blaming outside agitators or Communists because of ignorance of the activities of the colonized.[18]

There were other prescient trends marked by the Pan-African Congress. The *Chicago Defender* reflected a trend in the Black press when it noted both Du Bois' role and his lavish praise of the Soviet Union's material support for anticolonial movements. Years later, Du Bois commented on one demonstrative effect of this conference and, by inference, the effect of many of the other meetings he had occassion to attend. Though often castigated for simply generating talk and paper resolutions, conferences allow for the cementing of ties between and among individuals and organizations. Concerning Nkrumah, Du Bois notes that at Manchester: "there I first saw him and Kenyatta of Kenya and Johnson of Sierra Leone." Although his memory was a bit faulty here (Nkrumah, for one, had participated in the Harlem conference a few months earlier), the point is that the PAC helped to give structure to an anticolonial network; perhaps more importantly, it allowed for the embryos that bore fruit to develop quite rapidly. It was intended for the Manchester meeting to be "preliminary to a real Pan-African Congress of Delegates to take place in 1946 or 1947."[19]

This planned venture was stillborn, though not for lack of effort. If not greeted by sabotage, the PAC was certainly greeted with a blind eye in certain circles. Shortly after returning from England, Du Bois called on Henry Luce for "a little of your time" to discuss, among other things, how Africa is not getting a "fair share" of its riches and how this will "continue to frustrate the restoration and advance of civilization." If there was a reply by Luce, it does not survive. Lyman C. White of the Non-Governmental Organization section of the United Nations turned down the PAC's application for consultative status, though in many cases it was routinely granted. The rationale? "Your organization adopted a resolution in opposition to the Trusteeship System and that therefore you are opposing the aims of the charter of the United Nations." Du Bois deemed this a novel interpretation of international law and branded it "a lie" and "untrue," but the ability of the PAC to lobby within the community of nations was surely curtailed.[20]

The effectiveness of the PAC was also hampered by the attitude of leading circles of the NAACP itself. The *NAACP Branch Bulletin* gave full coverage to the meeting and its demands but implementation fell far short. After the fact Du Bois confessed, "against the desire of the secretary and several powerful members of the board, I was sent to the Fifth Pan African Congress." Why this reluctance? The reasons were to reverberate throughout the Cold War years. Du Bois wished to work more closely with the left-led Council on African Affairs (CAA) which has "a constituency and is doing good work"; the obstruction was the allegation that the council was "financed by the communists, which is probably true." Du Bois also wished to expand solidarity with African independence work in the nation with the largest Black population outside of Africa—Brazil. This would have been difficult and unwise to do apart from the leading organization in the field, the Council on African Affairs. But without the wherewithal of a mass organization like the NAACP, Du Bois' efforts could not be as extensive.[21]

After his sacking from the NAACP in the fall of 1948, Du Bois expanded on this contretemps in a discussion with the influential East African editor of the journal *Pan Africa,* T. R. Makonnen:

> The trouble has been that the secretary of the NAACP was not willing to cooperate with the Pan African movement, and a good many of the Board of Directors agreed with him. The result was that when I returned from the 1945 meeting I was unable to get any action whatsoever. My proposals for cooperating in a future meeting, for cooperating with the journal *Pan Africa,* for publishing pamphlets concerning Africa, were all met with a silence.[22] There was no vote but nothing was done.

Consequently, the NAACP thrust to support African liberation by producing literature, educating, and lobbying was aborted. The gathering Cold War windstorm played an important part, as the Association was hesitant to associate with the left-led CAA and with an issue that was increasingly associated with the left—African independence. The stage had been set for Du Bois' return but the script was changing as he entered.

CHAPTER 4

The World and Du Bois

A liberated Africa was an essential, but not the sole, priority for Du Bois on his return to the NAACP. In the letter inviting Du Bois to return, he was specifically requested to address the issues raised by the war's end, such as the peace settlement, the United Nations, and so on. But the aim was to insure that the interests of the African and colored peoples worldwide were represented. Long before the issue of Du Bois' ouster from Atlanta University and his return to the NAACP had arisen, Walter White had queried Du Bois concerning his possible service on a committee to present the cause of Blacks in the United States, West Indies, and Africa at the peace conference. A. Philip Randolph's militant March on Washington Movement had voiced the view of the NAACP and Afro-Americans when they announced:

> We demand representation for the colored and minority racial groups on all missions, political and technical, which will be sent to the peace conference so that the interests of all people everywhere may be fully recognized and justly provided for in the post-war settlement.

The war had been a watershed for civil rights, and it was manifest that the status quo of racism at home and colonialism abroad be unacceptable. George Padmore, who, along with Du Bois, was probably in the closest touch with Africans in the diaspora, was struck by the "obvious transmutation in the character of the movement [that] was precipitated by the second world war. The war years had brought a new kind of awareness to many old and young African leaders."[1]

In articles and in numerous speaking engagements, radio appearances, and the like, Du Bois tried to drive home the fact that opposing colonialism was not just altruistic humanitarianism but in the concrete interest of those in the West. He told the predominantly white readers of the *New York Post.*[2]

> But is it not barely possible that one of the reasons that human rights are not realized in Germany, England and the U.S. is just because they can be flouted at will in Nigeria, Java, Fiji and among the natives of South Africa?

These ideas of Du Bois were expressed not only on paper but in high policy-making circles. Secretary of State Edward Stettinius invited William Hastie, Mary McLeod Bethune, Du Bois, and representatives of over eighty other organizations to Washington for a meeting on the Dumbarton Oaks peace sessions. Interestingly, this meeting was called after the sessions had ended, though the purpose was meant to provide a means for the State Department to learn citizens' views. Du Bois subjected Dumbarton Oaks to withering criticism on the grounds that it contemplated colonialism's continuation, thereby paving the way for more war. Du Bois' views were in agreement with the Association's and they publicized them accordingly.[3]

At the March 12, 1945, board meeting, Du Bois drafted a strongly anticolonialist resolution that was a reprise of his *Color and Democracy* theses; it was adopted without opposition. At that same meeting, on the motion of Dr. Channing Tobias and seconded by Spingarn, Du Bois was appointed as representative of the NAACP at the San Francisco conference.[4]

This assignment did not simply involve attending a meeting and reporting back. Initially, Du Bois wrote the Secretary of State and inquired as to whether there would be Black representation at the conference. That the answer was in the affirmative was due in no small part to Du Bois' labors. But a product could not be fashioned if there was not cloth at hand and Du Bois had available a well-spring of support within the Afro-American community to draw on—it just required tapping. Thus, Du Bois proposed and

White quickly agreed to the idea of sending telegrams to Black labor, fraternal, community, and other organizations requesting their ideas on forming a Black agenda for San Francisco. Their tentacles extended beyond the Afro-American community. Du Bois reached out to the Committee to Study the Organization of the Peace, which had Claude Pepper, Philip Jessup, John Foster Dulles, Merle Curti, and others on its board and was directed by Clark Eichelberger. This committee had circulated a letter to be signed by leading organizations and was to be sent to the secretary of state. Du Bois cordially informed Eichelberger that the NAACP "would be glad to join in signing." But, indicating the militant role and influence of Afro-Americans, he added a quick caveat: "we believe that the second paragraph is not strong enough. We do not think that it should start with praising the [State] Department for a Division of Dependent Peoples." He went on to appeal for a strengthening of the anticolonial content of the letter and the United Nations itself.[5]

And it was Du Bois who, after observing in *The New York Times* that twelve representatives from national organizations would be playing key roles in San Francisco, immediately suggested to Roy Wilkins, "I think we ought to bring pressure . . . to see that the National Association for Advancement of Colored People is among those twelve."[6] Wilkins quickly followed through on this suggestion.

The telegram sent to Oscar Adams of the Supreme Lodge of the Knights of Pythias was similar to hundreds of others sent during that time. In going to San Francisco the NAACP was representing "not this organization but the whole body of American Negroes . . . If therefore you have passed any resolutions or come to any conclusions concerning what ought to be done at San Francisco . . . we will be glad to make representation to whatever authorities we have access." The range of Black organizations contacted by Du Bois on behalf of the association was broad and impressive. The March on Washington Movement, National Council of Negro Women, National Association of Colored Graduate Nurses, National Association of Deans and Advisers of Men in Negro Educational Institutions, National Association of Ministers' Wives, National Baptist Convention, National Bar Association, National Dental Association, and National Negro Insurance Association were just a few of the groups reached. Most replied affirmatively and with alacrity.

At the sessions in San Francisco, Du Bois was both a representative of the NAACP and consultant to the State Department.

There was a core committee of twelve organizations (including the American Bar Association, the American Federation of Labor, American Jewish Committee, National Association of Manufacturers, National Education Association, National Lawyers Guild) acting as a strategy committee, and Du Bois was the NAACP representative on this committee.[9]

White and Du Bois huddled constantly with other officials there. A bone of contention was whether the United States delegation should push for specific provisions on human rights. White pressed Stettinius on the issue of extending these protections to "colonials and other dependent people." According to White's confidential memorandum to his fellow Black delegates Du Bois and Mary McLeod Bethune, "Mr. Stettinius smiled somewhat embarrassedly and cryptically at this point." This was the extent of the NAACP's substantive headway on this point at this juncture.[8]

White, in particular, was roundly disappointed with the actions of Truman and the United States delegation. He communicated his disappointment to Wilkins in virulent terms:

> Its timorousness and political mindedness has caused the United States delegation to lose, perhaps beyond regaining, the bold moral leadership which it should have taken; Russia and China have taken the play away from the United States on the colonial trusteeship, while the smart boys like Eden appear to have outsmarted our delegation on purely political grounds.

He discussed how he had pressured Stettinius "by taking a bolder and more uncompromising stand," but to no avail.[9]

White was not alone in feeling that "Russia and China have taken the play away from the United States" on anticolonialism. Du Bois told the Black community, through the pages of the *Chicago Defender,* that Molotov, the Soviet delegate, was singular in his stress on the need to overcome racism, and discrimination against women, and ban colonialism.[10]

Du Bois was far from being shy about sharing this opinion with the United States delegation. He told them:

> We have allowed ourselves in this conference to be estranged from Russia by the plight of a dozen reactionary and Jew baiting Polish landlords, and have made no comment and taken no action on the great words spoken by Molotov.

He appealed for the delegation to press for a statement on equality of races along the lines of the Chinese proposal at Dumbarton Oaks and an anticolonial statement in the United Nations Charter. The general reaction from the United States delegation was studied indifference.[11]

Like the Fifth Pan-African Congress, the San Francisco meeting allowed for more intimate, personal contact among anticolonial advocates. Du Bois was able to cement relations with leading Soviet officials and others including "Mrs. Pandit, the sister, of Nehru." and "Mr. Singh, President of the Indian Association," with whom he had dinner. His relationship with his nominal leader, Walter White, showed little noticeable improvement, despite White's militance. In fact, his estimate of White may have plummeted even more:

> I think they put over certain decisions on Walter by reason of his unfamiliarity with the broader implications. In the end however I doubt if this made much difference.

His estimate of the other Black delegate was not much better: "Mrs. Bethune was rather a nuisance, but a harmless one." Walter White, at the same time, scored the *Pittsburgh Courier* for their "less than friendly coverage," in that they "tried to play [on] mythical differences" that allegedly pitted Bethune against White and Du Bois.[12]

Although Secretary of State Stettinius acknowledged the manifold effect of the Black community's pressure on the United States posture at Dumbarton Oaks and at the United Nations meeting, Du Bois left San Francisco disappointed. The Black community was not disappointed, however, with Du Bois' actions in San Francisco. Zore Neale Hurston expressed heart-felt "congratulations on your stand at San Francisco." The overflow crowds that greeted Du Bois' lecture tour on the United Nations after San Francisco, was revealing. He spoke to an audience of 2,000 in Oakland, 700 in San Francisco, and 1,000 in Los Angeles.[13]

The disappointment of San Francisco did not signal an end to anticolonial lobbying. Toward that end, immediately after the Bay Area conference, he met with the Liberian, Haitian, French, and Ethiopian delegations. He also met John Foster Dulles and union leader James Carey.[14]

This disappointment did not apply to the NAACP leadership's evaluation of Du Bois' role. The board felt so strongly about this that they voted a copy of Du Bois' *Color and Democracy* "be sent to each member of the American delegation at San Francisco." This reflected the fact that Du Bois' tract was rapidly becoming the Bible for anticolonial advocates in the United States. As Du Bois' publisher, Harcourt and Brace, effused, "requests have come for galleys for your book from various quarters, showing a lively growing interest, which bodes well for the book." Thus, when Eleanor Roosevelt asked Walter White for "guidance" in her role as delegate to the United Nations, he did not hestitate to admit the impact of Du Bois' ideas as expressed in *Color and Democracy* and elsewhere; he promptly forwarded a "combination of the ideas of Dr. Du Bois . . . and my own" that called for a somewhat radical program of banning colonialism.[15]

Du Bois took his campaign on the United Nations to the press and Congress. *The New York Times* interviewed him at Harcourt and Brace and he censured the "San Francisco Charter of World Organization" for deciding that it could not interfere with domestic matters such as colonies. When *The New York Times* quoted him as saying, "either the British Government will extend self-government in West Africa and the West Indies or face open revolt," it was not treated as an idle threat. Before the Senate Committee on Foreign Relations he conceded that the United Nations Charter was a "far step toward peace and justice" but that its provisions having to do with colonies were seriously deficient. In a letter to the editor printed in *The New York Times,* Du Bois prodded the United Nations to rectify this situation. He fumed about political repression directed against anticolonial movements in Nigeria, South Africa, Sierre Leone, and the Rhodesias. Hitting a familiar note, he linked the fate of 15,000,000 Negroes to the fate of Africa and posited that the enfranchisement of the former would held to liberate the latter.[16]

Du Bois devoted considerable time and energy to the United Nations, which he deemed a watershed development, and related events. This influence of the Father of Pan-Africanism was wide and recognized. White House aide Philleo Nash hurriedly wrote Du Bois: "former Commissioner of Indian Affairs . . . is most anxious to have a talk with you . . . [he] wants to draw on your deep knowledge of colonial and dependent problems". At the same time, Du Bois was not shy about calling on his network of influential colleagues to intercede on his behalf. He asked Gunnar Myrdal, "are you personally acquainted with Trygvie Lie, Secretary of the United Nations . . . I should like to become acquainted with him to talk with him about the question of colonies particularly in Africa." Myrdal used his good offices to set up this meeting.[17]

Du Bois took his campaign on the United Nations to the heartland of the United States. His schedule of public appearances had always been formidable and the continual crisis of the postwar years heightened his activism here. In the early postwar years, Du Bois' experience and knowledge in this area of racism and anti-colonialism was accorded due respect and deference by personages and policy makers of all backgrounds. But as the mercury in the political thermometer began to drop, Du Bois's popularity in certain circles fell accordingly.[18]

CHAPTER 5

When Push Comes to Shun

Du Bois and White could never be mistaken for bosom buddies. It was no secret that they did not get along personally, though this phenomenon also had clear political overtones and motivations. Du Bois saw White as a narrowly educated executive. White saw Du Bois as overbearing and arrogant. On the ideological level, there were fierce clashes that nurtured their personal difficulties.

Virtually from the moment that Du Bois returned to the NAACP there were differences between the two leaders. Though White had been trotting to the battlefronts across the globe, he objected to Du Bois' planned trip to Haiti in the summer of 1944. Du Bois disagreed and set off for Port-au-Prince though White expressed reluctance to start his salary while he resided in the Caribbean.[1]

When Du Bois returned to the Association, the whirlwind of personal difficulties continued unabated, ranging from the trivial to the sublime. The question of office space remained nettlesome throughout his second tenure with the Association. The contretemps over office space spawned a wider showdown with the NAACP board—the first of many Du Bois was fated to lose.[2]

Months before he was sacked, Du Bois complained to White and the board, "my present office is about 12′ × 20′. It houses 3 workers, 2500 books, 2 desks, a typing table, a dictaphone outfit and 6 four drawer file cabinets." He grumbled that this overcrowding meant that "much of my own work is done in my apartment." Explaining why he had remained mute about this problem for so long after his initial complaint, he conceded, "I did not complain further about office space for I realized that the failure to accommodate me was not necessarily personal."[3]

Office space was not the only divisive issue at NAACP headquarters. The ambiguity of Du Bois' position at the NAACP caused sparks to fly. White informed Du Bois' top aide, the scholar Irene Diggs, in the fall of 1944, "I would like to have you attend the monthly board meetings in the future." About six months later, probably as a result of deepening tension with Du Bois, he brusquely reversed field.[4]

Du Bois was allowed to attend board meetings but he frequently had to tell White, "I did not get the notice, reports and agenda of the last Board meeting." White was quick to tell Du Bois huffily, "you might put on your calendar that the Board meets every second Monday, with the exception of July and August." This did not answer Du Bois' complaint about not receiving notice of the meetings' substance. In a fit of exasperation less than a year before he was fired, he told Wilkins sarcastically, "for several months past I have received neither the agenda of the meetings of the Board of Directors nor a copy of the minutes . . . . May I enquire if there is any particular reason for this policy?" Du Bois continued to press for briefings on board agendas and meetings, thus underscoring the importance of the NAACP's major policy-making board. During this time, Du Bois was attempting to meld the NAACP with the Pan-African movement and engaging in related activities. The path would have been strewn with fewer obstacles if the board had been fully integrated in the direction of these efforts— and a minimum prerequisite for this would have been presentations and interactions at board meetings.[5]

A repeated problem for Du Bois was clerical assistance. The articles, books, speeches, etc. that he was turning out required this kind of aid. Once again, Du Bois beseeched Wilkins for a hand. But the former journalist from Kansas City was not convinced.[6]

A constant plaint of Wilkins was that Du Bois operated "as a sort of independent agency attached to the Association but suscribing to other departments." Carl Murphy, the powerful Black publisher, had occasion to wonder if Du Bois was leading an "individual office" that is autonomous or is his work "under the direction of the secretary." But all outside inquiries about Du Bois were not of this nature. White felt constrained to explain unequivocally to NAACP supporter Lillian Alexander: "First, with respect to your statement that there has been a 'plot' to get rid of Dr. Du Bois . . . there is not one scintilla of basis for such a statement as far as I know." He criticized Du Bois for not agreeing to have his mail opened along with that of other NAACP leaders; Du Bois felt that much of his correspondence—especially letters from abroad—was sensitive and that it would be politically unwise to have random eyes viewing it. White also blasted Du Bois about the office space issue while allowing that "it is true we promised Dr. Du Bois two offices." Alexander's inquiry moved White to an extended metaphor: "Suppose the quarterback of a team called for a forward pass which he and nine other men proceeded to execute while the eleventh member of the team without notification to the others, decided instead to plunge through the line."[7]

The core of Du Bois' conflict with the leadership rested with the executive secretary, Walter White. Du Bois saw this as both personal and political. In contrast, though political differences later set them far apart, Du Bois considered Arthur Spingarn and Louis Wright "close and loyal friends." The fact that Du Bois, White, Wilkins, and Thurgood Marshall all lived in the same Harlem apartment building, 409 Edgecombe Avenue, apparently did not increase their personal affections for one another.[8]

It should be stressed, however, that given the tension-ridden activity on the front lines of the battlefield—lynchings, bombings, and other frequent nerve-racking occurences in NAACP life—it was somewhat understandable how this atmosphere might detrimentally affect personal interaction; yet the NAACP probably had less turmoil of this sort than a similar sized union. One commentator has alluded to a Marshall-White rift; a rift between Marshall and the NAACP lawyer and future ambassador to Ghana Franklin Williams; a rift between Williams and NAACP attorney Marian Wynn Perry; a rift between Perry and NAACP lawyer and future federal judge Constance Baker Motley.[9]

But these proliferating rifts could not be separated from the office of the executive secretary. "There was the growing suspicion, too, that White was a white man passing as a Negro and using his marginal negritude as a passport to the white power structure . . . Walter White . . . inevitably lost touch with the colored masses and their needs." So says author Richard Kluger. The dynamics of skin color cannot be discounted as there was some suspicion that the white rulers of the nation preferred dealing with a lighter, nonradical Negro. Carl Murphy bitterly attacked White after he divorced his Afro-American wife and married a white South African, Poppy Cannon; nor were Murphy and others reassured when White was accused of advocating chemical skin lightening as a mode for ameliorating the so-called race problem.[10]

Oswald Garrison Villard was allowed to take to the pages of *Crisis* in denunciation of White's autobiography, *A Man Called White.* Villard was disappointed with White's inattention in his book to Joel Spingarn, Du Bois, Dr. Louis Wright, Mary White Ovington, and others. This was a reflection of White's tumultuous relationship with the NAACP leadership in general. The turmoil of the Du Bois sacking and Cold War tensions may have exacerbated this tendency but White and Spingarn were at each other's throats more than once. White was distraught about attacks on him because of his role in Du Bois' firing and he was disheartened by the board's attempt to force him to stop making public statements during a leave of absence. He considered resigning, partly because of his health, and actually sent Spingarn a frank letter of resignation; instead, he took another leave of absence.[11]

During White's frequent leaves and sicknesses, Wilkins took over the helm. His tenure was equallly stormy and his distaste for diplomacy seemed to be almost enzymatic at NAACP hedquarters.[12] Though popularly, Du Bois is focused on unduly when discussing personality problems there, the unpleasant fact is that dissension was rife at the NAACP. Personality and politics made for an often noxious brew at the NAACP.[13]

That this brew became noxious may have been due in part to the oft-criticized NAACP structure. At the time, many felt that too much power was invested in the office of the executive secretary and the Administration Committee that he controlled; and correspondingly, not enough power was invested in the convention and branches. Charles Toney, Acting Chairman of the Association, became dyspeptic in denouncing "totalitarianism" and what he saw as antidemocratic methods; these methods "have the effect of making the Secretary not only the Secretary of the Association, but President and Chairman of the Board of Directors." He was livid as he denounced to White the "totalitarian trend in your thinking" and fervently called for organizational democracy.[14]

Du Bois agreed with the analysis that the NAACP needed to strengthen the branches and convention. He said as much to Gloster

Current, who directed branch activities, and emphasized that more local autonomy and decentralization were needed along with less heavy-handed rule from the top. This harbinger of a New Left theme was a frequent battle cry of left and progressive voices within the Association. Frank Barnes, a postal worker who was an early victim of the red scare and militant leader of the Santa Monica, California branch, made what was considered the radical demand that the convention elect all members of the board rather than the self-perpetuating method. This call was taken up by Novella Watkins, secretary of the branch in industrial South Bend, Indiana, specifically asking White why Article 2, Section 3 of the NAACP Constitution couldn't be amended so that the board could be nominated and elected by the Annual Convention. The NAACP youth, a consistent voice for progress over the years, echoed the theme of Du Bois and company, and went further to demand "youth representation consisting of not less than four members of the Board of Directors."[15]

During this period, a disproportionate amount of NAACP activity was centered in the South and Midwest. Forces there carrying Du Bois' banner of less centralization pushed a resolution in 1946 for a national regional office based in these states with powers similar to those in New York and San Francisco. White and like-minded NAACP officials saw these issues as a cover for an unprincipled attack on the left flank and was able to portray the decentralization issue as a left issue. This ball of wax helped to motivate a directive forwarded to the branches:

> The Secretary read a draft of a letter to be sent to branches urging them to take care in joining with other organizations in conferences and avoiding involvement of the Association in any politically motivated movement.

The board acknowledged "general agreement with the thought behind it" though "there was some criticism of the wording of the letter." Left and progressive forces could and did play a substantial role in NAACP branches nationally, particularly in the Midwest, and would have been even more influential if power was redirected toward the convention; thus White's demarche was aimed at blocking those forces who wished to link the Association with other groups with common positions.[16]

Ella Baker, an unsung heroine of the civil rights movement who played a crucial role in the organization and direction of the Southern Christian Leadership Conference and Student Non-Violent Coordinating Committee, was, in 1940, director of NAACP branches and member of the staff of the national office of the NAACP. When the tremendous spurt in NAACP membership occurred in the 1940s, her peripathetic traveling and speaking tours were significantly responsible. Like Du Bois and others, she lambasted the NAACP structure and the lack of ballast in the allocation of leadership functions. She lamented the "inclination to disregard the individual's right to an opinion." Frustrated by lack of internal democracy, she mournfully recalled "an almost complete lack of appreciation for the collective thinking of the staff," as well as infrequent staff meetings. Apparently horrified at the erosion of civil liberties that characterized this period, she scorned "an indirectness that is more akin to espionage. Members of the staff are asked leading questions about the work of other staff members." One of those staff members whose activities NAACP higher ups were concerned about was their Director of Special Research with his ramified ties with the domestic and international left. It was not surprising then that Du Bois, along with the executive secretary and President Spingarn, received a copy of her resignation letter.[17]

As the vote on the ouster of Du Bois shows, there was no lemming-like unanimity on the board, with some favorable cries for decentralization voiced. Across the board there was discord. Earl Dickerson, the Black attorney who became president of the important National Lawyers' Guild and was a Progressive party leader, was an often angry voice for left and progressive causes; interestingly, the same could be said to an extent for the Vanderbilt heir, John Hammond.

At the same board meeting, the "Committee Investigating the influence of Paid Personnel upon Committees of the Board of Directors," gave a report pregnant with meaning for White's stewardship. Their report and its conclusion that there was undue interference in this area by "paid personnel . . . particularly in the years 1946, 1947, 1948 and some in 1949," was accepted by a vote of 11–2. The board split on other issues. Particularly controversial was the bitter battle to unionize NAACP employees. The employees eventually joined the Social Service Employees Union, Local 19 of the United Office and Professional Workers of America,

CIO, after an acrimonious dispute. This unpleasant turn of events was centrifugal in the direction of the board. Du Bois stood with the union across this 1946 chasm, inevitably, and many board members did not benignly view this.[18]

CHAPTER 6

Every Strike Is a Dress Rehearsal for Revolution

Du Bois' second tenure in the NAACP found him and this organization frequently grouped with labor on the other side of the barricades. The NAACP's startling rise in membership during the war years was inseparable from their ties with the Congress of Industrial Organizations (CIO)—as opposed to the more conservative American Federation of Labor (AFL); correspondingly, the Black advance during those same years was inseparable from their advance in the CIO unions. Consequently, the NAACP was an unblinking ally of the early target of the red scare—the CIO. Yet, such Du Bois-NAACP unity often ran aground as the Cold War deepened, with labor being only one of many points of difference.

The strike wars of 1946, and the politically divisive atmosphere it reflected and engendered, found certain board members at odds. With a thumbing of the nose at board conservatives, the board voted to "immediately" make up for lost time "by supporting the Electric Workers, Packing House Workers and General Motors and other strikes and urging our branches to take up collections to make these strikes more effective." This was a reward your friends policy because these unions were material allies of the NAACP and harbored both substantial numbers of NAACP members and relatively progressive, antiracist records. A month after this vote, presumably after a touch of arm twisting, the board changed "make up for lost time" to "immediately support." The thrust backing labor was still there though the rephrasing was both trivial and ominous.[1]

Labor advocates on the board found an unflinching ally in Du Bois. The strike wars of 1946 found him breathing fire in staunch support of the unions. He employed his widely read column in the *Chicago Defender* to mold and shape Black opinion. On the practical level, he stated flatly that "every American Negro ought to stand back of the strikes, give them their support and sympathy." On the theoretical level, he drew blood in attacking the "outmoded" wage fund theory of Ricardo that was at one time the inviolable line at Harvard University. He intimated that workers pushing for higher wages actually were essential to a healthy economy since otherwise goods and services being produced could not and would not be bought; as he saw it, if monopoly resisted labor's demands it could well lead to an economic collapse "as disastrous as that in the thirties." As the level of strikes reached a crescendo in the long hot summer of 1946, Du Bois went so far as to back the railway workers' strike even though they abjectly barred Black workers from their ranks.[2]

If queried, the Association leadership would have echoed "me too" to this prolabor aspect of W.E.B. Du Bois—at least before the onset of the Cold War. It would be one-sided, however, to unduly emphasize this aspect. For in actuality there were repeated and sharp differences between them throughout Du Bois' stay in the Wendell Wilkie Building. And if one were to plot a graph, there would be an unqualified incline represented in the year 1946.

This incline was right after the optimism generated by the Fifth Pan-African Congress in the fall of 1945. The volatile mixture of the political and personal was again stirred here. The Association was becoming less predisposed to align itself materially with an anticolonial movement that was often militantly left; and this trend was exacerbated by the waspish personal differences and jealousies that plagued the Du Bois-NAACP leadership tie.[3]

With evident regret, Du Bois recalled to White that "the NAACP has taken no stand nor laid down any program with regard to Africa." He advised collecting petitions, manifestoes on freedom by African anticolonial movements, a survey of labor conditions in Africa, and biographical notes on African leaders. He also underscored systematic correspondence and contact with Africans throughout the diaspora. Finally, in a board meeting a week later, just before the Christmas break, Du Bois formally requested that the Association materially fulfill this entire mandate. It was approved in principle. But there was little evident enthusiasm for speedy implementation, as a "committee" designated to flesh out the program wound up binding it all in red tape.[4]

That White felt overshadowed intellectually by Dr. Du Bois is no shocking revelation. His globetrotting during the war indicated that he had, in particular, foreign policy pretensions of his own. When Du Bois entered the spotlight with his frequent testimony on Capitol Hill, White curtly brought to his attention that "your appearance before the Senate Foreign Relations Committee without any information being given to the Association was objectionable." White claimed that a principal reason for his anger was that the appearance was a "household secret. No reporter from the Negro press was there." But, strikingly, that absence had apparently not bothered him on other occasions.[5]

These events transpired not long after Hiroshima, but in 1946 the differences began to fester like a raisin in the sun, finally exploding within hours of the new year. At this time Du Bois went to some length to air the controversies. White had complained bitterly about statements attributed to Du Bois which supposedly inflamed a desegregation battle in Dayton, Ohio. Du Bois pleaded staleness, noting that his 1940 autobiography had been quoted from, plus: "I was careful to add that I was passing no judgment on the current controversy." Regarding his congressional testimony, he countered a White objection by answering that it was given as an individual and not as an Association representative. He felt it necessary to recite a record of work and travel that would have withered most in response to White's veritable demand that there be a "careful reconsideration" of Du Bois' position in the organization.[6]

What may have prompted this request for a "careful reconsideration" was the gathering Cold War storm hovering on the horizon. All of a sudden, weeks after the Fulton speech, memos began to be circulated in the higher echelons of the NAACP drawing close attention to Du Bois' frequent dalliances with the organized left. Aghast, James Ivy, a future *Crisis* editor, asked Wilkins wondrously: "Do you know that W.E.B. Du Bois is now one of the contributing editors of the *New Masses?*" Roy Wilkins carefully filed away a news release from the National Council for American-Soviet Friendship which listed Du Bois as "executive board member" of the NAACP, side by side with "Andrei Gromyko, Soviet delegate to the U.N."[7]

Du Bois' friendship and alliance with the Black actor, singer, and activist Paul Robeson, was viewed with alarm as the year wore on. This was a bit ironic in light of his being awarded the NAACP's highest award, the Spingarn Medal, the year before. Robeson had formally requested Du Bois' support for his campaign to end lynching, which had been spurred by an unfortunately typical spate of antiBlack pogroms that had gripped the United States at the same time as the strike wars. Du Bois' agreement to join Robeson sparked a cyclone of protest. Franklin Williams at once grumbled to White, and acerbically noted that not only had the aging Black leftist climbed aboard but so had other key NAACP operatives, for example, James Egert Allen, president of the New York State Conference of NAACP branches. The gravamen of Williams' complaint was that Du Bois' signing of the call for a Crusade Against Lynching would lead some to believe that the Association supported Robeson's thrust, when, actually, the NAACP had its own committee that refused to join the Crusade. Williams was worried about the imputing of guilt by association with Robeson, an avowed believer in socialism. White was on all fours with Williams' opinion and did not hesitate to let Du Bois know. Du Bois felt it insane that in the face of ghastly mutilations of Blacks there would be roadblocks demarcated in the path of unity. He insisted that his endorsement of the Robeson-led effort "did not and could not have interfered with the NAACP program. The fight against mob law is the monopoly of no one person—no one organization." Besides, as he caustically indicated, the top brass of the Association did not bother to notify him about their antilynching effort.[8]

Williams intimated that in addition to political objections, he viewed the Crusade Against Lynching as akin to competition. This was another joker that popped up from time to time in the NAACP deck. They viewed the National Negro Congress (NNC) and the activities of "various Randolph organizations" with similar jaundice. The March on Washington Committee, the Lynn Committee to Abolish Segregation in the Armed Forces, and the Workers' Defense League were not viewed in practice as potential allies on an issue by issue basis. "They propose to duplicate the work of the NAACP in whole or in part" was how White put it to Thurgood Marshall—and this during the halcyon days of 1944. This also points up that in a manner that the Eastern European nations call "socialist emulation," the NAACP was spurred to greater heights by the existence of militant organizations attacking from the left, such as, the NNC.[9]

The left allergy of some of the Association's leadership reacted like ragweed in August in 1948, the year the Communist party directorship was put on trial. Time was to tell that this allergic reaction was not only to true blue reds but Progressive party activists as well. Du Bois was forced to react like a good soldier in telling Theodore Peck that he could not work more closely with the Henry Wallace campaign because of strictures.[10] But he then quickly put his finger in a loophole:

> If there could be a general meeting or a forum anywhere in which I could take part, I should be very glad to and to express my political opinions but I could not take part in a specific rally for any candidate.

Du Bois' persistent romance with the left infuriated many. And the Wallace campaign and the Southern Negro Youth Congress—two of his greater loves—rankled particularly. SNYC's assault on Jim Crow did not always meet the exacting standards of right-wing, racist anticommunists in the South. This led inexorably to a vicious attack on their ranks which made association with their cadre dangerous. This did not bar Du Bois, who admired and respected the Black activists and their spunk—particularly Esther Cooper Jackson, with whom he later founded the influential *Freedomways.* When Du Bois, in his *Chicago Defender* column, briefed Afro-America on this and more, tensions flared. His comparison of the origins of SNYC to the origins of the NAACP was notably galling to White.[11]

A similar objection was raised to Du Bois' contemplated signing of an antiwar statement in 1948 as Cold War hysteria reached belligerent proportions. Du Bois was executive board member of an initiating sponsor, the National Council of Arts, Sciences and Professions. Reluctantly, Du Bois told Harlow Shapley, "I do not, however, have the right to represent the NAACP officially" but agreed, with justifiable pessimism, to ask for White's endorsement. Du Bois was a leader of this talented coalition, NCASP. The response to these activities by the NAACP leaders was similar to the response to another Robeson-led venture: "The Administrative Committee, on May 24, 1948, directed me to write you that . . .

it disapproved your being an initiating sponsor of the March on Washington Movement for Civil Rights on June 2 . . . badly timed, contrary to the Association's strategy."[12]

It was precisely this legal strategy which was at issue, for Du Bois considered it insufficient. "The court cases are won but the whole social background is absolutely neglected." This strategy of the NAACP has also been questioned by others. The NAACP at that time was engrossed in more than litigation but litigation did play a preeminent role, as evidenced by the presence of Thurgood Marshall, William Hastie, Franklin Williams, Constance Baker Motley, and other lawyers in disproportionate number in the higher ranks of the NAACP. But one scholar has questioned the association's strategy in an area perceived to be a strength—the courts. Karen O'Connor has queried whether their tactics in administrating this strategy were wise given the conservative make-up of the court. Du Bois was quick to observe that Irene Morgan and her lawyers had won a juridical victory in 1946 on the question of segregated interstate bus travel—but this primitive throwback continued to persist. It should not be forgotten, as O'Connor reports, what the lack of the vote meant for the NAACP's limited "access to legislative or administrative arenas" which forced it "to concentrate its activities in the judicial arena." But the sort of militant direct action that Martin Luther King popularized and Robeson desired would have neatly sliced this gordian knot yet it was not viewed sanguinely by the more pallid NAACP strategies. The *Brown* v. *Board of Education* litigation "cost the NAACP over two hundred and fifty thousand dollars." It took two decades to win the restrictive covenant cases. Where Du Bois saw the militant rallying of popular support outside the courtroom as hand in glove with a militant defense inside the courtrooms (as his 1951 indictment and trial demonstrated), the Association has been criticized for deficiencies in the former area. Black lawyers were constantly harassed by white judges in the South and absences of visible demonstrations of mass strength cannot be discounted in explication. Du Bois saw the pointing up of the material interest that whites had in opposing racism as a *sine qua non* for any winning strategy. But "reddish" cadre, like Du Bois, were "black-baited" for unduly associating with whites (though this was unavoidable as the accusers' own records amply demonstrated), and Du Bois was balked on occasion when he wished to write on what many whites lose economically by racial discrimination.[13]

There was fear that Du Bois' influence and ideas would spread ineluctably if not damned. On an early 1946 lecture trip to California, Du Bois found himself telling San Francisco friend and NAACP leader Ethel Nance that because of pressure from on high; "I do not want to speak to branches of the NAACP. If, however, requests should come refer them directly to me." White particularly objected to his sowing the gospel in fertile NAACP territory—and elsewhere; he asked for a monthly list of Du Bois' speaking engagements whether at an Association branch or not.[14]

That Du Bois saw close coordination with the branches as a priority, complicated matters. Even Gloster Current, Director of Branches, and a leading redbaiter, conceded his value here. In closest touch with the grassroots of the right-wing NAACP directorate, Current was all too aware of the support in the regions for rejecting the straitjacketed NAACP structure. At the height of NAACP militance, and shortly after Du Bois had been hired, a resolution was submitted to the wartime conference by a number of branches. This broadly based initiative demanded an "amendment to NAACP constitution to allow branches greater political activity in order that members may more actively oppose both the Republican and Democratic parties, neither of which has lived up to the tenets of our constitutional democracy." This resolve could have been drafted by Du Bois himself. As for working with outcasts like Communists, they suggested that the Association should "disregard political affiliations and fight for those issues of paramount interest to our race in local, state and national affairs."[15]

The resolves of the NAACP annual conventions tracked Du Bois' militant footsteps. It was stressed in 1944 that "we seek the ending of imperialism," that "irrespective of party" the place for Blacks rested with those hewing to correct positions; the defeat of three members of the witch-hunting Dies Committee was hailed. In the summer of 1946, the resolutions adopted spoke distinctly in terms that Du Bois could have drafted, with ringing condemnation of colonialism and a call for freedom from India to Puerto Rico.[16]

The Progressive party was omnipresent politically at the 1948 NAACP conference in Wilkins' old home town, Kansas City, Missouri. The lead resolution spoke directly to the Du Bois/Wallace-White/Truman imbroglio:

> We uphold the right of any member or office to support the party or candidate of his choice. No member or officer of the NAACP should use or exploit his connection with the NAACP as a means of obtaining political office or preference.

This could be interpreted to be opposed to the White-Truman juggernaut recognized to be rambling through the convention. While a principal reason for Du Bois' ouster was his staunch refusal to play dead on his controversial United Nations petition, the conference foreshadowed Du Bois by calling on the American delegation at the United Nations to "reconsider its decision not to act upon the petition of the United Nations." The Mundt-Nixon bill was opposed, the abolition of HUAC was urged, and Taft-Hartley was condemned.[17]

For the first time in years there was no resolution on colonial peoples as such. The virtually rote resolution, reflecting *Color and Democracy,* on colonialism as a cause of war was conspicuously omitted. A doffing of the cap to prevalent tensions was marked by a veiled reference to certain "Big Powers" use of the "veto" in the United Nations Security Council; the United States was not the "big power" alluded to. The fact that, as ever, the liberal-left bloc in the branches tended to be more immersed in activism was marked by a resolve asking the branches "to consult with the National Office" before contributing or sending delegates to other organizations.[18]

There was opposition to this rightward line in the hustings, but the centralized control exercised by the executive secretary and certain board members was decisive. The self-perpetrating board liberally populated with fat cats and ideological biases was crucial in this process. The Faustian bargain entered into amounted to the Association higher-ups receiving a defined attitude and certain civil rights' concessions at home in exchange for steely eyed anticommunism abroad. The ousting of Du Bois in 1948 removed an impediment to this stampede; a stubborn voice that refused to stop insisting on peace, equality, and socialism at home and abroad was not stilled but moved.

CHAPTER 7

White on Black on Red

The Association's move, led by White, from militant anti-imperialism to virulent anticommunism, was a torturous path. In the heyday of Association militance, when membership rolls bulged, the NAACP was not shy about sparring in the political arena. The *Branch Bulletin* carried detailed listings of how members of Congress voted on major issues. There was no hesitation in attacking the seemingly eternal Dixiecrat-GOP alliance. The articles in the *Branch Bulletin* were not idle mumbling. Leslie Perry, who spearheaded this thrust from the Capitol, sounded a popular battle cry—to "elect better men to Congress"—after viewing the legislative knockouts inflicted by the 79th Congress. In a broad grapeshot attack on the GOP-Dixiecrat axis, Walter White told the branches that "the 1946 and 1948 elections will unquestionably be the most important in the history of America . . . no job you can do is more important than this. . . ." By 1948 those performing this important job were being persecuted by erstwhile advocates.[1]

There was an inordinate amount of pressure placed on the NAACP by anticommunists and led by Dixiecrats. Like the NAACP, the Communists opposed Jim Crow—which, like an associative law of mathematics, made the former equally red. This was no myth-induced chimera as evidenced by a flyer filed away by a NAACP staff member. On a sheet put out by Friends of Democracy on how to identify Communists, the association's name was placed besides two of the categories: "Continually receiving publicity in such Communist publications as the *Daily Worker* and *New Masses*"; and "arguing for a class society by pitting one group against another, putting special privileges ahead of community needs, as for example, claiming that labor has privileges but no responsibilities in dealing with management." The NAACP, which pitted one group of antiracists against another of racists, which put the privilege of Blacks being free of racism ahead of the racist community's needs, and which supported labor against management down the line was prime raw material for a witch-hunt.[2]

Thus, in March 1946, leading NAACP attorney and litigator Charles Houston worridly informed Springarn about racist Senator James Eastland of Mississippi basically accusing Hastie of being a "communist sympathizer" at confirmation hearings on his appointment as governor of the Virgin Islands.[3]

Particularly damaging and opinion molding in the anticommunist counterattack against the NAACP was the bile unleashed by the press. When Arthur Schlesinger, Jr., commented in *Life* magazine, the popular mass circulation magazine, that the Communist party was "sinking tentacles into the National Association for the Advancement of Colored People," it sent fear and trembling cascading through the New York office. Not to be left behind, *Newsweek* repeated the charges. White formally protested both smears at length but their conceptions dovetailed with the mood that was being fashioned. Indicative of the curiously mimetric nature that tends to arise in leading United States institutions was the fact that the Navy took up the cry in their "Communism in Action" pamphlet.[4]

As the climactic year of 1946 wound into 1947, the red scare attacks intensified. The New York office was not the only target. The California legislative committee headed by the former leftist Senator Jack Tenney created an outcry when he cast aspersions on the West Coast Regional Office and the state branches generally. Noah Griffin, regional secretary, harriedly told White about the "charges that had been made that the NAACP's ranks in California were being filled with communists." Legislative interest in the Association was not new. Martin Dies himself, Tenney's putative mentor, was fanatically concerned about Black Communists "infiltrating" Black organizations, even the Black church, and operating as a Black column in the "Trojan Horse": "Moscow realizes that it cannot revolutionize the United States unless the Negro can be won over to the communist cause." The interest expressed by politicians in NAACP affairs was not without effect. A flurry of interest also suddenly arose in NAACP branches about national policy on endorsement of political candidates. The San Francisco branch endorsed candidates for election, including Archie Brown, Communist write-in candidate for governor. The Boston Youth Council was investigated by the Association after it accepted a paid political advertisement from Communists. Representatives of the two major parties, Democratic and Replublican, were concerned about inroads made in the recently influential Black vote by another political party, the Communist Party. Du Bois, who eagerly co-operated with the Southern Negro Youth Congress, *New Masses,* National Council For American-Soviet Friendship, and other groups identified as "Communist Fronts," and who was the prime NAACP founder and most popular leader, gave credence, in certain eyes, to notions of Communist "infiltration of the NAACP."[5]

Rather quickly the charges of Communist "infiltration" of the NAACP was intoned as repeatedly as a popular song. Governor Kim Sigler of Michigan crowed that the Association was no more than a "communist front". The NAACP struck back with a hard-hitting press release but such an attack by the governor of a major industrial state was damaging. The charges that were being made were not just hot air without effect. White was forced to admonish both Attorney General Tom Clark and FBI Director J. Edgar Hoover after Dr. Herbert Marshall was refused selection as a member of a new five-man Slum Clearance and Development Agency in Washington, D.C. "His name was withdrawn after the FBI informed the Commissioner that Dr. Marshall had pinkish tendencies." The FBI was paradoxically not viewing the Association at all through rose colored glasses and "pinkish tendencies" were seen even in the opaque. The beating of one slave was enough to keep the entire plantation in line: "What has happened to Dr. Marshall may frighten a lot of less courageous Negroes [from] the fight for first class citizenship in America." White could have added that the fire aimed at the NAACP helped to keep other progressive-minded organizations in line.[6]

It was recognized by the NAACP that the public sector was critical in Black advancement, as evidenced by Black college graduates having trouble finding work except with the post office in urban centers. Clarence Mitchell sadly informed White of a letter received from a young man in Atlanta who, when applying for a post office job, was asked in his "loyalty test" if he belonged to a subversive organization known as the NAACP. Frank Barnes, militant president of the Santa Monica, California, branch, was suspended from his post office job on loyalty charges for organizing a picket line for jobs at a local Sears Roebuck store. In the charges filed pursuant to Executive Order 9835, it was alleged that he had been and was at that time "affiliated or sympathetic with an organization, association, movement, group, or combination of persons designated by the Attorney General as subversive." White insisted that a miscarriage of justice had been committed, but his words fell on ears more attuned to respecting the rights of employers rather than aggrieved colored employees. Finally the board, many of whose members fervently backed the Truman Administration, was forced to excoriate his regime in a strongly worded communique:[7]

> Charges of disloyalty based on flimsy and prejudiced information have been filed against colored government employees. . . . In each instance most of those cited have long records of vigorously fighting against segregation and discrimination in Federal Service itself. . . . At least five nationally known colored government employees have been charged with disloyalty on the basis of information assembled by the House Un-American Activities Committee and other questionable sources. The House Committee . . . is heavily dominated by John Rankin of Mississippi . . . not one of the more than 150,000 colored government employees throughout the country will be safe if the present trend continues.

They went on to ask Truman to review and rectify this situation. But their proposed remedy ironically highlighted the shortcomings of their approach. They limited their interventions to loyalty cases where "the whole charge or a part thereof" is based on factors such as race, NAACP membership, or membership in any coordinating group approved by the Association's national office. Euro-American members of the Association who supported the Progressive party of the former secretary of commerce and agriculture were particularly vulnerable under this formulation. In practice, so were Blacks of a similar category, particularly those college-educated government workers in northern urban centers who were in the forefront of NAACP militance. They were the first targets of the red scare, and the assumed object of protection outlined by this resolution. A grenade of anticommunism had been detonated in the NAACP by right-wing legislators and their supporters, and wounded many. During 1948, the year that Du Bois was ousted, it was becoming *de rigeur* for White to receive messages like the one he received from the Reverend John Brigham, a pastor in Sioux City, Iowa, who reported that at a meeting of the Sons of the American Revolution one "Milton Lory" denounced the NAACP as a "Communist Front Organization."[8]

But Association leaders picked up a similar grenade and tossed it into the rank and file. Even before the Cold War, there had been some trepidation within the leadership about associating with Communists. R. J. Simmons of the Philadelphia branch informed White in 1940 of his proposed anticommunist resolution pledging that "this organization . . . go on record as taking no part with public communistic activities whatsoever and that we renounce and condemn the same on the part of any member of the race." Singing a similar tune, Wilkins strongly advised a member "against any delegate in the Association's name attending Free Browder Congress."[9]

Yet it must be stressed, and will be demonstrated, that the tremendous pressure exerted on the Association, and the Black community generally, helps to explain, in large part, the rabid internal anticommunism that created a frenzy. The November 1948 resolution of the board singled out John Rankin, congressman from Mississippi, for particular attack. With the anti-Hitler war substantially discrediting racist ideology, Rankin, Bilbo, Eastland, and others found it useful to score Black activists as being as red as their blood in their campaigns of bigotry. Blacks and their organizations were an early and repeated target of the red scare offensive. Alan Harper mentions that in the Eleventh Congressional District of Indiana, "128 of 139 postal employees questioned by loyalty investigators . . . had been Jews and Negroes." Philip Foner observes that "the black tobacco workers were the first to feel the sting of the CIO's red-baiting drive" and notes that 65 percent of longshoremen in the International Longshoremen and Warehousemen's Union "screened" from the waterfront for decidedly "pinkish tendencies" were not white but Black. Black Communists were disproportionately hit. Richard Freeland records that Ferdinand Smith, Black communist leader of the National Maritime Union—a key ally of Du Bois—was one of the first victims of the Justice Department's effort to deport Cold War opponents of alien descent.

Indeed, it is no longer possible to adequately comprehend the Cold War itself without comprehending its sharp racist edge.[10]

The Association and its leadership did not go willingly into that dark night of anticommunism. The red scare offensive was launched in 1946 and accelerated in 1947, and even during the latter year a good fight was put up against the onslaught. White's opinion was that for the Attorney General's subversive list to be complete, it should include the Ku Klux Klan, Kingdom Gospel Institute, and the America First Party of the Fascist Gerald L. K. Smith. In the spring of 1947, White put his finger on the paradoxical conundrum of anticommunism: "If we go around denying that we are Communists, there will be suspicious people who will say where there is smoke there must be fire."[11]

It could be argued that an event a few days before was connected to White's insight. A regional conference of 237 delegates representing 85,000 association members from the deep south convened in Charleston, South Carolina, and the "delegates [went] on record as opposed to communism or communistic tactics." This resolution did not emerge from the North and West where Black-red activities were more extensive but from the Deep South where southern racists, scrambling to mold a new ideological weapon from the ashes of Hitlerism, found the red scare congenial and Southern NAACP members, feeling the heat strong and hot, were quicker to give organized expression to anticommunism.[12]

Even this organized expression was not an unqualified endorsement of anticommunism. Their lawyer-like resolution did not root for the red scare with vigor but conceded that because of pressure generated, "we feel it necessary" to make the obligatory anticommunist vow.[13]

Wilkins was aware of this general phenomenon. Though flames of the red scare were licking at him, he did not hesitate to extend his democratic embrace. He reproved Milton Morray, president of the embattled American Newspaper Guild, after he had raised the familiar charge that the NAACP was dominated by Communists:

> We have no bar to any person who subscribes to the principles and program of the NAACP becoming a member. We do not ask his political, racial or religious affiliations. We ask only that prospective members subscribe to the principles of the NAACP. Naturally, Communists, Socialists, Democrats, Pro-

> hibitionists, Free Thinkers and what have you are members of our Association.

The position of Du Bois was similar to Wilkins', that "Democrats, Prohibitionists, Free Thinkers and what have you" could and should be aligning with the Association.[14]

This rationale was reflected in a mid-1947 *Crisis* editorial entitled, with exasperation, "The D.A.R. Again." The Daughters of the American Revolution were condemned for attacking communism at their convention while remaining mute about the "barring of Negro artists from Constitution Hall." The editorial sardonically issued a veiled warning and implicitly sought unity with the harried Communist party: "Isn't it tragic that some of our Negroes are rumored to be bending an attentive ear to the Communists who go around preaching the subversive doctrine of equality and no discrimination."[15]

This rationale was reflected in the branches' voice, the *Branch Bulletin.* Leslie Perry, Washington lobbyist, was unequivocal: "The Ku Klux Klan and similar native American fascist groups enjoyed a free hand to spread their germs of hate and terror while the Dick Tracys in Congress trailed down New Dealers and 'reds.' " These right-wing members of Congress were branded as "servant of the few" and their supporters as "high financed lobbyists for the real estate interests" who "scuttled rent control and housing for veterans." HR–3813, which created the Loyalty Review Board, and related agencies was harpooned:[16]

> Disloyal conduct according to the standards of the Civil Service Commission and the FBI has, in the past, included the expression by white persons of views favorable to the Negro, or their entertainment of Negro friends in their home.

The November board meeting of the Association found the Association still battling anticommunism, though their tactics were questionable. A telegram was sent to Truman and the Civil Service Commission at White's suggestion, asking that there be a Black appointed to the Federal Loyalty Board. The telegram indicated that the desperate plight of Blacks "caused" Negroes to join organizations which promoted action against job discrimination and which may later be classified as "subversive". This, of course, struck a revealing chord in observing how reds or "subversives" might be in the vanguard of the struggle against racism on the job. But the divergent tendencies of the leadership was seen in their response to branch ties with groups of "pinkish tendencies". It was voted that "no branch take a position on any matter involving national or foreign affairs that has not been decided upon by the Association or the Annual Conference or that is against the position of the Association or the Annual Conference." This reining in of branches of necessity impacted the basic civil rights issues that were the NAACP's speciality. For it induced a passivity and reluctance on the part of branches to aggressively handle job discrimination and other basic issues of concern to Blacks. There were powerful forces opposing the NAACP, and fighting with their left arm tied behind their back was not a sure path to success.[17]

The pressure to back the Marshall Plan, initiated in 1947, was important in explicating NAACP leadership adherence to Cold War dictates. At the same board meeting where a proposal was floated to add a Black to the Federal Loyalty Board, a wire was received from Henry Stimson asking White to serve on a Citizens Committee For the Support of the Marshall Plan. There was spirited debate on this controversial point; it was well recognized that there was widespread opposition within the ranks to this foreign policy departure. There were objections made but White was allowed to serve with the understanding "that we do not consider the Marshall Plan perfect." Shortly thereafter, *Crisis* editorials that once sounded the clarion against the Cold War as a dominant theme had a change in emphasis. "The way the Communists took over Czechoslovakia" was seen as a warning to Blacks. It was suggested that Communists not be banned from the NAACP "but to out-work them and out-vote them in meetings." Symptomatic of the pervasively corrosive political atmosphere was the editorial's espousal of ideas of its chief adversaries. It was strongly implied that those Euro-Americans most opposed to Jim Crow and racism were Communists and should be carefully watched in the branches. Naturally, this heavy-handed approach caused a wail of protest and was "corrected" in a subsequent editorial. But this episode was indicative of how far anticommunism had reached since apparently there was sentiment for routing white members of the Association—who often were influential and sizeable financial contributors—in a spurious anticommunist crusade.[18]

Support for the Marshall Plan also signalled a shift away from the fiery language of old about colonialism being a prime cause of war. There was a shift to accommodation with the precepts of United States foreign policy. White and William Hastie, who was to become the top official in the Virgin Islands, "both agreed that the Virgin Islands is a laboratory experiment indicative of a more enlightened colonial policy, which makes it unique in the light of our participation in the formation of an American Committee on West Indian Freedom." Du Bois' plan for anticolonial pamphlets, manifestoes, and an all-around offensive were balked. Yet White found time to conduct an almost single-handed fight to obtain the approval of the State Department for a loan to Haiti, and not so much because of benign concern for the huddled masses of the economically depressed Caribbean island but, as White pointed out, "that one of the advantages of such a loan would be that it would help to answer the charges being made in other part of the world that the United States has imperialist designs on smaller and weaker countries, particularly if they are inhabited by persons of dark skin." Formerly, the conventional wisdom was that the United States ineluctably had such imperialist designs, but now there was an abrupt recasting of wisdom and past ideas no longer held sway. This led inexorably to an attempt to hamstring the resentment to these policies within the branches.[19]

The desire for Cold War conformity, particularly as it concerned United States foreign policy, had immediate impact on the branches and within the board. A frenzied hysteria was generated that handcuffed the Association during a time when their opponents were experiencing heightened political organization, and as signs of a Fascist-minded Dixiecrat party began to emerge throughout the South. Not surprisingly, the most sustained concern with Communists in the NAACP was initiated in the spring of 1946. Wilkins fretted constantly about Communist party activity, not just within the branches but outside the branches as well. Just as he and others were concerned in an invidious sense with the growth of movements led by Robeson and Randolph, he was also unhappy when the Washington, D.C. branch did not picket the United States Senate on issues of moment to Black veterans when the "Veterans Committee Against Discrimination (which some people suspect is a C.P. front) had done it." In this lengthy memo to White he was most concerned about the Communists stealing the thunder of the Association and Blacks' imagination along with it.[20]

Alfred Baker Lewis was not shy about pursuing a witch hunt. With barely concealed asperity, he knocked Springarn for supporting a nomination of John Hammond to the board despite the fact that the nominee had been a member of the Young Communist League in college. His somewhat bizarre logic was that since he was not now in the Communist party, but was not being attacked by the party, then he must be suspect politically. But as Lewis inadvertently confessed, his sudden concern was precipitated more by the prevailing political atmosphere than weariness about pinkish pedigree: "Now that Russia's course is more and more openly imperialist . . . it therefore is necessary for genuine progressives to be on their guard more than ever before."[21]

But Lewis' paralogisms were a mirror image of a rabid preoccupation with "Communist infiltration" of the branches. Horace Mann Bond, president of Lincoln University, spoke from his vantage point of the leftist American Youth for Democracy chapter disbanding and "they have moved enthusiastically into the NAACP and taken it over. It occurs to me that similar tactics may face you in other localities" A few months later, in early 1947, White felt compelled to tell Morris Ernst that "out of 1497 branches, youth councils and college chapters, we have found only eight instances where there seems to have been an attempt by Communists to gain control of these units." But days later evidence was circulating in NAACP headquarters that White's alleged relaxed attitude was not shared universally. Ruby Hurley, NAACP official, informed White that chapters targeted by the Communists included those at Cornell University, University of Wisconsin, Lincoln University, Cleveland Youth Council, Los Angeles Youth Council, and other chapters in Riverside, Vallejo, and San Diego; "since it is apparent that the Communists are going underground, we can reasonably expect them to get into our groups" Note that the alleged targets were in the North, disproportionately within comparatively liberal campuses and youth councils while the racists pressuring for ideological conformity were disproportionately in the South. The campuses had especially strong white memberships.[22]

As White implicitly revealed, he and others were looking over their shoulder at these southern racists as they conducted the anticommunist crusade. White felt it necessary to reemphasize that "the Annual Conference and the Board, and *no one else* determine policy for the NAACP" (emphasis in original). But the point was that White could repeat and prove this obvious point into infinity and men like Bilbo and Talmadge would continue to paint the Association red. Their aim was to destabilize the NAACP, drive friendly whites from it on the grounds that they were likely to be reds, and intimidate Blacks from joining on similar grounds. Wittingly or unwittingly the NAACP witch-hunt played right into the hands of Bilbo and Talmadge, as they attempted the nonsensical task of extinguishing an anticommunist fire fueled by racism with that same flame, while ironically mouthing Black nationalist rationales that were to arise again in the 1960s.[23]

The actual extent of so-called Communist infiltration, or democrat infiltration or Free-thinker infiltration of the NAACP is difficult to precisely determine. White did not reveal the exegesis that led to the revelation that there had been eight instances by the Communist party to "gain control" of branches. Maynard Dickerson, president of the Ohio State Conference of Branches, may have been a source. He told White early in 1947 that in the branch in the steel mill town of Youngstown, "there are probably 20 Communists or their sympathizers in branch membership and a less number of Trotskyists." He added with no delight that "the Communists were bending every effort to project their ideologies." With utmost concern, White reported "an almost complete taking over of the Executive Committee of the branch by the Communists" in the virtually lily-white Salt Lake City branch. Appropriate action was taken but the winner of these antired, antiwhite, and, ultimately, antiBlack purges were men like Bilbo and Talmadge. The Communists, like any political party seriously interested in attaining power, maintained an intense concern in NAACP affairs. Aware of the explosion in Association membership, particularly of workers from the auto, steel, aircraft, shipyard, packing, and tobacco industries during the war years, the Communists' policy of industrial concentration meant that Black workers in urban centers like Detroit, Chicago, the San Francisco Bay Area, Cleveland, and so on, who in many instances were NAACP members, were a top priority for recruitment. Thus, Black Communist leader Henry Winston, sensing the gathering opposition to this Black-red tie, recommended a strengthening of the "forces of unity and integrity in the National Board" and that in general "support be given to the NAACP." Adam Clayton Powell, Jr., knowledgeable about Communist party activity in building the CIO unions, a prime engine for Black progress, observed that "there is no group in America including the Christian church that practices racial brotherhood one-tenth as much as the Communist Party." While Communists were far-reaching in their attacks against racism and were a natural ally of the NAACP, their out-stretched hand of cooperation was scorned.[24]

This turning of the back was not without consequence on policy. A long-standing goal of the NAACP, and civil rights advocates generally, was to reduce congressional representation of the states, for example, South Carolina, Alabama, Mississippi, where Blacks were denied the right to vote; this was explicitly demanded of Congress. This was consonant with and obligatory pursuant to the Fourteenth Amendment. Eugene Dennis, Communist party general secretary, raised as a point in his appeal against conviction for contempt of Congress that the HUAC was illegally constituted because of the fact that its members, John Rankin of Mississippi, for example, sat in Congress in violation of the Fourteenth Amendment. Dennis' appeal made justiciable and a live case in controversy, a critical NAACP objective. But the association leadership abjectly refused to ally with the Communists for their long-standing goal, though the Communist party's thrust meshed neatly with their aims. Thurgood Marshall, when confronted with the request of Arnold Donawa and the Committee to Enforce the Fourteenth Amendment, scribbled feebly in the margin, "I do not oppose form letter to the Chief Justice of the Supreme Court." As it turned out, due to prodigious effort, the NAACP and the Communist party were failing to connect and unite. Black Communist leader Benjamin Davis at one point exclaimed of his party's "failure to give main attention to aiding and supporting the NAACP." Evidence why arose when the executive secretary of the New York City Communist party requested that White send him information on the United Nations petition organized by Du Bois. White told his secretary to place this correspondence in the "file no reply" cabinet.[25]

The practical impact of Black shunning red was crystallized by the controversial Hollywood Ten case of popular screenwriters and directors coming under fire from HUAC and other arms of the state. The Los Angeles branches had long been a bulwark of material and political support of the NAACP and figures from the film community played a prominent role in the case. Thus when Herbert Biberman of the ten asked for Du Bois' support, it came willingly. Initially, the NAACP was in accord with this view. A nationally circulated press release quoted White's rebuke of J. Parnell Thomas, HUAC's New Jersey leader. White knew that Trumbo, John Howard Lawson—Communist leaders in Hollywood—and the other defendants were singular in their positive portrayals of Blacks on the silver screen. Thus, he followed this up by sharply instructing Jack Warner, Universal Studio, and others in the film community:

> the "communists" issue is used as a means of expressing vicious anti-semitism, just as in 1941 it was the chief motivation of the Senate probe of the motion picture industry for making anti-Nazi pictures.

White's acute historical sense was also projected in his analysis of this critical case in the *Chicago Defender.* White had tipped his hand by conceding to Warner and others that he was adamantly opposed to "totalitarianism," which was left undefined, and communism. Shifting the balance from opposition to the persecution of artists to the safer opposition to totalitarianism was not impossible. But as late as November 8, 1947, White courageously declared:

> microscopic number of Communists have been industriously trying to propagandize Hollywood for a long time. But so has the Legion of Decency, the National Association of Manufacturers . . . and many other non-Communist organizations . . . Certain others in Hollywood who are viciously anti-Negro have been quick to charge those who want to see better roles for Negroes as being "communist."

These comments were prescient and perceptive, and could be applied not just to the film industry but to virtually every industry; getting better jobs for Negroes, as the FEPC fight was to show, was a casualty of the red scare.[26]

White did not consistently adhere to his words. Earlier in the year he was quite reluctant to join the Conference For Free Expression in the American Arts to Build the Cultural Division of the National Negro Congress. This may have been due to organizational jealousies but considering that Paul Robeson, Aaron Copland, Oscar Hammerstein II, Langston Hughes, Fannie Hurst, Garson Kanin, Rockwell Kent, Eve Le Gallienne, Alain Locke, Robert Motherwell, Zero Mostel, S. J. Perelman, Jerome Robbins, Thornton Wilder, and other artistic luminaries were involved, ignoring this meeting was hard to justify. Eventually this shunning of potential allies cropped up in the Hollywood Ten struggle after an anticommunist barrage by HUAC. Leslie Perry of the Washington office vainly tried to keep a finger in the dike by urging White and the Association to "do everything possible to head off the defeat contempt citations . . . because of the serious threat involved to freedom of speech, thought expression and political belief." He suggested that John Howard Lawson, in particular, should be aided and that the branches should flood Washington with telegrams opposing contempt citations. But White, despite his valiant words days earlier, would have none of it: "I question whether this is properly a matter for the Association to take action on" because "there is no doubt that some of the men who have been cited are unquestionably members of the Communist Party." After periodically telling the Black readers of the *Chicago Defender* that "getting better jobs for Negroes" was a primary consideration in this battle, White sheepishly declared that after discussing the matter with Spingarn and Marshall it was decided that the "kind of action suggestion" for the branches was "somewhat outside [the] scope of [the] Association's program."[27]

Getting better jobs was one possible goal of the long struggle for a Fair Employment Practices Committee (FEPC). But it ran aground during the red scare. Even before March 1946, the National Council For FEPC tended toward excluding Communists, or at least so Wilkins told Black board member Judge Hubert T. Delany. The judge, a board member who was frequently found in Du Bois' corner, took strong exception to all this:

> I have been definitely informed that the National Council for FEPC would not work with Sidney Hillman and Sidney Hillman is no Communist . . . furthermore, I think the time has come when the NAACP and its officers and directors who still indulge in red-baiting have got to put an end to it. . . . I think that any organization attempting to pass legislation that is as important as this legislation should accept the whole-hearted cooperation of all groups which sincerely want to see the bill passed and will lend their earnest effort in that direction. I have never advocated working with Communists but I have always maintained as I do now maintain that among the people whom I know and among the organizations with which I have worked closely there are no Communistic groups which can get in and "dictate strategy at all times." The strategy for the passage of the Permanent FEPC bill should properly be outlined by those progressive forces in labor and the NAACP and other

> similar organizations. If this is done with a will and if we can forget red-baiting for a while, I do not see there would be any danger of anyone dictating our strategy except those of us who really want to see the bill passed.

Delany's sage advice was incontestably accurate and designed as a rebuke to Wilkins' anticommunist tendencies—tendencies that plagued not only the FEPC fight but labor problems closer to home. Delany also rebuked the association's second in command "for the defensive attitude that you take toward unionization of the office and dealing with the union representative, gives one the feeling that you are not happy that the union has come to our office." Delany was not alone in the NAACP hierarchy when he announced to Wilkins "I sharply disagree with you in principle" on FEPC (and anticommunism) but their voices were often drowned out.[28]

The National Council for a Permanent FEPC was wracked with dissension. It was a high-powered group with A. Philip Randolph serving as co-chair and Senators Robert Wagner and NAACP ally Arthur Capper serving as honorary chairs. The weighty authority did not bar internal wrangling that, along with right-wing obstruction, helped to slow down perhaps the most important legislative effort of Afro-America in the cancerous area of job discrimination. The tendency of Wilkins to exclude certain groups on questionable grounds, organizations much tamer than the Communists, no doubt contributed to its inability to affect the enactment of this legislation. "Everyone has recognized that one of the prime weaknesses of the National Council For a Permanent FEPC was the fact that it was a socialist committee directed by A. Philip Randolph."[29]

With Wilkins and others fanning the anticommunist flames so vigorously, it was preordained that it would ignite in other circles. Southern and nonsouthern elites castigated the FEPC on anticommunist grounds that weakened the overall struggle; by going along with the prevailing concensus, the NAACP leaders strengthened the very forces they were ostensibly striving to weaken. This old red herring, often spawned by Wilkins himself, also haunted local FEPC tussles. Such was the case in industrial Michigan where job segregation was epidemic. Gloster Current was told, "I am sure as I am alive that FEPC is dead for this session of the legislature . . . mainly because the Governor and the legislature don't want to do anything and have found the Commie issue a good smoke-screen."

The Michigan press would have supported FEPC "if they could do so without seeming to be on the same side with the communists."[30]

Gloster Current was a principal player in anticommunist politics in Detroit. In 1945 he attended the conference that established the left-center World Federation of Democratic Youth (WFDY). He reported favorably on this meeting where Soviet input was substantial. He went so far as to lash "disgruntled elements in Britain who did not participate [and] labeled the conference 'communistic,' a familiar tactic used to discredit." He acknowledged Communist participation but was insistent that "the aims of the World Federation of Democratic Youth are laudable and are the aims of all of us." His report on the Soviet delegation's activities was favorable and urged that the Association collaborate with WFDY.[31]

Despite this, Du Bois was criticized soundly by White for adopting a similar posture on the WFDY meet. "I was disconcerted at Du Bois' reference to Miss Esther Cooper and his failure to make any mention of Gloster Current, the delegate from the NAACP to the world youth conferance" Contrary to Current, White was hostile: "You know that we suspected at the beginning that this youth conference and particularly the American delegation might be a communist front group and Mr. Current's analysis of the delegation at the 4-day training period they had before sailing bore out our suspicions" Current may have been taking a different stance than behind the scenes; perhaps the temperate political climate dictated this apparent hypocritical opportunism. White was vitriolic in denouncing the good friend of Du Bois, "Miss Cooper, the delegate from the Southern Negro Youth Congress, long recognized as a Communist front organization." White was so upset with all this that he formally requested that Du Bois alter his published references to Current and Esther Cooper.[32]

There were complaints in the branches about the tightly centralized structure, the self-perpetuating board, and why such a high percentage of membership fees should go to the national office. There were complaints in the branches about the entire panoply of Truman administration policies. Frequently these campaigns were led by progressive, antired scare leaders like the Reverend Charles Hill of Detroit and Dr. Carlton Goodlett of San Francisco. The internal witch-hunt within the NAACP may have been sincerely motivated but coincidentally or not one major result was the purging of those opposed to White-Truman policies or their being placed on the defensive. This battle was a necessary precondition to the sacking of Du Bois. It disarmed his potential allies and served as a model when the time came to oust the NAACP founder. There were contrary trends. Leslie Perry of the Washington office continually attacked the unholy alliance between reactionary Republicans and Dixiecrats. He denounced HUAC for ignoring the KKK. This was more than a straw in the wind. The internal attack on Du Bois and his ideological confreres weakened the NAACP and paved the way for racist attacks on the Black community, generally with a sharp anticommunist edge.[33]

CHAPTER 8

Human Rights—and Wrongs

The National Negro Congress petition to the United Nations, and the massive stir it created, helped to generate invidiousness within the NAACP leadership. The NNC's effort to internationalize the question of United States racism, to bring it before the world community as a threat to international peace and security, had wide impact. NAACP attorney Charles Houston spoke favorably of the petition. And as John Hope Franklin has pointed out, "the new stance of the United States government that sought to improve its racial policies in order to win support from [Africans] in the continuing rivalry with the communist bloc" meant that probing the sensitive underbelly of United States racism was bound to embarrass the Truman administration and conceivably lead to concessions, such as, establishing a civil rights commission or banning Jim Crow in the armed forces.[1]

These typically diverse considerations meant that Du Bois' initiative to introduce a United Nations petition in this area would be facilitated to a degree, though the rapidly dropping political mercury also had an effect. Further, the foundation for this submission to the United Nations had been laid in his positively received *Color and Democracy.* The militant atmosphere combined with the challenge of the NNC thrust meant that in August 1946, when Du Bois formally proposed to White that a petition be submitted, there was relatively speedy approval. By September it had been sanctioned by the board. They were persuaded by Du Bois' rationale: "The necessity of a document of this sort is emphasized by the fact that other groups of people, notably the Indians of South Africa, the Jews of Palestine, the Indonesians and others are making similar petitions . . . . It would be, I am sure, an omission not easily to be explained if the NAACP did not make a petition and statement of this sort." Like dominoes falling, the high administrative brass signed on. "I approve the proposal heartily," Wilkins enthused and White, Ruby Hurley, Leslie Perry, and key board member Channing Tobias concurred.[2]

With typically efficient haste Du Bois set in motion this momentous project. On August 25 he consulted with United Nations Secretary General Trygvie Lie on the substantive procedures of filing a petition. He enlisted the editorial assistance of such luminaries as Ralph Bunche, William Hastie, Rayford Logan, Earl Dickerson, and others. This work, *An Appeal to the World: A Statement on the Denial of Human Rights to Minorities in the Case of Citizens of Negro Descent in the United States of America and an Appeal to the United Nations for Redress,* despite its lengthy title, was a tightly written ninety-four-page indictment covering historical, legal, political, economic, and related matters. Unavoidably, those who ruled the United States came under heavy fire.[3]

Du Bois recognized that the success of the petition absolutely pivoted on the amount of domestic and international support that could be generated for it—a posture somewhat at variance with the NAACP leadership's practice. Hundreds of organizations were solicited and massive support was obtained. Du Bois did not flinch about seeking the endorsement of the NNC, which gave its approval. The Black fraternity Kappa Alpha Psi, Negro Newspaper Publishers Association, National Medical Association, National Bar Association, and a host of other Black groups signed on. D. V. Jemison, president of what may have been the largest Black organization, the National Baptist Convention, endorsed it; so did W. H. Jernagin, director of the Washington bureau of the National Fraternal Council of Negro Churches. Dr. C. B. Powell, publisher of the Black weekly *Amsterdam News* and Adam Clayton Powell, Jr., co-chairs of the Non-Partisan Interfaith Citizens Committee, after a mass meeting of nearly 3,000, ratified the petition.[4]

Du Bois did not shun the Black left and welcomed the Council on African Affairs and Southern Negro Youth Congress aboard. He also consulted with Noah Griffin, James Egert Allen, president of the New York State Conference of NAACP Branches, George

Parker, president of Phi Beta Sigma, and the Black fraternity Alpha Phi Alpha. Dutton Ferguson, editor of the decidedly non-leftist journal of the National Urban League was effusive in acclaiming the petition. Mary McLeod Bethume was equally impressed. Her colleague in leadership of Black women, Mrs. D. S. Smith, president of the fifty-year-old National Association of Colored Women, agreed to cooperate. Mae Downs of the leading Black sorority asserted that the petition "has the unqualified approval of Delta Sigma Theta." Du Bois was instrumental in galvanizing and channeling this torrent of support. He organized and spurred the organization of mass meetings in support of the petition, such as the packed October 5, 1946, meeting at Harlem's famous Schomburg Library.[5]

Before and after the filing of the petition, Du Bois closely coordinated his efforts with the trade union movement. Henry Lee Moon, who later became a top NAACP official, on behalf of the CIO Political Action Committee, early in the process agreed to cooperate with the NAACP. In fact, his only criticism was that the submission did not go far enough. Willard Townsend, International President of the United Transport Service Employees of America—and perhaps the nation's leading Black labor leader—expressed similar interest. The CIO unions were especially supportive and the National CIO Committee to Abolish Discrimination spearheaded their effort.[6]

Even William Green, president of the American Federation of Labor, and one not known for backing anti-imperialist thrusts, sent Du Bois a list of unions "in order to help you secure endorsement of the petition." Such high-level support had a ripple effect among comparable strata. Carl Van Doren endorsed the petition as did Senator Arthur Capper.[7]

Though the amount of domestic support the petition received was formidable, it could well be argued that equally important, or more so, was the substantial international backing it received. With the Truman administration embroiled in a Cold War and in search of allies—particularly in an increasingly colored world—allegations about deprivations of human rights of racial minorities did not go over well in Washington. The leading work on civil rights and the Truman administration acknowledges that initiatives such as the Du Bois petition, pushed the White House and Congress toward a posture more favorable to Blacks. Not the least reason for this was the "petition [which] created an international stir as the foreign press and foreign governments gave it great attention. The document also had an impact at home." The petition made quite a splash in the colonial world. Padmore related, "I have seen a number of colonial newspapers with a report of the resolution which you sent to UNO claiming representation there for the colonial peoples." This was not accidental as Du Bois consciously sought to bring his petition to the eyes of the world. His goal, as he expressed it, was to have "this book report printed eventually in English, French, Russian, Spanish, Portugese and Chinese."[8]

The petition received wide endorsement abroad from among others, the Trades Union Congress of Jamaica, Jomo Kenyatta of the Kikuyu Central Association of Kenya, Caribbean Labor Congress, Kenyan African Union, and the National Council of Nigeria and Cameroons. Nnamdi Azikiwe of this latter organization threw the powerful support of his forces behind the petition "without any qualification." Like Kenyatta, Azikiwe, after some travail, was to become the leader of his nation. Another future leader of an African nation, Kwame Nkrumah, reported that the organization he then headed, the West African National Secretariat, unanimously approved the petition; the same came from C. Matinga, President-General of the Nyasland African Congress. One of the few independent African nations, Liberia, lent its voice to Du Bois' effort. A similar statement was made by both Ken Hill, vice-chair of the Trades Union Congress of Jamaica and Joseph France, general secretary of the St. Kitts-Nevis Trades and Labor Union.[9]

The support for the petition was not limited to Africans in the diaspora. India, a nation whose sons and daughters resided in great numbers in racist South Africa, weighed in heartily in support. As Madame V. L. Pandit of the Indian delegation told Du Bois, "I shall certainly do what I can [to] help you place this before the Assembly of the United Nations or the Economic and Social Council."[10]

A number of other delegations indicated they would give the petition "sympathetic consideration," as the secretary general of the Pakistani delegation put it. The secretary of the Polish delegation promised to accord the petition "full consideration" after reviewing it. In a similar vein were the responses of Egypt, Ethiopia, Belgium, Haiti, Mexico, Norway, China, and the Soviet Union; the Dominican Republic's permanent representative saluted Du Bois for his labor on the United Nations petition, and he was not alone.[11]

The assistance of these nations was valuable in bringing the petition before the international community. Their visibility in this area was difficult to ignore and helps to explain the steady stream of press coverage, in the United States and abroad, thus marking its importance. The *Des Moines Register* noted that "it has accomplished its purpose of arousing interest in discrimination." Hugh Smythe, Du Bois' chief aide after Irene Diggs departed and later a professor of social sciences at Brooklyn College, did a comprehensive survey of press reaction. He found that the *New York Herald Tribune* "covered it fully" and "featured it in their largest circulation issues, the Sunday edition." Associated Press and United Press International "both carried notice . . . on their wire reports." Reporters for Greek, Russian, French, Italian, Indian, Danish, Chinese, English, and Norwegian newspapers requested petitions so as to do stories.[12]

Editorial reaction was revealing. As Smythe phrased it, reaction was "generally favorable, although some showed displeasure." The *San Francisco Chronicle* was puzzled by the petition. The *Morgantown Post* was displeased. Typical of Black press reaction was the enthusiastic response of the *Chicago Defender.* Ben Davis, in the *Daily Worker,* expressed the unanimously ecstatic viewpoint of Communists and the left. Both the *New York World Telegram* and *New York Post* spoke positively.[13]

The New York Times, the so-called newspaper of record, covered the petition and its aftermath extensively. One of their few Black reporters, George Streator, quoted at length from the petition, for example, the portion that said, "not Stalin and Molotov but Bilbo and Rankin" threaten United States national security. Similar articles were printed in the *Nation, Crisis,* and *New Republic.* Bruce Bliven, of this latter liberal publication, told White privately that the petition was a "magnificent historic document. The information in it ought to have the widest possible publicity."[14]

Not unexpectedly, all responses from the press were not glowing. The *Morgantown Post* of West Virginia blasted the NAACP for alienating "public support" and "furnishing Soviet Russia with new ammunition to use against us." This was a charge Du Bois repeatedly had to answer. The southern journalist Jonathan Daniels, who was also a member of the United Nations subcommission on Discrimination and Protection of Minorities, issued a criticism similar to the *Post*'s. Du Bois abrasively responded with his own view:[15]

> The NAACP is not "defending Russia" or anybody else; it is trying to get men like Mr. Daniels to stand up and be counted for the decent treatment of Negroes in America. . . . The Russian proposal ought to have had the wholehearted cooperation of American liberals.

The fact that it was the Soviet Union that brought the NAACP petition before the United Nations caused consternation in many besides Mr. Daniels. This was apparent in the widely covered speech of Attorney General Tom Clark before the National Association of Attorneys General, where he candidly admitted that he was "humiliated" by the Du Bois-Soviet Union collaboration. Nevertheless, his concrete response was to enlarge and strengthen the Civil Rights Section of the Justice Department, thus reinforcing the notion that this kind of collaboration was eminently useful. Du Bois was forced to go to the Soviets because of the refusal of the United States delegation to be helpful. Du Bois attended the first meeting of the Commission of Human Rights, escorted by Ralph Bunche, the director of the Division of Trusteeship. The petition was handed over to John Humphrey, director of the Commission on Human Rights, who was asked to take action on the petition. But Humphrey was unable. Nonetheless, he added that the commission was formulating "an International Bill of Rights" and was drawing up for the United Nations "clearer definitions" of "human rights and fundamental freedoms"; surprisingly, he asked the NAACP to continue its efforts, noting that the Human Rights Commission would be meeting soon and that the "subcommission on the prevention of discrimination and the protection of minorities will meet for the first time on November 24." Du Bois took the cue and engaged in intense lobbying but the subcommission voted down the proposal made by the Soviets to investigate discrimination against Blacks; the vote was 4–1 with the United States delegate Jonathan Daniels voting no and seven nations abstaining.[16]

It was not overly surprising that the subcommission would vote down this proposal since there was opposition within the NAACP's own ranks. Du Bois felt that White and others were unsettled by the frank exposé of racism in the United States and the fact that the principal Cold War antagonist—the Soviet Union—was sponsoring the petition. He complained directly to White about what he perceived as foot dragging and stalling on the printing of the petition and attempts to alter it. Uncomfortably feeling the heat from the right, White testily termed Du Bois' allegation "utterly without foundation [and] is additionally annoying in view of the fact that I had to spend most of the past two days answering the attack by George Schuyler in Plain Talk on the petition that your being on the editorial board of the New Masses makes the NAACP a Communist Front organization because of the presentation of this petition." Begun in the afterglow of the United States-Soviet collaboration from 1941–1945, Du Bois' petition became bogged down in the quagmire of Cold War politics.[17]

Complicating the entire process was Eleanor Roosevelt, who was a member of the United Nations Economic and Social Council in addition to being a board member of the NAACP. In attempting to get the petition before the international community, Du Bois beseeched her to help. When informed by Du Bois that "one or two . . . nations had expressed the possibility of putting item on agenda," Roosevelt tried to discourage him saying that it would be embarrassing and would only be grist for the Soviet mill. Du Bois did not allow this meeting to deter him as he fired off the petition to her requesting that she intervene with Trygvie Lie to get it before the Economic and Social Council. Du Bois was not startled when she did not reply and simply sent her a more strongly worded note. White was aware of these developments, as he was forwarded copies of this correspondence.[18]

This conglomeration of events surrounding the petition played a principal role in greasing the skids for Du Bois' departure. Bringing the ugly sore of United States racism before the eyes of the world was bound to be viewed with enmity in Washington, where the State Department was vieing with the Soviets for the hearts and minds of the soon to be free and already independent nations of what came to comprise the nonaligned movement. But Du Bois' efforts were not without effect. Without conceit he told Warren Austin, United States delegate to the United Nations, "it seems to me that the report of the President's Civil Rights Committee, substantiated practically all that we say in this petition." Du Bois' actions, and those of the left generally, such as the Progressive and Communist parties, were indispensable in helping President Truman to see the light on civil rights. Time was to prove that these activities in the arena of international human rights were a prime agent in catalyzing Du Bois' ouster. Years later Du Bois spoke wistfully of his petition's purpose of getting the "status of the American Negro discussed in the Assembly of the

United Nations." He recounted that in a meeting where "only" Roosevelt "was present," she said she "would feel compelled to resign" if the matter were debated. Instead, Du Bois was, so to speak, "compelled to resign" and the grounds were his obstinance in pushing racism as an international issue and his growing association with the Progressive party.[10]

CHAPTER 9

Gideon's Black Army

Du Bois was not much of a party man. Looking back in 1960, on the threshold of his joining the Communist party, he recalled that "the only parties of which I have been an actual member are the Socialist Party for about two years, the Democratic Party for perhaps four years and the Progressive Party for two years." He saw the evolution of his political thought as moving from seeking "completely to divorce politics from the mass of social activity and brought me to the much truer idea that a basis of political life is and must be economic." But as his joining the Socialist party in 1910, and his support for the third party effort of Senator Robert LaFollette demonstrated, political independence held no terror for Du Bois.[1]

His political independence and ties with the left were no secret when he returned to the Association in 1944. Nor was his opinion on the two-party system and its perceived detrimental impact shrouded in mystery. This outlook did not prevent Du Bois from speaking highly of President Franklin D. Roosevelt, particularly during the 1944 election. He told the predominantly Black audience of the *Chicago Defender*, that in evaluating candidates, "never mind what he calls his party or what he says his platform, follow his record." Adhering to his own advice, he found Roosevelt superior to Republican candidate Thomas Dewey. This led the owner of the *Amsterdam News*, a Black Harlem weekly that he had been writing for since 1939, to excise commentary from his columns; it seems that the owner was a staunch Republican. This incident dramatized how importantly Du Bois viewed the election, which he saw as a turning point for the nation.[2]

With FDR's death and the ascension of Harry S. Truman to the presidency, Du Bois began drifting away from the Democrats—along with other Roosevelt supporters. Actually, this process had begun just before Roosevelt's final sleep; early in 1945 he was invited to join the Executive Committee of the Independent Committee of Arts and Sciences. This impressive group, which included many luminaries, was viewed by some as a stalking horse for the left. At the same time, he took up the cudgels against the Union for Democratic Action, a precursor of the Cold War liberal Americans For Democratic Action, which was chaired by Reinhold Niebuhr and included Eleanor Roosevelt and A. Philip Randolph. He reproved them for their Dumbarton Oaks pamphlet which had "no mention . . . of the more than seven hundred million colonial people . . . Your picture . . . carefully omits colored people . . . I am not enthusiastic over your efforts." He turned a cold shoulder to the ideologically similar Liberal party of New York when they requested his membership and felt constrained to tell them, "I think I may want to join it, but I am writing to be sure that in inviting me, you are quite aware that I am of Negro descent." He did not join but, in the summer of 1945, he accepted the invitation of Elmer Benson, former governor of Minnesota, to join the executive council of the National Citizens' Political Action Committee; this organization was oriented toward the left and included Sidney Hillman, Gifford Pinchot, Dorothy Parker, Freda Kirchwey, and Mrs. Marshall Field. Interestingly, also included were NAACP board member Channing Tobias and soon to be Communist party general counsel John Abt.[3]

While Du Bois was drifting away from the Democrats and toward the beckoning glimmer of a third party led by Henry Wallace, the NAACP was backtracking in the opposite direction. In the Saturnalian days of 1941–1945, there were few politicians more highly praised by the NAACP than Henry Agard Wallace. In a rare gesture, the thirty-third annual conference of the NAACP meeting in Los Angeles singled him out for florid praise. Consequently, when Wallace was dumped in 1944 as Vice President on the Democratic ticket, a *Crisis* editorial seethed with rage and termed it "as dirty a deal as has ever been put over on the plain people of America." They were angry about "ramming Truman down the throats of the country." Wallace was profusely lauded for his stand on racism, the poll tax, Jim Crow, and so on in a separate editorial entitled "Salute to Wallace."[4]

Wallace was included in the pantheon of white leaders who the NAACP viewed favorably. Indicatively, Churchill was contrastingly counterposed to Wallace and others. Wallace was commended for representing positive trends and those who sought to replace him with a southern senator, such as Truman, were taken to task.[5]

After Wallace's ouster became a fait accompli, the association did not lose interest in him. A telegram urging congressional affirmation of Henry A. Wallace for secretary of commerce, with authority over loan agencies, was sent by Leslie Perry of the Washington office to thirty-four United States senators. Similarly, eighteen NAACP leaders in key states were asked to mobilize sentiment behind Wallace by Roy Wilkins, acting NAACP secretary. As it was becoming clearer that a third party challenge to Truman would be mounted, the NAACP leadership initially did not waver. However, the board approved the signing of "A Call to Progressives" to attend a conference in Chicago in September to "discuss political action at the November elections [by] independent voters." White spoke at this landmark conference and also present were notables like Claude Pepper, Henry Morgenthau, Harold Ickes, and Philip Murray. Deftly countering the prevailing feeling in the air, White announced, "I do not think a third party is the answer either in 1946 or 1948." This was not because Truman was the answer but simply because of the arduous task of getting on the ballot. Still, White made his ideological preference clear when he affirmed, "we want no part of imperialism which is the chief cause of war."[6]

It was not astounding then that Du Bois' association with what was to become the Progressive party was not viewed with equanimity within leading circles of the association. Early in 1947, White queried Spingarn about one of Du Bois' *Chicago Defender* columns that heaped praise on the Progressive Citizens of America (PCA). It was ironic that what raised White's ire were words that he could have uttered a few months previously. Du Bois fully endorsed the "excellent program" of PCA; their program which was a replica of NAACP tenets, called for the "abolition of segregation . . . a Federal Civil Rights Act . . . a federal anti-lynching bill . . . elimination of HUAC . . . abolition of the poll-tax . . . Bilbo out of Congress . . . opposition to militarism and imperialism." As ever, Du Bois did more than take to the pen to express his thoughts, he hit the lecture circuit speaking at a Chicago rally on similar issues, sponsored by, among others, progressives like Earl Dickerson, Curtis MacDougall, Father Clarence Parker, and labor leader Ernest De Maio. Du Bois' prominence in this movement was underlined when Wallace began requesting his *Defender* columns for information and analysis; soon other progressives nationally began making similar requests as Du Bois assumed the status of both scribe and elder statesman of the progressives. Emboldened, Du Bois accelerated his proprogressive posture. Once again in the *Defender* he asked Wallace "to run for President on a Third Party ticket in the next Presidential election." Otherwise, the choice would be "between fools and demagogues."[7]

Du Bois not only pleaded for Wallace to run but made a plea to Blacks to do the same; he urged that they write Wallace and ask him to stand for president on a third party ticket. He also defended Wallace against his detractors. The readers of *The New York Times* were asked if it was logical to smear Wallace as being communistic when he advocated plans long argued for and in part implemented by people like Norman Thomas and Robert LaFollette and by England's Labour party?[8]

Many Blacks heeded Du Bois' call and flocked to the Progressive party banner. Du Bois (along with Paul Robeson) was probably the most prominent Black supporter of the Progressive Party ticket; hence, analyzing the relationship between Blacks and the party is revelatory of his influence and the value of his anti-Truman posture. It is unavoidable that the Democrats feared the attraction of the Black vote to Wallace. He and his vice-presidential candidate Glen H. Taylor spoke throughout the South before nonsegregated audiences—a precedent shattering maneuver. Taylor was one of the Senate's most determined proponents of civil rights though there were only "500 Blacks in the entire state" of Idaho. He led the fight to oust Bilbo from the Senate and demanded that Truman send troops to Mississippi "to protect the Blacks' right to vote if this is the only way that their rights can be assured." Taylor was arrested and tried in Birmingham after he addressed a nonsegregated audience during the campaign.[9]

Obviously, Black voters would be stirred by a party that backed up its words with actions, particularly when Truman was knee deep in the muck of racism. Hence, it was to be expected that the party would be subjected to a veritable reign of terror and exposed to tactics more familiar to Germany in the early 1930s. The going was particularly rough on college campuses where firings, beatings, hecklings, censorship, and even murder were not uncommon. Larkin Marshall, "first Negro to run" for the United States Senate in Georgia since Reconstruction days was exposed to systematic harassment, which included cross burnings on his lawn. Another Progressive party supporter, who was in the progressive National Maritime Union, was called "Communist and a 'n-gg-r lover' " by a fellow worker, and then stabbed to death. When the Tenney Committee held hearings in 1948, one-third of those subpoenaed were Progressive party members. Just after the Progressive party convention in 1948, many of their leaders were subpoenaed by HUAC.[10]

The Progressive party, spurred by the backing of prominent Blacks, such as Du Bois, made significant inroads in the Afro-American community. Indicative of the importance of the Black vote was the fact that Wallace chose to consult with fifty-one Black leaders, including Du Bois, Shirley Graham, Paul Robeson, and Gordon Hancock, the day before formally throwing his hat into the ring. This wooing of Blacks was not without result:

> It was Negro signatures that put the New Party on the ballot in virtually every southern state; and in other parts of the country. Negro petitioners and signers were among the most active. . . . The Progressive Party nominated proportionately more Negro candidates than did the other parties; and it nominated them for offices to which Negroes had never been named by either major party . . . the largest number of Negro candidates ever picked to run on a single ticket since the days of Thaddeus Stevens.

Future high Black leaders received some of their earliest political experiences in the Progressive party, for example, Margaret Bush Wilson, former chair of the NAACP, who was "the first Negro woman to ever run for Congress from Missouri." These actions had impact despite a literally murderous campaign of opposition: "What went on in Georgia most of the time seemed closer to guerilla warfare than an American political campaign. . . . The majority of Progressive petition signers in Georgia were Negroes [and] at least two Negroes are known to have been killed because they insisted on voting in Georgia in 1948." In response to the assumed power of the Black vote, Governor Herman Talmadge moved to introduce a new literacy test to bar Black ballots. Despite these setbacks, it would not be farfetched in the slightest to give credit to the Progressive party and its backers, such as Du Bois, for weakening the walls of segregation that came tumbling down years later, as Curtis MacDougall outlined:[11]

> the dramatic efforts of the Wallaceites to defy Jim Crow accelerated the broader movement for racial equality . . . Negro voting was stimulated, not only the Supreme Court rulings, but also by the Wallace campaign, . . . There seems no doubt that the Progressives' adament stand on segregation hastened the employment of Negroes as policemen in Memphis, Chattanooga, Baltimore and elsewhere.

Because of these pioneering efforts, the Progressives attracted broad and influential Black support. Lena Horne was elected to the national board of the Progressive Citizens of America, along with Du Bois, Robeson, Bishop R. Wright, the Black publisher Roscoe Dunjee, Dr. Carlton Goodlett, George Murphy, Shirley Graham, Charlotta Bass, Margaret Bush Wilson, and Dr. J. R. Johnson, dean of Howard University's Medical School. Joe Louis, perhaps the number one Black hero of that era, gave $100 to the Wallace campaign and termed the Iowan a "great American" whom he "admires." Coleman Young, later to become mayor of Detroit, was state director of the Progressive party and ran for the State Senate in 1948 on the Progressive party ticket.[12]

One careful student has noted the wide support in the Black press for Wallace: "They supported Henry Wallace and his ideas . . . and applauded his attempts to force the United States to extend its Black citizens their rights." One Black newspaper, the *California Eagle* of Los Angeles, edited by Charlotta Bass, the first Black woman to run for the vice-presidency, actually registered potential Wallace voters in its offices. But it was in the South that the party had its most dynamic effect. As the Black newspaper the *Pittsburgh Courier* noted:

> There were Negroes in greater numbers in this convention than in any major party in history. . . . At least eighteen Negroes addressed the convention and for the first time in American history, a Negro acted as Keynoter and temporary chairman. Attorney Charles P. Howard apparently voiced the

feeling of Negro members of the Progressive Party when he said, "for the first time in my life I am experiencing human dignity."[13]

But what set the Progressives apart did not impress the association leaders. There was a hasty retreat from the leftist euphoria of the early postwar years. At first this took the form of evenhandedness. White made a request to the board to participate in the activities of Americans For Democratic Action. But, on a motion by Oswald G. Villard, the board voted that the "Secretary retire from both committees [continuations committees of ADA and PCA] and that the Association withdraw from any political situations." The board mandate was implemented, at least so far as it related to the PCA. Simultaneously, a vile campaign was launched against Wallace and the Progressive party. Walter White singled out for attack "supporters of Henry Wallace" for "pouring billings-gate of the most filthy sort upon the President" and ignoring "the decent things he has done." Yet, Du Bois claimed that this went against the grain of the Black community, not to mention the wishes of the NAACP staff itself: "A poll in the NAACP office showed that 70% of the staff favored Wallace."[14]

This retreat from leftist euphoria is reflected in the *Crisis* editorials and articles of 1948. In February, though chiding Wallace for not acting aggressively on segregation while heading the Department of Commerce, it was said that he "has more warm-hearted good wishes and sentimental support from Negro Americans than any man of any party." Democrats and Republicans were warned that they better get "straight on our question," otherwise third party support for Wallace would swell. By June, Wilkins had advanced to terming a vote for Wallace a "futile protest" and implicitly linked this futility with an alleged similar failure of the Communist party. By August the words of February apparently had been forgotten as an article on the annual conference indicated: "Roy Wilkins paid tribute to President Truman for his courage on the civil rights issue." In the closing address "Walter White criticized the Henry Wallace third party, the Republican Party and the 80th Congress."[15]

The biggest blast at Wallace was propitiously reserved for October, the weeks immediately before the election. Interestingly, they called on the socialist Norman Thomas for ammunition. He praised Truman, faintly praised Dewey, and fiercely berated Wallace for "his party is dominated by the Communists . . . and . . . his foreign policy for America which might have been dictated by Stalin." Wallace's historic antisegregationist tour of the South was attacked editorially as trivial since he had "little or nothing to lose by campaigning against inequality and segregation." A month after the election, a *Crisis* editorial plunged the knife a bit deeper and charged that "non-Communist Negro Wallace supporters . . . had been merely used by a disciplined pro-Communist group." The *Crisis* devolution from "warm good-hearted wishes" for Progressives to vulgar redbaiting was insolently at odds with the position of the NAACP's Director of Special Research.[16]

Du Bois took every available opportunity to disparage President Truman. At the same time that White was addressing Progressives in Chicago, readers of the *Defender* encountered Du Bois' opinion that the main issues of the November election—labor and strikes, colonialism, foreign policy, rotten boroughs in the South, lynchings, and job discrimination—would not be meaningfully discussed by either Truman's party or the Republicans. Of this myriad of issues, Du Bois took particularly strenuous objection to White House foreign policy. Typically, Du Bois' efforts in Chicago were not limited to writing; with fervor the *Defender* reported "his bringing 6000 listeners to their feet several times" as he tore into the "Truman Doctrine" and "the proposed $400,000,000 loan to Greece and Turkey." Invoking the powerfully insistent response of Afro-Americans to the Cold War, he rhetorically queried "can we expect Democracy in Greece and not practice it in Mississippi?" As the ramifications of the Truman Doctrine unfolded, he launched more missiles. The Marshall Plan became a familiar punching bag; as he saw it, though lavishly praised in certain circles, it was essentially a plan to assure United States domination over the European market and economy: "It is no matter of philanthopy; we need to sell to Europe just as much as she needs to buy from us."[17]

The NAACP had narrowly focused a friendly gaze on Truman in a peculiar form of tunnel vision. This was something of a change from previous years when Truman was a reviled figure not only among the NAACP but Blacks generally. The historian William Berman has noted, "when Truman ran for local office in his town of Independence, Missouri . . . the Kansas City chapter of the National Association for the Advancement of Colored People (NAACP) refused to endorse him." The Missouri senator was catapulted into prominence as a result of hearings into the defense industry but the NAACP was not convinced; they harshly characterized the hearings as a "frenzied and hasty attempt to dodge the real investigation into discrimination against the Negro in defense." Bitterly they saw the purpose of the hearings as a way "to head off the scheduled March on Washington." The historian Andrew Buni said bluntly, "Negroes looked skeptically at the Democrat from Missouri." Buni cited Truman's past support for the poll tax. "It was claimed that Truman did not personally favor the stronger phrasing of the civil rights platform of the Democratic National Convention. In the more than two hundred [speeches] delivered after his nomination, he made no [mention of it]." There was not unaminity within the Association on this militant opposition to Truman and the forces he represented. Spingarn specifically disapproved of the forceful Declaration of Negro Voters issued before the 1944 election. But in the "Record on Senator Truman with Respect to Matters Vital to Negroes" certain aspects of his political philosophy were cited: "On July 14, 1944, (3rd Session. 76th Congress) the Senator spoke at National Colored Democratic Association in Chicago . . . [he said] 'Before I go further I wish to make it clear that I am not appealing for social equality for Negroes' " This document also raised the specter of alleged Ku Klux Klan membership.[18]

Truman's appointments were subjected to withering attack, particularly James Byrnes' move to Foggy Bottom. Anti-Byrnes press releases were a common staple of the Association. They encouraged others, such as the powerful labor leader Willard Townsend, to take anti-Byrnes stands. This censuring of Byrnes was part of an overall broadside against Truman's foreign policy.[19]

His domestic policies did not win plaudits either—at least not initially. Barton J. Bernstein and Allen Matusow initimate why:

> [Truman] allowed Congress to strangle the special wartime Fair Employment Practices Commission. Though he unsuccessfully asked Congress to create a permanent FEPC, he also restricted the powers of the temporary Commission.

A resolution by the board attacked Truman for giving only "lip service" to FEPC. Later in 1946, White assailed "President Truman's astounding proposal to break strikes by drafting strikers into the army." According to Leslie Perry, this "would create a dictatorship."[20]

As White himself saw it, the violence of 1946 was of special import. "The year just ended has been one of the grimmest years in the history of the National Association for Advancement of Colored People—Negroes in America have been disillusioned over the wave of lynchings, brutality and official recession from all of the flamboyant promises of post-war democracy and decency." Nonetheless, "the year just ended" saw a metamorphosis in the NAACP's official view of the chief executive officer of the United States and their relationship to him. Retrospectively, White interpreted Truman's 1946 executive order creating the President's Committee on Civil Rights as resulting not from adverse publicity on racism generated by the groundswell of support for the United Nations petition or mass pressure generally, but as a result of a particular huddle he had in the White House. This reflected the growing closeness of the NAACP leadership—particularly White—to Truman. In cooperation with the NAACP, Truman made a speech at the Lincoln Memorial, broadcast around the world by radio, with White on the platform alongside Eleanor Roosevelt. The price for Truman's support was steep—an abandonment of militant action, especially in the arena of foreign policy.[21]

Alonzo Hamby has pointed out that Americans for Democratic Action (ADA) did not mount an aggressive campaign for social welfare goals, for example, desegregation, because "under the pressure of right-wing anti-Communism, too many progressives were beginning to compromise their affirmative principles." Substitute the acronym "NAACP" for "ADA" and the analysis still holds. A conclave of the NAACP in January 1948 insisted that Blacks "must use their ballots wisely and unselfishly to the end that the best candidates are elected, irrespective of political party." The historical consensus has not characterized the leadership's electoral activities in 1948 in that manner; and the fact that the Progressives threatened to capture the Black vote, and had already attracted one of their working associates—Du Bois—added to their urgency. William Berman has articulated the prevailing view: "Walter White . . . particularly made the NAACP an informal affiliate of the national Democratic party" Thus, the image of Truman in NAACP literature was burnished.[22]

Much was made of Truman's pledge to establish a permanent Commission on Civil Rights as a result of tacit and explicit Association support; even without this bargain, Truman would have been forced to move in certain directions. As Berman put it,

"Truman moved only because he had no choice. Negro votes and the demands of the cold war, not simple humanitarianism . . . produced whatever token gains Negroes were to make in the years Truman inhabited the White House."[23]

This partisan fondness for the president not only riled Du Bois and the left but the GOP also found it unseemly. Val Washington, assistant campaign manager of the Republican National Committee, complained to Louis Wright "in behalf of myself and other Republicans, who are members" of the NAACP about White's violation of the stated policy on nonpartisanship. He pointed to the White column in the *New York Herald Tribune* on September 19 slamming Dewey and a column a week later caressing Truman. "I also cite the tour [Leslie Perry] is making of NAACP branches in key states, urging support of Democratic members of Congress." McCoy and Ruetten note: "White's public expression in favor of Truman challenged the credibility of the organization's claim to non-partisanship." The acerbic Black conservative columnist George Schuyler commented that Du Bois, "whatever his motives, is not wrong when he charges that Walter is on the Truman Bandwagon . . . of course, Walter replies that the NAACP is non-partisan, but the people who believe that should have their heads examined."[24]

The Black vote proved to be the balance of power in the 1948 presidential election, and the NAACP—the largest, most influential civil rights organization—was indispensable in this process. The academic observer Warren St. James emphasized that "their leadership in securing an almost solid bloc of Negro voters for Mr. Truman is an example long to be remembered in pressure group success." This pro-Truman mobilization was resented not only by Du Bois, but also by the left and the GOP; even some pro-Truman rank and file NAACP members felt that nonpartisanship should have been adhered to. Some members formally objected when board member Alfred Baker Lewis, assisted by others, sent a letter to members urging support for Truman in the election.[25]

The tireless efforts of the NAACP bore fruit with Truman's stunning victory propelled by a substantial Black vote. The 1948 campaign turned out the greatest numbers of Negro voters than ever before. This was generated largely by the thrust of the Progressives in the eleven states of the Old Confederacy where most of the Afro-American population still resided. Richard Walton has mentioned the high proportion of Black voters in the Progressive party, especially when compared to the Democratic. Du Bois was supposed to have given the major address at the Progressive party convention but he demurred and the honor went to Charles Howard. But it should not be gainsaid that despite Du Bois' efforts and the labors of other Black and white activists, the Progressive party did not receive as many votes as the Democratic party in the presidential race. There are many reasons for this, not the least of which was the Democrats' liberal borrowing from the Progressive's platform. Allen Yarnell has disputed this but his own evidence indicates otherwise, not to mention his undue reliance on interviews granted years after the fact. Even the so-called leftist writer James Weinstein who, ironically, has furiously redbaited the Progressive party, acknowledges "the taking over of much of the new party's platform by the major parties." And the Progressive's platform was similar to the NAACP's platform.[26]

Truman's skillful coopting of the Progressive platform was not the only reason that Du Bois' party did not receive as many votes as some expected. Edward and Frederick Schapsmeier underscore the baiting and attacks launched against the Progressives. The party was "not only [the] whipping boy for Dixiecrats, Democrats and Socialists but also the primary target of the Americans for Democratic Action." So-called liberals, such as Ralph McGill of the *Atlanta Constitution,* had a frenzied reaction to the Progressives' nonsegregated activities. Such elements were crucial in stampeding voters away from the party, particularly in states with substantial Black populations, like Du Bois' old home of Georgia. One study of the party there concludes, in explaining vote totals disappointing to some, that "fear was a very potent factor. Fear of loss of job and status . . . the reactionaries regarded the party as something dangerous and a real threat."[27]

Fear took a heavy toll nationally but was devastating in the South. Tennessee "was struck hardest by the red-baiting terror. The rank and file suffered well above the national average, economically and socially." The fact that civil rights leaders like Walter White and the National Urban League's Lester Granger—the "first outstanding Negro leader to attack Wallace"—redbaited the party vehemently influenced many. Allegedly, Charles Howard did not "believe that the Negro leaders who used the Red issue to smear the Progressive Party were sincere in the light of their previous association and friendship with many of the persons whom they thus attacked." This may have been true but their actions had effect irrespective of their presumed lack of sincerity. Their actions and those making similar charges were popular press items. It was alleged that at a Los Angeles radio station, employees were ordered to slant the news against "Henry Wallace . . . and the Jews." Whether true or not, the fact is that the press was quite unfriendly to the party. Perhaps, the most substantive reason for Wallace not receiving as many votes as expected was, paradoxically, the challenge from the right. When J. Strom Thurmond and the Dixiecrats entered the fray, Blacks and whites were driven to Truman as a four way split vote might have allowed the right to win solely due to their presumed 25 percent of the electoral base.[28]

Du Bois, as a leader of Gideon's Black Army, was clearly not in accord with the cresting pro-Truman posture of his fellow NAACP leaders. While they baited Wallace, he may have been Wallace's most prominent supporter. But whereas this represented a sharp reversal of their past political positions, Du Bois remained constant. What had changed were objective political conditions. And it was this change that made Du Bois' departure from the NAACP as inevitable as the sun rising in the east.

CHAPTER 10

Farewell to All That

Du Bois was ousted from the Association principally because of his leading role in the Wallace campaign and his persistence on pressing the issue of United States racism in the United Nations. With the pressure to conform politically reaching a crescendo in 1948—an election year—Du Bois' exit was virtually assured.

Those attending the dinner honoring Du Bois on his eightieth birthday at New York's Hotel Roosevelt may not have been aware that months later he would be reviled by some of the same people who cheered that night. Both Fisk University and the New York City Fisk Club jointly sponsored this well-attended event. On the dais were Arthur Spingarn, Mark Van Doren, and John Hope Franklin. A "popular front" of individuals were in attendance, such as Herbert Aptheker, Howard Fast, James Ford, W. Alphaeus Hunton, Carl Van Vechten and—Walter White. Greetings were received from anticolonial leaders like Nehru and Norman Manley. Du Bois' eightieth birthday, celebrated while ensconced in the NAACP, caused a gushing of affection to flow from friend and assumed foe alike. Urban League official Eugene Kinckle Jones complimented the octogenarian; Channing Tobias, director of the Phelps Stokes Fund, was equally expansive. Speaking for the masses he represented, NAACP Youth chairman W. W. Law said simply that Du Bois was "a blessing to three or more generations. Youth of this nation love you."[1]

This unabashed adoration was not the unrivaled theme of Du Bois' life in 1948. Walter White, his constant nemesis, in an unsent memo, written less than forty-eight hours after Du Bois' birthday celebration, to the powerful NAACP Committee on Administration, strenuously objected to Du Bois' political activities. He singled out his joining Robeson in an effort to secure passage of the FEPC, antilynching, antirestrictive covenant, and antipoll tax legislation. Indicative of the petard by which White was hoisted and possibly why this document was not sent, was the fact that NAACP board members, Roscoe Dunjee and Judge Hubert Delany were also allied with Robeson's campaign. But White did forward to the staff the long-standing NAACP resolution on nonpartisan political activity—a pointed warning to the many NAACP staff members who were pro-Wallace. Two weeks later he sent it out again for added emphasis.[2]

Not shrinking from the challenge, Du Bois replied with careful clarity. But White was not pleased. One of Du Bois' many pro-Progressive Citizens of America columns sparked White to threateningly ask Springarn, "do you think the Association should take any position on the enclosed column by Dr. Du Bois?" Du Bois was perplexed by these trends. With wonder he asked Spingarn whether he should turn down offers to work with the China Welfare Fund, American Council for Democratic Greece, and like-minded organizations.[3]

Du Bois' poignancy left White unfazed. His overall attack on activist NAACP members who leaned toward the Progressive party was pressed at the April 1948 board meeting. White presented a resolution barring branch officers from running for political posts. With bureaucratic deftness, a committee was formed to study the question. But for White the meeting was not a total washout as the admission was wrung from Du Bois that "since the decision of the Board I have followed its directions and refrained from organized political activity."[4]

This admission did not curtail the avid interest in Du Bois' burgeoning political activities. Louis Wright, on behalf of the Committee on Administration, "disapproved [of] your being an initiating sponsor of the March on Washington Movement for Civil Rights on June 2"; he said that the action should have been cleared beforehand. Exasperated by the mushrooming Progressive party support exploding all around him, White suggested that the annual conference call for "re-affirmation even more explicitly of our non-partisan political position." Of course, nonpartisanship did not apply to those who backed the Democratic party. The uproar this created at the annual meeting provoked White to formally respond. Acknowledging the presumed reach of the First Amendment, he added that the convention recognized "the right of freedom of speech by all persons who address our convention."[5]

Taking this admission seriously, Du Bois asked White to place on the agenda of the upcoming board meeting for a possible endorsement a letter that was bound to be controversial in July 1948. Directed to the president and the State Department and signed by Albert Einstein, Professor Thomas Emerson, Dean Christian Gauss of Princeton, Lillian Hellman, O. John Rogge, Mark Van Doren, Rexford Tugwell, and others, it was inevitable that its contents would be viewed with hostility given the prevailing political climate:

> Twice this year our government has rejected Soviet offers to enter direct negotiations aimed at understanding between the two nations. [We call for] immediate conferences between the USA and the USSR to reach agreement on basic differences . . . . [We] insist that capitalism and Communism can and must peacefully coexist. USA-USSR cooperation won the last war and abandonment of that cooperation led us to the present crisis.

This milestone in the battle for detente was perceived by the board as a red flag to a bull.[6]

Not surprisingly, the board failed to favorably pass on this resolution. Its bold presentation sealed Du Bois' fate. Despite their glaring pro-Truman bias, White and his allies continued to insist that Du Bois' party activities and opposition to the gathering Cold War was unacceptable. Days after Du Bois' demarche on detente, White asked him about an Associated Press dispatch that quoted Du Bois as urging "vote for Joseph Rainey for Congress and Henry Wallace for President." Peremptorily, White demanded, "before asking for a correction of this statement I would like to know if this statement is true." Du Bois did not hesitate in reacting:

> The Board of Directors . . . has forbidden political activity on the part of employees. It has not forbidden an employee to hold political views and to express them properly, as you are doing daily.

This last dig was punctuated by his attaching a separate account of his actual words at the speech in question on June 23 in Philadelphia at a mass meeting of the NAACP branch. He said there: "I think I ought to add, speaking as an individual and not in any way representing officially the National Association for the Advancement of Colored People" that "the Third Party" was worthwhile. "I trust, therefore, you are going to take advantage of these two opportunities to help remake the United States by seeking the election of Wallace and Rainey."[7]

To Du Bois, White vehemently denied urging anyone to vote for any candidate. The Committee on Administration received a different approach. He forwarded a copy of the disputed Philadelphia speech and requested their opinion. Du Bois was not pleased with this turmoil and the effect of the March 13, 1944, resolution on nonpartisan political activity. There was not unanimity within the NAACP on opposition to Du Bois' stance or his explanation thereof. NAACP staffer Madison Jones argued that taking action against Du Bois was problematic "since Dr. Du Bois stated in the excerpts from his speech that he was speaking as an individual. . . . To try to censure an employee speaking as a private individual when he has specifically stated he was speaking in that category would be difficult."[8]

But White continued to proceed; yet, he was being buffeted from both sides by contending forces. One NAACP member sent in his dues and added, "I am hopeful that many NAACP members will not follow Dr. Du Bois' lead and lend support to left-wing organizations." In response, White displayed an ironic ability to understand his Director of Special Research's argument. Defending his other flank, White denied to Fred Taylor of the *Birmingham Herald* that he himself was "openly campaigning for Truman," while generously praising him.

The Wallace-Truman campaign was not the sole issue complicating Du Bois' relationship with the NAACP leadership. There was also the lingering issue of the United Nations petition—an issue complicated by the presence of Eleanor Roosevelt, NAACP board member and staunch opponent of the Progressive party. The two senior leaders had profound political disagreements. While Du Bois bore no particular animus toward the Communists, Roosevelt despised them. While she defended the Truman Doctrine and Marshall Plan, Du Bois ridiculed both. While Du Bois was a prominent Wallace supporter, Roosevelt redbaited him mercilessly. Most importantly for present purposes, while Du Bois saw United States racism as an issue meriting international strictures, Roosevelt opposed human rights' formulations that would bind the United States to "honor the civil rights of its people or to guarantee full employment."[9]

At the September 8, 1947, board meeting, it was voted that Du Bois be allowed to present a petition to the United Nations. But he was quickly checkmated at the United Nations by Eleanor Roosevelt. Du Bois complained to White of her capacity with the United Nations Commission on Human Rights, "I have written to her twice and received no reply, nor even acknowledgements." Du Bois was irritated because he was writing in response to a request from Roosevelt for NAACP participation at the United Nations. Du Bois was livid. Already the soon to be controversial issue of White going to Geneva to participate in a human rights forum had arisen: "It would be a waste of money and time for the NAACP to be represented at Geneva for these meetings."[10]

This was not the end of the sniping between the two camps. For his part, Du Bois disputed asking why the United Nations could discuss Israel, Austria, Finland, and other countries but could not discuss U.S. Blacks. Roosevelt retaliated at the February 9, 1948, board meeting, complaining of left and Soviet attacks on the United States at Geneva. At the board meeting in March, Du Bois received another setback when the board voted not to support him on the issue of political nonpartisanship.[11]

Roosevelt had threatened to resign from the U.S. delegation to the United Nations if the petition was presented; and Du Bois found this unacceptable. This exposé of Roosevelt's role was also seen by the mostly white liberal constituency of the *New Republic.* This intense focus naturally discomfited her. Years later, "on her radio show, Mrs. Roosevelt recalled how the communist use of the racial issue embarrassed her in the United Nations." An inkling perhaps of why this embarrassed her is revealing:

> Mrs. Roosevelt was frequently asked in India to explain American racial practices. This proved embarrassing for her . . . back home, she cited racism as the single domestic issue that damaged American chances for winning Third World peoples to its side in the cold war[12]

Given Du Bois' well-known public and private view of the controversy surrounding presenting the petition at the United Nations, it was curious that White would ask the Committee on Administration to appoint Du Bois to represent the NAACP at the crucial meeting of the United Nations General Assembly, in Paris in September 1948. Forcing Du Bois' hand, White asked him to assist in framing NAACP positions for the General Assembly. As was his custom, Du Bois launched a broadside in reply. He suggested that the NAACP:[13]

> demand that the petition . . .be placed on the agenda of the Assembly for discussion . . . there should be more direct and clear effort to emancipate the colonial peoples.

But his recommendations were also explicit and specific:

> I have no suggestions with regard to the bill of Human Rights . . . general statements on rights are of no importance to us today; what we want is specific application of universally recognized rights . . . I think that we should ask for a radical revision [of trusteeship] . . . so that the colonial peoples or their representative could be represented on the Council.

Guaranteeing Du Bois' fate was the September 9, 1948, article in *The New York Times* which reported that Du Bois "accused the association yesterday of abandoning efforts to ease the world plight of the Negro peoples to serve the interests of President Truman's administration." A memorandum alleged to have been written by Du Bois, was cited extensively. Interestingly, Roosevelt, when reached at Adam Clayton Powell's Abyssinian Baptist Church, "praised the work of Dr. Du Bois in presenting a petition on Negro rights in the United States." This *New York Times* article no doubt weighed like an alp on the minds of the NAACP board when they met September 12; White's recommendation that Du Bois be sent to Geneva was not accepted as White himself was appointed. Du Bois placed festering issues on the table; he complained about White not sending him board minutes and agendas and the general lack of direction from the board. He noted that in the past, for the most part, this deficiency was unimportant but the situation no longer obtained since the NAACP was being pressed to take a stand concerning African and Asian colonies.[14]

The board had the benefit of a lengthy memo from their Director of Special Research, detailing his manifold criticisms. He pounced on the Truman administration, which the board preferred to collaborate with:[15]

> it has refused to bring the curtailment of our civil rights to the attention of the General Assembly of the United Nations; it has refused willingly to allow any other nation to bring this matter up; if any should, Mrs. Eleanor Roosevelt has declared she would probably resign. In the Trusteeship Council the United States has sided with the Imperial powers; it has sided with Italy in taking all but an unimportant part of Eritrea from Ethiopia; it has opposed the best interests of India, the only nation which has defended Africa before the Assembly; it has not defended Indonesia, and is clearly straddling on Israel. If we accept a consultantship in this delegation without a clear, open, public declaration by the Board of our position on the Truman foreign policy, our very acceptance ties us in with the reactionary, war-mongering colonial imperialism of the present administration. It is certain that no influence applied in Paris is going to have the slightest influence on our delegation. Their minds are made up and their policy set. The only change that can be made is in Washington and the United States. I do not know the attitude of the Board of Directors of the NAACP on these matters, nor, so far as I know, does anyone else. . . .
>
> Our international policy . . . is not only being determined without consultation or investigation, but even discussion of these matters here in public have in my case been met by five threats and warnings from the officials of the NAACP not to engage in "political activity." My request for clarification of what "political activity" consists has never been answered. On the other hand, the political activity of various members of this Association has been widely known. I thoroughly agree that no official of this organization, salaried or unsalaried, should commit the organization as such to any one political party. But I insist that this rule should apply to all officials and not to a few; and I also insist that it is not only the right but the bounden duty of every official and member of the NAACP as an American citizen to investigate, interrogate, vote and defend his vote in every election, and I deny the right of any official to tie this organization to the foreign policy of the present administration as long as it stands against the public discussion of our civil rights, for the despoiling of Ethiopia,

for the delaying of recognition to Israel, and, in general, against the interests of colonial peoples.

This lengthy dissertation exploded in the NAACP board room. As the minutes taker put it: "There was considerable discussion on the matter"; this was gross understatement. Both Hastie and Delany stressed the issue of Du Bois' allegedly releasing the memo to the press. In fact, as the attorney-dominated board somehow chose to ignore, copies were sent to the staff and board only—and the leak probably sprung there. This reflected, however, the prevailing atmosphere in favor of getting rid of the octogenarian leader. Spingarn perceptively stressed prompt action since the matter would be a "cause celebre in the Negro press." Sensing an approaching cataclysm, a motion was made to table the issue of Du Bois to the next meeting. This was defeated and the meeting wore on. Du Bois was invited to the meeting and at that point he denied giving the memo to the press. He disclaimed knowledge of how the press got hold of it. But the board was not appeased. Hastie then made a motion emphasizing Du Bois' alleged distribution of the memo and demanding that he be fired; the motion also emphasized Du Bois' alleged refusal to cooperate with the staff for the upcoming General Assembly meeting. The motion passed and, remarkably, the substance of Du Bois' contentions—concerning the Truman administration and foreign policy—were barely addressed. John Hammond abstained since he felt an infringement of Du Bois' civil rights and liberties had taken place. Channing Tobias, who months earlier had lavished praise on Du Bois, expressed regret at the board's action and asked that an appreciation for the contributions Dr. Du Bois had made be read into the board's record. "Mr. Spingarn stated that Dr. Du Bois had expressed his own feeling in the matter." Five days after they had kicked off this episode by printing Du Bois' memo, *The New York Times* recorded Du Bois' sacking.[16]

Spingarn's concern about the firing of the most prominent founder of the NAACP and Progressive party leader becoming a cause celebre was sagacious. Many wondered why the alleged leak should be given such weight when it was well known for some time that the NAACP was seriously in need of plumbers. After Du Bois left, this problem was still not solved. When George Schuyler speared White in one of his columns, the secretary told Hastie, "this kind of information came from inside the Association."

Prior to that, Judge Jane Bolin observed in a board meeting that Du Bois was fired supposedly for leaking to the press but her failure to be renominated to the board was leaked without retribution. Later, in another board meeting where Bolin resigned, a spate of articles in the *Amsterdam News* and *New York World-Telegram* that furiously redbaited the NAACP were discussed. Hammond was smeared as an alleged red. Earl Dickerson felt that the journalists collaborated with someone within the association in a plot to make Hammond and others uninfluential.[17]

These contradictions were apparent in the immediate wake of Du Bois' ouster. The response of the NAACP constituency—pro and con—is a useful barometer of sentiment on a critical signpost issue on the path to a cold war in the Afro-American community. Support for the sacking was not widespread, though the prediction that the ouster would create a cause celebre was prescient. Not surprisingly, much of the support for the board's action came from within the NAACP leadership. Roy Wilkins was busily active here defending the board and rallying support among the membership. But even Wilkins was plagued with self-doubt. While averring that "I recognize that Du Bois has never fitted in to the Association since he has been back," he confessed, "I was not happy about the action of the Board." Perhaps this was why Wilkins was concerned more than most with the verdict of history: "we ought to take into consideration that if his false statements are not answered they will come back on us in the years to come."[18]

Compared to the backing of the board's action, the opposition was substantial. This opposition was like an avalanche within the association itself. Though many may have been subliminally motivated by concern and affection for a highly regarded senior citizen, stated reasons for opposition were invariably political—which sheds light on Wilkins' admonition that the dismissal was administrative and not political. Henry Lee Moon, a NAACP staffer at the time who implicitly supported the forced retirement, confided years later that what was involved was only "a surface issue of insubordination and violation of procedures but in truth involving much deeper political factors."[19]

What Moon saw was seen by others in 1948. James Powers of the Brooklyn NAACP told Wilkins, "the membership voted, by a unanimous decision, to protest the dismissal of Dr. Du Bois." The board was asked to reconsider their "ill-advised and unwarranted" act. NAACP youth leaders were equally furious. "We stand one hundred percent with . . . other members of the NAACP who have denounced the prejudicial ousting of W. E. B. Du Bois from his national position in the NAACP."[20]

A substantial portion of Du Bois' support emerged from the industrial Midwest, the San Francisco Bay Area, and, of course, New York State—all areas that Henry Winston had seen as a happy hunting ground for Communist recruiters. There was also an uproar in the campus towns, traditional hotbeds for leftist activity and a favorite haunt of Du Bois. The comment of Alfred Cain, of the Columbia University chapter of the NAACP, was indicative when he told Louis Wright of the "strong protest" there where the sacking was seen as being indicative of the view that it was "inimical to the best interests of the Association." But New York State remained in the vanguard. A year after the fact, the *Amsterdam News* reported that at the "quarterly conference of [the] New York State Conference—some 19 of the state's 42 branches passed a resolution urging the election of Dr. Du Bois to the National Board of Directors."[21]

It was not solely those from the NAACP who rose to Du Bois' defense. His friends and compatriots from other organizations rallied to his side and gathered support in the process. C. B. Baldwin, secretary of the Progressive party, announced: "on behalf of the entire Progressive Party I express my shock at the summary dismissal of Dr. Du Bois for exercising his rights as a free American." The press release went on to detail the burgeoning support for Du Bois:[22]

> Earlier Wallace addressing 19,000 persons at Wrigley Field, said that "the firing of Dr. Du Bois is a tragic example of how American fascism is creeping into all facets of our life." Declaring that Dr. Du Bois was dismissed "because of his courageous stand on behalf of the colonial peoples of the world."

Paul Robeson told the screaming Chicago audience that Du Bois:

> refused to permit the NAACP to be utilized as a tool for the Truman Administration in the prosecution of a foreign policy that would enslave Negro peoples throughout the world while paying lip service to democracy at home. . . . Dr. Du Bois' faith in the Progressive Party . . . is the real basis of the anger against him.

Shirley Graham was a one-woman gang on her future husband's behalf, especially with the articles she wrote. With George Murphy, dissident member of the family that controlled the Afro-American press chain, she cobbled together an Emergency Committee for Dr. Du Bois and the NAACP. It included, in part, such dignitaries as E. Franklin Frazier, Alain Locke, Lorenzo Greene, Louis Adamic, Horace Mann Bond, and the president of Cheyney Teachers College in Pennsylvania, Leslie Pinckney Hill. In her capacity as New York State secretary of the Council of the Arts, Sciences and Professions (ASP), she helped to organize a rally that passed a pro-Du Bois resolution. The council was a high-powered organization. Linus Pauling was regional chairman; Lillian Hellman, John Howard Lawson, Father Clarence Parker, Paul Robeson, O. John Rogge, and Max Weber were vice chairs. Du Bois was not the only well-known figure in the council; members included Albert Einstein, Thomas Emerson, Howard Fast, Melville Herskovits, Langston Hughes, Albert Maltz, Thomas Mann, Frederick Schuman, and Studs Terkel. Sponsors of the rally included Robert Hutchins, Howard Mumford Jones, and Ira De A. Reid. That "the ASP Resolution speaks also for the following persons, most of them long time members of the NAACP," was affirmed by Professor F. O. Matthiessen of Harvard, Dr. Lorenzo Turner, Guy Brewer, and others. When the resolution was presented, a furor erupted. Alfred Baker Lewis immediately contacted Frank Graham and Zachariah Chafee of ASP and charged that the pro-Du Bois resolution was "being used as widely as possible by Communists and their fellow travelers and dupes to attack and weaken the NAACP . . . I believe although I cannot prove it, that [Du Bois] took such a stand in order that the Communists and their fellow travelers and dupes who are his political associates could be given a hammer with which to attack the NAACP." Chafee politely disagreed and limned a different approach to battling the common racist foe because "when one is fighting fire he does not inquire closely into the political views of the man who is carrying a bucket of water beside him." Wilkins was aware of this dialogue and, naturally, sustained Lewis' view deeming it "entirely worthwhile"; it was felt that this stone-walling had paid off for within weeks of the firing, Wilkins concluded, "the Du Bois situation has died down."[23]

It was unavoidable that the Du Bois dismissal would initiate a brouhaha in the black press. Newspapers lined up on both sides of the barricades. The Afro-American chain, with a combined circulation of over 240,000 weekly that included Washington, Baltimore, Philadelphia, New Jersey, Richmond, and a national edition, was a linchpin of pro-Du Bois commentary and the influence of this giant's position was viewed with apprehension at NAACP headquarters. Hot on the heels of the sacking, *Afro* president Carl Murphy immediately signalled, "I do not approve of the preemptory [sic] dismissal of Dr. Du Bois." Thurgood Marshall, injudiciously and intemperately lashed into the *Afro's* coverage of the Du Bois affair as "nothing more than a deliberate effort to becloud the issues and to give to the *Afro* readers a picture consisting of lies and distortions of facts." In any event, Murphy denied being part of the pro-Du Bois organization; yet, he struck at the "personal dictatorship" of White. Days later, the *Afro* revealed cracks in the NAACP anti-Du Bois front, when top NAACP lawyer Charles Houston straddled the fence by praising Du Bois and the leadership. Finally fed up, Wilkins hotly hit back at Murphy's weeklies; he alleged that the *Afro* did a "petty hatchet work based upon misinformation, gossip, personal spite and rumor" Wilkins also furiously denied the reported effort to pull the Washington, D.C. chapter out of the national NAACP in protest.[24]

The *Cleveland Call and Post,* known to be heavily influenced by the GOP, was also harsh in condemnation. The *Call and Post,* of the industrial Lake Erie metropolis, extensively reported the fallout from the firing, in particular the George Murphy-Shirley Graham effort to overturn the board's decision. Their readers discovered that the Des Moines publisher Charles Howard, Reverend Charles Hill of Detroit, the daughter of former Senator Burton Wheeler, Frances Saylor, and Carl Murphy (who of course denied it) had all joined this effort. Similar points were raised by the *California Eagle,* a newspaper aimed at southern California's growing Afro-American population and somewhat partial to Wallace. They allowed Du Bois' friend Dr. J. Alexander Somerville, whose home he tended to reside in during his visits to that area, to present a partisan viewpoint of the controversy.[25]

The *Shrevesport News* expressed sympathy, like Charles Houston, for both sides, though not without focusing on a familiarly sore point of overcentralization within the NAACP. The *Norfolk Journal & Guide* analyzed in a like vein and conjectured whether the dismissal would lead to a reduction of White's power. The *St. Paul Recorder* editorialized in favor of Du Bois and this brought Wilkins to the door of his old hometown's paper. He chided the editor for a serious "factual error in your editorial." Conversely, though the *Los Angeles Tribune* headlined provocatively on its front page, "Wallaceites Claim Dr. Du Bois was Crucified," Wilkins earlier had thanked their editor for their "fair treatment" of the disputation.[26]

The NAACP leadership was sensitive to the ramifications of the Du Bois affair. They collected favorable and unfavorable editorial comments and did not hesitate to make their opinions known. The weight they carried generally, and especially with many advertisers, was not a negligible factor. In any case, the *Atlanta Daily World* lined up with White, as did Lester Granger who was allowed to do so in the *Amsterdam News.* Though borrowing from Du Bois' ally Lillian Hellman in entitling their editorial "The Little Foxes," the authoritative *Chicago Defender* weighed in on behalf of the board. Sympathy was expressed for Du Bois but not for his allies, "the left wing enemies of the NAACP."[27]

Predictably, the *Daily Worker's* Abner Berry avidly upheld Du Bois' position and accused Hastie, Delany, Theodore Berry, Charles Toney, Alfred Baker Lewis, and Channing Tobias—members of Truman's Civil Rights Committee—of being "active in pro-Truman politics"; it was observed that this was essential to understanding the conflict. The *New York Star* was likewise indignant; they saw "clear indications of a 'willful leak' of the memorandum to the press . . . 'engineered' by leaders opposed to Du Bois' political activities." They described the lobbying of a Du Bois support committee active in sixteen states and counted among its members the prominent Washington, D.C., attorney Archibald Pinckett, Dr. Joseph Johnson, dean of the Howard University Medical School, William Harrison, editor of the weekly *Boston Chronicle,* Dr. W. D. Bowden of Atlanta University and others.[28]

The response of the community at large was strongly pro-Du Bois; Dr. Carey Eldridge, assistant professor of Romance Languages at George Washington University, adopted a pluralistic model: "The NAACP has room for people of all political convictions who are sincere fighters for Negro rights." Helene Sneed of Oklahoma City, where NAACP desegregation sit-ins occurred before Greensboro, symbolized the spirit of the era soon to come: "I am just one of the little people but I know that it takes us behind you to make actions successful. . . . Why should one man be fired for expressing his ideas?" Ada Butcher of the Women's Trade Union League of the nation's capital followed that line. So did Archie Weaver, a charter member of the NAACP who was also District Deputy Grand

Master of Most Worshipful Prince Hall Grand Lodge, the Free and Accepted Masons of Illinois. This legendary leader was for thirty years on the executive committee of the populous branch in Du Bois' stronghold and secretary for ten years.[29]

Again, GOP maneuvering may have contributed in part to pro-Du Bois sentiment in Chicago and elsewhere. Val Washington, GOP functionary, weighed in. He twitted White and the puissant Washington bureau for their partisan political activities. Like others before and after him, he cited White's widely read columns in the *New York Herald Tribune.* This issue was sharply joined in the October board meeting after Du Bois' September dismissal—and weeks before a hotly contested presidential election. In an apparent attempt at even-handedness, Du Bois supporter Earl Dickerson agreed that White's activities were politically partisan but felt that an individual should be able to state his views. This lawyer's interpretation of the First Amendment provided that the NAACP should promote freedom of expression and not deny it to either side. Weakly, the board passed a resolution restating the March 13, 1944, directive specifying that "employed executive officers . . . may not speak at meetings called by partisan political groups." This was reflected in a letter authorized to Washington which also drew attention to White's *Herald Tribune* articles; they "express Mr. White's personal evaluation. . . . The Association has made no evaluation." Dickerson balked. He felt that times had changed since 1944. He was overruled and the board asked White to leave out his NAACP title in his articles.[30]

This was hardly the only notable occurrence at this board meeting. The minutes of the previous meeting were approved with the proviso that Du Bois' contention that he did not know how the *Times* obtained his original lengthy memo be added along with his feisty and rebellious addition that he would have given the memo to the press if asked. These concessions were fueled by White's cable to the meeting from abroad predictably reporting "progress being made in face of many [sic] difficulties on human rights and colonies 'issue.' " He made reference to the same nettlesome issues that Du Bois had indicated the "West" would not yield on, such as the Italian colonies and South Africa's illegal occupation of Namibia. Evidently unaware of such glaring contradictions, on his return White continued unreconstructed down the same path. Barely after arriving home, he was forwarding multiple memoranda to Spingarn, Wright, and Wilkins—with White, the NAACP gang of four—confidentially informing them that in coming to work he saw advertised "a meeting at the Golden Gate Ballroom in Harlem for tonight, October 29th, listing Dr. Du Bois along with Henry Wallace, Paul Robeson, Larkin Marshall as speakers at a Wallace mass meeting."[31]

The Truman-Wallace contest divided Du Bois and the NAACP leadership. But it was not to be long before White and his colleagues were again speaking of the president in words that Du Bois himself could have ghostwritten. The Truman administration drummed up an anticommunist symphony that sought to isolate their most implacable Black opponents, such as Du Bois. This weakening of the left made the administration and Congress more susceptible to the strength of the right and the Dixiecrats. NAACP leaders were blithely ignorant of the consideration that their own anticommunism—domestically and internationally—as exemplified by their sacking of Du Bois because of disagreements on Truman foreign policy, paved the way for attacks on southern liberals and progressives.[32]

CHAPTER 11

Africa and Peace; Part I

Du Bois did not allow his forced removal from the NAACP to deter him from pursuit of the two major intertwined goals to which he wished to devote the rest of his life—the liberation of Africa and world peace. At the same time, these objectives were seen as a link between the major domestic objective of civil rights for Blacks, and a way to weaken the overarching foe—the right wing. Emblematic of this thrust was the fact that after leaving the NAACP Du Bois moved his offices to the headquarters of the Council on African Affairs (CAA). In the spring of 1948, before his sacking, Du Bois was caught up in a major anticommunist controversy—the ouster of Max Yergan from the council. This brouhaha may have contributed to an atmosphere that made Du Bois' own dismissal from the NAACP possible; at minimum, the incident got Du Bois off to a rocky start with the council.

After his departure from the NAACP, there was the bothersome matter of income, since the NAACP was not altogether forthcoming in providing pension and adequate severance pay to their venerable founder. At this juncture Henry Wallace filled the breach. He agreed to use his good offices to arrange for Du Bois to see Mrs. Anita McCormick Blaine, heiress and bankroller of a number of progressive causes. Du Bois took this opportunity to inform her of his lamentable financial situation. He expected to receive $1,200 from Atlanta University and $2,400 from the

NAACP. He proposed a stipend be allocated to him in part for his upcoming effort to interpret the history of Blacks to the United States from 1876 to 1949—picking up where his massive *Black Reconstruction* left off. Blaine responded quite graciously: "What I understood that you would let me do is to add five thousand dollars to your available funds." His agreement with Blaine gave him at least temporary economic peace of mind.[1]

Thus, Du Bois moved his books, files, and office materials further south to a building also occupied by the American Committee for the Protection of the Foreign Born, the Council for Pan-American Democracy, the Hungarian American Council for Democracy, the Abraham Lincoln Brigade, and other leftist organizations. He departed with Roy Wilkins' words in *The New York Times* ringing in his ears; the former journalist labelled him "never an organization man" and the *Times* itself termed him a "stormy petrel." Du Bois became vice chairman of the council and chairman of their Africa Aid Committee which, among other things, collected funds for families of slain and injured victims of the Enugu massacre of striking coal miners in Nigeria. His path to the council was circuitous and not as obvious a decision as it might appear. The council was organized in London in the late 1930s by Max Yergan of the Young Men's Christian Association and Paul Robeson and established in New York City. Its purpose was to push for decolonization and educate the United States populace about this important issue. It was not a mass membership organization; by mid-1948 its leadership consisted of Robeson, Yergan, Hubert Delany, Ralph Bunche, and Mordecai Johnson. At this point the latter two departed and a host of newcomers joined: Charlotta Bass, Earl Dickerson, E. Franklin Frazier, John Hammond, and Edith Field, wife of Frederick Field, and Hammond's successor as treasurer. W. Alphaeus Hunton, a scholar in English literature, came aboard during this reorganization. Described by Hollis Lynch as "quiet, radical and brilliant," Hunton was "the council's administrative and intellectual mainstay." Like so many other Black radicals of that era, he had received a higher education, receiving his doctorate in English Literature in 1938. He became a fast ally and comrade of Du Bois. The council was an ideal spot for Du Bois to settle, not just because of the presence of allies but also because of the resources and contacts the organization provided. The council received a long list of publications from Africa and elsewhere that he found indispensable.[2]

Still, it was not preordained that he would arrive at 26th Street, since his relations with Yergan were not the best. This was so although both the YMCA official and Mordecai Johnson, president of Howard University, had recommended him for the post with the NAACP in 1944. This cooperation was not a chimera. Du Bois agreed to cosponsor a council-organized conference addressing self-determination for Puerto Rico. But Du Bois was disappointed with the relationship. He would have liked to have joined the council, and expected to be invited, but the secretary, Max Yergan, did not seem to want his cooperation. Earlier, when the council was organized in 1937, he pointed the finger of accusation huffily at the YMCA official.[3]

At the same time, the NAACP was not pleased with developing any ties with the council. This was apparent during the organizing of the Pan-African Congress and the Harlem colonial conference. Du Bois wished to work closely with the council but, due to their leftist ties, he felt that White and the leadership would object. This was something of a change, given that Robeson had been lauded as Spingarn Medal winner (the NAACP's highest honor) in 1945, while the radicalism of Du Bois's *World and Africa* and *Color and Democracy* were received favorably. Du Bois had defied this sentiment to an extent by accepting Robeson's and Yergan's early 1947 invitation to join the major policy-making body of the council. This was at a time when the council was responding to the gathering Cold War onslaught by stepping up its radicalism and not retreating. Its publication, *New Africa,* was becoming increasingly anti-imperialist. It focused intensely on big business investment in colonial Africa.[4]

Though the council was becoming increasingly anti-imperialist, or at least less reluctant to suppress their anti-imperialism, their leader Max Yergan was moving frantically in the opposite direction. The growing and yawning chasm between the council and Yergan was symbolic of the Cold War split in the Afro-American community, not unlike the Du Bois-NAACP gulf. The constant in both was that Du Bois was involved. This flip-flop on Yergan's part was a radical turnabout from his past activities, particularly during his years in South Africa and during his tenure with the Communist-influenced National Negro Congress. Capitalists and trusts were his prime targets, notably in his *Gold and Poverty in South Africa.* He served on the board of trustees of the Jefferson School of Social Science as late as October 1946. But for some time there had been disenchantment with Yergan. Padmore told Du Bois that South Africans in Britain had a very low opinion of Yergan because while residing there he "identified himself as much as possible with the white church community" and "treated the Africans, even the intellectuals . . . with the greatest contempt." Hollis Lynch has criticized Yergan, "who had a virtual monopoly of executive power within the Council, did nothing to broaden its base," though the council "did succeed between 1943 and 1947 in attracting significant national and international attention." Why Yergan reversed field may be found in the fact that "early in 1947 [he] married a 'wealthy and attractive' bourgeois white woman." Lynch also commented on his conflict with Du Bois: "Yergan, who loved center stage, might well have feared that Du Bois would overshadow him within the Council." Simultaneously, Yergan had not been a favorite of the political-economic rulers of the United States during his radical phase. The council often had occasion to rally the masses against United States foreign policy. In April 1944 they sponsored a conference on Africa chaired by Robeson. The main resolution sharply questioned United States foreign policy. Such positions certainly played a role in inspiring House Un-American Activities Committees chair Martin Dies to severely assail Yergan.[5]

In 1948, the same year Du Bois was ousted from the NAACP, Yergan was fired by the council after he began attacking alleged Communist influence within the organization. In addition, Yergan made a one-sided move to circumscribe the power of the council's Executive Committee, the major policy-making body and ideologically dominated by the left. In short, the Yergan affair was the flip side of Du Bois' contretemps with the NAACP. In any case, Du Bois threatened to resign if Yergan's maneuvers were successful and expressed doubt about his influence. Yergan moved to call a council meeting before it was due with the aim of jamming through his dictate. Hunton was blunt in averring that "a coup [would] be attempted" at this meeting. Du Bois was pessimistic about altering this course: "Yergan has the right to call a meeting of the Council, legally his position is impregnable." Yergan was temporarily thwarted, as he was censured for having police on the premises at an earlier meeting that was quite stormy. Yergan walked out, but not before he was blasted for mishandling and diverting funds. At this juncture Du Bois stiffened his spine: "I am quite willing to do anything I can for the Council of African Affairs but it must be on one condition, and that is that Mr. Yergan be replaced." But reports of Yergan's demise were slightly exaggerated, as Hunton indicated to Robeson with chagrin: "I received notice of discharge from Dr. Yergan and was locked out of my office some three hours later, during my absence from the building." This brought down the wrath of Robeson, chairman of the Executive Committee of the council:

> quite the contrast to his former position, Dr. Yergan is now unwilling to challenge the imperialist policy of the U.S. Senate Department. He tries to hide his retreat by recourse to the threadbare device of yelling "communist."

Robeson boldly denied Yergan's claim of a pro- and anti-Wallace bloc within the council: "No such proposal whatever, either directly or indirectly, has been made at a Council meeting or by any officer of the Council." Regarding the putative sacking of Hunton, Robeson deplored "the disruptive tactics" of Yergan.[6]

These internecine skirmishes plunged the council into turmoil and gave, ironically, an impression of communist disruption during the first crucial election year of the newly inaugurated Cold War. Several members of the Exeutive Committee, William, J. Schieffelin, Hubert Delany, and John Hammond—apparently not wishing to be smeared with the red brush—resigned. Remaining members of this body, which at this point included Columbia University professor Gene Weltfish, labor leader Charles Collins, the historian Herbert Aptheker, Du Bois, and Estelle Osborn, assistant professor of Nursing at New York University, founder of the National Association of Colored Graduate Nurses, and vice president of the National Council of Negro Women, issued a stinging rebuke to Yergan, calling his actions "reprehensible and dictatorial."[7]

Council members weighed in against Yergan. Eslanda Robeson, present at the creation of the council and wife of Paul, had given the initial financial contribution of 300 pounds to start the organization. She waxed indignant. "Until now," she began, Yergan had not "challenged the political opinions of Paul Robeson, George Marshall, Doxey Wilkerson, Ferdinand Smith and others in the Council." She forswore all knowledge as to whether there were Communists in the CAA "nor do I consider it any of my business." She wondered why this issue nettled Yergan when "it was in his home on Hamilton Terrace that I first met Earl Browder; this very well-known Communist was the guest of honor there." Commingling and diversion of funds was a repeated accusation leveled against Yergan, and Eslanda Robeson alluded to it when she charged that whenever they asked for a "financial report . . . we are met with the irrelevant answer Communism." Her husband Paul was no less irate in briefing Du Bois. He reproached Yergan for meeting behind "locked doors with one or two of his supporters"; those present "elected a new set of officers replacing all the present ones except himself and 'dropped' sixteen of those persons who share my views on the Council." Because of the Yergan controversy, he continued, "the work of the organization—for three months now—has remained at a stand-still." He listed thirty other CAA members, who had either assigned their proxies to him or were present in person at a recent meeting. The Executive Board substained all the charges against Robeson, its chairman, and demanded that Yergan "relinquish all financial and other records" to Hunton and move out of CAA premises "as of May 27, 1948." They also recommended that Yergan be fired.[8]

Furthermore, the CAA's Finance Committee found that Yergan failed during 1947 to send any funds whatever to Africa, even though these funds were received by the council in response to urgent appeals for African famine relief. Scathingly, they blistered Yergan for failing to establish branches in other cities, enlarge the membership, form a permanent Africa Relief Committee, rally support for the South West Africa cleric, Michael Scott, who was campaigning in the United States or Sylvanus Olympio of beleaguered Togo. Despite repeated appeals, they alleged, he did not respond. One of the CAA members denouncing Yergan was Du Bois. Du Bois was always careful to appropriately convey his proxy directly to Robeson for those meetings he was unable to attend. Though staggering under the virtual unanimous repudiation of the council, Yergan did not yield in his attempt to pin charges of Communist domination on the council. In this he resorted to innovative tactics. As Hunton confided to Du Bois, Yergan had three people "arrested for alleged assault after they refused to let him break down the door to the Council office. Yesterday Magistrate John E. Pendergast . . . threw the charges out of court as unfounded."[9]

Yergan's primary charge that there were Communists not only dominating the CAA but stampeding the council toward Wallace was a hot item in the press. The New York-based *People's Voice,* which Du Bois wrote for weekly before it lurched to the right, was reputedly owned and published by Yergan. That may have influenced their view a bit: "Max Yergan is doing a distinct service in exposing, defying and denouncing the Communist dirty work he is facing." More representative was the sober view of the editorially conservative *Amsterdam News,* which alleged that Yergan's position "does represent a marked departure from the Council's past position." *PM,* though generally sympathetic to Robeson, was enlightening: "Yergan also revealed the 70-member board of the Council had split wide open on the Wallace issue. He identified the leaders of the anti-third party block as Rep. Adam Clayton Powell, Municipal Court Judge Hubert Delany, Dr. Alain Locke, John Hammond, Mrs. Mary McLeod Bethune and Dr. Channing Tobias." If this is true, it is striking that Delany and Hammond, who backed Du Bois during his difficulties with the NAACP, reversed field on this question. But Yergan's credibility, as subsequent events demonstrated, was open to question. He ultimately became a favorite anticommunist witness before Congress, in newspapers, and elsewhere and completely retreated from his previous leftism, exhibited so boldly in the National Negro Congress, the Jefferson School of Social Science, and the Council on African Affairs. This episode, a cause celebre in the Black community, was instrumental in shaping an image of Communist disruption that washed over to affect public perception of Du Bois' ouster; Du Bois, linked with Robeson and progressives in the attempt to sack Yergan, was weakened by whatever strength red smear accusations held, when the time for his axing came.[10]

Entangled as he was in bureaucratic wrangles in 1948, replete with spite and backbiting, it would not be surprising if Du Bois had decided to rest his eighty-one-year-old bones in 1949. The Progressive party had suffered what many considered to be a crushing defeat. The domestic political atmosphere had chilled substantially, and the chill could not be separated from the detailed war plans drawn up by the Joint Chiefs of Staff. Sensing a war danger, Du Bois and a number of other sturdy fighters, flung themselves headlong into a booming peace movement. This multifaceted effort to reduce East-West tensions, subsequently encapsulated in the rubric "detente," has not always received respectful attention. Lawrence Wittner, who exposes his predilections by employing notoriously inaccurate House Un-American Activities Committee reports to indict the lodestar Cultural and Scientific Conference, avers "from 1950 to 1956, then the peace movement consisted of little more than a small band of isolated pacifists." Merely tracing Du Bois' involvement, snaking like the Nile through the heart of the peace movement, incontestably refutes this widely held fallacy.[11]

The Cultural and Scientific Conference for World Peace was brought together under the auspices of the National Council of Arts, Sciences and Professions at the Waldorf-Astoria in Manhattan on March 25–27, 1949. Du Bois was hardly modest in confessing, "I helped to plan this program." Indeed he did play a large role and this did not endear him to many of his fellow citizens. The response of the New York press—which whipped up a severe public hysteria about this peace conclave—has attracted specific scholarly attention. Henry Singer, in an exhaustive examination, states that out of 2,062 items comprising headlines, feature stories, articles, editorials, cartoons, and captions that appeared in the New York press from March 23–30, 1949, there were 1,090 emotionally charged words and phrases, 205 unsupported charges, 139 outright falsehoods, 463 statements in opposition to the conference, 132 statements neutral in tone, and 28 statements in favor of the congress. And this particular effort was benignly viewed compared to other peace thrusts. The *New York Journal American* called for 100,000 pickets to ring the Waldorf—though only a few hundred showed up, some carrying that paper's front page. Du Bois' endeavors on behalf of peace were not appreciated by the major press organs of U.S. elites: "The public was in fact . . . the recipients of somewhat distorted or slanted articles, and in some cases, the victims of pure fabrications. The implications of this are quite sweeping when one considers the total impact of the New York press and news services upon national and international media and thought."[12]

It is not idle to conjecture about what could prompt such an avalanche of hostile propaganda and scurrilous attacks. This event was participated in by 2,800, with thousands turned away. The broad participation was a veritable all-star line-up of progressive forces from the arts, sciences and professions and is worthy of extended mention as evidence of antiwar sentiment at a critical turning point: Stella Adler, Leonard Bernstein, Marlon Brando, Lee J. Cobb, Jules Dassin, Albert Einstein, Jose Ferrer, Dashiell Hammett, Lillian Hellman, Judy Holliday, Arthur Miller, Scott Nearing, Eugene Ormandy, Dorothy Parker, Dimitri Shostakovich, Rexford Tugwell, Louis Untermeyer, Norbert Wiener, and Frank

Lloyd Wright were among the illustrious participants. Messages to the conference were received from such distinguished personages as Pablo Casals, Charles Chaplin, F. Joliot-Curie, Anna Magnani, Pablo Neruda, Martin Anderson Nexo, Alan Paton, Michael Redgrave, Diego Rivera, and David Siquieros. With the intellectual, artistic, and scientific cream of the United States and the world turning against policy emanating from Foggy Bottom and the Pentagon, it is little wonder that wholesale attempts were made to derail this gathering.[13]

The high point of this historic movement was reached at Madison Square Garden, as Du Bois told his wife: "There were 20,000 people there . . . and two or more thousand could not get in. . . . I opened the meeting." In actuality, Du Bois' words excited the throng at one of the largest peace rallies before or since, as he tackled the burning questions of the age.[14]

This Du Bois-led campaign, which severely roiled the waters in the press and public eyes, was not greeted with insouciance by all. Days after the conference's closing, apparently stung to the quick, HUAC issued a lengthy diatribe against those involved. Du Bois was singled out for unique vituperation. There was a detailed indictment of Du Bois' various political activities that was considered powerful evidence of why they considered him dangerous. This lengthy dissertation against Du Bois was noteworthy for a number of reasons. As a resume it signalled how, unlike White, Yergan, and others, he had moved (or was moved) closer to the Communist party, seeing the party's defense as the first line of defense of civil liberties generally. As a bill of charges, along with the flood of press coverage, it showed how seriously a revived, invigorated peace movement, led by the patriarch of the Black and left, was taken.[15]

In a sense, Du Bois' removal from the NAACP was liberating in that it allowed him to devote more time to peace activism unencumbered by a stifled tongue. He saw this activism as critical not only because of explicit United States war plans but also due to fissures separating erstwhile allies. Figures like Norman Thomas, A. J. Muste, Dwight MacDonald; organizations like the Socialist party, Fellowship of Reconciliation, and the War Resisters' League, all redbaited the Progressive party, the Waldorf Conference, and other Du Bois initiatives. Lawrence Wittner portrayed their motivation kindly: "Pacifist organizations exhibited extreme caution when dealing with Communists, and consequently shunned all participation in Soviet-sponsored peace initiatives." This lack of unity did not make Du Bois' job easier—(nor did it bar the persecution of these anticommunist "leftists," and probably hastened it)—but he plunged on. Contemporaneous with the Waldorf conference, Du Bois was active with the American Sponsoring Committee, which helped to organize the World Congress for Peace in Paris on April 20–23, 1949. Du Bois was cochair of this prestigious gathering and F. J. Curie was president. There were 2,192 delegates from over seventy countries representing 700 million people participating. Though it was caluminated as further evidence of the proverbial "Soviet plot," the idea for the congress originated in the International Liaison Committee of Intellectuals for the Peace and the Committee of the Women's International Democratic Federation; the appeal for the congress was launched on February 25. When Paul Robeson made pointed comments questioning whether Blacks would be enthusiastic about fighting an undoubtedly suicidal war against the Soviet Union, it was guaranteed that the Paris meeting would capture headlines at home. The *National Guardian* was not engaging in hyperbole when it announced, "None Who Saw Paris Will Ever Forget." Du Bois was no less modest when he termed the congress the "greatest meeting of men ever assembled in modern times to advance the progress of all men." Its saliency was revealed in that "the colored world was present . . . in full right with full participation," in contrast to the colonialism supported by the anticommunists. The same factor was visible at the American Continental Congress for World Peace in Mexico City in September 1949. Du Bois was vice president of this fiery event, as was Linus Pauling. The two, along with O. John Rogge, Uta Hagen, and John Clark were sparkplugs behind the United States organizing.[16]

Contrary to their many detractors, these peace meetings were not just star-studded soirees in exotic foreign climes. They were sharply political, more often than not implacably opposed to United States foreign policy, and thus not greeted with glee by Washington and Wall Street. This tendency became distinctly intelligible when Du Bois, the only United States delegate, traveled to the Moscow Peace Congress, a trip funded by Anita McCormick Blaine. He was invited to this August 25th conference in a hastily sent telegram forwarded by a Soviet peace committee. The Moscow meeting preceded Mexico City, where O. John Rogge sparked controversy when he delivered a speech caustically critical of the Soviet Union. His views on the Soviet Union were at variance with Du Bois' and one's view of the Soviets was not only a factor in taking a stand against the Cold War but, also, an ever-present factor at these peace meetings. Just prior to leaving for Moscow, Du Bois had spoken unequivocally on this cardinal question in testimony before the House Foreign Affairs Committee on behalf of the Continental Peace Congress in Mexico. "In 1850's . . . the word of exorcism is 'abolitionist,' . . . Today the word is communist."[17]

Du Bois did not shrink from the first nation led by Communists. Soviet postwar policy in Eastern Europe was a bone of contention at some of these peace meetings, but to Du Bois it was a nonstarter. As early as April 4, 1945, Oswald G. Villard had requested that Du Bois sign a statement attacking Soviet policy in Poland. But he adamantly refused. This coupling of "Black and Red" was not the only basis for the pro-Soviet views that informed his peace activism. Opposition to imperialism was another pillar—an opposition grounded in an analysis of the state. At the same time, he felt that there were common objectives uniting the United States and the Soviet Union, that is, abolition of war and the abolition of poverty. Still, he was dismissive of United States-based anti-Soviet propaganda since the biased press coverage against Blacks impinged on their credibility when analyzing their coverage of reds. In *Soviet Russia Today,* Du Bois returned to the question of democracy in the Soviet Union. He felt that countries like the United States are anti-democratic since basic questions of life—housing, transportation, health care, and how much is grown at what price—are all decided by corporate boards beholden only to shareholders. The Soviet Union was deemed different and, "if the threat of foreign interference were not so constant, the goal of complete democracy would be more quickly reached."[18]

Such were the bases of Du Bois' peace activism. He did not retreat from these views at the Moscow Peace Congress and, if anything, extended them. This visit to Eastern Europe included a trip to the Poland that had occupied so much of Du Bois' attention and this may have led to his views being heightened. He was stunned by the "incredible devastation," of the landscape and the people: "I never thought it possible that human beings could do to each other in modern days what the Germans did to Warsaw." Du Bois had an advantage over his fellow citizens in being able to actually visit the home of the assumed "Iron Curtain" countries. But visual acuity was only part of the reason why in 1949 Du Bois was being mentioned—mostly abroad—as a possible recipient for the Nobel Peace Prize. Du Bois was not sanguine about this and not solely because of his laying major blame for Cold War at the feet of United States rulers. Yet Du Bois' relentless toiling for peace and his alignment with the vibrant Council on African Affairs was certainly worthy of note and award in 1949, and even more so when in 1950 war descended on Korea.[19]

CHAPTER 12

Ban the Bomb

In 1950 Du Bois reached the age of eighty-two, but as a monument to venerableness, maintained a staggering pace. After peace was disrupted in the Asian "land of the morning calm," he had to accelerate more. Threats to peace, civil liberties, and civil rights did not emerge suddenly like a sunburst from the blue in the summer of 1950—though it could appear that way. In March 1950 Pablo Picasso, the Reverend Hewlett Johnson, Dean of Canterbury, and ten other eminent people were barred from the United States. They tried to come on behalf of the World Congress of Partisans for World Peace—an organization Du Bois had helped bring into being. The United States State Department stoutly resisted the pleas of outrage and the American Civil Liberties Union's request that the visitors be granted visas. The State Department termed the delegation "phoney." As the *Daily Worker* reported, Du Bois called their bar, "tragic." With Linus Pauling and others, he circulated an urgent appeal lashing out at the State Department for their refusal to grant visas to the delegation who wished to speak in the United States on peace proposals to be made to President Truman and Congress. Similar delegations had been received by the parliaments of France, Britain, Holland, Belgium, and Mexico but Washington would have none of it. Events like these reinforced the existing notion that an organization would be needed to resist the call for war and the deprivation of rights that ineluctably accompanied it.[1]

Accordingly, a few weeks after this troublesome incident, the Provisional Committee of Americans for World Peace convened. The thirty-seven present included James Aronson, C. B. Baldwin, Dr. Edward Barsky, Cedric Belfrage, Howard Fast, Mike Gold, Albert Kahn, Rockwell Kent, John Howard Lawson, Elizabeth Moos, Richard Morford, Anton Refregier, Joseph Starobin, Louis Weinstock, and Gene Weltfish; Du Bois chaired the meeting, which was an outgrowth of the controversial Paris peace gathering. Moos proposed the formation of a Peace Information Center (PIC), designed to supply information on peace actions to the press, issue fact sheets, arrange for American delegations to attend peace conferences abroad, and supply information on peace actions in the United States to peace groups abroad. The budget was six to eight thousand dollars per year. Moos' proposal was accepted with Du Bois chosen as chairman of the Advisory Council and Mrs. Moos as executive director. The Executive Committee of the information center held its first meeting at Du Bois' office with Shirley Graham, Paul Robeson, and Moos among those present. These meetings were not always unanimous in their conclusions. At the May 11, 1950 meeting, O. John Rogge "disagreed with statements placing the blame of the cold war solely on the United States."[2]

The PIC quickly became notorious for its sponsoring of the Stockholm Peace Appeal, the so-called ban the bomb petition. This internationally agreed upon document, though slandered and maligned, may have been signed by more people than any other appeal ever devised by human hand and brain. It was pithy in simplicity:

> We demand the outlawing of atomic weapons as instruments of intimidation and mass murder of peoples.
>
> We demand strict international control to enforce this measure.
>
> We believe that any government which first uses atomic weapons against any other country whatsoever will be committing a crime against humanity and should be dealt with as a war criminal.
>
> We call on all men and women of goodwill throughout the world to sign this appeal.

"Ban the bomb" entered the public lexicon and was a clear harbinger for the massive antinuke movement that was to emerge years later. This was not by accident or chance but by dint of the resolute and indefatigable labors of the Peace Information Center led by Du Bois. They developed innovative propaganda designed to appeal to special groups, for example, "Catholics Speak For Peace" (with a list of well-known signers) and "Israel Welcomes the World Peace Appeal" (with an impressive listing of signers that ultimately included the vice-president of the Knesset, twenty-two deputies representing four parties, and the former commander-in-chief of the Haganah).[3]

The Afro-American community was a conscious and special target of the Appeal and their response was similar to their disproportionately favorable greeting of the Progressive party. The breadth of the Appeal's attraction was evidenced by the avid support of musician Charlie "Yardbird" Parker. Marian Anderson, another popular Black musical artist, was supportive. So was Pearl Primus, the dancer and anthropologist, when she addressed a N.Y.-CASP meeting in "protest against the H-Bomb and World War III."[4]

PIC's campaign to attract trade union support was extensive. The Baker and Confectionary Workers, Local 13, American Federation of Labor, voted to support the appeal and to get 3,000 signatures in New York City. A flyer, "You Too Can Vote for Peace," reported that also endorsing the petition were the International Longshore and Warehousemen's Union, District 2 of the International Woodworkers, Ship Scalers and Dry Dock Workers, Cannery Workers 7-C, Hope Lodge 79 of the International Association of Machinists, Marine Cooks and Stewards, and the Office and Professional Workers Union. Du Bois coordinated the gargantuan effort that bore such fruit. The Executive Committee of the PIC meeting in August 1950 noted that 3,500 prominent persons had been sent letters requesting their endorsement of the Appeal; endorsing were, among others, Albert Maltz, Thomas Mann, E. Franklin Frazier, Professors Dorothy Brewster and Bernhard J. Stern of Columbia University, Marc Chagall, Ewart Guinier, the Reverend Milton Galamison and—interestingly—a disproportionate number of clerics. Leonard Bernstein signed the appeal and Du Bois wrote him to get a "brief statement of endorsement . . . for use among cultural leaders," that already included George Bernard Shaw, Henri Matisse, Arnold Zweig, and Pablo Picasso.[5]

By the summer of 1950, over 1.5 million people in the United States had affixed their signatures to the documents. The support of the religious community was significant in this process. The 131st Annual Conference of the Methodist Church called for banning the bomb, along with the 162nd General Assembly of the Presbyterian Church. But this outpouring of support was dwarfed by the international response. There were 10 million signatories in France, 60 million in China, 115 million in the Soviet Union. In Brazil, the nation with the largest Black community in the Western hemisphere, where there were 3.75 million signers, "2,000 illiterate peasants have signed by making thumb prints with the juice of crushed poppy leaves."[6]

This support in the United States could not be generated solely by letters to prominent figures. Thus May 29–30, 1950, the PIC worked with Dr. Willard Uphaus, executive director of the Committee for Peaceful Alternatives and sponsors like Thomas Mann, Linus Pauling, Benjamin Mays, and others in organizing the well-attended Mid-Century Conference for Peace. There were 719 delegates from twenty-nine states, the District of Columbia, and the Territory of Hawaii.[7]

Hopes for peace were being shattered as the PIC's Advisory Committee met on June 26, 1950. As usual, emphasis was being placed on mobilizing Blacks—a community more predisposed than most to oppose war in Korea and elsewhere. As one scholar put it, Blacks were "angered at being denied their civil rights at home while being ordered to fight for democracy abroad." This was compounded by the sensitive issue of "colored" United States troops being deployed against "colored" people in Asia, under the aegis of a United States military machine still bearing the stain of segregation. Ben Davis, Du Bois' intimate and Black Communist leader, was not alone in pinpointing this dilemma and the Truman Administration's trumpeting of the use of Black troops and desegregation in the armed forces in order to cover up the perceived racist character of the war and to win over Blacks who might oppose the war. Davis was quick to note the "wide publicity given to the use of Negro troops in Korea." The rampant racism leveled at Black troops was also of particular concern to Du Bois and this was no new development. Before his departure from the NAACP, Du Bois had worked with the radical lawyer Conrad Lynn on the defense committee of the Campaign to Resist Military Segregation, which had prodded Truman's earlier efforts toward desegregation.[8]

Du Bois was the logical choice to organize the smoldering antiwar sentiment in both the Black and white communities and he moved quickly to fill the bill. Days after the conflict had begun, W. Alphaeus Hunton suggested that Du Bois draft a statement against the war to be sent to 500 Negro leaders. Du Bois followed through and speedily crafted an eloquent manifesto entitled, "A Protest and a Plea." Signed by Aaron Douglas, *Afro* editor, Ralph Matthews, and many others, this "Protest and a Plea" was not greeted with sobriety in a United States society that was coming to equate dissent to this war with treason. Opposition to the war took courage, and retribution could be swift, as evidenced by the judge who deprived a mother of custody of her children when she termed the "police action" in Korea "an imperialistic adventure"; according to the court, this made her "unfit to raise her children." Du Bois and the Council on African Affairs were undeterred by this frequently intransigent opposition; to the contrary, it seemed to inspire them. The CAA's bulletin, *New Africa,* reported that antiwar opponents were not alone, as they quoted antiwar views from the Nigerian *Eastern Mail,* the *Takoradi Times* of the Gold Coast, the African League in London, and others.[9]

The NAACP remained the preeminent Afro-American organization in 1950 and it was one of the leaders in opposition to the antiwar movement led by Du Bois. This was true even though they, too, were keenly aware of the rank discrimination visited on Black G.I.s, the subject of a well-publicized tour of Korea by Thurgood Marshall. But symptomatic of their approach during the Cold War, they advocated desegregation so that the fight against communism could be waged more effectively. They cogently noted that those in countries where United States troops were stationed would have a window on a particular United States vulnerability through observations of the troops there, thus harming the national image—or more precisely, reflecting it all too well. In editorial after editorial, *Crisis* pleaded for United States leaders to become better anticommunists by getting the racial house in order. Yet, the NAACP board voted to support United States efforts "to halt Communist aggression in Korea," though not without a certain amount of uncertainty. "America will win the hot war in Korea . . . [but] Asia is in revolution," they intoned, and the United States must not back "reactionaries like Bao Dai in Indochina, Chiang Kai-shek . . . or Rhee in South Korea." The board was seemingly not cognizant that, like any unpopular war, Korea involved a curbing of civil and human rights and the strengthening of those same right-wing forces desiring to repress Blacks; the assassination of NAACP officials, for example, Harry Moore in Florida, was not a chance outgrowth of the war. Nevertheless, the

1951 convention of the association in Atlanta followed the anti-communist tendencies of the 1950 Boston gathering. There were strains. They called on the government to "explore all avenues of peace and to consider every proposal for peace." But they could not resist supporting the war against Korea and maligning peace organizations demanding "bring back our boys from Korea.[10]

There was no doubt that the W.E.B. Du Bois-led peace campaign was the principal target of this resolution that illustrated the deep division over the war that engulfed the Afro-American community. At the same time, those on the left and other Blacks—such as Norman Thomas and A. Philip Randolph—supported the war down the line and also clashed with Du Bois. M. E. Mantell has observed, in his comprehensive dissertation, that "by helping to formulate Black opposition to Korea, Dr. Du Bois provided an important link between black and white anti-war activists." Shortly after the war began, the Peace Information Center held a rally in New York City where Du Bois called for an end to "foreign intervention" and the beginning of "arbitration." At a rally of 300 in Buffalo, during his campaign for the United States Senate in 1950, he was vehement. This tour took him to Schenectady and Albany and included several radio broadcasts. After a fiery speech before a crowd of 200 at a Syracuse University political science club, the American Labor party announced that Du Bois "campaigned like a veteran politician. . . . He often set the pace for younger members of the party."[11]

These activities were to rile many in the United States. In such an atmosphere, Du Bois' concrete attempts to bring about peace were virtually guaranteed an unfriendly reception. Ernest A. Gross, deputy United States representative to the United Nations, "rejected Dr. Du Bois' proposal that the United States delegation receive representatives . . . to hear its views on Korea . . . the delegation had received representatives last April and . . . no useful purpose would be served by another meeting." Gross also rejected an offer for the United States delegation to meet with F. Joliot-Curie of the World Peace Council.[12]

One reason that explains why both antagonism and a cold shoulder were turned to Du Bois was that his antiwar organizing was exceedingly effective in the face of a hostile environment and continued to attract adherents. Du Bois' colleague Elizabeth Moos told Fred Stover, president of the Iowa Farmers Union that the "situation in South-East Asia" has caused "a tremendous increase in the number of people willing to sign the peace appeal" but "especially the women" are signing up. A measure of this support was noted when Du Bois proudly announced on September 23, 1950, that 2.5 million people in the United States had signed the Stockholm Appeal—more than 2 million since the war against Korea had started despite a campaign of intimidation that had begun in several communities.[13]

The effectiveness of the antiwar campaign led by Du Bois was not lost on those leading the charge against Korea. Secretary of State Dean Acheson bitterly flagellated the Peace Information Center in *The New York Times* on July 13, 1950. His charges exploded across the pages of the press and in the electronic news media. Du Bois was touched to the quick. In his monumental *In Battle for Peace* he rebuked Acheson. Du Bois' lengthy response to Acheson was given space in *The New York Times.* The *Syracuse Post-Standard* was among the papers publishing Du Bois' reply in full. The Columbia Broadcasting System (CBS) called for an interview; but, and this was to be the more familiar reaction, the Hotel Chelsea demanded that PIC vacate the premises. Still, Du Bois did not pull his punches in making his retort to the Secretary of State:

> 200,000,000 ordinary men and women who want peace, have signed their names to the World Peace Appeal. George Bernard Shaw, Arnold Zweig, former President Cardenas of Mexico, former Premier Vittorio Orlando of Italy (who was one of the Big Four at Versailles), Osvaldo Aranha, Brazilian statesman and former president of the U.N. General Assembly, M. Mongibeaux, Chief Justice of the French Supreme Court, M. Mornet, Attorney General of France, Dr. Sholem Treistman, Chief Rabbi of Poland, Edouard Herriot, President of the French Senate and former Premier, Mm. Sun Yat-sen, Jose Bergamin, renowned Catholic philosopher, Cardinal Sapieha, Roman Catholic Primate of Poland . . . Nobel Peace Prize winner Emily Greene Balch . . . Thomas Mann . . . the appeal has been endorsed by the Egyptian Council of State, by the Roman Catholic Episcopate of Poland, by eight Catholic Bishops of Italy, by the Prime Minister and Cabinet of Finland and by the Parliament of the Soviet Union . . . International Committee of the Red Cross statement pointed out, "Against the atom bomb protection is impossible" . . . by the Cardinals and Bishops of the Roman Catholic Church of France, the Methodists, Presbyterians and Quakers and other religious

> groups in the United States . . . all have called for the banning of atomic warfare in as simple and direct a manner as called for by the World Peace Appeal . . . Israel Galili, former commander-in-chief of the Haganah in Israel, declared upon signing the Appeal: "When the Soviet Union supported the struggle for the creation of the State of Israel, no one said that help to Israel should be opposed because the Soviet Union was supporting Israel, and Britain was attempting to destroy it." So too, no one has the right today to smear the campaign for peace because the Soviet Union and the communist movement support it. . . . Certainly hundreds of millions of colored peoples . . . conscious of our support of Chiang Kai-shek, Bao Dai . . . and mindful of the oppressive discrimination against the Negro people in the United States would feel that our intention also must be accepted on faith. . . . While there is yet time, Mr. Acheson, let the world know that in the future, the Government of the United States will never be the first to use the atom bomb, whether in Korea or in any other part of the earth.

Dean Acheson did not, and perhaps could not, reply to this formidable broadside. But his government did. *The New York Times,* which had noted Du Bois' reply, printed what might be considered the informally reply to the militant leader. The PIC and its officers, the *Times* said on August 25, 1950, were "directed by the Department of Justice to register as agents of a foreign principal. Although the Government did not specify the foreign principal the Center is said to represent, it was apparent that the order stemmed from the group's distribution of the so-called 'Stockholm Peace Petition.' "[14]

The United States government and other forces opposed to the Stockholm Peace Appeal counterattacked on a broad front; they apparently felt that the petition disrupted the unity necessary to prosecute a war that was not universally popular. On July 13, 1950, the House Un-American Activities Committee issued a stinging condemnation of this peace campaign. They scored the demand for the outlawing of atomic weapons and "strict international control." The HUAC was so eager to disseminate an attack against the petition that they published a three-page report as a "preliminary note of caution" before a larger report was issued. "The petitions are intended to confuse and divide the American people," said HUAC. Francis H. Russell, director of the Office of Public

Affairs of the Department of State, in a widely circulated letter, denounced the petition for trying to promote "unenforceable Soviet proposals concerning atomic energy . . . to center attention on the use of atomic weapons . . . ignoring the aggression in other forms presently being practiced by the Communists." That this was a coordinated, planned attack and not just a few idle comments was revealed by Russell's closing remarks: "I should be pleased to arrange for you to attend one of the Department's regular briefing sessions." When United Nations Ambassador Warren Austin termed petition signers as "traitors," this was the last straw for Du Bois who publicly denounced this rhetorical excess.[15]

Taking an evident cue from the United States government, organized and often violent opposition to the Stockholm Peace Appeal surfaced. This campaign had impact and made the millions of signatures collected on the petition that much more politically remarkable. The fate of petitioners in Houston, described in Don Edward Carleton's gripping dissertation, was not dissimilar from experiences in other cities:

> [Police] harassed the petition drive at every turn, picking up the petitioners "for questioning" whenever they appeared on Houston streets.

Not atypically, after two petitioners were jailed, other "prisoners severely beat both men as their jailers looked the other way."[16]

Another fiery battleground involving the appeal was the religious community. Albert Kahn, the writer, was featured on a PIC speaking tour from August 4 to August 12, 1950. His report to Du Bois first noted the organized campaign of opposition. Though sobering, this was not the main theme of Kahn's report, which focused on the enthusiasm of the religious community. In actuality, a virtual guerrila war had broken out amongst religious factions, for and against the appeal. In the list of "Prominent Americans Endorsing the World Peace Appeal," there were a disproportionate number of Protestant clergy. They were also in the forefront of opposition to the war. An "Interfaith Committee for Peace Action" was formed with twenty-eight Protestant and Jewish leaders as sponsors. This trend did not sail along without resistance. Professor Joseph Fletcher of the Episcopal Theological Seminary at Cambridge, Massachusetts, assailed the World Council of Churches for not supporting the Appeal. He ridiculed the idea of peace and the appeal as being a communist "ploy."[17]

It was to Du Bois' credit that he led a movement that attracted mass support during troubled times. This mass support was not just in the churches but also in the synagogues. The appeal had picked up tremendous support among Jewish people, especially in Israel. The PIC also raised a substantial amount of money in the Jewish community. But also similar to the churches, there was a determined, inflexible opposition dug in against the appeal in the synagogues. Ten Jewish organizations ranging from the American Jewish Congress to the American Jewish Committee, the Association of Jewish Chaplains in the Armed Forces, Jewish War Veterans, and the National Council of Jewish Women spoke out against the petition.[18]

The campaign for the Stockholm Peace Appeal led by Du Bois created an angry controversy nationally. From May through October 1950, it was difficult to open *The New York Times* without staring at an article on the appeal, particularly after the "police action" in Korea had begun. On July 15 it reported that four solicitors for the Appeal were held by police for allegedly disobeying an order to move from a street corner. On August 8, they noted that solicitors had been threatened. On August 24 the *Times* described a case in Durham, North Carolina, where a judge barred the collecting of signatures; on August 31, another case involving a seaman fired for signing the Appeal. On September 15, A. Philip Randolph's Sleeping Car Porters was reported to have come out against the Appeal. But unfortunately scant coverage was given to a serious deprivation of civil liberties involving Du Bois. On July 29 Du Bois protested to Mayor William O'Dwyer of New York City about the refusal of the police to give a permit for a peace rally in Union Square, a prohibition occurring for "the first time in 150 years."[19]

The denial of First Amendment rights to Du Bois and the PIC were not limited to New York. The controversy raged across the nation, according to a statement released August 14, 1950, by American Civil Liberties Union board chair Ernest Angell, General Counsel Arthur Garfield Hays, and Executive Director Patrick M. Malin. Petitioners were "subjected to violence" and "arrest" nationally. But even this erstwhile statement of support revealed why petitioners faced such extreme difficulties, as they made repeated reference to the "evil of communism" and the "communist menace." A petitioner from Atlanta discussed being accosted by Ku Klux Klansmen who ironically echoed the ACLU. The KKK hit at them with a morbid allegation: "You're both Communists. We've got a great mind to kill you both." In Baltimore, both the *Sun* and the *News-Post* refused to print an advertisement on peace; only the *Afro* would print it. In New York, not only did the NAACP urge its members not to sign the appeal but popular musician Duke Ellington threatened to "sue sponsors of the Stockholm 'peace' appeal if they do not withdraw his name from literature which they have circulated."[20]

Leading circles of the peace movement reflected this discord but only to a small extent. After it had been suggested that O. John Rogge be publicly assailed, Rockwell Kent informed Du Bois to hold back on this until after a subsequent international peace meeting. The group then elected Rogge and Kent felt that "he is now sufficiently discredited to have any influence." Despite these defections from the ranks of the peace movement, the PIC carried on. Planning for an upcoming peace gathering was on the agenda at the October 12 Executive Board meeting: "It was emphasized that there should be a large Negro delegation." This was a constant theme—the notion of stressing Black community participation—that was emphasized at most meetings. And it was realized at the Second World Peace Congress, scheduled to take place in Sheffield, England. This congress called for going beyond the Stockholm Appeal to reducing arms, barring "aggression and armed intervention," and banning bacteriological warfare. After passports were denied to Paul Robeson, Howard Fast, Ernest De Maio, and others wishing to attend, the congress was shifted to Warsaw. Du Bois was elected to the presiding committee along with Paul Robeson and Howard Fast, at this meeting of 2,025 delegates, guests, and observers from seventy-two countries—an assembly more representative than the United Nations since the colonial lands were represented. But problems continued after the congress, as the St. Nicholas Arena—reportedly under severe political pressure—cancelled the contract for Du Bois and others to report on what happened in Warsaw. Yet, that was not the only problem the immensely successful peace movement led by Du Bois faced. An indictment stared them in the fact and the minutes of October 12, 1950, reflected these tensions:[21]

> Mr. Simon reported that the Justice Department had refused to make an appointment for Dr. Du Bois to personally discuss the case with them. . . . In view of the severe and pressing financial difficulties, and many allied problems, it was felt that the Peace Information Center should terminate its activities and dissolve.

CHAPTER 13

The American Labor Party and the Progressive Party

In 1950, in the midst of his duties as leader of the Peace Information Center, Du Bois was persuaded to run for the United States Senate seat from New York held by Herbert Lehman. His motto and primary campaign theme was "Peace and Civil Rights" and he brought it to city and town throughout New York State. He tried to show how the war prevented fulfillment of civil rights responsibilities. He did not win the election but, as he submitted early on, "I do not expect to be elected as United States Senator, but I do expect to get a chance to talk. It is about the only way one can express one's opinion these days."[1]

Du Bois ran as the candidate of the American Labor party, the local counterpart of the Progressive party. After the 1948 presidential election, unlike many progressives, Du Bois did not go softly into the night but remained close to the banner. When the Young Progressives of America, led by Louis Burham of SNYC and the future chair of the NAACP board Margaret Bush Wilson, asked him to sponsor their nationwide Salute to FDR rallies, he readily complied. Particularly in 1949, before repression heightened as a result of the war against Korea, the party was quite popular in the Afro-American community of New York. The *Guardian* found "three New York Negro districts in which the American Labor Party emerged as the top party in 1949 from third place in 1948" and where there was a "significant shift of Negro voters to Progressive Party candidates" due to the "transparent betrayals of the civil rights promises of Truman."[2]

The overriding trend was unity between Du Bois and Progressive party members. As he indicated to Henry Wallace in an elaborate historical analogy and as he told readers of the *Chicago Globe,* he saw the Progressive party as a latter day Liberty party, just as he saw Communists as heirs to the abolitionists. This was justifiable. The American Labor party was a long-time advocate of a permanent FEPC, increased welfare allotments, and an opponent of housing discrimination in Manhattan's Stuyvesant Town. The American Labor party in Brooklyn worked quite closely with the local NAACP chapter—a not uncommon occurrence in other cities—on issues of civil rights and police brutality. The Progressive party called for home rule in heavily Black Washington, D.C., elimination of discrimination and segregation in the armed forces, all federal agencies, and the Canal Zone, and, like its New York affiliate, a permanent FEPC. But his words to Wallace may have been for naught, as the 1948 standardbearer, along with others, deserted the party after its electoral loss.[3]

These defections weakened the Progressive and American Labor parties, but in 1950, as Du Bois was beginning to seriously consider running for the Senate, his party still maintained strength. For example, on May 12, 1950, Vito Marcantonio of the American Labor party demanded that the Democrats and Republicans nominate a Negro for "the important 14-year, $28,000 General Sessions judgeship." Events were to illustrate this trend in the American Labor party's and the Progressive party's history; that is, their presence presented an alternative for Black voters and forced more concessions from the two major parties. The *Guardian* analyzed the situation thusly:

> If they refused the ALP would name its own candidate and enter him in the Democratic primary. On July 5, after vowing they would not be "bullied" by the ALP, [the Democrats] named Negro Assemblyman Harold A. Stevens as their candidate . . . the first such nomination in New York's political history. . . . The next day to counter the Democratic move, the Republicans named Larson Walsh, a Negro for justice of the City Court.

This effect was not limited to New York, or to Du Bois' Senate campaign. When the Progressive party convened in Chicago on

February 24–26, 1950, not only were there leading nonBlack personalities like John Abt, Elinor Gimbel, John Rogge, and Lillian Hellman but there also were Black leaders like Larkin Marshall, member of the NAACP executive body in his home state and chair of the Georgia Progressive party and Willard Ransom, chair of the Indiana NAACP (the first Black in the state's history to be nominated for Congress there). Du Bois was the first Black to run for the United States Senate from New York. The American Labor and Progressive parties helped to liberalize the political atmosphere in an era of conservative ascendancy and objectively forced the two major parties to grant more concessions to Blacks in order to compete more effectively for their votes.[4]

Not everyone was able to follow every aspect of this progressive tradition. About the time Du Bois was cranking up to run for office, the National Committee of the Progressive party was meeting in Chicago. "As a special order of business," John Rogge moved that the party call a "special convention . . . to reconsider all the positions taken with respect to foreign policy . . . from the time of the founding convention in July 1948 to the date of the Special Convention." This was soundly defeated 41–2, with only Rogge and Cecile Lund of Wisconsin voting yes. But this did not adequately reflect the dissension within the party engendered by the war. At this meeting, Thomas Emerson, Lillian Hellman, and Elinor Gimbel resigned from the National Committee. Shortly thereafter, Corliss Lamont resigned as treasurer because of the party's failure to condemn "North Korean aggression." Proposed to replace them were Vincent Hallinan, Robert M. Lovett, and Du Bois. Du Bois' commitments with the NAACP and other organizations had previously deterred him from taking a leading role in the party. Earlier in 1950 he had chaired the Resolutions Committee at the convention (with Emerson as secretary). Because of his preeminent role among Blacks, Du Bois was something of an ideal choice to head these stormy sessions.[5]

The Progressives called on Du Bois quite a bit; in the space of a few weeks in early 1951 he was asked to speak by Young Progressives of America chapters at the University of Chicago, Columbia University, Hunter College, New York University, and Swarthmore College. The campuses were a major source of opposition to Cold War trends and Du Bois' popularity there, attributable to his scholarly writings and lifetime of activism, reflected and fed this dissent. In addition, requests for speaking engagements flooded in from other sectors. Though the *Defender*, apparently under pressure, dropped his weekly column, he used the pages of the rival *Chicago Globe* to stiffen the posture of liberals, such as, Claude Pepper and Frank Graham, who were besieged by redbaiting.[6]

His lofty role meant that his entry into the 1950 Senate race against Herbert Lehman would be viewed with trepidation in certain circles. Though they engaged in their customary redbaiting of Du Bois, the *Amsterdam News* felt that his entry into the race "might cause the defeat of Senator Lehman." The conservative Harlem-based weekly knew that both the Republicans and Democrats took the Black vote for granted and suggested the reason:

> Negro voters have failed to throw their political weight around as some of the other minority groups are doing. This may be our year for decision. This may be the time to let the major party leaders know the campaign facts of life. . . . They're figuring the Negro vote [is] in the bag.

But, in an evident contradiction, they directed a special attack at the only Black candidate in the race and ruefully exclaimed: "Dr. W.E.B. Du Bois as a candidate against Mr. Lehman and Lt. Gov. Hanley, means practically nothing." In their editorial endorsements just before the election, they passed over the NAACP founder. In a page one column on September 11, 1950, *The New York Times* said that "Dr. Du Bois is expected to add strength to the Labor Party ticket in Harlem and other Negro sections of the city and state." A *Daily Worker* article agreed.[7]

The American Labor party grouped Du Bois with a field of candidates that were much more representative of the ethnic and sexual composition of the city and state than that of the two major parties; their ticket included women, Blacks, and Puerto Ricans. The American Labor party was a major political force in the state as evidenced by the substantial number of candidates fielded in every borough for positions from Congress to the State Assembly, from City Court to Surrogate Court. The party took advantage of Du Bois' star in their campaign propaganda to help bring the rest of the ticket along. He was termed "A Giant of the People" who would bring fear to the hearts of some: "Let bankers and their back-room politicians match the world-acclaimed greatness of . . . Dr. W.E.B. Du Bois." They emphasized, with an eye on New York's substantial Jewish and anti-Fascist community, Du Bois' adamant anti-Nazi views and condemnation of West German rearmament. Because of his outstanding commitments in other areas, his campaign got off to what some considered a relatively slow start. Nonetheless, in his opening campaign speech, reprinted in the *Guardian,* he came flying out of the starting blocks. He proclaimed the American Labor party as successor of the New Deal. He berated Lehman for sponsoring "legislation for concentration camps for Communists and those called Communist" while ignoring "the restoration to power in Germany of the same gang which killed 6,000,000 Jews and . . . their rearming." The donkey and the elephant were given a tongue-lashing. Two other favorite targets were seared, the "McCarran Bill, the Fugitive Slave Law of 1950."[8]

The American Labor party had high hopes that these campaign themes would swing votes to Du Bois' side, even in the midst of a war that required repression of many ideologically comfortable with their views. In an "Informal Memorandum for Discussion" on the Harlem campaign, Ewart Guinier, chairman of the Harlem American Labor party council, set a goal of 400,000 votes in the city since, "last year in New York City, our State Chairman, Representative Vito Marcantonio polled 356,000 votes." He too saw the sexual and ethnic balance of the ticket as a plus with candidates like Michael Jiminez for comptroller, Manuel Medina for assemblyman and Jacques Isler, the "first Negro candidate for the State Supreme Court, First Judicial District."[9]

Harlem residents and others proceeded to rally to the banner of the Non-Partisan Citizens Committee for Election of Du Bois. Bishop William J. Walls, head of the Second Episcopal District of the AME Zion Church, served as honorary chair and Ollie Harrington served as chair. Other members included the Black actress Fredi Washington and Nina Evans, president of the Domestic Workers Union. Paul Robeson was a prime fundraiser by virtue of his singing. The party's Woman's Council played a role in the campaign, stressing the rights of Black women, holding classes on the "History of the Struggle for Women's Rights," and raising many issues that did not gain currency until the women's movement of the 1970s. Du Bois received a number of endorsements, particularly from left-led unions and organizations. All was not sweetness and light in the campaign, however, as Frances Smith, of the American Labor party, felt compelled to contact Mayor Vincent Impellitteri of New York City about "threats of lawless attacks" against a Robeson fundraising concert at the Audubon Ballroom. The travail of Du Bois supporter, Dr. Robert Simmons, was not unusual. He quickly announced support and vowed to organize "a club . . . with . . . 100 members in Boston [with] plans of raising $1,000 in the state for your campaign." But days before the election he was admitting in horror to Du Bois' aide George Murphy, "we never dreamed that we would run into such a 'Red Scare.' We have fallen short of our goal." The same sorry fate befell other pro-Du Bois organizing efforts.[10]

At a well-attended press conference at Harlem's Hotel Theresa on September 24, 1950, Du Bois, amidst raging conflict in Korea, announced that the great issue of the day was peace. His words were all consonant with the party platform which also scorned big business, the military state, and praised the vision of Franklin D. Roosevelt. In that view the platform demanded the admission of the Peoples' Republic of China to the United Nations, immediate negotiation of the war in Korea through the United Nations Security Council, decolonization in Asia, Africa, and Puerto Rico, and the banning of atomic weapons. It also lambasted the arming of the Arabs against the "young state of Israel," the renazification and remilitarization of Germany, and demanded an immediate halt to witch-hunts, loyalty purges, contempt frame-ups, and inquisitions. Passage was urged of antilynch and antipoll tax laws and FEPC legislation, while repeal of the Taft-Hartley law was demanded along with steeply graduated taxes on the unprecendented corporate profits. Far ahead of their time, the platform called for equal pay for equal work, day care centers, and an end to discrimination against women in jobs and education.[11]

Du Bois campaigned tirelessly throughout Harlem spreading this message. At the Golden Gate Ballroom there was a major rally on October 5, 1950. Paul Robeson did the introduction, Charles White did a huge portrait of Du Bois for the platform, and Frank Silvera read a poem. Du Bois gave a typical speech: included was a brief history of Harlem, a caustic attack on Lehman and the GOP nominee Joseph Hanley, and a condemnation of the war in Korea. The crowd of 3,500 cheered as Du Bois expressed his political views.[12]

Perhaps the biggest crowd addressed by Du Bois was the 17,000 gathered at Madison Square Garden. As always, his main theme of peace and civil rights was stressed but possibly the enthusiasm of the audience also caused him to speak with a throaty fervor in challenging the conventional political orthodoxy.[13]

Du Bois launched an extensive campaign using the electronic news media. On October 8 on WPIX-TV's "Battle Page of the Air" he debated Lehman and Hanley. He was frequently heard on radio stations, most noticeably on WMCA, WEVD, and WOR. Here, his constant refrain of peace and civil rights was stressed. The corrosive effect of the Cold War on freedom of expression was also a recurrent topic for Du Bois, as WMCA listeners discovered on October 26, 1950. In his WEVD and WOR flaying of Lehman and Hanley, the incumbent was hit more. His family's firm of Lehman Brothers was accused of investing "in oil in South America and Arabia; in copper and lead in Africa, in rubber in Asia, sugar and fruit in the Caribbean . . . [and] it is closely connected with war industry in the United States." Du Bois charged that the pressure placed on these investments by residents of these lands interested in nationalization explained Lehman's flip-flop politically from the time he was governor and international issues were not as important.[14]

There was a wide difference between the press coverage allocated to Du Bois and that accorded to his opponents. *The New York Times* gave him some inches but it hardly measured up to the coverage given Lehman and Hanley. But on October 10 they did note that he "attacked the foreign policy position of the Democratic and Republican parties." On October 30 they cited his acid reply to United Nations Ambassador Austin's attack on peace advocates, which he termed a "vicious misrepresentation . . . [that] adds to the general impression of Austin as a neurotic, hysterical man, without self-control or logic whose representation of the United States is a disaster." Still, insufficient press coverage was a constant complaint from his supporters.[15]

Senator Lehman, not taking any chances, unleashed a barrage of media endorsements on Black-oriented radio stations, such as, WLIB-AM and WWRL-AM. As the day of the election approached, it was difficult to turn on these stations in the morning—tuned in regularly by hundreds of thousands of Black citizens—without hearing a Black pastor or Black trade union leader or Black civil rights leader or Black political leader speaking in dulcet tones about the opponent of the founder of the NAACP. Reverend Nathaniel Lawson was none too circumspect in his radio endorsement of the senator. Another pastor praised the senator's pro-Korea, pro-Marshall Plan views. Reverend Moran Weston stressed Lehman's position in favor of FEPC. Black clergy were figures of no small influence and their endorsements clearly carried weight.[16]

Also carrying weight with a Black community that was predominantly working class were the cheery endorsements of Black labor leaders. Mabel Fuller, of Local 62 of the International Ladies Garment Workers Union, in her message backed Lehman because of his support of "our Freedom Fight" in Korea. Like other union leaders, such as Ashley Totten, international secretary of the Brotherhood of Sleeping Car Porters, and B. F. McLaurin, international organizer of the same union, she underscored Lehman's position on FEPC. Others echoed her. A. Philip Randolph's union was the bulwark of support for Lehman among Blacks in the labor movement. He sponsored a luncheon for the senator's reelection in Harlem addressed by Paul Douglas. In the perilous political times of witch-hunt and betrayals, many were convinced that the better part of wisdom was to swing behind the incumbent.[17]

Senator Lehman found a well-stocked cache of support among civil rights leaders. Old Du Bois coworker Mary McLeod Bethune served as a member of the Executive Committee of the Lehman reelection campaign. Channing Tobias, after noting his NAACP board membership "for the past twenty years," observed, that "it was [Lehman] who appointed the first State Committee Against Discrimination." The value of civil rights endorsers was not only important for Black support but it could also convince white liberals of the worth of Lehman's political views. Thus, on WMCA, Tobias joined Judge Harold Stevens and Eleanor Roosevelt alleging that "communism found in Senator Lehman, a very formidable adversary." Both Mabel Staupers, former director of the National Association of Colored Graduate Nurses, and John Doles, National Bar Association representative to the United Nations, took the high road and praised Lehman's outlook on health care and certain United Nations agencies respectively. The landslide for Lehman was so massive that even Dr. Hugh Smythe, former chief aide of Du Bois, joined the bandwagon. Walter White was more cautious. Though he called Lehman's civil rights record "exceptional," the NAACP ban on political activity barred him from direct support.[18]

The 1950 campaign for the United States Senate was a vigorous, hard-fought battle and Democratic party stalwarts were in the vortex. The Black vote was a balance of power nationally, as shown not only by the 1948 presidential race but also in New York, so Black Democratic leaders were counted on heavily. Hulan Jack, who had served Harlem as assemblyman and later became Manhattan borough president, in discussing the Colonial Conference at the Schomburg Library in 1945, exhibited the current fashion by condemning "Imperialism" and "British Colonial policy." But by 1950 fashion had changed and Jack endorsed Lehman and, inferentially at least, "British Colonial Policy," though like many others—including Lehman himself—he did not attack or mention the American Labor party and Du Bois but concentrated on the GOP. District leader Joseph Ford and the consummate Harlem politician J. Raymond Jones all joined the chorus of cheers for Senator Lehman.[19]

In addition to this heavy-hitting line-up, swinging from the heels against Du Bois were other less well-known personages on the grounds that "the forces of world communist tyranny" were hysterically opposed to Lehman. Lehman echoed the views of his endorsers. At the same time, he was concerned that Du Bois would drain away liberal votes and, like the *New York Herald Tribune,* felt that the American Labor party candidate "may represent a serious threat." Hence, his special effort in the Black community is graphically represented by his separate but equal files. Like a few other so-called Cold War liberals, he opposed witch-hunt legislation, such as the McCarran and Mundt-Ferguson bills, not on grounds of their patent unconstitutionality or their skewed political effect but because they were not the best tools for extirpating and destroying the Communist party; he appeared unaware of the damaging effect these bills had on noncommunist liberals or even on himself. His viewpoint on civil rights was also informed by a Cold War perspective. He was sure to thoroughly publicize his sending of a telegram to President Truman requesting an "executive order barring discrimination in defense industries." But this was not based on outrage at rank racism but because he wished to "strengthen America's moral position in the world," in the face of a worldwide left upsurge. Days before the election, in a rhetorical flourish, he delivered a speech at a Queens rally broadcast on WJZ, saying "that ten years ago the greatest threat to western civilization was fascist imperialism" while in 1950 it was "communist imperialism." The FBI, a thorn in the side of civil rights advocates, was hailed along with other "responsible security agencies of the Federal Government."[20]

In the face of this Lehman juggernaut Du Bois went down to defeat, which was expected. His vote total was respectable, however; upstate, for example, Du Bois ran 2,000 votes ahead of the rest of the American Labor party ticket. Out of 5 million votes cast, he received roughly 37,094 in the Bronx, 52,453 in Brooklyn, 18,480 in Queens, 1,637 in Staten Island, 55,935 in Manhattan, and 29,000 upstate—not inconsiderable totals in the midst of a hot and cold war. In Harlem he received approximately 12.6 percent of the total vote cast in contrast to the American Labor party's gubernatorial nominee, who obtained 8.9 percent. Depending on whether a half-empty or half-full view is taken, Du Bois either did amazingly well given the adverse political terrain or horrendously awful given his status and name recognition in the Afro-American community and state-wide. But a major factor was the dearth of funds—the mother's milk of politics in the United States—available to Du Bois. He drolly commented on it:

> $600,000 spent by the Republicans, $500,000 by the Democrats and $90,000 by the Liberals. The American Labor Party spent $35,000. This almost looks as though the parties paid a dollar-a-piece for votes except the American Labor, which was charged but fifty cents.

His 1950 defeat for the Senate did not mean the end of his association with the Progressive party or its New York affiliate, the American Labor party. But there were ups and downs. He was displeased with the Progressives' 1952 presidential ticket of the fiery, fighting lawyer Vincent Hallinan and the Black woman journalist Charlotte Bass—another of the party's firsts, being the first woman of her race to aspire to this high office—as vice-president. He frankly conceded to his friend and ally Vito Marcantonio, "I am rather alarmed at the Progressive Party ticket, but perhaps we could do no better." He tried to do better by taking it upon himself to ask Earl Dickerson to join the ticket but Dickerson would have none of it.[21]

Du Bois' attempt at king making was further evidence of his influence in the party during the 1952 election year. In the spring of that year he spoke at the party's campaign dinner at the Hotel St. George in Brooklyn; his remarks, which "appeared in a prominent position in the *Brooklyn Eagle*, . . . had a significant effect on the local politicians." Weeks later, along with Bass, Hallinan,

Marcantonio, and others, he addressed a rally of 16,000 at Madison Square Garden. Familiar targets were assaulted; the National Association of Manufacturers (NAM) was called "the upper house" and the Chamber of Commerce "the lower" that controlled the major party candidates.[22]

The national party campaign received his unstinted attention. He replied comprehensively to the party's draft statement on "Negro Representation". Interestingly, in what some today might consider an attack on affirmative action, he objected to the idea that "there must be unqualified support of the candidacy of any Negro on any party platform where no such representation has been enjoyed in the past . . . [this is] Hitler racism in reverse and asks that Negro candidates must be supported regardless of their beliefs or qualifications." Other ideas were reflected in his keynote address at the third national convention of the Progressives in Chicago. At this three-day conference of 1,797 delegates from over forty states, Washington, D.C., and Puerto Rico, Du Bois' words set the tone.[23]

After the convention, Du Bois did not rest. With his new mate, Shirley Graham, he took off on a whirlwind speaking tour. October 7–10 was spent in Ohio where the response to this legendary figure was not overwhelming: "Most people employed or in any important position are afraid to take a stand. Our audiences were enthusiastic but small." But this was not the total picture, as they had an "interview with the editor of the *Plain Dealer* . . . short-wire recording for a city-wide broadcast . . . [a] meeting in a Negro church with about 250 persons . . . the colored paper *Call and Post* gave us some publicity." In Youngstown, the steel center and one-time hot-bed of Communist support, there was a "meeting of some 300 . . . much enthusiasm." This tour was followed by a foray through New Jersey, including Vineland and Paterson.[24]

As election day 1952 drew closer, Du Bois hastened his campaign against the two major parties. As was his habit, he took up his pen to express his attitude toward urgent questions. The *Guardian* was the recipient of his controversial, "The Negro Voter in the 1952 Elections." He spoke of the Black vote as the balance of power which explained why "today the promise of judicial or foreign service positions is being waved before colored men of prominence." This factor along with "fears and temptation" were seen as the main reasons that Blacks were casting votes for the two major parties. He ripped into Adam Clayton Powell but lobbed his primary salvos at those at the top of the pyramid. He carried these themes to a major American Labor party rally held on October 27, 1952, at Madison Square Garden. With obvious irritation, he indicted both Dwight Eisenhower and Adlai Stevenson for speaking at rallies bedecked with confederate flags. Yet his tireless campaigning, which reached thousands and may have influenced many, did not result in an electoral victory. This did not depress Du Bois, however, for he was aware of the conditions that made for this setback. Though Truman was not running in this election, he saved his most telling blows for "the hard-bit man in the loud shirts" in his postelection analyses.[25]

Truman was not the only object of Du Bois' wrath. After Senator Robert Taft died of cancer, he did not mince words in stating that if the GOP and others had spent more on cancer research than weapons, Taft may have lived. But he was less harsh—inexplicably and strangely—toward the Ohio congressman than other political figures of the day. Du Bois' surfeit of generosity toward a political foe may have been motivated more by respect for the dead than anything else. For he and his party were stringently critical of Truman's successor and Taft's counterpart, President Eisenhower. They urged Ike to make "his first official act after his inaugural . . . to eliminate segregation in the nation's capitol." They followed this up by sponsoring a national conference in Washington to eliminate Jim Crow in the nation's capitol.[26]

But all was not well with the American Labor party or its national affiliate. Even though the unfriendly political atmosphere was still a factor, though with Marcantonio, Du Bois was still able to don the respectability of the New Deal cloak, they appeared on television in a laudatory "Tribute to Franklin D. Roosevelt." Still, the continuing witch-hunt meant that certain party members would lurch to the right—a trend that Du Bois railed against vehemently. In a stern appeal for party loyalty and maintaining the faith, Du Bois addressed third-party advocates in the pages of the *Guardian* and at the annual dinner of the American Labor party:

> if the members of the party are not willing to follow party advice, they do not belong in the organization . . . unless the party can count on an undivided and loyal support its existence becomes impossible.

This reflected the outlook of Marcantonio, the "premature integrationist." The congressman from East Harlem was long in the vanguard, having introduced legislation to abolish the poll tax, led the antilynching fight, and supported a strong FEPC—though less than 3 percent of his district was Black. He introduced a resolution asking the secretary of commerce to investigate the barring of Blacks from professional baseball. He joined with Adam Clayton Powell in sponsoring legislation calling for desegregation in Washington. He championed the rights of Puerto Ricans. But, like Du Bois in the postwar period, the nation was moving away from Marcantonio. The progressive causes of the 1930s and 1940s were becoming the subversive activities of the 1950s. Thus, it was not surprising when he resigned from the American Labor party. Du Bois was not contrite about his friend's departure. "I expected it and agree entirely with your decision . . . the leader has [not] resigned but has been deserted."[27]

The Progressive party's National Committee, meeting early in 1954, listed, as the second point on the agenda—after "stimulating participation of workers and farmers in 1954 election campaigns"—"Negro and minority representation." Du Bois was present along with a dwindling number of comrades, such as John Abt, George Murphy, Hugh Mulzac, and Paul Robeson. The legislative program they called for was congruent with Du Bois' senatorial platform and was somewhat timeless—antipoll tax and antilynching legislation, executive action to ban discrimination in Washington, ousting of Byrnes as United Nations representative, and a strong FEPC. Virtually all of these points and Du Bois' 1950 platform were eventually realized—though the major parties opposed them at the time. In that sense, Du Bois' tireless campaigning as party activist and candidate in the nation's most important state was a beacon though, like many many others, he had to endure disparagement and eventual trial because of his convictions.[28]

CHAPTER 14

The Battle for Peace

The Peace Information Center (PIC) was operative from April 3, 1950, to October 12, 1950, when, in response to financial and governmental pressures, it ceased functioning. For Du Bois this was not totally unfavorable since he was in the midst of a race for the United States Senate during the autumn of that year. On February 9, 1951, he was indicted, along with others at the center, as an unregistered foreign agent; at about the same time he married his long-time friend and ally, Shirley Graham. The trial did not begin until November 18, 1951. Prior to the trial Du Bois traveled nationally campaigning against the indictment and for peace; an enormous domestic and international crusade of impressive proportions arose as a response to political repression—not spontaneously but through a determined drive—and was probably not matched in the United States during the Cold War. Even the Central Intelligence Agency (CIA) was forced to take notice.

Eric Goldman has observed that, "the fury against Communism [in the nation] was taking on . . . elements of vendetta against . . . all departures from tradition . . . against the new, the adventurous, the questing in any field." Du Bois' ideas on peace and civil rights were not new, but given the frigid political climate they were adventurous and questing. The PIC and its Stockholm Peace Appeal, with its sizeable display of peace sentiment in the midst of a war whose legality was questionable under international law, was bound to arouse anger among leading United States circles. His campaign for the Senate was not pleasing to some either. Though a Black candidate, he was difficult to pigeonhole. Though it might be seriously and intently questioned why he "made no appeal to the Negro vote as such," his political campaign, too, was a formidable talisman of peace sentiment. But despite his status as a veritable certified landmark and monument, Du Bois' herculean activities did not escape critical attention.[1]

There was undoubtedly evolution in the entire postwar thought of Du Bois. But this unavoidably collided with the oft-heard assumption that Blacks should speak solely on Black matters and nothing else—especially peace—particularly African liberation. "Slowly I began to realize that the cause of [Black] suffering was not primarily a matter of ethics, but of ease of exploitation; of the larger profit which could be had from low-paid Negro labor." This developing kaleidoscope of Black and red flashed brightly in 1950 when the powerful PIC was developed. They not only issued "Peacegrams" regularly but other organizations' declarations, for example, those from the Red Cross Appeal, the Friends, and many others. And this was being spearheaded by an elderly leader of Blacks, who was politically from the left.

The 2.5 million or more who signed the appeal in a fear-ridden United States must have come into contact with a bit of the 750,000 pieces of literature distributed—the petitions, stickers, and pamphlets crafted specially for children, Blacks, Jews, Catholics, Hispanics, and Italians. Their mailing list was only 6,000—with more than a modicum of organizational representation—but it reached further than it appeared.[2]

Du Bois expected some form of retribution, though he did not welcome it. It was ineluctable that his indictment would ensue so as "to stop peace propaganda which would interfere with the war scare; and to warn Negro leaders to go slow. . . . But, at the same time, the government was not prepared to press this too far, for fear of its effect on the elections of 1952. However, all purposes would have been served if, having been indicted and thus thoroughly scared, the case against me was dropped with my consent and connivance." He stood firm.[3]

Weeks after Korea became a hot war, William Foley, chief of the Justice Department's Foreign Agents Registration Section, requested that the PIC register as a foreign agent "under the terms of the Foreign Agents Registration Act of 1938 as amended." The foreign principal was presumed by many to be the Soviet Union, though that was conveniently left unstated. Appropriately, Du Bois was reached in Paris at a peace meeting about this latest demand and he jumped right on that point. Jail was a frightening prospect. Abbott Simon, Du Bois' coworker at PIC, hurriedly told Foley that Du Bois was out of the country and this might delay things, but the Justice Department would have none of that. Gloria Agrin, the lawyer engaged to confront Foley, reported to Simon the substance of her conversations with him:

> I inquired directly who the Department of Justice believed to be the alleged foreign principal. Mr. Foley seemed hesitant and unwilling to reveal this to me. He preferred the identifying formulation that I must surely be aware that a "number" of foreign organizations were "doing the same things" . . . [as PIC].

After a prolonged discussion, he mentioned the World Peace Congress, the Partisans for Peace, and others. Du Bois had associated with these groups on a regular basis since his departure from the NAACP. Some in Justice might have expected Du Bois to go off meekly into the mist of jail for Shirley Graham reported them as furious about the publicity given the case. Like many lawyers in the United States, they apparently felt that the courtroom was the only proper forum for the debate of these issues, but Graham decidedly felt otherwise: "We suspect that some under official didn't know who you are and that now all hell and damnation had broken out because of who you are." The interregnum between Foley's August 1950 correspondence and the February 9, 1951 indictment was seen by her as "a mere formality for them to have a conference with you and, please God, forget the whole thing." Graham was cocky and itching for battle, but the hiatus was seen by others as a sword of Damocles threatening Du Bois with mayhem if he did not calm his frenetic peace organizing. Foley piously disagreed and stressed that "registration under the act is in no way intended to interfere with the operation of the Peace Information Center in its present program."[4]

The publicity alluded to by Graham was the tidal wave of furor uncorked by the Justice Department's action. It gripped the Black community, and perhaps the world generally, like few other political prosecutions had done in some time. From a certain perspective the acquittal may have been the best thing that ever happened to the Truman administration's Justice Department. The celebration of Du Bois' proliferating birthdays was not novel but the February 1951 event became, in light of his indictment, a political indice. It was to be held at the ritzy Essex House on Central Park South. But four days before the dinner and nine days after his indictment, in a move seen as politically motivated, management cancelled. Others were forced to pull out. Charlotte H. Brown of North Carolina's Palmer Memorial Institute told the secretary of the testimonial, Alice Crawford, that an "important New York Trustee threatens resignation if I appear on Du Bois' program. . . . Great fear of Communist influence. Sorry." This cruel dilemma was thrust unwillingly on many others—Black and white. It is difficult to say if the hotel can be evaluated so benignly. Elizabeth Lawson indicated to Du Bois that from her research there was evidence of "concerted action on the part of hotels, to prevent peace organizations and other progressive organizations from getting accommodations," citing "Hotel World Review, a trade organ." No matter, Essex House vice president, V. J. Coyle, told Crawford, "pursuant to our rules and regulations and for other sufficient reasons" cancellation was ordained and that, the "deposit is being returned"; the objective effect was still wide, conspiracy or no.[5]

Charlotte H. Brown was not the only party bailing out. Rabbi A. H. Silver of Cleveland at first agreed to serve as honorary chairman and then abruptly told the event's chairman E. Franklin Frazier, that "in view of the unexpected and embarrassing developments I regret absence," but "should you decide to postpone the meeting until the situation is clarified I shall be very pleased to address it then." The rabbi further requested that an announcement of his withdrawal be made at the testimonial. His coreligionist, Rabbi Jack Cohen of the Jewish Reconstrictionist Foundation, Inc., concurred.[6]

The year 1951 was a difficult time to be associated with the leader of the Stockholm Peace Appeal. Arthur Spingarn informed the committee that he would not be able to serve as honorary chairman of the testimonial dinner. Arturo Toscanini also declined to serve as sponsor. Ralph Bunche, hitting Du Bois while he was down, contumaciously dissented:

> I cannot accept your invitation to serve as a sponsor. When I was in the midst of my difficult Palestine work in the late 1948,

> Dr. Du Bois made a vigorous and totally unjustified personal attack upon me in a mass meeting at Madison Square Garden. I would not consider this attack of any importance if it had been confined to a criticism of my policies and actions in Palestine. . . . It was an attack upon my integrity and my objectivity in the conduct of the Palestine assignment. It was, in fact, presented in the form of an apology to the world on behalf of Negroes for my identification with that group. . . . It would be sheer hypocrisy for me to pretend that I had forgotten this insult from a man, who, up to that time, I had considered to be a truly great personality, to be admired and deeply respected, and with whom I had always had the most cordial relations.

Bunche took care to elucidate his reasons for not being able to attend, while C. C. Spalding, president of the Black-owned North Carolina Mutual Life Insurance Company of Durham begged out because of "a previous engagement on that date."[7]

But a more typical response came from J. Finley Wilson, grand exalted ruler of the Improved Benevolent and Protective Order of Elks of the World:

> In honoring Dr. Du Bois you are honoring yourselves. He is the race's greatest scholar and . . . a champion of human rights . . . and has always been in the forefront when the battle was the hottest.

The musician Leonard Bernstein agreed in sending greetings. In this vein, endorsements of the testimonial were received from Aubrey Williams, publisher of the *Southern Farmer* of Montgomery, Alabama; Ella Stewart, president of the National Association of Colored Women; Oksen Sarian, secretary of the Armenian Progressive League of America; W. H. Jernagin, president of the National Sunday School and BTU Congress; Benjamin Mays and Mary McLeod Bethune; Marian Probyn Thompson, of Thompson and Thompson Realty Company of Brooklyn, sent in a check for tickets; as did Oliver T. Palmer, business agent of the United Cafeteria and Restaurant Workers.[8]

Greetings from international dignitaries poured in: Gabriel D'Arbussier, deputy from North Africa in the Assembly of France, waxed lyrical and historical in placing Du Bois in the pantheon.

Jorge Amado, the popular Brazilian writer, spoke similarly in praise of Du Bois for a "life devoted to the service of . . . progress."[9]

The testimonial dinner moved uptown from Central Park South and, despite obstacles strewn in the path, was a rousing financial and political success. Greetings were received from Hewlett Johnson, dean of Canterbury; Dmitri Shostakovich; Georg Lukacs; F. Joliot-Curie, president of the World Peace Council; Nikolai Tikhonov, chair of the Soviet Peace Committee; Langston Hughes; President Charles Johnson of Fisk University; and the Black publisher Roscoe Dunjee, among many others. Though Du Bois' fraternity, Alpha Phi Alpha, voted down a birthday greeting and accompanied the action by bitter criticism in its private debate on the matter, the head of the organization, Belford Lawson, accepted an invitation to speak. Besieged and bombarded, Du Bois and his allies circled the wagons in anticipation of a stepped-up offensive and his eighty-third birthday dinner fortified the forces for battles to come.[10]

The handcuffing of Du Bois before his appearance in court, as could well be expected even during the Cold War, caused an angry outcry—particularly in the Afro-American community. This reaction was adumbrated when Perry Howard, Jr., son of the Mississippi Republican National Committeeman, became personal bondsman for Du Bois; and his arraignment, prior to going on his Caribbean honeymoon, was an eye-opening experience for him; and the scene in which he was placed gave him an inkling as to how he was viewed by certain elites:

> It was my first visit to a criminal court. I was finger-printed, made to empty all my pockets, "frisked" for concealed weapons and hand-cuffed.

But Du Bois was not sufficiently taken aback to forget about issuing a fiery denunciation of his tormentors. He stressed the obvious flaws of the indictment's gravamen: "My interest in world affairs is long standing." Though the Black press and community tended to echo support for Du Bois in this crisis and authored many lines that could have been written by him, there was not a unanimous viewpoint among the press at large. *The New York Times* saw fit to print the fact, of questionable materiality, that the Labor Research Association's Robert Dunn, who was also treasurer of the Civil Rights Congress, "which put up $260,000 bond for the eleven convicted [Communist] leaders," were lodged in the same building as the PIC. Guilt by association may not have been their aim but it was certainly the objective of others during the stormy era. But Du Bois remained unbowed.[11] Judge James Cobb, a friend of Du Bois', answered his cry, showing him that he was not alone. In reality, there may not have been a larger protest against a political prosecution since the Scottsboro or Sacco-Vanzetti cases of years past. It was an island of victory in a sea of defeats for progressives during this period. Du Bois provides a useful survey of this process in his *In Battle for Peace,* though ultimately it can only provide a glimpse of the depth of the anger invoked. He discussed his not too fruitful effort to get support from liberals; he said that only "a dozen nationally prominent Negroes" could be found to sign a public statement of support, which was seen as not enough "to warrant its circulation." The press was not much better. "The white commercial press treated our case either with silence or violent condemnation . . . outside of the Negro press . . . I got support from radical periodicals alone, like the *Daily Worker,* the *People's World,* etc." On the other hand, a supportive statement issued by the National Council of the Arts, Sciences and Professions was signed by 220 leaders of the arts, sciences, clergy, and other professions from thirty-three states; the Methodist Federation for Social Action and the Executive Board of National Lawyers Guild acted similarly.[12]

Besides the international community, the support base for Du Bois rested among the Afro-Americans. "The response of Negroes in general was at first slow and not united, but it gradually gained momentum." Reflecting a familiar and prevalent reproach of himself, Du Bois acknowledged that many felt he committed the so-called crime and moved to the left "in retaliation for continued discrimination" and that he had "let myself be drawn into some treasonable acts or movements." At times the Black press perpetuated this general myth, yet "most of the Negro press from the first showed unusual leadership." But they were not necessarily representative of their class and strata. "The intelligentsia, the Talented Tenth, the successful business and professional men, were not for the most part, outspoken in our defense . . . as a group this class was either silent or actually antagonistic."[13]

Still, this was not necessarily the dominant trend, as Du Bois expressed it: "I am strengthened by the knowledge that a larger proportion of intelligent Negroes stood staunch in my defense than of intelligent whites in defense of the Hollywood Ten or other victims of the Un-American Committee." Nevertheless, it was the outpouring of support from the labor community that made him reappraise his view on class in the Black community: "Truman heard from the Fur and Leather Workers, Marine Cooks and Stewards; thirty locals of the United Electrical Workers and others" such as Ford local 600 of the United Autoworkers, "the largest local in the world." This was in addition to international trade union support from Africa, Australia, Eastern and Western Europe, and elsewhere. The impact of the trial among students was similarly significant. "North and South, in white and Negro colleges . . . on the campuses of the University of Chicago, of Wilberforce University in Ohio, of the University of Texas, of Fisk University, etc." there were protests. They "published pamphlets, sent letters and telegrams to the Department of Justice and to President Truman. Most of these organizations were quickly suppressed by the college authorities."[14]

Paul Robeson's Harlem-based newspaper *Freedom,* boldly reported on Du Bois' trial. This fact was striking because of the diversity of the editorial board and contributors; in the former category were Modjeska Simkins and Revels Cayton, with Lorraine Hansberry and John Oliver Killens in the latter. Old Du Bois allies like George Murphy, W. Alphaeus Hunton, Ewart Guinier, and Shirley Graham were naturally represented. They validated Du Bois' assertions about students in a March 1951 issue. With a banner headline "Southern Students Defend Du Bois," they broadcast this fact to the world. *Freedom* made the Du Bois case a constant, featured news item. One issue featured a front page picture of Robeson shaking Du Bois' hand and expressing solidarity. Editorially, they demanded his freedom. *Freedom*'s avidity for the case was further demonstrated by their special deal for subscribers to receive *In Battle for Peace.*[15]

Du Bois noted in this book and elsewhere that his trial led him to be more aware of class differences among Blacks. This was a realization that struck many as a by-product of the case. P. L. Prattis of the *Pittsburgh Courier* scorned those who shunned Du Bois:

> When they back down they betray their people and their country. They should remember this as they think upon the fate of the great Du Bois . . . a thousand Negroes should rise

> to take the place of Du Bois and other thousands for all those others "the terror" will soon clamp its ghost-like hands upon.

Lawrence D. Reddick, a close friend of both Du Bois and Martin Luther King, Jr., was of a similar persuasion:

> The deep concern of the Negro people in this case is nationwide. It ranges from the highest professional circles to the man in the street. . . . The Negro press has given wide coverage to the events and strong editorial support to Dr. Du Bois.

Reddick criticized some of Du Bois' views, like his controversial "Close Ranks" article on World War I, but, in common with so many others, he saw the government case against him as a frame-up. The novelist John Oliver Killens was able to distill the essence of these notions:

> Many Black folk who owed him so much failed him at this hour. Some were too busy scurrying for cover, only to find out ultimately that there was no real hiding place down here, nor is there now, nor will there ever be. . . . We Black folk must never again turn our back on our leaders just because the Establishment attacks them. A leader of the oppressed becomes suspect to his people when the oppressors take him to their bosoms.

Langston Hughes was equally poetic: "The Accusers' Name Nobody Will Remember but History Records Du Bois." If Du Bois were to be jailed, "the banner of American democracy will be lowered another notch, particularly in the eyes of the darker peoples of the earth."[16]

It was the question of class differentiation among Blacks that occupied the thinking of many Afro-Americans—and whites as well. M. E. Mantell's formidable study indicates that "for the most part the Black community reacted to Du Bois' indictment according to class." Du Bois raised his voice from time to time in a like manner, though by and large he recognized that though proportionately "big Negroes" were less supportive than Black working masses, they were still substantially represented in the defense and definitely more so than whites of a similar strata on behalf of himself or in cases like that of the Hollywood Ten. Shirley Graham notes how in the Caribbean, "Naussau's Black elite" were quite supportive and Blacks of similar class background in Chicago and California raised funds for his legal defense.[17]

Graham has described the pleasures and vicissitudinous incidents that accompanied their triumphant tour across the country for support in 1951. Although there was much pressure in Portland, Oregon, for the Black community to withdraw support from Du Bois, but there were stunning receptions in the San Francisco Bay Area and Los Angeles: "Festival air: dinner, receptions, photographs and always flowers." In Milwaukee, an affluent Bahai businessman, who was a supporter, arranged meetings with city editors of major newspapers and the mayor's Commission on Human Rights. In Detroit, plagued with fierce class battles, there was terror; for the first time they had a bodyguard. This turmoil that the Du Bois tour caused was an extension of the general controversy that the case itself sparked. Judge Hubert Delany, the maverick NAACP board member, captured some of these contradictions in a dialogue with E. Franklin Frazier:

> I did not sign the peace mobilization petition but . . . if an outstanding [man] like Dr. Du Bois . . . could be indicted . . . few of us are safe from an attack upon our loyalty.

Like the well-trained jurist, many were of the belief that the gunning down of Du Bois was only the first shot in an extended shooting war. But Delany also sensed what was apparent to others, that is, that the prosecution of Du Bois would not win friends in "South America, India, China, or Africa." It was the ramifications for himself and others to which the judge kept returning. Though Du Bois complained fitfully about the lack of support generated among the Black college community, the General Alumni Association of Fisk University reflected Delany's thinking by passing a resolution supporting Du Bois. Yet Du Bois' vitriolic designation of Howard's Mordecai Johnson as a "born liar" was symptomatic of his relationship to this constituency during the trial.[18]

The NAACP leadership saw the Scylla of pressure from on high and Charybdis of pressure from below—both with drastically differing opinions on W.E.B. Du Bois. This was the problem of Mordecai Johnson and the middle strata generally, though both Truman Gibson and Benjamin Mays contributed to the defense fund. The NAACP convention, meeting in a segregated Atlanta, deeply under the influence of the right wing, passed a resolution—considered tepid by many—that reverberated and reflected these strains. First it was noted that the NAACP board, "has expressed the opinion that this action against one of the great champions of Civil Rights lends color to the charge that efforts are being made to silence spokesmen for full equality of Negroes." Their resolve, however, disappointed many:[19]

> Therefore, be it resolved that this convention go on record as being unalterably opposed to such methods by any governmental instrumentality to silence spokesmen for full equality.

Du Bois was often a smash hit during his tours to garner support and his trip to Denver weeks before the trial validated this conception. This well-received journey was the "first meeting sponsored by an NAACP chapter since his indictment." The *National Guardian* reporter was euphoric about the reception. His press conference extended over two hours and resulted in friendly articles in the Denver press. Over two hundred people packed a reception. More precisely, during his stay, Du Bois met with the chair of the Urban League board, the director of the Jewish Community Center, the associate editor of the *Colorado Labor Advocate,* the president of the Oil Workers International Union (who interlocked with the CIO National Executive board), religious leaders, political leaders, the president of the National Farmers Union, the chair of the Mayor's Human Relations Committee, and other dignitaries.[20]

This was a response from the heartland and contrasted sharply with the attitude of the New York-based NAACP leadership. Herbert Aptheker is not off the mark in asserting that "the leadership of the NAACP adopted a hostile attitude toward Du Bois during his indictment and trial . . . some among the NAACP leaders affirmed belief in Du Bois' 'guilt.' " In an exasperated review of his *In Battle for Peace,* the *Crisis* mockingly derided Du Bois:

> How did this great warrior for human freedom ever get himself tied up with the American Communists and the "peace" pledge in the first place? *In Battle for Peace* brings its author the nearest to babblement [sic] he has ever ventured.

But the powerful New York State Conference of Branches probably better represented the rank and file view when it unequivocally condemned the "attacks upon . . . Dr. W.E.B. Du Bois." One angry citizen contacted Du Bois' defense committee and implored: "What I am unable to understand is why . . . the NAACP [is] not helping."[21]

The support generated within the NAACP and elsewhere did not arise spontaneously. A motivating force was the National Committee to Defend Dr. W.E.B. Du Bois and Associates in the Peace Information Center. Paul Robeson and Elmer Benson, former governor of Minnesota and Progressive party leader, exhibited the Black-white unity that earmarked the campaign, in their positions as cochairs. Vice-chairs included Charlotta Bass, Professor Henry Pratt Fairchild, Vito Marcantonio, and Leon Straus; members included Howard Fast, Dashiell Hammett, Richart Morford, Angie Dickerson, Rockwell Kent, Stetson Kennedy, Larkin Marshall, and Doxey Wilkerson. Abbott Simon was an energizer of this effort, along with Alice Citron. Weeks after the indictment came down, the kernel of the campaign was outlined: "The cultural and intellectual issue represented by the attack on you as an individual . . . was one prong; the other committee will be based on the advocacy of peace." This plowing and tending quickly bore fruit. "Press clippings . . . wonderful letters and expressions of support continue to roll in. . . . The feeling on this case is very deep."[22]

Simon knew that divine providence did not produce this impressive response. Their advertising, as demonstrated by an appeal in the *National Guardian,* was topical and effective:

> Frank Costello, gangster and underworld boss, is a free man. Even after his shameful performance before the Kefauver Committee, he has not been arrested, indicted or jailed. . . . But the man on the left [Du Bois] has been indicted, arrested, handcuffed, finger-printed and now faces a possible five-year prison sentence.

They printed postcards for supporters to mail to President Truman that termed the prosecution a "serious error" and demanded that the attorney general "drop this indictment." They printed petitions with return envelopes that had prepaid return postage. They made special appeals to designated constituencies, like labor, peace, Blacks, and others.[22]

The anticommunism engendered by the war against the "Communists" in Korea did discourage many. But there was an inordinate amount of local initiatives, as manifested by the Right to Speak for Peace Committee of San Francisco, which mobilized forces to write to the attorney general about dropping "the anti-peace persecution of Dr. Du Bois and his co-defendants." The latter notwithstanding, harassment of Du Bois case activists was no small issue. This makes the great number of those who decided to send petitions in support of the defendants even more impressive. Du Bois told Harriet Smith of the St. Paul Committee: "I have heard that the FBI annoyed your husband. If anything more comes of this please let me know." A great deal of harassment befell one New York City woman unlucky enough to have the same name as one of Du Bois' codefendants.[24]

The Progressive party national affiliates, the PIC contacts, the CASP remified network, the CAA ties, all congealed into a tight nucleus of vigorous activism. The Progressive party was particularly crucial since it was the common ground on which so many progressive forces met; it was a hub from which many spokes emanated. In New York, during February 1951, the American Labor party sponsored a boisterous rally of 500 at the Golden Gate Ballroom demanding swift dismissal of the indictment. At the defense committee meeting in May 1951, it was confidently announced, "ALP clubs will organize neighborhood activities to send wires of protest; contact local leaders for support, collect funds." Their activism helped to make possible other announcements at this crucial meeting, such as, "ASP has sent a statement to 22,000 professionals. . . . Full page in the NAACP Souvenir Journal for Josephine Baker Day." The Progressive party generated a windstorm of activity outside of New York as well. The Illinois party sent $63.15 "which was donated spontaneously by the delegates attending our 3rd Illinois PP State Membership Convention . . . each and every delegate present addressed a personal message to Attorney General McGrath." Walter O'Brien of the Massachusetts party invited Du Bois to speak to an expected 200 to 400 on the smoldering issue of "Negro liberation movement . . . as it is related to peace." The Irishman was sufficiently excited about this Boston engagement to exclaim:

> your courageous stand and loyalty to the principles of peace are so great that they are inspiring hundreds of thousands—yes, possibly millions—to stand up and be counted for peace.

Money for the defense was also sent from Minnesota, Montana, Idaho, Oregon, and from other regions.[25]

Du Bois' allies in peace activism were just as busy. The lineal descendant of the indicted PIC was the American Peace Crusade (APC), steered by the white-Black team of Willard Uphaus and Thomas Richardson. The APC passed a resolution supporting Du Bois and calling for organized delegations to visit "local legislators, congressmen and senators [to] . . . persuade them to urge that the Justice Department" drop the case. They suggested the distribution of literature, such as Du Bois' pamphlet "I Take My Stand for Peace," and that "letters and postcards" be rained on the nation's capitol; they reminded people that "specially printed postcards are available." Peace activists across the country sprung into action.[26]

The Du Bois campaign kicked up quite a bit of dust nationally, which helped to draw in many from the predominantly white organizations, ranging from the ideological adversary to the suspected apathetic. Joseph Hansen, of the Trotskyite Socialist Workers Party, gave guarded support. Du Bois' frequent foe in peace, A. J. Muste, termed the government's action "monstrous and dangerous." He sent a letter to the Justice Department's William E. Foley and pledged to support Du Bois. Some may have been surprised by the letter sent to Truman from "members of the Greenwich Village community" protesting the indictment, signed by thirty-two including Eleanor Leacock, "Mr. and Mrs. William Paley," and the actor Martin Wolfson. This broad reach of the defense committee was egged along by ASP, not only in New York but nationally. The ASP statement thrashing the indictment was signed by a celebrity-studded list that included Alexander Meikeljohn, Muriel Rukeyser, Dalton Trumbo, Charles White, Gene Weltfish, and Alexander Calder. If the indictment were not dropped, they said, "no person or organization, whose views on the crucial issue of war and peace differ from the administration in power, will be safe from calumny and attack." They followed this up with a meeting on peace at Town Hall featuring Du Bois. Their controversial views were not accepted with equanimity, however. When ASP officials invited Arthur Spingarn to speak on "The Right to Advocate Peace," he demurred: "I am convinced that no action taken at that meeting can be helpful to Du Bois' case."[27]

Spingarn's view was not accepted without equivocation within all sectors of the press. Favorable sentiment—particularly noticeable in the Afro-American press—was fueled by Du Bois' gentle stroking. Weeks after his indictment he found it wise to write Carl Murphy, *Afro-American* publisher. He was generous in his praise of I. F. Stone's "recent columns in the *Compass.*" He thanked W. P. Dabney of the *Cincinnati Union* for newspaper publicity on the case.[28]

Black newspapers, in particular, were relatively more independent financially than the Black colleges who were often dependent on niggardly state legislatures captivated by the racist notion of separate but equal; the press also had to contend more with the Black masses outraged by the manacling of their patriarch. P.L. Prattis of the *Pittsburgh Courier* stridently and vividly outlined the matter: "The handcuffs on Du Bois are meant to serve as a GAG on any Negro leadership that is disposed to 'shoot the works' for freedom." Not unlike others, he linked the fight for Du Bois' freedom to the fight for anticolonial freedom. The *Courier* put its finger on a contradiction seen by many:

> Now a government which has found itself unable to protect the rights of an entire people against criminal intrusion of a prejudiced majority finds the means to handcuff the man who has fought most insistently for these rights.

Across the state, the *Philadelphia Tribune* editorially contoured the situation in supporting Du Bois. The *Tribune* agreed with the *Courier*'s Marjorie McKenzie who said that "the indictment . . . is a symbolic act whose significance will not escape colored people here and abroad." The *National Baptist Voice* editorial also approached the international angle, but from a different perspective:

> if the devil circulates Peace petitions or love petitions, is that a crime? It is said that he was an agent of a foreign power. . . . On that basis then every Preacher should be in jail because Christianity originated with foreigners.

The *Afro-American,* the *Chicago Defender,* the *Oklahoma Black Dispatch,* the *Gary American,* the *Cincinnati Union,* the *Louisville Defender,* along with the progressive *Daily Compass,* concurred with the idea that Du Bois deserved unstinting support.[29]

Du Bois' and Graham's cross-country tours in search of support complemented and generated Black press support like one hand clapping the other. The raising of funds for the legal defense for an impecunious Du Bois was not a minor consideration. His journeys caused a rising tide of dollars to flow to the Defense Committee; there were also "contributors to Emergency Legal Defense Fund" with Paul Robeson, William Rix of the United Packinghouse Workers, and Oliver Palmer of the United Cafeteria and Restaurant Workers Union as the three top contributors.[30]

In September, Du Bois traveled to Milwaukee, Detroit, Denver, and Chicago. According to Du Bois, "Milwaukee was reactionary with no organized Peace or Progressive groups." Yet, he spoke to a meeting of 1,500 at a "colored church," albeit with a "timid pastor"; attendance was "half-white. . . . The *Journal* gave us a good column interview on the case and a half-column report on the meeting; but after our departure it ran a lead editorial, condemning me for encouraging race animosity. . . . The *Sentinel* was silent." As noted, Michigan featured these retrograde tendencies as well. Though apparently little effort was put into it, nearly one-third of the audience of 200 was white. "Unions were well-represented but upper class Negroes absent. . . . One local colored paper refused to run the advertisement of the meeting; the other and the local edition of the *Pittsburgh Courier* did. The white press was silent." Though on the positive side, local Black leaders Coleman Young and George Crockett (now a Detroit congressman) were among the sponsors. His well-received Colorado venture with NAACP support was next. In Chicago "we had about 700 persons crowding the hall." But events there were "not well organized . . . chief support came from the unions," not from Blacks.[31]

These multifaceted travels touched many. The Defense Committee was deluged with donations, letters of support, and copies of letters of protest sent to Washington. This breadth of support for Du Bois was inspiring to him. He was aware that much of it was sparked by the most formidable of Black institutions, the Black church. As noted, the *National Baptist Voice* came out flatly for Du Bois, even after word of the possibility of indictment emerged. The Louisville and vicinity Baptist Ministers and Deacons meeting "representing sixty-five churches with a constituency of over twenty-thousand persons" asked the government to drop the indictment. The Baptist Ministers Conference of Philadelphia and vicinity met and "unanimously endorsed a resolution" supporting Du Bois. With organizational channels often blocked in the NAACP, Black activists checked out and took their proposals to the Black church. This support for Du Bois was a complex mosaic of interlocking movements and individuals that wildly overlapped neat categories. J. Finley Wilson of the Elks, the "largest Negro fraternal order in the world" with 500,000 members in the United States, Canada, and the Canal Zone and the most Black followers since Marcus Garvey reported: "I have sent a telegram to the President and I am urging all of my friends to do likewise." Churchgoers were prominent in the Elks and also part of the multilayered delegations that saw fit to visit Washington. An American Peace Crusade (APC) group caught the eye of the House; it involved the Reverend Dudley Barr, congregational minister of Connecticut, the Reverend Edward Freeman, president of the Kansas City NAACP, Bishop H. H. Hooper of Holy Nazarene Church of Chicago, and Maurice Travis, secretary-treasurer of the International Union of Mine, Mill and Smelter Workers Union.[32]

The presence of a trade unionist in the predominantly church-based APC delegation to Washington was not a mindless blunder, for the unions were a bulwark of determination and staunchness behind Du Bois during this crisis. This labor support—particularly the support of the CIO unions—was a critical pillar in the pro-Du Bois edifice. Shirley Graham heard reports of work stoppages on the part of some unions in response to the indictment. In any case, it is accurate to report that certain labor unions demanded freedom for Du Bois in no uncertain terms. Local 197, Paper Bag and Novelty Workers Union, Huge Bryson of the Marine Cooks and Stewards, the International Mine, Mill and Smelter Workers Union, the International Fur and Leather Workers, Ferdinand Smith, executive secretary of the Harlem Trade Union Council, and John T. Gojack, president of District 9 of the United Electrical Workers (representing thirty local unions in Indiana and Michigan) were a few of these insistent voices. The Furriers Joint Council, composed of 15,000 members, complained about the indictment directly to Washington.[33]

Labor interlocked with the Progressive party as neatly as Black organizations did with the NAACP. This was noticeably true in California—Berkeley, San Diego, San Gabriel Valley, and Alameda County. Shirley Graham was told that Los Angeles "is now in the midst of establishing two committees for the defense of Dr. Du Bois." Labor was instrumental in this process of forming one broad committee and one based in the party. In October 1951, 50,000 leaflets on the case were distributed. Cleveland Robinson, Black vice president of District 65 of the Distributive Workers, took a special interest in "Sister Sylvia Soloff," his constituent and PIC office worker, indicted in what they perceived as a dangerous move of including nonprincipals within the prosecutorial dragnet. His union was a left-led one, as was the United Electrical Workers Union, and both were under tremendous pressure from the American Federation of Labor and the government because of red charges. Bert Washington, secretary of the union's Fair Practices Committee in District 7, told Defense Committee leader Alice Citron that his district "approved the recommendations of the Executive Board to call upon the local unions of the District for moral and financial support to" the Defense Committee. He sent money for the committee's pamphlets. When Du Bois spoke in Seattle, flanking him on the platform were Eddie Tangen of the Marine Cooks and Stewards, Karly Larson, president of the Northern District Council of the International Woodworkers of America—CIO, and Ed Carlson of Machinists Lodge #79, among others. Labor also played a big role in forming the Seattle and Tacoma defense committees.[34]

The left-led unions' most significant contribution may have been their organizing of a fundraising dinner on behalf of the Trade Union Committee to Defend Dr. W.E.B. Du Bois. Ben Gold of the Furriers was chair of this impressive grouping: the sponsors included the presidents of six international unions and other leading CIO, AFL, and independent union leaders. The dinner, which was Gold's idea, was held December 16, 1951; $2,300 was collected.[35]

In an era when Communist and left-led unions were under severe attack, it required a courageous profile to stand up for the most well-known critic of the war against Korea. It is not accidental that many of the unions and union leaders who stood beside Du Bois were gone from the scene, many times unwillingly, after a while. Huge Bryson, the Black union leader, was a key link in Du Bois' chain of support. Early in the campaign he had been one of the first trade unionists contacted by Alice Citron to initiate "defense committees, meetings, fund raising affairs." Bryson assumed the mantle and contributed unselfishly to the Du Bois campaign. On April 7, 1953, Bryson was indicted for perjury in signing a non-Communist affidavit. The union which Bryson served as president, the National Union of Marine Cooks and Stewards, had a disproportionately high percentage of Blacks—40 percent—and eight Black officials. Subsequently, this union was violently savaged, in part because they "condemned [the] indictment of Dr. W.E.B. Du Bois."[36]

Despite the penalties that were attached to support for Du Bois, he received a surprising amount of support from diverse sectors. The Manhattan District of the Jewish Peoples Fraternal Order, which was affiliated with the International Workers Order, gave to Gold's testimonial dinner. Soon after they were fighting an attempt by New York State to force their liquidation. Fred Stover's besieged Iowa Farmers' Union vowed that he would contribute to the defense effort. William Patterson's Civil Rights Congress was conspicuous in rousing opposition to the indictment, particularly in the Denver, Vallejo, San Francisco Bay, and Detroit chapters.[37]

The legal community was part of the multifaceted pro-Du Bois coalition. Not long after the indictment came down, Abbott Simon mentioned that a lawyer friend "volunteered to raise funds among sympathetic lawyers to take care of nearly $5,000 worth of legal expenses." Arthur Madison, Esq., offered free legal service for the trial; Theodore Schroeder, an attorney hailing from Cos Cob, Connecticut, offered a "large fund of . . . information [re] . . . all the modern psychologic *[sic]* theories and historical data pertinent to the constitutional issues" of the case—information that would be devastating on cross-examination. Professor Thomas Emerson of Yale Law School, derided as "Tommie the Commie" by some of his cruder colleagues, was solon-like though clear in support: "So far as I know the facts in the indictment of the Peace Information Center, I am strongly opposed to the action taken by the government." Du Bois felt sufficiently confident in his relationship with Harvard Law School's Zachariah Chaffee to seek his legal opinion in this controversial case.[38]

The American Civil Liberties Union (ACLU), which had ousted Communist Elizabeth Gurley Flynn from a leadership position, was not predisposed to be favorable to Du Bois' defense, despite the putative unconstitutionality and chilling effect of the act under which Du Bois was indicted. First of all, Arthur Garfield Hays suggested that Du Bois write a memorandum explaining the issues. Apparently, Du Bois' brief was not persuasive for the ACLU declined to render aid. Though they ousted Communists and would defend Nazis, after "very serious consideration . . . there is no indication that the trial would be in any way unfair . . . I am sorry because personally I should like to have helped in this case."

Hays was also on the NAACP Legal Committee and his anti-Du Bois attitude carried weight there. He made a financial contribution but refused to join the defense committee "because of my primary allegiance in civil liberties matters" to the ACLU board.[39]

Though his reception from the legal community may have been mixed and sputtering, support from abroad was torrential. It was to be expected that there would be discontent in Africa about perceived maltreatment of the Father of Pan-Africanism. C. F. Hayfron-Benjamin, solicitor of the Gold Coast Supreme Court, proclaimed: "All your friends, well-wishers and admirers in Africa are solid in their united support for victory over the forces of evil." The *West African Pilot* of Nkrumah's Gold Coast reported favorably the comment of J. A. Wachuku, noted barrister and founder of the New Africa party, that the indictment "shocks the conscience of humanity." Editorially, this prominent journal admitted, "we are alarmed." George Padmore fanned out from his British base to rally support and was a key participant in generating pro-Du Bois action. He informed his elderly friend, that it helped to spur into action prominent figures like Wachucku, who "was [a] delegate" to the Fifth Pan-African Congress and "has recently started a Pan-African Party in Nigeria to spread the ideas of which you are the worthy father." Padmore was instrumental in a Caribbean effort that "succeeded in getting some of the local political and trade union leaders to take an interest in your case. They plan to send protest resolutions to the State Department through the local U.S. consuls." As in the United States, Du Bois' African support cut across all lines. He received support from both the Federation of Madagascar and Dependencies Trade Unions and P. K. Crankson & Co., exporters, importers and general agents—not to mention Sam Kahn of the House of Assembly in Capetown.[40]

The Caribbean was another bulwark of dependable support throughout Du Bois' ordeal. This was most noticeably apparent in the trade union movement, as demonstrated by the solidarity evinced by V. Lamon, general secretary of the Departmental Federation of the Trade Unions of Martinique, the Manual and Metal Workers of Grenada, and the Caribbean Labour Congress, London branch.[41]

Du Bois recognized the value of broad international backing. In fact, he saw the acquittal emerging because the "eyes of the world were fixed on the case." This international support had to be filtered through a domestic press that was frequently hostile. Yet, despite this steeled opposition, support continued to roll in.

Latin America was not derelict, as demonstrated by the support rendered by public figures like Pablo Neruda and Jorge Amado. James Ivy, editor of *Crisis* and not prejudiced in favor of Du Bois, reported to the defendant on a dialogue he had with Edison Carniero, speaking from the largest Black community outside of Africa: "He wishes you to know that the Brazilian Negro community is 100 percent behind you and fighting in every manner possible to show the ridiculousness of the charges preferred against you."[42]

This was matched by support in Asia. Du Bois congratulated the editor of *Kaboutare-Solh* for his support. The editor of this journal of "progressive Iranian artists . . . published several articles on the . . . trial . . . and . . . has called upon eminent personalities, judges, artists, writers and peace loving people" to protest. They established a "provisional committee for defense of Dr. W.E.B. Du Bois." From Japan came word, "I have made public your case in the organ 'Buraku.' " The All China Students Federation protest prompted Du Bois to scribble, "from Asia comes many letters"; the fact that Du Bois was a good friend of Kuo Mo-jo, vice-president of Government Administration in Peking, helps to explain this encouragement from China. Panitera Peladjar dan Pemuda, an Indonesian youth and students group based in Amsterdam, soundly protested. All of these angry outbursts were not necessarily self-generated. At about the time that he was receiving word of protest from the Union des Etudiants du Vietnam, the All-India Peace Council invited him to speak at their conference; he informed them that his trial prevented it and added, "I would be glad if the Peace Council during its deliberations would take note of this prosecution and pass appropriate resolutions."[43]

Canada, the northern neighbor of the United States, weighed in heavily against the indictment. The Civil Rights Union of Toronto, the British Columbia Peace Council, and the London, Ontario, chapter of the Congress of Canadian Women vigorously denounced the indictment. The Canadian Peace Congress, which had on its Advisory Board deputies from Belgium and Sweden and a former cabinet member of Mexico, "lodged strong protests" with the United States attorney general. Their brothers and sisters in Great Britain were equally industrious. Ivor Montagu, of the British Peace Society, was solidly behind Du Bois, as was London's League for Democratic Rights. The Student Labour Federation in London announced "we have protested to the appropriate quarters in your country." The League of Colored Peoples based in London was adamant: "The situation is viewed in a very serious light indeed and the Coloured Community of this country will combine to take whatever action they can." Like George Padmore, Cedric Dover was a one-man whirlwind counteracting the United States government's action. From his British residence, the former Fisk professor sent indignant letters to forty newspapers across the globe (Padmore sent ten), besides those to prominent personalities world-wide. His letters appeared in the *Ashanti Pioneer* of West Africa, the *Beacon* of Barbados, and others. Dover had close ties to India and the Indian community and, not coincidentally, his letters were printed in the local papers of Northern India and Allahbad's *India Today.* Francois Joseph Cariglio of Edinburgh sent his protest letter to Truman, care of the London Embassy, which was signed by eighty-three peoples."[44]

Those from the British Isles were not alone in Europe in opposition to the prosecution. The National Peace Movement of Luxembourg, the powerful Communist-influenced General Confederation of Labor in France, and Bruno Frei, editor of *Der Abend* and *Tagebuch* in Vienna were among the dissenters. Nor were Britons isolated within the commonwealth. The Hotel, Club, Restaurant, Caterers, Tea Rooms and Boarding House Employees Union of Australia told Howard Fast of the Defense Committee that they would "write in protest to the State Department" on the indictment. The South East Asia Committee, a group of Asians based in London, sent copies of their protest to Secretary General Lie of the United Nations, the United States Embassy in London, and the international press.[45]

But it was from Eastern Europe that some of Du Bois' most determined sustenance emanated. He had traveled to Prague earlier and established ties with various organizations there. Anezka Hodinova, president of the Czechoslovak Peace Committee, the Council of Masaryk University of Brno, Czechoslovakia, Dr. J. Murkarovsky, rector of Charles University, and the Union of Czechoslovak Writers all stood by Du Bois. The Central Council of Trade Unions of Prague, "on behalf of three million members," told Defense Committee member Louise Patterson of their staunch advocacy of Du Bois' cause. The Fight for Peace Committee of both the Cluj and Iasi regions and the Permanent Committee for the Defense of Peace of Romania registered their opposition to the prosecution. The Union of Polish writers and the Association of Polish Lawyers acted similarly, as did the Hungarian National Peace Council, the

Comite al Banais Pour La Defense De La Paix in Tirana, Albania, "the Democratic Students and the Democratic Youth of the Free Territory of Trieste," and the Soviet Peace Committee. Communist Party, USA contacts were all valuable here. William Weinstone of the party wrote articles that circulated in the press of many Eastern European nations.[46]

These streams of support from Africa, Asia, Latin America, the Caribbean, Australia, Europe, and from every part of the globe, all came together in international fora. The International Democratic Federation of Women, the International Organization of Journalists, and the World Federation of Scientific Workers were just a few of the international groupings that engaged in lobbying on behalf of Du Bois. Louis Saillant signed the World Federation of Trade Unions resolution, "in the name of over eight million organized workers throughout the world." Paul Delanoue, secretary general of the World Federation of Teachers' Unions, told Alice Citron that they would publicize the case and rally against Truman and McGrath. Many of these organizations and individuals were affiliated with the Comite International De Defense Du Dr. W.E.B. Du Bois et de ses Colleagues. This broadly based committee, with members in both Germanys, Britain, Austria, Belgium, Brazil, Bulgaria, Columbia, China, Denmark, France, Holland, Iran, Italy, Libya, Martinique, Poland, Romania, Switzerland, and the Soviet Union, was top heavy with lawyers, law professors, judges, academics, and peace activists. Activists from this committee were tireless. Dr. Elia Erralgol, president of the Comite Nacional por la Paz y la Democracia—which included Lazaro Pena and Fernando Ortiz—and the Democratic Rights Council of Australia were among the like-minded that raised voices against the trial.[47]

It was inevitable that the decibel level of all these domestic and international raised voices would capture the attention of Washington, D.C.—or more precisely, Langley, Virginia. An acting chief of a Central Intelligence Agency (CIA) bureau reported to higher quarters:

> Attached herewith for the possible interest (deleted) is an outdated form letter recently received by the Chilean Student Federation (FECH) from the International Student Federation. The letter requests the aid of FECH in a campaign to free United States pro-peace leader [Dr.] W.E.B. Du Bois, who at the time the letter was written was apparently awaiting trial

> in the United States for his pro-peace activities. Included in the letter is a suggestion that the FECH send a student delegation to the United States Embassy in Santiago to protest the proceedings against Dr. Du Bois . . . such a protest at least to date, has not been made (deleted).

The CIA was also active in Belgium investigating the "communist propaganda campaign on behalf of Dr. W.E.B. Du Bois." From West Africa, Dr. R. E. G. Armattoe confided to Du Bois that "the United States Information Services had let loose a violent propaganda barrage against you out here." The CIA was so fascinated by the pro-Du Bois movement that it came to use association with these forces as a litmus test for redness.[48]

This outpouring of global concern about his fate heartened Du Bois. He knew that with the eyes of the world watching, the chances for a fair trial were improved. He also knew that generating support in the nation's heartland was critical, which is why he spent so much time in the industrial centers, where a disproportionate share of the nation's wealth was created. As the time for the trial rapidly approached, he was reinvigorated by the burgeoning signs of outraged opposition. After the labor and sweat put into building a Defense Committee which crossed the nation and circled the globe, the actual trial of Du Bois and his colleagues may have been anticlimatic to some. Du Bois was well aware that the implications of the trial stretched beyond him and his codefendants. Du Bois did not feel, in any event, that an indictment was warranted since PIC was non defunct. But this contention was not acceptable to the Justice Department which stated that: "Dissolution of an organization relieves neither the organization itself nor its officers from complying with the provisions of the Act." So the case went to court. The arraignment gave a hint as to what could be expected. Du Bois was accompanied to court by former judge James C. Cobb of the Washington Municipal Court; Dean George W. Parker of the Terrell School of Law; Barrington Parker, Dean Parker's son; and George Hayes. Perry Howard, Republican National Committeeman and a partner of Judge Cobb's was also on hand. Du Bois and the others were shunted to the criminal chute. The point-counterpoint of support for Du Bois in the face of determined antagonism toward him was to be a theme of the trial.[49]

A key tactical victory for the defense was securing postponement of the trial from May 14 to the fall. This gave the defendants important breathing space in which to organize and rally their forces. Prior to that, the defendants were lucky when, after Judge Alexander Holtzoff, formerly advisor to J. Edgar Hoover, a judge of strong right-wing and antiradical bias, heard the initial motion to dismiss, the case was assigned to Judge Matthew McGuire.[50]

Du Bois was not alone in this crisis, though there is some question as to the depth of support from among the Black middle class. When the trial began the courtroom was frequently visited by leading capitol activists and other members of the Washington, D.C., Black bar; it was also habitually visited by friends and allies. The Council on African Affairs sent seventy-five notices to contacts in the South and one hundred in New York alone requesting that the courtroom be packed. The American Peace Crusade, in a circular sent to local Peace Councils, called for delegations from community leaders, trade unions, Negro organizations, youth and women's groups, clergymen, and others to fill the courtroom and to visit their congressmen, senators, and the Department of Justice concerning the dropping of the case. A pillar of the Black bar, Judge James Cobb, suggested using the wide range of Du Bois' support in advocating an opening discussion with Congressman William Dawson, the phlegmatic Black politico from Chicago, when discussing his assistance in the defense with Du Bois: "I know he has a very high regard for you," was Cobb's considered analysis.[51]

The pretrial preparation by attorneys was thorough. There were three groups of witnesses to be interviewed, including Robeson, George Murphy, Rockwell Kent, Jessica Smith, C. B. Baldwin, John Howard Lawson, Henry Foner, James Aronson, Edward Barsky, Howard Fast, Mike Gold, and Anton Refregier. These witnesses all shared a certain familiarity with the peace movement and a common leftist political orientation. The direct examination of Du Bois was also worked out in advance. Counsel sought to indicate the reasonableness of their efforts by bringing out other activities done by PIC besides circulating the Stockholm Peace Appeal, such as disseminating the International Red Cross Appeal. This detailed single-spaced, legal size memo dealt with the forming of PIC, its independence, distribution of the appeal, and the change in PIC officers necessitated by Elizabeth Moos' departure. Moos was a big issue at this trial. This daughter of German-Jewish parents, whose mother was a member of the Daughters of the American Revolution and whose ancestors arrived in the United States in 1642, was regarded by some as a class traitor, along the lines of Alger Hiss and deserving of special opprobrium. She was the former mother-in-law of William Remington, convicted the Wednesday before the indictment of perjury in denying he was a Communist. It was felt by some that the indictment of PIC functionaries was a way for the government to display a more vigilant posture, since Remington had worked at the Department of Commerce. These factors were cited by some along with the fact that Moos was in Warsaw attending a peace meeting at the time of the indictment.[52]

Since the heart of the government's case was the legal absurdity of showing that the accused were agents of an unnamed, but well-known, foreign principal, the political climate was all important—which is why so much of the defense effort was devoted to rallying the masses. The prosecution was determined to slip in subtly or overtly presumed damaging evidence on world peace efforts. Because of the shakiness of their case, the prosecution deployed tactics considered questionable by some and unethical by others. Du Bois divulged to Judge Cobb information on that score:

> During the trial someone told me that the Department of Justice had hired [a] professor in the Howard Law School to prepare a dossier on my career; that he did this over the protests of many of his colleagues.

Relaying the intelligence, Cobb quickly revealed to Du Bois the mole's name and identity: "[he] works at DOJ and teaches at Howard. He is white, and claims to be interested in the Civil Rights of colored peoples." The fact that so many of Du Bois' supporters in the Black bar were close to Howard Law was apparently deemed a plus by Justice. These hardball tactics outside the court were duplicated in the courtroom.[53]

Some were disturbed by the prosecution's use of a prime witness, the apostate O. John Rogge. Fundamentally, whether Du Bois would spend what might have been the remaining years of his life in a prison cell turned on whether the jury believed Rogge's testimony. Rogge had been catapulted into prominence in the progressive movement of the 1940s when he linked United States businessmen of a certain stripe with Nazis. He was dismissed from his post in the government in a glare of publicity when he disclosed details of the investigation. So ended one stage of the career of Oetje John Rogge. Born on an Illinois farm on Columbus Day 1903, Rogge was precocious. He graduated from the University of

Illinois at 19, Harvard Law School at 21, and along the way worked for the Department of Justice and fought the Huey Long machine. Like so many others, the United States—Soviet alliance against fascism moved him to the left—at least for a while. Rogge, a former assistant United States attorney general in charge of the Justice Department's Criminal Divison, created an uproar with the 1949 publication of the prophetically titled *Our Vanishing Civil Liberties.* It was a formidable blunderbuss shot against the cutting edge of Truman's loyalty program, HUAC, and other aspects of the thought police. Yet, even before the trial, Du Bois had begun to sense the drift of Rogge to the right. Eventually, Rogge became notorious for his actions against the Rosenbergs and the Trenton Six and, in his *In Battle for Peace,* Du Bois lambasts him for this, being a paid agent agent of Tito's government in Yugloslavia, and for being chastised by a federal Court of Appeals for neglect of a labor client.[54]

Du Bois was not the only progressive disturbed by Rogge's political direction. The *Daily Compass* reported that he "appeared nervous, harried and worn" in court. I. F. Stone was decidedly harsh in his comments. Albert Kahn publicly ridiculed and mocked Rogge for having worked with the Yugoslavians; he painted him as a complete opportunist who joined the stampede to the right after the Progressive party failed to get more votes in 1948—a vote that was a telling indication to some of which way the wind was blowing.[55]

This was an unmasked political prosecution and many expected Judge Matthew McGuire to favor the prosecution, but this turned out to be an inaccurate perception. He proved to be fair and judicious. A turning point came when Judge McGuire asked government prosecutors whether they intended to show that the Soviet Union was behind the Paris committee. They said they did not. Along with Rogge's ineffective testimony attempting to link the defendants with the mystery principal, this spelled doom for the prosecution's efforts. The judge directed a verdict for the defense after the trial's sixth day, refusing to let the jury "speculate on a speculation." In her comprehensive report of the trial, Elizabeth Moos graphically outlined the courtroom scene. She was particularly praiseworthy of the defense counsel, the Black trio from Washington—George Hayes, James Cobb, and George Parker—and the four New Yorkers—Bernard Jaffe, Stanley Faulkner, Gloria Agrin, and Vito Marcantonio. The press section was amply populated, which assured coverage in Uganda, India, Scotland, and other parts of the globe. There were eight Blacks and four whites on the jury. After the trial, two Black jurors allegedly whispered, "we could see the government did not have anything on you." But Moos clobbered the press for reporting the exact opposite. She lamented how this threadbare indictment pulled all away from pressing political obligations. She too was drawn to that deathless moment in the trial when the prosecution asked Rogge on the witness stand if he knew Du Bois: "O. John peered helplessly about until Dr. Du Bois rose with impressive dignity . . . saying quietly, 'Here I am.' " Rogge continued a bit flustered and caused further affront when he contradicted himself on his assertion of the true principal by way of earlier admissions that the world peace movement was not dominated by one foreign country; nor did his own status as a paid agent enhance his credibility. Rogge was not the only witness deemed curious. Moos' admonitions about the press were reinforced when three *New York Times* reporters testified for the prosecution. Judge McGuire did not flinch in the face of this barrage; his initial ruling that just showing parallel lines between PIC and the unnamed principal was not enough, was critical. The prosecution was not operating with all guns blazing though because of an important constraint: "The government was particularly sensitive to opinion abroad in the colonial countries, among the colored peoples."[56]

The acquittal buoyed Du Bois beyond a range to be expected. He was only somewhat gracious toward Judge McGuire as he acknowledged that the prosecution was "utterly surprised by the fairness of the judge, who has been heretofore one of the worse judges on the bench. Of course he doubtless had his orders from above." He was more effusive in assessing his defense team—lavishing praise on all—but he was particularly grateful to Vito Marcantonio. Du Bois was equally, if not more, thankful to Gloria Agrin for her "extraordinary work [and] unselfishness in yielding without a word of protest or a moment of hesitation your rightful place as our chief counsel." This personnel shift caused a certain amount of strain that prompted Du Bois to score the "pre-historic prejudice that still obtains in the case of women." Du Bois was right to be grateful to Agrin, since it was her research and lawyering that was so instrumental in the victory. When Judge McGuire announced, "we are not trying the foreign policy of the Soviet Union or the foreign policy of the United States or the foreign policy of any government in the world," Agrin could take credit for providing the judge with the bricks that helped him form this legal foundation.[57]

The PIC victory was not just a victory for the defendants but it was perceived as a gain for all those concerned about the growing challenge to civil liberties, for example, the thousands of individuals, unions, churches, community organizations, and so on that rallied to the side of the defendants. Of this Du Bois was acutely aware:

> [the acquittal was] . . . not merely a victory for 5 persons and an organization, but much more a triumph for free speech and the right to defend peace . . . for nine months I and my associates have had to give up most of our normal work . . . this vindication did not come cheap . . . $35,000 in cash [was spent].

But even here, the situation extended beyond the PIC because such a sum could not have been raised for such a case at such a time without mass participation in the United States and abroad. Words of elation were echoed across the country and around the world. *Pittsburgh Courier*'s executive editor P. L. Prattis expressed the sentiments of many:

> In those days to come, future historians will measure off the dimensions of Dr. Du Bois and discover the stature of one of the greatest protagonists of peace and of the poor, of this and all times. This bit of history, denied me, will be the pleasure and inspiration of my children and grand-children.

The *Daily Compass* echoed these prophetic words and termed the acquittal:

> "[the] biggest victory for peace and civil liberties to be seen around these United States in many months."

The *National Guardian* underlined the far-reaching political significance of the case: "For the first time since Harry S. Truman set off the greatest witch-hunt of modern times with his loyalty purge in March 1947, the government last week took a stunning defeat."[58]

This stunning victory, so rare for progressives in an otherwise dismal string of losses, flung Du Bois like never before into the forefront of anti-Cold War heroes; unlike others, he slew the dragon. Du Bois was too experienced and savvy to let this lofty role go to his head, as he was sensible enough to recognize that there was a correlation between his freedom and the mass participation in his defense committee. His thanks to Albert Einstein could have been expressed to any of millions across the continents and not just the world famous.[59]

Du Bois was far from being intimidated by the indictment and trial. It did not cause him to tack his sails to the prevailing winds. G. V. Banks of Prairie View State College in Texas warned him after the acquittal to "hush now and just be glad to live." Du Bois, addressing the wife of the vice president of the college as "My dear Krazy Kat," admonished her and Banks gently, "you know perfectly well that I am not going to stop talking. . . . If we are near you we will call in, unless you think it would frighten your trustees and teachers too much."[60]

Du Bois was magnanimous after the trial and, as his comment to Banks showed, sensitive to compromising his friends because of his heralded status. After the trial he immediately resigned from the Sigma Pi Phi fraternity and specifically from Zeta Boulé, New York City. Du Bois was upset because "of the thirty or more Boulés in the United States only one has sent me a single word of sympathy or offer of help." The action of the isolated Washington, D.C., chapter was not enough to sway Du Bois.[61]

Du Bois also had a bone to pick with the NAACP leadership after the trial. On the day of the acquittal Walter White, speaking in Milwaukee, was asked why the Association did not support Du Bois. He was alleged to have said that the government showed him irrefutable proof (not evidence) of Du Bois' guilt; specifically Peyton Ford of the Justice Department had said there was definite evidence nailing Du Bois. Du Bois was livid. Du Bois accused Roy Wilkins of warning the Detroit branch " 'not to touch' this matter," that is, his case, and inveigling to get Judge Delany to speak at the same time and hour as his appearance in the Motor City; but Delany foiled these elaborate plans by talking about the Du Bois case. The NAACP was also accused of nonfeasance: "[The] Legal Department of the NAACP, which is under the control of Arthur Spingarn, Walter White and Thurgood Marshall . . . refused to take part in my defense . . . although appealed to." Walter White continued to be a bone in Du Bois' throat. He threatened to sue him for libel for his comments on his "guilt" and termed him "the most unpopular leader among Negroes." Du Bois saw White as conspiring against him on more than one front:

> During the election, White secured funds from the Democratic National Committee to pay the debts of the owner of the Defender. Soon after my column was dropped. White's column continues.

But most nettling to Du Bois was the attempt by the NAACP to cut off his pension despite the known financial strain caused by his legal defense. When after the indictment the NAACP cut his pension in half without notice, Du Bois perceived this as outright economic warfare. It was claimed that this was purely a move of economy due to lack of funds but a few months later White's salary was increased significantly, in addition to his being allotted a large personal expense account. This move was supported by Spingarn. Du Bois considered going to court over this but possibly because of the negative backwash of publicity that would have swept the NAACP, the leadership chose to reconsider and reach an agreement with their founder.[62]

Loss of erstwhile friends and associates and loss of funds was not the only result of Du Bois' trial. Trials of this nature pull activists away from political activism, as energies have to be concentrated on defense. After the acquittal, William Patterson of the Civil Rights Congress encouraged Du Bois to fly to Paris to present his controversial and historic *We Charge Genocide* petition. But the trial had taken its toll and Du Bois' physicians resisted the idea of his departure; perhaps being overly cautious, his lawyers resisted as well, feeling that it might not sit well with the government that had just tried him. Patterson was infuriated and unforgiving, but Du Bois did not budge. Neither could he lend a hand when he was asked a few days later to speak at a fundraiser for Patterson, who himself was being tried by the government. In this sense, though, the directed verdict in his favor was a boon, the government had won at least a small victory since the ordeal of the trial had caused Du Bois' wings to be cropped a bit.[63]

The trial caused other strains. Du Bois, though he received wide support, was displeased with the efforts of some quarters. After Dean Martin Harvey of Southern University of Louisiana sent him congratulations on his acquittal, Du Bois replied acidly: "Of all the Negro colleges in the United States, I have heard from the officials or students of only two. You are the third." Apparently, Du Bois was unmindful of the outpouring of support from Black students that greeted his indictment. Nonetheless, the sourness did not always travel in one direction. Years afterwards, Du Bois was compelled to explain to his Washington friend Eugene Davidson why he had not mentioned his hospitality in the book about the trial. Du Bois gently explained:

> I was very careful not to mention your name and not to say too much where I had stayed because I was afraid that it might [hurt] you in your business.

On further reflection, Davidson agreed: "Frankly, I think it is wise that you did not do so merely because there are so many bigots who could and would misinterpret our basic reason." Davidson expressed a view shared by quite a few when he proclaimed that "a possible difference in ideologies" could not sever their "friendship." Going along with this outlook was Belford Lawson, Washington attorney and president of the Alpha Phi Alpha fraternity. Addressing an Alpha banquet at Morgan State during the Christmas season of 1951, he observed that the United States government could not have afforded to convict Du Bois. He presciently praised Ben Davis, Paul Robeson, and others of like mind: "Who are we to say these men are wrong. We do not know that one day history may find them right."[64]

CHAPTER 15

Africa and Peace; Part II

After the hiatus caused by having to spend time fighting the indictment, Du Bois resumed his two major dialectically intertwined goals—fighting for colonialism's death in Africa and peace. From his office at the Council on African Affairs, he planned and wrote lectures, articles, and carried on his wide correspondence; he raised funds for the liberation movements; and he mobilized and organized mass support against colonialism. Most of all, he influenced masses, despite an adverse political climate. Shirley Graham has portrayed this well in discussing the "many Africans who were studying at various colleges in the city," who took his classes at the leftist Jefferson School of Social Science, and who were entertained at their home; "During these recent years I have met more than one now highly placed African official who told me how much he appreciated such evenings in our Brooklyn home." This influence was observed by Du Bois' and the CAA's adversaries, and it was not long before the council was run out of business. Government fury was understandable. The council hit hard at United States investments abroad, United States military collaboration with colonialism, United States votes in the United Nations, the fraud of anti-communism, and other issues not designed to curry favor in Washington or on Wall Street. *The New York Times* recognized with typical prescience the importance of Africa for United States strategic planners in a revealing editorial:

> Africa is the continent of the future. We learned its strategic value in the second World War. Its economic potentialities are the hope of Western Europe . . . as well as the rest of the world. . . . The United States need not be afraid of the label of reactionary if [we] oppose too hasty "independence."

Du Bois and the Council were rooting on a hasty independence for the continent and the fact that he was both Black and influential was guaranteed to cause tensions. It was important that those of African ancestry in the United States be brought into line in support of United States foreign policy, but Du Bois and the Council were not cooperative. Rayford Logan was also denounced for his speech at the fortieth NAACP convention by Du Bois and his associates; they felt that his asking Blacks to "join forces with those who want to make Point Four truly a bold program" was symptomatic of a dangerous trend whereby United States Blacks would be trotted out as spokesmen for United States foreign policy.[1]

A primary role for Du Bois at the Council was as chair of the African Aid Committee, which raised funds for those besieged on the continent by repression. With Du Bois in the driver's seat, and with the usual assortment of allies assisting, funds were raised and sent to the Nigerian National Federation of Labor. He arranged for Dean Dixon, the Afro-American composer, musician, and conductor, to do a benefit concert. The Council's January 1950 newsletter featured a front-page picture of Du Bois handing over a $200 check to Dr. Nnamdi Azikiwe for aid to Enugu strike victims in Nigeria; miners there had been slain during a violent labor conflict. Du Bois' committee sent $100 more to help establish the first free school for girls in Sierra Leone. Aid of another kind was rendered to Seretse Khama of Bechuanaland, leader of the Bamangwato people, who was exiled by the British colonialists after he married a European woman. The CAA telegraphed Sir Oliver Franks of the British diplomatic corps and Tygve Lie to protest. Du Bois, Robeson, and Hunton—the CAA troika—were able to get sixty-five signatories to the telegram, including Mary Church Terrell, Bishop J. A. Gregg of Jacksonville and numerous pastors. The future leader of Botswana was grateful.[3]

This harassment did not force Du Bois or the council to cower. In the same month that Du Bois was entering the dock as a defendant, the council's newsletter was blasting United States foreign policy with both barrels. Subsequently, they noted critically growing United States investments in Africa and scored them as bolstering colonialism. They rhetorically asked a question on the minds of many: "Will Negroes be called upon to suppress in blood the African peoples."

Apartheid was a primary concern of both Du Bois and the council. When the African National Congress (ANC) of South Africa launched its Campaign of Defiance of Unjust Laws in South Africa, Du Bois and his associates quickly sprung into action. Over a six month period in 1952, $2,422 was raised for them. In April, they organized a rally in Harlem to support the ANC's civil disobedience campaign and a picketing of the South African consulate in New York. Also, at the council's initiative, there was "an observance of silence in Negro churches and communities" in solidarity with antiapartheid forces; messages of support were sent to the leaders of the South African struggle. Simultaneously, the CAA launched a campaign to get 100,000 signatures by September 15 of that year in support of the ANC; but by the time that date rolled around only 3,800 signatures had been collected and only $835 collected, but this was seen as a victory during difficult political times. It was also seen as a victory in South Africa itself. Both Dr. J. S. Moroka, president-general of the ANC and Dr. Y. M. Dadoo, chair of the South African Indian Congress, took time to send the council a message of thanks and solidarity. Walter Sisulu, secretary-general of the ANC, also thanked the council for their support.[3]

Despite the fact that 1952 was a bleak year for progressives, the Council was flourishing. Their newsletter was coming out every two to three weeks rather than monthly. The best and the brightest were flocking to their banner. The talented novelist and screenwriter John Oliver Killens joined the staff. The skilled writer Alice Childress, who also wrote for *Freedom,* alluded to the defiance campaign in her popular play *Gold Through Trees,* produced by the left-center Committee for the Negro in the Arts. This too was a reflection of the Council's myriad efforts to instill a consciousness of the struggle in Africa.

CAA support for the struggle in South Africa was not a one-way street. When Max Yergan unleashed another wave of redbaiting against the council, ANC leaders did not stand by silently. Nelson Mandela, volunteer-in-chief of the Defiance Movement and president of the ANC Youth League, was extensively quoted in *Freedom* attacking Yergan. Z. K. Matthews, chairman of the Cape Province section of the ANC and former Henry Luce Visiting Professor at

Union Theological Seminary, spoke in a like manner. Perhaps because of the immediate, fiery reaction of prominent South African Blacks, Black leaders in the United States who otherwise would not be found on the same side of the barricades with Du Bois and Robeson, mightily condemned Max Yergan; this also illustrates how the African liberation struggle moved United States Blacks to the left. Lester Granger and Walter White were among those who reproved Yergan. These Black leaders still paid at least lip service to the notion of anti-colonialism and would have lost credibility if they had not united with the ANC, even on so controversial a point as Yergan's redbaiting. At the same time, in the ANC, as a message from Z. K. Matthews attested, there was high regard for the CAA's work throughout Africa. Thus, despite a prevailing Cold War atmosphere, the Council was able to have influence not only domestically, but also internationally.[4]

In the midst of this fruitful activity there were strains within the CAA. When in the fall of 1952, Hunton suggested moving the CAA office from downtown Manhattan to Harlem, Du Bois called it a "calamity. . . . No international agency belongs today in Harlem. It has neither the contacts nor the inspiration there." From his point of view, the move would mean the loss of Frederick Field's "magnificent library" and too much distance from the United Nations at nearby Turtle Bay. Du Bois was also upset about Robeson's other activities: "He cannot support the Council, conduct a monthly newspaper, sing, and lecture and cooperate with other activities." Nevertheless, he saw the merit in Hunton's position that their office should be moved to Harlem, since it was the "main base of our work." But these strains were far from being a constant refrain in the Du Bois-CAA relationship. His criticism of Robeson was in a fit of pique and he recognized that progressives had to do more than their share because of intense political repression.[5]

Most of all Du Bois recognized that whatever differences he may have had with his colleagues, they paled in significance when compared with the differences and conflicts he had with the United States government and its patrons. The CAA newsletter, prepared by Hunton with assistance from Du Bois, continually listed a tally of United States votes on key issues in the United Nations concerning colonialism in Africa. During one period the record showed that while the United States abstained or voted no on sample anticolonial measures, the Soviets voted yes on all.[6]

The harpoons tossed at leading political and economic targets were not greeted with diffident calm. Association with the "subversive" CAA was not designed to keep the FBI away from one's door. Weeks before the epic *Brown v. Board of Education* decision, Du Bois confidentially informed Hunton, "A friend of mine sent this contribution to the Council. Do not acknowledge it or use her name." Prior to that, Du Bois caustically told Elizabeth Lawson that the Voice of America broadcast Dean Dixon's fundraising concert for the CAA "without mentioning the fact that if the Council had not been on the Attorney-General's subversive list," the effort would have made more money. The Voice of America was not the only arm of the United States interested in the council's work. The deputy director of Plans of the Central Intelligence Agency (CIA) told the FBI director:

> It was reported in December 1953 by a source of unknown reliability (deleted) that a Pan African Conference which was scheduled to be held in Cairo during 1954 "is the brainchild of the American Negro, Dr. Du Bois. . . ." Therefore, your Bureau is requested to transmit to this Agency and information which indicates that W. E. B. Du Bois or the Council on African Affairs had had any connection with either project or any other recent project for a Pan-Africanist nationalist conferance.

It is striking that there was this avid interest in Du Bois and the CAA's activities. Yet, they were not alone for during this same period Attorney General Herbert Brownell requested that the Council register as a "Communist-front organization."[7]

The council was charged with having positions identical or similar to those of the Communist party, USA on such topical issues as the war against Korea, the House Un-American Activities Committee, the seating of the Peoples Republic of China at the United Nations, NATO, the riot against Robeson and other progressives at Peekskill. By this standard, of course, any dissent to the prevailing consensus made one liable to smear and censure. But this was not the only accusation:

> The Council seeks to create and further hostility among the negroes in this country to the United States for the purpose of rendering this segment of the population susceptible to communist indoctrination.

Hunton was subpoenaed to appear in court and produce all correspondence and communications between the CAA and the African National Congress from 1946 to the present; the same was requested regarding the South African Indian Congress. Also requested was all "correspondence and communication" and "any individual outside the United States . . . affiliated with a foreign government, foreign political party and/or any organizations." Demanded also was "all materials published and/or disseminated" and "all books and records of accounts." Through this the government learned that the CAA did not have much of the fabled Moscow Gold, showing a total income of $8,007.55 in 1952, $4,857.15 in 1953, and $11,700 in the first ten months of 1954; but the government was not deterred. A prime witness against the council was the ubiquitous Max Yergan,who again was trying to show that the ANC and CAA were "Communist controlled." The council did not cut and run in the face of this onslaught, although its scope was comprehensive. Du Bois addressed the United Nations community seeking support for the CAA, now under attack for "collecting funds to aid the people's resistance struggle abroad." But ultimately the CAA could not overcome pressure from above and was forced to liquidate its operation, though Du Bois and the council did not go down quietly, but in flames.[8]

The council was not only sharply critical of the State Department and United States-based transnational corporations but they also turned their microscope on potential friends and allies. They commended the NAACP for their resolution on colonialism in 1953 but criticized the use of the term "natives" and the equating of the "persecution" of Britons in South Africa with Blacks; they questioned their lack of forthright support for specific organizations—like the ANC—and United States votes in the United Nations on Africa. A specific reference to East Africa by the Association—"we view with alarm the terrorist methods of the Mau Maus in Kenya"—was strenuously attacked.[9]

Those in Africa were not free from the council's searching eye. The government of Liberia was assailed in late 1952 for engaging in political repression and sanctioning economic exploitation, such as through their dealings with Firestone Rubber Company. Mary McLeod Bethune, Carl Murphy, and Ambassador Edward Dudley were scored for failing "to tell the truth" about this situation. Even Kwame Nkrumah, a personal friend and protegé of Du Bois, could not escape condemnation from time to time. In early 1954 he was assaulted for ousting labor leaders Anthony Woode and Turson Ocran because of "their association with the World Federation of Trade Unions" and other sundry leftist influences. They needled him when he invited United States investors into Ghana and continued harassing the left. Nkrumah was also criticized for the "banning of Communists" from public office and alleged Communist publications from the country. Du Bois refused to write an article on Liberia in September 1954 because "anything that I said would not be too kind and perhaps there is no reason for stirring up unpleasant things on the occasion of the President's visit.[10]

The Council was not as discreet when the Ethiopian leader Haile Selassie decided to visit the United States. In an open letter, they urged Selassie "on the day of his official visit" to the United Nations to "establish a commission composed of representatives of non-colonial powers to investigate the conflict in Kenya"; he was asked to urge this on "American opinion" as well. Their old friend Azikiwe was also assailed. He was scorned when he was alleged to have said that outside investment would be welcomed in Nigeria. He was knocked for opportunism when he averred that "it doesn't matter what political party is in power, the same standards will remain."[11]

But the main focus of Du Bois and the CAA was not criticism of their allies but repeated attacks on colonialism and imperialism. As the stuggle in Kenya heated up, this British colony became a familiar object of attention. A high point in this process was the April 1954 Conference in Support of African Liberation at Friendship Baptist Church. There a proposal was made to establish a Kenya Aid Program and a Kenya Aid Committee which it was hoped would initially raise $5,000 in the two month period following the conference; milk, vitamin pills, and first aid supplies were also to be gathered and forwarded to representative of the Kenya African National Union (KANU) in London. Here was set down the most comprehensive view of what the CAA stood for at a crucial moment in their history. Their extensive "Declaration in Support of African Liberation," demanded, among other things, the "right of Africans to assemble freely," be guaranteed, that there be a ban on "racial discrimination," a "guarantee that economic planning and development" be for the "progress of the African masses, returning the land to the Africans," and a "specific time-limit" for "self-government in every colonial teritory" be established; on this latter point specific reference was made to Namibia (Southwest Africa), the "Federation of Rhodesia and Nyasaland," and South Africa's "annexation of Bechuanaland, Bautoland and Swaziland." There were other demands put forward: "full suffrage rights and genuine representative government, . . . stop the jailing and exiling of leaders in Kenya, Uganda, Morocco and other territories," a ban on military bases of any foreign power and a bar on "technical, financial, or military" aid to such countries as, Kenya, Morocco, Tunisia, or South Africa. Above all the declaration proclaimed; "We declare that Africa must be free.[12]

This statement was widely circulated for endorsement. A specific resolution on Kenya was sent to the United Nations, the State Department, and the British Colonial Office. There were 114 courageous delegates and observers attending the conference gathered in Harlem. The CAA troika was ever-present and was the heart of this conference. Du Bois gave the keynote address, Hunton presented the CAA report,and Robeson made the concluding statement. Their words and the conference resolutions did not just remain on paper. A few months after the meeting, Hunton happily told Du Bois; "We have received a warm letter of thanks from the Kenyatta Defense Fund in London for $500 collected and recently sent them by our Kenya Aid Committee."[13]

There were Communists present at this CAA function and they were present at many other CAA-sponsored events. This did not endear the Council or Du Bois to the United States government. Nor was the government pleased when influential African opinion concurred with Du Bois' approach. The *West African Pilot* berated the notion that the battle against colonialism was "Communist inspired":[14]

> The Communists [could] not be as bad as their enemies say they are. Are they not practically the only white nation [USSR] that has voted consistently in the United Nations for the right of colored peoples? . . . We have every cause to be grateful to the Communists for their active interest in the fate of colonial peoples and for their constant denunciation of the evils of imperialism.

When the Bandung Conference of 1955, which brought together the Afro-Asian countries in an historic meeting signalling the rise of the nonaligned and the third world, was held, it received favorable coverage not only from the CAA newsletter but from the Black press generally, while the white-owned press was generally indifferent or hostile. The *Afro-American* and the *Oklahoma City Black Dispatch* were among the papers that endorsed the meeting. In any event, the council was not around too long after the Bandung Conference to comment on the development or revelation of Black public opinion; for the court action begun in 1953 led to the dissolution of the council in 1955. This too marked a watershed for Du Bois and at this juncture he decided to move his office to his Brooklyn Heights home.[15]

The dissolution of the Peace Information Center did not spell the end of Du Bois' peace activism. Indeed, many of those who were formerly associated with PIC quickly surfaced in the newly organized American Peace Crusade. Du Bois was honorary chair of the APC, organized in 1951. Abbott Simon presented the rationale for the APC's basic thrust:

> Petitions no longer held the value they once had for a national campaign, it was felt; therefore, the proposal for a people's referendum.

The APC campaign, based on this novel notion, quickly caught fire: "There has been an overwhelming and enthusiastic response to the announcement of the Peace Crusade . . . an initial printing of 50,000 ballots has been completely exhausted." Though he was in the midst of preparing for a trial in March 1951, Du Bois had time to consult on the APC's peace pilgrimage of 2,500 from forty states—though most were from Du Bois' home state of New York—that presented an anti-war statement to Secretary of Defense George Marshall. This all-out assault on Washington, D.C., included a visit to the Department of Justice and a visit of the American Women for Peace to Senator Margaret Chase Smith. The APC was also involved in the formation of the National Committee for Peaceful Alternatives which developed "more than one hundred local committees . . . throughout the country" and had Thomas Mann and Bishop W. J. Walls as cochairs. That such burgeoning peace activism could flourish in a hostile political atmosphere made the accomplishment that much more extraordinary. For example, *The New York Times*, the *New York Post*, and *Herald-Tribune* plus the *Washington Post* all turned down paid ads from the APC in the thick of the drive against the war.[16]

Paradoxically, the indictment of Du Bois may have provided a shot in the arm for the peace movement. It was no doubt the opinion of many that if a world renowned figure like Du Bois could be handcuffed and tried, few dissenters were safe; and this realization probably spurred some into activism as a matter of self-interest, if nothing more. The apex of this effort may have been reached June 29 to July 1, 1951, at the People's congress and Peace Exposition in Chicago. Du Bois' appearance there was sandwiched in between speeches on a cross-country tour rallying support against his prosecution. More than 7,000 heard him speak in Chicago on a program that included Eslanda and Paul Robeson, Philip Morrison, Willard Uphaus, and E. Franklin Frazier. Thousands cheered and clapped rhythmically as he declaimed on the issues. Like this mass outpouring of anti-war sentiment in Chicago, Du Bois was not far from wrong when he told his fellow New Yorkers, "The press treated this significant resolution very quietly."[17]

Though little press coverage was given to the APC's successes, there was an intense fascination in the press with their setbacks and cleavages. The celebrated author Thomas Mann bolted from the APC early in 1951 after a *New York Times* article linked him with the Communists. Du Bois and other APC officials were quick to reply. Professor Philip Morrison acerbically lashed out at the *Times* for distortion and omission:[18]

> Our release listed about sixty-five names . . . four men bore the title of bishop . . . scholars and scientists like Professors Panofsky, Sorokin, Pauling, or Dr. Du Bois. There were AFL and CIO leaders, ministers and physicians, farm leaders and writers. The *Times* mentioned none of this . . . it mentioned only ten names. These were the four or five persons as you said "generally identified with communistic leanings" a few others known for partisan political activity and your name and mine. This story could have been no accident.

This was not the only difficulty faced by the APC. Du Bois had reason to feel set upon. He had been indicted and earlier he had been ousted from the NAACP. But even after this acquittal in November 1951 there was no let-up. On November 17, 1952, he told Elizabeth Moos that he wanted her to personally deliver a letter to Jean Laffitte, his European co-worker in peace activities, since "in the past I have rather suspected that some of my leters to him have not reached him. At any rate, no answers have come." If postal authorities were in fact tampering with Du Bois' correspondence, they may have been taking their cue from the House Un-American Activities Committee, which denounced Du Bois at length in their *Report on the Communist "Peace Offensive": A Campaign to Disarm and Defeat the United States.* They noted that the *Daily Worker* sided with Du Bois in his dispute with the NAACP and Walter White. "Lest it be thought that Dr. Du Bois is really representative of the great mass of Negro people." This naked attempt to redbait Du Bois was not without effect, as it was designed to isolate him politically. The forty-third annual convention of the NAACP meeting in Oklahoma City in 1952 proclaimed; "We warn our branches and youth councils against so-called 'peace organizations.' "[19]

Canada apparently took heed of admonitions emanting from their southern neighbor as they prohibited Du Bois' entry for the Canadian Peace Congress, May 10–11, 1952. Isabel Blume, the Socialist deputy from Belgium, was to join Du Bois on the platform for this much awaited event. Canadian peace activists expected obstacles to Du Bois' entry, so they suggested that Du Bois travel by train since it was "much less conspicuous." The Canadian activists went to such lengths because his presence guaranteed that a crowd of at least 2,000 could be expected. Du Bois was not optimistic though. The Canadians were not deterred and defiantly upped the ante: "We have changed our original plans and have rented the largest public hall in the city—capacity about 17,000." Thumbing their nose at the United States government, they suggested as a peace topic: "We won the fight to speak for peace in the United States. Now, no one, anywhere in the world, can take it away."[20]

But these well laid plans proved awry. Du Bois and Shirley Graham "arrived . . . Friday . . . at 10:30 noon Standard Time" in Toronto and were questioned immediately. Shortly thereafter, an "Order for Deportation" was issued. C. E. S. Smith, Canadian Director of Immigration, claimed in *The New York Times* that Du Bois and Graham "had been sent back to the United States from Toronto for refusing to undergo an examination." This was hotly refuted by Du Bois: "This is a flat lie to which we both will take oath . . . we both answered fully every question asked us." Though he was barred, the thousands that gathered at the rally heard a tape recording of Du Bois denouncing United States foreign policy and the United States government's presumed role in his banning. The reaction in Toronto was outrage. They were no more incredulous than Du Bois himself, as he told Jean Laffitte of the World Council of Peace:

> This exclusion was undoubtedly done at the suggestion of our State Department, just as some time ago the State Department refused us a visa to go to the Peace Congress called for . . . Rio de Janeiro and later transferred to Montivideo. . . . In some cases we have not been able to send representatives to your bureau meetings, as was the case in the meeting at Oslo held recently.

But the prevailing political conditions were not eternal. The February 8, 1960, *Toronto Globe & Mail* featured, on page one, a picture of Du Bois addressing a 2,000 strong peace rally there.[21]

The promise of thousands rallying for peace under the banner of the APC and following Du Bois' leadership was flickering out in 1952 and almost extinguished in 1953; all this with the ample assistance of powerful political and economic forces in the United States. Du Bois adumbrated this dilemma in his remarks sent to the Continental Cultural Congress in Santiago, Chile, in April 1953: "If the United States government would permit we would be very glad to be in attendance, but no American who has been outspoken for peace and cultural freedom is allowed to leave under present restrictions." Cutting off the United States peace movement from international allies and sustenance was the aim and it was pursued by mail restrictions, travel restrictions, and general harassment. Sometimes this was not adequately understood among Du Bois' coworkers abroad. Continually he had to remind Jean Laffitte that because of the McCarran law which required registration, no peace organization in the United States could affiliate with the World Peace Council (WPC).[22]

Their reluctance to affiliate with the WPC did not save the APC from searching inquiries from the Justice Depatment. From the attorney general the APC received an incredibly detailed interrogatory; like the Council on African Affairs, Du Bois' other base, the APC was receiving the probing scrutiny of law enforcement agencies. The Department of Justice charged that the APC was established as a front for the Community party and succeeded the Peace Information Center. They demanded the names and addresses of virtually anyone who could have been connected with the APC. They asked about the peace pilgrimage of March 1951, the People's Congress and Exposition for Peace held in the summer of 1951, and related events. There were a number of questions asked about named individuals, such as, Paul Robeson, Howard Fast, Gil Green, Abbott Simon, Ernest De Maio—and Du Bois. The APC fired back an angry response to Assistant Attorney General Warren Olney's attempt to list them as a subversive organization. "We shall not answer" these interrogatories, they began, because they considered it "unconstitutional"; but they decided to "attach hereto all available statements, declarations, resolutions, announcements and pronouncements" issued by the APC. They strove valiantly to deflect the Communist issue by claiming that they "welcome into its membership persons of all political faiths who agreed with its objectives for honorable peace." But Justice was not persuaded and the same legal trap that snap shut and wiped out the CAA similarly extinguished the APC.[23]

This unremitting pressure on the APC inevitably had effects. It reenforced and spawned strains within the organization. Du Bois touched on this question in comments he made to Abbot Simon about APC activities:

> The plan is good and I have approved of it, but I am unhappy about the Peace Crusade as an organization. I do not think that we have an effective executive, and I do not think that long mimeographed communications are of much use. . . . We have no effective publicity. We have had very little field work and local and regional organization, and . . . I do not like the way in which finances are being handled. . . . What we need is wide personal correspondence and personal contact. As compared with other countries like Canada and Mexico our efforts suffer tremendously. . . . There has got to be one responsible head, and he must work and not simply talk and write.

It could be pointed out that though there were strong right-wing forces in countries like Canada and Mexico, comparing organizing for peace there with a country that may have been the major threat to world peace—and the repressive state apparatus that involved—was questionably apposite. Du Bois was not convinced, however, and he informed Huge Bryson, Herbert Aptheker, Howard Fast, and other APC supporters of his concerns, particularly an implication of corruption in his allegation that via the APC, a house had been purchased for Thomas Richardson." Despite the denial by Richardson, Du Bois was not assured. He strove to obtain information on the "previous history" of Richardson, and told Richardson that he would resign from his high post in the APC unless his request concerning an accounting of income and expenditures was fulfilled. Du Bois remained unhappy with the administration of the APC and was so angry that when he was to receive an international peace prize, he chose to receive it in Chicago so as to not involve the APC. He continued to criticize the APC in his correspondence. Du Bois did recognize that there was more reason than the inefficiency of the APC that explained the sorry state of the United States peace movement; yet he remained critical.[24]

It should not be thought that the APC was totally consumed with internal dispute. In actuality there was a plethora of activities in which they were involved. Du Bois and other peace activists sponsored a National Delegates Assembly for Peace on April 11, 1952; they demanded no "rearming and renazification of Western Germany . . . an immediate truce in Korea, full recognition of the right of self-government for the colonial peoples . . . rejection of the UMT" and ratification of the five-power peace pact. This Washington assembly of 800 included visits with congressmen and presentation of 500,000 signatures collected in various congressional districts in support of their objectives. A delegation led by Charlotta Bass visited the South African legation and presented their concerns. Du Bois was ever-present in this scenario. At the afternoon plenary, he "brought the delegates to their feet" with his fiery remarks. Du Bois had reason to be optimistic about prospects for peace despite heavy government repression. There was still powerful propeace sentiment internationally, as evidenced by the World Peace Council announcement earlier that year that 596,302,298 signatures had been collected on a petition calling for a peace pact among the five great powers.[25]

Du Bois and the APC were able to attract a disproportionate number of clergy to their ranks. This had been true for the Stockholm Peace Appeal and it continued to be true. The bulletin of the World Council of Peace reported that nine of America's leading Protestant churchmen had written an Open Letter inviting the American people to join them in using a Prayer for Peace in church services, private meditation, and public meetings. This forthright appeal, which was forwarded to President Truman, attracted ecumenical support. The same applied to their long planned National Referendum for Peace in 1952, which starkly posed the question: "I want a 'ceasefire' in Korea now with all open questions settled at an immediate peace conference." A substantial number of the clergy joined these two initiatives; some of these and others joined in the gala eighty-fourth birthday celebration for Du Bois, sponsored by the APC, that grossed $8,273.21.[26]

As 1953 dawned, Senator Joseph McCarthy was riding high and blacklist was a term being unduly applied to United States Blacks. Yet Du Bois struggled on with the peace movement despite the roadboocks strewn about; and the year culminated with his receiving the International Peace Prize of the World Council of Peace that consisted of a gold medal, a diploma, and $6,500 in cash.[27]

Du Bois' stature within the peace movement meant that his words would be carefully weighed. There were thirteen United States members of the World Council of Peace, including Du Bois. Though he was barred from traveling to Europe, it was not unusual for recorded remarks from Du Bois to be heard at international gatherings, for example, at a major peace congress in Helsinki in July 1955. The attempt to resume formal ties between the APC and international peace forces accelerated in the 1953 to 1955 period. Du Bois proposed formal affiliation with the WPC, despite the "McCarran law . . . even if we have to register, report receipts and label our literature." This was not a minor matter, as the PIC indictment flowed from their tie with the international peace movement. Undaunted, Du Bois proceeded. In 1955 he addressed a lengthy memorandum to Scott Nearing, Anton Refriegier, Rockwell Kent, and other comrades in the peace movement proposing reaffiliation. There was a mixed response with Kent being the most adamant in refusing. Du Bois' powers of persuasion were evidently still keen, as Kent reversed field and joined Robeson, Uphaus, Fast, and the rest in exploring the notion of WPC affiliation. Yet there was no unanimity on the question of whether the APC should register as a foreign agent and avoid the PIC's pitfalls. Kent unequivocally rejected this proposition. He felt that registration would bring on a "stigma" and make the United States branch a "little private club." Scott Nearing agreed in rejecting registration, though he noted that his difficulty in obtaining a passport showed the limitations of the Geneva spirit.[28]

Du Bois' proposals here cannot be separated from his forlorn view of the APC. He could not avoid pointing the finger at his old nemeses—Simon and Richardson. Du Bois, as he saw it, sought to rectify this by proposing more formal affiliation with the WPC, writing the Department of Justice and informing them of this reality, while reserving that there would be registration if Justice insisted—though Du Bois and his associates would fight it out in court. They would also "expect the right" to go to meetings abroad—a point viewed as urgent and imperative. There was not overwhelming support for Du Bois' proposal. Even Shirley Graham, who was taking Russian lessons at Columbia, scribbled "Nyet" at the bottom of Du Bois' crafted document. Fast, Robeson, and John Darr met at Du Bois' office to discuss the idea. Fast expressed the feeling that he rejected Du Bois' demarche, since he saw the fight for peace as "services for my country" and not service for a foreign power and did not care to accede. Fred Stover did not care to become embroiled in yet another draining court battle since he was already involved in two law suits, both growing out of, or at least related to, his connection with the peace movement.[29]

The questioning of Fast and Stover was an aspect of a widespread dissatisfaction with Du Bois' proposal, as directly expressed in the meeting with him. There was spirited discussion on this with some saying, according to Du Bois, that the "peace movement must take place outside our ranks and be led by the church or trade unions." Du Bois was a bit irritated with the wrangling and at that particular political viewpoint: "I shall do nothing further in the matter. When and if the church and the trade unions or any other groups starts a peace movement, I will join if invited. Otherwise, I am taking no further action."[30]

Pressure from outside combined with centrifugal forces weakened the peace movement to the point of virtual evanescence. Looking back at Elihu Burritt, Victor Hugo, Andrew Carnegie, and other historical figures who had been involved in various sectors of the peace movement, Du Bois waxed glumly. He lamented the fact that in the United States "peace is synonymous with 'Communism.' " Concomitant with this strange reality was the unavoidable actuality that "from 1949 until today, all over the world except in the United States there has spread a movement for peace on earth." Like others of the era, Du Bois could have been accused of paying undue attention to centrifugal forces within the APC. But Du Bois' concern was justifiable, as evidenced by the fact that

Shirley Graham was one of the few women high in the leadership of the peace movement, and despite well-known propeace sentiment "there is only one representative west of Iowa." But perhaps more representative of the reasons why not only the American Peace Crusade but also the Council on African Affairs eventually bit the dust was revealed in the HUAC's "Investigation of the Unauthorized Use of U.S. Passports." Willard Uphaus, then executive director of World Fellowship, Inc., was relentlessly examined by acting counsel Richard Arens about the peace movement and its international ramifications. One of the few persons of African descent queried about was Du Bois, as Uphaus was asked if the elderly champion of anticolonialism was one of the directors of the "Vienna peace parley that you set up." The answer was obviously yes, as Arens must have known, but the incident is cited to illustrate what harried fate might befall peace activists. Uphaus was eventually jailed because of his activism and his example and the sight of his comrade Du Bois in handcuffs chilled potential dissent on the peace and anticolonial fronts.[31]

W.E.B. Du Bois at 81 and Paul Robeson at the World Peace Conference in Paris in 1949

CHAPTER 16

Du Bois and Cold War Repression

It was not accidental that the name W.E.B. Du Bois would be on the lips of HUAC's counsel. One should be reminded that during the course of the Cold War he was one of the most highly regarded dissenters to the obtaining consensus.* Du Bois was cited more often in the HUAC index than some leading Communists—the ultimate target of domestic repression—such as, Henry Winston, James Jackson, and others. Most HUAC members were from the South and the Midwest, areas particularly unsuited to Du Bois' brand of political engagement. HUAC was not alone, however, in their interest in Du Bois. The Central Intelligence Agency, the United States Information Agency, and even leaders of the NAACP joined the witch-hunt that bedeviled Du Bois and others who were remiss in toeing the line.[1]

HUAC found it fit to devote an inordinate amount of attention to Du Bois' political activities, especially his politicking for peace. HUAC noted the June 1951 APC-sponsored Peace Congress and Exposition in Chicago, the April 1952 National Assembly for Peace in Washington, and Du Bois' role in each; they also noted his keynote address at the Chicago area conference, World Peace Through Negotiations.

---

* Files recently released from the FBI pursuant to the Freedom of Information Act show that the surveillance of Du Bois was greater than could have been imagined. See, for example, FBI File 100-99729, 100-20789, and so on.

This attention to Du Bois and its use as a litmus test for redness continued to plague even after his passing. This was a weapon deployed frequently against Blacks, as Reverend James Robinson, pastor of the Church of the Master, director of Operation Crossroads Africa, member of the National Advisory Council of the Peace Corps, found out in his 1964 HUAC appearance. He tried to parry their thrust by brandishing his anticommunist credentials, casting Operations Crossroads Africa as a trojan horse for certain United States interests on the continent. But the committee would have none of that. He was pressed on his association with Du Bois' African Aid Committee:

> Moreover, Dr. W.E.B. Du Bois, the Chairman of this group . . . joined the Communist Party in 1961 and for many years prior thereto was extremely active in Communist causes—so much so that in 1948 or 1949, as I recall, he lost his position as research director for the NAACP.

Reverend Robinson was asked not only to testify about Du Bois, but also about Coleman Young, Henry Winston, Robeson, and the National Committee to Defend Negro Leadership. Openly, Reverend Robinson confessed that his involvement with the left flowed from his relationship with Harry Ward of the Civil Rights Congress. But Congressman Richard Ichord was after something else more important, which became a theme of the 1960s—as Du Bois eventually foresaw:

> Do you feel that a Negro in the Peace Corps working in Africa will generally be more effective. . . . You inferred that, I thought, from your statement?

Meekly, Reverend Robinson replied affirmatively.[2]

While HUAC was busily ferreting out details of Du Bois' political life, he was not resting supine. It is not farfetched to allot the Afro-American community substantial credit for helping to put HUAC out of business, and Du Bois was not absent from this process. In 1947 he came forward with a vigorous protest of the opinion of the United States Court of Appeals, Second Circuit, in *U.S.* vs. *Leon Josephson;* he praised the potent dissenting opinion of Judge Charles Clark which questioned the raison d'etre of HUAC. On January 26, 1948, the National Institute of Arts and Letters passed a hotly debated resolution drafted by Allan Nevins and others that blasted HUAC by the lopsided vote of 109–30–8. Du Bois was in good company in fighting for this resolution and was joined by Walter Lippman and many others. There was trepidation that Du Bois could not altogether allay, "that the resolution may be construed as berating the activities of the Communist Party in the United States."[3]

Du Bois' role in these struggles was a facet of the overall unease of the Black community with HUAC. These efforts often reflected the influence of Du Bois, as an article on Hvac by J. A. Rogers in the *Pittsburgh Courier* of January 8, 1954, indicated:

> What has this committee done against an un-American activity older than Communism and far more galling to Negroes, namely Jim Crow—the economic robbing of citizens based on color or skin? Nothing. And not only that—some of the members actually owed their place in Congress to their support of this injustice. The committee can take no credit to itself for the Negro's loyalty.

Rogers and other Blacks saw, like Du Bois, that no matter how recumbent or compliant, Blacks could come under attack. The United States Information Agency removed from their libraries abroad, not only books by Du Bois and Langston Hughes, but those of Walter White as well. HUAC reflected these trends and when activists like Coleman Young came before them, a constant grilling about not only Communists but also about the Progressive party could be expected. Yet it was not only domestic leftist ties with Blacks that captured the attention of HUAC. In 1955 they quoted from Charlotta Bass' *California Eagle* which noted that Blacks have a "special stake in protesting the right to disagree." An Afro-American community that often found it expedient to depart from the consensus on, for example, rope and faggot justice, of necessity was in the forefront in the fight to protect the right to dissent. This was duly observed by HUAC. "Negro leaders have been in the front ranks in the battles against McCarthyism—Dr. Du Bois, Paul Robeson, William Patterson."[4]

In the opinion of many, the death knell for HUAC was sounded when it brought its traveling roadshow to Atlanta in 1958. The decision by 180 Black leaders, many of them Du Bois' comrades in arms—E. Franklin Frazier, Charles Gomillion, Andrew Simkins,

Oliver Cromwell Cox, and others—to publicly attack the committee was the initial and most organized confrontation with which HUAC had to contend. The Black leaders were incensed that most of those subpoenaed to appear and deemed subversive were white supporters of integration, like Frank Wilkinson, Anne Braden, and Carl Braden. Strikingly, when the House voted 365–1 to cite the trio for contempt, the lone dissenter was Black Congressman Robert Nix. When the Ad Hoc Committee to Eliminate HUAC was organized, Du Bois was quick to add his weight. He joined with 340 others from thirty-two states in signing a petition to be presented to Congress on HUAC's abolition. Until he moved to Africa, Du Bois remained active against HUAC. After a June 5, 1961 court decision validating the membership clause of the Smith Act and the registration provision, Du Bois was asked to speak at a September rally where 3,200 attended. Twelve hours after the rally HUAC subpoenaed key organizers to come to Washington immediately for interrogation. Earlier Du Bois had joined James Baldwin in a ban HUAC rally. But this dangerous 1961 turn of the courts and HUAC convinced Du Bois that the trials of 1951 would be replicated and this factor catalyzed his departure for Ghana, days after the September rally. Still, though Du Bois was gone, he was far from forgotten. In 1967, when HUAC was inevitably investigating "Subversive Influence in Riots, Looting, and Burning," Du Bois remained on the lips of committee members, as his association with the left-center *Freedomways* magazine and his name being taken by the young Marxist-Leninist-oriented youth of the nationwide Du Bois Clubs were noted.[5]

It was not extraordinary that HUAC would devote such grueling attention to the minutiae of Du Bois' life. Du Bois was seen as a double threat—as a Black and as a leftist leader. Complicating the matter was the presence in heavy numbers within HUAC and the machinery of political repression of southerners not enchanted with the kind of Blackness and redness Du Bois represented. Charles Cheng, writing "The Cold War; Its Impact on the Black Liberation Struggle Within the United States" for one of Du Bois' favorite publications, *Freedomways,* quoted Martin Luther King, Jr.'s aide Jack O'Dell on this point:

> Every organization in Negro life which was attacking segregation per se was put on the subversive list by Attorney General Tom Clark.

Approaching the issue from another angle, was Barton, J. Bernstein, who has written:[6]

> [Truman's] loyalty-and-security program, in its operations discriminated against Negroes and Federal investigators, despite protests to Truman, apparently continued to inquire into attitude of inter-racial sympathy as evidence relevant to determination of loyalty.

Racism ineluctably accompanied anticommunism. Du Bois was aware of this and put great stock in a heralded article by the veteran Nazi hunter Charles Allen, entitled "McCarthy Enemy of the Negro People." This article was important not only for its content but also for its impact on Du Bois' thought. McCarthy was accursed as working closely with "Gerald L. Smith . . . and . . . the Christian Nationalist Crusade." Smith had "spoken of . . . making . . . a Federal crime for intermarriage." In barring books from USIA libraries abroad, McCarthy was accused of singling out antiracist writings, including works by Aptheker, Robeson, Gunnar Myrdal, and Du Bois. Du Bois came to see anticommunist repression as ineradicably stained and intertwined with racism, which provided him with even more reason to oppose it. At the same time, the anticommunists were prone to oppose Du Bois, not only because he was Black and "red", but, as their book burnings showed, they were apprehensive about the influence of intellectuals who were also disproportionately hit—and the elderly patriarch remained a leading intellectual light.[7]

The pressures created by the changing political atmosphere were apparent early on. In mid-1948 Du Bois had contacted P. L. Prattis, executive editor of the *Pittsburgh Courier,* about placing a letter, from Howard Fast concerning his perceived unjust conviction in the widely read paper. Prattis' metaphor-laced response caught the tension of the era:

> I do not know just what I can do in the Courier without creating an issue. There is so much dust in the air these days your motives are obscured and impugned. I shall mull over the Fast letter for a few days and do whatever I can with the hope of not making bad matters worse.

Fast's irate reaction dramatized the widespread perception of betrayal that would drive many from political movements:[8]

> What does he mean when he says that he does not know what he can do in the Courier without creating an issue. He cannot create an issue. The issue is there. He reminds me of people who say it is wicked to take up the struggle for Negro rights since you thereby create problems.

Du Bois' ouster from the NAACP coincided, not accidentally, with an escalation of domestic repression. At this historic juncture Du Bois proved to be ubiquitous in contributing more than his share to the counterattack. To Lasker Smith he offered a rationale for resisting the blandishments of what came to be called "Cold War liberalism." But unlike many other intellectuals, Du Bois was engaged in the vortex of activism in implementing his ideas. In 1949, he did not hesitate to join John Rogge's legal defense of the National Federal Employees Defense Committee in their court challenge to Truman's Executive Order 9835 on loyalty; he also agreed to sponsor a conference against repressive legislation introduced by Senator Mundt. And during this same spring Du Bois received a personal taste of the bitterness of the new era. Martin D. Jenkins, president of Morgan State University, abruptly withdrew an invitation for Du Bois to make the 1949 commencement address because of his appearance with Robeson at the World Peace Congress in Paris; and "your failure to condemn his treasonable statement made at that meeting have linked you in the public mind with the Communist movement. I think that Mr. Robeson's views and approach are to be severely condemned."[9]

Robeson's controversial remarks created an early firestorm and cause celebre in the Afro-American community and the United States generally. He was alleged to have said: "The Black folk of America will never fight against the Soviet Union." In an atmosphere of *Dropshot* war plans being actively contemplated against the Soviet Union, Robeson's commentary outraged and infuriated many. Du Bois did not tarry in rushing to the defense of his friend, and ally in taking the unusual step of issuing a press release which said: "I agree with Paul Robeson absolutely, that Negroes should never willingly fight in an unjust war." Carrying the banner for the other wing of the Black community, Walter White vigorously assailed Robeson. In the popular Black magazine, *Ebony,* he harshly discussed "The Strange Case of Paul Robeson." He followed and engendered a similar approach to the issue within the NAACP. A *Crisis* editorial, revealingly entitled, "Robeson Speaks for Robeson," attempted to isolate Robeson: "Today Mr. Robeson, if he represents any group at all, speaks for the fellow traveller of communism." They let out all the stops in their barrage, as Robeson was accused of elitism, while dismissing his Council on African Affairs, "Long ago labeled a Communist Front." They hit him from the right and the left, implying that he was more interested in African than in United States Blacks and that he "has none except sentimental roots among American Negroes." The NAACP, a group that had theretofore been known for stressing interracial unity, adopted the tack of their racist critics and took an ultranationalist line against "mixed and all-white left groups"; according to this view, these latter were aided by Robeson but not by "ordinary American Negroes."[10]

Concretely symbolizing their respective roles as leader of the left and the right within a torn Afro-American community, Du Bois and White debated each other in the pages of *Ebony*'s sister publication, *Negro Digest.* Du Bois, with typical eloquence, defined the issues and bombarded Robeson's critics. White's tersely titled reply, "Paul Robeson: Wrong," was an unusually personal attack on the singer-activist. White was also opportunistically pragmatic: "minorities like the Negro would be insane to cast their lot with the Communists."[11]

Philip S. Foner has noted that as a result of Freedom of Information Act revelations, light has been shed on the conscious effort by United States government agencies to shape an unfriendly and definite reaction to Robeson. "Robert Alan," the "pen-name of a well-known New York journalist," was actually a mole in the service of the FBI whose *Crisis* article helped to fashion an image of Robeson, which was carried over to characterize other well-known Black dissenters, like Du Bois; Robeson's love for socialism was seen as being motivated not by a desire to see a more just and equitable world but because of "slights" that left him "embittered." At a 1955 HUAC hearing investigating Communist activities in San Diego, California, the witness Anita Schneider was examined by Chairman Francis Walter about a prior comment on Wall Street's drive to war. "Now one of those people is Dr. W. E. B. Du Bois. He is an educated man. Does he believe that sort of tripe, too?" The witness replied evasively nd shiftily: "I met Dr. Du Bois. I don't believe he does. His wife, Shirley Graham, however, I think, does." Walter then leapt to drawn a distinction between the "hard-boiled Communist politician" and a "frustrated idealist," like Du Bois. The attraction of so many to the image of Du Bois and Robeson was so strong that it could not be met by head on attacks of the sort that hit other leftists, derisively dismissed as hard-boiled Communist politicians. Like Robeson, Du Bois was a special case that had to be treated gingerly and delicately in the cruel sport of disinformation.[12]

Du Bois stood by the side of his friend Paul Robeson through his tribulations. When the bloody right-wing outrage directed at Robeson's concert in Peekskill, New York, occurred, Du Bois joined the protest to Truman, Governor Thomas Dewey, and Attorney General J. Howard McGrath. When the State Department seized Robeson's passport in 1950, at Du Bois' urging, Helen Mangold, president of the Social Service Employees Union, and others complained to Secretary of State Dean Acheson. In contrast, the NAACP continued their savaging of Robeson. When the National Negro Labor Council was formed in 1951, *Crisis* almost laughably disregarded it: "Just the name of Paul Robeson on the convention program stamped the NNLC as red-inspired." The NAACP was riding high on a wave of anti-Robeson sentiment, characterized by the countretemps surrounding the publication of Langston Hughes' book *Famous Negro Music Makers.* The book had been sent to Du Bois for his comments and he asked why Robeson was excluded. Edward H. Dodd, Jr., president of the publisher Dodd, Mead and Company, responded candidly:

> [Hughes] was told by experts of his acquaintance and probably also told by our library advisors that the inclusion of Paul Robeson would probably eliminate the book from acceptance by a good many school libraries, state adoption lists, etc.

Even the militant writer Langston Hughes had to accede to demands "to be non-controversial," a telling comment on the depth of the overriding of the First Amendment that engulfed Robeson and Du Bois.[13]

Robeson was not the only Black ally Du Bois had to defend and who, in turn, defended him at his time of crisis. Charlotta Bass, editor of the *California Eagle* for forty years, came under heavy fire in 1949 when she sought to attend an important women's conference in Peking; her trip was foiled when she failed to get a British visa for Hong Kong. Like Du Bois, she was a fervent partisan of the Soviet Union. Naturally, the "little HUAC" committee of

State Senator Jack Tenney took an interest in Bass; she felt that the committee was in search of people who fought discrimination and segregation. In her battles with Tenney and in her other activities, such as her 1950 congressional race on the Progressive ticket against Sam Yorty where she soundly captured the Black vote, she had the firm support of Du Bois. When her honorary membership in Iota Phi Lambda sorority, awarded in 1948, was rescinded on August 16, 1956, because she was listed in the "Sixth Report on Un-American Activities in California, 1951," Du Bois did not approve.[14]

Temperatures rose not only as a result of the war against Korea and the PIC indictment but because of Du Bois' zealous defense of Ethel and Julius Rosenberg and Morton Sobell. There was a certain parallelism between their two cases. William A. Reuben has observed that, "in August 1950, on the very day that Ethel and Julius Rosenberg were indicted on charges of espionage," the Department of Justice ordered Du Bois to register as a foreign agent. Both cases received a similar reception from the NAACP. Roy Wilkins bluntly told Ben Bell of the Chicago branch, "under no circumstances is the NAACP to be affiliated with the 'Committee to Secure Justice for the Rosenbergs.' " Not atypically, Bell informed Wilkins inferentially that there was no need to worry since he had "checked with the FBI." Though NAACP officials did not hesitate to touch base with the FBI, they were not as forthcoming in their reception of the Rosenberg defense efforts. When Clemens France of the Emergency Committee of the Arts and Professions to Secure Clemency for the Rosenbergs reached Thurgood Marshall and requested assistance, the civil rights' lawyer scribbled "File—no answer."[15]

At a time when most were fleeing in horror of being associated with the real reason for the Rosenberg indictment—the Soviet Union—Du Bois put forth the issue squarely at a rally on the defendants' behalf organized by the Civil Rights Congress and in his remarks reprinted in the *Daily Worker.* He traced the evolution of anti-Sovietism, the past pro-Soviet statements of Douglas MacArthur and Winston Churchill, the treatment of the issue in high school textbooks and how once the American ambassadorship to Moscow was highly sought. Du Bois went to such lengths to sketch this portrait because he saw it as necessary background to the Rosenberg trial. He spoke for the New York City Committee for Clemency for the Rosenbergs and the Committee to Secure

Justice in the Rosenberg Case; with others he tried to file a friend of the court brief with the United States Supreme Court, but their motion was denied; he was also in touch with the support committee in Britain, trying to build solidarity.[16]

The appeal of Du Bois, Robeson, and other popular Black leaders was not without effect. Black labor leaders like William Hood, Coleman Young, Asbury Howard, and Vicki Garvin were active in the Rosenberg defense. The *Pittsburgh Courier* reported that "thousands of Negroes have joined the cries for clemency . . . [Negro] Baptish ministers of Washington, Chicago, Camden, San Francisco, along with Mary Church Terrell have joined in the pleas." Ever vigilant, HUAC kept tabs on Du Bois' political activities and defense efforts generally.[17]

Du Bois did not neglect the defense of Morton Sobell either. Helen Sobell had asked him to write the director of Prisons so Morton Sobell could be transferred from Alcatraz. Promptly on December 10, 1954, Du Bois wrote Director James V. Bennett. He closely collaborated with the New York Committee to Secure Justice for Morton Sobell and allowed a powerful statement to be read at a June 16, 1955, rally at Carneige Hall.[18]

Government authorities were not ecstatic about Du Bois' role as a veritable one-man seat of opposition. This factor may have had a correlation with Du Bois' constant complaint about tampering with his mail. His complaint blossomed in 1953. His secretary Lillian Hyman sent Padmore a second message for F. Joliot-Curie; the first message was sent to its intended recipient "but some of his mail is tampered with and he is afraid it may not get through." The complaint that his mail might not be getting through accelerated in 1955. He grumbled that "much of mail from abroad goes astray these days" in explaining why contact may have been lost with Dr. Armattoe's wife in Hamburg. The problem with mail involved both sending and receiving and was designed apparently to isolate Du Bois. He indicated this and more in a discussion with Robert Benchley:[19]

> It is almost impossible for me and I am sure the same thing is true of Paul Robeson either to get anything published or to communicate with our friends abroad or to get communications through to us. Our mail is regularly disturbed and all we can do is to sit still and make gestures.

Du Bois' complaints were especially focused on the socialist bloc of Eastern Europe. He was unhappy that copies of the Soviet publications "New Times" and "The Soviet Union" were not arriving.

Finally Du Bois wrote Postmaster General J. Edward Day when a manuscript he had sent to Seven Seas Publishers in the German Democratic Republic did not arrive for months; it can be assumed that this letter arrived safely. In any event, months later the manuscript arrived in Berlin.[20]

The year 1953 saw an acceleration of the witch-hunt process. Early in the year, Du Bois was disinvited from an Inter-School Conference held annually by some twenty-five private schools in the metropolitan area. It was deemed that the program was too weighted with controversial figures. Days hence Mrs. A. S. Hancock of the Trenton NAACP refused to accept consignment of his *In Battle for Peace* since they "do not wish to involve . . . controversial matters." "Controversial matters," "controversial figures," these two categories touched Du Bois and induced him to be gun-shy. On February 9, 1953, he asked his long-time friend Ethel Ray Nance for advice on his California speaking engagements. "I would like to have you look them over and tell me if there is anything I had better be careful of or that would be unpleasant. Of course, keep this all under your hat." Du Bois was being besieged constantly by victims of repression and he was not always up to dealing with this. The year before, he had told Alice Citron in a huff, "Shirley and I have decided that we will not, for the time being, head any more petitions or appeals. We are willing to sign with the crowd, but we are not going to ask them to sign." But this was hardly the trend of his response. He informed Cedric Belfrage, only somewhat facetiously: "I am beginning to feel that unless I get in jail very soon I have not been doing my duty towards my nation and times."[21]

These signs, no matter how faint, of Du Bois' shrinking a bit from certain questions, were uncommon. The actual trend was his staunchly standing in the way of repression. He had been active with the heavily bombarded Council of the Arts, Sciences and Professions. He was nominated for another term as vice chairman and graced his selection by speaking of the "menace of McCarthyism . . . our members who have stood firm for democratic principles" were to be congratulated. It was little wonder that Du Bois stood with the council. Their "proposed policy and program" opposed "thought control . . . loyalty oaths" and spoke of the "extension of full political, social and economic rights and equalities to our Negro population." With ASP members and comrades like William Patterson, he came to the aid of the Citizens Emergency Defense Conference, which was proposed as well for the subversive list by the attorney general.[22]

He was not always in accord with ASP, particularly on the controversial issue of book banning. The State Department's International Information Administration issued a directive in 1953 placing Du Bois' *Color and Democracy* and Shirley Graham's *Paul Robeson: Citizen of the World* as unacceptable and not to be stocked at libraries abroad. This firsthand experience made Du Bois sensitive to this question and he therefore adamantly opposed an ASP letter to the president on this general question. The ASP proposed that books could be barred which were "advocating the destruction of the freedoms by which we live as Americans." They alleged that book prohibitions were "standard Communist procedure." Du Bois was infuriated: "Your . . . paragraph on legislating freedom into existence or censoring it into existence is a contradiction of your red-baiting." He objected to their "obsequious gratitude" to Eisenhower. Louis Kronenberger replied curiously, averring that the response to the letter "was small . . . it has been decided not to send it—even though more than required 75% of those voting were in favor of it." Apparently, in these frightened times, the positive response was so tepid that ASP leadership decided that the better part of valor was not to take on the formidable Dr. Du Bois.[23]

Du Bois' appeal among the masses and the concomitant desire by some to quarantine him came to a confluence in the effort to prevent his travels abroad. Du Bois was consistent on this point. As early as April 7, 1948, he signed a "statement to Secretary Marshall protesting the refusal to grant me a passport"; the "me" in this case being A. B. Magil of the *Daily Worker.* Before the statement was sent, the decision was rescinded by "the fact that the statement was being circulated became known to the State Department and it may have played a part in winning a reversal." Not surprisingly, when the Sheffield, later Warsaw, Peace Congress was scheduled, Du Bois was a bit hesitant:

> I . . . did not apply for [a] passport, and I have a sneaking suspicion that if I had applied, I might not have gotten permission either here or in England, I trust I am wrong.

Barriers to Du Bois' travel were not all externally imposed. The Inter-Continental Peace Conference in Rio de Janiero in 1952, sponsored by Salvador Allende among others, beckoned Du Bois but he was unable to make it:[24]

> I had hoped to be present, but . . . this is impossible, not only on account of my teeth . . . because of the cost involved and the probability that I could not get a passport, although this last is not certain.

Du Bois finally applied for a passport renewal and cited his record. Ultimately, the response from the chief of the Passport Division, Ruth B. Shipley, in February 1952 was negative. Early in 1953 he applied for documentation in order to travel to Hungary and India. Shipley cited a prime reason for her action here:

> if you and Mrs. Du Bois are communists, the Department under the new regulation, copy of which is enclosed, would be obliged to refuse to provide you with a passport.

Du Bois was not alone in being denied; Hunton let him know in August 1953 that Robeson's latest passport application had been turned down.[25]

This denial was a major setback for Du Bois, cutting him off from a source of support that proved formidable when he was on trial. He was unable to attend the Vienna Peace Congress and told Uphaus so on November 3, 1952, but he sent an audio tape and film of peace activists instead. He was also unable to attend the National Conference of the Convention of the People's Party of Nigeria and the Cameroons, December 31–January 7, 1952–1953. Lack of a passport prevented Du Bois' mixing with and passing on his radicalism to many West Africans and it was a loss regretted on both sides.[26]

Du Bois tried a different tack in a March 28, 1953, letter to Shipley. He proposed attending a World Peace Congress meeting in Budapest but also threw in an Inter-Continental Conference of the Bahai Faith in New Dehli. Shipley remained unimpressed and refused papers to him, despite the religious component of the proposed trip. Nor did Shipley budge when Robeson wished to travel abroad to receive the Stalin Peace Prize.[29]

The virtual imprisonment of Du Bois in the "Free World" came to a head in 1955 when he wished to travel to Europe for a youth meeting. First he had to turn down an invitation to the December 1954 preparatory meeting in Austria because of no passport. When on June 8, 1955, he applied for permission to go to the World Federation of Democratic Youth meeting in Poland and the warm baths of Carlsbad, Frances Knight of the Passport Division turned him down pursuant to Section 51.135 of Title 22 of the Code of Federal Regulations, specifically "it is alleged that you are a Communist and as the Congress which you wish to attend is Communist inspired." Du Bois angrily replied, terming her reasoning "illegal and personally insulting. . . . I maintain that it is none of your business what I believe or think so long as I transgress no law . . . you are resting your hope for continued illegal procedures on the cost of litigation which you assume only the rich can afford. . . . Nor will I be intimidated by secret 'allegations' of unnamed informers which have no status in law." Du Bois' response was indicative of how strongly he felt about attending this forum where 30,000 youths from 100 countries were expected to attend. But 1955 was the year of the "spirit of Geneva" and this helped to propel Du Bois to fight. He was reluctant to fight their decision in court because it "could cost more time and money that I have." Nevertheless, he consulted attorney James Cobb who suggested that he simply capitulate and file a noncommunist affadavit. Du Bois resolutely refused, and declared "principles and rights . . . are involved here." Finally Gloria Agrin and attorney Joseph Forer of Washington, D.C., became counsel in his case.[28]

Du Bois was also unable to attend a peace meeting in Belgium and an invitation to Peking at their expense to commemorate Benjamin Franklin's 250th birthday. But the most weighty and significant loss was the barring of his visits to Africa. Ultimately this ban was undone in a process that revealed much about how United States competition with socialism for the hearts and minds of Africa led to an unraveling of McCarthyite procedures and even Jim Crow. The backdrop was Ghana's coming to independence in 1957. In October 1956, Cedric Belfrage reported to Du Bois that "Padmore is urging Nkrumah to make representations on the highest level to Washington for you to be graciously 'permitted' to come." Washington was in a quandary. On the one hand, Du Bois, the dangerous 'communist,' had to be prevented from traveling abroad; on the other, Du Bois, the Father of Pan-Africanism, was revered and not being allowed to see the birth of his child would not go down well on the continent and elsewhere. The *Evening News* of Ghana sharply raised these issues in an editorial, which caught the eye of the CIA. A CIA report of May 5, 1957, on "Reprints of National Guardian Articles in Ghana Evening News, CPP Newspaper," expressed concern with a *National Guardian* article about the refusal of a passport to Du Bois. While noting the invitations extended to Cheddi Jagan, Emile Burns, and Jomo Kenyatta, the CIA operative wrote worriedly: "The primary significance to thse articles lies in the fact they appear in the Ghana Evening News, official organ of Nkrumah's party, the CPP."[29]

Du Bois knew that barring his travel would be a major diplomatic setback for the United States. At the same time, the criticisms expressed earlier by the CAA against certain Nkrumah policies indicated to him that United States influence in Ghana could override his. He questioned to Padmore the sincerity of Nkrumah's lobbying for his passport:

> I doubt if any such appeal has been made. Meantime, Mr. Eisenhower, mindful of the important Negro vote, has shrewdly designated Vice-President Nixon to represent the United States on March 6. He stands, as you know, for the most reactionary right wing of arrogant capital. . . . I am pretty sure, then, that Dr. Nkrumah has given up all hope of my presence.

His pessimism did not mean that Du Bois was sitting on his hands awaiting for an invisible hand to intercede on his behalf. With a flurry of action, he launched a lobbying effort on his own behalf. He fired off letters to Mohammed Awad of the Subcommittee on Protection of Discrimination and Protection of Minorities, Secretary of State John Foster Dulles, Black Congressmen William Dawson, Charles Diggs, and Adam Clayton Powell, Senator Thomas Hennings, Richard M. Nixon, and the Membership of the Third Committee of the United Nations General Assembly. Shortly thereafter, the *Daily Worker* headlined: "Nkrumah Cables Regrets at Ban on Du Bois' Trip."[30]

However, the State Department remained obstinate. They turned down Du Bois' request for limited passport facilities for a trip to the Gold Coast. Thus, Du Bois had to simply file away his formal invitation to Ghana's independence celebration, March 3–10, 1957. The repercussions were immediate. Nkrumah termed his absence a "great and bitter disappointment" in a touching note:

> You will have some consolation in the fact that not [only] was your name on almost every tongue . . . I want to ask you to keep in touch with me and not to hesitate [to] let me know of any ideas which you have. The advice you gave in Padmore's letter, for instance, is most valuable. I hope that we will be able to meet some day soon.

Nkrumah's words were echoed by the *National Guardian*'s James Aronson. Belgrage had told him "that several Ghana newspaper men wanted to picket Nixon with signs reading 'We Want Du Bois.' . . . In any case I got the feeling that your absence created a tremendous stir among the people of Ghana. And out of negation sometimes comes progress." Aronson's dialectic proved to be accurate as African countries getting up in arms about Du Bois, helped to force the rescinding of the travel ban that drew all within its ambit. Nkrumah's words to Bernard Reswick for conveyance to Du Bois epitomized the strong feelings for him:

> Africans and people of African descent the world over owe a great debt of gratitude to Dr. Du Bois. . . . It therefore gives me great pleasure to ask you to convey to Dr. Du Bois felicitations of the highest esteem on behalf of myself and my Government.

This process was helped along by again stroking the press; Shirley Graham asked Roscoe Dunjee, a Black publisher, to publicize the passport denial and its implications. Reflecting on this, George Padmore wrote from Ghana:[31]

> The refusal of the U.S. to give you a passport has certainly made them very unpopular. They have been attacked in the press and I can assure you that if you ever get a passport to Ghana will give you more than a royal welcome. . . . Even your FBI are all around.

The press reaction, particularly among Blacks and the left, was almost uniformly critical of the State Department. Martin Luther

King, Jr., was allowed to go but I. F. Stone denigrated the passport refusal and predicted that it would harm United States-African relations. With his usual eloquence, the *Pittsburgh Courier*'s Prattis expressed his regret to Shirley Graham:[32]

> It seemed almost unbelievable to me tht officialdom would be so cruel as to deny the Father of African nationalism the chance to see the birth of his first child.

Nkrumah was not the sole African interested in the matter, Gabriel D'Arbussier was also in touch with Du Bois. Nor was Ghana the only country barred to Du Bois; his attempts to make the Third World Conference Against Atomic and Hydrogen Bombs for Disarmament in Japan was foiled. But his long-time friend Kwame Nkrumah was the person Du Bois turned to with pungent political analysis:

> What the United States is trying to do is to keep anybody from going abroad who will dare testify as to conditions in the United States. Nothing would please me better than to make a trip to your country. But if I do make such a trip, I will say what I please and not what I am ordered to.

A year after Du Bois' abortive effort to reach Ghana, Nkrumah continued to be effusive about his mentor and thus, inferentially indicated why the travel ban had to end.[33]

Even after the political climate began to change and some passports were issued, Du Bois continued to encounter difficulties in traveling abroad. E. J. Hickey of the Passport Division told Du Bois' attorney that they would withhold action on revoking his passport pending Supreme Court decisions in the cases of Waldo Frank and William Worthy. But "in the meantime," he asked Du Bois and Graham to "surrender their passports, as requested, or agree in writing not to use them until this matter is resolved." A few months after, Du Bois was compelled to write disappointingly to Umberto Campagnolo of the Societe Euripeane de Culture who had invited him to a meeting in Rome in February 1960:

> it would be impossible for me to attend. In the first place it would be impossible for me to obtain a passport from the United States Government because I visited China last year.

Inevitably the CIA took an intense interest in the matter of Du Bois' travels. A CIA functionary in a memorandum on passport legislation exhibited frenzied concern about travel abroad of "American Communists." He singled out Du Bois' and his wife's travels, "[one of the] more notorious recent instances where U.S. passports were used to further the interest of the Soviet Union or the International Communist movement." Attached was a lengthy summary of Du Bois' speeches abroad in the Hague, Tashkent, Peking, and Stockholm, and Graham's delivery of a speech for Du Bois in Accra.[34]

The CIA's concern about Du Bois' activities was in a sense not unjustified at least from their point of view, for he continued to be a burr under the government's saddle. He interceded on behalf of other victims and his proved to be troublesome to some. He gave a piece of his mind to the prime minister of Ceylon, Sir John Kotelawala, opposing "methods by which Madame Rhoda Miller de Silva was forcibly separated from her husband and brought to America." Miller, married to a Ceylonese, charged that in 1954 she was expelled at the behest of the United States Ambassador and that United States Embassy officers assisted in the deportation. The reason alleged for her ouster was her writing of "The Rosenbergs—What Was Their Crime," and her journalistic "exposure of American policy" in Ceylon. Trans World Airlines was also charged with complicity in this affair. Along with Aronson, Uphaus, Annette Rubinstein, and others, Du Bois helped organize the Provisional Committee for Rhoda Miller de Silva. They carried her battle to the public; they publicized Britain's refusal to allow her to join her husband there because "it has been alleged that you were a Communist." This was denoted as "divorce by decree of the Passport Office." Du Bois wrote the State Department and campaigned for her. She was eventually allowed to join her husband and the intensive lobbying was given credit for this. The State Department was worried about the peals of outrage generated by the campaign, as evidenced by a report from the embassy in Colombo filed by the secretary. The effort spearheaded by Du Bois forced their retreat.[35]

Winning justice, even partial justice, for Lee Lorch was something Du Bois was not able to pull off. This young professor of mathematics was called before HUAC, cited for contempt, and then, with little pretense toward due process, was ousted from his post at Fisk University. Their board's Executive Committee fired him forthwith and never asked if "[I] had ever been a Communist" until after the sacking. Official Fisk policy was broken by inquiring into his beliefs. When called before the committee, he was assured it would be confidential but soon found it presented one-sidedly and released to the press, including the allegation by two paid informers that he was a Communist in 1941—an allegation made two weeks after he tried to enroll his daughter in a Black school. Lorch was fired though he took the First, and not the Fifth, Amendment at the hearing. Lorch saw his integration efforts as the basis for HUAC's interest in him; this effort, "the only one [of] this kind reported anywhere in the South," was bound to be frowned on by a House committee dominated by racists inflamed by the issue in light of the *Brown* decision. Du Bois did not procrastinate when asked for assistance and quickly circulated a letter of support. Du Bois was appalled by the facts of this case. Lorch was a long-time foe of racism; he took a leading part in the battle against Metropolitan Life's policy of excluding Negroes from Stuyvesant Town. He was a NAACP chapter vice-president for two years. At the hearing Lorch denied party membership but refused to say if he were a member at the University of Cincinnatti in 1941 or City College in 1946. Other members of the Fisk faculty, in a unanimous resolution, backed Lorch, one of only two white teachers there.[36]

The Fisk alumni, spurred by Du Bois, came to Lorch's defense pointing to piercing issues of race. They noted that during his NAACP tenure he led a "successful campaign which prevented a frame-up of a 12-year old Negro boy for alleged 'rape' of a 47-year old white divorcee." But they also pointed to his integrationist efforts as a cause for his dismissal, as did the *Oklahoma City Black Dispatch.* The *Dispatch* did not stand alone in defending Lorch. Dunjee's paper noted pro-Lorch statements and editorials in the *Arkansas State Press, Louisville Defender, Nashville Globe, Atlanta Daily World,* and other Black papers. This favorable press deluge was fueled in part by Lorch's own keen analysis, amply assisted by Du Bois. Like Du Bois, Lorch noted the relatively new development of racists attacking antiracists, not so much on traditional race grounds but on grounds of being red, which allowed them to shroud their own antiBlack views, which had largely been discredited by the war against Hitler.[37]

Lorch was similarly damnatory of the Fisk board. Resembling Du Bois, he complained of Blacks who "front for whites, such as is increasingly attempted in the field of international relations" though he did observe that "every member present of the white majority on the Board voted for dismissal; most of the Negroes on the Board opposed dismissal." Nevertheless, in an action that could easily be described as racist itself—and to which Du Bois pointedly did not respond—Lorch was particularly and singularly censorious of Blacks who he felt should have spoken out. Perhaps Lorch felt that Blacks, above all, should have stood with him and their failure deserved special reproach. But the fact was that it was the Afro-American community that was staunchest in solidarity. The Black sector of the board, for example, L. Howard Bennett and prominent Black alumni like Du Bois, were his most devoted supporters.[38]

The cases of Lee Lorch and Rhoda Miller de Silva are examples of the hundreds of persons under siege assisted by Du Bois. Seeing so many of his friends jailed, harassed, persecuted, and even murdered did not drive Du Bois into fits of manic depression. Nonetheless, Du Bois' own experience at that time could be construed as contradicting his optimistic assessment. In March 1956 he was arbitrarily banned from entering a Levittown hall, even as a guest, where he was scheduled to speak on desegregation in the United States. Du Bois' feeling was that in the face of this all-sided attack, maximum unity was the key; yet, as he sadly conceded to Rockwell Kent, "It is astonishing to see so many good and reasonable men rushing off in contrary directions and wasting their strength against each other, rather than against the common enemy."[39]

During this period, Du Bois' friend and literary executor, Herbert Aptheker, linked the escalation of repression with deprivation of Blacks' civil rights. And from Du Bois' point of view it often seemed that Blacks were a disproportionate victim of repression in a manner only equalled by the white allies of Blacks. Carl and Anne Braden reported from Kentucky on their oppressive trial, where "after a struggle with the attorney general and local prosecutor" their books—were returned. They had been held for over three years. Included "among 562 books and pamphlets" snatched was Du Bois' "I Take My Stand for Peace" and "Government Exhibit No. 57." Like so many other persecuted victims of this era they were thankful for his timely aid, so they sent this exhibit to Du Bois "as a small token of our appreciation for your help in helping us to win a final and complete victory in our struggle."[40]

Du Bois found the political atmosphere not only oppressive but stultifying. This was so all pervasive that even Black communications media could be similarly directed. The *Afro-American* had informed his friends Ethel and Ray Nance that his contract with the *National Guardian* barred his writing for them. Du Bois was acerbic in return: "The *Afro-American* lied, as is natural. I am under no contract to any paper." He pointed to the press generally as a major instrument for enforcing conformity. The ethos they reflected and created produced a situation where, as he told the Soviet publication *New Times,* even a courageous individual like "Bishop Walls [could be] . . . frightened into silence."[41]

Du Bois' presence brought, as Willard Uphaus phrased it, "cheer and courage," to many who felt compelled to swim against the prevailing political tides. By the same token, others viewed him as a decided menace who disrupted United States relations with the developing nations and pointed United States Blacks in a direction contrary to United States foreign policy.[42]

Du Bois' constant needling of the United States government may help to explain why his CIA file was so bulky and voluminous. As noted, both HUAC and the FBI took an inordinate interest in his activities. But the CIA, whose mission was ostensibly international affairs and was bound by its charter from becoming involved in domestic matters, outdid their brethren in displaying an unseemly interest in the minutiae and detritus of Du Bois' life. In pages of small print in excruciating detail they listed the scores of organizations with which Du Bois worked. They were particularly concerned with his visits to socialist countries—China and the Soviet Union—and his broadcasts on Radio Moscow and Radio Peking. They virtually shadowed him on his trips abroad. "Subject . . . was to have been sent to Germany two weeks ago for Medical Treatment. No further details." "We would appreciate any information you might be able to obtain on subject . . . who plan to travel in East Germany . . . and in Rumania." They requested "any pertinent information which might come to your attention concerning subject." This CIA surveillance, a palpable violation of its charter and presumptively illegal, was just one more aspect of the Cold War repression visited not only on Du Bois, but Blacks and progressives in general. This repression hampered, but could not still, the onrushing surge for civil rights, in which Du Bois played a surprisingly—to some—substantial role.[43]

CHAPTER 17

Du Bois and the Civil Rights Movement

The principal biographies of Du Bois, as previously noted, have helped to perpetrate the myth of Du Bois' isolation from the mass of Blacks and their movement for equal rights from the early 1950s until his death. Nothing could be further from the truth. First of all, there was an evolution—a particular trait of the course of history—in how Du Bois was viewed during this period. The fierce repression of the early part of the era could not but affect how he was seen and presumably scare the timid and even the brave away from this leader of the much-reviled left. But, especially with the coming to independence of Ghana in 1957, there was a noticeable shift in the perception and treatment of Du Bois; apparent is a reversion to the idea of Du Bois as revered statesman. Evidently his closeness to the new Nkrumah regime and the hero worship of him in Africa generally was noted by leading circles in the United States and apparently by the much-hounded Afro-American community. Thus, in the last years of his life, he basked in the glow of the heroism to which he had long since grown accustomed.

Further, it is difficult, if not unwise, to discuss Du Bois' impact on the civil rights movement apart from the impact of the left and anticommunism on this movement. For if there was admiration and affection for Du Bois among his people or a lessening of his influence on the movement he had led for decades, manifestly it was attributable to the overall political climate more so than any radical shift in his thinking. Again, how this was played out within the NAACP and within the organizations that either emerged or grew—perhaps as a result of the Association's weaknesses—during this time must be examined.

Nevertheless, as Du Bois himself often admitted, there were perceptible shifts in his thought concerning the Afro-American community during this time. Re-examined critically was a notion of his that had spawned charges of his perpetuating "elitism" and class division: "If I were writing today about [the] 'Talented-Tenth' I should still believe in the main thesis but I would make rather different emphasis." He averred that his assumption was that educated Blacks would work for the masses but, as he indicated in 1947, he now saw that educated Negroes have produced "a large number of selfish and self-seeking persons, who will not work for the best interests of the masses of the people."[1]

In 1956 in "How United are Negroes?" he developed this troublesome topic further. Obviously, this was an issue that occupied Du Bois' thought and bothered him to a large extent. Upon receiving an honorary degree at Prague's historic Charles University in 1958, he, not accidentally addressed the issue of "The American Negro and Communism" and sharply raised the issue again:[2]

> [During the 1930s] I repudiated the idea that Negroes were in danger of inner class division based on income and exploitation. Here again I was wrong. Twenty years later, by 1950, it was clear that the great machine of big business was sweeping not only the mass of white Americans . . . it had also and quite naturally swept Negroes into the same maelstrom.

Another major pillar of Du Bois' thought was altered during this period. In a 1953 article in the *Guardian,* he recalled his 1920 line in *Darkwater* that "the problem of the 20th century is the problem of the Color Line."

> [But] there is but one aspect of this deepening world rift along the Color Line which saves it from being complete, and that is the peoples of the Soviet Union and her sister group of states. . . . For this fact, Britain, France and the U.S. ought to be thankful to Russia and her refusal to be "white."

Du Bois was edging away from this hallowed view and edging toward the view that the twentieth century's problem was labor.[3]

There were certainly variations in Du Bois' thought but there were also constant themes from which he rarely diverged. In July 1946 he provided a perspective on the civil rights movement that time has not eroded:

> time will prove, if it has not already proven that the fight which descendants of American slaves have made in the United States is one of the most significant in the world; and that its results are of importance not simply for themselves and for Americans but for all peoples of the world who are today in contact and commerce with the darker races.

He pointed out how Haiti earlier and Ethiopia later came to realize that they must unite with the United States's Blacks because of cultural ties and political influence. Pankhurst picked up on this theme later: "The Italian American vote has been a menace to Ethiopia throughout, and the Negro vote would be larger if the Negroes could vote. This is but one instance in which the destruction of Negro rights is very hurtful to world affairs, as well as to domestic affairs." Both Du Bois and Pankhurst realized that there was a close connection between events abroad and at home; and this was one of the many factors that separated Du Bois from the organization he founded—the NAACP—which tended to go along with United States foreign policy in return for concessions on the home front.[4]

Du Bois also had firm and decided views about the basis for race discrimination. He continually pointed to the wage differential between Black and white workers as the material basis for racism. In addition to this solid base for racism, Du Bois saw other props for it, legal enactment, current custom, and ancient folk-ways. Correspondingly, remedies would involve repealing laws, attacking custom, mass education, and, ultimately, elimination of wage differentials. In the same *Monthly Review* article where he explored the economics of racism, he elaborated on the fight involving those fearless enough to go against the prevailing consensus. Simultaneously, there was the potential shangri-la facing those who wished to go along. He predicted the fall of segregation in public accommodations and schools, which would mean Blacks "will be divided into classes even more sharply than now."[5]

Du Bois continually outlined how racism disfigured the political landscape and chained Black and white. He returned to this critical issue in a 1956 *Guardian* article:

> Mississippi and Kansas had about the same population in 1950 and each had in Congress six representatives based on that population. Yet Kansas needed 600,000 votes to elect her Congressmen, while only 150,000 votes were needed in Mississippi. Practically each voting Mississippian went to the polls with four ballots in his hand, where the Kansan had one.

He demanded federal action and saw, like Martin Luther King, Jr., that Black voting rights were an absolutely critical need. He recognized that obliterating the stain of racism from the United States escutcheon was no simple task and the persuasiveness of white skin privilege was a principal reason. White males were called "Mr." by Blacks whatever their age; whites were allowed to sit in front of the bus, use segregated public parks, libraries, and so on. "In return for this empty and dangerous social bribery the white laborer fared badly," being deprived of effective child labor laws, long work days, and poor education.[6]

Du Bois spoke to other concerns of the Black community. Long before the Black Studies controversy of the 1960s flared, Du Bois had concluded that "Negro History . . . [should] be taught as a separate subject . . . until all are familiar with the main facts." In 1954, years before the controversy erupted among Blacks, he had written at length on the question of what his people should be called; "Negro" was "not . . . the logical name" though Afro-American "was somewhat awkward." And it was Du Bois who sounded the trumpet call for the Southern Negro Youth Congress (SNYC), the militant forerunner of the Student Non-Violent Coordinating Committee (SNCC), in his frequently reprinted "Behold the Land" address at their Columbia, South Carolina, conference. Foreshadowing the upheaval soon to come, he said the "future of American Negroes [is] in the South" and advised the young Blacks not to flee to New York and Chicago but to "grit your teeth" and fight it out in the South.[7]

Because Du Bois remained such a towering figure, and because of the disproportionate southern racist influence in the anticommunist upsurge, it was unavoidable that attempts would be made to isolate him from the civil rights movement. The entire question of the links between anticommunism and racism is worthy of extended elucidation, not least because it sheds light on Du Bois' last years. Mississippi's John Rankin, a man of "monumental prejudices," according to Robert Carr, was perhaps more closely identified in the mind of the average person with the Un-American Activities Committee than any other individual. He made subversive influence among Blacks one of HUAC's favorite areas.[8]

Shockingly, this question of the intersection between anticommunism and racism has received little scholarly attention. Wayne Addison Clark has penned the most comprehensive study and it reveals the political context in which Du Bois was forced to operate. He observes how Dixiecrats achieved maximum mileage out of labelling civil rights advocates subversive and red since the war against Nazism undercut, somewhat, outright racist appeals. Politicians such as Senators James Eastland, Herman Talmadge, and Strom Thurmond and organizations such as the Citizen's Councils promoted a southern variation of McCarthyism. Many of the measures, for example, the Internal Security Act, used against the reds nationally were adopted on the state level by the South to use against Blacks. The fact that so many argued that Jim Crow must end to combat the Soviets demonstrated the "extent to which the Cold War shaped American racial and political thought." Moreover, the fact that the *Brown* ruling came in the midst of a concerted governmental campaign against international and domestic communism is one of the most overlooked aspects of the decision.[9]

The fact that the NAACP itself could at one time counsel Blacks to be suspicious of whites who wished to work with them, showed the effectiveness and pervasiveness of the racist's propaganda. Racists wishing to slow down and halt the Black drive for rights found it convenient to raise the red scare—and the presence of Du Bois facilitated this slick maneuver.

Donald R. McCoy and Richard T. Ruetten have cogently stated that "the drive for minority rights in America, regardless of its many forms, had roots. It was not launched from scratch." Like Philip S. Foner, they point to the militance of the war years as a golden era of Black progress. It was Black-white, left-center unity that propelled these gains, and the NAACP was a prime mover of these efforts. With the rise of the Cold War, Black-white unity was seriously shaken by the imputation of red to those whites who moved in that direction and left-center unity was virtually broken. Though Du Bois and others continued to call for the wartime alliances that produced so many significant gains, it was no longer de rigeur. The authors note a slackening of progress after 1954 partially due to the fact that "traditional Negro leadership seemed to sit back and wait for something to happen and little did." While their opponents continued to link the battle against Blacks and reds, many civil rights advocates failed to see the connection between fighting racism and fighting anticommunism—a prescription suggested by Du Bois but ignored by many.[10]

From the time of his return to the NAACP to the day of his death, Du Bois was in the thick of the fight for civil and human rights. Though some saw his peace activism as supplanting this interest, his idea was that they were complementary in that funds necessary to improve Black health, education, and welfare would not be available as long as there was a draining war budget; not to mention that social progress would be difficult in an atmosphere of bellicosity. This interest in rights did not only extend just to Blacks. In 1944, at a time when they were being shunned by most, Du Bois was not afraid to say, "I have every sympathy with the Japanese American Citizens League and if my [name] will help, you are at liberty to use it." The same held true for the struggle for women's equality, an issue he spoke to on more than one occasion.[11]

It was the civil rights of the Black community—an issue to which he had devoted most of his adult life—that continued to be a primary focus of his activism; he did not simply drop the question in the postwar period. In 1945 he resigned from the American Association of University Professors because of their penchant for holding meetings in places where Blacks "are not allowed to stand." He continued to write for the Black press and address these issues therein. He also continued to break down the barriers of segregation, as he informed Marshall Bidwell in late 1947: "I think that probably this is the first time that Princeton University ever had a Negro lecturer."[12]

Some of Du Bois' activities in this arena were questionable. At the same time that he was about to address many of the Black youth of the rural South at the SNYC meeting, he issued a contrary and wrong-headed declaration to Cleo Hamilton:

> I think it is very unwise for you to form an organization of rural youth. You must remember that Negro youth in the rural districts are too ignorant to form an intelligent organization. Organizations which desire to help them must be form *[sic]* by outsiders.

This was not the warp and woof of his civil rights thought fortunately—and his remarks in Columbia, South Carolina, earlier explicitly contradicted these words.[13]

Publicly, as in a 1948 letter to the editor of *The New York Times,* he continued to complain vociferously about Jim Crow, for example, segregated interstate travel. He coupled his angry words with action, joining Lester Granger, Charles Drew, William Patterson, and others at the 1949 Legislative Assembly for Civil Rights, attended by 1,200 delegates from thirty states in Washington, D.C. This was only one of many joint projects he worked on with the Civil Rights Congress.[14]

Another CRC project that Du Bois worked on was the case of Rosa Lee Ingram, a Black widow with twelve children, living in Georgia who killed a white man in self-defense; he had begun to beat her when two of her sons joined her in repelling the attack; all three were convicted. In 1949 Du Bois informed Shirley Graham of his activities on the case:

> I have written a petition on the Rosa Ingram case for a committee of colored women headed by Mary Church Terrell. I think it's a pretty good document and they thought so too. It is going to be presented to the United Nations.

It was presented to the United Nations and received quite a bit of attention. The Ingram case received worldwide attention on October 12, when Dr. Jan Probojowski referred to it as the "most flagrant violation of human rights."[15]

In addition to his addresses and ties to the Black church, Du Bois was also involved with Black colleges—a long time source of employment for him. At the same time that Morgan State, under pressure, was withdrawing their invitation for him to give a commencement address, President Raphael O'Hara Lanier of Houston's Texas State University for Negroes asked him if he would be interested in being visiting professor for the summer or entire year. A few months later, in 1950, he and Mary McLeod Bethune received the 1950 Alpha Medallion from the Lincoln University Nu Chapter of Alpha Phi Alpha fraternity. This of course signifies Du Bois' continuing ties with the Black community, even during the stormy year of 1950.[16]

These ties to the Black community were often parlayed into advances for the reds. In 1952, the Lehigh Valley Progressive

Forum invited him to speak on the case of "the Communist Steve Nelson." Strikingly, the meeting was to take place in a Black church, Shiloh-Baptist in Easton. It was this rare ability to unite Black and red that fomented so much outrage. But Du Bois' efforts were not always successful. P. L. Prattis of the *Pittsburgh Courier* refused to be associated with a Du Bois project due to fear of redbaiting:

> I can only unite and be effective as long as I can maintain my personal invulnerability. All that the "patriots" would have to know would be that I had some associations, affiliations, and what not. If they could get hold of such a "past" and publish it, I would be done for. I do not own the Courier. I only work for the publisher.

This, he regrettably declaimed, despite his admiration and respect for Du Bois.[17]

The continued high regard for Du Bois among Afro-Americans was evidenced in 1952 by a series of testimonials for Du Bois read at a reception for him. It is worth noting that such gushing prose could be issued in the immediate aftermath of his indictment and at a time when association with him would bring few encomia from the nation's rulers, especially when one considers the perilous, parlous role of college administrators. The presidents of Kentucky State, Langston, Fisk, Wiley, and Ohio's Central State strained rhetorical excess in their praise.[18]

Another feature of Du Bois' multifaceted activity was his mass of speaking engagements, particularly before heavily Black audiences. Du Bois, despite what "big white folks" might say about him or do to him was still a Black hero of major stature; indeed, attacks by these elements—like later attacks on Adam Clayton Powell, Jr., in the 1960s—if anything, increased his stature. For many Blacks felt he must be doing his job if he was the object of so much scorn and wrath. Early in 1953 he spoke in L.A. at the largest church in the Negro community (1,800 capacity) on behalf of the Southern California Peace Crusade. The welcoming committee was broad, replete with lawyers and many pastors. Du Bois himself was impressed: "It was the best planned lecture trip that I have ever taken and I [have] been lecturing for some 50 years.' " Du Bois was referring as well to the San Francisco Bay Area component of his trip. In San Francisco the Committee to Welcome Dr. W.E.B. Du Bois consisted of officials from the American Federation of Labor, International Longshore and Warehousemen's Union, National Lawyers' Guild, and National Negro Labor Council. In Oakland a separate but equally representative committee was formed and Du Bois spoke at one of the large Negro churches, Taylor Memorial Methodist Church. Du Bois was able to introduce the controversial issue of peace into the heart of the Black community and this both reflected and reinforced prevailing sentiments. This multiclass appeal of Du Bois was also seen when he spoke to the Progressive party of Maryland in February 1954 at the "home of the Negro doctor's association."[19]

Du Bois was involved in some of the most passionate battles of the 1950s civil rights movement. When Carl and Anne Braden got into hot water for trying to sell their home to Andrew Wade IV, a college-educated Black, racists erupted in protest. The Bradens, who had been active in the NAACP and the National Negro Labor Council, ultimately were indicted for sedition. The case quickly became a cause celebre, as the National Lawyers Guild, units of the NAACP, Black churches, and unions joined in what was an emotionally charged episode that defined Cold War racist tension. Both Bradens and Wade were active in the Progressive party and the indictments were seen as stemming from their political activity. The inevitable result, as the Black lawyer Louis Redding explained it, was that both whites and Blacks drifted away from the party and allied activity because of fear of the red smear. In the midst of the harried defense effort, the Bradens told Du Bois about the prosecution list of their involvement with thirty subversive organizations: "three of the organizations on the list were ones you were connected with—the National Committee to Defend Dr. Du Bois, the Council on African Affairs and the Stockholm Petition." They desperately wanted Du Bois to come and testify on their behalf. But the pressure of events and financial difficulties prevented it.[20]

Throughout the 1950s Du Bois was in touch with Black leadership nationally despite his departure from the NAACP. In 1955 he thanked the usually moderate Dean Gordon Hancock of Virginia Union University for an article favorable to him that had been written for the *Indianapolis Recorder.* This was part of Du Bois' continued effort to influence the Black press, the chronicle of the civil rights movement and an often accurate barometer of Black public opinion. On May 2, 1955, he forwarded a letter to a number of Black papers requesting that they report more on peace activities, the threat of nuclear war, and so on. Though this appeal did not bear immediate fruit, the lessening of international tensions detected in 1955 combined with the increasing prestige accorded Du Bois as a result of Ghana's independence did mean that his political activities in this area received increased coverage. This tendency was reflected in a critically received television program on Du Bois broadcast in the New York area that moved the literary scholar Annette Rubinstein to congratulate Du Bois directly:

> I have, since June 4, seen literally almost a hundred people who spoke of the very great pleasure they also had in watching you that night. In fact, I don't believe I have been with a single group during the last ten days in which someone didn't mention what a thrilling experience it was.

James Ivy, editor of *Crisis,* told Muriel Symington he was affected similarly:

> Did you see Dr. Du Bois on "Nightbeat" week before last? He mentioned his break with the NAACP and why he still stands for Socialism. He was magnificent!

In 1960, Du Bois' venerability and unflinching consistency assured him of favorable treatment in the Black press. The *Afro-American* of February 22, 1960, featured a full page on "Dr. Du Bois at 92—A Living Legend." In contradistinction to negative articles by certain white writers, Hubert Delany penned a four-part series for the *San Francisco Sun-Reporter* on Du Bois entitled "A Prophet with Honor."[21]

Du Bois' increasingly favorable and frequent treatment in the Black press was a facet of the changing political climate and his strengthened ties to Black leaders. Delany's articles were not the returning of a favor though the judge did thank Du Bois for support concerning "allegations and innuendos made against me by the Mayor." In late 1955, Du Bois joined with Raymond Pace Alexander, Arna Bontemps, and other leaders in sponsoring the Alain Locke Memorial Workshop at New York University. His trip to southern California during the spring of 1956 highlighted these trends. Dr. Jack Kimbrough, "a strong civic leader not only in the Negro population but city-wide," hosted Du Bois in San Diego; "ministers of about all Negro churches . . . (were) scheduled to announce" Du Bois' visit there; a "front page display" of Du Bois in the only Negro newspaper in the city was arranged.[22]

Du Bois' involvement in the civil rights fight was witnessed most clearly during the crisis surrounding Emmett Till, one of the most crucial and important yet little known events of the 1950s that galvanized civil rights activists nationally. Till, a Black youth in Mississippi, was lynched for allegedly whistling at a Euro-American woman. *Crisis* devoted a number of articles and editorials to this outrageous tragedy. A feature article on "L'Affaire Till" in the French press concluded that the press from "right to left" condemned the incident, "it raised sharp doubts about the sincerity of the United States in posing as a defender of human rights and of oppressed peoples throughout the world." Du Bois was quick to speak and place the events in a political context. Hence, the meaningful memorial to the memory of Till would be a massive push for voting rights—a point he had been stressing for years. Again, this was not just a theoretical point to be raised and forgotten for he moved swiftly to channel the angry sentiment around the Till murder. With Lyman Beecher Stowe and others he formed the Provisional Committee for Justice in Mississippi. They played a pivotal role in the holding of a protest rally with 20,000 people in New York, which Du Bois addressed, again stressing voting rights. The NAACP was hesitant because of the role of left-influenced unions like District 65 in mobilizing for the rally. This despite the favorable view of indigenous Mississippians; the Mississippi Regional Council of Negro Leadership, for example, based in the Black town of Mound Bayou, worked toward Du Bois' efforts.

This Till incident outraged Du Bois. *Crisis* noted that "with the exception of William Faulkner no prominent American spoke out in public condemnation of this monstrous crime and the shameful verdict." This was not enough for Du Bois. *The New York Times* reported that Du Bois "challenged William Faulkner . . . to a debate on integration . . . he suggested that the debate take place on the steps of the Court House at Summer, Mississippi where the Emmett Till murder case was tried." The subject would be the novelist's "Go Slow Now" advice to Negroes in a recent *Life* magazine article. The novelist did not accept the invitation. But Du Bois and the Provisional Committee continued their efforts despite a vicious redbaiting attack, sending a ton of clothes and food to the beleaguered Blacks of Mississippi.[23]

Another major crisis of the civil rights movement of the 1950s involved desegregation of public schools in Little Rock, Arkansas, and the violent reaction to it. President Eisenhower, in *Crisis,* echoed the NAACP in underscoring the international implications of the controversy: "Our enemies are gloating over this incident and using it everywhere to misrepresent our whole nation." The cartoonist Herb Block, in a popular illustration of the day, showed people in Africa and Asia unbelievably reading the headlines about racial turmoil in Arkansas. It was the Little Rock crisis and the blow it gave to United States prestige that as much as any other factor accelerated the dismantling of Jim Crow.[24]

The confluence in 1957 of Little Rock, Sputnik, and the refusal to allow Du Bois to travel to Ghana exposed serious strains in United States domestic and foreign policies, causing international outrage that would eventually spell changes in domestic policies. The NAACP was revealing the impact of the anticommunism it had supported and generated which made moderates and liberals view desegregation as a red-tinged issue. Du Bois had warned that stampeding away potential allies would be the inexorable result of going along with the purges and the NAACP's complaint here he saw to an extent as chickens coming home to roost. But that did not bar his issuing a similar indictment of United States foreign policy. He asked plaintively, "does 'all deliberate speed' mean 338 years?" After a speech by AFL-CIO head George Meany before the United Nations Human Rights Committee duirng the height of the crisis where he termed the Black condition, "one phase of a great advance," Du Bois demurred. In a letter widely carried in the Black press but addressed to the committee, he questioned Meany's right to speak for Blacks and deemed Little Rock "threatening evidence of a great retreat."[25]

The cry from the NAACP about the desertion of moderates and liberals during the height of civil rights battles may have been the most unfortunate effect of the anticommunist purges on the civil rights movement. The NAACP participation in these purges made it ill-suited to take an aggressive leadership role as the modern civil rights era dawned. The most comprehensive recent study has observed that "from the very beginning, many of the Southern Blacks wanted to move faster than the NAACP." This view is not false. Aldon Douglas Morris has pointed to the Southern Christian Leadership Conference (SCLC) as the main engine of the civil rights movement and leftist organizations such as the Highlander

Folk School and SCEF, along with the sit-in movement as the other main forces. He criticizes the NAACP for being "one-dimensional" and "legalistic"—complaints frequently made by Du Bois. The NAACP objected to the formation of the SCLC, just as "the NAACP became one of the most zealous participants in a broad attack by liberals and liberal groups [on] an alleged communist influence in SNCC." Both SNCC and SCLC were influenced by Du Bois and the left. SNCC refused to bar Communists for, as one militant put it, "I don't feel that we as [a] minority group fighting for the right to freely speak and think can take such a position." Unlike its white counterpart, Students for a Democratic Society (SDS), SNCC refused to "insert a totalitarian disclaimer" in its constitution.[26]

These factors are striking because it is difficult to speak of Du Bois as being isolated from the civil rights movement because of his leftism, when the major arms of the movement were equally, if not more so, to the left. The Highlander Folk School (HFS) was crucial, as Morris explains, in the organizing of civil rights protest. HFS's leader, Myles Horton, studied Marx, had known Du Bois since the early 1930s, and insisted that Communists not be barred from another organization he had worked with—the Southern Conference for Human Welfare (SCHW). Communists were welcome at HFS and freely participated. Many of the original leaders of the student nonviolent movements had attended Highlander workshops. "We shall overcome" was a legacy from Highlander Folk School. Rosa Parks, before refusing to relinquish her seat on a bus in Montgomery, had attended workshops at HFS. Horton had been associated earlier with Du Bois' colleague James Dombrowski as a member of Commonwealth College, an avowedly Marxist labor college; the decidedly non-Marxist Orval Faubus was also allied in this effort. Large numbers of future sit-in leaders attended HFS sessions. Morris pointed to HFS as a mode by which many began moving away from NAACP's court orientation and into direct action. Martin Luther King, Jr., maintained a direct link with Highlander, although it was scored as "a communist training ground." HFS influenced King aide Andrew Young to leave the National Council of Churches and join the civil rights movement as an activist. Such was the influence of the left. Assuming that Du Bois would be isolated from the civil rights mainstream because of his leftism reveals an ignorance of the dynamics of Black politics.[27]

SCEF was another left-oriented organization with widespread impact on the civil rights movement. Morris says it had the major role in convincing southern whites to join the movement. The Reverend Fred Shuttlesworth was both a top leader of SCEF and SCLC. Pressure was placed on King to keep a respectful distance from SCEF but this effort met with little success. James Dombrowski was director of SCEF at this time, Aubrey Williams was president, and Morehouse College president Benjamin Mays was vice-president. Ella Baker, former executive director of SCLC and a principal founder of SNCC, worked closely with SCEF. Floyd McKissick, former leader of the then militant Congress of Racial Equality (CORE), worked closely with SCEF's parent, SCHW.[28]

That the NAACP might be missing the boat in terms of galvanizing the upsurge of civil rights activity dimly occurred to the leaders. The *Crisis* issue of April 1958 featured an article on the "changing structure of Negro leadership" which was highly critical of Association policies; particularly their legalistic strategy and their presumed slow response to events in Montgomery. This trenchant attack, so reminiscent of Du Bois' allies, was answered quickly in the following issue. Rosa Parks' role in the NAACP was mentioned and E. D. Nixon, NAACP leader in Montgomery, was accurately described as boycott leader. But this begged the question in a sense because both had long-standing ties with the left, Nixon having worked hand in glove with the SNYC. Yet these articles did underscore a level of discontent within the association, and the rebuttal's branding of the critique as "totalitarian" was revelatory of how deeply redbaiting had seeped into the marrow of the NAACP.[29]

The NAACP was not the only civil rights organization grappling with the question of left influence. CORE chapters, particularly in Chicago and Columbus, Ohio, included Communists despite ritual avowals of anticommunism. But if Morris is correct—and most likely he is—SCLC was the engine of the civil rights movement and examination of the left's role here would reveal much about the dynamics of Black politics and Du Bois' assumed isolation. The Montgomery Bus Boycott was the crucial event that eventually led to SCLC's creation. The first person called by E. D. Nixon after hearing of Parks' arrest was former Progressive party leader attorney Clifford Durr, the second person was Ralph Abernathy, and lastly Martin Luther King. Nixon, former SNYC activist, was the man who convinced King to assume a leadership role. Parks had been recommended for HFS by former Progressive party activist Virginia Durr; Parks later recalled how this experience gave her sustenance to struggle in that she "had never before experienced interracial living." Carey McWilliams, editor of the left-liberal *Nation* was in close touch with King, consulting with him on numerous issues and lending support to his fundraising activities. Each spring until his death, King sent the *Nation* an annual report on the state of the civil rights movement. Jack O'Dell, an editor of *Freedomways* magazine, founded by Shirley Graham, was a top advisor to King: "It was John Kennedy himself who took Martin Luther King Jr. aside during a White House conference and told him SCLC had to get rid of O'Dell." Anne Braden adds, King "himself always rejected the witch-hunters' attempts to isolate SCEF. He defied a barrage of criticism to initiate a clemency petition as a protest when Carl went to prison in the HUAC case . . . after Carl left prison in 1962, I was invited to speak at the annual SCLC convention in Birmingham." Not surprisingly, when the Montgomery Bus Boycott was launched, "the White Citizens Council announced that the boycott had been planned in Moscow and was communist inspired."[30]

Perhaps many scholars have ignored the role of the left and, correspondingly, Du Bois' influence on the civil rights movement because the contemporary press did not pay sufficient attention to the relationship. In the spring of 1959 there took place a youth march for integration with over 20,000 comprising 134 busloads of students from more than 100 campuses. *Guardian* reporter and Du Bois intimate Louis Burnham reported that as A. Philip Randolph called on the United States "to give Negroes their civil rights today" as "one of the best ways to halt the progress of communism in Africa and Asia," the youth "sat in silence and seeming bewilderment as he inveighed against the Fascist and communist enemies of democracy at home and abroad." The NAACP had "opposed the First Youth March for Integrated Schools last October and discouraged participation by its youth councils . . ." These mass marches of youth coming years before Berkeley and prior to Greensboro, augured the youthful discontent of the 1960s that came as a surprise to some. The *New York Herald Tribune* did not cover this march at all and *The New York Times* gave it cursory coverage on page sixty-four. The NAACP had lost its preeminent role in the Black political movement precisely because it failed to follow the path set out by Du Bois.[31]

In fairness to the NAACP, it should be observed that there was inordinate pressure on it to stay in line. Its forty-fourth annual convention in St. Louis in 1953 spoke directly to this issue. But continuing their post-World War II pattern, the NAACP went on to emulate their victimizers by conducting their own internal witch-hunt. They begged the United States rulers to ban Jim Crow so as to heighten the battle against communism. Their anticommunist policy, violently opposed by Du Bois and others, did not save them from the most virulent redbaiting attacks; and by chasing away some of their more militant and determined cadre, they virtually insured segregationists a certain amount of success. After the NAACP helped to rout the reds, priority then shifted in the mid-1950s—notably after *Brown* v. *Board of Education*—to routing the Blacks—that is, the Association itself. Georgia Attorney General Eugene Cook, who earlier had been inveighing against "subversive" reds, asked the state legislature to investigate the NAACP "for possible subversive influence." Just as Communist party membership lists had been sought earlier, by 1956, the NAACP was complaining about southern states seeking their lists. Just as there had been efforts to ban the Communist party, by the mid-1950s, there were efforts to ban the NAACP. At the forty-seventh annual convention in 1956, the NAACP appeared desperate: "First of all, practically all of our branch presidents in the Deep South have been the victims of the most vicious threatening tactics." Again, Wilkins wistfully tried to convince others that attacks on the NAACP harmed the United States image abroad. Their 1950 ritual anti-communist resolution was belatedly amended, to no avail, to cover their true antagonists; it was "reaffirmed and extended to include a ruling that Communists and/or persons who are prominently identified with the Ku Klux Klan, White Citizens Councils, or Communist-front or Communist-line organizations, are ineligible for membership in the NAACP." There had been no reports of a rush of KKK members to take out membership cards in the NAACP. The anticommunist whirlwind that the NAACP had helped to sow boomeranged and smacked the Association itself. Soon thereafter, there were reports in *Crisis* about Catholics and others reluctant to join the NAACP because of its alleged subversive nature. On the other hand, militants like Cleve Sellers tried to enlist the local NAACP in the early sit-ins but were told that "marches and demonstrations were too provocative" and that the "courts will decide these matters." When the watershed Mississippi

Freedom Democratic party arose, Aaron Henry, of the Mississippi NAACP, wanted to accept a compromise that the rest of the delegation "voted almost unanimously to reject." Worse, Wilkins arrogantly castigated legendary Black heroine Fannie Lou Hamer: "You don't know anything, you're ignorant, you don't know anything about politics. I've been [in] the business over 20 years." This insolent display did not endear the NAACP to militant activists and drove a continuing wedge between them and those who saw the Du Bois tradition as worthy of emulation.[32]

It was unavoidable that the militants of the civil rights era would look to Du Bois as a symbol of resistance. James Forman, one of the key operatives in SNCC, freely admitted, "I was greatly influenced by the call of Du Bois." He acknowledges that a step in his radicalization process was the NAACP refusal to invite Du Bois to their fiftieth anniversary celebration. H. Rap Brown admits that he read and was influenced by Du Bois. The participants in the first Greensboro sit-ins discussed the writings of Du Bois in and after class. John Lewis, another key SNCC operative, observed that "the masses and the Negro academic community really feel a great deal of understanding and love for people like Robeson and Du Bois." It was not just the younger militants who were devotees of Du Bois. Coleman Young was an ally of Du Bois and was grilled before HUAC because of his ties to the Council on African Affairs and the Progressive party.[33]

Du Bois remained in touch with the developing civil rights movement. He had a direct link to Martin Luther King, Jr., through their mutual friend L. D. Reddick, who sent him a blow by blow description of the developing battle. Du Bois' opinion of Dr. King varied. In Reddick's biography of the militant cleric, Du Bois calls him "honest, straight forward, well-trained and knowing the limits." But in Du Bois' view of the book he found the portrait of King:

> a little disturbing. . . . His doctor's thesis is on a vague theological problem about the power of God as pictured by two of his theological teachers. . . . I was sorry to see King lauded for his opposition to the young colored man in North Carolina who declared that in order to stop lynching and mob violence, Negroes must fight back . . . it is a very grave question as to whether or not the slavery and degradation of Negroes in America has not been unnecessarily prolonged by submission to evil.

He compared King to his mentor Gandhi and averred that the latter had an economic program but he was not sure about the former.[34]

Du Bois' view of King varied, just as Du Bois' views generally varied over the years. In a 1957 *Guardian* article he reviewed both aspects. He conceded that in his early youth he thought war brought progress and "that if my people ever gained freedom and equality, it would be by killing white people." Then came a sort of pacificism interrupted by his support of World War I. And now in Montgomery not "Negro professional men, merchants and teachers but the black workers: the scrubbers and cleaners; the porters and seamstresses" are fighting led by one "who had read Hegel, knew of Karl Marx" and used Gandhi's methods. Yet, Du Bois saw King's problems as being perhaps an insufficient realization that the whites he was trying to sway with moral fortitude were diseased with racism and maybe unreachable by this method. Ominously, he remarked, "it is possible any day that their leader will be killed." On another occasion he expanded his perspective on the turbulent events in Montgomery:

> it had no connection originally with the NAACP and was a mass movement of workers with no leadershp from the Negro intelligentsia or bourgeoisie . . . it received rather unexpectedly leadership from the Negro church. . . . The question is whence does it go from here? This is not clear. It is now taking uncertain refuge in prayer meetings and following Gandhi techniques. It should emphasize the right to register and vote and get better jobs . . . for ordinary Negro workers. . . . This requires an understanding of socialism. . . . So long as the Negro voter supports the current effort to oppose socialism and overthrow communism by force and starve the welfare state in order to prepare for world war, the Negro worker will be forced below a decent standard of life.

Du Bois went on to point out that Nkrumah, Azikiwe, and others are all declared socialists, so why not United States Black leaders? He went on to detail the perils of anticommunism and described "a concerted effort to lessen color caste and make Black folk the allies of Big Business by bribe or better jobs. The partial breaking of the color line was used to answer the stand of the Soviet Union against color discrimination. . . . This was aimed to split American Negroes from union with or sympathy for colonial peoples." Du

Bois knew that some criticized his strident views as unrealistic but his query was why had these attempts to lessen color caste, come during the Cold War in the 1950s and not, say, in the 1930s. In any event, his analyses of the movement were widely read and influenced a generation of civil rights activists, particularly those of SNCC and others on the cutting edge of social change. At the same time, Martin Luther King—as his 1968 comments weeks before his assassination showed—evaluated Du Bois highly and their tie was even closer than exhibited by the March 30, 1956, *San Diego Lighthouse* front page that told of Du Bois speaking there, flanked in the next column by an article on a guilty verdict against King.[35]

As might be expected, Du Bois' leftism, which would captivate SNCC militants and fascinate Martin Luther King, Jr., would not find favor within the NAACP, but even here a certain evolution can be detected; for after Ghana's independence and a lessening of Cold War tensions, it is possible to detect a softening in attitude toward Du Bois. There had been conceptual differences between Du Bois and NAACP leaders for some time on how militant the NAACP should be. As early as 1913, he had put forward the notion of the association as a central headquarters for vigilance committees that would defend Black communities against racist violence. After his sacking this type of militance continued to strike a responsive chord among NAACP chapters. In 1949 alone, he was deluged with invitations to speak at branches in Easton and New York City and college chapters at Columbia, Brooklyn College, Hunter College, Pennsylvania State University, and elsewhere. The Urban League of Greater New York invited him to speak on discrimination in education. During his 1953 West Coast tour he pulled back from associating with the branches because he felt his presence might cause undue opprobrium to be leveled at them. He also was leery of certain elements within certain chapters which he sensed were too close to the state apparatus. In late 1953, despite an invitation, he informed one correspondent, "it would not be ethical for me at this time to evaluate publicly the NAACP." NAACP leaders and certain chapters returned the favor and, save a pointed potshot from time to time, they converted him into a nonperson.[36]

But there was an evolution in this trend, noticeable in late 1956, though visible as early as 1953 when he spoke at the dedication of a high school named after Joel Spingarn. Early in 1956 the Westwood, Los Angeles, NAACP had invited him to speak at UCLA during their controversial Academic Freedom Week. Then on November 16, 1956, Roy Wilkins himself invited Du Bois to a luncheon in honor of Jackie Robinson, 1956 Spingarn Medal winner. He added gratuitously: "Your presence will add luster to the event and will be a source of real gratification to us." One reason for this sudden recognition of his "luster" was the NAACP's growing pretensions to assume an international role, particularly in Africa, and finding that their ignoring of, and hostility toward, Du Bois did not make many friends on the continent. Nevertheless, Muriel Symington bitterly complained about Du Bois' conspicuous absence from the special issue of *Crisis* devoted to Ghana. Wilkins retreated a step but basically held his ground: "there is no policy to exclude Dr. Du Bois . . . however I would be less than frank if I did not say that the present views of Dr. Du Bois are not deemed fitting . . . I learned my 'NAACP' at the feet of Du Bois as did many of my generation . . . though I cannot go with him in his conviction that reformism here will not do, and that a socialist revolution in the Soviet pattern must ensue." Just as James Forman complained about the NAACP failure to include Du Bois in its fiftieth anniversary celebration, T. F. Sellers, former copy-desk editor at the *Norfolk Journal and Guide,* city editor at the *Afro-American,* and managing editor of the *Amsterdam News,* protested to the NAACP's Henry Moon about this lack of recognition.[37]

Wilkins' overture to Du Bois in 1956 was symptomatic of a new trend but backing and filling was also present because of pressure from the right. But there was also pressure from the other side, as evidenced by the brouhaha over the ignoring of Du Bois during the NAACP's fiftieth anniversary. Garfield Hinton added his name to the burgeoning protest list, saying absence of the founder of the NAACP "was inexcusable." He suggested awarding Du Bois the Spingarn Medal. Sufficiently prompted, Du Bois was invited to the Spingarn Medal presentation and the convention of 1959. This did not quell or satisfy the critics. Covering the 1959 convention, Louis Burnham launched a mighty broadside against the NAACP for not insuring Du Bois' attendance and the political philosophy that undergirded the perceived pusillanimousness: "The concept of integration as meaning that Negroes should adopt the prevailing political prejudices which big business imposes on the majority citizenry with whom Negroes seek equality is not new with the NAACP." Like many others he stressed that the new initiative—

the Montgomery bus boycott, the Tallahassee boycott—did not emerge from the NAACP. This atmosphere created by the largest civil rights organization made it possible for Martin Luther King to allege that Blacks should be given civil rights since they fought "in good wars and bad."[38]

The year 1959 marked an acceleration of Du Bois' invitations from the chapters. Even Roy Wilkins sent him warm greetings and ended with the salutation, "yours in the Society for the Propagation of the Old Days." Apparently, the executive secretary was not referring to the "old days" of Du Bois' ouster or the redbaiting they had heaped on him from time to time. Subsequently, Arthur Spingarn, who had ignored and baited him for years, wished Du Bois a speedy recovery during a sickness and signed off ironically as "your old friend."[39]

Du Bois and the NAACP leadership provide a useful point-counterpoint vis-à-vis the labor movement. Both recognized that there were more dues-paying Blacks in the labor movement than in the NAACP. Moreover, the labor movement—particularly the CIO—provided material and political support to the civil rights movement. But where Du Bois supported and was not adverse to the left-led and Communist-led unions, the NAACP treated them with disdainful hostility. This is unfortunate because recent scholarship has noted that Communists within the United Auto Workers, the Electrical Workers, the National Maritime Union, and so on played a significant and leading role in fighting racism, despite the fulminations of historians who have distorted the history. Du Bois himself was a member of Local 3 of the American Newspaper Guild and a firm believer in labor solidarity. It was not particularly extraordinary when he was sent "congratulations on your having recently joined the New York City Western Union pickets." This kind of labor solidarity in action led to formal recognition: "at a recent Executive Board meeting of the Social Service Employees . . . you be invited to accept an honorary, life-time membership in our Union."[40]

The relationship of the association with the unions was not always so felicitous. While Du Bois got on well with the militant International Union of Mine, Mill and Smelter Workers—they invited him to address their 1950 convention—the association frequently attacked this staunch foe of racism. This stance in opposition to such unions often led the NAACP into bizarre positions. Contrary to the view of many unions then and the contemporary cry of

Blacks, NAACP leader Herbert Hill bitterly opposed super seniority, quotas, and affirmative action to overcome the past and present effects of racism. Hill termed such measures "nothing more than a sugar coated form of segregation and in the last analysis it would do serious harm to the Negro community." Such views did not enrapture many progressive trade unionists or many Blacks. Du Bois, on the other hand, adopted a somewhat different posture. During 1950 when the war against Korea began, Du Bois stepped up his contact and addresses to unions in recognition of their crucial role within the body politic. He spoke in Chicago at the Packing House Workers Center, the United Electrical Workers, the Teachers Union of Philadelphia, and elsewhere during this critical year.[41]

White-collar unionists, particularly, looked up to Du Bois. In 1952 he joined past winners Franz Boas, George Washington Carver, Harlow Shapley, and Albert Einstein as recipient of the award for "Distinguished Service in the Cause of Education for Peace and Freedom" from the New York City Teachers Union. This fete was attended by 1,800 and addressed by filmwriter Lester Cole and Corliss Lamont and covered by *The New York Times.* But white-collar unions were not alone in lauding Du Bois. The National Negro Labor Council, mainly led by Black factory workers, looked to both Robeson and Du Bois for leadership. From the other side of the ledger, the NAACP scored the NNLC and other trade unionists who, ironically, were the most determined opponents of the racism the Association was designed to stamp out. At the same time, *Crisis* was graphically describing how the backlash of red-baiting they had helped to generate was smacking them. Fair employment practices and attacks on Jim Crow in New Mexico were seen as "Kremlin-sponsored and written by Joe Stalin" and stymied.[42]

Du Bois also became involved when Frank Graham, Arthur Schlesinger, and Mordecai Johnson asked for his support in a campaign of elderly educators against low pensions and benefits. Du Bois replied forthrightly and positively. He saw this involvement in labor issues as part and parcel of his involvement with the civil rights movement generally, not only because of labor's material and political support for Blacks, but also the working class make-up of the Black community. The NAACP from time to time was dimly aware of these factors, especially at certain junctures, for example, when Westley Law, NAACP board member and president of the Georgia State Conference of Branches and the Savannah chapter, was dismissed from his position as letter carrier because of his Association activities. This point was sharply drawn in a *Crisis* article describing how racebaiting was used to prevent unionization in Mississippi.[43]

The NAACP and Du Bois not only diverged in their relationships with laborers but with lawyers as well. Just as the Association ousted Du Bois when the Cold War heated up, they also attempted to break off ties with the National Lawyers Guild (NLG). This was part of an effort to shun the left that was ironic since it was the progressive Garland Fund that contributed $100,000 to the NAACP to instigate litigation culminating in the *Brown* decision and NLG lawyers played a substantial role in this entire process. The Communist Party had played the lead role in forming the Guild and, according to Percival Roberts Bailey, exhibited "sensitivity to mass social injustice that was extraordinary." Because of the racist and discriminatory policies of the staid American Bar Association, Black lawyers flocked en masse to the NLG. Thurgood Marshall served as secretary of the Guild. Charles Houston was vice-president of the New York City chapter. Simultaneously, a number of Guild leaders were active in the NAACP. There was close collaboration between the two allies during the war on such issues as treatment of Black soldiers, government hiring of Black lawyers, FEPC, and so on.[44]

After the war, the NAACP and their Director of Research continued to work closely with the NLG. Du Bois addressed the issue of "Civil Rights Legislation—Before and After the 14th Amendment" at an important Howard University conference in 1947 on the use of federal power to protect civil rights cosponsored by the National Bar Association, NAACP, and NLG. The guild called for the unseating of Bilbo, challenged separate but equal facilities, and intervened in important civil rights cases. Joseph Forer, Houston, and other NLG members fought the action that led to the desegregation of Washington. Marshall continued to be active with the guild in opposing Truman's loyalty security program and Houston served as defense counsel for the Hollywood Ten.[45]

But as the Cold War ossified, this Gibraltar-like alliance disintegrated despite Du Bois' clamorous protestations. According to Roberts, NLG opposition to the war and United States foreign policy "would not be obsolete a quarter century later"; like Du Bois, they advocated a policy later to be known as "detente." A

September 1950 HUAC report on the NLG had a devastating impact on the organization and its relationship with others. Yet, a Black newspaper in Cleveland took a poll of two dozen Black lawyers and found that all but one had "a high regard for the Guild's work in championing the cause of civil rights." But the pressure cooker was heating up. Louis Redding, one of the guild's most eminent Black members, resigned after his home state, Delaware, enacted a law requiring members of organizations on the attorney general's list to register with the state police. NLG leader Earl Dickerson was a boon companion of Du Bois and denounced his arrest and trial. This NLG backing was a continuation of their tie with Du Bois that had continued—if not quickened—after his NAACP sacking. In 1950, at the urging of future attorneys Mark Lane, Oliver Sutton (one of the first Blacks to serve in New York State's higher courts), and Alan Westin, he agreed to address the NLG student division.[46]

The NAACP was not as eager about working with the guild after the Cold War began. SNCC, the shock troops of the civil rights movement and the organization most partial to Du Bois, was in constant conflict with the NAACP over their refusal to disavow the guild. Both the NAACP and the NAACP Legal Defense Fund threatened to withdraw from an alliance with SNCC in Mississippi if legal assistance from the NLG was accepted—despite the dearth of progressive lawyers willing to work pro bono to retrieve protesters from the grim reality of southern jail cells. The NAACP was not alone in this sectarianism, as CORE took a similar position. Du Bois, contrarily, valued their tireless devotion to civil rights and saw retreat from the guild as playing into the none too merciful hands of racists.[47]

Du Bois recognized that many of the legal cases that the NAACP put so much effort into could not be won without progressive legal assistance because of the timidity and racism of the bar combined with an ingrained, inculcated reluctance to challenge the status quo—along with a studied preference for stare decisis, i.e., following—perhaps racist—precedent. Two of the most important court cases of the era involved Du Bois' cronies: *Dombrowski* v. *Pfister* and the southern voting rights case involving Charles Gomillion. Gomillion, dean of students at Tuskeegee, supported Du Bois during his trial and belonged to SNYC. As early as 1944, he had been in contact with Du Bois about his study of voting in Tuskeegee. He worked with guild lawyers and wrote for *Lawyers*

Guild Review. These supposedly subversive ties were, of course, attacked by the racists. But the lesson of the Tuskeegee victory, apparently lost on the NAACP leadership, was that no matter how non-red a civil rights fighter, such charges would be dredged up anyway so that, like Gomillion, there might as well be a reliance on allies—despite their "pinkness"—so desperately needed to win difficult battles.[48]

Du Bois most certainly did not shun the left in participating in the civil rights struggle. But this did not at all signal a retreat from the Afro-American community, as some of the more wrong-headed critics have alleged. His concerns remained in the main-stream of Black politics. He continually condemned segregated education and was ecstatic about *Brown* v. *Board of Education:* "I have seen the impossible happen. It did happen on May 17, 1954." On the occasion of the 27,000 strong Prayer Pilgrimage in Washington, D.C., Du Bois saw the "watchword" as "register to vote." In a "Petition of Right to the President, the Congress and the Supreme Court of the United States of America," drafted by Du Bois in 1957, he again stressed the primacy of civil rights but buttressed it with other pillars, for example, public ownership, old age pensions, and other social welfare measures.[49]

With Sputnik and, especially, the coming to independence of Africa, the father of Pan-Africanism took on a new stature and he used the opportunity to push recurrent themes. For the first time in years, he was invited to give a commencement address and did so at South Carolina's Allen University in 1957; he repeated the idea that United States Blacks cannot lead Africa but must follow them since they were socialists. This commencement invitation was an opening wedge that spurred on other Black colleges. On April 12, 1958, the *Afro-American* editorialized:

> The Department of Social Sciences of Howard University deserves a great deal of credit for its courage in bringing the distinguished sociologist, author and scholar, Dr. W.E.B. Du Bois to deliver an address to the students. . . . Critics of Dr. Du Bois accuse him of being pro-communist and his speech Monday night did little to allay their suspicions but there is one important factor which his critics overlook. Dr. Du Bois is not saying anything now which he was not saying 40 years ago, long before the Russian revolution became a fait accompli.

> . . . As a scholar and thinker, he is one of the darker men whom the white man fears.

Soon thereafter S. J. Wright, president of Fisk University, bestowed an honorary degree on their most distinguished alumnus, garnished with high praise. In rapid succession the Fisk class of 1935 sponsored and organized the "Du Bois Lectures" and the university named a dormitory in his honor.[50]

The lifting of the travel ban on Du Bois allowed him to visit China, the Soviet Union, and other lands; the warm and excited receptions he received abroad increased his stature in the United States, as it revealed to the uninformed that he was a world figure of heroic proportion. Thus, when Harry Belafonte, Jackie Robinson, and Sidney Poitier of the African American Students Foundation sought to raise money for Kenyan students to study in the United States, they requested the advice and aid of Du Bois. Symbolic of the changing line on Du Bois was the awarding, in 1960, of an honorary degree to him by the same President Martin Jenkins of Morgan State who in the early 1950s had capitulated to Cold War pressure and reneged on inviting him to the campus for a commencement address.[51]

This increasingly popular recognition of Du Bois did not blunt his sharp tongue and trenchant sociopolitical analyses. In the *National Guardian,* he did not backtrack away from the new militance, confessing unabashedly, "of course I am especially uplifted by the revolt of Negro students in America"; this militance was necessary because Blacks faced not only "lynching, mob-law . . . poverty and disease" but also a "daily, unending series of petty, senseless insults carried out almost everywhere." Nor were alleged allies spared his spear: "Already in New York alone we have four 'African' organizations financed by Big Business and officered by Negroes supposed to give 'information' on Africa." Weeks after the sit-in movement had broken out on February 1, 1960, in North Carolina, Du Bois was on the scene witnessing his ideological disciples, as he told the future Communist party leader Ishmael Flory: "We have just returned from Johnson C. Smith College in Charlotte, North Carolina, where I spoke to the Association of Negro Deans and saw some of the student sit-ins. It was a very inspiring trip." Du Bois' remarks to this gathering reflected the inspiration, as he discussed matters domestic and foreign. He observed that with the advent of voting rights and other forms of equality, the end of the problem is not met "but a beginning of even more difficult problems of race and culture" would be emerging. He also reminded them that from 1950 to 1958 he was unable to get a passport and travel. Those upset with sit-ins were no doubt displeased with his plea for radicalism and his urging of educators to visit the Soviet Union and teach what they learn, "even if they lose their jobs."[52]

The dissolving of the stain attached to Du Bois meant that invitations to speak, awards, and the like would be showered on him, notably in the post-1957 period. It also meant that civil rights leaders would increasingly seek him out for advice and assistance. This was the case in March 1960 when the embattled Dr. C. O. Simpkins of the United Christian Movement of Shrevesport asked Du Bois about the United Nations petition of 1947 and its applicability to the situation in Louisiana and the South. Du Bois referred him to the NAACP for the document and added words of encouragement to the civil rights leader. Similarly, when Martin Luther King, Jr., was arrested around the same time, it was not surprising that Du Bois would receive an appeal for funds. Du Bois was a frequent guest at New York solidarity gatherings with the southern crusaders, for example, at a reception for SCEF and at a reception in late 1960 for Ruby Shuttlesworth in Brooklyn.[53]

Evidence of Du Bois' popularity was rife in the 1960s. L. R. Perkins, field representative of the United Negro College Fund, sent Du Bois a copy of a speech made by Dr. Harlan Hatcher, president of the University of Michigan, at a UNCF kick-off dinner where he liberally referred to Du Bois' *Souls of Black Folk.* The Fisk president asked him for information and pictures to be posted in the dorm in honor of his being named "Alumnus of the Week." At Houston's Texas Southern University, Du Bois was asked to participate "with a deep sense of pride" in a tribute to their president Dr. W. R. Banks, who the once-scorned radical had instructed in college. Times had changed and Du Bois, in these changed times, was being courted enthusiastically. Alpha Phi Alpha of Morehouse, students at Amherst College, and others stood in line to request Du Bois' presence. Along with Nkrumah, he was asked to address the All-African Students Conference in London—a request that got them into hot water with the United States and Britain.[54]

His growing popularity was not limited to the campuses. John Procope, future head of the National Newspaper Publishers Association and future publisher of the *Amsterdam News,* invited Du

Bois to address the Bedford Branch YMCA Club, a luncheon club for business and professional men. Du Bois' fraternity, Alpha Phi Alpha, honored Du Bois, along with Channing Tobias and Lester Granger. Clarence B. Jones, yet another future publisher of the *Amsterdam News,* and civil rights lawyer Arthur Kinoy, who were drafting a law review article, asked Du Bois for his comments and expressed the view of many who were then sparking the civil rights battles of the South: "Since every writer on civil rights owes his inspiration to you for your pioneer work, we would be deeply appreciative of receiving, if you have the time, any of your thoughts, comments or criticisms of the article."[55]

Du Bois' increased popularity did not abate his often bitter critiques of Black politics and leadership. He refused to bite his tongue:

> The Robesons can hardly come to America just now . . . King, Abernathy and Shuttlesworth lack intelligent interest in colonialism. The people connected with CORE are doing good work but largely confined to the South. Mordecai Johnson is not willing to take any further steps beyond that which he has taken. Mercer Cook is in the pay of the State Department. Killens and Baldwin are good material but if they go [too] far will lose their chance to earn a living by writing. Hughes is quite impossible. Randolph is a red-baiter. Ben Davis is a brave man but quite alone without means of earning a living and what Howard Thurman really believes I have never been able to find out. Yet, in the long run and not too far off, people like these are going to be driven into some sort of unity.

This unalloyed militance did not alienate him from the larger Black community, as some have maintained, but, if anything, solidified his ties with the surging combativeness of the civil rights movement. A letter from Janet Stevenson was indicative of his effect on the civil rights protesters. She described the 1960 Democratic National Convention in Los Angeles and the militant effect of the "Nashville and Montgomery" elements on it, a militance traceable to Du Bois: "Come back before we all get too worn out. I mean come back here and pump us up again." This militance was also evidenced when the NAACP leader from North Carolina, Robert Williams, was forced to go underground after he was alleged to have used weapons and engaged in a kidnapping. He was rapidly repudiated by the NAACP leadership but when the FBI came to Du Bois' home looking for Williams, they did not give him away though Shirley, and presumably Du Bois, knew he was "safe in Canada."[56]

One of Du Bois' last political acts before his departure for Africa is representative of why he continued to be venerated among Blacks. His petition, drafted for President John F. Kennedy in February 1961, stated the present problems of Blacks and outlined their future demands. He requested an end to discrimination, appointment of a Black to a cabinet post "to be known as Secretary of Civil Rights," special aid to "Negro Ghettoes," an end of aid to all segregated colleges and universities, the calling of a national "End Segregation Conference," cancellation of contracts with discriminatory government contractors, full voting rights, an end to housing discrimination, the ordering of all federal agencies to end discrimination, the acceptance of all recommendations of the United States Civil Rights Commission concerning racial discrimination, and so on. This distillation of one of his last expressions on civil rights was far from being outlandish and, in actuality, was firmly in accord with the movement of the day.[57]

The factors that contributed to a more favorable assessment of Du Bois were synergistic and interactive, that is, United States competition for the hearts and minds of the colored world was hampered by racism at home and unappreciated by this increasingly decolonized world that saw an option in socialism; this in turn gave a boost to the civil rights movement and necessitated a lessening in restrictions on Du Bois, which created favorable conditions for an improvement of his public image. Jake Miller, in his *The Black Presence in American Foreign Affairs,* commented on Du Bois' singular impact on this area:[58]

> While it appeared that the words of the controversial Black scholar had had a very minor impact upon foreign policy-makers, his status among Blacks, both in and out of the United States, caused the American Government to view him with great concern. In the attempt to minimize the influence of Du Bois, American policy-makers were willing to listen more attentively to the demands of more "moderate" Blacks—although yielding very little on matters of substance.

Anne Braden, one of the more prolific writers and determined activists of the era, who admits to Du Bois' sizeable impact on her own life, has spoken of how the elderly radical and other Blacks similarly inclined, were the force that broke the back of McCarthyism: "For in truth it was the new Black liberation movement—arising in Montgomery . . . that broke the pall of the 1950's. . . . The beginning of the end of HUAC came . . . when it was foolish enough to go South in 1958 and attack people active in the civil rights movement." The May 1960 turbulent student demonstration against HUAC was "inspired by the Black students who had launched the sit-in movement in the South." By the time of Montgomery in 1955, "radical organizations of Blacks—and those that brought Black and white together . . . had been destroyed," for example, SNYC, NNLC, PP, SCHW, CAA, etc. The wiping out or handcuffing of such experienced cadre meant that those who rose to leadership, from SCLC to SNCC, were relatively youthful and politically inexperienced—despite the continuity of the cadre from these groups—E. D. Nixon, James Dombrowski, Charles Gomillion, Anne Braden, and others. In addition to HUAC, aiming fire at the movement was Senator James Eastland's investigating committee, state investigating committees like LUAC in Louisiana, FUAC in Florida, the Georgia Education Commission, the Mississippi Sovereignty Commission, and so on. "All of them went after the civil rights movement, labeling it as Communist [which] enabled the Southern segregationists to tie their knots to [a] national windstorm. It made it possible for them to pose not as defenders of a corrupt Southern way of life . . . but as guardians of the national security and all that was patriotic." Most importantly, this complicated the left's aligning with the civil rights movement and hindered the movement's move left.[59]

This tangled melange of factors was compounded by the widespread acceptance by many liberals of the precepts of anticommunism and the extravagant financing of the right wing by affluent businessmen. Inevitably this affected the pace, direction, and gains of the civil rights movement. Charles Alexander has observed that "after 1952, for the first time since the depression era, overall black income began to decline in relation to white income. . . . In the period 1957–1960 the Department of Justice brought only ten suits to secure voting rights for black people." Allan Wolk has acknowledged the "wide gap between the law as written and actual compliance with it." This was because, he says, the civil rights forces' "achievements in the administrative area of civil rights enforcement have been quite limited in comparison to their success in the legislative realm." Whatever the case, the anticommunist strategies pursued by the NAACP, the leading civil rights organization, was a drag on the entire movement, even leading to demonstrators rotting in jail because of a reluctance to align with the progressive National Lawyers Guild. Unavoidably, the NAACP was supplanted by SCLC as the engine of the movement. The backward political attitudes of Walter White's mate, the white South African Poppy Cannon—viewed by some as the First Lady of the civil rights movement—symbolized much of what was wrong with the civil rights forces. And, correspondingly, for many of the SCLC and SNCC activists, Du Bois symbolized much of what was right with the movement.[60]

CHAPTER 18

Du Bois as an Intellectual Force

Du Bois' ultimate significance during the Cold War may be counted as an intellectual and political force on a generation of intellectuals and political activists. The previous chapters should have made this fairly clear, but just as some have portrayed Du Bois as alienated from the civil rights movement, many of these same elements have pictured him as isolated from the intellectual and political activists that flowered in the 1960s. During the Cold War era, for example, Elliott Rudwick claims that "only the far left continued to claim this man whom one observer described as a 'Prophet in Limbo.' " Francis Broderick, Rudwick's colleague, has termed Du Bois "a lonely and tragic Negro. Once a national audience, black and white, heard his plea for Negro equality. Now few listen and fewer still heed him." Another popularized view of Du Bois has been propagated by Harold Isaacs who has alleged that "Du Bois . . . had despaired twenty-five years before of winning through to Negro integration in American life." These ill-considered analyses are at war with the evidence. Most revealing is that in assessing why some may have turned away from Du Bois, all of these writers turn a blind eye to the machinations of HUAC, FBI, CIA, and other government arms whose analyses strangely echo theirs.[1]

The popular image of Du Bois as disseminated by these writers and others is worthy of evaluation. Herbert Aptheker, friend of Du Bois and a fellow historian, has spoken ill of the biographies of Du Bois by both Rudwick and Broderick. According to Aptheker, Du Bois' literary executor and former custodian of his papers, Broderick does not "give enough attention to impact upon a Negro of the indecencies and violence and constant pressures of a Jim Crow society." Like others, Broderick has devoted substantial attention to Du Bois' personality while not recognizing that the scholar was "given very much to shyness than to conceit." Moreover, Broderick does not note that Du Bois tended "to shy away from affiliations, committees, organizations, high positions—a feeling that all these require some compromise of individual principle." Aptheker's opinion is that Rudwick's effort is poorer than Broderick's. Rudwick blames the victim in excoriating Du Bois for publishing mostly in left journals after 1948, while ignoring pressure from on high that led to this result; most of all, Rudwick pushes the line of Du Bois' lost influence during the Cold War, which Aptheker adamantly rejects. The flawed views of Rudwick and Broderick have been perpetrated to the detriment of Du Bois and the evidence.[2]

Understandably, Du Bois was reluctant to allow Broderick to rummage through his files, when he was approached in 1951. Eight years later, Du Bois negatively evaluated Broderick's work in a letter to Dr. W. M. Brewer of the *Journal of Negro History.* He indicated a lack of completeness on Broderick's part which may help to explain the inadequacy of his understanding and his proselytizing of the myth of Du Bois' waning influence. August Meier, reviewing his friend Elliott Rudwick's book in *Crisis,* agrees with the view of Du Bois as an "arrogant, egotistical individualist" by throwing in his own language and calling him an "irascible and egotistical personality." Yet, writing in 1962—presumably when Du Bois' influence was at its nadir—Meier concedes, "he is now . . . despite his espousal of an unpopular ideology . . . even more than Martin Luther King a symbol of Negro aspirations and the Negro protest."[3]

Contemporary writers have varied in their evaluation of Du Bois. Writing, significantly, in the first issue of *Black Scholar*—the Rosetta Stone of contemporary Black intellectuals—Lenneal Henderson, Jr., called him, "the most discredited and maligned black scholar in the twentieth century." Why? "Perhaps because he identified with socialism and eventually joined the Communist Party." According to Henderson, a weakness of the scholarshiip on Du Bois is a lack of "examination of the role he actually played in predicting and pushing the modern civil rights movement." In sum, Du Bois "deserves the title of Father of Black Scholarship . . . Father of Pan-Africanism, Dean of the Civil Rights Movement . . . Leader of Black journalists . . . fathered what we know as Black Studies." James Turner, from the other shore, has scored Du Bois' "inconsistency," while pointing to a perceived evolution of his views.[4]

During the height of the Cold War, Daniel Wynn, who taught at Tuskeegee and was involved with Charles Gomillion, succinctly analyzed the disciples of Du Bois' thought:

> Followers of Dr. Du Bois . . . were found in most of the large cities of the North and East. Although they were very few, those that talked were very outspoken and well informed. Even those that were obviously not well educated were well informed.

One does not have to posit that Du Bois' opponents were not well informed in order to be impressed by Professor Wynn's point. George Murphy, then a special deputy in the Elks' national office also commented insightfully on possibly why a flaming radical like Du Bois would not be isolated among Blacks, contrary to the opinion of some:

> many progressives, some Negro progressives too, have never understood the Negro people's all-class attitude toward communism. As a persecuted and proscribed people they have been quite determined, it seems to me, to decide on the merits and demerits of Communism for themselves and they have done this, despite their being an island in a "white sea."

Murphy also spoke specifically to why a leftist like Du Bois would continue to be a major force, despite the malediction of him, by citing an anecdote from J. Finley Wilson, grand exalted ruler of the Improved, Benevolent and Protective Order of Elks of the World for over thirty years, being treated at John Hopkins Hospital by "Dr. Wilson," who says:

> "I have been asked to ask you whether you would [help] us to stop communistic influence among Negroes by going before the House Committee to testify against Paul Robeson and Dr. Du Bois. . . ." I said "why Doc . . . you got the wrong man. I'm just a little ole leader of a small group of colored boys

> and girls . . . but when you come to Mr. Robeson and Dr. Du Bois, well these men are so great I'm not even worthy to unlatch their shoelaces. They got Phi Beta Kappa keys, been all around the world and have got a lot of degrees too. My folks would run me ragged if I said anything against them."

Some analysts have not sufficiently recognized that simply because the rich and powerful would deprecate and blacklist Du Bois did not automatically mean that the Afro-American community would fall into line lockstep. If anything, the exact opposite effect would be more likely to occur with Blacks circling the wagon around the besieged, as happened in the 1960s during so many elections involving Adam Clayton Powell, Jr.[5]

The fact is that Du Bois had a tremendous effect on the Black scene, most notably the artistic community. It was not surprising that J. Finley Wilson would link Du Bois' name with that of Robeson, the artist cum revolutionary. Paul Robeson never hesitated to cite his intellectual and political debt to Du Bois. Personally, unlike the scholars who did not know him, Robeson found Du Bois "down-to-earth . . . [a] delightful and ready wit, a keen and mischievous sense of humor . . . [a] gay spontaneous laughter." Unlike his political opponents, Robeson found it "logical, and deeply moving" when Du Bois joined the Communist party. Like Du Bois, Robeson's image was shaped by government agencies, as the vice-consul in Accra-sponsored articles in *Crisis,* which fabricated an image similar to that forged of his elderly comrade—that is, that he moved sharply to the left out of bitterness and despair. But the viewpoint expressed in *Crisis* did not necessarily reflect the viewpoint of the Black masses. At the Cold War's apex in 1952, Senior Bishop W. J. Walls at the thirty-fourth quadrennial conference of the A.M.E. Zion Church, with 3,000 present, was quoted as saying: "Everyone here who is in favor of having Mr. Robeson's passport returned to him—stand up on your feet." According to a reporter, "Only two persons . . . remained seated." That the hero of Black masses, Paul Robeson, was influenced by Du Bois, speaks volumes about the scholar-activist's "isolation" during the Cold War.[6]

Perhaps the greatest Black women fiction writers of the twentieth century, Alice Childress and Lorraine Hansberry, both came under Du Bois' spell. Hansberry studied under Du Bois at the Marxist Jefferson School, worked as a journalist at Robeson's newspaper *Freedom,* and kept in touch with him after she had attained success as a playwright. Alice Childress, before achieving prominence as a novelist, was an actress of some note, who also was a scribe with *Freedom.* Indicative of the ties between Du Bois and the artistic community was the "Cultural Reception in Honor of Dr. Herbert Aptheker, Historian," organized by Childress and others. Among the special guests for this April 1953 event were Du Bois, Robeson, and the artist Charles White; hostesses included Mrs. Leon Bibb and Mrs. Sidney Poitier.[7]

Robeson, Childress, Hansberry, Sidney Poitier, Harry Belafonte, and others were all banded together in the Committee for the Negro in the Arts, an organization designed to press for Black rights in artistic fields. Earlier, Du Bois and Dorothy Parker had been involved in the Voice of Freedom Committee, which had a similar purpose of trying "to dramatize [the] shameful lack of adequate employment for Negroes in the radio industry." They conducted a "nation-wide poll to ascertain . . . whom the people would like to hear" on the networks and the result of this 1949 survey revealed that Mary McLeod Bethune, Robeson, and Du Bois were the names most cited. The Committee for the Negro in the Arts picked up where the Voice of Freedom left off and strove strenuously not only for more jobs but for better roles and positions for the Black artist. The committee was not unsuccessful in their efforts and attracted considerable support. At their March 5, 1952, brunch, Du Bois was the guest of honor. The committee was eventually destroyed and redbaited out of existence, like so many other progressive groups of the era. But it is ineradicable that its example of left influence on the arts was indicative of how Du Bois affected artists.[8]

New York was not the only site of Du Bois' impact on the artistic scene. In Chicago, the politically progressive Du Bois Theater Guild, brought within its ambit such talents as Oscar Brown, Jr., and Richard Durham, future official biographer of Muhammad Ali. Langston Hughes, in a book written on the NAACP at the Cold War's zenith that featured a foreword by Arthur Spingarn, did not budge from a pro-Du Bois position, citing his impact on manifold facets of Black life. In 1954, when association with him would bring sharp censure, Du Bois remained in contact with the Black intellectual and historian Lorenzo Greene and suggested that the publication he edited, the *Midwest Journal,* print a Louis Aragon comment on a poem by the Communist V. J. Jerome. It should not be assumed, however, that Du Bois' relationship with other

Black writers and intellectuals was not without incident and contradiction. In 1956, he sent a message to the First International Congress of Colored Writers in Paris that brought together sixty delegates from twenty-four nations, including Aime Cesairé, James Ivy, Mercer Cook, Horace M. Bond, Richard Wright, and other Afro-Americans sufficiently in the good graces of their governments to be awarded a passport. Du Bois' message to this meeting did not go over well with the United States delegation, since Du Bois accused those assembled of being bought. This message was simply one facet of a larger attack by Du Bois on anticommunism that swept up Black intellectuals, like Richard Wright. Wright openly admitted collaborating with the CIA-sponsored Congress for Cultural Freedom. Wright's stature as a leading Black writer and apostate led Du Bois to severely indict him, and in particular his best-selling book *Black Boy,* where Du Bois found "the Negroes whom he paints have almost no redeeming qualities" and that the "total picture" was unconvincing. At a time when *Crisis* was praising Wright's *The Outsider* as "the most shattering evidence against Communism yet recorded," Du Bois was reproaching Padmore for his praise of the writer's *Black Power:*[9]

> Naturally I did not like Richard Wright's book . . . his logic is lousy. He starts out to save Africa from Communism and then makes an attack on British capitalism which is devastating. How he reconciles these two attitudes I cannot see. . . . The Communists of America started him on his career. It is quite possible that some of them presumed on this help and tried to push him around. They, like most human beings, are often narrow and ignorant. But because of that to slur communism as such, to slander Russia, and above all, to spit on American Negroes is too much for an honest artist. Wright has great talent and his descriptions of West Africa are literature; but to write a book to attack Communism in Africa, when there has been no Communism in Africa, and when the degradation of Africa is due to Capitalism which Wright is defending—this is sheer contradiction.

Sheer contradiction also describes the relationship Du Bois had with intellectuals as disparate as Langston Hughes and Richard Wright.[10]

Du Bois' steady jabs at Wright and others who took the fashionable anticommunist route kept them off balance and hindered their gathering of further adherents. The fact that Du Bois, the premier Black intellectual, adopted such an uncompromising position was of substantial meaning and helped to create an atmosphere that allowed artists like William Marshall, Oscar Brown, Jr., Lorraine Hansberry, and others to run the risk of blacklisting and deprivation in order to align with the progressive movement. Du Bois was not omnipotent, however. The Black woman intellectual Pauli Murray tersely informed Du Bois when he reached out to her: "Would you be kind enough to have my name removed from your mailing list."

The revering of Du Bois among Black college presidents is well established; for example, Horace Mann Bond, president of Lincoln University—and no acolyte of communism—stated in 1948 that he "held" Du Bois in "great esteem."[11]

This kind of florid admiration from the Black scholarly community escalated after Cold War tensions lessened. John Hope Franklin, who Du Bois refused to denounce in the Lee Lorch affair, was a devoted admirer of the leftist leader and was not afraid to admit it. In 1956, on the occasion of his eighty-eighth birthday, the historian sent "heartiest birthday greetings. May you continue to live and thrive and be an inspiration to all of us who try to maintain the high standards of truth and honesty." He went public in 1957 in the pages of *Crisis,* a journal not so accustomed at this time to such grandiloquent praise of Du Bois: "It is W.E.B. Du Bois [who has been] . . . providing intellectual inspiration to a despairing people and charting the course for the future." Du Bois, said Franklin, "provided the grist for the Negro history mill." Dr. Elliott Skinner, future United States ambassador to Upper Volta, wrote Du Bois on May Day 1957:

> I want to see and speak to the person who started to fight for me before I was even born. You can even say that I want to make a pilgrimage to see, who is to my mind, one of the most important men in the world today. . . . I am the second Negro to be appointed to the faculty of Columbia University. I am sure that all this is possible only because people like you have struggled for our rights. My seeing you can spare me a great deal of embarrassment when, on any future trip to Africa, I am asked by a barely literate African whether I know one Dr. Du Bois.

Another Black West Indian Columbia University professor, Hollis Lynch, expressed similar admiration. While still a student, he corresponded with Du Bois in 1959 to 1960. At first he was interested in doing research on Du Bois' life for a thesis. Subsequently, like so many other eager students, he inquired of Du Bois about his influence on Nkrumah, Pan-Africanism, and so on. Professor Gwendolen Carter of Smith College, well-known Africanist, also sought out Du Bois to confer with him on similar topics.[12]

The evaluation of Du Bois by the Black community at large and his corresponding influence on them was substantial and conspicuous, before and after the Cold War. Certainly there were attempts to frighten Blacks and others away from Du Bois, and these tireless efforts were not totally unsuccessful; yet, only a crude obtuseness could not fathom the high regard in which Du Bois was held by Afro-Americans during his latter years. In 1947, Mervyn Dymally—presently a leader of the Congressional Black Caucus—had recently arrived from Trinidad, where he was secretary of the Press and Printers Union and sub-editor of the *Vanguard*, official organ of the Trinidad and Tobago Trades Union Council. Though he did not know him, one of the first persons he sought out was Du Bois for advice on his prospects in the United States. That same year, the United Negro and Allied Veterans of America, with Black hero Joe Louis as honorary commander and future Detroit mayor Coleman Young as vice commander, sought to make a political statement by honoring Du Bois. This action, as the Cold War was dawning, epitomized the clinging and rallying around Du Bois as a symbol of opposition.[13]

Du Bois' influence among Blacks was diverse and manifested itself in many ways. In a major study of the Black press, Roland E. Wolsley has noted his broad impact on this formidable institution. For example, in 1954, Mel Tapley of the relatively conservative *Amsterdam News* was so impressed with Du Bois' comments on *Brown* v. *Board of Education* that he sought to make a recording of it for mass distribution. Also indicative of the wide reach of Du Bois' influence was that he even had impact on Blacks—presumably conservative—who chose to throw their lot in with the administration. John Davis, director of Operations of the United States Mission in Liberia, in 1954, mentioned in birthday greetings how Du Bois had influenced him. From his vantage post as a teacher at the Jefferson School before it was shut down, Du Bois had the opportunity to impress his ideas on diverse personages from budding writers like Lorraine Hansberry to African students, many of whom later became leaders in their own countries.[14]

Again, one can detect the flowering of Du Bois' manifold impact in the mid- to late 1950s. On March 19, 1956—as the bus boycott raged—Martin Luther King, Jr., reached out to Du Bois after he had expressed solidarity with the struggle in Montgomery:

> This is just a note to express my deepest gratitude to you for your kind letter. Such letters from friends sympathetic with our momentous struggle for justice give us renewed vigor and courage to carry on.

One year later, George Edmund Haynes of National Urban League fame warmly approached Du Bois and frankly noted how the press of world events may have strongly swayed his words:[15]

> This note is to emphasize our love and admiration for you . . . we would like to come and visit you at home . . . Mrs. Haynes and I have thought and spoken of you and Mrs. Du Bois so often. Especially is this true in these days of world events coming to pass for which you worked and about which your eloquent voice and pen gave prophecy.

Du Bois was aware of his role as a leading intellectual force and his pen, particularly, was employed to point the way to others. In his review of his friend E. Franklin Frazier's book *Black Bourgeoisie,* a book he generally liked, he issued stringent criticism of the stratum he led. But Du Bois was also encouraging to intellectuals, as his review of Frazier's book shows and as is demonstrated in his foreword to W. Alphaeus Hunton's *Decision in Africa: Sources of Current Conflict.*[16]

The intellectual shadow of Du Bois reached not simply artists, scholars and civil rights leaders. In Baltimore, where he had maintained a home, there was a Du Bois Circle, which met the third Tuesday of each month. There were approximately thirty members, mostly women, all but three of whom were married. They studied his works and the works of others. This kind of popular sentiment for Du Bois reached an apogee in 1957 when a bronze sculptured head of Du Bois was presented to the Schomburg Library. Both Judge Jane Bolin and Van Wyck Brooks spoke at the presentation. The event received wide and favorable press coverage; even *Crisis* gave it full page coverage and hailed him as "founder of the *Crisis* magazine." This prepossession with Du Bois heightened as time wore on. In the spring of 1960 Howard Zinn, chair of the Department of History at Spelman College invited Du Bois there to speak: "how much enthusiasm there is among faculty and students here about the possibility that you might come." This included, said Zinn, faculty and others who were there during Du Bois' tenure. But since his unceremonious bouncing from Atlanta University in 1944, Du Bois had been loathe to return there, not to mention any of the Atlanta colleges. Hence, he told them that there was "small chance" that their wishes would be satisfied. It should not be assumed that the enthusiasm for Du Bois in Atlanta was replicated in all quarters. In 1959 a controversy erupted in the *Saturday Review* when Carl Rowan, in a review of Broderick's book, denounced Du Bois as an "irascible black racist." Rowan repeated the fabricated view perpetrated by Broderick and other anticommunists that Du Bois' bitterness at treatment accorded him by whites pushed Du Bois leftward. His friend L. D. Reddick protested and termed Rowan's review "maddening" but his words could not deflate that view set afloat and held aloft by influential forces.[17]

Du Bois did not just carry weight with Black artists, scholars, and intellectuals but with Euro-American ones as well. As such, his prestige in these circles was high. Marshall Field called Du Bois "one of the great Americans of our generation." Just as Black veterans had honored Du Bois in 1947, Du Bois was informed, "you have been unanimously selected by the National Administrative Committee of the American Veterans Committee as 'AVC Man of the Year for 1948.' " Going further, Van Wyck Brooks effusively termed Du Bois a "truly Jeffersonian figure, as thinker, scholar, teacher and writer . . . one of those men who unite great charm of personality with depth of intellect."[18]

Du Bois was a well-respected figure among the hearty band of left and progressive students brave enough to raise their voices during an epoch of conformity. He spoke frequently in their fora, be it the National Lawyers Guild-Student Division, Young Progressives of America, Labor Youth League, and so on. After a lecture in Eric Goldman's class, the Princeton professor thanked him profusely: "your lecture has certainly left a profound impression on the students who heard you . . . how thoroughly stimulating they found your remarks." His impact extended throughout the

Cold War. In 1952, he addressed the National Student Conference for Academic Freedom at the University of Wisconsin. In 1960, after an urgent appeal from organizers, he agreed to lend his name to the new left journal *Studies on the Left.* Frankly, they told Du Bois: "We . . . want to borrow some of your prestige to help us make the journal self-supporting." As Richard W. Evans' major study indicates, this publication had a sizeable effect on younger leftist historians; Eugene Genovese, James Weinstein, and Staughton Lynd all served as editors. Bettina Aptheker, one of the leaders of the student rebellion at Berkeley in 1964, studied at the knee of Du Bois during her years in Brooklyn and was not an infrequent correspondent.[19]

Du Bois was not only an aid to leftist scholars and writers. When Orlando Ward, United States Army Major-General and Military History Chief, was working on *The U.S. Army in World War II* series, he did not hesitate to forward to Du Bois for comment the draft of a volume entitled *The Employment of Negro Troops in World War II;* remarkably, this took place in August 1950 at a time when the United States Secretary of State was frequently lashing Du Bois in the press because of his antiwar efforts. Equally striking was the inquiry at the same time from John Russell of the United States Office of Education's Federal Security Agency requesting a Du Bois recommendation in filling the specialist for higher education of Negroes vacancy. August Meier, ideologically distant from Du Bois, still sought Du Bois' advice in researching the point about Booker T. Washington owning and subsidizing Black newspapers. Eleanor Flexner, when seeking information on Black women for an upcoming book, contacted Du Bois.[20]

Du Bois was a bulwark of assistance for students, especially after the thaw of Geneva. Lawrence Howard, doing a dissertation at Harvard on United States foreign policy toward Africa in the 1945 to 1952 period, tried to draw on Du Bois' wealth of practical and theoretical knowledge in this area. Kathleen Long, a graduate student at Bryn Mawr, consulted with Du Bois on Wilson's policy toward Blacks. Harvey Wachtel received Du Bois' assistance in doing his honor's thesis at Howard on George Washington Carver, as did Nathaniel Tillman, Jr. The difficulties of many of these students was neatly encapsulated by Eugene Genovese. In 1955 he told Du Bois that "members of the history department at Columbia are something less than adequate in economics and the economics department is not at all interested in history, at least of the Old

South." He complained of being "hampered by having to use the definitions and concepts of Weber rather than of Marx . . . discretion being the better part of valor, it would be best to omit direct mention of Marx's work." Du Bois took time out to criticize his master's essay for its "entire omission . . . of all reference to the domestic slave trade in the South"; he recommended the work of Frederic Bancroft to him and added, "your dependence on Weber, while defensive, is too great." In the spring of 1956, Genovese returned to the issue at hand: "following your advice, I greatly reduced the dependence on Weber and tried to relate the essay more directly to Marx." Du Bois' influence on this would-be Marxist was clear. But this was one aspect of his enormous effect on leftist writers of the era generally.[21]

Creative writers did not escape the grasp of Du Bois either. Henry Miller was frank about this, as he told Carey McWilliams: "When I was a very young man I attended his lectures, read his books. I owe a great deal to him—he was one of the truly deep influences in my life." Until his apostasy and defection from politics, Du Bois was quite friendly with Howard Fast. They collaborated on a number of projects and worked closely together. He wrote a foreword for *Freedom Road* and called *Spartacus* "a most unusual and fascinating work of art." Du Bois was close to the Council of Arts, Sciences and Professions and in 1951 was asked to serve as honorary chairman of the Writing and Publishing Division; this provided him the opportunity and vantage point to influence many a writer. In October 1959, Truman Capote turned to Du Bois when he needed help in getting to the People's Republic of China. This was an example of both the changing political times and Du Bois' sizeable impact.[22]

And his sizeable impact was manifested and translated mostly through his intellectual endeavors—writing and public speaking. He rarely spoke extemporaneously and most often from a prepared detailed text; even the speech he gave on the most current topic had an historical aspect. As for his writings, their popularity with the publishing houses ebbed and flowed along with the vicissitudes of the Cold War. Du Bois worked long and hard on a provocative, thoughtful book on the Soviet Union that never saw the light of day. Weeks after the war against Korea had broken out, Robert Firoux, of Harcourt, Brace and Company, brusquely informed him: "We do not find your book the balanced interpretation we had hoped. . . . It seems to us an uncritical apology for Soviet Russia and an excessive condemnation of the United States." A few days later Du Bois conceded to Jessica Smith, editor of *Soviet Russia Today:* "The Korean War not only held up but frightened my proposed publishers."[23]

An examination of this book is important for the light that it sheds on Du Bois' intellectual and ideological development up to 1950. He had asked Herbert Aptheker to review it and Aptheker approached it with caution: "My remarks are made with deference." Du Bois had written, "Socialism is state control of industry through a planned economy." Aptheker, a Communist in good standing, took sharp issue with this analysis: "This typifies . . . a serious error and one which recurs throughout the MS—i.e., ignoring of the class character of society. The facing of the question—who owns the state." He blasted Du Bois' assertion that Nazism "adopted theoretically" Soviet policy. "Another complete error," Aptheker countered, which "stems from a failure to probe . . . the question [of] . . . fascism as the opposite of socialism." Aptheker continued his searing indictment. "I disagree strongly" with the notion of placing the "onus of failure of democracy . . . on ignorance and lethargy of voters. . . . Who is responsible for ignorance; who is responsible for lethargy? Is lethargy altogether bad in the face of lack of reality of choice? Ignorant of what?—of their real needs, or of the surface posing and demogogic characteristic of our elections as conducted by major parties?" In rapid fire fashion, Aptheker shot down other points made by Du Bois. Du Bois alleged that "wages must be taken from profits." Aptheker replied sharply, "no—profits [are] taken from labor." On another point, the historian doubted the contentment of the Japanese working class. On the central point of the study, Aptheker was adamant: "May one with full confidence assert that most Americans wanted Russia to lose early in World War II—doubt it—certainly most of the press did but doubt that most of the people did." Du Bois had said also: "Russia is not today a democracy and elections are influenced by the Communist Party." Aptheker: "This seems to me to be a non-sequitur." Despite these pointed barbs tossed by his friend, Du Bois' work was nonetheless extraordinary for attempting to present a balanced view of the Soviet Union, distilled from decades of experience with this land. Aptheker himself was unequivocal on this score, "as for the work as a whole, my one fear is that it is much too good and clean to gain publication in our country today. I hope I'm wrong." Yet, Aptheker's critique points up not only the intellectual influence he had on Du Bois but, as well, the patriarch's departures from Marxism-Leninism at a late stage in his career.[24]

From Johannesburg the Indian author and journalist P. S. Joshi praised his *The World and Africa.* In 1955, the Reverend Stephen Frichtman of Los Angeles sent him a copy of his January 23 sermon on "the challenge of Africa," which relied heavily—"great dependence" were the pastor's words—on Du Bois' book so heavily praised by Joshi.[25]

In 1955, Du Bois approached Dr. A. M. Townsend, secretary of the Sunday School Publishing Board of the National Baptist Convention about the printing of a jubilee edition of *The Souls of Black Folk.* He refused, but this demonstrates that contrary to the assertion of some, how Du Bois first turned to Black and center organizations before seeking out other sources, inevitably left. There was still a demand for this classic that Du Bois estimated in 1953 had gone through twenty editions and had sold nearly 100,000 copies. In 1957, Du Bois received word that Presence Africaine-Editions Africains would publish the entire book and Temps Modernes would publish excerpts. Earlier another correspondent from Western Europe, Giongiacomo Feltrinelli of Milan expressed a similar interest and also, after noting John Oliver Killens' *Youngblood,* asked Du Bois "to propose [to] us young Negro writers who are now emerging." This foreign interest in Du Bois' writings was widespread, his works being translated in India, China, the Soviet Union, and elsewhere. This interest abroad was matched by a corresponding lack of domestic interest—except in certain leftist circles. After the *New Republic, Harper's, Atlantic Monthly, Saturday Review,* and others had turned thumbs down on articles written on his worldwide journey of 1958, Jessica Smith of *Soviet Russia Today* expressed interest.[26]

Lawrence Lader, in his *Power on the Left: American Radical Movements Since 1946,* has commented on the NAACP's treatment of Du Bois during this period: "The NAACP harassed him further by prohibiting local branches from sponsoring his lectures and pressuring black newspapers to turn down his articles and boycott his name." They were not altogether successful in this. In fact, they were not altogether successful in accomplishing this goal in their own journal, *Crisis.* He was too highly regarded among Blacks to be totally ignored or subjected to a total hatchet job. In the fortieth anniversary issue of *Crisis* in 1951, Roy Wilkins paid homage to Du Bois' editing of the journal. When they sought to sell past bound volumes, they did not hesitate to advertise Du Bois prominently as being among the contributors. In 1953, Wilson Record published in the *Crisis* his usual pastiche of half and quarter truths on the "Role of the Negro Intellectual"; he approached Du Bois gingerly, noting his "fine moral courage and scientific sociology." But in 1954 Arthur Spingarn, in his annual review of books by Black authors, noted the reprint of Du Bois' book on the African slave trade; he castigated Du Bois' alleged unclear view of the class struggle for income and power.[27]

Particularly after Ghana's independence, the varying kaleidoscope of hostility, diffidence, and friendliness toward Du Bois was transmuted into the latter factor. In May 1958, an article by Du Bois appeared in the pages of *Crisis* for the first time in years. He reviewed Abram Harris' *Economics and Social Reform* and did not equivocate in criticizing it. In the previous issue of *Crisis,* a full page picture of Du Bois was featured and, lest anyone had forgotten, identified him as founder-editor of the journal. In an article exploring the NAACP's history, Du Bois was pictured as "the brilliant leader of the 'talented tenth.' " In an innocuous article penned by former NAACP official August Meier on Du Bois' ideological development, he was praised as "one of the famous trio of Negro leaders," along with Booker T. Washington and Frederick Douglass.[28]

Crisis was a major shaper of the intellectual firepower of the Black community and being the organ of a mass organization is more useful than the Black press as a measure for determining the perception of Du Bois; given its conservatism and latterly positive attitude toward Du Bois, it becomes even more useful to examine the journal. Though Broderick may have looked at Du Bois as a "prophet in limbo," *Crisis,* when it reviewed his biography, tended to see Broderick as the one in "limbo." It was termed a "disappointment," characterized by "unevenness." The reviewer delicately handled Du Bois' leftism: "Though Du Bois' star of destiny was to lead him through the camps of . . . the NAACP, Socialism and Communism, he was never anyone's disciple but his own." In 1961, after he had left the United States, he was termed "the most internationally distinguished alumnus of Fisk University." He was lauded as "the noted Negro scholar." In 1962, a *Crisis* article went so far as to criticize certain Blacks for being "ashamed to speak of such great Negroes as W.E.B. Du Bois and Paul Robeson."

Perhaps emboldened by his good press in *Crisis,* Du Bois decided to reestablish contact with the NAACP board; he requested that they mark the centenaries of Dred Scott, John Brown, and the Emancipation Proclamation. The NAACP did not take up Du Bois' suggestions but *Crisis'* treatment of him from the mid-1950s onward calls into question the notion of his abject isolation from Afro-Americans. His voluminous writings and numerous speaking engagements alone help to refute this assertion.[29]

Du Bois is known mostly for his nonfiction writings but during the 1950s he spent an inordinate amount of his time—"four or five hours a day"—writing a trilogy of novels that attained a modicum of popularity. Du Bois considered *Black Reconstruction* his most important book and had spent most of his writing time on history and sociology projects. But he had long been attracted to fiction and had once told Professor R. B. Garrett of Bradley University, "I certainly hope you will not learn [to write] like a social scientist, for most social scientists I know are unable to write." So, he used this trilogy—*The Ordeal of Mansart, Mansart Builds A School,* and *Worlds of Color*—to weave a complex tapestry of United States history from the nineteenth century to the present. Through the vehicle of fiction, he attempted to convey his political ideas to that vast audience which perhaps did not read history but soaked up novels. Du Bois, through his trilogy, subtly attempted to link the fates of the Soviets and Afro-Americans, the early years of the NAACP, Blacks, and trade unions, socialism and the Communist party. Though certainly not runaway best sellers, as one of the few Black novelists of that era and as a monumentally influential public figure, of necessity these novels carried weight and reached an audience that otherwise might have missed his message.[30]

Though his trilogy were works of fiction, Du Bois approached their sale and distribution like the political works they in fact were. His numerous speaking engagements were used to sell these books, as they were frequently on display in the halls where he spoke. Hence, he was using fiction to build the movement and inform, similar to how *In Battle for Peace* was used to strengthen peace forces. A list of organizations, political parties, and unions was developed worldwide for contact about sales. With George Murphy as his assistant, he sought out a publisher; Murphy insisted, "this book must come from a Negro publisher." He mentioned a number of lawyers, doctors, and judges, including Dr. Henry A. Callis (founder of Alpha Phi Alpha), who might be inclined to help fund publication. According to Murphy, this development would "once more resume the even tenor of his way in believing that middle class Negro folk are not all such a bad lot." But this optimism was a bit premature. The Association of Negro Life and History was approached but to no avail. Thus, Du Bois was forced to turn left toward Joseph Felshin, Herbert Aptheker, and Mainstream Publishers.[31]

The mainstream was not totally recalcitrant here, as one colleague offered him a mailing list of 1,500, including nearly fifty libraries. But it was Mainstream that performed yeoman service in publishing and promoting the trilogy. Du Bois complained about his work not being in stores: "Of course . . . this is a matter not of advertising, but of keeping certain books from being published and certain authors from being read." Thus, despite the energetic promotional efforts of Aptheker and Felshin, Du Bois sadly reported to Leo Huberman that the *Ordeal of Mansart* "has sold poorly, perhaps 1500 copies, and has not been reviewed by any respectable publication." Du Bois was angry, and not just at the ruling class, about the disappointing sales.[32]

Perhaps one reason for the disappointing sales was the novels' appeal as creative fiction. Truman Nelson, in the *National Guardian,* was critical: "It is not . . . 'fictiony' enough. There is not enough of minute description of purely external experience, of faces, clothes, gestures, the tones of individual voices, the shifting scenes in which the characters and occurrences germinate." Some readers may have been put off by this alleged quirk, others by political biases; James Ivy said that *Worlds of Color* was an "over-simplification." Nevertheless, critical comment was generally favorable. Alice Childress, a woman with credentials in the field, was quite complimentary: "The writing was beautiful, the characters were exciting and the work held me from beginning to end." Van Wyck Brooks found *The Ordeal of Mansart* "absorbingly interesting." Eslanda Robeson in the *National Guardian* found *The Ordeal of Mansart* "a book of very great importance in our time," powered by "insight . . . clarity . . . [and] enormous scholarship." J. Saunders Redding praised *Mansart* in the *Afro-American.* A review of Du Bois' fiction in *Crisis* brought forth this analysis of his history as fiction: "Dr. Du Bois has seen it and he has so importantly influenced it."[33]

One of the more provocative analyses of Du Bois' trilogy is by Keith Eldon Byerman. He termed the trilogy "the most complicated, if not sophisticated, of his writings." On Du Bois' controversial views, as expressed in his novels and elsewhere, Byerman concurs with the position that it was not so much that Du Bois had changed—as Broderick, Rudwick, and others have maintained—but more so that the times in which he lived had changed: "The difficulty that Du Bois faced, then, was not the novelty of the stance he took; it was rather the historical circumstances in which he took it."[34]

Du Bois' trilogy may have received a not too promising reception, as Byerman indicates, because of the historical times. This may not have been true for his play *Black Man and the Moon.* Arnold Perl, of the Carnegie Hall Playhouse, turned it down because "it made more interesting reading than performing. I doubt its value as a play on stage." Even V. S. Bogatyrev, chief of the American Department of the USSR Society for Cultural Relations with Foreign Countries, was unfavorable. Bluntly and candidly he told Du Bois, it was not suitable.[35]

Though his fiction received mixed reviews, Du Bois' efforts in the area of journalism were better received. He was associated as a writer and in other capacities with three independent publishing efforts—*People's Voice, National Guardian, Freedom* (and its lineal descendant *Freedomways*). The *People's Voice* was a Harlem-based newspaper; Doxey Wilkerson served as editor and Max Yergan as president, with Adam Clayton Powell, Jr., also playing a leading role. Initially the paper was fervently opposed to the red scare and attacks on Communists. Most articles, amidst tons of ads for hair straighteners, stores, and restaurants, were progressively slanted. Du Bois wrote a regular column called "Pan-Africa" on African events with an accompanying map of the continent. Indicative of the paper's breadth and slant was a column by Lena Horne heavily praising the writer Howard Fast, then under attack by anticommunists, and another by popular Black actress Fredi Washington execrating HUAC. But after the red scare got underway, the leftist Wilkerson was discharged as editor and Du Bois' regular column was ended—and not long thereafter so did the paper.[36]

Freedom was another recipient of Du Bois' pen and time. Because of the leading role played by Paul Robeson, the paper was able to attract the cream of Black artistic talent. Sidney Poitier, Harry Belafonte, William Marshall, Alice Childress, Beulah Richardson, Donald McKayle, and Charles White were featured at the paper's first anniversary celebration. John Henrik Clarke, Kenneth Clark, and Oscar Brown, Jr., were among the contributors. Robert

Williams, then a student at Johnson C. Smith College and before fame was thrust on him for his armed resistance of racist whites, was also a contributor. John Oliver Killens wrote for the paper and condemned Ralph Ellison's *Invisible Man* for redbaiting. Lorraine Hansberry wrote articles supportive of Labor Youth League leader Roosevelt Ward and other piquant subjects. She was one of the more uncompromising leftists on the staff, scoring Richard Wright's *The Outsider* for anticommunism and Langston Hughes' book for children for omitting the names of Du Bois and Robeson. Thus, during the height of the Cold War, a bevy of Black talent—many of whom played key roles during the civil rights upsurge of the 1960s—surrounded Du Bois and Robeson at *Freedom*, contradicting the notion of their isolation; and when the paper was forced to close in the mid-1950s, these Black talents spread their artistic messages—laced with Du Bois' influence—across the country.[37]

Shirley Graham, who also played a leading role with *Freedom*, explained that from its embers there arose like a phoenix *Freedomways*, a quarterly still publishing. Du Bois was frequently invited to give advice and counsel to this publication, which he gave generously. *Freedomways* became not only a major cultural but a political force as well.[38]

The *National Guardian*, a leftist weekly begun in the late 1940s, was another beneficiary of Du Bois' time and thought. He began writing for the paper in 1948 and, as the founders Cedric Belfrage and James Aronson stated in their memoir, he "introduced our first Negro History Week section and, in our first financial crisis [helped out]. . . . In all, he wrote 130 articles for the *Guardian* in fifteen years. Almost no one else would publish him." Not only did he write for the paper but, similar to his other efforts, he acted in other capacities, in this case as fund administrator. Belfrage and Aronson have spoken in detail of Du Bois' multifaceted role. He also served on the Board of Trustees and exercised a "dictatorship" over speakers at their various political and fundraising efforts. They recognized that Du Bois did not agree with every word printed in the paper, but they praised his lack of sectarianism. Du Bois continued to be a close associate of Belfrage after he was deported, he acted as forwarding agent, sending him material in Europe. Despite frequent attacks, the *Guardian* remained an authoritative paper that was able to achieve a none too piddling circulation of over 29,000 weekly in 1959. Through all his journalistic efforts, just as in his fiction efforts, Du Bois was striving to get across his partisan political viewpoint on the Cold War, Pan-African liberation, and socialism.[39]

Further evidence of Du Bois' influential reach and lack of isolation during the Cold War were the celebrations surrounding his ninetieth birthday in 1958. Public affairs marking the event were held in New York City and in Chicago. Messages of greetings were received from across the globe. Dr. Nnamdi Azikiwe, Prime Minister of Eastern Nigeria; V. V. Kuznetsov, deputy Foreign Minister of the Soviet Union; Cheddi Jagan, premier of British Guyana; and Mayor Richard Daley of Chicago were among those congratulating Du Bois. This message from the mayor is significant, for most certainly it was sent not as a result of ideological compatibility with Du Bois but because of pressure from the Afro-American community. Messages were received from the presidents of a number of Black colleges, including Langston, Fisk, Philander Smith, St. Augustine's, Livingstone, Morehouse, LeMoyne, Shaw, Tennessee State, Spelman, Tuskeegee, and others. The Chicago celebration was particularly noteworthy. The sponsoring committee included Earl Dickerson, Truman Gibson, Dr. St. Clair Drake, Judge Fred Slater, and future Congressional Black Caucus member Gus Savage. Du Bois did not pull back from his political beliefs at this gathering, defending communism and the Soviet Union. Even the NAACP got involved in this effort. The New York celebration was equally extraordinary with 2,000 in attendance at the Hotel Roosevelt. John Hope Franklin spoke and acknowledged the debt he and other scholars owed to Du Bois.[40]

These birthday celebrations were just the beginning of a flood of Black press coverage on Du Bois. The *Afro-American* covered the New York dinner and even *The New York Times* could not ignore it. When he spoke at Howard University, the Veterans of Foreign Wars protested but the school administration did not retreat; the *Pittsburgh Courier* headlined "Socialism is Inevitable—Du Bois" and reported that 800 persons packed the Howard University chapel. The press took notice when on the seventieth anniversary of his 1888 graduation, Fisk had an annual lectureship named in Du Bois' honor and they wrote of the NAACP's snub of him during their fiftieth anniversary. The *Afro-American* gave page one coverage to his return from Europe and later pictured him at a Washington reception with Premier Nikita Khrushchev of the Soviet Union.[41]

This explains why any portrayal of Du Bois as a prophet in limbo during his latter years shows an abysmal and perhaps willful ignorance of the evidence. Afro-Americans knew that Du Bois was a world figure who had clout, who was sought out by Mao Zedong, Cheddi Jagan, Kwame Nkrumah, Nikita Khrushchev, and other world leaders. His lack of recognition in the white press, ironically, only certified in many minds that he was on the right track. The bloody history of racism in this country has undoubtedly created a certain nationalism among Blacks that tends to reject those who are too cozy with the power brokers of this country. Hence, scholars like John Hope Franklin, artists like Lorraine Hansberry, intellectuals like Alain Locke, continued to look to Du Bois for leadership, no matter the opinion of the swells and those whites affiliated with them.

Meeting with Soviet Premier Nikita Khrushchev in Moscow, 1959

CHAPTER 19

Du Bois and Foreign Affairs

Du Bois' unyielding opposition to the main direction of United States foreign policy—an opposition not universally accepted in the United States during his time—may help explain why some have portrayed him in his later years as a prophet in limbo. His tireless labor for world peace and African liberation are well established. But the fact is that opposition to colonialism, imperialism, and worldwide racism was quite strong in the Afro-American community—so strong that even the NAACP had to at least pay lip service to it. Du Bois' long years of international experience and recognized international stature meant that his foreign policy views would be given increasing respect among Black and progressive forces, domestically and internationally.[1]

To a certain extent Du Bois was not plowing new ground in pushing his radical foreign policy course, since the Black community had historically been to the left of other sectors of the United States polity on these issues. He perceived an intimate connection with the court victories of the NAACP and the international situation:

> No such decision[s] would have been possible without the world pressure of communism led by the Soviet Union. It was simply impossible for the United States to continue to lead a "Free World" with race segregation kept legal over a third of its territory.

Though it may be surprising to some, this was a view basically in accord with that of the NAACP leadership and its allies; shortly after White had passed away in 1955, a memorial to him underlined this: "He always stressed the influence of foreign relations upon domestic problems, racial, and otherwise." Walter Reuther, speaking at the fiftieth anniversary meeting of the NAACP, warned that segregation "can be American democracy's achilles heel in Asia and Africa where the great millions of the human family lives." The Department of International Justice and Goodwill of the Churches of Christ in the United States observed that, "racial discrimination and segregation in the West, particularly in the United States, has become a powerful factor in world affairs . . . [it] undercut[s] our moral position among the darker-skinned peoples of Asia and Africa." Conversely, Marion Wright, of the Southern Regional Conference, warned of the attempt by segregationists to proclaim "that desegregation is a Communist device and that the Supreme Court is a tool of Moscow."[2]

The historians have been unusually perspicacious in detecting various facets of this trend. In explicating the civil rights thrust during the Truman administration, Mary Frances Berry has pointed out that, "the Cold War, the struggle for economic and social development in the non-white nations . . . were factors which made this new reform politically expedient." Carl Solberg quotes James Baldwin as saying that "the rise of Africa in world affairs" had "everything to do" with the civil rights thrust of the 1950s, if only by providing United States Blacks a militant example to follow. The beginning of the end for Jim Crow "seems to have begun with Kwame Nkrumah," Du Bois' prime pupil. William Leuchtenburg has conceded that President Eisenhower "understood, too, that in a struggle with the Soviet Union for the allegiance of the Third World evidence of racial discrimination in the United States was a decided handicap." Carl Brauer has graphically described how these forces beset President Kennedy:

> The Birmingham crisis touched another sensitive Kennedy nerve when it attracted a great deal of publicity abroad. . . . In several countries, particularly in Ghana and Nigeria, the media poured out caustic denunciation of the racial outrage. Radio Moscow, after a hesitant beginning was currently devoting a quarter of its output to Birmingham, much of it beamed to African audiences. Given Kennedy's expansionist

> view of his country's role in the world, the damage Birmingham had done to America's image undoubtedly concerned him.

In article after article and editorial after editorial, *Crisis* also drove such points home.[3]

The NAACP was not afraid to raise these sensitive issues in the context of explosive international events. They agreed with Soviet Ambassador Jacob Malik when he asked how Governor James Byrnes could hit at "inequality" in Eastern Europe when it festered in South Carolina. Continuously they repeated words of public figures like George Meany to similar effect and carped about emphasis on "denial of democracy" in Eastern Europe by raising the same issue in reference to the South. The repeated condemnations of United States foreign policy were complemented with resolutions of action. The NAACP resolved, for example, "to organize an international department." Illustrative of how these words were translated into action became clear in 1951 when the NAACP sponsored a testimonial dinner for Ralph Bunche. The words of the invitation, directed at the affluent, seemed straight from a *Crisis* editorial:

> at this critical juncture of world history when Russia is playing up in Asia, Africa and South America every incident of racial discord . . . it can thereby demonstrate that a majority of Americans are actively opposed.

This appeal was persuasive and the dinner a rousing success. Henry Ford II headed the committee sponsoring the dinner; the invitation was signed by Eleanor Roosevelt, Eric Johnston, and Herbert Lehman—a major funder of the association.[4]

The volatile flip side of this coin was that Afro-Americans—because of, among other things, the disproportionate level of their oppression—were in the forefront of opposition to United States foreign policy; and southern leadership of the Cold War meant—opposition to foreign policy or not—Blacks would be disproportionately victimized by the red scare. The NAACP was aware of all this, knew how it roiled the Black community, and responded accordingly. Conservative NAACP board member Alfred Baker Lewis told rank and file members:[5]

> If there is . . . a group interested in the discussion of foreign policy, they might take a speaker on the bad effect of racial discrimination on our foreign relations . . . [they] should be able to answer questions about . . . our exclusion of Communists and our support of anti-Communist foreign policy measures.

Thus, the NAACP was trying to run with the hares and hunt with the hounds; attempting to tweak Uncle Sam, they hammered on the hypocrisy of foreign policy when it came to race while eagerly supporting the glue that held this policy together—anti-communism. But they were not alone in this and the tendency of certain Blacks to be vocally anti-communist bothered Du Bois to no end.[6]

Particularly galling to Du Bois was the tendency of certain Blacks to travel on behalf of the State Department to third world countries in a vain effort to rebut charges of the United States being a racist hellhole for peoples of color, then returning and writing wide-eyed books about their adventure. J. Saunders Redding traveled to India under the auspices of the Department of State. At the request of the State Department, Du Bois' detractor Carl Rowan ventured to India, Pakistan, and Southeast Asia "to try to convince Asians that they should keep faith in democracy." Needless to say, there was considerable and vocal skepticism about Rowan's ingenuous defense of the Black condition. When Black United Nations delegate Edith Sampson traveled to India embarrassing questions were asked about the plight of Afro-Americans. Said one; "We will believe in America's altruistic motives after we see the American government raise the living standard of the Negroes and extend to them full justice and equality." On one occasion, she was asked why she omitted the names of Du Bois and Robeson when she was listing noted Blacks. Significantly, in India "both the left and the right press have commented unfavorably against the denial of civil rights to the American Negro." P. L. Prattis in the *Pittsburgh Courier* said flatly that her being appointed was "Truman's recognition of the disturbing influence of race and color in the current world struggle," while the *New York Herald Tribune* said Sampson's tenure "serves as an answer to Russian propaganda that Negroes in the United States are an oppressed people deprived of opportunity, influence and position." Sampson's verbal boners made her a bugaboo, of sorts, among Blacks. She was quoted as saying that freeing "subject people . . . before they are prepared . . . might result in their subjection to the 'new colonialism of the Soviet Union.' " She was heckled in Vienna when she "denied that the color bar is typical in the U.S." *Freedom* noted the trip of the Reverend James Robinson to India and lashed into Channing Tobias for his anti-Soviet statements at the United Nations Assembly in Paris. *Freedom* editorialized that Black "leadership must decide whether its mission in life is to 'foil the Russians' or to free the Negroes."[7]

Du Bois decisively took public, well-publicized positions in opposition to United States foreign policy. The cornerstone of the Truman Doctrine was assistance to anticommunists in Greece coupled with repression of Communists at home. In 1948, while still with the NAACP, he cochaired the National Conference on American Policy in Greece which mobilized sentiment against these policies. His prominence as a foreign policy critic caused Florida's Senator Claude Pepper to seek his backing for his resolution opposing United States policy to "support foreign soldiers as part of a global policy of power politics which can only lead to war." The Black press was firm in opposition to the Truman Doctrine as well. The *Los Angeles Sentinel California Eagle, St. Louis American, Afro-American, Philadelphia Independent* and others cursed with hostility this foreign policy turn.[8]

In formulating and articulating his opposition to Cold War foreign policy, Du Bois echoed *Crisis* by zeroing in on the hypocrisy of calling for democracy abroad when it did not exist in the South. In August 1949, when testifying in opposition to the Military Assistance Bill before the House Committee on Foreign Affairs, he was adamant. The NAACP was quite sensitive to the issue of racism among the allies the United States had pledged to defend. There were complaints about the treatment of Blacks in the western zone of Germany, Britain, France, Denmark, and the United States Navy's observance of apartheid laws when docking in Capetown. At the same time, they zestfully reported information from the European press: "Even the European men in the street sensed the incongruity of a 'democratic' equality that condemned Negroes to service batallions and segregated outfits. . . . To preach democratic equality while making distinctions of color and race strikes Europeans as bizarre, if not perverse."[9]

In 1949 Du Bois helped to pull together a Washington Conference on Foreign Policy that focused on the North Atlantic pact;

surprisingly, expressing "willingness to take part in our deliberations [were] . . . Senators J. W. Fulbright, Margaret Chase Smith, Herley M. Kilgore, Glen H. Taylor; Congressmen John A. Blatnik and George G. Sadowski." Traveling in such notable company did not cause Du Bois to back off from his positions. He castigated, for example, NATO General Lucius Clay as a "prominent investor and exploiter of labor," director of General Motors, Marine Midland, Newmont Mining, which owns "Zelida mine of lead and zinc in Morocco," who gave $1 million to the anticommunist Crusade For Freedom. But such assaults on leading lights were not out of line with Blacks' orientation. In a hard-boiled editorial, *Crisis* struck at the entire United States policy in Europe. They pooh-poohed the notion of liberating "enslaved peoples" in Eastern Europe while "Washington, the capital of the Free, for instance, is the most thoroughly jim-crow capital in the world." The reality was that the fact of colonized Africa meant that congenitally Blacks could not list to the right as far as other sectors. Cold War liberals may have been on the left side of the political spectrum among whites but were on the right among Afro-Americans.[10]

Europe was not the only battleground where Du Bois came into conflict with United States foreign policy, nor was it the only foreign arena with which he kept up. In 1948, when he wrote the Library of Jewish Information of the American Jewish Committee asking to be placed on their mailing list to "receive regularly issues of articles of interest in Current Problems and other literatures," it was just a further expression of a long-standing interest in the Middle East. This relationship with Zionist organizations was not always smooth. In 1944 he gave a sharp reply to the AJC's president when they sought his endorsement of their proposed Declaration of Human Rights:

> you appeal for sympathy for persons driven from the land of their faith; but how about American Negroes, Africans and Indians who have not been driven from the land of their birth but nevertheless are deprived of their rights. . . . You want redress for those who wander the earth but how about those who do not wander and are not allowed to travel and nevertheless are deprived of their fundamental human rights. . . . In other words, this is a very easily understood declaration of Jewish rights but it has apparently not thought of the rights

> of Negroes, Indians, and South Sea Islanders. Why then call it the Declaration of Human Rights?

Nor did Du Bois balk in 1947 in criticizing David Ben-Gurion, chairman of the Jewish Agency in Jerusalem, for saying "Palestine is now the only place in the civilized world where racial discrimination still exists in law." He drily asked Ben-Gurion if he had heard of South Africa. Yet, throughout his later years, Du Bois—like so many other leftists and progressives—was amazingly friendly to the Zionist entity of Israel and surprisingly reticent about the rights of the Palestinians.[11]

Du Bois not only worked behind the scenes but used his considerable stature and contacts to lobby for the creation of Israel. He criticized Arabs for their alleged "widespread ignorance, poverty and disease and a fanatic belief in the Mohammedan religion." This overstating of the case against the Arabs was combined with machine gun fire attacks on Ernest Bevin and Harry Truman as perpetrators of the crisis. He spoke frequently before the American Jewish Congress on such topics and it was not surprising that he was contacted to participate in the Emergency Conference to Repudiate the Betrayal of Jewish People through the Administration's withdrawal of support of Palestine partition which was held in Cleveland, Ohio. These speeches often stressed the theme of the unity of the Black and Jewish peoples. He noted:[12]

> the way in which African and Jewish history have been entwined for 3,000 years. . . . I wish to apologize in the name of the American Negro for the apparent apostasy of Ralph Bunche . . . even when loaned to the Secretariat of the United Nations, he has consistently followed the directives of the State Department, whose appointee he continues to be in fact if not in law.

In his speeches to the Jewish community, he often focused on the dangers of nazism. This was the case in his 1951 address to the American Jewish Labor Council protesting German rearmament. Prior to this in 1950, he spoke at length on this issue in a speech before the Jewish People's Fraternal Order:

> It has been said more than once that if and when fascism comes to America . . . it will be the Negro people followed by the Jewish people who will feel the fury of barbaric sadism

> . . . The Negro people have an obligation to support the fight for a free Israel as the Jewish people have an obligation to support the fight for a free Africa.

In the 1952 edition of *The Souls of Black Folk,* first published in 1903, there were changes made to eliminate possible anti-Semitic connotations. His defense of the Rosenbergs was often placed in the context of the fight against anti-Semitism and fascism. These themes were raised once more when he addressed the rally organized by the United Committee to Commemorate the Tenth Anniversary of the Warsaw Ghetto Uprising.[13]

As Israel's policies came under heavier bombardment from progressives internationally, Du Bois, like his United States comrades, remained surprisingly soft-spoken. His 1956 poem on the Suez crisis is evidence of this. He scored United States intervention in Lebanon in 1959—according to the *Guardian,* the "Negro Press [was] silent or critical of intervention in Lebanon"—but again did not highlight the Israeli role. Interestingly, throughout his career, Du Bois took a soft line on Israel and was virtually mum about the Palestinians.[14]

The Caribbean islands were another area of intense interest for Du Bois. Their proximity to the United States and their heavily Black populations guaranteed this would be the case. However, even during the height of the Cold War when lack of a passport barred visits elsewhere, it was possible to journey there. As the Father of Pan-Africanism, Du Bois was well known and popular, particularly in the British colonial possessions. He received inquiries about his books from there and in 1948 Jamaica's anticolonial leader Norman Manley again spoke glowingly of Du Bois.[15]

Despite the fact that it was easier to travel to the Caribbean then, say, Europe or Africa, even Du Bois was surprised at times with the fluidity of the situation. In 1953 he told Ben Davis in amazement, "I expected to be turned back from my trip to Haiti but was not." He also vacationed in Grenada in 1955 and was met at the airport by a sizable delegation led by T.A. Marryshow, national hero and member of the Legislative Council for 30 years—"said to constitute a record for the . . . so-called Colonial Empire," he proudly told Du Bois. His forays to the Caribbean were not always so well received. Though he had known Eric Williams from the time when he taught at Howard University, the prime minister did not meet with him when he visited Trinidad and Du Bois surmised that pressure was the reason. Williams' secretary wrote Du Bois afterwards and apologized, but Du Bois was unconvinced and speculated that this signalled a demise of the radicalism of the author of the angry *Capitalism and Slavery*.[16]

Du Bois' closest relationship with Caribbean leaders was probably with Guyana's Cheddi Jagan, Marxist and general secretary of the People's Progressive Party, who served as prime minister during the mid-1960s. Jagan's wife Janet, United States born and a political leader in her own right, told Du Bois in 1956, "your name is known and beloved by our members." Jagan visited the United States on numerous occasions and in 1961 Jagan (an "East Indian" in a country where this ethnic group was the majority) complained to Du Bois about the sabotage of the case for independence by his Black rival Forbes Burnham and his machinations with the British. He spoke to Du Bois of Burnham's race politics and how he was encouraged by the British to split the Party. In a country rocked by the Marxism of Fidel Castro, Jagan's presence in the United States charged emotions. He told Du Bois of how the John Birch Society objected to his speaking engagements and tried to "block this function." He asked Du Bois' advice about asking Nkrumah, Sekou Touré, and other well-respected African leaders to come to Guyana "to emphasize the fact that the fight today is between classes and not between races." Indicative of his great respect for the elderly leftist, he made a forthright request: "I would greatly like to discuss this matter with you and to seek your advice on a number of other problems which arise out of our impending independence."[17]

Du Bois' interest in the Caribbean was a facet of his interest in Western Hemisphere affairs generally. Again, the NAACP went along with this focus. Du Bois' radicalism here, for example, his support for the Cuban revolution, was not unusual, as Martin Luther King, Jr., too shared this viewpoint. Du Bois joined with Marianne Moore, John Ciardi, Alan Lomax, and others in protesting the visit of Chilean General Gonzalez Videla to the United States and the driving of Pablo Neruda into exile. Like other areas of the globe, he closely followed events in the region and, for example, when Peronism surged in 1955, he began receiving information directly from Buenos Aires on this phenomenon.[18]

An issue that concerned both the NAACP and Du Bois was the question of racial discrimination against Black workers in the United States controlled Canal Zone. In 1948, just before his ouster from the NAACP, Du Bois agreed to "aid in the initiation of the National Citizens Committee to Abolish the Jim Crow 'silver-gold' system on the Panama Canal Zone." Du Bois served as cochairman along with his usual partners Robeson and Charlotta Bass. In *The New York Star* he slashed at policies there:

> They lived in hovels, with poor food and wretched sanitation; their schools were poor and teachers underpaid. . . . All this was taking place under the army rule of the United States Government which was discriminating against colored workers (called silver workers) and paying white workers (Gold workers) wages often 100 percent highter, with good homes, schools and opportunity for promotion.

He recounted the remarks of a Black Panamanian worker he heard speak in New York: "Finally he turned to his neighbor, a white editor and said: 'And they call me Communist? What do they mean by that?' " The committee's efforts did somewhat ameliorate conditions of discrimination there but, like so many other efforts of this era, it fell by the wayside as repression intensified.[19]

Given his interests in Europe, Africa, and the Western Hemisphere, it would have been unusual if Du Bois had ignored the most populous continent—Asia—and, of course, he did not. Indonesia, China, Vietnam, and India were just a few of the objects of his attention. As the liberation struggle against Dutch colonialism heated up in Indonesia in 1947, he joined Uta Hagen, Louis Burnham, and others in sponsoring an action conference on this matter. Thus, when the triumphant President Sukarno visited the United States he naturally was introduced to Du Bois. As ever, he was hyperactive on behalf of his favorite causes. In the *Chicago Globe* alone, in the year of the Korean War's inception, he wrote articles on the culture and art of Indonesia, and religion in India, Burma, and Malaya.[20]

His work with the peace movement meant that Korea and the somewhat related issue of China would be not far from his mind. As in other areas, he galvanized dissent to United States policy by joining activists in a 1948 National Conference on American Policy in China and the Far East. During a time when the "yellow hordes" of China were a frequent target for organized anger, he joined the Board of the relief agency, China Welfare Fund. Symbolic of the difficulties involved in such political work, just after the triumph of the revolution a major point on the agenda of the board was the "visit of FBI representative."[21]

The smoldering war against Vietnam was, obviously, not supported by Du Bois. During the early stages of the war in 1954, veteran and militant journalist William Worthy was allowed to publish an article sharply critical of western interests there in *Crisis.* Worthy's condemnation of Cold War liberalism was unallayed. Worthy's view was not an isolated one among Afro-Americans, disgusted as they were with their country's firm support of colonialism, but it was a bit much for the NAACP. In an unusual move, the NAACP subsequently sought to refute the thrust of Worthy's article. Even more unusual, they lashed out at anticolonial organizations that remain "mute and conscienceless when faced with the crimes of the rival imperialism of the Soviet Union." This redbaiting of Worthy was followed by a ritualistic recitation of past Association resolutions backing United States policy. Years later there was little change in this orientation, as Roy Wilkins joined Carl Rowan and Whitney Young in condemning Martin Luther King's opposition to that same war against Vietnam.[22]

But the fact that *Crisis* printed Worthy's article, despite the condemnation they knew would inevitably rain down, was indicative of their catering to a mass viewpoint they knew existed among Blacks. Du Bois, of course, was the living symbol of this trend—both in the United States and abroad. This became clear in 1955 with the landmark meeting in Bandung, Indonesia, of Afro-Asian countries—a signal development in the evolution of third world nonalignment. Du Bois was not allowed to travel to this mass gathering but he sent a message. Du Bois also drafted a lengthy "Memorandum on the Bandung Conference" which was unmistakeably directed at Adam Clayton Powell, Jr., Carl Rowan, Richard Wright, and other Afro-Americans allowed to travel to Bandung for the purpose of refuting charges of United State racism. To the Bandung conferees, Du Bois was a vivid symbol of anti-imperalism and anticolonialism and they openly showed their respect.[23]

India played a large role at Bandung and other Afro-Asian assemblages of the era. Du Bois was a friend of India and cited the day of their independence as "the greatest historical date of the nineteenth and twentieth centuries." On Du Bois' eightieth birthday Nehru sent warm greetings. Du Bois was friendly with Babindranath Tagore and the Indian poet had occasion to complain to him about the racism he found in the United States. The Du

Bois-Indian relationship was not always smooth. In 1949, he joined in "An Open Letter" to Nehru protesting alleged "widespread violations of civil liberties."[24]

Despite his criticisms of Nehru's regime, they remained friendly and Du Bois provided him with useful intelligence on world conditions. He informed Nehru about why the barriers of segregation in the United States fell: "for this we have to thank the rise of the Soviet Republics and the rise and growth of free India." Still, their relationship was frank enough for him to tell the prime minister: "At first I was deeply disturbed at the jailing of Communists"; Du Bois' closeness to Nehru was just one feature of his formidable stature on the world scene—a stature that could allow for candor in his dealings with other leading public figures.[25]

It is essential to recognize that Du Bois' radical views on foreign affairs struck a responsive chord among an Afro-American community that was not pleased about Africa being chained by colonialism. This tendency was so strong that even the NAACP had to pay obesiance to it; though on the left-liberal side of the overall United States spectrum, the NAACP was on the other side of the Black political spectrum.

CHAPTER 20

Du Bois and the Communists

Du Bois had read Marx quite thoroughly by the 1930s and gave a course on Marxism and the Negro during the 1933 summer session at Atlanta University. He studied Lenin and his schooling in Berlin in the 1890s involved more than a passing acquaintance with the ideology of socialism. Still, the Cold War did cause Du Bois—and recall that he was in his eighties— to deepen his study of Marxism-Leninism. In 1954, he was "reading again Lenin's *Imperialism*" and looking for the "best logical follow-up of this argument." Aptheker suggested that he examined works by the Soviet economist Eugene Varga, R. Palme Dutt, Victor Perlo, and others. In any case, Du Bois' joining the Communist party in 1961 was—contrary to the opinion of many—not a radical departure from his past praxis and, in actuality, a logical continuation.* The trip from the NAACP in 1944 to the Communist party in 1961 was not as convoluted as some might suspect; their immediate goals were closely congruent, despite the frequent sniping of the former at the latter. The Black community

* When asked late in life why he had not become a Communist earlier, he replied: "I suppose one of the chief reasons that I didn't become a Communist as a young man was that nobody asked me to." "The Reminiscences of William Edward Burghardt Du Bois," No. 517, Category 1A, PRCQ, Columbia University, Oral History.

was probably the most left sector of the United States polity, and Du Bois was a leader of both Blacks and the left.[1]

As might be surmised, an oppressed Afro-American was susceptible to arguments that both explained their subjugation and pointed the way toward its demise. Though an apparently logical and sound deduction, there are those who have railed against it. Loren Baritz has deftly articulated this widely accepted view:

> Black radicalism was slow to gather, slower even than white. Racial oppression combined with economic repression effectively submerged Black Americans to a pre-political level [sic]. Their struggle was one of sheer survival, and there can be only occasional politics in the jungle. The consequence was atomization, a sensible attachment to the techniques of personal endurance, and deep distrust of organized activity, black or white, except for the church.

This position is both bizarre and inaccurate though subscribed to by all too many. Perhaps wishful thinking is the motivating factor here but, in any case, Nathan Glazer—no great friend of Blacks or the left—has presented a more balanced view:[2]

> It is commonly said that the American Negroes resisted the appeal of Communism [but] . . . there was perhaps less antipathy than elsewhere in American society . . . the party was the only institution in American life in which Negroes commonly worked with whites on a level of equality, which was really indifferent to issues of race. . . . A Negro who knew the party could see the simple fact that if a Negro became a true Bolshevik, there was no limit to the position to which he might rise in the party; indeed he might rise higher than a white of the same ability.

At the time Du Bois' relationship with the party was admittedly checkered but there was more that united them than divided them. In 1935 Du Bois, Communist leader James Ford, Walter White, representatives of Marcus Garvey's Universal Negro Improvement Association (UNIA), and the Brotherhood of Sleeping Car Porters were on the platform at Madison Square Garden as 10,000 clamored against Italian aggression against Ethiopia. The party was heavily involved in Black life. Jabari Onaje Simama has gone so far as to say: "The CPUSA was never a success in America when it was not successful in the Black community." Professional anticommunist Phillip Abbot Luce phrased it differently but meant the same thing: "All American Communists, regardless of their particular theoretical persuasion are adamant in their belief that the Negro people are the essential catalyst for the projected revolutionary situation in the United States." Nathan Glazer has averred: "The Communist Party devoted more resources, more attention, more effort, to the recruitment of Negro members than it expanded on any other social group, except perhaps for industrial workers and trade unionists." William D. Andrew, in his study of Ford's giant Local 600, has observed: "the Party desired to bring Black workers into union offices. The left wing became a consistent advocate for the election of Negroes to office and made this a major issue." Roger Keeran has pointed this out as being true of the Communist party within the auto workers' union generally. Mark Naison has outlined the effectiveness of the party and its leaders in Harlem and their acceptance among Blacks. Harvard Sitkoff has echoed this modern historiographical view of the party:

> It sparked and financed new civil rights groups whose radicalism, ironically made the established Negro organizations more militant. . . . Many liberals, moreover, out of the need to compete with the Communists or the desire to emulate them, joined with the left. . . . Among the accolades bestowed on the Communists by Afro-Americans, none appeared more frequently than praise for the party's overt interracialism.

The party's affirmative action policies won many adherents among Blacks. Thus,it was not surprising that a *Negro Digest* poll in 1944 found an overwhelming majority of Blacks praising the party's policies.[3]

This relative popularity of the party among Blacks has had special features. The Communist party journal *Political Affairs* has long been aware that "fear of unity with the left is not so influential a factor among the Negro people as it is among the mass of white workers, farmers, middle classes." A 1955 Columbia University dissertation found 61 percent of the Blacks interviewed sympathetic to communism and found the more educated (who presumably were more informed) were even more sympathetic. A recent analysis of the party's leadership is revealing: "by 1961 one-quarter of the Central Committee members were Blacks. . . . Blacks . . . were far less likely than whites to leave the CPUSA by either resignation or expulsion." Thus, Blacks were far more dedicated to the party and better represented at the highest levels than in the Democratic or Republican parties or virtually any other United States insitution for that matter. But like the study just cited, it is revealed in other studies that educated Blacks were more likely than many other ethnic groups to flock to the party's banner. The influence of the party among Blacks was pervasive. Ralph Bunche, generally regarded as the premier establishment Black, was at one time alleged to have "personified a neo-Marxist disposition." And W. E. B. Du Bois, the first Black to receive a doctorate from Harvard, was quite in the tradition of Black Communist leaders like the lawyers Ben Davis and William Patterson or the college graduates Doxey Wilkerson, James Ford, and others—all this at a time when going to college for Blacks was not an ordinary occurrence. Strikingly, just as Black Communists influenced the civil rights movement, women Communists deeply influenced women's struggle for equality; and a number of them, for example, the legendary Mother Bloor who had a degree in biology from the University of Pennsylvania, were college educated.[4]

One reason for the distorted perception of the party that has been passed down—and the infamy attached to Du Bois for joining—has been the distorted intepretations passed down by historians. Bernard Sternsher has shown how Cold War pressure affected the writing of history. William D. Andrew has noted that the traditional image of "fellow travellers," and "dupes," led by a "totalitarian Stalinist organization . . . leaves much to be desired." Roger Keeran has decisively rebutted the constructs of Irving Howe, Philip Taft, Benjamin Stolberg, Max Kampelman, and a passel of others that Communists' ties to the Soviet Union meant they could not be, for example, "legitimate trade unionists." His recitation of the loaded language used by certain historians is instructive:

> non-communists win union elections but Communists "capture" a union. Non-communists join unions; Communists "infiltrate" or "invade" them. A non-communist states his or her position; a Communist "peddles the straight party line." Non-communists influence or lead groups; Communists dominate them. A non-communist political party passes resolutions or makes decisions, but a Communist party invariably issues "directives."

Actually, it was the right and the center, not the left, which used undemocratic means to expel Communists. Anti-communism was a convenient tool for getting rid of troublesome critics and solidifying power grabs. Increasingly this is the view of the more recent studies.[5]

Nevertheless, Du Bois' joining the party did require no small amount of courage. The ruling parties of the United States feared the Communist party and its potential impact on the body politic. A day after the opening of the Progressive party convention in 1948—where the Communist party played a large role—the Smith Act indictments came down. David Jacob Group has outlined the horrid story of legal repression that befell the party. Truman's loyalty security program was typical—where neither loyalty or disloyalty was explicitly defined. The attorney general's list of subversive organizations was an official political blacklist, which seriously impaired the functioning of the groups it cited—as Du Bois could well attest—especially in the area of membership and funds. Many had their tax exemptions cancelled; housing units constructed under the Housing Act of 1937 could not be occupied by someone who was a member of a listed organization; education and retirement benefits were denied pursuant to the list, as well as hiring from state and local government to private industry. Not only was membership actionable but also affiliation and sympathetic association. This legal barrage was accomanied by an ideological barrage, for example, equating fascism and communism through the term "totalitarianism." Results were predictable. The left movement was left in disarray. Talented artists like John Garfield and Canada Lee were driven to heart attacks. Too many others, such as, F. O. Matthiessen, were driven to suicide. Du Bois' closeness to the party and his decision to take out membership, therefore, required extraordinary courage.[6]

So intended, the attack on the party extended beyond card-carrying Communists, as the pre-1961 career of Du Bois exemplified. Peter Lincoln Steinberg put it succinctly: "The American Communist Party was the first victim of political repression, but society as a whole eventually suffered the consequences of the minority suppression." This Cold War attack was world-wide, with parties and progressives in South Africa, the Caribbean, the Middle East, Europe, and Asia under siege simultaneously. There were also similar worldwide consequences.[7]

Du Bois often acknowledged that the attack on the Communists was just the opening shot in an overall assault on progressive forces. I. F. Stone has articulated the inextricable intertwining of these issues:[8]

> if it had not been for the Communists there would have been no Progressive Party, and if they are ever purged the Progressive Party will disappear . . . I see no way to wage an effective and principled fight without fighting for their rights and with their help. Everywhere in Western Europe we see that when the non-communist left is split, reaction takes power. When the Communists go under, the popular fronters will follow and when we have been taken, the ADA-ers and the liberals will be next in line of fire.

Just as Roger Keeran, William D. Andrew, and others have complained about distortions of the relationship between the trade union movement and the Communists, a similar plaint could be issued about Blacks and the Communist party, especially the NAACP and the party. Indeed, misinformation on this score is a major reason why the interpretation of Du Bois' joining the party has been so distorted. Employing the laughable language cited by Roger Keeran, Thomas R. Brooks has intoned with no mock seriousness:

> [The party] quietly dumped the [National Negro] Congress for a policy of infiltration of the NAACP, following the end of World War II, largely in the hopes of securing the NAACP's endorsement of the Progressive Party, presidential candidate Henry A. Wallace.

Naturaly, there was no footnote or documentation for this assertion. In discussing party policy, many have assumed that the rules of evidence are inapplicable. Wilson Record, a sociologist attempting to write history, has been the most notorious example of this trend. Robert Zangrando blasted one of his works saying it was a "disappointment," "stiff and repetitious," "inadequate footnotes," "not tightly organized." On the other hand, Herbert Hill, who penetrated to the highest levels of the NAACP leadership, somehow found the gumption to praise Record's *The Negro and the Communist Party* for its "wealth of documentation *[sic]*." In an article for *Phylon,* founded by Du Bois, Record rendered a typical performance, managing to excoriate Black Communists—in particular—Henry

Winston, James Jackson, and Claude Lightfoot—without benefit of a single footnote.[9]

The fact is that there was a clear congruence between the programs of the NAACP and the Communist party, as the latter's 1948 election platform demonstrated. Certain *Political Affairs* articles, such as one on "American Imperialism and the Colonial World," in 1947, could have appeared in *Crisis.* In fact, the similarities betwen the two organizations on the "Negro" spurred the fury of Dixiecrats and HUAC. Du Bois' journey from the NAACP in 1944 to the Communist party in 1961 was not a labyrinth. Yet, the party was one of its own most severe critics in assessing their impact on the civil rights movement.[10]

The party constantly implored Blacks and the NAACP to recognize that anticommunist laws were also meant for them. Around 1955 it is possible to detect at least a slight alteration of party rhetoric and policy on the NAACP. This may have been due to the fact that "the influence of our Party on the ranks of the Negro people has not kept pace with the rapid growth and development of the Negro people's freedom movement itself." Like many party analyses of the era, this one discounted the impact of political repression on the Communist party ranks on this process. There was still focus on the petit bourgeois character of the NAACP and how they needed movement in order to wring concessions for themselves. By 1957 the party's "Black Belt" thesis was well on its way to being junked and the result and emphasis on Blacks as a national minority seeking equality was reflected in their analysis of the NAACP. James Jackson, friend of Du Bois and principal architect of the new policy, presented this amended analysis of the NAACP in 1957:

> The leading organization of the Negro people of the South, as elsewhere, remains the NAACP . . . It exerts the main influence on the social programs of all other Negro organizations. It is the only organization of the Negro people's movement with a regularly appearing monthly journal, *The Crisis.* It has more or less formalized cooperation bonds and fraternal relationships with all the major Negro civic, fraternal, scholastic and religious organizations. . . . It has the general backing of almost the entire Negro press.

This positive evaluation of the NAACP was not in line with past attacks on their "reformist" leadership and, coincidentally, occurred at a time when the lessening of international tensions and the decolonization process were moving the NAACP closer to Du Bois. This did not wipe out the NAACP's anticommunism but it did soften past references to Communist party attempts "to use the Negro . . . to infiltrate and disrupt . . . to rook the Negro masses and smear Negro leaders" and their general "ideological flap-doodle.[11]

Du Bois' formal casting of his lot with the Communists was not an aberration. He had never been particularly close to the Democrats or Republicans and had flirted with third paties, such as, LaFollette's 1924 effort. After he came to the NAACP in 1944, he associated with the Communists, Progressives, and even took the time to address the Social Democratic League for Industrial Democracy, Student Division. But what really stirred controversy was his refusal to vote in the 1956 election, which he termed a "sit-down strike." He found the Democrats and Republicans unacceptable and longed for a third party. Many could agree with his forthright indictment of the so-called two-party system; but virtually all of those who responded to his idea of sitting out the election, vociferously disagreed.[12]

A significant token of Du Bois' practical political activity was a rare and unusual Carnegie Hall meeting in this election year. This gathering featured on one platform (besides Du Bois) Communist General Secretary Eugene Dennis, Socialist Norman Thomas, civil libertarian Roger Baldwin, and Charles Lawrence of the Fellowship of Reconciliation. The *Guardian* headlined; "The disunited left meets on one platform." Baldwin puckishly but notably said that present were representatives of "the Socialist way, the Communist way, the Pacifist way—and Dr. Du Bois." The debate was a verbal brawl and something of a free-for-all. Thomas, for example, lashed into Du Bois for not voting for him in earlier election years and trounced the Soviet Union. Du Bois was nonplussed: "He gets terribly excited and hysterical. He yells and what he's talking about I really don't know." One thing he did know about, however, and addressed forcefully: "We need to discuss ourselves, not, the USSR." Still, this gathering did lead to the creation of the American Forum for Socialist Education (AFSE), spurred by Du Bois, A. J. Muste, Sidney Lens, Doxey Wilkerson, and others—an event not welcomed by certain leading political quarters. Black lawyer Conrad Lynn was sharply queried about it in an appearance before HUAC;

Senator James Eastland inquired directly of Muste about AFSE's Communist ties.[13]

The AFSE was not the only leftist political form with which Du Bois worked. He spoke at a centennial meeting for Eugene Debs. Du Bois was asked to withdraw from the program due to Trotskyite (Bert Cochran, *American Socialist* editor) and the anti-Soviet *Monthly Review* influence. This was a recurring theme presented to Du Bois, though he demurred. He also would not budge from his stance on not voting. He recounted his past votes involving compromises, for example, voting for Norman Thomas in 1928 "although the Socialists had attempted to Jim Crow Negro members in the South."[14]

Though some of his Communist friends vocally objected to association with some elements within the AFSE and related forms, Du Bois continued this relationship. During January 1958 he met with Corliss Lamont, Ben Davis, Paul Sweezy, Joseph Starobin, Leo Huberman, James Aronson, Annette Rubinstein, Conrad Lynn, and others to discuss a proposal for a "united Independent-Socialist" ticket in the November election in New York. Later, a conference was held with many of the same people plus Joyce Cowley of the Socialist Workers' Party, Rockwell Kent, and others to concretize the proposal. Subsequently, Ben Davis condemned these activities and the "viciously anti-Soviet Trotskyists" who were involved. Again, Du Bois demurred. He stressed their agreement, for example, concurring on peaceful coexistence, banning the color line, and so on, and downplayed their differences. For example, "the Socialist reveres Trotsky, hates Stalin and declares that the Soviet Union is not really a Socialist state" but Du Bois strongly disagreed. Du Bois wound up standing apart from the Communists on this ticket and became an initiating sponsor of the Independent Citizens Committee for Corliss Lamont's United States Senate campaign.[15]

Du Bois' estrangement from the Republicans and Democrats was also a factor widespread among Blacks, even the NAACP. He termed the 1960 election between "the pleasant young son of a stock gambler who hates Communists and the impossible politician who crucified Hiss" a disaster. Speaking of the thirty-sixth anniversary of the *Worker*, he reiterated his notion that taking votes from Blacks made the southern vote worth seven times the North's; thus, "the South rules the nation and big business rules the South." But he also issued unstinting praise of the *Worker* and the party it represented, lauding it as "the newspaper of a third party." Though they did not go as far as Du Bois, traditional political alliances were also becoming less tasteful to the NAACP. Wilkins was not at ease over John F. Kennedy's endorsement by Governor John Patterson of Alabama. At a 1960 rally of 6,000 in Los Angeles to pressure Democrats on their platform, Kennedy was booed, Lyndon Johnson did not come for fear of a hostile reception, and Truman's name was hooted, "[this] stemmed from this assertion that the 'sit-ins' were 'communist inspired.' "[16]

In his *Chicago Defender* column of February 8, 1947, as the red scare was gathering steam, Du Bois strongly indicted redbaiting as a classical device "to distract the thought of the people of the United States from the main issues which can confront them and the world." He was quick to assail the likes of John Temple Graves II, Virignius Dabney, and Ralph McGill, "these men are professional liberals but they are not willing to stand up for principles." This indictment of liberals was a recurrent theme. Du Bois implemented these noble words in practice. In February 1950, he contacted his good friend Dr. Vada Somerville in Los Angeles about an upcoming speaking engagement: "Tell me something about this bookshop. I am sure it is run by the Communists, but that makes no difference to me, if it is a good effort and if you think I should respond favorably to this invitation.[17]

Du Bois looked benignly and positively on the Communists and this tendency increased as time wore on. He compared the terror and repression directed at both groups and concluded, "the analogy between treatment of abolitionists yesterday and the communists today is strong." Consequently, it was not surprising when Du Bois scored Douglas Stuart Moore, Pulitzer Prize winner, who, in his capacity as president of the National Institute of Arts and Letters (Du Bois was the first and only Black member), had reassured the authorities that it was not procommunist. That same year, Du Bois severely took to task the American Association of University Professors for its statement on "Rights and Responsibilities," which questioned the use of the Fifth Amendment. Du Bois was outraged: "We condemn Russian Communism,' declare the very persons who have just affirmed that colleges can take 'no official policy' on 'political questions or matter of public policy.' " He was not pleased with those who, like Howard Fast, flip-flopped and gave succor to the anticommunists. In his *Color, Communism and Common Sense* (foreword by Archibald Roosevelt), Manning Johnson, the leading Black professional anticommunist cum informer, castigated Du Bois fiercely through a strange historical prism, and praised Booker T. Washington, since his industrial education policy would have better prepared Blacks for the atomic age. He quoted an anticommunist attack by Kelly Miller on Du Bois and James Ford, then threw another blow: "Many Negroes realize that Du Bois was wrong then, as he is today in his attempt to steer them down the road to Communism."[18]

Du Bois' support for the Communists was not just rhetorical. He testified at their trials, attempted to lobby on their behalf, signed their petitions, spoke on their behalf, and generally lent his good offices on their behalf. Most of all, he collaborated directly with them. He was close to the American Youth For Democracy and though he was unable to make it to all of their efforts, for example, their 1946 venture featuring Jackie Robinson, Bess Myerson, and Leonard Bernstein—he allowed his name to be used by them. The Black Communist Harry Haywood shortly thereafter requested a copy of Du Bois' United Nations petition for use for his book *Negro Liberation.* After Eugene Dennis was convicted, Du Bois joined the National Defense Committee and their innovative effort to invoke the Fourteenth Amendment on his appeal. He agreed to sign a telegram to Congress protesting a HUAC bill requiring registration of the party or Communist party "fronts" as designated by the attorney general, the barring of government employment and passports to them, and so on. He joined a "Statement of American Educators," a week later on April 15, 1948, "concerning the blacklisting of a number of Marxist and labor schools by the Attorney-General." At this early stage of the red scare, 254 signed or "more than 25% of those appealed to."[19]

Much of this early procommunist activity was occurring while he was an NAACP officer and was a factor leading to his dismissal. Walter White and company did not appreciate the flowery messages from Communists that often passed across Du Bois's desk. But more so did the NAACP leadership object to a paid advertisement appearing simultaneously in the Black press that came out July 28, 1948, weeks before Du Bois' ouster. This "Statement by Negro Americans to the President and Attorney-General of the United States" did not pull any punches in its defense of the Communist party. Joining this ad were Paul Robeson, Oliver C. Cox, St. Clair Drake, Coleman Young, John O. Killens, Canada Lee, George Murphy, Jr., Hugh Mulzac, Hope Stevens, Bishop Reverdy Ransom, and others. The NAACP's director of research's association with indicted Communists was not greeted magnanimously and the leadership did not react magnanimously. A year later, in 1949, when Du Bois and others asked Thurgood Marshall to join them in protesting excessive bail for Communist leaders, he abruptly refused.[20]

Du Bois did not learn the lesson of staying away from the Communists after he was fired. But when Herbert Aptheker attempted to get him to testify for the Communist party Eleven he declined: "of the accused persons I have only met two and only know one well [referring here to Eugene Dennis and Ben Davis] . . . I have no information at all as to the action of the Party . . . a good attorney might elicit from me a confession that force and violence have been used by Communists and certainly may be used." Du Bois regretted this declination, still the year's end found him sponsoring a "reception in honor of Harry Sacher . . . one of the defense attorneys who are now facing imprisonment for their courageous defense of the eleven Communist leaders."[21]

At the same time that he was leading the peace movement, Du Bois somehow found the energy to be active in the National Non-Partisan Committee to Defend the Rights of the Twelve Communist Leaders. They drafted a petition to Trygvie Lie and Carlos Rumulo, president of the United Nations General Assembly, Eleanor Roosevelt, chair of the United Nations Human Rights Commission, and Lester Pearson, chair of the Political Committee protesting the indictment and citing Article 19 of the Declaration on Human Rights ("Freedom of thought and conscience and religion") and Article 21 ("Freedom of peaceful assembly and association"). Later he joined Wilkerson, Earl Dickerson, and other Black leaders in filing a friend of the court brief on the case which argued that the denial of Communists' rights weakened democratic rights and harmed pursuit of Black rights generally; the brief attempted to link the antired and antiblack drive. Subsequently, Du Bois joined other "undersigned Negro citizens" in filing a friend of the court brief in the case of John Gates, then Communist leader. Du Bois was also active with organizations with Communist party leadership that were coming under siege. He was on the dais with Gypsy Rose Lee and Dorothy Parker for the Joint Anti-Fascist Refugee Committee-Spanish Refugee Appeal Tribute to Edward Barsky. Also, in 1950, he consented to serve as honorary president of the Harlem chapter of the Civil Rights Congress.[22]

During the year when Du Bois was indicted, he was not sufficiently intimidated to back away from support for indicted Communists. He signed a joint telegram greeting Eugene Dennis on his birthday, with Philip Foner he protesed the Smith Act indictment of Alexander Trachterberg, he served as sponsor of the June 14, 1952, National Conference to Win Amnesty for Smith Act Victims, but a good deal of his effort went into the National Committee to Defend Negro Leadership. Naturally, Walter White called the Committee a "Communist Front" and warned NAACP branches to shun it. Ted Poston, Black reporter for the *New York Post* also redbaited it. This was of necessity a busy committee, for at one time or another they were defending Du Bois, Ben Davis, and a host of others. But even Du Bois had limits. James Ford had asked him to write a recommendation for indicted Communist Marcus Murphy of St. Louis, even though he did not know him. Du Bois replied brusquely, "it is going a little too far for one man to send a commendation about an entire stranger." But requests for assistance were not a one-way street. After one of their rallies in early 1953, Ford forwarded funds to him on behalf of the committee.[23]

The party also assisted in the sale of *In Battle For Peace,* advertising it in *Political Affairs* and giving heavy, torrential praise to it by Aptheker in the same journal. Nevertheless, Du Bois' assistance to the party's victims of the red scare was formidable. He sent detailed letters to his numerous contacts abroad in Africa, France, Cuba, India, and elsewhere. His message was in support of Smith Act victims, suggesting they write Eisenhower. This rallying of support was typical and demonstrated that he gave more than formal support. Yet, the replies he received, as he told Celia Zitron, were not always promising. On the other hand, Du Bois' letter came as a revelation to Hewlett Johnson, dean of Canterbury: "I did not know that it was being operated in the way you state . . . this is disasterous *[sic]*." This campaign by Du Bois did lead to greater awareness abroad of Smith Act persecutions that no doubt was translated into protest.[24]

But Du Bois did more than simply write letters and lend his name, he put himself directly in the line of fire. As he told the readers of *Jewish Life* magazine, "for the first time [I] took [the] oath as a witness" in the trial of Ben Gold, Communist labor leader whom he had known for twenty-five years and who had mobilized support for Du Bois when he was on trial three years earlier.

William Patterson's wife had asked him to head up the defense committee for her recently imprisoned husband and he quickly entered the fray. He condemned the "injustice" done to Patterson "because he refuses to be a stool pigeon." The wife of Communist leader George Meyers was highly appreciative of how positively Du Bois' writings had affected her jailed husband. The wife of jailed Communist poet Walter Lowenfels added her name to the growing list of those seeking Du Bois' assistance. She asked that he help "secure a lenient sentence for Walter, the first poet to be convicted under the Smith Act." Lowenfels had written eight books, mostly poetry, and was Pennsylvania editor of the *Daily Worker.* Du Bois was sympathetic but was unsure about what he could do, perhaps due to false modesty:[25]

> I protest, and have protested but I have come to realize that my name on any petition hinders rather than helps. However, if there is anything that you think that I could do I would be only too glad to do it.

The Eleventh District of the Un-American Activities Committee of the American Legion had scored Du Bois, not only for his defense of the twelve Communist leaders but for his belonging to fifty organizations that were "subversive". The number was probably understated. *The New York Times,* for example, reported that when the *Daily Worker* tried in court to obtain books, papers, and correspondence seized by the Internal Revenue Service, Du Bois was in the forefront of the "Independent Emergency Committee for a Free Press" formed "to give moral and financial support to the Worker"; they denounced the seizure as "a tyrannical and illegal act." Du Bois' interventions, false modesty aside, were not uniformly baneful nor fruitless. The wife of Alexander Bittelman, yet another jailed Communist, thanked Du Bois for his "support in getting the permission of the government to write a book while he is in the Atlanta Penitentiary"; this success emboldened her to ask his help in resisting the attempt to take away his old age pension because he was a Communist. This same year, 1955, Eugene Dennis sent "very special and deep-felt" thanks to Du Bois for the letters he had sent to the authorities about the general secretary's imprisonment: "It undoubtedly helped to facilitate my release and that of several of my co-defendants after 44 months in prisons—the statutory 'good time' limit on a five year sentence." But there was no need to be estatic: "My co-defendants and I were re-arrested upon our release . . . and now another trial under the 'membership' section of the Smith Act." When Vincent Hallinan was released from prison, it was Du Bois who addressed a crowd of 1,500 that welcomed him home. It was Du Bois, along with Pete Seeger, Robeson, and others, who sponsored a testimonial for Hugo Gellert, the progressive artist. But as he had told James Ford, his time and inclinations were not inexhaustible. He was forced to tell the besieged Communist William Albertson that he could not testify for the Civil Rights Congress before the Subversive Activities Control Board since it would be "neither necessary nor logical."[26]

It was clear that testifying and the like was a heavy burden, which helps to account for the somewhat testy response to Albertson. Du Bois' experience when testifying in the 1956 trial of Alexander Trachtenberg, James Jackson, and others in the United States District Court, Southern District of New York, reflects the nature of this burden and the United States government's approach to the non-Communist left. The first day on the witness stand, Du Bois testified to knowing Alexander Trachtenberg since "1910 or 1911" but he was not allowed to fulfill the defense's wish to speak on his loyalty and patriotism until the next day. But he was allowed to speak about the character of Jackson whom he had known since 1935 and visited at his father's house in 1935. Du Bois denied being a member of the party though he had been asked to join by Jackson in 1946 or 1947. Du Bois testified, perhaps a bit disingenuously, that he had no active affiliations with any organizations at this juncture. At that point the prosecutor announced that he would try to discredit Du Bois by showing he was procommunist by linking him to different organizations. The judge, interestingly, said: "This fellow is obviously a scientist and he doesn't care what anybody thinks about an organization. He makes his independent study and comes to his individual conclusion and if he concludes that the reputation is ill-founded, he associates himself with the organization." The prosecution was dumbfounded by this and quickly alleged that Du Bois belonged to over fifteen different groups on the attorney general's list; thus, the judge assented to the prosecution's submission. The prosecution then proceeded to ask Du Bois about the American Peace Crusade, China Welfare Appeal, Civil Rights Congress, International Workers Order, Jefferson School, Peace Information Center, and so on, in an attempt to discredit him. George Charney, who later left the party, recalled years later:

> I remember fidgeting uneasily when on cross-examination [Du Bois] was presented with a list of front organizations on which he served as chairman or vice-chairman. The effect, I thought was unfavorable.

The prosecution inquired about Communist party participation in these "front" organizations, "I don't know . . . I don't see how one can determine whether there is a Communist participation or not. I can't look out in this audience and say whether there is or not. I don't recognize Communists by their face or dress." Du Bois' acid comment did not elicit laughter from the prosecutor, as he pressed on doggedly. He asked about Robeson's Paris statement on Blacks' unwillingness to fight the Soviets, the Progressive party and the Committe for Protection of the Foreign Born. The prosecutor tried to use Du Bois' split with the NAACP in 1948 to discredit him. Then he asked the $64 question: "Doctor, is it or is it not a fact that you are a member of the Communist Party." Under oath and on pain of perjury, Du Bois firmly answered no. Though Charney may have been disappointed with Du Bois' effort since all the defendants were convicted, they were released on bail pending appeal; they were finally acquitted in May 1958. Charles Duncan, Jackson's lawyer—a Black graduate of Dartmouth and Harvard Law School whose wife was subsequently murdered mysteriously—was no less thankful for Du Bois' effort.[27]

After the thaw of Geneva and the independence of Ghana, when Du Bois' stock nationally improved, he did not flee in horror from the Communists—nor did they flee from him. He joined with the Committee to Defend Grady and Judy Jenkins, young Communists from New Orleans arrested for violating Louisiana's criminal anarchy statute and subversive activities control law. The Communist party journal *Political Affairs* in turn devoted respectful attention to Du Bois. He was termed a "True Prophet among us"; Aptheker listed him with George Washington, Abraham Lincoln, Frederick Douglass, and William Z. Foster as one of the "Five Who Made History." Du Bois's selfless toiling on behalf of the party caused the leadership of the People's Republic of China in 1962 to formally communicate their own thanks for his and Shirley Graham's energetic effort in spearheading opposition to the attempt by the United States government to outlaw the Communist party.[28]

Du Bois was personally close to a number of Communists, Herbert Aptheker and James Jackson to name a few. But James Ford, fellow Fisk graduate, 1932 Communist vice-presidential candidate, and a Black man with the abstemious personal habits that Du Bois possessed and admired was one of his closer friends in the party. Du Bois' 1957 eulogy of Ford says as much about himself and what he valued, as it does about the fallen leader:

> He was a man of good manners . . . [and honesty] . . . He was neither loud nor rude but courteous and dignified. He regarded women neither as playthings to be pawed over nor beasts of burden but co-workers with whom he did his share of work. He was a man who did an honest job of toiling long and thoroughly until the end. . . . He had manners.

Ford and Du Bois had a mutually respectful relationship. In 1945, after the *Daily Worker* had hit hard at Du Bois' view on the colonial question, Ford indicated similar disagreement with his fellow Fisk alumnus but apologized: "Nevertheless, I want you to know that I disagree entirely with the manner and content of the criticism expressed in the *Daily Worker* article by Max Gordon who incidentally expressed his own individual opinion." Despite Ford's disagreement, his *Daily Worker* reviews of *Color and Democracy* and *World and Africa* were generally favorable—favorable enough to be clipped by the FBI and placed in Du Bois' file.[29]

Ford was an unashamed admirer of Du Bois and frankly acknowledged his elder's influence on him, especially his writings, for example *The Souls of Black Folk:* "I have treasured [it] over the years. In fact it was among the first basic books on the social problems of Negroes that I read, and I am sure it will be fresh and valuable for the present generation." Ford felt sufficiently confident in his relationship with Du Bois to discuss with him the sensitive matter of the deportation of his comrade Claudia Jones, but, as so often happened during this era, their efforts did not bear fruit and Jones was deported to Trinidad. Shortly thereafter Ford passed away, just after he had written Du Bois from the hospital concerning a brochure they were working on. His widow passionately thanked Du Bois for speaking at his funeral service and being there when needed.[30]

Du Bois was also friendly with Ford's 1932 running mate, red patriarch William Z. Foster, long-time Communist party chairman. He lent him books, for example, one on Haiti, for Foster's own complex historical studies and praised him highly. But the comrade to whom Du Bois probably had the closest relationship was Foster's ideological compatriot, the Amherst and Harvard-trained Black lawyer, Ben Davis. This, too, was a mutual admiration society with Davis calling Du Bois on his eightieth birthday, "one of the most distingished scholars that America has produced, irrespective of race, creed or color." In turn, Du Bois tendered his support for Davis' city council races, who did not fail to advertise this fact. In 1949 he was chairman of the Independent Non-Partisans Citizens Committee for the Re-Election of Councilman Davis, and Shirley Graham was secretary. He campaigned for Davis and spoke at a number of his rallies and spoke out forcefully against the successful effort to railroad out of office a duly elected Communist, whose holding office put the lie to red scare shibboleths: "he has constantly been on the side of the people—so much so that the political machines of three other parties have united to defeat him."[31]

Du Bois was a tower of strength for imprisoned Communists like Davis. At a December 1953 rally against the Smith Act he was adamant in his support. He ruefully compared the amnesty given to the Confederate traitor Jefferson Davis with the harsh treatment accorded communists. From the Allegheny County Jail in Pittsburgh, Davis wrote Du Bois at length in appreciation. He recounted how Du Bois' 1951 legal victory was "celebrated by us" in prison. He related his laborious attempt in August 1953 to obtain certain books to use when testifying in Pittsburgh "in behalf of 5 Smith Act defendants"; at the time he was imprisoned in Terre Haute "under close custody." He requested *In Battle For Peace* and added proudly that getting the book was "worth all the incredible red tape . . . though it had to be read under the eyes of a special guard."[32]

Davis was free in that fateful year of 1955 and not long afterward,he initiated a dialogue with Du Bois about the party's controversial Black Belt thesis, which allowed for self-determination, including secession, for Blacks in the Black Belt South. Ex-Communist leader John Gates was not alone in averring that the Black Belt thesis "made ample use of the historical studies of Dr. W.E.B. Du Bois." Thus, Davis formally asked Du Bois:

> What do you think of our party's theoretical position on the Negro question in the South—involving the question of self-determination for the Black Belt—in the light of the direction of the Negro peoples movement in the South today, particularly in Montgomery.

Du Bois had expressed a veiled dissatisfaction with the thesis and, after considerable wrangling, the position adopted by Du Bois—stressing Blacks as a national minority struggling for equality—was eventually reflected in the party's theses. William Z. Foster, chief ally of Davis in the factional fights that gripped the party in the mid-1950s, signalled a shift reflecting Du Bois' *Freedom* view in a *Political Affairs* article at variance with past pieces that graced this journal: "In the past . . . we have made serious leftist sectarian errors, by advancing the slogan of self-determination too much as a slogan of active agitation or even of action." Foster analyzed Blacks, including so-called Black reformists as generally less hawkish and more anti-McCarthy than whites: "The Negro people already are the most international-minded section of the working class and American democratic forces." He criticized a perceived past Communist party policy of downplaying race and elaborated on the dynamics of antiracism: "A powerful organizing force in development of this world condemnation of Jim Crow has come from the progressive elements of the American Negro people . . . [e.g.] Dr. W. E. B. Du Bois."[33]

Benjamin Davis similarly campaigned extensively for an alteration of the Black Belt thesis and added, "our Party has properly apologized to various individuals over the last months for wrong judgments upon them which were unjust." Eugene Dennis joined him. But his view was not universally accepted within the party. Cyril Briggs heavily polemicized against the new position but his efforts were for naught. Foster and Davis in a joint article acknowledged past errors concerning the Negro question and placed their imprint on the new policy, influenced by Du Bois and adumbrated by him years before. This evolution of the party's position was further evidence of Du Bois' growing closeness to and impact on the Communists. Thus, in 1959 after a lengthy tour abroad, Du Bois and Shirley spent time the day after their arrival with Davis and William Patterson.[34]

Another Black communist who Du Bois spent time with was Dr. James Jackson, who was also a college graduate, having studied pharmacy at Howard University. In fact, Jackson claims credit for recruiting Du Bois to the party. In any event, they became particularly close during the early years of the Southern Negro Youth Congress, particularly when Du Bois gave his famous "Behold the Land" address in Columbia, South Carolina, in 1946. Du Bois withstood substantial pressure and consented to descend into the bastion of segregation; Adam Clayton Powell and Mike Quill, New York transit leader, pulled out at the last minute. Leading lights of the 1960s civil rights movement—Charles Gomillion, James Dombrowski, Arthur Shores, Benjamin Mays, and others—were affiliated with SNYC. Both the FBI and CIA took note of his ties to SNYC, but Du Bois was not deterred. He told Jackson's wife and SNYC compatriot, "I think that your organization is the most promising organization of young people which I know." Jackson thought highly of Du Bois as well, taking time during the latter stages of World War II to write from the Burma-China border that "the name of Du Bois will be topped only by that of Douglas." But Jackson's typical effervescence in this case could not top Du Bois' whose positive evaluation of the left-led SNYC knew no apparent bounds.[35]

The SNYC was not the only Communist-led organization with which Du Bois collaborated. He was a frequent instructor at the Jefferson School for Social Science. In 1945 he was asked to speak there on what Blacks could expect from the San Francisco Conference; this was one of the few occasions on which he could not comply, but he spoke at their fourth anniversary dinner on February 9, 1948, where $10,000 was raised. His classes through the years at the school drew packed crowds, particularly African and other foreign students. When in 1953 the attorney general petitioned the Subversive Activities Control Board to order the school to register under the McCarran Act, almost 10,000 students were enrolling each year. Du Bois joined Rexford Tugwell, Oliver Cox, Robert Lynd, Philip Foner, Thomas Emerson, and others in protest. At the SACB hearing, Du Bois testified for the school, along with Broadus Mitchell and Professor Robert Cohen of Wesleyan University, but under pressure from government authorities, it was voted in late November 1956 to liquidate, and a powerful institution was removed from the scene. Hence, Du Bois' classes on Reconstruction, African History, and so on, where students were asked the "cause of war," "will workers fight each other if capitalist wars cease," and other probing questions went down the drain.[36]

It was natural that Du Bois would be attracted to other intellectuals. On his return from the comparative intellectual backwater of Atlanta, it was inevitable, in a sense, that he would fall in with the likes of Wilkerson, Davis, Aptheker, and others with a similar interest in social change and matters cerebral. His writings began to appear in the Communist-edited weekly *New Masses* in 1945. His relationship with *New Masses* began to deepen at this point, as he spoke at their meeting honoring Romain Rolland and agreed to be honored at their Cultural Awards Dinner sponsored by a diverse crew. Thereafter he joined the publication as contributing editor and maintained that title after it became *Masses and Mainstream.* They were involved in publishing his novels and also gave a favorable review of *In Battle For Peace,* as he thanked Wilkerson for "his very appreciative review. . . . You read it thoroughly, and I agree with your judgment."[37]

Du Bois also gave his time and energy to other left publications; *Soviet Russia Today,* which eventually became *New World Review,* and its sister organization, the National Council of American-Soviet Friendship. When Du Bois returned to the NAACP in 1944, in that balmy political day, the council had an unusually broad board that included, among others, Adam Clayton Powell and sponsors, such as, Charles Chaplin, Thomas Mann, and Max Yergan. As late as May 1946, when Du Bois spoke for the council in Madison Square Garden, this group remained intact. When *Soviet Russia Today* requested permission to reprint his well-received remarks, they had a circulation of close to one hundred thousand. As time passed Du Bois continued to comply with their requests, for example, endorsing "Get Together with Russia" month and in response to an urgent appeal, agreed to speak on their conference concerning United States-Soviet relations. He joined Corliss Lamont on the Advisory Council of *Soviet Russia Today* and, with 150 prominent Americans, joined the protest against the release of the 20th Century Fox film "The Iron Curtain." In 1950 he accepted an invitation to join the NCASF's central body, the National Council, at a rather desperate hour. By that time Lillian Hellman had resigned, but Adam Clayton Powell remained. Unlike the Jefferson School and *Masses and Mainstream, Soviet Russia Today* and NCASF did not disappear. Du Bois played a personal role in prolonging this longevity.[38]

Given his close relationship to so many Communists and organizations within the party's orbit, it was inevitable that certain government agencies would strongly suspect that he was a card-carrying member. On August 26, 1948, the Atlanta Bureau of the FBI wrote J. Edgar Hoover directly on this point and also adressed his ties to the Progressive party; the bureau's informant listed participants in a New York meeting that he/she had infiltrated. Considering the time frame of these memoranda, it is interesting to speculate on whether the FBI communicated directly to the NAACP leadership about Du Bois' redness and whether this helped to spur his dismissal. In any case, Du Bois' fondness for the party during a time when it was probably the most reviled institution in the United States, cannot be denied. In 1954, when Senator McCarthy was still riding high, Du Bois was heaping praise upon his nemesis, the *Daily Worker.* When his friend James Jackson became editor, his ties to the paper became closer. In 1960 he spoke at a Carnegie Hall rally sponsored by the *Worker* focusing on Negro History Week and the thirty-sixth anniversary of the paper.[39]

Consequently, when Du Bois finally joined the party, "on this first day of October," 1961, it was an anticlimax for the FBI, albeit a surprise to others. The announcement was a significant political coup for the party and it broadcast his association widely. Once one posits Du Bois' longstanding relationship with Communists and Communist-led organizations, his decades-old affiliation as a "socialist of the path," and the fact that highly educated Blacks tended to be both more sympathetic to communism and to be represented in the party's highest circles, allegations about "senility" or "bitterness" leading to his membership only exemplify how anticommunism has blinded certain writers and historians to the diversity of reality. Du Bois' widely circulated message explaining his decision, as much as anything else, helps to explain his move. As early as his stay in Berlin in the 1890s, he ackowledged, "I attended meetings of the Socialist Party and considered myself a socialist." He freely admitted past differences with the party's "tactics in the case of the Scottsboro boys and their advocacy of a Negro state." Then he went to the heart of the question:

> Capitalism cannot reform itself; it is doomed to self-destruction. . . . Communism . . . this is the only way of human life. It is a difficult and hard end to reach—it has and will make mistakes. . . . On this first day of October 1961, I am applying for admission to membership in the Communist Party of the United States.

Certainly, Du Bois was not joining the party because it was fashionable; actually, this may have been the Communist Party's darkest hour, as *The New York Times* reported:

> The announcement came at a time when the party faced penalties of $10,000 a day for failing to register under the 1950 Internal Security Act. . . . If its officers do not register by November 30 and members then fail to register by December 20, each individual becomes liable to a similar fine and five year's imprisonment for each day of noncompliance.

The *Times* inadvertently rebutted any notion of an addled brain by referring to Du Bois as "still a spry man." Years later, Aptheker commented on his motivation: "Du Bois decided that it might be some contribution to peace and sanity if he were not only to join that Party but to do so with a public announcement of the fact." Aptheker was not that far from the truth in saying his choice "represents the logical culmination of his fabulous life."[40] Though Du Bois departed to reside in Africa after joining the party, he remained high in the firmament for the Communist Party and the world communist movement generally. Ellie Bowles of the *African Communist,* journal of the South African Communist party, breathlessly informed Du Bois that the "political appreciation" on Du Bois' life they published, spurred "numerous letters . . . from our readers all over the African continent." When the *Worker* celebrated its thirty-ninth anniversary, there were three themes stressed: one hundredth anniversary of the Emancipation Proclamation, International Women's Day, and Du Bois' ninety-fifth birthday. Du Bois was also honored when the young Communists of the United States reorganized and named themselves the "Du Bois Clubs." Though some may have found him a prophet in limbo, isolated and alone, harmless and ineffectual, apparently this was not the idea animating some United States government agencies, the CIA and FBI among others, to take note of his joining the party and the Du Bois Clubs being named after this much hunted man.[41]

Du Bois with Party Chairman Mao Zedong in Peking, 1959

CHAPTER 21

Du Bois and the Socialist Countries

Du Bois had traveled to Eastern Europe as early as the 1890s and had seen the poverty and hunger there; thus, he greeted the overthrow of the ancient regimes in the post-1945 period and the development of socialism there with satisfaction. Du Bois' idea of socialism, however, may have been disputed by Marxist-Leninists, as he had occasion to speak of the socialism of the Scandinavian countries. He was a firm believer in socialism as "the one hope of American Negroes." He conceded that he had once "stressed Nego private business enterprise," then "group economy"; he had hoped to establish cooperatives but they failed "because without the support of the state [they] cannot succeed." He noted that even in Western Europe the state owned "railroads and means of communications . . . hospitals" and called for increased public ownership in the United States.[1]

This was not the view of the NAACP, whose views on the Socialist countries ranged from the serious to the sublime. Henry Moon, director of public relations for the NAACP, broadcast over Radio Free Europe "to the captive people behind the Iron Curtain," according to *Crisis*. *Crisis* also reported that the men of Socialist Bulgaria were "Europe's least handsome men." This antagonistic viewpoint clashed with Du Bois' own outlook. Du Bois invited so many Eastern European diplomats to his Brooklyn home that the United States closed off the entire borough to them. When he was finally granted a passport, he traveled to Eastern Europe—a trip that had an admitted dramatic impact on his life. He confessed more than once afterwards that, "my whole attitude toward life has been changed," after he had seen socialism in practice. He was grandly feted during his trip, being awarded honorary doctorates from the universities of Humboldt, Charles, Moscow, and Sofia.[3]

Just as the NAACP's view of socialism evolved from the World War II era to the Cold War, so did the attitude of that dominant shaper of the United States body politic—United States business. Jonathan Boe has pointed out that their hostility toward socialism in Eastern Europe developed and escalated once the "trend toward state trade and bilateralism which forced out the American entrepreneur" became clear. Thus, in 1947, there was a decisive shift in attitude toward the rather quaint notion that a "planned economy necessarily led to aggression and that with socialist countries" negotiations were practically useless. The Marshall Plan was, as a consequence, presented "to the public—including businessmen—as an anti-Communist measure, and it was accepted as such." Once big business adopted its line, all others began to fall into place like ten-pins—or dominoes—the NAACP included.[3]

But not Du Bois. In 1946, at a time when an hysterical propaganda campaign was being whipped up against the Soviet Union in particular, Du Bois was using his column in the *Chicago Defender* to counter it. By the same token, during a time when the Communist party of France was under considerable pressure and being chased out of the government with the able assistance of the CIA, Du Bois was sending a message in his own hand and in French to be broadcast over the air, wherein he bitterly attacked anticommunism.[4]

At a 1949 speech in Madison Square Garden reprinted in the *Daily Worker,* Du Bois directly contradicted press reports about an "Iron Curtain" being forced down over a window on capitalism in Eastern Europe. "I wonder if what is called aggression in the Balkans may not be liberation of landless serfs and giving their ignorant masses in 25 years such education as American Negro slaves have not received in 75." He continued by stating that the press "has lied about American Negroes for three hundred years," which unavoidably damaged their credibility and he "for one will condemn neither Russia nor Communism on such testimony."[5]

The Soviet Union was much on Du Bois' mind at this time and not just because of the recurrent, ever-present crisis it was embroiled in with the United States. At this point he was at work on his book on the Soviet Union—*Russia and America: An Attempt at Interpretation*—the manuscript of which Aptheker had leveled withering criticism. It was based on his several trips there in 1926, 1936, and 1949, sent to several publishers, one of whom accepted it. At this juncture, in 1959, Du Bois considered the United States-Soviet contradiction to be primary—determining the course of events in the world—and the contradiction between the colonial powers and colonies, secondary. But Du Bois' comprehension of major social phenomena, for example, fascism, still reflected a disturbing naivete:[6]

> [Fascism is] leadership by a small group with total power supported by the capitalists and run for their benefit but allaying the complaints of the workers by full employment, better wages and many social gifts like housing and social medicine.

Joseph Hansen, Trotskyite and Socialist Workers party candidate for the United States Senate in 1950 against Du Bois, did not hesitate to attack what he perceived to be one of Du Bois' more controversial positions:

> I have challenged you repeatedly to use your influence to hasten shipments of food from America to drought-stricken Yugoslavia, thus publicly disassociating yourself from Moscow's policy of trying to bring the Yugoslav people to their knees. . . . Your continued silence leaves no other conclusion possible—you are acting as respectable front of Moscow's local representatives. You are permitting the local agents of the Kremlin police regime to exploit your good name and distinguished reputation for reactionary ends. In the twilight of a career of service to the people of America you have permitted Stalinism, "the syphilis of the labor movement," in Leon Trotsky's words, to place its hideous sore on your name.

This accusation of "Stalinism" was frequently tossed at Du Bois during this period but it did not faze him since he saw it as a reflection of United States government propaganda. Thus, he did not hesitate to ask that the Yugoslav Information Center remove his name from "the list of persons receiving your publications, I am not interested."[7]

Du Bois met head on the inflammatory issues of the day pertaining to the Soviets. In 1953, after accounts had appeared in the press concerning "Jewish purges," a correspondent of Du Bois coldly roared, "as a Jew I will certainly regard Russia [in] a much different light than I have up to now." Du Bois stubbornly balked: "It is the policy of those who are now in control of the United States to spread every charge possible against the Soviet Union, whether it is true or not." He spoke of "$200,000,000 to be used for subversion, bribery and revolt" by the United States in Eastern Europe for disruption and plotted allegations of "Jewish purges" along that line of the graph. Six years later he raised the same point concerning alleged Soviet anti-Semitism:

> Personally I have found no evidence of injustice toward them and I have met large numbers of Jews who agree with me. I am sure that there would be in the Soviet Union as there has been elsewhere, strong opposition to the assumptions of the Jewish Orthodox church. . . . I am opposed to the most of that which is called religion.

As for the other inflammatory issue of so-called Soviet interference in the internal affairs of other nations, Du Bois was equally forthright: "There has been in the United States much less evidence of communist plotting and propaganda than there has been of American plot and propaganda in Europe, Asia and Africa."[8]

Perhaps no person was more controversial in the United States than Joseph Stalin and Du Bois did not shirk from defending him and eulogized him on his death in 1953:

> [he] was a great man. . . . He was attacked and slandered as few men of power have been. . . . He early saw through the flamboyance and exhibitionism of Trotsky, who fooled the world and especially America . . . our naive acceptance of Trotsky's magnificent lying propaganda . . . deep worship of Stalin by the people [in the USSR].

When the revelations of Stalin's misdeeds were revealed by the Communist Party Congress in 1956 in Moscow, Du Bois did not change his mind. John Kingsbury was dissatisfied with the National Council of American-Soviet Friendship statement on the issue, feeling it was far too critical. He told this to Shirley Graham, who concurred in his view. Du Bois elaborated on this point when John

Biddle, publisher and president of the *Daily News* of Huntingdon, Pennsylvania, specifically asked him in 1956 to change his mind: "may I say that I do not at present see any reason to change my words of 1952." He said his praise was based on his "carrying out of the Revolution initiated by Lenin in the face of attack of all sorts. . . . That Stalin was a hard dictator is true but if he had not been Churchill and Truman would have crushed the Soviets. I still believe that Stalin's attitude at Yalta and Potsdam showed calmness, courage and clear thought." He was also critical of the principal perpetrator of the revelations: "I am not at all satisfied with Khrushchev's *[sic]* testimony. It seems to me irresponsible and muddled. He lumps together Stalin's fight against Trotsky and the various victims of the great purge. . . . I am not in the least cast down. The Soviet state is great and progressing. . . . Not even upheaval in Poland disturbs me. I saw Poland in 1893 and in 1950. Its progress, contentment and peace is unquestionable. Of course the old landlord and military clan bribed by the United States is going to make trouble for a long time to come." But he remained incorrigible on the issue of Stalin: "I still regard [him] as one of the great men of the twentieth century. He was not perfect; he was probably too cruel; but he did three things." And the three elements that Du Bois found that redeemed Stalin was his role in establishing the first socialist state, his breaking of the Kulaks and collectivizing agriculture, and his leading of the struggle that whipped Hitler.[9]

Du Bois took to the pages of *New World Review* (formerly *Soviet Russia Today*) to elucidate his controversial evaluation of the Georgian and the state he helped to build. With typical broad brush strokes, he castigated the "smallness of [Negro] intelligentsia" for going along with the "current witch-hunt" and its "devastating" effect on black literature, music, and so on; all this, according to Du Bois, because of a deep hatred of the Soviet Union defiling the United States. Furthermore, in a review of Anna Louise Strong's *The Stalin Era* he restated his unalterable view:

> That many persons, including herself suffered in this process was regrettable and even in cases terrible, but the total result was a glorious victory in the uplift of mankind.

He then quoted a decidedly noncommunist source, Howard K. Smith: "Had Russia not liquidated a few thousand bureaucrats and officers, there is little doubt that the Red Army would have collapsed in two months."[10]

Simultaneous with the Stalin revelations was another event that rocked the United States left—Hungary. The uprising against socialism there shook the confidence of many progressives, but not Du Bois. He did feel the pressure of taking a position not in line with the conventional wisdom: "of course just not every progressive, not to mention other people, must be expert on Hungary whenever he opens his mouth." With his usual thoroughness, he studied various reports and sources, then took the opportunity of a memorial meeting for Vito Marcantonio, two years after his death, to speak out publicly:[11]

> I do know that the Hungary which I saw in the last decade of the nineteenth century was the most cruelly exploited nation in Europe. On the backs of a poverty-stricken, ignorant and superstitious peasantry rode a flamboyant, impudent, aristocracy, rich, privileged and shrill; on the backs of these lazy, lecherous tyrants, perched a growing host of British, French and American investors eager for "high society" and rich profits . . . and now among . . . the proposed rescuers of the Hungary which they once destroyed is the same gang of titled nobility, the same flock of rapacious landlords and an increased host of American capitalists seeking to sink their claws again into the mines and oil wells, soil and serf labor of ten million Hungarians. The folk who itch to go to Hungary and investigate have billions of [dollars] invested in the old regime which they hope now to get back.

The response of the Black community to events in Eastern Europe was diverse. Naturally, the NAACP tried to use the crisis in Hungary for its own purposes: "Is the Federal government going to continue to have more concern with civil rights in the Russian satellite countries than in our own South." Roy Wilkins, per usual, struck out with unrestrained vigor:

> In Hungary the Soviets used tanks to beat down freedom. . . . Our opponents have been seeking to label the NAACP . . . as communist but their . . . dictatorship in their own Deep South is a true blood-brother to bolshevism.

Other Blacks raised this contradiction of penultimate concern about white Hungarians and not too benign neglect of United States and other Blacks, but without Wilkins' anticommunist hue. James Hicks in the *Amsterdam News* confessed to being "pretty well fed up with Hungarians and the Hungary problem." He recalled when hurricanes blew through the Caribbean leaving thousands of Blacks homeless:

> I didn't see anyone here get up on the rooftops and say: "Let's bypass the McCarran Act and let 21,000 West Indians into this country to ease their suffering." . . . I don't know. I suppose I'm just a maladjusted Negro. But it looks mighty funny to me that we Americans can sit back and watch Black people from Ethiopia to Mississippi get their brains beat out by anyone who has enough guns to do the job without getting "charitable" or "excited."

P. L. Prattis in the *Pittsburgh Courier* was equally concerned with the contrast in treatment of Blacks, in this case oppressed and down-trodden Kenyans:

> [Britain] strafed and bombed bands of natives wherever they could find them. Thousands were killed and injured. Other thousands—some 72,000—were captured and placed in concentration camps. . . . The slaughter in Kenya has been quite as sanguinary as any in . . . Eastern Europe.

New York City Councilman Earl Brown in the *Amsterdam News* said that while "our government [was sending] airplanes to Austria to whisk [Hungarians] to freedom in the U.S. by the thousands," he queried whether the same would be done for Blacks being "brutalized" in Clinton, Tennessee. Even conservative NAACP leader Clarence Mitchell observed in the *Afro-American* that the attention given to Hungary was well and good but what about Africa? Thus, it was not altogether shocking when a Du Bois correspondent criticized him for being soft on Stalin but then declared to the Black patriarch: "As to the Hungarian rebellion and its smash, I am in complete agreement with you. And I congratulate you on your courage to state it."[12]

At the same time it appeared that the NAACP leadership was becoming progressively anticommunist, Du Bois was steadily singing the praises of socialism at every opportunity. When he spoke at

Howard University in March 1958, he spit in the face of right-wing opposition to his appearance by addressing the impact of socialism from 1917 to 1957. His message to the All-African People's Congress in Accra, Ghana, in December 1958 basically directed the Africans that their only hope for true freedom was building socialism. In a Chicago speech in late 1959 he graphically described the low prices and quality of life under socialism. In his remarks to the Wisconsin Socialism Club at the University of Wisconsin, he spoke of "Socialism and the American Negro."[13]

Finally, in 1958, months after Ghana's independence celebration, Du Bois was granted a passport and allowed to travel abroad to see the socialism he had been carrying the torch for for so long. From August 1958 through July 1959, he and Shirley Graham were out of the United States virtually the entire time. In 1960 they did not relent, traveling to Ghana, Western Europe, the Virgin Islands, Canada, and to Nigeria for their independence celebration. His being granted a passport was not directly the result of a case fought before the Supreme Court, but as outlined earlier, a result of a massive outpouring of international and national criticism over his virtual house imprisonment in the United States. The *Accra Evening News* was candid:

> we are weeping over the denial of a passport to Dr. Du Bois. . . . That the position remained unchanged after our Prime Minister's personal intervention is the first serious slap in the face of Pan-Africanism since our emergence to Independence . . . the treatment meted out to Dr. Du Bois is a Black page which we will never forget.

This direct challenge from such a politically and strategically important nation could not be easily dismissed. And, as Shirley Graham has described, the rallying around Du Bois on his nintieth birthday spoke with equal clarity and eloquence. The special messages from Britain, France, the Soviet Union, German Democratic Republic, Italy, Ghana, Kenya, Nigeria, People's Republic of China, India, Cuba, Brazil, Japan, and the British West Indies, the special issues of the *Afro-American* and *Pittsburgh Courier,* the special celebrations in New York, Chicago, San Francisco, Los Angeles, Nashville, Baltimore, and Detroit, all attested to Du Bois' unflagging and continued popularity and the discontent with his house arrest.[14]

Thus, in 1958 Du Bois, now viewed as something of a dangerous radical, was allowed a passport for the first time since 1950. In London he was greeted triumphantly, particularly by the substantial African and Caribbean community. He spoke to African students (addressing events in South Africa particularly), met with the Soviet Ambassador, China's chargé, and members of Parliament. He gave two lectures and made two broadcasts and resided in Robeson's apartment while he was there. In Amsterdam he was similarly received. In Paris he gave an electrifying speech at a rally against the war in Algeria. His reception in France was no less honorific: "I attended the Joliot-Curie memorial and sat on the red-draped rostrum at the right hand of the presiding chairman, Thorez." Du Bois and Graham spent two weeks as guests of the Czechoslovakian government and the six-hundred year old Charles University in Prague, one of the oldest institutions of higher education in the world, awarded him an honorary degree. Continuing the tenor of his speeches in the United States, the theme of his acceptance remarks was, "the salvation of American Negroes lies in socialism." Shirley Graham caustically noted that Harvard never invited Du Bois to lecture and the Harvard Club in New York barred his entrance, but while abroad Du Bois was treated like a touring potentate.[15]

After his fervent defense of the Soviet Union in the face of biting criticism in the United States, his visit there was redemptive in spirit and perhaps, the high point of his travels. New Year's eve of 1958 he spent in Moscow celebrating with Nikita Khrushchev, the Robesons, and embassy personnel from India, Ceylon, and elsewhere. but most heartening was his visit to the Afro-Asian Cultural Conference in Tashkent, Uzbekistan, in Soviet Central Asia. There he and Shirley were honored guests at this meeting of African and Asiatic authors. Du Bois "drew the only standing ovation to an individual," and was "elected to the [presidium] and made a speech." In an informal discussion of African unification problems with writers from Nigeria, Madagascar, Ghana, Somaliland, Senegal, and Angola he said "a socialist Africa was inevitable." This infecting of Africans with a radical vaccine was precisely what the denial of his passport was designed to prevent. However, the 140 delegates from thirty-six countries did not seem to object to his peroration: "He was fervently applauded for his insistence that 'village socialism' in Africa would be skipped." The renowned writers present—for example, Burma's U Kyaw Lin Hyunt, China's

Mao Tun, India's Yash Pal, Cambodia's Ly Theam Teng, Indonesia's Amanta Toer, Vietnam's Pham Huy Thong, and the famed Turk Nazim Hikmet—listened attentively to Du Bois' measured denunciation of United States imperialism and explication of the noncapitalist stage of development.[16]

Du Bois was appreciative of the honorary degree from Charles University—"the most gorgeous honors ever bestowed on me"—and the German Peace Medal he received in East Berlin, but few events pleased him more than Premier Khrushchev's acceptance of his "Proposal to the Soviet Union to Undertake a Scientific Study of Africa." Herein he suggested establishment of an Institute for Study of Africa, an idea quickly snapped up by the Soviets, approved and established in Moscow. Subsequently, he met with prominent Soviet Africanists, such as Professor I. Potekhin, who endorsed his idea of preparing an Encyclopedia Africana. Du Bois was charmed by his two hour meeting with the Soviet premier:

> It was so informal and friendly. . . . We just sat on opposite sides of a table and talked together. We talked about peace and ways to develop closer and friendlier relations with the United States. . . . I talked about Africa. . . . I thought the best way the Soviet Union could help would be to study African history, African culture, African environment and make the results of their studies available to the African people.

Similarly, as Wilfred Burchett reported, Moscow was quite charmed with Du Bois: "Dr. Du Bois has charmed everyone here by his vitality, his penetrating observations of the world and by his quiet, ripe wit." Later, the Soviet academician M. F. Nesturkh complimented Du Bois directly on how he and Shirley Graham had made a "profound impression on our anthropologists' audience" on their visit to the Moscow State University and Anthropological Institute and Museum. The CIA was also a bit charmed by Du Bois' trip and took note of an interview with him in an obscure magazine where he praised the Soviet Union and Sputnik as a testament to Communism.[17]

Du Bois' trip to the Soviet Union took place at a time, perhaps not coincidentally, when—as Louis Burnham put it—the "U.S.-Soviet thaw [was reaching] into [the] Negro community." He contrasted the Soviet and United States positions on Africa and highlighted the generous aid from the former with the exploitative and tight-fisted policies of the latter. Different delegations of Black bankers, journalists, and students were visiting the Soviet Union at this juncture and returning with favorble comment:

> Throughout the Cold War period Negroes have had perhaps less reason than some other groups to embrace the foreign and domestic policies of the Truman and Eisenhower administrations . . . for many years such [positive] appraisals of Soviet life could be heard in the Negro community only from W.E.B. Du Bois, Paul Robeson, or other partisans of socialism. . . . With the current thaw there has begun a call for the reappraisal of the role of these two outstanding leaders.

The thaw likewise had a positive effect on Du Bois: "Then in 1959 . . . I came to Moscow again and spent six months in the Soviet Union. They healed my body; translated my books. . . . They opened their periodicals and press to my writings." In a lengthy letter to S. A. Dangoulov in the Soviet Union expounding his views on the proletarian movement, and the role of the left, he returned to the impact of his 1958–1959 journey; "it was not until my last trip to Europe in 1958 that I felt that from my own life and experience I was a member of the working group." The experience of Du Bois and the Black community with socialism had a profound impact on both; it was unavoidable that intimate contact with a different way of life, where antiracism and anticolonialism was stressed, where medical care was free and prices low, of necessity would lead to this result; it was just a short step from the visits of the late 1950s to the widespread civil rights protests of the early 1960s stressing precisely these things—antiracism and anticolonialism.[18]

It should be understood that W.E.B. Du Bois was one of the few United States citizens with sufficient clout to be given a private audience with the leader of the Soviet Union. Similarly when he traveled to China, he was not just accorded audiences with Mao Zedong,* Chou En-lai, and Madame Sun Yat-sen but, in the first

---

* On meeting Du Bois, Mao said, "You are no darker than I. Who could tell which one of us is darker?" There was sharp argument between the two over United States foreign policy, principally concerning Mao's benign view of the United States that reached fruition in the post-1971 period. Tracy B. Strong and Helene Keyssar, *Right in Her Soul: The Life of Anna Louise Strong* (New York: Random House, 1983), 298, 301.

place, was one of the few from the United States to be allowed in the country during this period of difficult relations with Washington over Quemoy, Matsu, and related matters. Moreover, Du Bois' journey to China took a certain amount of courage. The Black journalist William Worthy had been one of the first to violate the State Department's travel ban, which was upheld in district court. Hence, *The New York Times* report of February 14, 1959 rang ominously:[19]

> [W.E.B. Du Bois] was reported by the Peking Radio to have arrived in Communist China today. The State Department declared that Dr. Du Bois had no authorization to go to Communist China.

This was not Du Bois' first visit to China. He noted that when he had traveled there in 1936, "I saw a little English boy of perhaps four years order three little children out of his way on the sidewalk of the Bund. They meekly obeyed and stepped into the gutter. It looked like Mississippi." In *Freedom* he had addressed a troublesome issue dividing Washington and Peking: "By what far-fetched logic can Formosa, on the opposite side of the earth from us, be regarded as necessary for the protection of our western border. . . . Do we simply pretend to own the earth. . . . Of [China's] legal right to Formosa there is no doubt." He did not try to hide his partisanship on behalf of China. Not recognizing the Peking regime and barring it from the United Nations, he said, "is not only against diplomatic usage, it is against common sense, it is against ethics and philanthropy. . . . With our noses in the mud we are trying to find the spy who betrayed us in China. We need look no further. We ourselves were the scoundrels.[20]

Because he was such a determined partisan of Peking, at a time when this was regarded as veritably traitorous in the United States, Mao Zedong spoke highly of Du Bois:

> Du Bois [is] a great man of our time. His deeds of heroic struggle for the liberation of the Negroes and the whole of mankind, his outstanding achievements in academic fields and his sincere friendship toward the Chinese people will forever remain in the memory of the Chinese people.

His 1959 jaunt to China was seen as vindication of Peking's then energetic opposition to United States foreign policy. Du Bois was given an official state reception by Chou En-lai, prominently covered by the Chinese press; the *People's Daily* placed it on page one. On February 23, 1959, Du Bois gave a birthday address to thousands at Peking University faculty and students. Then there was the Chinese-style party to celebrate the ninety-first birthday of Dr. W.E.B. Du Bois held at Peking Hotel with Vice Premier Chen Yi and other Chinese prominent in many fields of work attending. Du Bois was ecstatic about this signal honor: "Ministers of state were there, writers and artists, actors and professional men; singers and children playing fairy tales. Anna Louise Strong came." This was not the extent of his China trip:

> I travelled 5,000 miles by railway, boat, plane and auto . . . [I] lectured and broadcast to the world . . . I was on the borders of Tibet when the revolt occurred. I spent four hours with Mao Tse-tung and dined twice with Chou En-lai . . . China has no rank nor classes; her universities grant no degrees; her government awards no medals . . . [but] China is no Utopia.

Again, one senses Du Bois' naivete in being seduced by certain precursors of the disastrous cultural revolution. Nevertheless, it is doubtlessly true that the Chinese people and leadership took Du Bois to their heart. He was the first American ever allowed to observe the National Day Parade on October 1 from the central rostrum with Mao and other Chinese leaders.[21]

Du Bois' experience in China only served to deepen his anti-imperialist and prosocialist commitment:

> This . . . has been a far greater experience than all the rest of my travels put together. I have seen to an extent that I never expected to see, the practical possibility of changing what we call human nature from dog-eat-dog to cooperation. It is being done and it is working. I am afraid that most Americans either will not listen or won't believe if they do, but that doesn't alter the fact.

Du Bois was right, as Shirley Graham had difficulty in placing her fascinating account of the journey in the mainsteam press but wound up inserting a version of it in *Political Affairs.*[22]

Du Bois' extended tour of Europe and Asia had a broad impact on Du Bois' outlook. He told E. Franklin Frazier; "It was a most extraordinary journey and has changed my outlook on current affairs." His closeness to the Soviet Union was manifested when he was awarded the Lenin Peace Price in 1959—past award winners had been Howard Fast and Paul Robeson.[23]

Du Bois had long seen the battle against United States racism as "a continuation of a world movement" and, from his point of view, this would eventually override any Black dalliance with anti-Sovietism. This was part of the message he took to the airwaves of the world. On WBAI-FM in New York he discussed China; on Bulgarian Radio he made remarks on Eisenhower, the Soviets, DeGawlle, and the upcoming summit of 1960—all to be "broadcast in [their] Home Service as well as in all the foreign language transmissions of Radio Sofia." On Czechoslovakian radio, similar statements were made.[24]

This collaboration with Czechoslovakia signaled a developing rapprochement between the regime in Prague and Du Bois. Years previously they had arranged a Czech translation of *In Battle for Peace* that earned Du Bois no piddling amount of royalties, despite the post office's attempt to stymie these arrangements. Du Bois was a frequent guest of United Nations representatives from Eastern Europe but the Czechoslovaks were in the vanguard as they went so far as to organize a special buffet dinner honoring him in 1955. Hence, it was natural when in 1960 they offered to subsidize his coming to Prague; Du Bois took this opportunity to piggy-back trips to Rome, Ghana, and Western Europe. For the first time in years, the man who continued to be a vigorous swimmer in his nineties, began to show the seam of age: "I got a shock in the true sense of the word, that is a fairly mild attack of apoplexy—bad arteries in a small area of the brain—which warned me that my work is about finished." Thus, on his return to New York, he decided "not to go out very much." But Du Bois was peripatetic and he could not be kept down; yet, this time, his visit to Eastern Europe was to a famous sanitorium for the elderly in Romania, renowned for its frontier research in gerontology:

> I am very glad I went, I am in better health and it was a marvelous privilege to live in a little country, like Romania, which has just about the same number of people there are Negroes in the United States and yet has 25,000 physicans and is graduating 1,000 each year. . . . In the sanitorium where I was there were 26 doctors, over 50 medical assistants,

> besides trained nurses and helpers. I had visits from at least two doctors every day and every kind of analysis and measurement to see just what the state of my health was . . . I got so that I was afraid to express any wish or desire, because I knew they would immediately go and arrange for it.

This blissful respite was brought to a rude awakening on his arrival back in the United States: "The Customs officials were curious about my correspondence and papers and held me up an hour or so but were quite polite, and I still have my passport."[25]

The Cuban Revolution was in its infancy during Du Bois' last years but it did not escape his attention. The Fair Play for Cuba Committee invited him to visit there in September 1960 but he declined because of reasons of health. Still, he remained unbowed: "I hope some time in the near future to be able to visit Cuba to see for myself this brave and courageous country." After the abortive invasion at the so-called Bay of Pigs (Playa Giron), engineered by the CIA and Cuban exiles, he was quick to join William Worthy, Emmett Bassett, and other Afro-Americans in a resolute protest. Personally, he bitterly denounced the invasion:

> It was crazy, ill-judged scheme. The work that Castro is doing in Cuba is marvelous and inspiring and the mass of people utterly support it. . . . We secretly planned an invasion while publicly righteously denying it. Then to our own surprise, but to that of no one else, we were roundly beaten . . . the young president . . . was utterly astonished.

Hard on the heels of the Bay of Pigs invasion, *Crisis,* in a move that probably was not unintentionally timed, featured a virulently anticommunist broadside against the Havana regime and Fidel Castro—"this master of deceit" (to quote J. Edgar Hoover) and "dictator."[26]

Du Bois' frequent travel to Socialist countries during the last years of his life admittedly changed the texture of his existence and marked a growing closeness to these regimes. Rather than depositing his historically significant papers on the Pan-African Congress in a United States institution, he sent them to Moscow for microfilming. He gratefully accepted his selection as an "honorary member of the Moscow Society for Experimentation in Nature," and various other awards, memberships, and honors showered on him by Socialist states world-wide. When asked by Radio Moscow to list the signal events of the 1960s, his response mirrored his Eastern orientation:

> The highlights of 1960 are the rise of the peoples of Africa toward independence and socialism; the continued progress of China as a leading Communist state; the unbreakable cooperation of China and the Soviet Union; the successful fight of the Soviet Union in the United Nations against colonialism; the successful revolt of the people of Cuba.

When asked what his primary wish would be, he said, "peace . . . disarmament . . . abolition of nuclear weapons." After he moved to Ghana in 1961, his outlook in word and deed did not change. In 1962 he traveled to Peking to celebrate the eighteenth anniversary of the People's Republic of China, met with Mao and Chou once more, and assumed a place of honor in Tien An Men Square during the October 1 parade of 500,000—which was seen as a gesture toward his party, the Communist party, and toward America's progressives generally. United States government agencies were also consumed with Du Bois' visits East. The embassy in Bucharest faithfully reported on his stay there while the CIA forwarded to the FBI a "clipping from the Accra (Ghana) Evening News, dated 8 October 1962, describing Chou En-lai's reception of Mr. W.E.B. Du Bois and his wife, Shirley Graham, during their trip to Communist China. Mr. Du Bois is an American residing in Accra and is well-known for his Communist sympathies."[27]

Given his solidarity with the Socialist camp, it was natural that Du Bois would be disturbed by Peking's breaking away from the world Communist movement. Shirley Graham appeared to be more taken with Peking than Moscow—"inside China the straight line towards the ultimate goal is clearer and simpler than inside the USSR"—but it does not seem that this attitude was shared by her husband. In 1963 he drafted a letter to leaders of both Peking and Moscow setting forth his dimly understood grasp of the issues; yet he sincerely tried to bridge the gap:

> The Russians must remember that the Chinese have suffered long and are very sensitive. The Chinese must remember that the Russians first made Communism a workable form of society.

> . . . The joy of the imperialist is great as they see differences arising in Communist leadership.

Du Bois did not live to see the gaping chasm that separated Peking from other Communist parties. In any case, it cannot be denied that as an aspect of his travels to Socialist countries his life was unalterably changed, his commitment was deepened, and, in his mind, his move to join the Communist party was foreshadowed.[28]

Du Bois with Kwame Nkrumah, President of Ghana, at celebration of Du Bois' 95th birthday in 1963

CHAPTER 22

Du Bois and Africa

The importance of Du Bois to Africa and the importance of Africa to Du Bois was dramatized when his passport, seized after his 1959 visit to China, was returned to him after the intervention of the Ghana Embassy in Washington when he wished to travel to Accra in 1960. This was clear recognition of both the importance of Du Bois and the power of newly independent Africa. The early 1960s brought great concern with whether a free Africa, no longer blocked from independence, would go "Communist." Part of this was fueled by rampaging guilt over the notion that Africans would be so discontented with the ravaging of imperialism and colonialism, that they would turn East. Du Bois, friendly with Nkrumah, Toure, Azikiwe, Nyerere, Banda, Ben Bella, and other African leaders, was viewed as a dangerous beacon of radicalism. John Hennings, a colonial attaché in Britain's Washington Embassy, in his *The Attitudes of African Nationalism Toward Communism*—a title neatly summarizing the fears of the era—while acknowledging Du Bois as the Father of African nationalism, still severely berated him because of his left politics. Not only Mr. Hennings but a number of others in the "West" were concerned that Du Bois would use his vast influence among the Africans to nudge them leftwards. And they were right; Du Bois was as whirling and contrapuntal as a Bach fugue in doing this. The NAACP, reflecting its petit bourgeois leadership, trapped between those on high and the masses below, pursued a schizophrenic policy; engaging in its usual redbaiting while warning that racism was destabilizing the battle against communism.[1]

One of the most well-known facts about Du Bois is his role in the development of Pan-Africanism on an anti-imperialist and anti-colonial basis. His Pan-Africanism was not the exclusivist model so popular among a narrow stratum of Afro-Americans during the 1960s. He was quite cognizant of oppression of colored peoples generally. He conceded that his 1934 departure from the NAACP was tied to their lack of internationalism. "They will have nothing to do with Africa or the Negroes outside the United States and I could not agree with them." His return to the NAACP in 1944 and his later years generally coincided with an upsurge in all anti-colonial struggles, but particularly those in Africa, which culminated in the "year of Africa"—1960—when so many Black states achieved formal independence. A particular concern of United States policy makers was the possibility that these nations would go left. Zbigniew Brzezinski, in his 1963 opus, *Africa and the Communist World*—yet another title encapulating the tensions of the epoch—nervously discussed the problem: "no Communist state has ever been a colonial power on the African continent. . . . It is not surprising that African statesmen visiting the Soviet Union even if they consciously attempt to avoid identifying themselves with the USSR in international affairs . . . do express admiration for the way the Soviet Union is carrying out its modernization." With utmost concern, he quoted a 1962 poll taken by *Jeune Afrique* which found that 57 percent of the students from Guinea and Mali preferred the "Soviet model" while 38 percent in Cameroun, Congo-Brazzaville, and Gabon felt likewise—this despite the barrage of anticommunist propaganda and the assumption that education and contact with the "West" was a sound purgative for leftist ideas; but, like Blacks in the United States, it seemed that education may have increased the seductive allure of socialism. And, just as Du Bois' example gave succor to progressives in the United States, this man, who was probably the most well-known North American and Afro-American, played a similar role among progressives in Africa.[2]

Much of Du Bois' support activities for African liberation were carried out under the auspices of the Council of African Affairs. He also used his prolific pen to detail the massive strikes and boycotts sweeping Africa and stressed the growth of trade union militancy on the continent. He was also instrumental in rallying Afro-American sentiment against colonialism. In 1952, at his initiative, Sidney Poitier, Coleman Young, Paul Robeson, and others filed an angry petition with President Truman denouncing "our government's policy toward colonial and subject peoples, especially Africa. . . . As Negroes we have a deep bond of sympathy, growing out of a common experience of suffering and struggle, with the two thirds of the world that is called colored." Among their demands were that the United States "withdraw . . . military force and installations from all foreign territories where their presence is not authorized by agreement of all the major powers." They submitted their petition, which was signed by 160 Blacks from twenty-eight states—including a disproportionate number of clergy—to the Democrats, Republicans, and Progressives; naturally, their concerns were more amply represented in the latter's platform. They held a well-attended press conference on June 30 to publicize their effort.[3]

This petition was further confirmation of Du Bois' continuing stature in the Pan-African world, despite the Cold War attempt to isolate him. In 1953, Walter Sisulu, secretary-general of the African National Congress (ANC) of South Africa suggested that Du Bois was the person to convene another Pan-African Congress. That same year Alphaeus Hunton reported on African press coverage of Du Bois: "the *West African Pilot* has recently carried a front-page report of a speech by you on the Rosenbergs and your message (and also Paul's) to the people of Africa on the occasion of the last World Peace Congress." A recurrent theme promulgated by Du Bois was the basic unity between Africans and Afro-Americans, though he scored United States Blacks for not aiding Africa more.[4]

Du Bois remained a close student of NAACP activities over the years, even after his departure, and recognized the duality of their support of, and retreat from, African liberation. That the NAACP was interested in Africa cannot be denied. Virtually no issue of the *Crisis* did not pass without either an article or book review that touched on the continent; this was especially so after Ghana's independence in 1957 and during the year of Africa, 1960. In 1951 the World Assembly of Youth—which was patterned after the United Nations—was held at Cornell University and with NAACP participation. "African delegates vigorously objected to the holding of the assembly in the United States because they were afraid they would be lynched as soon as they disembarked." It was noted that Africans had a wide knowledge of racial discrimination cases: "Ironically enough the Civil Rights Congress or some other left-wing group had been involved in almost every one of the cases mentioned." The NAACP's participation in this effort was not singular. In 1952 they invited twenty-five organizations to join with them in a statement asking the United States to take a stronger stand on Africa, particularly Tunisia, Morocco, and South Africa. At the fifty-first annual convention Dr. Mlaheni Njisane of South Africa spoke and compared the ANC of South Africa to the NAACP; and the film on South Africa, "Come Back Africa," was shown. In 1959, they joined the American Committee on Africa in sponsoring a dinner for the visiting Sekou Touré, soon to be pummeled by the United States press for his fervent anti-imperialism. Wilkins' message to the All-African People's Conference in Ghana in December 1958 resonated soundly and could have been authored by Du Bois.[5]

A particular concern of Du Bois, the NAACP, and the State Department was the often dastardly treatment dished out to Caribbean and African Blacks in the United States: "The Mayor of Kingston, Jamaica says she was grossly insulted yesterday when refused service in Louisville drugstore." Ferdinand Oyono, Cameroun delegate to the United Nations complained of the racist treatment he had received at the hands of New York police. In 1961 the Nigerian ambassador Julius M. Udochi was refused service at a restaurant in Charlottesville, Virginia. H. V. H. Sekyi, Ghanaian diplomat, was subjected to racial indignities while observing election procedures in Mapletown, Georgia. These were just a few of the reported incidents, and the proverbial tip of the iceberg, for it was clear that racism was hindering the execution of United States foreign policy. John Owen, who had served as a visiting professor at the University of Helsinki during 1951 to 1952, had observed that race was the topic most students wanted to hear about when the United States was discussed. He warned that if "future leaders . . . return home with tales to tell of the discrimination they observed, or perhaps painfully encountered, it is not likely to help our democratic cause in the eyes of the world."[6]

At times the NAACP rhetoric on Africa flew so hot and heavy that it could be easily mistaken for a Du Bois essay in the *National Guardian.* In 1952, not long after they had balked in aiding Du Bois during his trial, the *Crisis* editorialized: "Imperialism has been weakened in Africa, but it has not been liquidated. Europe still expects Africa to supply foodstuffs, raw materials, big African armies and to provide military, naval and air bases." Here, the

NAACP leadership was responding to entreaties from the Black masses below. Thus, from 1944 to 1963, few issues, including FEPC, received more attention in the *Crisis* than South Africa. Blacks generally saw parallels in their struggle and that of Black South Africans. Even Thurgood Marshall, the sober attorney, in 1960 compared the struggle in the South to the "cry against apartheid in South Africa . . . [and] one man, one vote in Kenya." Yet, when Du Bois complained of the lack of Afro-American support for anticolonialism, he no doubt did not refer to the frenzied demonstration at the United Nations February 15, 1961, protesting Patrice Lumumba's assassination and led by militant Afro-Americans. Roy Wilkins denounced the protesters and redbaited them mercilessly: "Belgium colonizers should not be replaced with Soviet Union colonizers." Here, the NAACP leadership was responding to entreaties from the white rulers above.[7]

Du Bois, unlike the NAACP leadership, was not one to condemn militant demonstrations against rape of the continent and this is what endeared him to Africans. At the meeting of African and Asian writers in 1958 in Tashkent, which had a far larger representation from Africa than was present at the Bandung Conference in 1955, Du Bois was lionized. The same thing happened at the Sixth Conference of the All African Students Union of the Americas held in Chicago in June 1958.[8]

Du Bois' contribution to Africa was substantially political and intellectual. In early 1961 he again attacked the line popularized by the NAACP, that Jim Crow should be abolished so the left and socialism could be beaten back. Du Bois' considered opinion was that because Africans were less prejudiced toward socialism, Afro-Americans would wind up following them rather than the reverse, as many earlier suspected. The Rowans, the Whites, and others were seen as agents, like King Canute, trying futilely to halt a rising tide of socialism.[9]

Du Bois was not only harsh in his assessment of Blacks who he perceived as trodding the incorrect path. He sharply criticized a paper on Pan-Africanism written by Professor Immanuel Wallerstein of Columbia University, forwarded to him for his comments weeks before his departure to live in Ghana:

> The Communists did not oppose Pan-Africanism. They did not, for some time, realize its existence and did not pay proper attention to advice of men like Padmore, especially in the early

> 19th century *[sic]*. In the 20th century, however, they began to recognize the Pan African movement and to cooperate with it. Just before his death Padmore entertained a number of prominent Russians in Ghana; and I am convinced that had he lived, he and the Soviet Union would have come to closer understanding. . . . Pan-Africanism was not dormant between the Manchester meeting in 1945 and the Accra meeting in 1958. It was alive in the plans of Nkrumah, Padmore and many others; but the question was where it could meet and how far its program could go. The meeting in 1958 at Accra was really the 6th Pan African Congress. The only speech there delivered by a non-African was my speech. It was read to the Congress by special vote by my wife as the physicians decided that I was not in good enough health to come.

This revision of Wallerstein's analysis also revealed Du Bois' conscious determination to set the historical record straight as he approached the end of his life. It also revealed that his powers of critical perception had not diminished. Around the same time, Du Bois told the future leader of the Illinois Communist party, Ishmael Flory, of his distaste for the American Society for African Culture: "they have investment in mind or personal position instead of scientific work. . . . The president is Horace Mann Bond. I have heard of nothing yet worthwhile that they have done."[10]

Du Bois was able to speak so confidently about events and organizations because he had remained in close contact with correspondents on the continent. Alphaeus Hunton, who came to work in Guinea early in May 1960 at the direct invitation of President Touré, kept him posted on continental developments. Du Bois was also in contact with the white South African Communist leader Ray Alexander, also a feminist heroine and writer. Alice Citron told him that Alexander had written her about his article in the *National Guardian* on the Congo and Ghana, and that "you are greatly admired and inspire those who carry on in Capetown and Johannesburg."[11]

Du Bois continued to be in close touch with events and personalities in Nigeria, the continent's most populous nation. He went there in November 1960 "to see Azikiwe made Governor-General . . . I feel it my duty to be present since I was so urgently invited." "Transport and accommodation will be borne by this government" was the word he received from Lagos. W. O. Goodluck, secretary-general of the Nigerian Trade Union Congress in 1960 and present leader of the left forces there dubbed Du Bois "Father of Pan-Africanism" and invited him to visit Nigeria "as the NTUC *special guest.*" NTUC, he continued, "would very much [like] to seize this very rare opportunity which may not be repeated in view of the difficulties you have faced for so many years before you were granted your passport to leave the U.S.A. . . . You can be assured that there awaits you a tremendous welcome from the Nigerian workers, the progressives, intellectuals and a large section of the Nigerian community."[12]

At the request of Nnamdi Azikiwe, he drafted a pamphlet, "A Path for Nigeria," which was "a sort of guide from the Socialist point of view of the steps which Nigeria ought to take." The pamphlet was drafted after private conversations with the Nigerian leader in Lagos; he also drafted a pamphlet, *Africa and the French Revolution,* published in Nigeria.[13]

Similarly, Du Bois kept abreast of developments in troubled Kenya. As with so many other African countries, students from there were wont to pen him poignant letters requesting assistance in studying in the United States. Jomo Kenyatta wrote him from prison, singing his praises and later also asked for assistance in helping his children. After events in Kenya had normalized to an extent, the African and the Afro-American kept in touch. As in Nigeria, Du Bois' contacts extended beyond the leader of the nation. While in Lagos, he met Tom Mboya, a member of the Kenya Legislative Council, general secretary of Kenya's Federation of Labor, member of the International Confederation of Free Trade Unions, and widely touted as Kenyatta's eventual successor. Du Bois was in touch with another possible Kenyatta successor, the leftist Oginga Odinga, vice-president of KANU (Kenya African National Union), the leading party there. Testimony to how valued Du Bois' opinions were came shortly. Odinga wrote him in 1961 with a bit of irritation showing requesting Du Bois' opinion of Kenyatta's release from prison: "I am extremely disappointed to note that I have not as yet received your opinion. . . . Your opinion is considered as one of greatest importance and I am . . . looking forward to receive it for publication in [my] book."[14]

Du Bois' unrivaled stature as Father of Pan-Africanism and mentor to liberators of Africa meant that his words carried no small weight. Thus, the negative attitude of Tanganyika's (now Tanzania) Julius Nyerere toward United States foreign aid and the Peace Corps may be traced to his correspondence from Du Bois:

> I am however, a little alarmed at the American Peace Corps which I understand is about to come to your country. I hope you will watch these persons carefully. Most of them will be trained "nigger" haters and filled with ideas of white superiority. Of course, there may be some exceptions.

Du Bois' trips abroad and eventual residing in Ghana as the honored guest of Kwame Nkrumah, acknowledged leader of African anticolonialism, meant that he would meet and speak with other African leaders along similar lines. He "had the pleasure of meeting" Dr. Hastings Banda, future leader of Malawi, in Lagos and discussed with him assistance on the Encyclopedia Africana project. When Algeria's leftist, anti-imperialist ruler Ben Bella visited Accra, he proudly posed for a photograph with the Father of Pan-Africanism. It was also not surprising when Professor V. Chkivadze of the International Institute for Peace in Vienna asked Du Bois to lead a delegation to Africa with representatives from India, the Soviet Union, and the Arab countries. Du Bois' hurried departure for Ghana aborted this journey but it signified his continuing importance as a recognized world leader. Also signifying this trend were the frequent requests from United States-based technicians who would ask Du Bois to use his influence to assist them in finding jobs and using their skills on behalf of an independent Africa. Du Bois would recommend some, mostly those he knew, but his experience with United States intelligence and police agencies made him suspicious of unsolicited requests.[15]

Du Bois' clout and his impact on Africa is reflected in his relationship with Ghana and Kwame Nkrumah. In essence, it would not be outlandish to suggest that Ghana's receiving its formal independence in 1957—years before 1960, the year of Africa—may have been due in large part to Du Bois' predominant influence on Ghana's leader. At the same time, there were those in the United States who expressed concern over a perceived leftward tilt of the Accra regime. Though not traditionally regarded as such, Nkrumah's Svengali from the right may have been Du Bois' frequent correspondent George Padmore, who, according to one scholar, "exercised considerable influence on Nkrumah's policy." Padmore "seemed to have preferred collaboration with the West as opposed to his former associates." Following Padmore's policy would have "brought that continent closer to American control. . . . Until 1960, and certainly as a result of Padmore's influence,

Ghana's non-alignment greatly favored the West . . . it was no accident that the development of closer relations between Ghana and the socialist countries occurred after his death in 1959." Du Bois' opinion was that Padmore was approaching a detente with the Socialist camp but it is clear as he forcefully stated in his curiously titled *Pan-Africanism or Communism?*, that Padmore was no firm advocate of socialism, his militant verbiage notwithstanding.[16]

Though Du Bois and Padmore disagreed on a number of points, from the importance of the Soviet Union to the value of Richard Wright's writing, the Afro-American leader valued him as a repository of information even as he doubted his advice to Nkrumah. Du Bois also received intelligence on Ghana from Dr. R. E. G. Armattoe—an avid enemy of Nkrumah. In this 1951 letter to Padmore, he indicated by inference why he was such a valuable correspondent:[17]

> There is no doubt [that] African mail to America is tampered with. Letters do not reach their destination. We can keep up with occurrences in British West Africa, and with some difficulty in French West Africa. We can get no information from the Sudan or Yuganda *[sic]* or Portugese Africa, very little from Kenya and . . . Tanganiyka, something but not much from Nyasaland, the Rhodesias and the protectorates, nothing from the Belgian Congo. A good deal of information from the Union of South Africa but nothing from Southwest Africa. We ought to get all of these areas together with the United States and the Caribbean into a mutual exchange of information and thought.

"A mutual exchange of information and thought" was the kind of Pan-Africanism in action that Du Bois advocated. But the kind of exchange of information that Du Bois was receiving from Dr. Armattoe about Nkrumah's Ghana, though somewhat discounted, had to be unsettling:

> intimidation of political opponents . . . victims are not white but Africans . . . they are being victimized by a group of people who loudly claim that they alone represent the country. These victims . . . are responsible educated men whose stand against imperialism is of long standing. . . . Today Nkrumah has become the friend of imperialists . . . I am fully aware that George Padmore, after dragging your name and mine in

> the mud as communists or crypto-communists now has the effrontery to assure you that Nkrumah is a savior of our country. . . . By no stretch of the human imagination can one label the CPP as a nationalist movement, although it began as such. . . . Already our names have [figured] on the assassination lists of Nkrumah. . . . No word of mine can paint Nkrumah worse than he is. . . . We have now formed the Ghana Congress Party to save the country.

Padmore responded in kind, denying his allegations about the CPP and Nkrumah himself as a "travesty of the truth." As for Dr. Armattoe, Padmore characterized him as "one of the most reactionary supporters of the chiefs and an enemy of the people." Padmore went on the offensive, and after labeling Du Bois the "foremost Afro-American scholar," used language in the *Crisis* to rebut Nkrumah's detractors that was quite similar to Armattoe's indictment of Nkrumah:[18]

> In order to discredit them and scare away the people from supporting the CPP, Dr. Nkrumah was denounced as a "communist." This move fitted in with the international "Cold War"; for if this Joseph Goebbelsian lie was believed, the government would be able to justify its repressive measures against the CPP leaders on the ground of "Defending Democracy" against "Communism."

Du Bois was disturbed by the political sniping, but what was interesting was how all sides found it necessary to present their Rashomon versions to him for his approval. This was simply one aspect of the respect in which he was held in Africa generally and in Ghana particularly, despite the world-wide propaganda barrage of Cold War warriors. The stature of Du Bois was also reflected in a 1953 *Accra Evening News* editorial which quoted generously from *In Battle for Peace* to greet a visiting delegation of the British Labour Party:

> This message of Dr. Du Bois, the greatest humanist . . . must come as an eye-opener to those British Socialist advocates of the well-conceived Afro-Asian "Third Front" who are ruining their cause, and creating further bitterness in the world by attempting to woo colored Nationalists and leftist leaders against Communists in the East-West Cold War.

This blunt message was also a shot over the bow at the United States Cold War liberal counterparts who propounded policies similar to the Labourites. Du Bois' prestige allowed him to rise in defense against the fulminations of opponents of unity with the Communists. On West African Regional Radio it was not unusual during this era of the red scare for Du Bois to be featured in the "Famous Folk of Colour" series.[19]

Du Bois did not remain mute about developments in Africa and the opinions of Padmore and Nkrumah that he considered faulty. In 1954, after Padmore had called Richard Wright's book on the Gold Coast "very good," Du Bois countered by terming it "lousy." Du Bois went on to say that he was a "little afraid . . . of the policy of you and Dr. Nkrumah. . . . The power of British and especially American capital when it once gets a foothold is tremendous." Padmore responded that Afro-Asian nations were spurning both capitalism and communism but "striving to find a middle road adopting features from both systems." Du Bois considered this poppycock: "I realize what Nkrumah is trying to do . . . but it is also dangerous and wrong to attack communism in other lands and among other groups . . . let Africans and West Indians seek the 'middle way' and refuse at least now to adopt communism. . . . But let them also steadfastly refuse to join in the lying chorus attacking Russia. . . . There is a grave danger in the 'middle way' when it comes to capital." He stated that an independent economy could only come through Soviet aid, which served to build the public sector, and not the West's aid. Du Bois feared that Nkrumah and Azikiwe "will think that they can save West Africa by a species of reformed capitalism in which benevolent white industrialists will have a philanthropic share. In that direction I am convinced lies disaster." Du Bois' portentous words were met with a well-worn attack by Padmore on Britain's Communists and Armattoe, but he failed to meet the thrust of Du Bois' arguments. Still, in 1955, Du Bois conceded, "I am satisfied that Nkrumah is doing a good job." As for Padmore, Du Bois was unclear about his dispute with the Communists and the Soviets; "Just what these points of differences were I do not know." In this eulogy to Padmore, he continued this inquiring posture: "I was hoping that when I went to Ghana I would have opportunity to discuss these matters with Padmore. . . . Unfortunately we never had a chance to discuss this difference of view face to face."[20]

Though Du Bois was barred by his government from going to Accra in 1957 to celebrate Ghana's independence, it did not prevent him from proffering advice on the new nation's path. He proposed to Nkrumah that he initiate "a new series of Pan African Congresses. . . . It should stress peace and join no military alliance . . . and should try to build . . . socialism." He suggested that Ghana should act as an advocate for sub-Saharan Africa, which "should avoid subjection to and ownership by foreign capitalists [and] should try to build socialism." Since he again made reference to soi-dissant, British and Scandinavian socialism, his advice was subject to misinterpretation. He concluded with a drumroll flourish: "I hereby put into your hands, Mr. Prime Minister, my empty but still significant title of 'President of the Pan African Congress' to be bestowed on my duly elected successor." Du Bois, like a doting father, after passing on the torch, counseled Prime Minister Nkrumah to look after his health. Now ever conscious of the decline that age brings, he announced, "pardon this sermon; but don't neglect it." But the thrust of his advice was given to Padmore for passing on to the Ghanaian leader: "I hope you will emphasize the necessity of his getting close to Nasser and the Sudanese. With Northeast Africa behind him and Central Africa lined up Ghana can face the Cape."[21]

Nkrumah, followed up on Du Bois' advice, sponsored what might have been called the "Sixth Pan-African Congress," the All-African People's Conference in Accra, December 1958. He dearly wanted Du Bois to attend but the patriarch would not yield to his suggestion to sign the non-communist affadavit in order to obtain his passport. The prime minister interceded on his behalf; Du Bois was finally granted a passport but was unable to travel to Accra because of fragile health, so his wife delivered his message for him. Du Bois' militant message to this historic gathering of future African prime ministers, presidents, cabinet members, ambassadors, and others, was not tailored to be greeted with a paroxysm of euphoria in the White House. He made a strong plea for all these nations to strive for socialism and for cooperation with the Soviet Union, and he warned against a creeping neocolonialism implanted by the West which "offers to let some of your smarter and less scrupulous leaders become fellow capitalists with the white exploiters if in turn they induce the nation's masses to pay the awful cost. . . . A body of private capitalists, even if they are black, can never free Africa."

With a vigorous nod at Karl Marx, he concluded, "you have nothing to lose but your chains. 'You have a continent to gain.' "[22]

Du Bois was hailed as free Africa's mentor at this crucial assemblage. British MP Fenner Brockway, chairman of the Movement for Colonial Freedom, proclaimed that the conference "may change the face of Africa"; he deemed it "appropriate" that "this idea should be taking practical form in the year when Dr. Du Bois, the American Negro 'Father' of the idea is celebrating his 90th birthday." Nkrumah went to great lengths to stress Du Bois' role; he "paid tribute at the very beginning of his talk, to the pioneering of Dr. W.E.B. Du Bois" and lauded him as "America's foremost son of Africa" and as the "moving spirit in those Congresses." He emphasized this again during his closing speech. At the conclusion of the congress a permanent secretariat was set up to coordinate continent-wide political activity, an embryonic Organization of Africa Unity.[23]

By the time of Ghana's formally joining the Commonwealth as a republic in 1960, Du Bois had his passport and he and Shirley were duly invited by Nkrumah to the inauguration ceremony as his personal guests. Du Bois attended the opening of the first session of the first Ghanaian Parliament: "There was about it a certain magnificence." He was impressed:

> a black man carried the new mace in the presence of 104 members of Parliament, the drums of the chief rolled the ancient call; a paramount chief gowned and crowned in gold poured libations in the doorways to his gods; women danced in solemn rhythm. President Nkrumah entered, robed and alone. The Golden Stool was unveiled and the national anthem roared. This black man, whom a free white American once dared to spit on when he asked a drink of water in Maryland.

The journey was punctuated by a festive dinner honoring Du Bois organized by the Ghana Academy of Learning and attended by the new nation's leaders and leading academics from the western hemisphere like St. Clair Drake, C. L. R. James, and Hugh Smythe. As ever, Du Bois did not restrain himself in addressing the gathering where he prescribed a path for Ghana:

> If you can get capital from the Soviet Union and China at two per cent and nothing attached, it would be crazy of you

> to borrow from the United States and Britain at 4, 5, or 6 per cent with the resultant industry under their control.

Stormy applause greeted his remarks in these piping times and even Rockwell Kent back in New York heard about it: "We have read about the ovation accorded the Doctor on the occasion of his address in Ghana."[24]

Given his worshipful, esteemed status in Ghana and the difficulties that afflict any elderly Black person in New York City, exacerbated by the hostile and racist climate that hounded his controversial views, it should not be startling that Du Bois would decide to spend his last days in tropical, verdant Accra. Yet, some have pointed to his October 1961 departure as evidence of Du Bois' "isolation," or "bitterness and frustration" or even "senility," as if he were fleeing like a fugitive from justice. With a peculiarly United States-style national chauvinism, the underlying assumption appears to be that anyone who would choose to leave the United States and live elsewhere must somehow be deranged. Looking through the wrong end of the telescope, these critics do not examine the special opportunities available to Du Bois in Accra, for example, directing the organization of a major work, the Encyclopedia Africana—a project Du Bois had contemplated and longed for for at least fifty years.

Moreover, it is curious that many who speculate on Du Bois' departure from the United States somehow fail to mention that the nonagenarian felt there was an imminent chance that he would be placed under virtual house arrest—deprived of his passport—again. This would not only have aborted the Encyclopedia Africana project but would have jeopardized something that had brought him sustenance, education, and joy—foreign travel. In early October 1961 a lawyer friend told Graham that the Supreme Court was soon "going to hand down an adverse position on the Communist Party and Dr. Du Bois will most certainly be one of the citizens of this country who will be prevented from travelling anywhere." Du Bois himself told Professor Potekhin of the Soviet Union that he had planned to go to Ghana in the spring of 1962. "However, the United States Supreme Court handed down a decision which made it doubtful if we could travel in 1962." Du Bois and Graham arrived in Ghana October 7, 1961, and the much awaited adverse court decision was rendered October 9, 1961. For a senior citizen receiving free expert medical care in Eastern Europe, inability to travel may have been all too deadly. Similarly, Du Bois' decision to take out Ghanaian citizenship has been shrouded in misinterpretation. Herbert Aptheker, who drove Du Bois to the airport on the day he left the United States for good, has noted: "In Ghana, the U.S. Consulate refused to renew Dr. Du Bois' passport—under the terms of the McCarran Act, then still in force, it was a crime subject to ten years' imprisonment for a Communist to have a passport." Hence, he obtained Ghanaian citizenship and a passport. Graham sheds another beam of light on this controversial decision: "I am sure that the many signs of Ghana's growth and development and its forward looking vision impelled my husband to become a Ghanaian citizen." As for signs of senility, this certainly was not reflected in his continuing prolificacy and recognized sharp tongue. Graham, who was closer to him and knew him better than anyone else, confirmed what others had noted, that in his ninety-fifth year, "there was no diminution in his mind; his articulation was clear, his eyes keen and his hearing unimpaired." As for bitterness, few Black persons living in apartheid America in the early 1960s were heartily pleased with the political and economic situation. Du Bois was no exception, but the ability to suffer Ghandian torment is not necessarily the beau ideal or beau geste. Some apparently see it as strange or perhaps "un-American" for Blacks to express discontent with the United States but Blacks had been fleeing to Mexico, Cuba, and Africa for centuries. Weeks before he departed for Ghana, Grace Goens had informed him of the racist difficulties she had encountered in securing decent housing. Du Bois exploded:

> Your letter of Sept. 7th makes me so mad . . . I just cannot take anymore of this country's treatment. We leave for Ghana October 5th and I set no date for return. . . . Chin up, and fight on, but realize that American Negroes can't win.

This was uncharacteristic pessimism from the good doctor; but like many Blacks he saw that whether the anti-imperialist struggle was fought from Accra or New York was, to a point, of small moment. In any case, bitterness in a twentieth century Afro-American should be taken as normal and natural, not an aberration.[25]

Bitterness aside as a factor in Du Bois' departure (which rings, in any event, of the FBI-inspired hatchet job done on Robeson in the *Crisis*), a primary reason for his traveling to Ghana was to direct the organization and completion of the Encyclopedia Africana. He initiated the idea as early as 1909, then dropped it; revived it in 1934 with assistance from A. Phelps Stokes but again dropped it in 1944 due to lack of funds. In 1947 he expressed pessimism to an inquiring correspondent about the project:

> You are wrong about the *Negro Encyclopedia* being "well along"; all we have been able to do is publish a preliminary volume, with subjects and bibliography. The main work has not yet obtained enough for its plans, I doubt it will be begun in my day.

Thus, when Nkrumah offered to subsidize this ambitious project, Du Bois quickly snapped up the offer and moved abroad to an attractive house buffeted by a verdant atmosphere. His proposed plans for an Encyclopedia Africana focused on human life. Biographies of virtually all European explorers, missionaries, colonial officials, and so on were to be excluded, since they all could be found elsewhere; from Du Bois' point of view, it was not to be an ethnographic dictionary. The estimated length was to be 10 million words and was to touch on art, politics, economics, and agriculture from the prehistory to the present. The CIA was well aware of why Du Bois moved to Africa, even though scholars and historians may not have been: "In Ghana [he] had number of people around him but he is an elderly man, was more inter *[sic]* in prod *[sic]* African Encyclopedia than anything else, and did set it up before his death."[26]

John Blassingame, yet another Black scholar who has been praiseworthy of the Black Communist, has condemned United States-based foundations for not giving more support to Du Bois' encyclopedia. Though these establishments did not come through, Nkrumah's Ghana most certainly did. Du Bois issued instructions for the University of Ghana faculty to take charge of the project, set up a Ghana University Press, and amply fund the encyclopedia—and Nkrumah strained to comply. Du Bois also sought—and this was the hallmark of this entire effort—to involve scholars from across the globe for this gargantuan effort. Early on he contacted Melville Herskovits, W. Arthur Lewis, Eric Williams, L. B. S. Leakey, Cedric Belfrage, John Bernal, Richard Pankhurst, Bertrand Russell, and the Academy of Sciences in Lisbon, Rome, and Madrid. A. A. Kwapong, acting secretary of the Ghana Academy of Learning, informed Du Bois: "I am happy to observe that, with the exception of Professor Arthur Lewis who considers the project premature at this stage, all the others are in complete agreement with your major proposals." In reply, Du Bois was in rare feisty form. After proposing that Kwapong contact French, Spanish, Portuguese, and Arab scholars about the project, he rebutted his suggestion that Horace Mann Bond come on board. He's "a scholar of ability," Du Bois began, but "he is in the pay of the United States State Department and of the Rockefeller interests." He likewise execrated the American Society of African Culture, "which purports to study African history and culture." The Ghanaians were undeterred by Du Bois' combativeness; the academy met May 13, 1961, under Nkrumah's chairmanship, appointed Du Bois director of the secretariat and invited him to move to Ghana. With his usual historical optimism, the ninety-three-year-old Du Bois noted that this would be at least a ten-year project but agreed to come. In his initial reply he was apprehensive and cited his age as a barrier. But after his visit to Romania, he was much more optimistic: "I feel improved in health and I think that I will be able to give one or two years service to the planning of the Encyclopedia. Also the situation in the United States is such that I have changed my plans in other matters." This latter comment was an obvious reference to the gathering Cold War freeze and his impending house arrest, a point he made clearer to the Ghanaians in September 1961. They wanted him to delay his arrival because Nkrumah was out of the country and Queen Elizabeth was to arrive shortly, but he was adamant in following his plans.[27]

The Encyclopedia Africana was no minor, trifling matter. In 1961 it was estimated that the budget would rise from $43,000 in the first year of operation to $74,600 in the fourth. Du Bois had started the ball rolling even before he moved across the sea. In March 1961, the Committee of African Organizations based in London, which was comprised of the leading national liberation forces of Africa, such as, the African National Congress of South Africa, the National Council of Nigeria and Cameroons, Somali National League, Uganda Peoples Congress, Uganda National Congress, West African Students Union, United National Independence Party of Northern Rhodesia, and so on eagerly agreed to assist the project. Richard B. Morris, head of Columbia University's History Department, was enthusiastic about the effort led by the Black radical: "I should be very glad to call to the attention of the Department your exciting plan . . . [it is an] extremely worthwhile project. . . . With every good wish on your project which I know will crown a long and distinguished scholarly career." Professor G. M. Johnson of the University of Nigeria concurred. Kuo Mo-Jo of China tendered "heart-felt support for such an effort." Roy Nichols, vice provost and dean of the University of Pennsylvania expressed great interest. Professor R. R. Palmer of Princeton University, in a lengthy response, deemed the project "important and necessary." The leading Africanist, Dr. Kenneth Dike of University College of Ibadan, Nigeria, joined in. The leading United States Africanist, Professor David Apter of the University of California-Berkeley, was asked to do a similar encyclopedia for the Free Press but deferred after he heard of Du Bois' effort:

> there is no one more appropriate for that most difficult enterprise than yourself. Indeed, I would feel it presumptuous to continue . . . knowing that your work is under way . . . I wish you every success in this undertaking which should provide a fitting capstone to your years of hard work on Africa's behalf.

Claude Barnett, director of the Associated Negro Press National News Service was equally interested: "This channel—as it always has been—is at your disposal."[28]

Of course, a project led by a Black Communist, even if it was Du Bois, would not receive a unanimous shout of approval. Professor Robert Byrnes, chair of Indiana University's History Department, was reluctant to cooperate and pessimistic about eventual success; not surprisingly, therefore, he suggested that it be done in England not Africa. Chester G. Starr, chair of Illinois University's History Department, was similarly skeptical. Professor R. I. Rotberg of the Harvard Center for International Affairs (where Henry Kissinger was on staff) gently warned Du Bois to avoid "ethnocentrism"—though he did not bother to mention the ethnic diversity of the staff he headed. Symptomatic of the Cold War atmosphere, even the Association for the Study of Negro Life and History was reluctant; they "finally answered after a long silence. I understood that he had presented the matter to the Board of the Association for the Study of Negro Life and History and they had debated for a long time and come to no conclusion."[29]

Overall, however, the response to the encyclopedia was tremendous, particularly outside of the United States. Du Bois gave a special effort to dredging up support from world leaders. He reached Sekou Touré about assistance: "I did not have the opportunity of meeting you at Accra, although we dined on either side of President Nkrumah at the state dinner." A. K. Mayanja, minister of education of Uganda was enamored:

> I must say there has been tremendous response from throughout this country and even outside Uganda. The Prime Minister of Tanganyika for example, has expressed very keen interest in the project and a number of leading Africans in Kenya and Uganda have given full support to the project.

The Sudanese ambassador to Ethiopia, Jamal Mohammed Ahmed, was among the African leaders to approve the project and pledge aid. Academics from Italy, the Ivory Coast, Paris, Federal Republic of Germany, Britain, and elsewhere were among those who donated materials for the encyclopedia. The zenith of world-wide support was reached when an International Congress was held December 11–18, 1962, at the University of Ghana with over 500 participants in support of the encyclopedia's aims. There were participants from the Ford Foundation, China, Brazil, and Australia. Virtually all of the embassies represented in Accra, including those of the United States and Israel, were there. Press coverage was substantial, including that from the various news services and Radio Ghana. As usual, Du Bois was an honored participant.[30]

Though he was ninety-three when he moved to Ghana, the fire had not disappeared from Du Bois' belly. He came into conflict with E. A. Boateng, secretary of the Ghana Academy of Sciences, Dr. D. A. Ackaah, and Professor D. G. Balta of the academy over the pace and progress of the project. Du Bois' projections may have been a bit long term for the Standing Committee of the academy to perceive. Du Bois felt that, "if we can begin publication in 10 years, we will be doing very well. . . . If we are able to publish a first volume of the Encyclopedia by 1970, I think we would do well." Yet, in April 1961, he complained that "the project is still nebulous." And by March 1963, months before he passed away, he complained to George Murphy, "in theory, I am working on the Encyclopedia Africana, as a matter of fact, I am not accomplishing very much. I am too old and weak to do much effective work. Nevertheless, I am doing something." After his death, Alphaeus Honton, who came to the staff after Du Bois made a personal appeal to Sekou Touré, carried on the project, but the 1967 coup that ended Nkrumah's reign basically ended the Encyclopedia Africana.[31]

The Du Boises were provided with commodious living arrangements in Accra. Those who were familiar with Du Bois' Brooklyn residence probably did not wonder why he left there. The journalist Charles Howard was expansive:[32]

> [The Ghana government] provided him and his wife . . . a beautiful seven-room residence high on a hill in an area called the cantonment. . . . Situated in the center of an acre of ground, the house is a typical tropical one with windows everywhere; Dr. Du Bois' room has windows on three sides. The grounds are divided, English style, by hedges and blooming trees. Two scarlet red flamingo trees guard the entrance driveway. . . . Under the main roof is a main library, living room, dining room, two bedrooms with private baths, a study room for Mrs. Du Bois and a screened porch of nylon netting. The household help consists of a steward, cook, driver and night watchman. The Du Boises have two cars, a Chike (Russian) and a . . . Minor (English) for Mrs. Du Bois. They brought along much of their household furnishings from their former home in Brooklyn. President Nkrumah in presenting the home to the Du Boises, said, "I want my father to have easy, comfortable and beautiful days." I spent a day with them. He has breakfast about nine, goes to the office about ten and stays until about noon. He comes home and takes an afternoon nap. He likes to go for a daily drive, especially to the commanding hills surrounding Accra. The Du Boises love Ghana. He told me: "Accra is definitely the Capital of Africa. It is the headquarters of many different African groups. There is no rivalry here with other places, only broad austerity." Ghana loves Dr. Du Bois; the people here adore and revere him. A few days ago, when President Nkrumah addressed the Accra Assembly [on] "The World Without the Bomb," his first act on entering the Assembly Hall was to go directly to Dr. Du Bois and warmly greet him. President Nkrumah is a constant visitor at the Du Bois home. Last week he and Mrs. Nkrumah with the two Nkrumah children . . . spent the afternoon with the Du Boises.

The Du Bois residence rapidly became a focal point for political activity and Du Bois himself rapidly became a focal point as well. The ambassador from British Guiana wrote him in early 1962:

> I have today received a letter from Dr. Cheddi Jagan, Prime Minister of . . . British Guiana, asking me to represent our affairs in Ghana on an Honorary level. (Since we are not yet independent we cannot as yet have embassies abroad). Cheddi has asked me to seek your advice in a number of questions and I should be grateful for an opportunity to meet with you.

Du Bois was friendly with the Chinese ambassador, Huang Hua, now foreign minister, and when figures like Dr. Banda were in the "capital of Africa," they always sought out the Father of Pan-Africanism.[33]

But Du Bois was an old man and could not fulfill all of his social obligations. He was forced to tell the ambassador from British Guiana, "I have been critically ill, had an emergency operation Jan. 30th. I have pulled through this successfully, but am leaving Ghana February 22nd for some weeks of convalescence in a Romanian sanatorium." On February 6, 1962, Du Bois' wife sadly told the International Institute for Peace, "without warning on January 30th Dr. Du Bois was compelled to undergo an emergency operation relating to the prostate gland." A few months later after specialists from the Soviet Union and Romania had come to Accra to treat him, Du Bois could report, "I am progressing fairly well. I have had no special urological attention since coming here and had one attack of malaria but I am doing pretty well." But in July 1962 he was admitted to University College Hospital in London for a transurethal section of the prostate. According to the doctor, "his present condition is excellent for a man of his age." He stayed in London and in Switzerland for a good while convalescing as his doctors prescribed. His stay in Western Europe was not all bad news; he had a pleasant time talking with Charles Chaplin, just as he had enjoyed meeting with Pablo Casals. However, he complained that the "recovery is slow and tedious and it has taken me a long time to be myself again."[34]

Du Bois may have been an elderly, sick man but United States government agencies acted as if he were a robust revolutionary in the trenches. The formation of the Organization of African Unity in May 1963, where homage again was paid to Du Bois, gave evidence as to why there might still be nosy interest in this Afro-American. The independent and increasingly militant African countries were judging the United States not by long-winded declarations but by how their brethren across the sea were treated; and Du Bois was a living, visible symbol of that treatment. Thus, close tabs were kept on Du Bois' every move after he left the United States. William B. Edmondson, second secretary in the United States Embassy in Accra, filed a confidential report on Du Bois just after Du Bois arrived and related that he had written in the *Accra Evening News* "advising Ghana to join the Soviet Union and China in ushering in the world." He faithfully reported that "Chinese Communist Ambassador to Ghana, Mr. Huang Hua" often called on Du Bois. Days later, Edmondson worriedly forwarded Washington another article by Du Bois in the *Accra Evening News* praising socialism and added:[35]

> Because Dr. Du Bois is still greatly respected by many Ghanaians and to other Africans as "the Father of Pan-Africanism" articles by him may carry somewhat greater weight here and elsewhere in Africa. . . . "What you have been told about the evils of Communism is wrong" the article seems to be saying—which is mighty potent propaganda for those who wish to see for themselves but rarely have the chance to do so.

No aspect of Du Bois' life was too trivial for the CIA to investigate. Du Bois' French teacher was a CIA plant, wittingly or unwittingly. Earlier, the CIA station chief in Accra filed this report:

> My French teacher, Madame Bassguy told me that she is now giving Dr. Du Bois and his wife French lessons. The couple contacted the French Embassy for a teacher and they were referred to her. Madame Bassguy said that Dr. Du Bois stated that he had come to Ghana on the invitation of the government to remain two years to write an antique encyclopedia on Africa. . . . Madame Bassguy stated that Dr. Du Bois is 93.

Another CIA source reported that Du Bois came to Africa to work on the encyclopedia and because he felt the FBI might pick up his passport. Asked why he waited so long to join the Communist party, according to the source, he said, "he could no longer be identified with such a society of philosophy *[sic]*. Communism, as a philosophy and a way of life, offers a new vehicle and new beginning for mankind to rediscover himself, said Dr. Du Bois." This same memo was sent to the FBI director and six other "deleted" officials in March 1962. Another source in December 1962 "noted the presence in Ghana of a number of members of the Communist party who are known to have engaged in activities embarrassing to American interest. The following is a resume of such persons." All names were deleted, except Du Bois'.[36]

Du Bois' Communist party connections kept a bevy of government agents on the payroll justifying their salaries by filing reams of memos about him; his egging on independent Africa to socialism created concern in Washington and on Wall Street. Virtually to his dying day, this so-called prophet in limbo was one of the most closely watched of the much monitored United States citizenry.

CONCLUSION:

The Death of Du Bois

With his usual fastidiousness, Du Bois had planned his funeral. In 1957, motivated by the ceremony for James Ford, he set out for Shirley Graham a scenario:

> I want the ceremony short and simple. I would prefer it not in a church, unless Howard Melish is still at Trinity. . . . I would prefer no flowers but perhaps one large evergreen wreath. . . . The music might be: Two or three Negro spirituals. . . . Then Schiller's Ode to Joy, Beethoven's music. . . . Finally one, certainly not more than three short talks; colored and white . . . perhaps a woman if you think of one . . . don't stress religion or immorality or Jesus Christ or the Good God. The good life at present and progress in the future are what I want stressed.

In 1961 he appointed his wife as executrix of his will. Du Bois' descent into death was not painful for him, though emotionally painful—inevitably—to his wife:

> Our dear William's health has become such an uncertain element that my days and nights go "up and down." I believe now, however, we have come to a kind of level which we must accept as remaining consistent. He is very weak, must be cared for patiently and tenderly. But he is not really sick, suffers no pain and all his faculties retain their efficiency. Now, that he

> has accepted the fact that his body is weak and his activities therefore curtailed, he is beginning to take some beauty in the enjoyment of his surroundings and the loving attention he receives on every side.

Then the fatal day came: "My Dear One passed away without suffering or pain. He steadily grew weaker, but was able to go for his accustomed afternoon drive up until two days before he left us."[1]

Du Bois in death symbolized prestige and stature as he did in life. His burial took place August 29, 1963. The tribute to him by Nkrumah was front page news in Ghana. Members of Parliament and the diplomatic corps participated. The *Amsterdam News* reported that he was buried with full honors. His widow said "she had received messages of sympathy from every embassy in Accra but one: that of the USA." The coffin, sealed with the red, green, and gold flag of Ghana, was followed by the masses as it was carried along a three-mile route. Ironically, Du Bois died on the same day as the historic March on Washington, where 250,000 gathered in Washington, D.C., to press for jobs and equality. James Aronson wrote that when Du Bois' passing was announced at the sweltering manifestation, "an old woman wept on hearing the news—'It's like Moses,' she said. 'God had written that he should not enter the promised land.' In the moment of silence that followed the announcement, there was a bond of understanding in that assembly—a bond of [pride] among the Negroes that one of their race should have lived to this great age to become one of America's greatest scholars." John Oliver Killens has noted the anguish of James Baldwin, Sidney Poitier, and himself in Washington when they heard, " 'The old man died' . . . and not one of us asked 'What old man?' We all knew [who the old man was] because he was our old man. He belonged to every one of us. And we belonged to him. To some of us he was our patron saint, our teacher and our major prophet. There was here a kind of poetic finale that made sense to us, that he should die on the very eve of this historic occasion."[2]

Du Bois' death was mourned world-wide with regrets pouring in from Chou En-lai, Gus Hall, the left, the center, Black, and white. The *Philadelphia Tribune* represented the sentiment of much of the Black press by hailing him as "Truly a Great American." *The Wall Street Journal* quickly formulated the line that was to dog the Du Bois legacy to this day: "his former associates saw little of him and today they dismiss his Communism as an eccentricity of his old age. 'You really have to forget about the last years of Du Bois' life,' one of his old friends remarks." Herbert Aptheker penned a worshipful eulogy for *Political Affairs,* while *Crisis* was a tad less awe struck:

> Although in recent years, Mr. Wilkins said the venerable scholar had chosen a different path than that of the NAACP, his contributions helped pave the way to the present upsurge of Negro demands for equality now.

Yet, even in death Du Bois, epitomized left-center unity. The sponsors for the 1964 memorial honoring him included Daisy Bates, Dr. Kenneth Clark, the Reverend Milton Galamison, Staughton Lynd, Jacob Javits, A. Philip Randolph, Sidney Poitier, and Roy Wilkins. At the mass gathering at Carnegie Hall, John Hope Franklin provided the eulogy, Godfrey Cambridge did a dramatic presentation of his life, while Arthur Spingarn and Bishop Stephen Gill Spottswood spoke.[3]

The ultimate comment on Du Bois and his significance, even in death, emerges from the press. The CIA quietly filed away the *Washington Star* and *Washington Post* obituaries of him. Across the ocean, the *Accra Evening News* in the same issue that put his burial on the front page carried these headlines: "Ghanaian Scientists Visit USSR," "Soviet Science Equipment for Ghana Schools," "Afro-Americans Will Press for Civil Rights." But in the United States they remembered the words of *The Wall Street Journal* when Du Bois' name was recalled: "You really have to forget about the last years of Du Bois' life."[4]

NOTES

Introduction

1. V. I. Lenin, *Imperialism, the Highest Stage of Capitalism* (New York: International Publishers, 1939); Gus Hall, *Imperialism Today* (New York: International Publishers, 1972); J. A. Hobson, *Imperialism, A Study* (Ann Arbor: University of Michigan Press, 1965).
2. See John Lukacs, *A New History of the Cold War* (Garden City, N.Y.: Doubleday, 1966).
3. Edward F. Sharp, "The Cold War Revisionists and Their Critics: An Appraisal" (Ph.D. diss., University of North Carolina, 1979); L. K. Adler, "The Red Image: American Attitudes Toward Communism in the Cold War Era" (Ph.D. diss., University of California, Berkeley, 1970); A. T. Golden, "Attitudes to the Soviet Union as Reflected in the American Press, 1944–1948" (Ph.D. diss., University of Toronto, 1970); Mary Atwell, "Congressional Opponents of Early Cold War Legislation" (Ph.D. diss., St. Louis University, 1974).
4. A. L. Patti, *Why Vietnam? Prelude to America's Albatross* (Berkeley: University of California Press, 1981); for a keen analysis see Mark Solomon, "Black Critics of Colonialism and the Cold War," in *Cold War Critics,* edited by Thomas Paterson (Chicago: Quadrangle, 1971), 22–56.
5. See C. A. Chick, Jr., "American Negroes' Changing Attitudes Toward Africa," *Journal of Negro Education* 31 (Fall 1962), 531–635; Rupert Emerson and Martin Kilson, "The American Dilemma in a Changing World; The Rise of Africa and the Negro American," *Daedalus* 94 (Fall 1965), 1055–84; Robert Weisbord, "Africa, Africans and Afro-Americans: Images and Identities in Transition," *Race* 10 (January 1969), 305.
6. For alternative views, see Gar Alperovitz, *Atomic Diplomacy: Hiroshima and Potsdam* (New York: Simon and Schuster, 1965); Gar Alperovitz (ed.), *Cold War Essays* (New York, 1976); D. F. Fleming, *The Cold War and Its Origins* (Garden City, N.Y.: Doubleday, 1961); Leo Okinshevick, *U.S. History and Historiography in Post-War Soviet Writings, 1945–1970* (Santa Barbara, Ca.: Clio, 1976).
7. Quoted in Richard Kluger, *Simple Justice: The History of Brown* v. *Board of Education and Black America's Struggle for Equality* (New York: Knopf, 1976), 253.
8. Robert Griffith, *The Politics of Fear: Joseph McCarthy and the Senate* (Lexington: University of Kentucky Press, 1970), 205.

9. Donald F. Crosby, *God, Church and Flag: Senator Joseph McCarthy and the Catholic Church, 1950–1957* (Chapel Hill: University of North Carolina Press, 1978), xii, 243, 238, 202. See also Michael Paul Rogin, *The Intellectuals and McCarthy: The Radical Specter* (Cambridge, Ma.: M.I.T. Press, 1967), 248, 255, 256.
10. Alfred L. Hero, *American Religious Groups View Foreign Policy: Trends in Rank and File Opinion, 1937–1969* (Durham: Duke University Press, 1973), 85, 90–91; Alfred O. Hero, "American Negroes and U.S. Foreign Policy: 1937–1967," *Journal of Conflict Resolution* 8 (June 1969), 220–51.
11. See Mary Sperling McAuliffe, *Cold War Politics and American Liberals 1947–1954* (Amherst: University of Massachusetts Press, 1978); John Steinke and James Weinstein, "McCarthy and the Liberals," in *For a New America: Essays in History and Politics From Studies on the Left, 1959–1967,* edited by James Weinstein and David Fakins (New York: Random House, 1970), 180–96; Robert Booth Fowler, *Believing Skeptics: American Political Intellectuals, 1945–1964* (Westport: Greenwood Press, 1978); Thomas C. Reeves, *Freedom and the Foundation: The Fund for the Republic in the Era of McCarthy* (New York: Alfred A. Knopf, 1969); Marian J. Morton, *The Terrors of Ideological Politics: Liberal Historians in a Conservative Mood* (Cleveland: Press of Case Western Reserve, 1972); Bernard Sternsher, *Conflict, Consensus and American Historians* (Bloomington: Indiana University Press, 1975).
12. Francis Broderick, *W.E.B. Du Bois: Negro Leader in a Time of Crisis* (Palo Alto, Ca.: Stanford University Press, 1959), 229; Elliott Rudwick, *W.E.B. Du Bois: Propagandist of the Negro Protest* (New York: Atheneum, 1968).
13. W.E.B. Du Bois to "Dear Madame," October 25, 1957, Reel 72, #1070, *The Papers of W.E.B. Du Bois.* University of Massachusetts, Amherst, Ma., hereinafter cited as *Du Bois Papers;* Du Bois to Arna Bontemps, November 3, 1952, Reel 68, #280, *Du Bois Papers;* W.E.B. Du Bois, *In Battle for Peace* (Millwood: Kraus-Thomson, 1976), 10.
14. Quoted in Broderick, *W.E.B. Du Bois,* 28; Harold Isaacs, "Pan Africanism as Romantic Racism," in *W.E.B. Du Bois: A Profile,* edited by Rayford W. Logan (New York: Hill and Wang, 1971), 210–48, 314; Martin Luther King, Jr., "Honoring Dr. Du Bois," in *Black Titan: W.E.B. Du Bois,* edited by John H. Clarke, et. al. (Boston: Beacon, 1970), 176—83.
15. Du Bois to John Slater Fund, March 10, 1893, in Herbert Aptheker (ed.), *The Correspondence of W.E.B. Du Bois, Volume 1, Selections: 1877–1934* (Amherst: University of Massachusetts Press, 1973), 23; hereinafter cited as *Du Bois I.*
16. *Crisis* 4 (August 1912), 180.

17. William Boyd, "Affirmative Action in Employment—The Weber Decision," *Iowa Law Review* 66 (October 1980), 1–62.
18. Du Bois, "Sociology and Industry in Southern Education," *Voice of the Negro* 4 (May 1907), 170–75; *Boston Chronicle*, January 20, 1926.
19. *The New York Times*, December 22, 1929; W.E.B. Du Bois, "Memorandum to the Labor Party of England on the American Negro," December 21, 1918, *Freedomways* 5 (Fourth Quarter 1965), 113–15.
20. *Fisk Herald*, November 1877.
21. Du Bois, "The Color Line Belts the World," *Collier's* 28 (October 20, 1906), 20.
22. Ibid.
23. Du Bois, "World of Color," *Foreign Affairs* 20 (April 1925), 423–44.
24. *Crisis* 2 (August 1911), 154–55, 157–59.
25. Du Bois to Mildred Scott Olmsted, January 20, 1932, in *Du Bois I*, 449, 450.
26. W.E.B. Du Bois, "The African Roots of War," *Atlantic Monthly*, May 1915, 707–14; Du Bois, "Of the Culture of White Folk," *Journal of International Relations* 7 (April 1917), 434–47; Du Bois, *Color and Democracy: Colonies and Peace* (Millwood: Kraus-Thomson, Ltd., 1975).
27. Du Bois, "A Re-Statement of the Negro Problem," Reel 80, #1237, *Du Bois Papers; National Guardian*, September 26, 1960.
28. Du Bois, "The Talented Tenth Memorial Address," *Boulé Journal* 15 (October 1948), 1–13.
29. Ibid.
30. Du Bois to Robert Bennett, February 16, 1954, Reel 70, #470, *Du Bois Papers.*
31. Du Bois to George Streator, April 17, 1935, in Herbert Aptheker, (ed.), *The Correspondence of W.E.B. Du Bois, Volume II: Selections, 1934–1944*, (Amherst: University of Massachusetts Press, 1976), 87; hereinafter cited as *Du Bois II;* Du Bois to Kirby Page, June 24, 1930, in *Du Bois I*, 425.
32. Du Bois, "My Evolving Program for Negro Freedom," in *What the Negro Wants*, edited by Rayford Logan (Chapel Hill: University of North Carolina Press, 1944), 31–70.
33. *Crisis* 18 (September 1919), 235.
34. "Negro Editors on Communism: A Symposium of the American Negro Press," *Crisis* 39 (April–May 1932), 117–19, 154–56.
35. *Crisis* 32 (July 1926), 59–64; see also William Scott, "A Study of Afro-American and Ethiopian Relations, 1896–1941," (Ph.D. diss., Princeton University, 1971).
36. *Crisis* 39 (March 1932), 93–94, 101.
37. Du Bois, "Democracy's Opportunity," *Christian Register* 125 (August 1946), 350–51; Du Bois, "Common Objectives," *Soviet Russia Today* 15 (August 1946), 13, 32–33.

38. *Crisis* 35 (December 1928), 401; see also John Diggins, *Mussolini and Fascism: the View from America* (Princeton: Princeton University Press, 1972).
39. Du Bois to Anna Graves, November 17, 1934, in *Du Bois II,* 27.
40. Du Bois to Andrew Allison, Feburary 2, 1941, in *Du Bois II,* 272.
41. Du Bois to Waldo McNutt, February 25, 1939, in *Du Bois II,* 185.
42. Du Bois to the editor of *Fortune,* May 21, 1942, p. 325.

CHAPTER 1. DU BOIS UP CLOSE

1. Du Bois had a relative at Shay's Rebellion. He initially wanted to be an attorney and it is interesting to speculate what would have been his impact if he had followed this career path. ("The Reminiscences of William Edward Burghardt Du Bois," No. 517, Category 1A, PRCQ, Columbia University Oral History.
2. Du Bois to Louis Burnham, August 29, 1954, Reel 70, #625, *Du Bois Papers;* Elizabeth Lawson to Du Bois, undated, Reel 69, #943, *Du Bois Papers;* Shirley Graham, "W.E.B. Du Bois: 82 Years Alive," *Harlem Quarterly* 1 (Spring 1950), 117; Du Bois to Dr. Louis Wright, November 27, 1946, Reel 59, #824, *Du Bois Papers.*
3. Du Bois to Anita McCormick Blaine, December 1948, in Herbert Aptheker, (ed.), *The Correspondence of W.E.B. Du Bois, Volume III: Selections, 1944–1963* (Amherst: University of Massachusetts Press, 1978), pp. 230–232 (hereinafter cited as *Du Bois III*).
4. Dr. Louis Wright to "Whom it May Concern," August 31, 1944, Reel 56, #88, *Du Bois Papers;* Truman K. Gibson to Du Bois, July 26, 1946, Reel 59, #585, *Du Bois Papers.*
5. Du Bois to Life Extension Examiners, July 16, 1953, Reel 69, #955, *Du Bois Papers; Du Bois III,* 350.
6. Du Bois to Paul Trilling, April 3, 1952, Reel 67, #1068, *Du Bois Papers.*
7. Du Bois to William Patterson, October 13, 1952, Reel 68, #114, *Du Bois Papers.*
8. "Individual Income Tax Return," 1953, Reel 70, #109, *Du Bois Papers;* Du Bois to Dr. Walter Beekman, November 30, 1951, Reel 66, #208, *Du Bois Papers;* Du Bois to Yolanda Du Bois, February 11, 1952, Reel 70, #129, *Du Bois Papers.*
9. *Brooklyn Heights Press,* March 6, 1958.
10. Shirley Graham, "W.E.B. Du Bois: 82 Years Alive," 117–19.
11. Du Bois to B. B. Powell, October 16, 1957, Reel 72, #532, *Du Bois Papers.*

12. Du Bois to Roy Wilkins, January 4, 1945, Reel 57, #744, *Du Bois Papers;* Du Bois to Dean of Makerere, January 9, 1948, Reel 62, #338, *Du Bois Papers;* East Africa Ltd. to Du Bois, March 1, 1945, Reel 47, #127, *Du Bois Papers;* "Invoice," October 1945, Reel 57, #429, *Du Bois Papers;* Julian Ladson, September 26, 1957, Reel 72, #418, *Du Bois Papers;* The *Beacon,* February 7, 1957, Reel 72, #418, *Du Bois Papers; I. F. Stone's Weekly,* February 20, 1956, Reel 72, #233, *Du Bois Papers;* Du Bois to Publisher of *New Republic,* Reel 56, #500, *Du Bois Papers;* Du Bois to New Press, Inc., Reel 69, #1124, *Du Bois Papers.*
13. Program of Harlem Opera Society, November 3, 1960, Reel 74, #332, *Du Bois Papers;* Shirley Graham Du Bois, *Du Bois: A Pictorial Biography* (Chicago: Johnson Publishers, 1978); Shirley Graham Du Bois, *His Day is Marching On* (Philadelphia: Lippincott, 1971); Du Bois to Shirley Graham, October 15, 1947, Reel 60, #67, *Du Bois Papers;* Du Bois to Stephen Frichtman, June 30, 1959, Reel 73, #657, *Du Bois Papers;* Du Bois to James Ford, June 5, 1953, Reel 69, #1047, *Du Bois Papers.*
14. Du Bois to B. P. Moreno, November 15, 1948, Reel 62, #381, *Du Bois Papers.*
15. Given that in 1985 another Afro-American (Muhammad Ali) is often said to fit this characterization, it is not unusual that this could be said of Du Bois—especially after his trip to China in 1959.
16. Du Bois to Jawaharlal Nehru, November 7, 1946, *Du Bois III,* 126; Du Bois to Georgia Johnson, September 18, 1950, Reel 65, #151, *Du Bois Papers;* Albert Kahn to Du Bois, March 17, 1950, Reel 67, #1138, *Du Bois Papers.*
17. Thomas H. Bresson, Chief, Freedom of Information-Privacy Acts Branch, Records Management Division—Federal Bureau of Investigation, to Eric McKitrick, November 5, 1980, "Confidential," Air Force Office to Special Investigations (1964). (In possession of author); I. Sabel to Du Bois, January 26, 1951, Reel 67, #465, *Du Bois Papers;* Du Bois to I. Sabel, September 18, 1950, Reel 65, #617, *Du Bois Papers.*

Chapter 2. A Militant, Anti-Imperialist Afro-American Community

1. Philip S. Foner and George Walker (eds.), *Proceedings of the Black State Conventions, 1840–1865,* 2 vols. (Philadelphia: Temple University Press, 1979–1980); Willard Gatewood, "A Black Editor on American Im-

perialism: Edward Cooper of the *Colored American,* 1898–1901," *Mid-America* 57 (January 1975), 3.

2. Charles Kellogg, *NAACP* (Baltimore: Johns Hopkins Press, 1967), 44, 250; see also Arnold Shankman, "Brothers Across the Sea: Afro-Americans on the Persecution of Russian Jews, 1881–1917," *Jewish Social Studies* 37 (Spring 1975), 14; Willard Gatewood, "A Black Editor on American Imperialism: Edward Cooper of the *Colored American,* 1898–1901," *Mid-America* 57 (January 1975), 3; James Ivy, "Traditional NAACP Interest in Africa (as reflected in the pages of *Crisis*), in *Africa as Seen by American Negro Scholars,* edited by American Society of African Culture (New York: ASAC 1963), 229–46; see also Hollis Lynch, "Pan Negro Nationalism in the New World Before 1862," *Boston University Papers on Africa,* vol. II (1966), 149–79.
3. Richard Dalfiume, "The Forgotten Years of the Negro Revolution," in *The Negro in Depression and War: Prelude to Revolution,* edited by Bernard Sternsher (Chicago: Quadrangle, 1969), 298–316; Wayne Addison Clark, "An Analysis of the Relationship Between Anti-Communism and Segregationist Thought in the Deep South, 1948–1964" (Ph.D. diss., University of North Carolina, 1976).
4. A. Russell Buchanan, *Black Americans in World War II* (Santa Barbara: Clio Books, 1977); A. M. Osur, *Blacks in the Army Air Force During World War II: The Problem of Race Relations* (Washington, D.C.: Government Printing Office, 1977); T. N. Dupuy (ed.), *Documentary History of the Armed Forces of the United States* (Washington, D.C.: GPO 1978); Minutes of NAACP Board Meeting, September 11, 1944, *NAACP Papers,* Library of Congress, Washington, D.C.
5. "Press Release," *India News,* February 12, 1943, *NAACP Papers; Crisis* (May 1945), 141; Thomas Hachey, "Walter White and the American Negro Soldier in World War II: A Diplomatic Dilemma for Britain," *Phylon* 39 (Third Quarter), 241–49.
6. Walter White to Winston Churchill, February 20, 1943, *NAACP Papers;* S. Chandrasekhar, "I Meet the Mahatma," *Crisis* 49 (October 1942), 312–13, 331–34; H. P. Howard, "The 'Negroes' of India," *Crisis* 49 (December 1942), 377–78, 392–93; S. Chandrasekhar, "Indian Immigration to America," *Crisis* 50 (March 1943), 73–75.
7. *Crisis* 53 (January 1946), 17; George Padmore, "The Sudanese Want Independence," *Crisis* 54 (June 1947), 176–80; George Padmore, "Anglo-American Plan for Control of Colonies," *Crisis* 51 (November 1944), 355–57; L. D. Reddick, "Africa: Test of the Atlantic Charter," *Crisis* 50 (July 1943), 202–4, 217–18.
8. Jonathan Boe, "American Business: The Response to the Soviet Union, 1933–1947" (Ph.D. diss., Stanford University, 1979); George Schuyler, "A Long War Will Aid the Negro," *Crisis* 50 (November 1943), 328–29, 344; *Crisis* 51 (January 1944), 16–17.

9. Lee Finkle, "Forum for Protest: The Black Press During World War II" (Ph.D. diss., New York University, 1971).
10. Mark Naison, "The Communist Party in Harlem: 1928–1936" (Ph.D. diss., Columbia University, 1975); *Crisis* 50 (December 1943); Thurgood Marshall to Ben Davis, June 8, 1945, *NAACP Papers;* Dalton Trumbo, "Black Face, Hollywood Style," *Crisis* 50 (December 1943), 365–67, 78; Minutes NAACP Board Meeting, March 13, 1944, *NAACP Papers;* Randall W. Bland, *Private Pressure on Public Law: The Legal Career of Justice Thurgood Marshall* (Port Washington, N.Y.: Kennikat, 1973), 40.
11. Doxey Wilkerson, "Freedom-Through Victory in War and Peace," in *What the Negro Wants,* edited by Rayford Logan (Chapel Hill, 1944), 193–216.
12. "Resolutions Adopted at War-Time Conference," July 12–16, 1944, *NAACP Papers; NAACP Bulletin* 3 (September 1944), 9, *NAACP Papers.*
13. Richard Dalfiume, "The 'Forgotten Years' of the Negro Revolution," 298–316.
14. Ralph Levering, *American Opinion and the Russian Alliance, 1939–1945* (Chapel Hill: University of North Carolina Press, 1976), 97.
15. Philip S. Foner, *Organized Labor and the Black Worker* (New York: International, 1976), see notes 69, 72; Merze Tate (ed.), *Trust and Non-Self-Governing Territories: Papers and Proceedings of the Tenth Annual Conference of the Division of the Social Sciences,* Graduate School, Howard University, Studies in the Social Sciences, vol. 6, no. 1, April 18–19, 1947, Washington, D.C., 1947.
16. *Chicago Defender,* March 16, 1946; *Crisis* 53 (April 1946), 118.

Chapter 3. Color and Democracy

1. Annual Report of the Director of Special Research, October 4, 1944–July 1, 1945, Reel 57, #912, *Du Bois Papers; Amsterdam News,* August 19, 1944.
2. Du Bois, *Color and Democracy: Colonies and Peace,* 12–13; Report of the Director of Special Research, June 12–September 9, 1945, *NAACP Papers.*
3. Du Bois to George Finch, February 11, 1941, in *Du Bois II,* 277; Du Bois to Rayford Logan, April 26, 1941, in *Du Bois II,* 283–284.
4. Du Bois to Paul Robeson, April 7, 1944, in *Du Bois II,* 378; Du Bois to Amy Jacques Garvey, April 8, 1944, Reel 56, #110, *Du Bois Papers.*
5. George Padmore to Du Bois, August 17, 1945, Reel 57, #1040, *Du Bois Papers.*

6. Du Bois to Walter White, July 5, 1944, *NAACP Papers;* Minutes of NAACP Board Meeting, September 11, 1944, *NAACP Papers.*
7. Du Bois to Committee on Pan African Congress, July 10, 1945, in *Du Bois III,* 68; Rayford Logan, June 21, 1945, Reel 57, #572, *Du Bois Papers;* William Hastie to Walter White, July 17, 1945, *Arthur Spingarn Papers.*
8. Du Bois to Walter White, August 15, 1945, *NAACP Papers;* Walter White to Du Bois, August 22, 1945, *NAACP Papers.*
9. Du Bois to Norman Manley, October 10, 1944, Reel 56, #383, *Du Bois Papers;* Du Bois to George Padmore, September 12, 1945, in *Du Bois III,* 82.
10. Du Bois to George Padmore, September 18, 1945, in *Du Bois III,* 86.
11. Du Bois to Jean de la Roche, March 8, 1945, Reel 57, #208, *Du Bois Papers;* Du Bois to Rene Pleven, May 7, 1945, Reel 57, #204, *Du Bois Papers;* Jean de la Roche to Du Bois, March 14, 1945, Reel 57, #209, *Du Bois Papers;* Jean de la Roche to Du Bois, June 2, 1945, Reel 57, #216, *Du Bois Papers.*
12. Reverend Harry Emerson Fosdick to Du Bois, January 11, 1945, Reel 57, #202, *Du Bois Papers;* Du Bois to Reverend Harry Emerson Fosdick, January 17, 1945, Reel 57, #203, *Du Bois Papers;* A. Phelps Stokes to Melville Herskovits, May 5, 1943, Reel 55, #562, *Du Bois Papers;* Ralph Bunche to Du Bois, January 31, 1945, Reel 56, #1251, *Du Bois Papers;* Senator Arthur Capper to Du Bois, June 9, 1945, Reel 56, #1263, *Du Bois Papers.*
13. "Colonial Conference," April 6, 1945, Reel 57, #79–796, *Du Bois Papers.*
14. Du Bois, et. al. to President of Liberia, circa 1945, Reel 57, #562, *Du Bois Papers;* Du Bois to George Padmore, October 5, 1945, Reel 57, #1050, *Du Bois Papers;* A. Phelps Stokes to Lord Halifax, October 6, 1945, Reel 57, #1108, *Du Bois Papers.*
15. "Report of the Department of Special Research," October 8–December 3, 1945, Reel 57, #963, *Du Bois Papers.*
16. James Hooker, *Black Revolutionary: George Padmore's Path from Communism to Pan-Africanism* (New York: Praeger, 1967), 95.
17. Ibid., 96.
18. Ibid., 97.
19. *Chicago Defender,* November 17, 1945; *National Guardian,* July 30, 1946; Du Bois to Acting Secretary General-West African Students Union, September 17, 1945, Reel 58, #203, *Du Bois Papers.*
20. Du Bois to James Coleman, February 18, 1950, in *Du Bois III,* 276; Du Bois to Henry Luce, December 17, 1945, Reel 57, #578, *Du Bois Papers;* Lyman White to Du Bois, April 14, 1947, Reel 60, #923, *Du Bois Papers.*

21. *NAACP Branch Bulletin* 4 (November 1945) 2, *NAACP Papers;* Du Bois to George Padmore, December 30, 1946, Reel 59, #375, *Du Bois Papers;* Du Bois to George Padmore, January 28, 1946, Reel 59, #351, *Du Bois Papers.*
22. Du Bois to T. R. Makonnen, November 9, 1948, Reel 62, #1068, *Du Bois Papers.*

Chapter 3. The World and Du Bois

1. Walter White to Du Bois, May 17, 1944, *NAACP Papers;* Walter White to Du Bois, June 19, 1943, Reel 55, #475, *Du Bois Papers;* Herbert Aptheker (ed.), *Documentary History of the Negro People in the United States,* vol. III (Secaucus: Citadel, 1974), 421; George Padmore (ed.), *History of the Pan-African Congress* (Manchester: Pan African Service Ltd., Manchester, 1946).
2. *New York Post,* May 9, 1945; *New York Post,* May 15, 1945.
3. *Pittsburgh Courier,* October 28, 1944; "Du Bois Hits Colonial Issues at State Department Conference," Press Release, October 19, 1944, *NAACP Papers;* Minutes of NAACP Board Meeting, December 1, 1944, *NAACP Papers;* Minutes of NAACP Board Meeting, November 13, 1944, *NAACP Papers.*
4. Minutes of NAACP Board Meeting, March 12, 1934, *NAACP Papers.*
5. Du Bois to Secretary of State Edward Stettinius, March 10, 1945, *NAACP Papers;* Du Bois to Walter White, April 12, 1945, Reel 57, #861, *Du Bois Papers;* Du Bois to Clark M. Eichelberger, March 9, 1945, Reel 56, #1047, *Du Bois Papers.*
6. Du Bois to Roy Wilkins, March 30, 1945, Reel 57, #781, *Du Bois Papers;* Roy Wilkins to Clark Eichelberger, March 30, 1945, Reel 57, #782, *Du Bois Papers.*
7. "Consultants and Associates" to San Francisco Conference, circa 1945, Reel 58, #119, *Du Bois Papers.*
8. Walter White to Du Bois and Mary McLeod Bethune, May 1, 1945, Reel 57, #872, *Du Bois Papers.*
9. Walter White to Roy Wilkins, May 14, 1945, Reel 57, #877, *Du Bois Papers.*
10. *Chicago Defender,* May 26, 1945.
11. Du Bois to the U.S. Delegation, May 16, 1945, in *Du Bois III,* 10.
12. Du Bois to Nina Gomer Du Bois, April 28, 1945, Reel 57, #75, *Du Bois Papers;* Du Bois to Nina Gomer Du Bois, May 17, 1945, Reel 57, #87, *Du Bois Papers;* Du Bois to Arthur Spingarn, May 30, 1945, in *Du Bois III,* 13; Walter White to Roy Wilkins, May 14, 1945, Reel 57, #877, *Du Bois Papers.*

13. Du Bois to Lawrence Spivak, May 22, 1945, in *Du Bois III,* 12; Zora Neale Hurston to Du Bois, June 11, 1945, Reel 57, #395, *Du Bois Papers;* "Report of the Director of Special Research to the Board of Directors of the NAACP," May 11, 1945, Reel 57, #874, *Du Bois Papers.*
14. "Activities of W.E.B. Du Bois, May 16 to June 4, 1945," Reel 57, #885, *Du Bois Papers.*
15. Minutes of NAACP Board Meeting, June 11, 1945, *NAACP Papers;* John Woodburn to Du Bois, March 23, 1945, Reel 57, #305, *Du Bois Papers;* Minutes of NAACP Board Meeting, May 14, 1945, *NAACP Papers;* Walter White to Eleanor Roosevelt, December 28, 1945, Reel 57, #971, *Du Bois Papers.*
16. *The New York Times,* June 6, 1945; *The New York Times,* November 28, 1945; U.S. Senate, Committee on Foreign Relations, 79th Cong., 1st Sess. (Rev.), *Hearings on the Charter of the United Nations,* July 9–July 13, 1945 (Washington, D.C.: Government Printing Office, 1945), 391–93; *The New York Times,* November 12, 1946.
17. Philleo Nash to Du Bois, April 2, 1946, Reel 59, #13, *Du Bois Papers;* Du Bois to Gunnary Myrdal, July 29, 1946, Reel 58, #1304, *Du Bois Papers.;*
18. Du Bois to Luther Foster, November 26, 1946, Reel 59, #678, *Du Bois Papers;* Du Bois to John Davis, November 30, 1946, Reel 59, #706, *Du Bois Papers.*

CHAPTER 5. WHEN PUSH COMES TO SHUN

1. Walter White to Du Bois, August 28, 1944, *NAACP Papers;* Walter White to Roy Wilkins, August 10, 1944, *NAACP Papers;* Walter White to William Hastie, August 25, 1944, *NAACP Papers.*
2. Walter White to Du Bois, September 22, 1944, *NAACP Papers;* Du Bois to Walter White, April 10, 1945, *NAACP Papers;* Du Bois to Walter White, June 26, 1945, *NAACP Papers;* Walter White to Du Bois, June 27, 1945, *NAACP Papers;* Du Bois to Walter White, July 2, 1945, *NAACP Papers;* Du Bois to NAACP Board, July 5, 1945, *NAACP Papers;* Walter White to NAACP Board, July 7, 1945, *NAACP Papers.*
3. Du Bois to Walter White and NAACP Board of Directors, January 28, 1948, *NAACP Papers.*
4. Walter White to Irene Diggs, November 28, 1944, *NAACP Papers;* Walter White to Irene Diggs, June 4, 1945, *NAACP Papers.*
5. Du Bois to Walter White, September 17, 1945, *NAACP Papers;* Walter White to Du Bois, September 29, 1945, *NAACP Papers;* Du Bois to

Walter White, September 19, 1946, *NAACP Papers;* Du Bois to Roy Wilkins, May 20, 1947, *NAACP Papers;* Du Bois to Roy Wilkins, September 22, 1947, *NAACP Papers.*

6. Du Bois to Roy Wilkins, January 4, 1945, *NAACP Papers;* Roy Wilkins to Du Bois, January 25, 1945, *NAACP Papers;* Du Bois to Roy Wilkins, January 26, 1945, *NAACP Papers;* Roy Wilkins to Du Bois, January 27, 1945, *NAACP Papers.*
7. Roy Wilkins to Walter White, June 7, 1945, *NAACP Papers;* Carl Murphy to Walter White, September 26, 1945, *NAACP Papers;* Walter White to Lillian Alexander, November 29, 1945, *NAACP Papers.*
8. Du Bois to George Padmore, April 7, 1949, Reel 64, #208, *Du Bois Papers;* Du Bois to Cedric Dover, December 18, 1947, Reel 59, #1349, *Du Bois Papers;* List of "NAACP Staff Members," December 18, 1946, Reel 59, #283, *Du Bois Papers.*
9. Richard Kluger, *Simple Justice: The History of Brown* v. *Board of Education and Black America's Struggle for Equality* (New York: Knopf, 1976), 271.
10. Ibid., 139; Carl Murphy to Arthur Spingarn, August 27, 1949, Box 12, *Spingarn Papers,* Library of Congress, Washington, D.C.
11. *Crisis* 56 (January 1949), 18–19; Walter White to Arthur Spingarn, April 20, 1949, Box 12, *Spingarn Papers;* Walter White to Arthur Spingarn, May 2, 1950, Box 12, *Spingarn Papers;* Walter White to NAACP Board of Directors, October 19, 1948, *NAACP Papers;* Walter White to William Hastie, Thurgood Marshall, et. al., May 28, 1948, *NAACP Papers;* Walter White to Spingarn, May 5, 1949, Box 12, *Spingarn Papers;* Arthur Spingarn to Walter White, April 11, 1949, Box 12, *Spingarn Papers.*
12. Alfred Baker Lewis to Spingarn, February 28, 1950, Box 12, *Spingarn Papers;* John Hammond to Roy Wilkins, October 8, 1943, *NAACP Papers;* Roy Wilkins to John Hammond, October 9, 1943, *NAACP Papers;* Roy Wilkins to Walter White, December 13, 1946, *NAACP Papers.*
13. Du Bois to Oswald G. Villard, February 13, 1946, in *Du Bois III,* 108.
14. Charles Toney to Walter White, October 8, 1946, Box 11, *Spingarn Papers;* Allan Nevins, *Herbert Lehman and His Era* (New York: Scribner, 1963); "Members of the National Board of Directors: 1948," Reel 62, #907, *Du Bois Papers.*
15. Du Bois to Gloster Current, July 17, 1947, Reel 60, #533, *Du Bois Papers;* Frank Barnes to NAACP, April 29, 1947, *NAACP Papers;* Novelia Watkins to Walter White, May 9, 1949, *NAACP Papers; NAACP Bulletin* 5 (December 1946), 2, *NAACP Papers.*

16. "Resolution to Establish a National Regional Office Within an Area Comprising Twelve Central States," June 26, 1946, *NAACP Papers;* Minutes of NAACP Board Meeting, May 13, 1946, *NAACP Papers.*
17. Ella Baker to Walter White, May 14, 1946, Reel 59, #188, *Du Bois Papers;* Ella Baker to Walter White, May 14, 1946, Box 11, *Spingarn Papers.*
18. Minutes of NAACP Board Meeting, June 12, 1950, *NAACP Papers;* Franklin Williams to Arthur Spingarn, March 5, 1946, Box 11, *Spingarn Papers.*

CHAPTER 6. EVERY STRIKE IS A DRESS REHEARSAL

1. Minutes of NAACP Board Meeting, February 11, 1946, *NAACP Papers;* Minutes of NAACP Board Meeting, March 11, 1946, *NAACP Papers.*
2. *Chicago Defender,* February 2, 1946; *Chicago Defender,* March 16, 1946; *Chicago Defender,* June 22, 1946.
3. Du Bois to Walter White, May 15, 1946, *NAACP Papers.*
4. Du Bois to Walter White, November 14, 1946, *NAACP Papers;* White to Du Bois, November 14, 1946, *NAACP Papers;* Du Bois to Walter White, December 2, 1946, *NAACP Papers;* Minutes of NAACP Board Meeting, December 9, 1946, *NAACP Papers;* Du Bois to George Padmore, December 30, 1946, in *Du Bois III,* 159.
5. Walter White to Du Bois, July 12, 1945, Reel 57, #923, *Du Bois Papers;* Walter White to Du Bois, July 18, 1945, Reel 57, #930, *Du Bois Papers.*
6. Du Bois to Walter White, January 3, 1946, *NAACP Papers.*
7. "JWI" to Roy Wilkins, May 3, 1946, *NAACP Papers;* Roy Wilkins File, June 4, 1946, *NAACP Papers.*
8. Paul Robeson to Du Bois, August 30, 1946, in *Du Bois III,* 112; Walter White to Du Bois, September 1946, in *Du Bois III,* 113; Walter White to Du Bois, September 19, 1946, Reel 59, #219, *Du Bois Papers;* Du Bois to Walter White, September 23, 1946, Reel 59, #219, *Du Bois Papers;* Du Bois to Walter White, September 23, 1946, in *Du Bois III,* 114–15.
9. Walter White to Thurgood Marshall, September 23, 1944, *NAACP Papers;* Du Bois to George Padmore, September 23, 1947, Reel 60, #718, *Du Bois Papers.*
10. Du Bois to Theodora Peck, April 4, 1928, Reel 62, #549, *Du Bois Papers.*
11. Walter White to Arthur Spingarn, November 21, 1946, Box 11, *Spingarn Papers.*

12. Du Bois to Harlow Shapley, July 2, 1948, Reel 62, #462, *Du Bois Papers;* Jack Kamaiko to Du Bois, December 30, 1948, Reel 62, #474, *Du Bois Papers;* Louis Wright to Du Bois, May 28, 1948, Reel 62, #822, *Du Bois Papers.*
13. W.E.B. Du Bois, "The Problems of Negro Organization" (Speech Before the NAACP Branch in Roanoke, Virginia), November 17, 1948, Reel 80, #1140, *Du Bois Papers;* Karen O'Connor, "Litigation Strategies and Policy Formulation: An Examination of Organized Women's Groups Use of the Courts, 1869–1977" (Ph.D. diss., State University of New York at Buffalo, 1979); see also, Ann Fagan Ginger, "Litigation as a Form of Political Action," *Wayne Law Review* 9 (Fall 1963), 463–68; Richard Cortner, *The Supreme Court and Civil Liberties Policy* (Palo Alto, Ca.: Stanford University Press, 1975); Charles Toney to Du Bois, November 14, 1946, Reel 59, #599, *Du Bois Papers.*
14. Du Bois to Ethel Nance, January 4, 1946, Reel 59, #1, *Du Bois Papers;* Walter White to Du Bois, October 4, 1946, Reel 59, #227, *Du Bois Papers.*
15. Gloster Current to Du Bois, December 19, 1947, Reel 60, #648, *Du Bois Papers;* Resolution Submitted for Wartime Conference of NAACP, July 12–16, 1944, Chicago, Ill., *NAACP Papers.*
16. Resolutions Adopted by the 35th Annual Conference, June 1944, *NAACP Papers;* Resolutions Adopted by the 37th Annual Conference, June 29, 1946, *NAACP Papers.*
17. Resolutions Adopted by the 39th Annual Conference, June 26, 1948, *NAACP Papers.*
18. Ibid.; Resolutions Adopted by the 40th Annual Conference, July 16, 1949, *NAACP Papers.*

Chapter 7. White On Black On Red

1. *NAACP Branch Bulletin* 11 (October 1943), 5, *NAACP Papers;* Draft Annual Report, January 4, 1944, *NAACP Papers; NAACP Branch Bulletin* 4 (February 1945), 2; *NAACP Branch Bulletin* 5 (August–September 1946), 1, *NAACP Papers; NAACP Branch Bulletin* 5 (March 3, 1946), 1, *NAACP Papers.*
2. "Friends of Democracy," undated flyer, *NAACP Papers.*
3. Charles Houston to Arthur Spingarn, March 28, 1946, Box 11, *Spingarn Papers.*
4. Walter White to Henry Luce, July 29, 1946, *NAACP Papers;* Walter White to John Shaw Billings, August 16, 1946, *NAACP Papers;* Walter White to John Shaw Billings, August 15, 1946, *NAACP Papers;* John Shaw Billings to Walter White, August 6, 1946, *NAACP Papers;* Walter

White to Editorial Board of *Newsweek*, June 2, 1947, *NAACP Papers;* Walter White to James Forrestal, August 20, 1947, *NAACP Papers.*

5. Noah Griffin to Walter White, November 1, 1946, *NAACP Papers;* Martin Dies, *The Trojan Horse in America* (New York: Dodd Mead, 1940); Gloster Current to Walter White, December 18, 1946, Reel 59, #285, *Du Bois Papers;* Edward Barrett, Jr., *The Tenney Committee: Legislative Investigation of Subversive Activities in California* (Ithaca, N.Y.: Cornell University Press, 1951).
6. Walter White to Governor Kim Sigler, March 3, 1947, *NAACP Papers;* NAACP Press Release, March 30, 1947, *NAACP Papers;* Walter White to Tom Clark and J. Edgar Hoover, February 14, 1947, *NAACP Papers.*
7. Clarence Mitchell to Walter White, January 12, 1948, *NAACP Papers; NAACP Branch Bulletin* 7 (May 1948), 4, *NAACP Papers;* Minutes of NAACP Board Meeting, November 8, 1948, *NAACP Papers;* Clarence Mitchell to Walter White, January 12, 1948, *NAACP Papers.*
8. Minutes of NAACP Board Meeting, November 8, 1948, *NAACP Papers.*
9. R. J. Simmons to Walter White, June 20, 1940, *NAACP Papers;* Roy Wilkins to George Dozier, March 18, 1942, *NAACP Papers.*
10. Jane Cassels Record, "The Red Tagging of Negro Protest," *American Scholar* 26 (Summer 1957), 325–33; Alan Harper, *The Politics of Loyalty: The White House and the Communist Issue, 1946–1952* (Westport, Ct.: Greenwood Press), 49; Philip S. Foner, *Organized Labor and the Black Worker* (New York: International, 1982), 282, 283, 286; Richard Freeland, *The Truman Doctrine and the Origins of McCarthyism: Foreign Policy, Domestic Policies and Internal Security, 1946–1948* (New York: Schocken, 1974).
11. Walter White to Tom Clark, April 14, 1947, *NAACP Papers;* Walter White to Roy Wilkins, April 16, 1947, *NAACP Papers.*
12. *Crisis* 54 (May 1947), 150.
13. *NAACP Branch Bulletin* 6 (April 1947), 3, *NAACP Papers.*
14. Roy Wilkins to Lt. W. P. Riley, May 29, 1947, *NAACP Papers;* Roy Wilkins to Milton Murray, April 2, 1947, *NAACP Papers;* Milton Murray to Roy Wilkins, April 13, 1947, *NAACP Papers.*
15. *Crisis* 54 (June 1947), 169.
16. *NAACP Branch Bulletin* 6 (October 1947), 1, *NAACP Papers.*
17. Minutes of NAACP Board Meeting, November 10, 1947, *NAACP Papers.*
18. Minutes of NAACP Board Meeting, November 10, 1947, *NAACP Papers; Crisis* 55 (April 1, 1948), 104; *Crisis* 55 (June 1948), 169.

19. Walter White to Roy Wilkins, June 18, 1947, *NAACP Papers; NAACP Branch Bulletin* 6 (April 1947), 4; Clarence Mitchell to Roy Wilkins, July 6, 1948, *NAACP Papers.*
20. Roy Wilkins to Walter White, March 13, 1946, *NAACP Papers.*
21. Alfred Baker Lewis to Arthur Spingarn, June 19, 1946, Box 11, *Spingarn Papers.*
22. Horace Mann Bond to Walter White, November 7, 1946, *NAACP Papers;* Walter White to Morris Ernst, January 3, 1947, *NAACP Papers;* Ruby Hurley to Walter White, January 7, 1947, *NAACP Papers.*
23. *NAACP Branch Bulletin* 6 (February 1947), 1.
24. Maynard Dickerson to Walter White, February 16, 1947, *NAACP Papers;* Walter White to Gloster Current and Thurgood Marshall, October 24, 1947, *NAACP Papers;* Henry Winston, "Party Tasks Among the Negro People," *Political Affairs* 25 (April 1946), 349–61; Adam Clayton Powell, Jr., *Marching Blacks* (New York: Dial, 1973), 69.
25. *NAACP Branch Bulletin* 5 (March 1946), 2, *NAACP Papers;* Arnold B. Donawa to NAACP, October 22, 1948, *NAACP Papers;* Benjamin Davis, "The Negro People's Liberation Movement," *Political Affairs* 27 (September 1948), 880–98.
26. Du Bois to Herbert Biberman, January 12, 1948, in *Du Bois III,* 175; Press Release, October 16, 1947, *NAACP Papers;* Leslie Perry to Walter White, November 11, 1947, *NAACP Papers;* Walter White to Nicholas Schenck, Jack Warner, November 7, 1947, *NAACP Papers; Chicago Defender,* November 8, 1947.
27. Call to Conference for Free Expression in the American Arts to Build the Cultural Division of the National Negro Congress, March 16, 1947, New York City, *NAACP Papers;* Leslie Perry to Walter White, November 1, 1947, *NAACP Papers;* Walter White to Arthur Spingarn, November 13, 1947, *NAACP Papers.*
28. Hubert T. Delany to Roy Wilkins, February 19, 1946, *NAACP Papers.*
29. Minutes of National Board of Directors, National Council for Permanent FEPC, August 2, 1946, *NAACP Papers;* Roy Wilkins to Walter White, October 18, 1946, *NAACP Papers.*
30. Shad Polier to Roy Wilkins, April 25, 1947, *NAACP Papers;* Minutes of NAACP Board Meeting, October 13, 1947, *NAACP Papers;* George Schermer to Gloster Current, April 7, 1947, *NAACP Papers; Crisis* 54 (November 1947), 329.
31. Gloster Current, "World Youth Meets for Peace," *Crisis* 53 (February 1946), 41–43, 60; Minutes of NAACP Board Meeting, December 10, 1945, *NAACP Papers.*
32. Walter White to Roy Wilkins, December 6, 1945, *NAACP Papers.*

CHAPTER 8. HUMAN RIGHTS—AND WRONGS

1. John Hope Franklin, *From Slavery to Freedom: A History of Negro Americans* (New York: Knopf, 1974), 461–62.
2. *Crisis* 52 (June 1945), 205; Du Bois to Walter White, August 1, 1946, in *Du Bois III,* 163; Walter White to Du Bois, September 17, 1946, *NAACP Papers;* Du Bois to Walter White, August 1, 1946, Reel 59, #199, *Du Bois Papers;* Roy Wilkins to Walter White, September 3, 1946, Reel 59, #209, *Du Bois Papers;* Thurgood Marshall to Walter White, August 31, 1946, Reel 59, #208, *Du Bois Papers;* Ruby Hurley to Walter White, August 29, 1946, Reel 59, #209, *Du Bois Papers;* Channing Tobias to Walter White, August 30, 1946, Reel 59, #210, *Du Bois Papers;* Leslie Perry Memo, September 10, 1946, Reel 59, #213, *Du Bois Papers.*
3. Chronology of "NAACP Petition to the United Nations," Reel 62, #935, *Du Bois Papers.*
4. Dorothy Funn to Du Bois, August 22, 1946, Reel 59, #63, *Du Bois Papers;* Frank Stanley to Du Bois, November 5, 1946, Reel 59, #74, *Du Bois Papers;* Earl Dickerson to Du Bois, October 3, 1946, Reel 59, #18, *Du Bois Papers;* D. V. Jemison to Du Bois, October 22, 1946, Reel 59, #18, *Du Bois Papers;* Dr. C. B. Powell to Du Bois, August 20, 1946, Reel 59, #134, *Du Bois Papers;* Non-European Unity Committee to Du Bois, October 26, 1946, Reel 59, #132, *Du Bois Papers.*
5. Noah Griffin to Du Bois, October 3, 1946, Reel 59, #324, *Du Bois Papers;* James Egert Allen to Du Bois, October 1, 1946, Reel 59, #320, *Du Bois Papers;* George Parker to Du Bois, October 17, 1946, Reel 59, #417, *Du Bois Papers;* Dutton Ferguson to Hugh Smythe, October 20, 1947, Reel 60, #420, *Du Bois Papers;* Mary McLeod Bethune to Du Bois, September 21, 1946, Reel 59, #27, *Du Bois Papers;* Mrs. C. J. Smith to Du Bois, October 17, 1946, Reel 59, #17, *Du Bois Papers;* Mae Downs to Du Bois, September 24, 1946, Reel 58, #811, *Du Bois Papers;* "Organizations and Persons Who Have Accepted Membership on the Pan African Committee," undated, Reel 59, #348, *Du Bois Papers; The New York Times,* October 6, 1946.
6. Henry Lee Moon to Du Bois, August 10, 1946, Reel 58, #1297, *Du Bois Papers;* Willard Townsend to Du Bois, September 23, 1946, Reel 59, #609, *Du Bois Papers;* George T. Guernsey to Du Bois, April 10, 1947, Reel 59, #1240, *Du Bois Papers;* Estelle Robbins to Roy Wilkins, October 31, 1947, Reel 60, #113, *Du Bois Papers.*
7. William Green to Du Bois, September 25, 1946, Reel 58, #483, *Du Bois Papers;* Carl Van Doren to Du Bois, September 21, 1946, Reel 59, #668, *Du Bois Papers;* Senator Arthur Capper to Du Bois, February 3, 1948, Reel 63, #332, *Du Bois Papers.*

8. Donald McCoy and Richard Ruetten, *Quest and Response: Minority Rights and the Truman Administration* (Lawrence, Kan.: University of Kansas Press, 1973), 67; George Padmore to Du Bois, December 12, 1946, in *Du Bois III,* 157; Du Bois to Milton Konvitz, August 28, 1947, Reel 60, #201, *Du Bois Papers.*
9. Nnamdi Azikiwe to Du Bois, October 9, 1946, Reel 59, #29, *Du Bois Papers;* Kwame Nkrumah to Du Bois, November 4, 1946, Reel 59, #703, *Du Bois Papers;* C. Matings to Du Bois, October 20, 1946, Reel 59, #148, *Du Bois Papers;* Gabriel Dennis to Du Bois, October 10, 1947, Reel 60, #242, *Du Bois Papers;* Ken Hill to Du Bois, October 6, 1946, Reel 60, #610, *Du Bois Papers;* Joseph France to Du Bois, November 8, 1946, Reel 59, #486, *Du Bois Papers.*
10. Hugh Smythe to Cedric Dover, November 3, 1947, Reel 60, #788, *Du Bois Papers;* A. M. Wendell Malliet to Du Bois, January 23, 1947, Reel 60, #288, *Du Bois Papers;* V. L. Pandit to Du Bois, September 25, 1947, Reel 60, #130, *Du Bois Papers.*
11. M. Ayub to Du Bois, September 30, 1947, Reel 60, #698, *Du Bois Papers;* M. V. Mara to Hugh Smythe, October 7, 1947, Reel 59, #1300, *Du Bois Papers;* H. Jaccard to Du Bois, October 9, 1947, Reel 60, #752, *Du Bois Papers;* M. T. Doss to Du Bois, October 9, 1947, Reel 59, #1390, *Du Bois Papers;* Deborah Bennett to Du Bois, undated, Reel 59, #1391, *Du Bois Papers;* Henrik Kauffman to Du Bois, October 13, 1947, Reel 59, #1322, *Du Bois Papers;* "Nations Acknowledging the NAACP Letter of September 29, 1947, Concerning the Association's United Nations Petition to be Presented to the General Assembly, 1947," September 29, 1947, Reel 60, #572, *Du Bois Papers;* Albert Fenn to Du Bois, October 16, 1947, Reel 59, #1150, *Du Bois Papers;* T. Tokina to Hugh Smythe, October 10, 1947, Reel 60, #920, *Du Bois Papers.*
12. Hugh Smythe, Press Reaction to the NAACP United Nations Petition," undated, Reel 60, #789, *Du Bois Papers.*
13. Ibid.
14. *The New York Times,* October 12, 1947; *The New York Times,* October 24, 1947; "Annual Report, Department of Special Research, 1947," December 23, 1947, Reel 60, #659, *Du Bois Papers;* Bruce Bliven to Walter White, December 11, 1947, Reel 60, #634, *Du Bois Papers.*
15. Du Bois to Editor of *Morgantown Post,* October 27, 1947, in *Du Bois III,* 185–86; Du Bois to A. G. Mezerik, January 23, 1948, in *Du Bois III,* 187.
16. *People's Voice,* November 8, 1947; "NAACP Petition to the United Nations—Chronology," undated, Reel 62, #935, *Du Bois Papers;* John Humphrey to Du Bois, October 9, 1947, Reel 60, #973, *Du Bois Papers; The New York Times,* October 24, 1947; Du Bois to William Stoneman, October 16, 1947, in *Du Bois III, 181; Du Bois to Warren*

Austin, October 14, 1947, in Du Bois III, 182; *People's Voice,* December 13, 1947.

17. Du Bois to Walter White, December 15, 1947, Reel 60, #640, *Du Bois Papers;* Walter White to Du Bois, December 16, 1947, Reel 60, #641, *Du Bois Papers.*
18. Du Bois to Walter White, July 1, 1948, Reel 62, #835, *Du Bois Papers;* Du Bois to Eleanor Roosevelt, September 19, 1947, Reel 60, #809, *Du Bois Papers;* Du Bois to Eleanor Roosevelt, October 14, 1947, Reel 60, #810, *Du Bois Papers.*
19. Du Bois to Warren Austin, February 4, 1948, Reel 63, #336, *Du Bois Papers;* Du Bois Memorandum on Biography of Himself by Clark Foreman, March 24, 1955, Reel 71, #382, *Du Bois Papers.*

CHAPTER 9. GIDEON'S BLACK ARMY

1. Du Bois to Robert Moore, June 8, 1960, Reel 74, #569, *Du Bois Papers;* W.E.B. Du Bois, "From McKinley to Wallace: My Fifty Years as a Political Independent," *Masses and Mainstream* 1 (August 1948), 3–13.
2. Du Bois to Anna V. Brown, February 23, 1937, in *Du Bois III,* 138; *Chicago Defender,* September 30, 1944; *People's Voice,* October 21, 1944; *Amsterdam News,* August 19, 1944; W.E.B. Du Bois, "What He Meant to the Negro," *New Masses* 55 (April 24, 1945), 9.
3. Henrietta Buckmaster to Du Bois, February 12, 1945, Reel 57, #413, *Du Bois Papers;* Du Bois to James Loeb, Jr., March 27, 1945, Reel 58, #4, *Du Bois Papers;* Du Bois to John Childs, July 3, 1945, Reel 57, #556, *Du Bois Papers;* Du Bois to Elmer Benson, July 19, 1945, Reel 57, #649, *Du Bois Papers.*
4. Resolutions of 33rd Annual Conference of the NAACP, July 14–19, 1942, Los Angeles, California, *NAACP Papers; Crisis* 51 (August 1944), 249.
5. *NAACP Branch Bulletin* 3 (September 1944), 9, *NAACP Papers.*
6. *NAACP Branch Bulletin* 4 (March 1945), 3; Minutes of NAACP Board Meeting, September 9, 1946, *NAACP Papers; NAACP Branch Bulletin* 5 (October 1946), 1, *NAACP Papers.*
7. Walter White to Arthur Spingarn, March 11, 1947, Box 11, *Spingarn Papers; Chicago Defender,* March 1, 1947; Eve Abraham to Du Bois, April 17, 1947, Reel 59, #1130, *Du Bois Papers;* Hugh Smythe to Henry Wallace, November 24, 1947, Reel 60, #440, *Du Bois Papers;* Dorothy Blake to Du Bois, January 15, 1948, Reel 62, #960, *Du Bois Papers; Chicago Defender,* January 3, 1948.

8. *Chicago Defender,* January 3, 1948; *The New York Times,* August 10, 1948.
9. F. Ross Peterson, *Prophet Without Honor: Glen H. Taylor and the Fight for American Liberalism* (Lexington, Kentucky: University of Kentucky Press, 1974), 56, 69, 113; F. Ross Peterson, "Glen H. Taylor and the Bilbo Case," *Phylon* 31 (Winter 1970), 344–50.
10. Curtis D. MacDougall, *Gideon's Army,* 3 vols. (New York: Marzani & Munsell, 1965), 387–88, 393, 395, 400, 406, 407, 686.
11. Ibid., 662–65, 741–45, 864.
12. *People's Voice,* January 31, 1948.
13. Charlotte G. O'Kelly, "Black Newspapers and the Black Protest Movement, 1946–1975," *Phylon* 44 (Winter 1980), 312–24; Charlotta Bass, *Forty Years: Memoirs From the Pages of a Newspaper* (Los Angeles: Bass Publishers, 1960), 142; Karl Schmidt, *Henry A. Wallace: Quixotic Crusade 1948* (Syracuse: Syracuse University Press, 1960), 137, 182; *Pittsburgh Courier,* June 23, 1948.
14. Minutes of NAACP Board Meeting, February 10, 1947, *NAACP Papers;* Madison Jones to Walter Liebman, February 28, 1947, *NAACP Papers;* Walter White to Prof. Miller, March 1, 1948, Reel 62, #752, *Du Bois Papers;* W.E.B. Du Bois, *The Autobiography of W.E.B. Du Bois: A Soliloquy on Viewing My Life From the Last Decade of Its First Century* (New York: International Publishers, 1971), 334.
15. *Crisis* 55 (February 1948), 41; *Crisis* 55 (June 1948), 178; *Crisis* 55 (August 1948), 245.
16. *Crisis* 55 (October 1948), 291; *Crisis* 55 (December 1948), 361.
17. *Chicago Defender,* October 5, 1946; *Chicago Defender,* April 19, 1947; *Chicago Defender,* April 26, 1947; *Chicago Defender,* August 9, 1947; *Chicago Defender,* September 27, 1947.
18. William C. Berman, *The Politics of Civil Rights in the Truman Administration* (Columbus, Ohio: Ohio State University Press, 1970); *NAACP Branch Bulletin* 1 (July 19, 1941, 1; Andrew Buni, "The Negro in Virginia Politics, 1902–1950" (Ph.D. diss., University of Virginia, 1965); Arthur Spingarn to Walter White, August 2, 1944, Box 11, *Spingarn Papers;* "Record on Senator Truman with Respect to Matters Vital to Negroes," undated, *NAACP Papers.*
19. Walter White, "Memorandum to Editors," June 4, 1945, *NAACP Papers;* Walter White to Willard Townsend, July 3, 1945, *NAACP Papers; NAACP Branch Bulletin* 4 (June 1945), 1, *NAACP Papers.*
20. Barton J. Bernstein and Allen Matusow (eds.), *The Truman Administration: A Documentary History* (New York: Harper & Row, 1966), 95; *NAACP Branch Bulletin* 5 (January 1946), 3, *NAACP Papers; NAACP Branch Bulletin* 5 (June 1946), 1.
21. *NAACP Branch Bulletin* 6 (January 1947), 1, *NAACP Papers; NAACP Branch Bulletin* 6 (August 1947), 1, *NAACP Papers.*

22. Alonzo Hamby, *Beyond the New Deal: Harry S. Truman and American Liberalism* (New York: Columbia University Press, 1973), 400; *NAACP Branch Bulletin* 7 (January 1948), 1; Berman, *Politics of Civil Rights,* 217.
23. Berman, *Politics of Civil Rights,* 85, 134, 240.
24.. *Crisis* 55 (September 1948), 264; Val Washington to Louis Wright, September 27, 1948, *NAACP Papers;* McCoy and Ruetten, 139; *Pittsburgh Courier,* October 19, 1948.
25. Warren St. James, *The National Association for the Advancement of Colored People: A Case Study in Pressure Groups* (New York: Exposition Press, 1958); Douglas John McAdam, "Political Process and the Black Protest Movement, 1948–1970," (Ph.D. diss., State University of New York at Stony Brook, 1979); Minutes of NAACP Board Meeting, November 8, 1948, *NAACP Papers.*
26. Harvard Sitkoff, "Harry Truman and the Election of 1948: The Coming of Age of Civil Rights in American Politics," *Journal of Southern History* 37 (November 1971), 597–616; Richard Walton, *Henry Wallace, Harry Truman and the Cold War* (New York: Viking Press, 1976), 235; Allen Yarnell, *Democrats and Progressives: The 1948 Presidential Election as a Test of Post-war Liberalism* (Berkeley: University of California Press, 1974), 34, 72–73, 85; James Weinstein, *Ambiguous Legacy: The Left in American Politics* (New York: New Viewpoints, 1975), 110.
27. Edward and Frederick Schapsmeier, *Prophet in Politics: Henry A. Wallace and the War Years, 1940–1965* (Ames: Iowa State University Press), 189; Richard Walton, *Henry Wallace, Harry Truman and the Cold War,* (New York: Viking, 1976), 169; Samuel Williams, "The People's Progressive Party of Georgia," *Phylon* 10 (Third Quarter 1949), 226–29.
28. MacDougall, *Gideon's Army,* 734, 659, 693, 696–702.

CHAPTER 10. FAREWELL TO ALL THAT

1. Eugene Kinckle Jones to E. Alexander, February 13, 1948, Reel 62, #196, *Du Bois Papers;* Channing Tobias to Du Bois, February 24, 1948, Reel 63, #230, *Du Bois Papers;* W. W. Law to Du Bois, February 23, 1948, Reel 62, #244, *Du Bois Papers.*
2. Walter White to Committee on Administration, January 24, 1948, *NAACP Papers;* Walter White to NAACP Staff, February 25, 1948, *NAACP Papers;* Walter White to NAACP Staff, March 13, 1948, *NAACP Papers.*

3. Du Bois to NAACP Board of Directors, March 8, 1948, *NAACP Papers;* Walter White to Arthur Spingarn, March 11, 1947, *NAACP Papers;* Du Bois to Arthur Spingarn, April 2, 1948, *NAACP Papers.*
4. Minutes of NAACP Board Meeting, April 12, 1948, *NAACP Papers.*
5. Louis Wright to Du Bois, May 28, 1948, *NAACP Papers;* Walter White to Roy Wilkins, June 16, 1948, *NAACP Papers;* Statement by the Secretary, June 26, 1948, *NAACP Papers.*
6. Du Bois to Walter White, July 2, 1948, *NAACP Papers.*
7. Walter White to Du Bois, July 2, 1948, *NAACP Papers.*
8. Walter White to Du Bois, July 12, 1948, *NAACP Papers;* Walter White to Committee on Administration, July 12, 1948, *NAACP Papers;* Du Bois to Secretary, Chairman and President of the NAACP, July 15, 1948, *NAACP Papers;* Madison Jones to Walter White, July 20, 1948, *NAACP Papers;* Warren Dix to Walter White, August 10, 1948, *NAACP Papers;* Walter White to Warren Dix, August 13, 1948, *NAACP Papers;* Walter White to Fred Taylor, September 2, 1948, *NAACP Papers;* Du Bois to Godfrey Cabot, October 13, 1948, *NAACP Papers.*
9. Du Bois to Du Bois Williams, October 18, 1946, Reel 59, #742, *Du Bois Papers;* Jason Berger, "A New Deal for the World: Eleanor Roosevelt and American Foreign Policy, 1920–1962" (Ph.D. diss., City University of New York, 1979).
10. Minutes of NAACP Board Meeting, September 8, 1947, *NAACP Papers;* Du Bois to Walter White, November 24, 1947, Reel 60, #615, *Du Bois Papers.*
11. W.E.B. Du Bois, Untitled Essay, circa 1947, Reel 60, #128, *Du Bois Papers;* Minutes of NAACP Board Meeting, February 9, 1948, *NAACP Papers;* Minutes of NAACP Board Meeting, March 1948, *NAACP Papers.*
12. Du Bois to Walter White, July 1, 1948, *NAACP Papers.*
13. Walter White to Committee on Administration, July 13, 1948, *NAACP Papers;* Walter White to Du Bois, August 20, 1948, *NAACP Papers;* Du Bois to Walter White, August 23, 1948, *NAACP Papers.*
14. *The New York Times,* September 9, 1948; Du Bois to the Secretary and Board of Directors of the NAACP, September 7, 1948, in *Du Bois III,* 243.
15. Ibid.
16. Minutes of NAACP Board Meeting, September 12, 1948, *NAACP Papers; The New York Times,* September 14, 1948.
17. Walter White to William Hastie, July 26, 1950, *NAACP Papers;* Minutes of NAACP Board Meeting, October 10, 1949, *NAACP Papers;* Minutes of NAACP Board Meeting, March 13, 1950, *NAACP Papers.*
18. George McCray to NAACP, September 29, 1948, *NAACP Papers;* Senator Arthur Capper to Walter White, September 16, 1948, *NAACP*

Papers; Roy Wilkins to Walter White, September 14, 1948, *NAACP Papers.*

19. Henry Lee Moon (ed.), *The Emerging Thought of W.E.B. Du Bois* (New York: Simon and Schuster, 1972), 28.
20. James Powers to Roy Wilkins, September 24, 1948, *NAACP Papers;* Nathaniel Bond to W. W. Law, October 26, 1948, *NAACP Papers;* W. W. Law to Louis Wright, October 23, 1948, *NAACP Papers.*
21. Alfred Cain to Louis Wright, December 27, 1948, *NAACP Papers; Amsterdam News,* November 19, 1949.
22. Progressive Party News Release, for release week of September 20, 1948, *NAACP Papers.*
23. Shirley Graham, "Why Was Du Bois Fired?" *Masses and Mainstream* 9 (November 1948), 5–26; George Murphy, Jr. to Shirley Graham, October 8, 1948, Reel 61, #1064, *Du Bois Papers;* "People to White Concerning W.E.B. Du Bois," September 1948, Reel 62, #878, *Du Bois Papers;* Shirley Graham to Arthur Spingarn, October 11, 1948, *NAACP Papers; The New York Times,* October 11, 1948; Minutes of NAACP Board Meeting, October 11, 1948, *NAACP Papers;* List of Supporters of Council of Arts, Sciences and Professions Backing Du Bois on Firing, October 11, 1948, Reel 62, #882, *Du Bois Papers;* Alfred Baker Lewis to Frank Graham and Zachariah Chafee, October 21, 1948, *NAACP Papers.*
24. Carl Murphy to Louis Wright, September 20, 1948, *NAACP Papers;* Thurgood Marshall to Carl Murphy, September 24, 1948, *NAACP Papers; Washington Afro-American,* October 2, 1948, *Washington Afro-American,* October 5, 1948; *Washington Afro-American,* October 9, 1948; Roy Wilkins to Carl Murphy, October 26, 1948, *NAACP Papers.*
25. *Cleveland Call and Post,* September 25, 1948; *Cleveland Call and Post,* October 2, 1948; *California Eagle,* September 23, 1948; *California Eagle,* September 30, 1948.
26. *Shreveport News,* October 2, 1948; *Norfolk Journal & Guide,* October 9, 1948; *St. Paul Recorder,* October 8, 1948; Roy Wilkins to Cecil Newman, October 15, 1948, *NAACP Papers; Los Angeles Tribune,* October 25, 1948; Roy Wilkins to Editor of *Los Angeles Tribune,* October 11, 1948, *NAACP Papers.*
27. *Atlanta Daily World,* September 29, 1948; *Chicago Defender,* October 23, 1948.
28. *Daily Worker,* September 26, 1948; *New York Star,* October 4, 1948.
29. Dr. Corey Eldridge to NAACP, September 17, 1948, *NAACP Papers;* Helene Sneed to Roy Wilkins, September 23, 1948, *NAACP Papers;* Ada Butcher to Arthur Spingarn, November 30, 1948, *NAACP Papers;* Archie Weaver to NAACP Board, October 23, 1948, *NAACP Papers.*
30. Minutes of NAACP Board Meeting, October 11, 1948, *NAACP Papers.*

31. Ibid.; Walter White to Arthur Spingarn, Louis Wright, Roy Wilkins, October 29, 1948, *NAACP Papers.*
32. Minutes of NAACP Board Meeting, February 14, 1949, *NAACP Papers;* Minutes of NAACP Board Meeting, April 11, 1949, *NAACP Papers.*

Chapter 11. Africa and Peace: Part I

1. Henry Wallace to Du Bois, November 29, 1948, Reel 63, #376, *Du Bois Papers;* Du Bois to Anita McCormick Blaine, January 7, 1949, Reel 63, #743, *Du Bois Papers;* Anita McCormick Blaine to Du Bois, April 7, 1949, Reel 63, #746, *Du Bois Papers.*
2. *The New York Times,* December 31, 1948; Du Bois to C. B. Baldwin, April 6, 1949, Reel 63, #722, *Du Bois Papers;* Hollis Lynch, "Black American Radicals and the Liberation of Africa: The Council on African Affairs, 1937–1955," Unpublished paper in possession of author, p. 19; List of Publications Received by Council on African Affairs, undated, Reel 63, #927, *Du Bois Papers.*
3. Max Yergan to Walter White, August 21, 1944, *NAACP Papers;* Du Bois to Max Yergan, November 29, 1945, Reel 56, #1389, *Du Bois Papers;* Du Bois, *Autobiography,* 344; Du Bois to Ruth Ann Fisher, March 12, 1949, Reel 63, #1052, *Du Bois Papers.*
4. Du Bois to George Padmore, July 12, 1946, *Du Bois III,* 141–44; Minutes of NAACP Board Meeting, September 10, 1945, *NAACP Papers; Crisis* 54 (March 1947), 90; Paul Robeson and Max Yergan to Du Bois, February 7, 1947, Reel 59, #1255, *Du Bois Papers; New Africa* 6 (December 1947), 3–4, Reel 59, #1283, *Du Bois Papers.*
5. *Official Proceedings and Resolutions of the National Negro Congress* (Chicago, 1936); Max Yergan, *Gold and Poverty in South Africa* (The Hague and New York: International Industrial Relations Institute, 1938); Du Bois to Harold Collins, October 28, 1946, Reel 46, #1092, *Du Bois Papers;* George Padmore to Du Bois, August 9, 1946, Reel 59, #369, *Du Bois Papers;* Hollis Lynch, *The Council on African Affairs,* 17, 43–44, 50; Dies, *The Trojan Horse,* 128.
6. Du Bois to Hugh Smythe, February 14, 1948, Reel 62, #737, *Du Bois Papers;* W. A. Hunton to Du Bois, undated, Reel 61, #736, *Du Bois Papers;* Du Bois to Hugh Smythe, March 7, 1948, Reel 61, #737, *Du Bois Papers;* Minutes of Council on African Affairs Meeting, March 25, 1948, Reel 61, #748, *Du Bois Papers;* Du Bois to W. A. Hunton, March 26, 1948, Reel 61, #750, *Du Bois Papers;* W. A. Hunton to Paul Robeson, March 27, 1948, Reel 61, #751, *Du Bois Papers;* Paul Robeson to Du Bois, April 6, 1948, Reel 61, #757, *Du Bois Papers;*

Du Bois, *Autobiography,* 344–47; Du Bois, *In Battle for Peace;* Paul Robeson, *Here I Stand* (Boston: Beacon Press, 1972), 126–28.

7. Council on African Affairs Executive Board to Council on African Affairs Members, April 15, 1948, Reel 61, #761, *Du Bois Papers;* Press Release from Council on African Affairs, April 21, 1948, Reel 61, #763, *Du Bois Papers;* Paul Robeson to Du Bois, undated, Reel 61, #763, *Du Bois Papers.*
8. Eslanda Robeson, "Open Letter to Fellow Members of the Council on African Affairs," April 17, 1948, Reel 61, #762, *Du Bois Papers;* Paul Robeson to Du Bois, April 26, 1948, Reel 61, #764, *Du Bois Papers.*
9. Du Bois to Paul Robeson, May 26, 1948, Reel 61, #768, *Du Bois Papers;* "Resolution of the Executive Board on the Case of Dr. Max Yergan," May 26, 1948, Reel 61, #769, *Du Bois Papers.*
10. "A Postscript of Newspaper Excerpts," concerning ouster of Max Yergan, undated, Reel 61, #735, *Du Bois Papers; People's Voice,* April 17, 1948; *Amsterdam News,* February 17, 1948; *PM,* April 16, 1948; *New York Herald Tribune,* April 6, 1948; *The New York Times,* April 6, 1948.
11. "War Plan: U.S. vs. USSR (Short Title: Broiler), 1947"; "War Plan: U.S. and Allies vs. USSR (Short Title: Bushwacker), 1948"; *Records of the Joint Chiefs of Staff: Part II, 1946–1953,* Washington, D.C.: GPO 1978; Lawrence Stephen Wittner, "The American Peace Movement, 1941–1960" (Ph.D. diss., Columbia University, 1967).
12. Du Bois to Nina Du Bois, March 30, 1949, in *Du Bois III,* 260; Henry A. Singer, "An Analysis of the New York Press Treatment of the Peace Conference at the Waldorf Astoria," *Journal of Educational Sociology* 23 (January 1950), 258–70; Walter White to Roy Wilkins, March 24, 1949, *NAACP Papers;* see also Reel 65, #1101, *Du Bois Papers.*
13. Daniel S. Gillmoor (ed.), *Speaking of Peace: An Edited Report of the Cultural and Scientific Conference for World Peace* (New York: National Council of Arts, Sciences and Professions, 1949), 15, 34–35, 23–25, 70–72, 83, 85–87, 92, 105.
14. Du Bois to Nina Du Bois, March 30, 1949, Reel 63, #1017, *Du Bois Papers; New Africa* 8 (April 1949), 2.
15. "Review of the Scientific and Cultural Conference for World Peace arranged by the National Council of the Arts, Sciences and Professions and held in New York City on March 25, 26, and 27, 1949," prepared and released by the U.S. House of Representatives, House Committee on Un-American Activities, *Communism in the Detroit Area—Part 1.* Hearings Before the Committee on Un-American Activities, 82nd Cong., 2nd Sess., February 25–29, 1952, Washington, D.C., 1952; *Crisis* 58 (March 1951), 192.

16. Wittner, "The American Peace Movement," 292, 319; Albert Kahn to Du Bois, April 8, 1949, Reel 64, #527, *Du Bois Papers;* "Background Information Notes," April 15, 1949, Reel 64, #530, *Du Bois Papers;* "In Defense of Peace," August 1949, Reel 64, #56, *Du Bois Papers;* Du Bois, et. al. circular, July 20, 1949, Reel 63, #665, *Du Bois Papers.*
17. Du Bois to Anita McCormick Blaine, September 27, 1949, in *Du Bois III,* 268; *National Guardian,* September 26, 1949; *The New York Times,* September 8, 1949; *The New York Times,* September 10, 1949; *National Guardian,* August 22, 1949; Memo from Du Bois, Reel 64, #615, *Du Bois Papers.*
18. Oswald G. Villard to Du Bois, April 4, 1945, Reel 58, #147, *Du Bois Papers;* Du Bois to Anna Melissa Graves, July 9, 1946, Reel 58, #969, *Du Bois Papers;* W.E.B. Du Bois, "Common Objectives," *Soviet Russia Today* 15 (August 1946), 13, 32–33; W.E.B. Du Bois, "The Most Hopeful State in the World Today," *Soviet Russia Today* 16 (November 1947), 24; W.E.B. Du Bois, "Russia: An Interpretation," *Soviet Russia Today* 17 (November 1948), 15, 32.
19. Du Bois to Anita McCormick Blaine, September 27, 1949, Reel 63, #748, *Du Bois Papers;* R. E. G. Armattoe, October 15, 1949, Reel 63, #699, *Du Bois Papers;* Du Bois to R. E. G. Armattoe, October 28, 1949, Reel 63, #700, *Du Bois Papers.*

Chapter 12. Ban the Bomb

1. *New York World Telegram and Sun,* March 3, 1950; *Daily Worker,* March 3, 1950; *Compass,* March 3, 1950; *New York Post,* March 3, 1950; *Daily Worker,* March 5, 1950.
2. "Minutes Provisional Committee, Americans for World Peace," April 3, 1950, Reel 64, #934, *Du Bois Papers;* Minutes of Peace Information Center Executive Committee, April 18, 1950, *Abbott Simon Papers;* Minutes of Peace Information Center Executive Committee, May 11, 1950, *Abbott Simon Papers* (hereinafter noted as *Simon Papers,* in possession of Mr. Simon).
3. Copy of World Peace Appeal Petition, circa 1950, Reel 65, #491, #514, #517, *Du Bois Papers.*
4. Pamphlet for Black Community on Peace Appeal, circa 1951, *Simon Papers;* Henry Pratt Fairchild to Du Bois, May 4, 1950, Reel 65, #331, *Du Bois Papers.*
5. "Peace Activities in the U.S.," undated, *Simon Papers;* "You Too Can Vote for Peace," circa 1951, *Simon Papers;* Peace Information Center Executive Committee, August 3, 1950, *Simon Papers;* Peace Appeal

Endorsers, undated, *Simon Papers;* Du Bois to Leonard Berstein, July 31, 1950, Reel 64, #988, *Du Bois Papers.*

6. *Peace-Gram* 1 (Summer 1950), 5, *Simon Papers; Peace-Gram* 1 (May 12, 1950), 6, *Simon Papers; Peace-Gram* 1 (May 31, 1950), 1, *Simon Papers.*
7. "Call to Mid-Century Conference for Peace," May 29–30, 1951, Reel 64, #1087, *Du Bois Papers;* Robert Havighurst to Sponsors of Peace Conference, June 19, 1950, Reel 65, #254, *Du Bois Papers;* Willard Uphaus to "Dear Friend," May 24, 1950, Reel 65, #253, *Du Bois Papers.*
8. M. E. Mantell, "Opposition to the Korean War: A Study in American Dissent" (Ph.D. diss., New York University, 1973); Benjamin Davis, "On the Use of Negro Troops in Wall Street's Aggression Against the Korean People," *Political Affairs* 29 (October 1950), 47; Samuel Banks, "The Korean Conflict," *Negro History Bulletin* 36 (October 1973), 131–32; Conrad Lynn to Du Bois, September 10, 1948, Reel 62, #321, *Du Bois Papers.*
9. W. A. Hunton to Du Bois, July 7, 1950, Reel 64, #1157, *Du Bois Papers; The New York Times,* July 24, 1950; *New Africa* 9 (July–September 1950), 7.
10. Thurgood Marshall, "Summary Justice—the Negro G.I. in Korea," *Crisis* 58 (May 1951), 297–304, 350–55; *Crisis* 58 (March 1951), 181; Colonel George C. Reinhart, "No Segregation in Foxholes," *Crisis* 60 (October 1953), 457–63, 508–11; *Crisis* 58 (February 1951), 102; *Crisis* 57 (October 1950), 586; *Crisis* 57 (August–September 1950), 511; Minutes of NAACP Board Meeting, November 13, 1950, *NAACP Papers; Crisis* 58 (August–September 1951), 491.
11. Mantell, "Opposition to the Korean War," 28–29, 41, 54; "Statement by Dr. W.E.B. Du Bois," July 12, 1950, Reel 54, #445, *Du Bois Papers;* Du Bois Statement re: "The Truman-MacArthur Meeting," October 12, 1950, Reel 65, #445, *Du Bois Papers;* Press Release, October 16, 1950, Reel 64, #848, *Du Bois Papers;* Press Release, October 18, 1950, Reel 64, #850, *Du Bois Papers.*
12. *The New York Times,* June 21, 1951.
13. Elizabeth Moos to Fred Stover, July 6, 1950, *Simon Papers;* Peace Information Center Press Release, September 23, 1950, *Simon Papers;* "Facts on Korea," issued by Committee for a Democratic Far Eastern Policy, circa 1951, *Simon Papers;* Text of Du Bois Speech, June 29, 1951, *Simon Papers.*
14. *The New York Times,* July 13, 1950; Du Bois, *In Battle for Peace,* 39; *The New York Times,* July 17, 1950; Minutes of Peace Information Center Executive Committee Meeting, July 17, 1950, *Simon Papers; The New York Times,* July 13, 1950; *Syracuse Post-Standard,* July 26,

1950; Du Bois to Dean Acheson, July 14, 1950, *Du Bois III,* 303–6; *The New York Times,* August 25, 1950.

15. *The Communist "Peace Petition" Campaign,* issued by the Committee on Un-American Activities, U.S. House of Representatives, July 13, 1950, Washington, D.C. 1950; Associated Press news item, August 12, 1950, Reel 65, #1094, *Du Bois Papers;* Francis H. Russell to Dear Friend, July 27, 1950, Reel 65, #453, *Du Bois Papers;* Peace Information Center, Organizing Letter #9, September 18, 1950, *Simon Papers.*
16. Mantell, "Opposition to the Korean War," 111; Don Edward Carleton, "A Crisis of Rapid Change: The Red Scare in Houston, 1945–1955," (Ph.D. diss., University of Houston, 1978); Paul Meyerson to Du Bois, undated, Reel 65, #251, *Du Bois Papers;* Flyer, circa 1953, Reel 69, #1161, *Du Bois Papers.*
17. "Report of Albert E. Kahn Speaking Tour (August 4–12, 1950)," Reel 65, #448, *Du Bois Papers; The New York Times,* October 8, 1951; Prof. Joseph Fletcher to an official of Federal Council of Churches, undated, Reel 65, #494, *Du Bois Papers.*
18. Press Release, July 14, 1950, *Simon Papers; The New York Times,* August 18, 1950.
19. *The New York Times,* July 14, 1950; *The New York Times,* July 15, 1950; *The New York Times,* August 8, 1950; *The New York Times,* August 24, 1950; *The New York Times,* August 31, 1950; *The New York Times,* September 15, 1950; Du Bois to Mayor William O'Dwyer, July 29, 1950, Reel 65, #369, *Du Bois Papers;* Press Release, July 13, 1950, *Simon Papers.*
20. Fred Stover to Du Bois, August 7, 1950, Reel 65, #130, *Du Bois Papers;* Statement of American Civil Liberties Union, August 14, 1950, *Simon Papers;* "From Our Mail," September 14, 1950, Reel 65, #474, *Du Bois Papers;* Ruth Bleier to Du Bois, January 30, 1951, Reel 66, #1126, *Du Bois Papers;* Minutes of NAACP Board Meeting, September 11, 1950, *NAACP Papers; Amsterdam News,* September 30, 1950.
21. Rockwell Kent to Du Bois, July 13, 1950, Reel 65, #192, *Du Bois Papers;* Minutes of Peace Information Center Executive Board, October 12, 1950, *Simon Papers;* Minutes of Peace Information Center Executive Board Meeting, August 31, 1950, *Simon Papers;* Press Release, October 19, 1950, Reel 64, #916, *Du Bois Papers;* Press Release, November 12, 1950, Reel 64, #919, *Du Bois Papers;* "Report" on Congress, November 17, 1950, Reel 64, #920, *Du Bois Papers;* "Report", December 6, 1950, Reel 64, #926, *Du Bois Papers; National Guardian,* November 22, 1950.

CHAPTER 13. THE AMERICAN LABOR PARTY AND THE PROGRESSIVE PARTY

1. Du Bois to Mae Ovings, September 18, 1950, Reel 65, #418, *Du Bois Papers.*
2. Paul Draper to Du Bois, February 2, 1949, Reel 64, #595, *Du Bois Papers; National Guardian,* December 12, 1949; *National Guardian,* December 26, 1949.
3. Du Bois to Henry Wallace, December 2, 1949, in *Du Bois III,* 272.
4. *National Guardian,* July 12, 1950; Progressive Party convention, February 24–26, 1950, Reel 65, #554, *Du Bois Papers.*
5. "Minutes of Meeting of National Committee," Progressive party, September 16–17, 1950, Chicago, Reel 65, #575, *Du Bois Papers;* Convention Committees, 1950, Reel 65, #556, *Du Bois Papers;* C. B. Baldwin to Du Bois, March 7, 1950, Reel 65, #567, *Du Bois Papers.*
6. Jack Kroner to Du Bois, February 27, 1950, Reel 65, #1041, *Du Bois Papers;* Sidney Socolar to Du Bois, February 27, 1950, Reel 65, #1041, *Du Bois Papers;* Jack Kroner to Du Bois, February 27, 1950, Reel 65, #1041, *Du Bois Papers;* Frances Murray to Du Bois, April 8, 1950, Reel 65, #1043, *Du Bois Papers;* Norman Pelver to Du Bois, April 13, 1950, Reel 65, #1045, *Du Bois Papers;* Myron Sharpe to Du Bois, February 9, 1950, Reel 65, #1046, *Du Bois Papers.*
7. *Amsterdam News,* September 9, 1950; *Amsterdam News,* September 16, 1950; *Amsterdam News,* November 4, 1950; *The New York Times,* September 11, 1950; "DuBois Research Material", *Daily Worker,* September 14, 1950, Series I, Ac. 2245, A–D, 1950, *American Labor Party Papers.*
8. "Biographical Data on American Labor Party Candidates," September 5, 1950, Reel 64, #802, *Du Bois Papers;* "Literature-Memos" File, Series I, Ac. 2245, Li–M, 1950, *American Labor Party Papers; National Guardian,* October 4, 1950.
9. "Informal Memorandum for Discussion," September 7, 1950, Reel 64, #795, *Du Bois Papers.*
10. Press Release, circa 1950, Reel 64, #801, *Du Bois Papers;* Frances Smith to Mayor Vincent Impellitteri, October 24, 1950, Series I, Ac. 2245, A–D, 1950, *American Labor Party Papers;* "Women's Committee" File, Series I, Ac. 2245, S–Z, 1950, *American Labor Party Papers;* Perry V. Knight to American Labor Party, October 7, 1950, Reel 65, #193, *Du Bois Papers;* Resolution of Joint Board Fur Dressers and Dyers Union, October 11, 1950, Reel 65, #168, *Du Bois Papers;* Robert A. Simmons to Du Bois, September 27, 1950, Reel 65, #627, *Du Bois Papers.*

11. Press Conference, September 24, 1950, Reel 64, #816, *Du Bois Papers;* "Platform" of American Labor Party, September 15, 1950, Reel 64, #805, *Du Bois Papers.*
12. Press Release, October 4, 1950, Reel 64, #829, *Du Bois Papers;* Du Bois Speech at Rally, October 5, 1950, Reel 64, #833, *Du Bois Papers; The New York Times,* October 6, 1950.
13. Du Bois Speech at American Labor Party Rally, October 24, 1950, Reel 64, #856, *Du Bois Papers.*
14. Press Release, October 3, 1950, Reel 64, #828, *Du Bois Papers;* Text of WMCA Radio Broadcast, October 9, 1950, Reel 64, #842, *Du Bois Papers;* Text of WMCA Radio Broadcast, October 26, 1950, Reel 64, #860, *Du Bois Papers;* WEVD and WOR Radio Broadcast, "Lehman and Hanley," October 22, 1950, Reel 80, #1461, *Du Bois Papers.*
15. *The New York Times,* October 10, 1950; *The New York Times,* October 30, 1950.
16. Transcript of Endorsement by Reverend Nathanial Lawson, WLIB Radio 9:45 A.M., File C238, Folder 121, *Herbert Lehman Papers;* Transcript of Endorsement by Reverend Walter Pinn, WWRL Radio, 5:15 P.M., File C238, Folder 134, *Herbert Lehman Papers;* Transcript of Endorsement by Reverend Moran Weston, WWPL Radio, 5:15 P.M., File C238, Folder 105, *Herbert Lehman Papers.* (Circa 1950).
17. Transcript of Endorsement by Mabel Fuller, WWRL Radio, 9:30–9:45 A.M., File C238, Folder 86, *Herbert Lehman Papers;* Transcript of Endorsement by Ashley Totten, WWRL Radio, 9:30 A.M., File C238, Folder 65, *Herbert Lehman Papers;* Transcript of Endorsement by B. F. McLaurin, WLIB Radio, 9:15 A.M., File C238, Folder 90, *Herbert Lehman Papers;* Transcript of Endorsement by Leo Stoute, WWRL Radio, 9:30 A.M., File C238, Folder 115, *Herbert Lehman Papers;* A. Philip Randolph to Herbert Lehman, February 10, 1950, Special File 732, *Herbert Lehman Papers.* (Circa 1950).
18. Transcript of Endorsement by Channing Tobias, radio recording, Fall 1950, File C238, Folder 101, *Herbert Lehman Papers;* Transcript of Endorsement by Mary McLeod Bethune, WQXR Radio, October 11, 1950, File C233, Folder 17, *Herbert Lehman Papers;* Transcript of Endorsement by Channing Tobias, Eleanor Roosevelt, Harold Stevens, WMCA Radio, File C238, Foler 99, *Herbert Lehman Papers;* Transcript of Endorsement by Mabel Staupers, WLIB Radio, October 31, 1950, 9:45–10:00 A.M., File C238, Folder 122, *Herbert Lehman Papers;* Transcript of Endorsement by John Doles, WWRL Radio, October 25, 1950, 9:30–9:45 A.M., File C238, Folder 98, *Herbert Lehman Papers;* Transcript of Endorsement by Hugh Smythe, WWRL Radio, 9:30 A.M., File C238, Folder 50, *Herbert Lehman Papers;* Walter White to A. Philip Randolph, October 26, 1950, Special File 931e, *Herbert Lehman Papers.*

19. Allan Nevins, *Herbert Lehman and His Era,* 312–331; Assemblyman Hulan Jack to Du Bois, April 4, 1945, Reel 57, #444, *Du Bois Papers;* Transcript of Endorsement by Hulan Jack, WLIB Radio, October 29, 1950, File C238, Folder 109, *Herbert Lehman Papers;* Transcript of Endorsement by Joseph Ford, WWRL Radio, November 1, 1950, 9:30 A.M., File C238, Folder 123, *Herbert Lehman Papers;* Transcript of Endorsement by J. Raymond Jones, WWRL Radio, November 1, 1950, 9:30 A.M., File C238, Folder 124, *Herbert Lehman Papers.*
20. Transcript of Endorsement by Mr. Pinkney, WLIB Radio, October 29, 1950, 9:30 A.M., File C238, Folder 110, *Herbert Lehman Papers; New York Herald Tribune,* August 27, 1950; Speech of Herbert Lehman, September 5, 1950, File C238, Folder 17, *Herbert Lehman Papers;* Press Release, October 16, 1950, File C238, Folder 51, *Herbert Lehman Papers;* Address of Senator Herbert Lehman delivered at Queens Rally, WJZ Radio, November 2, 1950, File C238, Folder 129, *Herbert Lehman Papers.*

    Amsterdam News, November 11, 1950; Du Bois to Du Bois Williams, December 4, 1950, Reel 65, #846, *Du Bois Papers;* Arthur Schutzer to Du Bois, January 28, 1952, in *Du Bois III,* 331; *The New York Times,* December 15, 1950; *The New York Times,* November 29, 1950; Du Bois to Arthur Schutzer, December 5, 1950, Reel 64, #873, *Du Bois Papers.*
21. Du Bois to Vito Marcantonio, March 10, 1952, Reel 67, #1045, *Du Bois Papers;* Du Bois to Earl Dickerson, February 12, 1952, in *Du Bois III,* 333.
22. Paul Trilling to Du Bois, April 24, 1952, Reel 67, #1069, *Du Bois Papers; National Guardian,* May 22, 1952.
23. Du Bois Reply to Draft Progressive Party Statement on "Negro Representation," June 26, 1952, Reel 68, #866, *Du Bois Papers; National Guardian,* July 4, 1952; *National Guardian,* July 10, 1952; *The New York Times,* July 5, 1952.
24. Du Bois to Lillian Baldwin, "Memorandum on Ohio Trip of W.E.B. Du Bois and Shirley Du Bois, October 7–10, 1952, Reel 68, #895, *Du Bois Papers;* Lillian Baldwin to Du Bois, October 15, 1952, Reel 68, #896, *Du Bois Papers.*
25. *National Guardian,* September 11, 1952; Text of Du Bois Speech, "The Confederate Flag" (circa 1952), Reel 81, #497, *Du Bois Papers; National Guardian,* January 22, 1953.
26. *National Guardian,* August 10, 1953; Progressive Party Press Release, November 19, 1953, Reel 69, #1201, *Du Bois Papers.*
27. Louis Kopecky to Du Bois, April 16, 1953, Reel 69, #938, *Du Bois Papers;* American Labor Party Television Broadcast, WABD-TV, Channel 5, April 13, 1953, 9:30 A.M., Reel 81, #629, *Du Bois Papers; National Guardian,* October 19, 1953; Alan Schaffer, *Vito Marcantonio:*

Radical in Congress (Syracuse; Syracuse University Press, 1966); Du Bois to Vito Marcantonio, November 10, 1953, Reel 69, #461, *Du Bois Papers.*

28. Herbert Holdridge to Du Bois, May 20, 1954, Reel 70, #685, *Du Bois Papers;* Du Bois to Herbert Holdridge, January 6, 1955, Reel 71, #439, *Du Bois Papers;* Progressive Party National Committee Meeting, January 16–17, 1954, Reel 80, #997, *Du Bois Papers;* Progressive Party Legislative Program for 1954, Reel 70, #1008, *Du Bois Papers.*

Chapter 14. The Battle for Peace

1. Eric Goldman, *The Crucial Decade and After: America 1945–1960* (New York: Vintage, 1960), 214; Du Bois, *In Battle for Peace,* 46, 49.
2. Ibid., *In Battle for Peace,* 180, 109, 37, 40.
3. Ibid., 87, 27–28.
4. William E. Foley to Peace Information Center, August 11, 1950, Reel 65, #463, *Du Bois Papers;* Peace Information Center Press Release, August 24, 1950, *Simon Papers;* Abbot Simon to William Foley, August 18, 1950, Reel 65, #463, *Du Bois Papers;* William Foley to Peace Information Center, August 23, 1950, Reel 65, #464, *Du Bois Papers;* Gloria Agrin to Abbot Simon, August 31, 1950, Reel 65, #466, *Du Bois Papers* William Foley to Gloria Agrin, September 19, 1950, Reel 65, #477, *Du Bois Papers;* Shirley Graham to Du Bois, September 1, 1950, Reel 65, #70, *Du Bois Papers;* William Foley to Gloria Agrin, September 19, 1950, Reel 65, #477, *Du Bois Papers.*
5. Charlotte H. Brown to Alice Crawford, February 21, 1951, in *Du Bois III,* 324–325; Elizabeth Lawson to Du Bois, undated, circa 1951, Reel 66, #1019, *Du Bois Papers;* V. J. Coyle to Alice Crawford, February 19, 1951, Reel 66, #606, *Du Bois Papers.*
6. Rabbi Abba Hillel Silver to E. Franklin Frazier, February 15, 1951, Reel 67, #507, *Du Bois Papers;* Rabbi Jack Cohen to E. Franklin Frazier, January 27, 1951, Reel 66, #356, *Du Bois Papers.*
7. Arthur Spingarn to Alice Crawford, January 19, 1951, Reel 67, #538, *Du Bois Papers;* Walter Toscanini to E. Franklin Frazier, February 5, 1951, Reel 67, #588, *Du Bois Papers;* Ralph Bunche to E. Franklin Frazier, January 29, 1951, Reel 66, #279, *Du Bois Papers.*
8. J. Finley Wilson to E. Franklin Frazier, January 27, 1951, Reel 67, #790, *Du Bois Papers;* Leonard Bernstein to Du Bois, February 23, 1951, Reel 66, #227, *Du Bois Papers;* Aubrey Williams to E. Franklin Frazier, January 30, 1951, Reel 67, #761, *Du Bois Papers;* Ella Stewart to Du Bois, February 20, 1951, Reel 67, #38, *Du Bois Papers;* Oksen

Sarian to E. Franklin Frazier, February 16, 1951, Reel 67, #580, *Du Bois Papers;* W. H. Jernagin to Du Bois, January 22, 1951, Reel 66, #941, *Du Bois Papers;* Mary McLeod Bethune to E. Franklin Frazier, February 6, 1951, Reel 66, #229, *Du Bois Papers;* Marian and Probyn Thompson to Dr. Walter Beekman, February 16, 1951, Reel 67, #580, *Du Bois Papers;* Oliver Palmer to Du Bois, February 23, 1951, Reel 67, #645, *Du Bois Papers.*

9. Gabriel D'Arbussier to Du Bois, February 14, 1951, Reel 66, #449, *Du Bois Papers;* Jorge Amado to Du Bois, February 16, 1951, Reel 66, #31, *Du Bois Papers.*
10. E. Franklin Frazier to Officers, Sponsors and Guests of Du Bois Testimonial Dinner, undated, Reel 66, #541, *Du Bois Papers;* Du Bois, *In Battle for Peace,* App. B, p. 64.
11. Du Bois, *In Battle for Peace,* 65; "The Case of Dr. W.E.B. Du Bois and His Associates for Peace," undated, Reel 67, #191, *Du Bois Papers; Du Bois III,* 310; Du Bois to Elizabeth Moos, May 21, 1952, Reel 68, #573, *Du Bois Papers; The New York Times,* February 10, 1951; *New York World Telegram,* February 9, 1951; *New York Journal American,* February 9, 1951; *New York Herald Tribune,* February 10, 1951; Du Bois to James Cobb, April 10, 1951, Reel 66, #349, *Du Bois Papers.*
12. Du Bois, *In Battle for Peace,* 72.
13. Ibid., 74–75.
14. Ibid., 178, 101, 107, 104.
15. *Freedom,* March 1951; *Freedom,* December 1951; *Freedom,* November 1951; *Freedom,* May 1951.
16. *Morning Freheit,* December 21, 1952; *National Guardian,* March 7, 1951; Address of Lawrence D. Reddick, Town Hall, at National Council of Arts, Sciences and Professions meeting, September 28, 1951, *Simon Papers;* W.E.B. Du Bois, *An ABC of Color,* intro. by John Oliver Killens (New York: International Publishers, 1969); *Chicago Defender,* October 6, 1951.
17. Mantell, "Opposition to the Korean War," 96; Harry Roberts to Du Bois, December 5, 1951, Reel 67, #442, *Du Bois Papers;* Shirley Graham, *His Day is Marching on* (Philadelphia: Lippincott, 1971), 146–147, 157.
18. Graham, *His Day is Marching On,* 160, 164–165; Hubert T. Delany to E. Franklin Frazier, February 16, 1951, Reel 66, #462, *Du Bois Papers;* Hubert T. Delany to Du Bois, November 27, 1951, Reel 66, #464, *Du Bois Papers; Du Bois III,* 315; Du Bois to Thelma Dale, October 27, 1951, Reel 66, #446, *Du Bois Papers;* Thelma Dale to Du Bois, September 26, 1951, Reel 66, #446, *Du Bois Papers.*
19. *Crisis* 58 (August–September 1951) 483; NAACP Resolution, June 26–30, 1951, Reel 67, #11, *Du Bois Papers.*

20. *National Guardian,* October 3, 1951; Helen Gordon to Alice Citron, undated, Reel 66, #700, *Du Bois Papers.*
21. *Du Bois III,* 322; *Crisis* 59 (December 1952), 673; *Crisis* 59 (November 1952), 48; Roy Andrews to Du Bois Committee, October 23, 1951, Reel 66, #147, *Du Bois Papers.*
22. National Committee to Defend Dr. W.E.B. Du Bois and Associates in the Peace Information Center, May 23, 1951, Reel 66, #57, *Du Bois Papers;* Abbott Simon to Du Bois, March 10, 1951, Reel 66, #86, *Du Bois Papers.*
23. *National Guardian,* May 16, 1951; Exhibits of Defense Committee, circa 1951, Reel 67, #82, *Du Bois Papers.*
24. "Right to Speak for Peace Committee," flyer, circa 1951, Reel 65, #604, *Du Bois Papers;* Du Bois to Harriet B. Smith, November 29, 1951, Reel 67, #515, *Du Bois Papers; The New York Times,* March 14, 1951.
25. *The New York Times,* February 22, 1951; Minutes of Du Bois Defense Committee Meeting, May 16, 1951, Reel 67, #63, *Du Bois Papers;* M. L. Allen to Shirley Graham, October 2, 1951, Reel 67, #398, *Du Bois Papers;* Walter O'Brien to Du Bois, February 3, 1951, Reel 67, #398, *Du Bois Papers;* Walter O'Brien to Du Bois, November 2, 1951, Reel 67, #400, *Du Bois Papers;* Progressive Party of Minnesota to Defense Committee, October 19, 1951, Reel 67, #403, *Du Bois Papers;* John Rideout to Defense Committee, February 20, 1951, Reel 67, #406, *Du Bois Papers; The New York Times,* November 10, 1951.
26. American Peace Crusade, to Dear Friend, August 20, 1951, Reel 66, #109, *Du Bois Papers;* Isabel M. Cerney to Alice Citron, November 21, 1951, Reel 86, #304, *Du Bois Papers.*
27. Joseph Hansen to Du Bois, October 17, 1951, Reel 67, #535, *Du Bois Papers;* A. J. Muste to Du Bois, September 1, 1950, Reel 65, #5, *Du Bois Papers;* Undated copy of letter from "Members of the Greenwich Village Community," circa 1951, Reel 66, #719, *Du Bois Papers;* William Meek to "Dear Citizen," Reel 67, #239, *Du Bois Papers;* Council of Arts, Sciences and Professions Statement on Du Bois, et. al. indictment, May 29, 1951, Reel 67, #221, *Du Bois Papers;* Robert M. Lovett to Arthur Spingarn, September 21, 1951, Reel 66, #1081, *Du Bois Papers;* Arthur Spingarn to Robert M. Lovett, September 21, 1951, Reel 66, #1081, *Du Bois Papers.*
28. Du Bois to Carl Murphy, April 11, 1951, Reel 66, #12, *Du Bois Papers;* Du Bois to I. F. Stone, July 19, 1951, Reel 67, #545, *Du Bois Papers;* Du Bois to W. P. Dabney, October 8, 1951, Reel 66, #440, *Du Bois Papers;* Thomas Dabney to Du Bois, February 23, 1951, Reel 66, #439, *Du Bois Papers.*
29. *Pittsburgh Courier,* March 3, 1951; *Pittsburgh Courier,* March 10, 1951, *Philadelphia Tribune,* February 22, 1951; *National Baptist Voice,* Feb-

ruary 15, 1951; *Afro-American,* February 24, 1951; *Chicago Defender,* February 24, 1951; *Gary American,* June 8, 1951; *Cincinnatti Union,* May 31, 1951; *Louisville Defender,* August 25, 1951; *Daily Compass,* May 22, 1951; Michigan Council for Peace, flyer, circa 1951, Reel 66, #1168, *Du Bois Papers* (see also Reel 67, #47, #66, #67, #78, #220); "They Have Spoken For Dr. Du Bois and Associates," circa 1951, *Simon Papers.*

30. "Incomplete Financial Report on Cross Country Trip," July 5, 1951, Reel 67, #71, *Du Bois Papers;* Du Bois to Cedric Dover, July 10, 1951, Reel 66, #508, *Du Bois Papers;* Pauline Watkins to Defense Committee, May 20, 1951, Reel 67, #638, *Du Bois Papers;* "They Have Spoken for Dr. Du Bois and Associates," undated, *Simon Papers;* Du Bois to John Brown, Jr., July 10, 1951, Reel 66, #265, *Du Bois Papers;* "Contributors to Emergency Legal Defense Fund," June 30–August 11, 1951, Reel 67, #75, *Du Bois Papers.*
31. W.E.B. Du Bois, "The September Trip," 1951, Reel 67, #91, *Du Bois Papers;* Du Bois to Lawrence Hautz, September 27, 1951, Reel 66, #756, *Du Bois Papers.*
32. J. Pius Barbour to George Murphy, October 3, 1950, Reel 65, #282, *Du Bois Papers;* Resolution by Louisville and Vicinity Baptist Ministers and Deacons Meeting, circa 1951, Reel 67, #83, *Du Bois Papers;* Marcus M. Boulware, "J. Finley Wilson, Fraternal Orator," *Negro History Bulletin* 27 (December 1963); 67–69; J. Finley Wilson to Jerome Rush, November 24, 1951, Reel 67, #793, *Du Bois Papers; Peace Crusader* 1 (March 26, 1951), 3; Sylvia Sticht to Alice Citron, October 23, 1951, Reel 67, #544, *Du Bois Papers.*
33. Graham, *His Day Is Marching on,* 170; "They Have Spoken for Du Bois," undated, *Simon Papers;* Statement by Ferdinand Smith, undated, Reel 66, #744, *Du Bois Papers;* John T. Gojack to Defense Committee, October 23, 1951, Reel 67, #649, *Du Bois Papers;* Furriers Joint Council to Harry S. Truman, May 10, 1951, Reel 66, #890, *Du Bois Papers.*
34. Jack Berman to Shirley Graham, August 3, 1951, Reel 66, #872, *Du Bois Papers;* Jack Berman to Shirley Graham, October 6, 1951, Reel 66, #872, *Du Bois Papers;* Cleveland Robinson to Shirley Graham, May 23, 1951, Reel 66, #647, *Du Bois Papers;* J. W. Gable to Shirley Graham, August 30, 1951, Reel 67, #648, *Du Bois Papers;* Thelma Slappy to Slyvia Soloff, October 3, 1951. Reel 67, #648, *Du Bois Papers;* Isidore Rubin to Defense Committee, June 25, 1951, Reel 67, #567, *Du Bois Papers;* "Report of the Fair Practices, Director of Local 600, UAW-CIO," September 9, 1951, Reel 67, #640, *Du Bois Papers;* Platform Guests for Du Bois Seattle Speaking Engagement, 1951, Reel 67, #179, *Du Bois Papers;* Volunteers for Committee, Washington, circa 1951, Reel 67, #130, *Du Bois Papers.*

35. Press Release, October 19, 1951, Reel 67, #592, *Du Bois Papers;* Wendell Thrower, May 31, 1951, Reel 66, #421, *Du Bois Papers;* Leon Straus to Du Bois, February 21, 1952, Reel 66, #399, *Du Bois Papers;* Du Bois to Ben Gold, December 19, 1951; Reel 66, #902, *Du Bois Papers.*
36. Alice Citron to Hugh Bryson, May 1, 1951, Reel 66, #277, *Du Bois Papers;* Circular, June 1, 1953, Reel 69, #1112, *Du Bois Papers.*
37. Manhattan District Jewish Peoples Fraternal Order to Defense Committees, February 20, 1951, Reel 66, #914, *Du Bois Papers;* Fred Stover to Defense Committee, May 1, 1951, Reel 66, #914, *Du Bois Papers;* Statement and Greetings, Civil Rights Congress Chapters, February 21, 1951, Reel 66, #337, *Du Bois Papers;* Civil Rights Congress Chapters, March 23, 1951, Reel 66, #336–338, *Du Bois Papers.*
38. Abbott Simon to Du Bois, March 10, 1951, Reel 66, #86, *Du Bois Papers;* Arthur Madison to Du Bois, February 20, 1951, Reel 66, #1098, *Du Bois Papers;* Theodore Schroeder to Defense Committee, June 27, 1951, Reel 67, #593, *Du Bois Papers;* Thomas Emerson to David Robinson, May 4, 1951, Reel 66, #600, *Du Bois Papers;* Du Bois to Zacharish Chaffee, April 10, 1951, Reel 66, #306, *Du Bois Papers.*
39. Du Bois to Arthur Garfield Hays, April 20, 1951, Reel 66, #821, *Du Bois Papers;* Arthur Garfield Hays to Du Bois, April 26, 1951, Reel 66, #822, *Du Bois Papers;* Corliss Lamont to Paul Robeson, April 23, 1951, Reel 66, #1012, *Du Bois Papers.*
40. Hafron-Benjamin to Du Bois, October 31, 1951, Reel 66, #817, *Du Bois Papers; West Africa Pilot,* April 5, 1951; Shirley Graham, "For the Defense," circa 1951, Reel 66, #538, *Du Bois Papers;* George Padmore to Du Bois, January 8, 1952, Reel 68, #764, *Du Bois Papers;* Du Bois to George Padmore, April 11, 1951, Reel 67, #307, *Du Bois Papers;* George Padmore to Du Bois, May 29, 1951, Reel 67, #308, *Du Bois Papers;* Federation of Madagascar and Dependencies Trade Unions to Defense Committee, November 7, 1951, Reel 66, #619, *Du Bois Papers;* Sam Kahn to Defense Committee, June 8, 1951, Reel 67, #178, *Du Bois Papers;* Tidone to Du Bois, November 19, 1951, Reel 67, #547, *Du Bois Papers;* P. K. Crankson to Du Bois, July 27, 1951, Reel 66, #430, *Du Bois Papers.*
41. V. Lamon to Leon Straus, November 10, 1951, Reel 66, #472, *Du Bois Papers;* Manual and Metal Workers Union of Grenada to Harry Truman, December 22, 1951, Reel 66, #721, *Du Bois Papers.*
42. Du Bois, *In Battle For Peace,* 124, 83, 79; James Ivy to Du Bois, August 7, 1951, Reel 67, #12, *Du Bois Papers.*
43. Du Bois to J. Behrouz, June 20, 1952, Reel 68, #460, *Du Bois Papers;* J. Behrouz to Du Bois, December 1, 1951, Reel 66, #911, *Du Bois*

Papers; Shozo Kojime to Du Bois, February 23, 1952, Reel 68, #478, *Du Bois Papers;* All China Students Federation to Defense Committee, November 28, 1951, Reel 66, #24, *Du Bois Papers;* Painters Penladjar dan Penuda, October 24, 1951, Reel 67, #312, *Du Bois Papers;* Du Bois to All-India Peace Council, October 11, 1951, Reel 66, #25, *Du Bois Papers;* Union des Etudiants du Vietnam Statement, undated, Reel 67, #632, *Du Bois Papers.*

44. Civil Rights Union to Defense Committee, December 21, 1951, Reel 66, #343, *Du Bois Papers;* Resolution of British Columbia Peace Canadian Women to J. Howard McGarth, November 15, 1951, Reel 66, #416, *Du Bois Papers;* Canadian Peace Congress to Defense Committee, August 21, 1951, Reel 66, #291, *Du Bois Papers;* Ivor Montague to Defense Committee, February 2, 1951, Reel 66, #1188, *Du Bois Papers;* League for Democratic Rights to Defense Committee, November 14, 1951, Reel 66, #1022, *Du Bois Papers;* League of Colored Peoples to Howard Fast, June 23, 1951, Reel 66, #1023, *Du Bois Papers;* Cedric Dover to Du Bois, June 11, 1951, Reel 66, #506, *Du Bois Papers;* Cedric Dover to Du Bois, July 14, 1951; Reel 66, #509, *Du Bois Papers;* Mulk Rj Anand, Mahomed Ashraft, et. al., letter of protest, October 2, 1951, Reel 66, #521, *Du Bois Papers;* Association of Scientific Workers to Defense Committee, October 2, 1951, Reel 66, #525, *Du Bois Papers;* Francois Joseph Cariglioli to Citron, November 11, 1951, Reel 66, #301, *Du Bois Papers.*
45. National Peace Movement to Attorney General McGrath, September 10, 1951, Reel 66, #1203, *Du Bois Papers;* General Confederation of Labor Statement, November 7, 1951, Reel 66, #685, *Du Bois Papers;* Bruno Frei Statement, undated, Reel 66, #669, *Du Bois Papers;* F. Davis to Howard Fast, July 31, 1951, Reel 66, #844, *Du Bois Papers;* South East Asia Committee Resolution, September 21, 1951, Reel 66, #518, *Du Bois Papers.*
46. Anezeka Hodinora to Du Bois, February 22, 1951, Reel 66, #434, *Du Bois Papers;* Council of the Msasryk University Statement, Juluy 10, 1951, Reel 66, #1131, *Du Bois Papers;* J. Mukarovsky to Du Bois, February 16, 1951, Reel 66, #308, *Du Bois Papers;* Central Council of Trade Unions of Prague to Louise Patterson, February, 13, 1951, Reel 66, #303, *Du Bois Papers;* Fight for Peace Committee of Cluf Region, July 31, 1951, Reel 66, #538, *Du Bois Papers;* Fight for Peace Committee of Iasi Region, July 31, 1951, Reel 66, #539, *Du Bois Papers;* Union for Polish Writers Statement, February 21, 1951, Reel 61, #665, *Du Bois Papers;* Association of Polish Lawyers to Defense Committee, November 22, 1951, Reel 66, #176, *Du Bois Papers;* Hungarian National Peace Council Statemenmt, February 21, 1951, Reel 66, #857, *Du Bois Papers;* Comite Al Banais Pour La Defense De La Paix, July 28, 1951, Reel 66, #366, *Du Bois Papers;* Trieste

Youth Statement, February 22, 1951, Reel 66, #434, *Du Bois Papers;* William Weinstone article, September 28, 1951, Reel 67, #718, *Du Bois Papers.*

47. Jiri Hronsek to Defense Committee, undated, Reel 66, #405, *Du Bois Papers;* World Federation of Scientific Workers Resolution, May 22, 1951, Reel 67, #804, *Du Bois Papers;* International Federation of Democratic Women, June 6, 1951, Reel 66, #887, *Du Bois Papers;* World Federation of Trade Unions Resolution, undated, Reel 67, #814, *Du Bois Papers;* Paul Delanoue to Alice Citron, May 18, 1951, Reel 67, #64, *Du Bois Papers;* "Comite International De Defense Du Dr. W.E.B. Du Bois et des Colleagues," circa 1951, Reel 66, #374, *Du Bois Papers;* Du Bois to Paul Demeulenaere, December 3, 1951, Reel 66, #374, *Du Bois Papers;* Elias Entralgo to Defense Committee, June 15, 1951, Reel 66, #387, *Du Bois Papers;* Democratic Rights Council of Australia to Defense Comittee, circa 1951, Reel 66, #468, *Du Bois Papers.*
48. "Via: Air Pouch To: Chief (deleted) From: Acting Chief (deleted) Subject: General-Miscellaneous Matters Specific-Pro Peace Correspondence Date: 13 February 1952, "Central Intelligence Agency; "Via: Air Pouch to: Chief (deleted) From: Deputy Chief (deleted) Subject: General-Operational Specific-Meeting of Congress of Peoples Against Imperialism Date: 26 February 1952, "Central Intelligence Agency; Report From Belgium, November 21, 1951, subject: "Communist Propaganda Campaign in Behalf of Dr. W.E.B. Du Bois," Central Intelligence Agency; (in possession of author) 201–7123; R. E. G. Armattoe to Du Bois, August 27, 1951, Reel 66, #165, *Du Bois Papers.*
49. Du Bois, *In Battle for Peace,* 151; Du Bois to William Foley, undated, in *Du BoisIII,* 308–9; William Foley to Du Bois, February 2, 1951, in *Du Bois III,* 309; *Daily Compass,* February 16, 1951.
50. Du Bois to Eugene Davidson, May 11, 1951, Reel 66, #456, *Du Bois Papers; National Guardian,* November 14, 1951; *Daily Compass,* November 22, 1951.
51. Council on African Affairs circular, November 18, 1951, Reel 66, #425, *Du Bois Papers;* Thomas Richardson and Willard Uphaus to "Dear Friend," October 18, 1951, Reel 66, #115, *Du Bois Papers;* James Cobb to Du Bois, August 24, 1951, Reel 66, #350, *Du Bois Papers.*
52. Gloria Agrin to Alice Citron, May 28, 1951, Reel 66, #15, *Du Bois Papers;* "Matters to be Elicited on Direct Examination of Dr. Du Bois," circa 1951, Reel 67, #349, *Du Bois Papers;* Biography of Elizabeth Moos, circa 1951, Reel 67, #142, *Du Bois Papers; Daily Compass,* February 1, 1951.

53. Du Bois to James Cobb, December 19, 1951, Reel 66, #352, *Du Bois Papers;* James Cobb to Du Bois, December 22, 1951, Reel 66, #352, *Du Bois Papers; Daily Compass,* February 11, 1951.
54. *The New York Times,* March 23, 1951; O. John Roggs, *Our Vanishing Civil Liberties* (New York: Gaer, 1949); Du Bois, *In Battle for Peace,* 109, 110, 111.
55. *Daily Compass,* November 15, 1951; Albert Kahn article, undated, Reel 68, #566, *Du Bois Papers.*
56. *The New York Times,* November 21, 1951; Elizabeth Moos Report on Peace Information Center Trial, December 13, 1951, Reel 66, #1189, *Du Bois Papers.*
57. Du Bois to Metz Lochard, November 27, 1951, Reel 66, #1068, *Du Bois Papers;* Du Bois to Vito Marcantonio, February 29, 1951, Reel 66, #1111, *Du Bois Papers;* Louis Untermeyer to Du Bois, October 13, 1948, Reel 61, #591, *Du Bois Papers;* Du Bois to Gloria Agrin, November 29, 1951, Reel 66, #17, *Du Bois Papers; National Guardian,* November 21, 1951.
58. Du Bois to Thomas Richardson, November 30, 1951, Reel 66, #123, *Du Bois Papers;* Du Bois to Harold Mason, December 5, 1951, Reel 66, #1135, *Du Bois Papers;* P. L. Prattis to Alice Citron, November 26, 1951, Reel 67, #376, *Du Bois Papers; Daily Compass,* November 22, 1951; *National Guardian,* November 28, 1951.
59. Shirley Graham Du Bois, *His Day is Marching on,* 210; Du Bois to Albert Einstein, November 29, 1951, Reel 66, #591, *Du Bois Papers.*
60. G. V. Banks to Du Bois, November 30, 1951, Reel 66, #193, *Du Bois Papers;* Du Bois to G. V. Banks, December 5, 1951, Reel 66, #194, *Du Bois Papers.*
61. Du Bois to Arthur Flames, November 27, 1951, in *Du Bois III,* 321; Du Bois to Hubert Delany, November 30, 1951, Reel 66, #465, *Du Bois Papers;* John Brown to Du Bois, December 29, 1951, Reel 67, #503, *Du Bois Papers;* Du Bois to John Brown, January 7, 1952, Reel 68, #997, *Du Bois Papers.*
62. Du Bois to Vito Marcantonio, December 6, 1951, Reel 66, #1112, *Du Bois Papers;* Du Bois to Hubert Delany, November 30, 1951, Reel 66, #465, *Du Bois Papers.*
63. William Patterson to Du Bois, November 30, 1951, Reel 66, #335, *Du Bois Papers;* Du Bois to Arthur McPhaul, December 3, 1951, Reel 66, #342, *Du Bois Papers.*
64. Du Bois to Martin L. Harvey, December 19, 1951, Reel 67, #535, *Du Bois Papers;* Du Bois to Eugene Davidson, April 18, 1955, in *Du Bois III,* 382; Eugene Davidson to Du Bois, April 27, 1955, Reel 71, #307, *Du Bois Papers; Afro-American,* December 22, 1951.

Chapter 15. Africa and Peace; Part II

1. Shirley Graham Du Bois, *His Day is Marching On,* 213; Hollis Lynch, "The Council on African Affairs," 53; *The New York Times,* November 22, 1949; *New Africa* 8 (July–August 1949), 1.
2. Du Bois to "Dear Friend," January 5, 1950, Reel 64, #740, *Du Bois Papers; The New York Times,* May 21, 1950; *New Africa* 9 (January 1950), 1; *New Africa* 9 (April 1950), 1; Du Bois, Paul Robeson, and W. Alphaeus Hunton to Trygve Lie, undated, Reel 65, #725, *Du Bois Papers; New Africa* 9 (April 1950), 1, Reel 64, #1151, *Du Bois Papers.*
   Du Bois to Elizabeth Sturten, October 8, 1951, Reel 66, #473, *Du Bois Papers; Afro-American,* July 21, New Africal; Du Bois circular, August 8, 1951, Reel 66, #862, *Du Bois Papers.*
   New Africa 10 (November 1951), 10.
3. *New Africa* 10 (November 1951), 10; Council on African Affairs information on "Campaign of Defiance of Unjust Laws in South Africa," July 24–December 31, 1952, Reel 68, #203, *Du Bois Papers;* W. Alphaeus Hunton to Du Bois, April 2, 1952, Reel 68, #187, *Du Bois Papers;* Council on African Affairs Press Release, July 25, 1952, Reel 68, #198, *Du Bois Papers;* W. Alphaeus Hunton circular, September 17, 1952, Reel 68, #199, *Du Bois Papers.*
4. *Freedom* (October 1952); *Freedom* (June 1953); *Spotlight on Africa* 12 (June 11, 1953), 4; Minutes of Council on African Affairs Meeting, February 17, 1954, Reel 70, #528, *Du Bois Papers; New Africa* 9 (May–June 1950), 3, Reel 64, #1155, *Du Bois Papers.*
5. Du Bois to W. Alphaeus Hunton, September 26, 1952, Reel 68, #200, *Du Bois Papers;* Du Bois to Council on African Affairs, undated, Reel 66, #426, *Du Bois Papers;* W. Alphaeus Hunton to Du Bois, October 29, 1952, Reel 68, #201, *Du Bois Papers.*
6. *Spotlight on Africa* 12 (January 8, 1953), 3; Reel 69, #686, *Du Bois Papers; 195* 11 (June 24, 1952), 1.
7. Du Bois to W. Alphaeus Hunton, March 2, 1954, Reel 70, #531, *Du Bois Papers;* Du Bois to Elizabeth Lawson, December 13, 1951, Reel 66, #1018, *Du Bois Papers;* Deputy Director, Plans of Central Intelligence Agency to Director of Federal Bureau of Investigation, April 1, 1954 (in possession of author); Petition by U.S. Attorney General, April 20, 1953, Reel 69, #692, *Du Bois Papers.*
8. Subpoena to W. Alphaeus Hunton, October 7, 1954, Reel 70, #549, *Du Bois Papers;* Council on African Affairs press release, October 7, 1954, Reel 70, #550, *Du Bois Papers;* Du Bois to United Nations community, June 18, 1953, in *Du Bois III,* 348; Du Bois to W. Alphaeus Hunton, July 29, Reel 69, #706, *Du Bois Papers.*
9. *Spotlight on Africa* 11 (July 14, 1953), 1.

10. Council on African Affairs Press Release, November 8, 1952, Reel 68, #181, *Du Bois Papers; Spotlight on Africa* 13 (January 21, 1954), 3; *Spotlight on Africa* 13 (May 18, 1954), Reel 70, #539, *Du Bois Papers;* Du Bois to W. Alphaeus Hunton, September 29, 1954, Reel 70, #548, *Du Bois Papers.*
11. *Spotlight on Africa* 13 (May 18, 1954), 1; Council on African Affairs Press Release, June 2, 1954, Reel 70, #543, *Du Bois Papers;* Du Bois to W. A. Hunton, June 8, 1954, Reel 70, #544, *Du Bois Papers; Spotlight on Africa* 13 (June 22, 1954), 5; W. Alphaeus Hunton to Du Bois, September 27, 1954, Reel 70, #547, *Du Bois Papers.*
12. "Conference in Support of African Liberation at Friendship Baptist Church," April 24, 1954, New York City, Reel 70, #533, *Du Bois Papers.*
13. Ibid.; W. Alphaeus Hunton to Du Bois, September 27, 1954, Reel 70, #547, *Du Bois Papers.*
14. *West African Pilot,* May 20, 1953; *West African Pilot,* June 30, 1953; *Spotlight on Africa* 12 (July 14, 1953), 5.
15. *Spotlight on Africa* 14 (May 1955), 1; *Afro-American,* May 14,1955; *Oklahoma City Black Dispatch,* April 23, 1955.
16. Abbott Simon to Du Bois, January 31, 1951, Reel 66, #64, *Du Bois Papers;* Report of the Sponsors Meeting of the American Peace Crusade, February 11, 1951, Reel 66, #80, *Du Bois Papers;* Statement of APC Delegation Presented to Secretary of Defense George Marshall, March 15, 1951, Reel 66, #87, *Du Bois Papers;* Robert J. Havighurst to "Dear Friend," February 1, 1951, Reel 67, #39, *Du Bois Papers;* Statement by APC, April 11, 1951, April 11, 1951, Reel 66, #91, *Du Bois Papers.*
17. *National Guardian,* July 11, 1951; "Tentative Program and Agenda," of People's Congress and Peace Exposition, June 29–July 1, 1951, Reel 67, #364, *Du Bois Papers;* Du Bois and Clementina Paolone to "Dear Fellow New Yorker," May 2, 1951, Reel 66, #98, *Du Bois Papers; National Guardian,* June 13, 1951.
18. *The New York Times,* February 2, 1951; Philip Morrison to Thomas Mann, February 13, 1951, Reel 66, #1107, *Du Bois Papers;* Du Bois to *The New York Times,* undated, Reel 66, #285, *Du Bois Papers.*
19. Du Bois to Elizabeth Moos, November 17, 1952, Reel 68, #574, *Du Bois Papers;* U.S. Congress, *House Report on the Communist "Peace Offensive": A Campaign to Disarm and Defeat the United States,* April 1, 1951, prepared and released by the Committee on Un-American Activities, Washington, D.C. (82nd Cong. 1st Sess.); *Crisis* 59 (August–September 1952), 2.
20. Canadian Peace Congress press release, circa 1952, Reel 68, #73, *Du Bois Papers;* Mary Jennison to APC, January 13, 1952, Reel 68, #68, *Du Bois Papers;* Du Bois to Mary Jennison, April 30, 1952, Reel 68,

#70, *Du Bois Papers;* Mary Jennison to Du Bois, April 30, 1952, Reel 68, #71, *Du Bois Papers.*

21. "Via phone to Toronto, May 11, 1952," Reel 67, #1096, *Du Bois Papers;* "Order for Deportation, The Immigration Act, Section 33," Reel 68, #65, *Du Bois Papers; The New York Times,* May 10, 1952; Bruce Mickleburgh to Du Bois, June 10, 1952, Reel 68, #79, *Du Bois Papers;* Ivy Stoetzer to Du Bois, May 12, 1952, Reel 68, #1021, *Du Bois Papers;* Du Bois to Jean Laffitte, May 14, 1952, Reel 69, #83, *Du Bois Papers; Toronto Globe and Mail,* February 8, 1950, Reel 74, #112, *Du Bois Papers.*
22. Du Bois to Continental Cultural Congress, April 21, 1953, Reel 69, #676, *Du Bois Papers;* Du Bois to Jean Laffitte, April 24, 1953, Reel 69, #677, *Du Bois Papers.*
23. "In the Matter of the Proposed Designation of the American Peace Crusade, Pursuant to Executive Order 10450," circa 1953, Reel 69, #486, *Du Bois Papers;* American Peace Crusade to Herbert Brownell, September 29, 1953, Reel 69, #503, *Du Bois Papers.*
24. Du Bois to Abbott Simon, August 4, 1952, Reel 67, #1121, *Du Bois Papers;* Du Bois to Abbott Simon, Hugh Bryson, et. al., December 1952, Reel 67, #1137, *Du Bois Papers;* John Kingsbury to Du Bois, December 18, 1952, Reel 67, #1139, *Du Bois Papers;* Thomas Richardson to Du Bois, December 19, 1952, Reel 67, #1142, *Du Bois Papers;* Du Bois to Edward Bearsley, November 1, 1952, Reel 68, #29, *Du Bois Papers;* Du Bois to Thomas Richardson, February 2, 1953, Reel 69, #465, *Du Bois Papers'* Du Bois to Marjorie Milton, September 22, 1953, Reel 69, #652, *Du Bois Papers; National Guardian,* April 25, 1954.
25. Press Release, February 28, 1952, Reel 67, #1081, *Du Bois Papers;* Press Release, undated, Reel 67, #1150, *Du Bois Papers;* "Communique" from "The Secretariat of the World Council of Peace," January 1, 1952, Reel 60, #27, *Du Bois Papers.*
26. "The Bulletin of the World Council of Peace," May 2, 1952, p. 11, Reel 69, #60, *Du Bois Papers;* Willard Uphaus to Du Bois, August 26, 1952, Reel 67, #1127, *Du Bois Papers;* Financial Report of Du Bois Birthday Celebration, June 11, 1952, Reel 67, #1100, *Du Bois Papers.*
27. American Peace Crusade Press Release, circa 1953, Reel 69, #518, *Du Bois Papers.*
28. Paul Robeson to U.S. members of World Council for Peace, June 23, 1951, Reel 67, #839, *Du Bois Papers;* "A Speech recorded for the World Peace Congress," July 1955, Reel 81, #1001, *Du Bois Papers;* Du Bois to Jean Laffitte, April 24, 1953, Reel 69, #58, *Du Bois Papers;* Du Bois to Scott Nearing, et. al., May 10, 1955, Reel 71, #471, *Du Bois Papers;* Du Bois to Rockwell Kent, May 16, 1955,

Reel 71, #477, *Du Bois Papers;* Rockwell Kent of Du Bois, May 25, 1955, Reel 71, *Du Bois Papers;* Rockwell Kent to Du Bois, December 3, 1955, Reel 71, #479, *Du Bois Papers;* Scott Nearing to Du Bois, November 29, 1955, Reel 71, #621, *Du Bois Papers.*

29. Du Bois to Holland Roberts, November 29, 1955, Reel 71, #343, *Du Bois Papers;* Howard Fast to Du Bois, December 19, 1955, Reel 71, #343, *Du Bois Papers;* Fred Stover to Holland Roberts, December 22, 1955, Reel 71, #647, *Du Bois Papers.*
30. Du Bois to Gloria Agrin, January 4, 1956, Reel 71, #981, *Du Bois Papers.*
31.. W.E.B. Du Bois "The World Peace Movement," *New World Review* 23 (April 1955), 9–14; Holland Roberts to Du Bois, October 20, 1955, Reel 71, #666, *Du Bois Papers;* U.S. Congress, House Comittee on Un-American Activities, *Investigation of the Unauthorized Use of U.S. Passports,* Part I, 84th Cong. 2nd Sess., Washington, D.C. 1956.

CHAPTER 16. DU BOIS AND COLD WAR REPRESSION

1. Walter Goodman, *The Committee: The Extraordinary Career of the House Committee on Un-American Activities* (New York: Farrar, Straus, Giroux, 1968); U.S. Congress, House Committee on Un-American Activities, *Hearings Before the Committee on Un-American Activities,* 80th Congress, 1st Session on H.R. 1884 and H.R. 2120, Bills to Curb or Outlaw the Communist Party in the U.S., Public Law 601 (§121, Sub Q (2)), July 2, 1947, Washington, D.C. 1947, pp. 34, 42, 93, 96; U.S. Congress, House Committee on Un-American Activities, *Communist Political Subversion,* Part 2, Appendix, 84th Congress, 2nd Session, Washington D.C., 1957, pp. 7702, 7810, 7814, 8312, 8083, 7934. U.S. Congress, House Committee on Un-American Activities, *Investigation of Communist Infiltration of Government—Part 3, Hearings Before the Committee on Un-American Activities,* 84th Congress, 2nd Session, February 14–16, 1956, Washington, D.C., 1956, p. 3240; *Investigation of Unauthorized Use of Passports,* Part 2, May 25, 1956, p. 120; U.S. Congress, House Committee on Un-American Activities, *Communist Propaganda—Part 9—Student Groups, Distributors and Propagandists,* Hearings Before the Committee on Un-American Activities, House of Representatives, 85th Congress, 2nd Session, June 11–12, 1958, Washington, D.C., 1958; U.S. Congress, House Committee on Un-American Activities, *Communist Activities in the Minneapolis Area,* Hearings Before the Committee on Un-American Activities, House of Representatives, 88th Congress, 2nd Session, June 24–26, 1964, pp. 1795, 1797; Ibid., *Communist Political Subversion—Part 2,* p. 7712;

U.S. Congress, House Committee on Un-American Activities, *Investigation of Communist Activities, New York Area—Part VIII* (Entertainment), 84th Congress, 1st Session, October 4, 1955, Washington, D.C., 1955; U.S. Congress, House Committee on Un-American Activities, *Investigation of Communist Activities, New York Area—Part III,* Hearings Before the Committee on Un-American Activities, House of Representatives, 84th Congress, 1st Session, May3–4, 1955, Washington, D.C., 1955, p. 965. U.S. Congress, House Committee on Un-American Activities, *Communist Activities in the Chicago, Illinois Area, Part 2, Appendix to Hearings Before the Committee on Un-American Activities,* 89th Congress, 1st Session, May 25–27, and June 22, 1965, Washington, D.C., 1965, p. 583; U.S. Congress, House Committee on Un-American Activities, *Communist Training Operations, Part 1,* Hearings Before the Committee on Un-American Activities, 86th Congress, 1st Session, July 21–22, 1959, Washington, D.C., 1959, p. 977; U.S. Congress, House, *Hearings Before the Subcommittee to Investigate the Administration of the Internal Security Act and Other Internal Security Laws of the Committee on the Judiciary,* 84th Congress, 1st Session, Pursuant to S. Res. 58, March 9, 1955, Part 1, Washington, D.C., 1955, p. 720, p. 729; Ibid., *Communist Political Subversion, Part 2,* Appendix, p. 7163; Ibid., *Communist Political Subversion, Part 2,* Appendix 7235; U.S. Congress, House Committee on Un-American Activities, *Investigation of Communist Activities in the Seattle, Washington Area—Part 1,* Hearings Before the Committee on Un-American Activities.

2. U.S. Congress, House Committee on Un-American Activities, *Testimony of Reverend James H. Robinson,* hearings before the Committee on Un-American Activities, House of Representatives, 88th Cong. 2nd Sess., May 5, 1964, Washington, D.C., 1964, pp. 1939, 1961, 1968, 1972; U.S. Congress, House Committee on Un-American Activities, *Violation of State Department Regulations and Pro-Castro Propaganda Activities in the United States,* Part 2, Hearings Before the Committee on Un-American Activities, House of Representatives, 88th Congress, 1st Session, August 5, 1963, Washington, D.C., 1963.
3. Court Opinion, December 2, 1947, Reel 59, #1162, *Du Bois Papers;* National Institute of Arts and Letters, January 26, 1948, Reel 62, #504, *Du Bois Papers.*
4. *Pittsburgh Courier,* January 8, 1954; *National Guardian,* January 31, 1955; *Crisis* 60 (June–July 1953), 353; *Communist Political Subversion,* Part 2, Appendix, p. 8186.
5. *National Guardian,* August 4, 1958; C. E. Pickett to Du Bois, December 31, 1960, Reel 74, #61, *Du Bois Papers;* National Assembly for Democratic Rights, August 31, 1961, Reel 75, #459, *Du Bois Papers;* U.S. Congress, House Committee on Un-American Activities, *Subversive Influence in Riots, Looting, and Burning, Part 1,* Hearings Before the

Committee on Un-American Activities, House of Representatives, 90th Cong., 1st Sess., October 25–26, 31, and December 28, 1967, Washington, D.C., 1968, pp. 893, 1277.

6. Charles Cheng, "The Cold War: Its Impact on the Black Liberation Struggle Within the United States," *Freedomways* 13 (Fall 1973), 184–189; Barton J. Bernstein, "America in War and Peace," in *Towards a New Past,* edited by Barton J. Berstein (New York: Random House, 1968), 308; Charles Allen, "McCarthy: Enemy of the Negro People," *Jewish Life* 8 (November 1953), 9–11, Reel 69, #911, *Du Bois Papers;* Jane Sanders, *Cold War on the Campus: Academic Freedom at the University of Washington, 1946–1964* (Seattle: University of Washington Press, 1979), passim.
7. Ibid.; Du Bois to Karl Mundt, January 22, 1945, Reel 58, #29, *Du Bois Papers;* Clarice Claps to Du Bois, April 12, 1947, Reel 59, #1004, *Du Bois Papers;* Herbert Biberman to Du Bois, December 29, 1947, Reel 59, #1051, *Du Bois Papers.*
8. P. L. Prattis to Du Bois, June 29, 1948, Reel 62, #1146, *Du Bois Papers;* Howard Fast to Du Bois, July 7, 1948, Reel 61, #969, *Du Bois Papers.*
9. Du Bois to Lasker Smith, March 9, 1949, Reel 64, #311, *Du Bois Papers;* B. A. Washington, to Du Bois, April 7, 1949, Reel 63, #1049, *Du Bois Papers;* Stanley Isaacs to Du Bois, May 17, 1949, Reel 63, #1049, *Du Bois Papers;* Martin D. Jenkins to Du Bois, April 29, 1949, in *Du Bois III,* 259.
10. Press Release, May 10, 1949, Reel 64, #611, *Du Bois Papers;* Walter White, "The Strange Case of Paul Robeson," *Ebony* 6 (February 1951), 79; *Crisis* 56 (May 1951), 137.
11. W.E.B. Du Bois, "Paul Robeson: Right," *Negro Digest* 3 (March 1950), 10–14; Walter White, "Paul Robeson: Wrong," *Negro Digest* 8 (Mrch 1950), 14–18.
12. Philip S. Foner (ed.), *Paul Robeson Speaks: Writings, Speeches, Interviews, 1918–1974* (New York: Brunner-Mazel, 1978); Robert Alan, "Paul Robeson—The Lost Shepherd," *Crisis* (November 1951), 569–573; U.S. Congress, House Committee on Un-American Activities, *Investigation of Communist Activities in the San Diego, California Area,* Hearings Before the Committee on Un-American Activities, 84th Cong., 1st Sess., July 5–6, 1955, Washington, D.C., 1955, p. 1919.
13. Du Bois, Paul Robeson, et. al. to Harry S. Truman, October 12, 1949, Reel 63, #934, *Du Bois Papers;* Helen Mangold to Dean Acheson, August 10, 1950, Reel 65, #640, *Du Bois Papers; Crisis* 10 (December 1951), 671; Edward H. Dodd, Jr. to Du Bois, October 4, 1955, Reel 71, #327, *Du Bois Papers.*
14. Charlotta Bass, *Forty Years: Memoirs From the Pages of a Newspaper* (Los Angeles: Bass Publishers, 1960), 156, 161, 134, 175, 182, 188.

15. William A. Reuben, *The Atom Spy Hoax* (New York: Action Books, 1954), 291; Roy Wilkins to Ben Bell, August 14, 1952, *NAACP Papers;* Clemens France to Thurgood Marshall, December 16, 1952, *NAACP Papers.*
16. *Daily Worker,* November 16, 1952; Du Bois Speech at "Rosenberg Rally," January 8, 1953, Reel 81, #536, *Du Bois Papers;* Aaron Schneider to Du Bois, January 12, 1953, Reel 69, #636, *Du Bois Papers;* Walter and Miriam Schneir, *Invitation to an Inquest: Reopening the Rosenberg "Atom Spy Case,"* (Baltimore: Penguin, 1973), 178; Du Bois to National Rosenberg Defense Committee, June 12, 1954, Reel 70, #906, *Du Bois Papers.*
17. *National Guardian,* July 6, 1953; U.S. Congress House Committee on Un-American Activities, *Investigation of Communist Activities: The Committee to Secure Justice in the Rosenberg Case and Affiliates,* Part 1, Hearings Before the Committee on Un-American Activities, 84th Cong., 1st Sess., August 2 and August 3, 1955, Washington, D.C., 1955.
18. Helen Sobell, December 1, 1954, Reel 70, #1073, *Du Bois Papers;* Du Bois to James V. Bennett, December 10, 1954, Reel 70, #468, *Du Bois Papers;* Statement to New York Committee to Secure Justice for Morton Sobell, June 11, 1955, Reel 71, #633, *Du Bois Papers.*
19. Lillian Hyman to George Padmore, May 11, 1953, Reel 69, #1179, *Du Bois Papers;* Du Bois to Mrs. H. Ragosin, February 16, 1955, Reel 71, #662, *Du Bois Papers;* Du Bois to Robert Benchley, April 18, 1955, Reel 71, #245; *Du Bois Papers.*
20. Du Bois to K. Chugnov, May 31, 1955, Reel 71, #754, *Du Bois Papers;* Du Bois to V. V. Kuznetsov, May 28, 1956, Reel 72, #72, *Du Bois Papers;* Du Bois to J. Edward Day, May 15, 1961, Reel 75, #704, *Du Bois Papers;* Du Bois to Veb Verlag Der Kunst, April 3, Reel 75, #711, *Du Bois Papers.*
21. John Brooks to Du Bois, January 15, 1953, Reel 69, #1123, *Du Bois Papers;* Joseph Felshin to Du Bois, January 28, 1953, Reel 69, #1116, *Du Bois Papers;* Du Bois to Ethel Ray Nance, February 9, 1953, Reel 60, #1023, *Du Bois Papers;* Du Bois to Alice Citron, April 23, 1952, Reel 68, #107, *Du Bois Papers;* Du Bois to Cedric Belfrage, May 21, 1953, Reel 69, #106, *Du Bois Papers.*
22. H. P. Fairchild to Du Bois, April 16, 1953, Reel 69, #1064, *Du Bois Papers;* Du Bois to H. P. Fairchild, April 21, 1953, Reel 69, #1065, *Du Bois Papers;* Information on ASP Rally, September 27, 1953, Reel 69, #1069, *Du Bois Papers;* Sam Kanter to Du Bois, January 12, 1953, Reel 69, #611, *Du Bois Papers.*
23. *The New York Times,* July 16, 1953; Du Bois to National Council of Arts, Sciences and Professions (NCASP) Secretary, July 28, 1953, Reel 69, #1102, *Du Bois Papers;* Louis Kronenberger to Du Bois, August 26, 1953, Reel 69, #1103, *Du Bois Papers.*

24. A. B. Magil to Du Bois, April 7, 1948, Reel 61, #818, *Du Bois Papers;* Linus Pauling to Du Bois, circa 1950, Reel 65, #431, *Du Bois Papers;* Du Bois to Ruth Anna Fisher, November 28, 1950, Reel 65, #20, *Du Bois Papers;* Circular letter from Du Bois, et. al., January 9, 1952, Reel 61, #1029, *Du Bois Papers;* Du Bois to Mario Rosa Oliver, January 14, 1952, Reel 61, #1030, *Du Bois Papers.*
25. Du Bois to Department of State, August 1, 1950, Reel 65, #767, *Du Bois Papers;* Ruth B. Shipley to Du Bois, February 12, 1952, Reel 68, #1099, *Du Bois Papers;* Ruth B. Shipley to Du Bois, April 6, 1953, in *Du Bois III,* 346; W. Alphaeus Hunton to Du Bois, August 25, 1953, Reel 69, #711, *Du Bois Papers.*
26. Du Bois to Willard Uphaus, November 3, 1952, Reel 68, #1140, *Du Bois Papers;* M. A. Oki to Du Bois, December 15, 1952, Reel 68, #169, *Du Bois Papers;* Du Bois to M. A. Oki, January 6, 1953, Reel 69, #1175, *Du Bois Papers.*
27. Du Bois to Ruth Shipley, March 28, 1953, Reel 70, #106, *Du Bois Papers;* "Paul Robeson Receives Stalin Peace Prize," October 1953, Reel 69, #1139, *Du Bois Papers.*
28. Du Bois to Jiri Pelikan, October 29, 1954, Reel 70, #701, *Du Bois Papers;* Du Bois to Frances Knight, June 8, 1955, Reel 71, #731, *Du Bois Papers;* Frances Knight to Du Bois, July 1, 1955, Reel 71, #732, *Du Bois Papers;* Du Bois to Frances Knight, July 13, 1955, Reel 71, #733, *Du Bois Papers;* Du Bois to Jacques Denis, June 6, 1955, Reel 71, #780, *Du Bois Papers;* Gloria Agrin to Du Bois, March 14, 1956, Reel 71, #984, *Du Bois Papers;* Du Bois to James Cobb, June 27, 1955, Reel 71, #291 *Du Bois Papers.*
29. Du Bois to R. Holender, June 6, 1956, Reel 72, #243, *Du Bois Papers;* "1956 Committee for Commemoration of Great Figures in World Culture," to Du Bois, October 12, 1956, Reel 79, #50, *Du Bois Papers;* Cedric Belfrage to Du Bois, October 30, 1956, Reel 72, #156, *Du Bois Papers;* Report of Central Intelligence Agency, May 1957, Subject: Reprints of National Guardian Articles in Ghana Evening News, CPP Newspapers (in possession of author) 201–7123.
30. Du Bois to George Padmore, Februry 7, 1957, Reel 79, #1085, *Du Bois Papers;* Du Bois to Mohammed Awad, February 24, 1957, Reel 72, #1042, *Du Bois Papers;* Du Bois to John Foster Dulles, February 22, 1957, Reel 72, #1042, *Du Bois Papers;* Du Bois to William Dawson, Charles Diggs, Adam Clayton Powell, February 22, 1957, Reel 72, #1042, *Du Bois Papers;* Du Bois to Thomas Hennings, march 26, 1957, Reel 72, #1051, *Du Bois Papers;* Membership of the Third Committee, United Nations General Assembly, October 10, 1957, Reel 72, #1042, *Du Bois Papers.*
31. Invitation to Ghana Independence Celebration, March 3–10, 1957, Reel 72, #596, *Du Bois Papers;* Kwame Nkrumah to Du Bois, April

4, 1957, Reel 72, #597, *Du Bois Papers;* James Aronson to Du Bois, March 29, 1957, Reel 72, #887, *Du Bois Papers;* Kwame Nkrumah to Bernard Reswick, April 25, 1957, Reel 72, #920, *Du Bois Papers;* Shirley Graham to Roscoe Dunjee, March 10, 1957, Reel 72, #921, *Du Bois Papers;* George Padmore to Du Bois, undated, Reel 72, #926, *Du Bois Papers.*

32. I. F. *Stone's Weekly,* March 11, 1957, Reel 72, #1011, *Du Bois Papers;* P. L. Prattis to Shirley Graham, March 12, 1957, Reel 72, #973, *Du Bois Papers;* P. L. Prattis to Shirley Graham, March 14, 1957, Reel 72, #972, *Du Bois Papers.*
33. Du Bois to Gabriel D'Arbrussier, September 27, 1957, Reel 72, #508, *Du Bois Papers;* Du Bois to Saburo Yamada and Hideki Yukawa, May 22, 1957, Reel 72, #696, *Du Bois Papers;* Du Bois to Kwame Nkrumah, February 12, 1958, Reel 73, #330, *Du Bois Papers.*
34. E. J. Hickey to Blanche Freedman, October 8, 1959, Reel 73, #666, *Du Bois Papers;* Du Bois to Umberto Campagnolo, January 25, 1959, Reel 74, #800, *Du Bois Papers;* "Memorandum for: John W. Hanes, Jr., Administrator, Bureau of Security and Consular Affairs, August 10, 1960, Central Intelligence Agency" (in possession of author).
35. Du Bois to Sir John Kotelawala, December 6, 1954, Reel 70, #501, *Du Bois Papers;* Rhoda Miller to President Eisenhower, July 24, 1954, Reel 70, #572, *Du Bois Papers;* "Provisional Committee for Rhoda Miller De Silva," February 25, 1955, Reel 71, #318, *Du Bois Papers;* Press Release, June 16, 1955, Reel 70, #318, *Du Bois Papers;* Du Bois to U.S. State Department, August 16, 1955, Reel 70, #321, *Du Bois Papers;* Report by James H. Boughton, July 28, 1955, 246–1111–da Silva 19–2855, U.S. Embassy-Colombo, Department of State (in possession of author).
36. Statement by Lee Lorch, November 13, 1954, Reel 70, #784, *Du Bois Papers;* Lee Lorch to "Dear Friend," December 14, 1954, Reel 70, #786, *Du Bois Papers;* Lee Lorch to Du Bois, December 14, 1954, Reel 70, #780, *Du Bois Papers.*
37. Fisk Alumni to "Dear Fellow Alumnus," October 1954, Reel 0, #783, *Du Bois Papers; Oklahoma City Black Dispatch,* October 2, 1954.
38. Lee Lorch to Du Bois, February 16, 1955, Reel 71, #530, *Du Bois Papers;* Lee Lorch to Du Bois, February 12, 1955, Reel 71, #526, *Du Bois Papers;* Lee Lorch to Du Bois, March 12, 1956, Reel 72, #65, *Du Bois Papers; Pittsburgh Courier,* May 14, 1955; Press Release, Reel 71, #537, *Du Bois Papers.*
39. Levittown American Labor Party Press Release, March 22, 1956, Reel 71, #999, *Du Bois Papers;* Du Bois to Rockwell Kent, January 7, 1957, Reel 72, #707, *Du Bois Papers.*
40. Herbert Aptheker, *History and Reality* (New York: Cameron, 1955), 138; Carl and Anne Braden to Du Bois, November 3, 1957, Reel

72, #443, *Du Bois Papers;* Clark Foreman to Du Bois, May 6, 1957, Reel 72, #537, *Du Bois Papers;* Emergency Civil Liberties Committee, June 8, 1960, Reel 74, #210, *Du Bois Papers;* Emergency Civil Liberties Committee Press Release, March 16, 1956, Reel 71, #1128, *Du Bois Papers.*

41. Du Bois to Arthur Huff Fauset, June 30, 1958, Reel 73, #132, *Du Bois Papers;* Du Bois to Ethel Ray Nance, March 26, 1957, Reel 72, #852, *Du Bois Papers;* Du Bois Speech, February 12, 1960, Reel 81, #1279, *Du Bois Papers;* "Africa Awakened," circa 1959, Reel 82, #663, *Du Bois Papers.*
42. Willard Uphaus to Du Bois, March 15, 1960, Reel 74, #854, *Du Bois Papers.*
43. Reports of Central Intelligence Agency (in possession of author).

Chapter 17. Du Bois and the Civil Rights Movement

1. Du Bois to Cecil Peterson, January 6, 1947, Reel 60August 47, *Du Bois Papers.*
2. Du Bois Speech, St. Cyprian's Church, May 18, 1952, Reel 81, #404, *Du Bois Papers.*
3. *National Guardian,* January 23, 1956; Du Bois Speech, October 23, 1958, Reel 81, #1203, *Du Bois Papers; National Guardian,* February 12, 1953.
4. Du Bois to Estelle Pankhurst, July 31, 1946, in *Du Bois III,* 133; Estelle Pankhurst to Du Bois, November 17, 1948, Reel 62, #1101, *Du Bois Papers.*
5. W.E.B. Du Bois, "Negroes and the Crisis of Capitalism in the United States," *Monthly Review* 4 (April 1953), 478–485; Du Bois to Abraham Chapman, October 4, 1947, Reel 60, #47, *Du Bois Papers.*
6. W.E.B. Du Bois, "Bound by the Color Line," *New Masses* 58 (February 12, 1946) 9–12; *National Guardian,* March 15, 1956; W.E.B. Du Bois, "Georgia, Torment of A State," *New Masses,* 60 (September 10, 1946), 3–7.
7. W.E.B. Du Bois, "Should Negro History Be Taught As A Separate Subject," unpublished article, circa 1950, Reel 83, #522, *Du Bois Papers;* Du Bois to Estelle Pankhurst, March 31, 1954, in *Du Bois III,* 358; W.E.B. Du Bois, "Behold the Land," *New Masses* 62 (January 19, 1947), 18–20.
8. Robert Carr, *The House Committee on Un-American Activities, 1945–1950* (Ithaca: Cornell University Press, 1952), 222–231.

9. Wayne Addison Clark, "An Analysis of the Relationship Between Anti-Communism and Segregationist Thought in the Deep South, 1948–1964" (Ph.D. diss., University of North Carolina, 1976).
10. Donald R. McCoy and Richard T. Ruetten, "The Civil Rights Movement: 1940–1954," *Midwest Quarterly* 11 (October 1969), 11, 15.
11. Du Bois to Clarence Pickett, April 29, 1944, Reel 56, #261, *Du Bois Papers;* Du Bois Speech, "Marion Bachrch," October 1957, Reel 81, #1094, *Du Bois Papers;* Du Bois, "The American Negro Woman," circa 1949, Reel 83, #467, *Du Bois Papers.*
12. Du Bois to Ralph Himsteed, March 13, 1945, Reel 56, #1059, *Du Bois Papers;* Metz Lochard to Du Bois, January 2, 1947, Reel 59, #1140, *Du Bois Papers;* Du Bois to Marshall Bidwell, December 18, 1947, Reel 59, #1057, *Du Bois Papers.*
13. Du Bois to Cleo Hamilton, September 10, 1946, Reel 58, #984, *Du Bois Papers.*
14. *The New York Times,* December 11, 1948; Dr. J. F. Wilson to Du Bois, January 24, 1949, Reel 63, #1040, *Du Bois Papers;* Esther Cooper Jackson to Du Bois, January 25, 1949, Reel 63, #, *Du Bois Papers.*
15. Du Bois to Shirley Graham, June 24, 1949, Reel 63, #1108, *Du Bois Papers;* "Ingram Newsletter," November 1949, Reel 64, #41, *Du Bois Papers.*
16. Raphael O'Hara Lanier to Du Bois, February 16, 1950, Reel 65, #705, *Du Bois Papers; The New York Times,* May 1, 1950.
17. James Lipsett to Du Bois, August 6, 1952, Reel 68, #485, *Du Bois Papers;* Du Bois to P. L. Prattis, October 1, 1952, Reel 68, #832, *Du Bois Papers.*
18. R. B. Atwood to Oscar Greene, November 11, 1958, Reel 68, #34, *Du Bois Papers;* G. L. Harrison to Oscar Greene, November 8, 1952, Reel 68, #135, *Du Bois Papers;* J. S. Scott, Jr., to Oscar Greene, November 19, 1952, Reel 68, #136, *Du Bois Papers;* Charles Wesley to Du Bois, November 1952, Reel 68, #136, *Du Bois Papers;* Oscar Greene to Du Bois, December 5, 1952, Reel 68, #137, *Du Bois Papers.*
19. Peter Hyun to Du Bois, January 22, 1953, Reel 70, #18, *Du Bois Papers;* William Kerner to Du Bois, February 3, 1953, Reel 69, #1152, *Du Bois Papers;* Du Bois to Milton Bates, February 7, 1954, Reel 70, #1035, *Du Bois Papers.*
20. Anne Braden, *The Wall Between* (New York: Monthly Review Press, 1958), 10, 186–90, 278; Louis Redding, *Louisville Tragedy* (New York: Emergency Civil Liberties Committee, 1955), 232, 236; Carl and Anne Braden to Du Bois, November 24, 1954, Reel 70, #483, *Du Bois Papers;* Du Bois to Carl and Anne Braden, December 1, 1954, Reel 70, #484, *Du Bois Papers.*
21. Du Bois to Dean Gordon Hancock, March 23, 1955, Reel 71, #438, *Du Bois Papers;* Du Bois letter to Black press, May 2, 1955, Reel 71,

#937, *Du Bois Papers;* George Murphy to Du Bois, October 29, 1957, Reel 72, #845, *Du Bois Papers;* Shirley Graham to Carl Murphy, February 8, 1957, Reel 722, #344, *Du Bois Papers;* Annette Rubinstein to Du Bois, June 15, 1957, Reel 72, #99, *Du Bois Papers;* James Ivy to Muriel Symington, June 14, 1957, Reel 72, #10222, *Du Bois Papers; Afro-American,* February 22, 1960; *San Francisco Sun-Reporter,* June 11, 1960.

22. Hubert Delany to Du Bois, October 14, 1955, Reel 71, #313, *Du Bois Papers;* Alain Locke Memorial Workshop, October 29, 1955, Reel 71, #521, *Du Bois Papers;* E. M. Mahoney to Du Bois, February 2, 1956, Reel 72, #247, *Du Bois Papers;* Alice B. Hoskins to Elmer Mahoney, April 2, 1956, Reel 79, #57, *Du Bois Papers.*
23. *Crisis* 62 (October 1955), 481; *Crisis* 62 (December 1955), 596–97; *Crisis* 62 (November 1955), 546; *National Guardian,* January 2, 1956; Lyman Beecher Stowe to Du Bois, January 25, 1956, Reel 72, #190, *Du Bois Papers;* Du Bois Speech, "The Senators From Mississippi," February 8, 1956, Reel 81, #1003, *Du Bois Papers;* Du Bois, "A Political Program," June 1956, Reel 81, #1015, *Du Bois Papers;* Committee for a Free South Announcement, November 28, 1952, Reel 68, #129, *Du Bois Papers;* Dr. T. R. M. Howard to Lyman Beecher Stowe, November 8, 1956, Reel 72, #191, *Du Bois Papers; The New York Times,* April 16, 1956; *National Guardian,* February 20, 1956.
24. Gloster Current, "Crisis in Little Rock," *Crisis* 64 (November 1957), 523–35, 580; *Crisis* 64 (November 1957), 555; *Crisis* 64 (December 1957), 625–27; *National Guardian,* September 30, 1957; *Crisis* 65 (December 1958), 619.
25. *Crisis* 64 (November 1957), 535; *National Guardian,* November 4, 1957; *National Guardian,* January 23, 1956.
26. Aldon Douglas Morris, "The Rise of Civil Rights Movement and Its Movement: Black Power Structure, 1953–1963" (Ph.D. diss., State University of New York at Stony Brook, 1980), 19, 34, 163; Emily Stoper, "The Student Non-Violent Coordinating Committee; Rise and Fall of Redemptive Organization," *Journal of Black Studies* 8 (September 1977), 13, 25; Howard Zinn, *SNCC: The New Abolitionists* (Boston: Beacon Press, 1964), 227; Harvard Sitkoff, *The Struggle for Black Equality, 1954–1960* (New York: Hill and Wang, 1981).
27. Thomas Bledsoe, *Or We'll All Hang Separately: The Highlander Idea* (Boston; Beacon Press, 1969), 50, 63, 115, 221; Frank Adams, *Unearthing Seeds of Fire: The Idea of Highlander* (Winston-Salem, n.g.: Blair, 1975), 16; Aldon Douglas Morris, 385, 398, 415, 418; Clayborn Carson, *In Struggle: SNCC and the Black Awakening of the 1960's* (Cambridge: Harvard University Press, 1981).

28. Aldon Douglas Morris, 442, 308, 458; Southern Conference Education Fund, *Discrimination in Higher Education* (New Orleans: SCEF, 1950).
29. Frank F. Lee, "Changing Structure of Negro Leadership," *Crisis* 65 (April 1958), 197–200, 251; John A. Morsell, "Comment on Frank Lee's Changing Structure of Negro Leadership," *Crisis* 65 (May 1958), 61–65, 365.
30. August Meier and Elliott Rudwick, *CORE: A Study in the Civil Rights Movement, 1942–1968* (New York: Oxford University Press, 1973), 31; *Southern Exposure* 9 (Spring 1981) 13; Carey McWilliams, *The Education of Carey McWilliams* (New York: Simon and Schuster, 1978), 206; Anne Braden, "A View From the Fringes," *Southern Exposure* 9 (Spring 1981), 68–74; Eugene P. Walker, "A History of the Southern Christian Leadership Conference, 1955–1965: the Evolution of A Southern Strategy for Social Change (Ph.D. diss., Duke University, 1978), 91.
31. *National Guardian,* April 27, 1959; *National Guardian,* May 11, 1959; *National Guardian,* May 25, 1959.
32. *Crisis* 63 (April 1956), 232–33; *Crisis* 63 (June–July 1956), 356–58; *Crisis* 63 (August–September 1956), 420–29; *Crisis* 66 (December 1959), 618; Walter White, *A Man Called White* (New York: Viking Press, 1948), 133, 316; Wilson Record, *Race and Radicalism: The NAACP and the Communist Party in Conflict* (Ithaca, N.Y.: Cornell University Press, 1964), 116; *Crisis* 63 (June–July 1956), 325–27, 380; *Crisis* 64 (May 1957), 292–93; Cleveland Sellers, *The River of No Return: The Autobiography of A Black Militant and the Life and Death of SNCC* (New York: Marrow, 1973), 26; "Interview with Fannie Lou Hamer," *Southern Exposure* 9 (Spring 1981), 45–48.
33. James Forman, *The Makings of Black Revolutionaries* (New York: MacMillan, 1972), 30, 177; H. Rap Brown, *Die Nigger Die'* (New York: Dial Press, 1969), 59; William Chafe, "The Greensboro Sit-Ins," in *America Since 1945,* by Robert D. Marcus and David Burner (New York: St. Martins Press, 1981); August Meier, Elliot Rudwick, and Francis Broderick (eds.), *Black Protest in the Twentieth Century* (Indianapolis: Bobbs Merrill, 1971), 357–58; U.S. Congress, House Un-American Activities Committee, *Communism in the Detroit Area-Part 1,* Hearings Before the Committee on Un-American Activities, 82nd Cong., 2nd sess., February 225–29, 1952, Washington, D.C., 1952, pp. 2887–8.
34. L. D. Reddick to Du Bois, April 11, 1659, Reel 72, #204, *Du Bois Papers; National Guardian,* November 9, 1959; L. D. Reddick, *Crusader Without Violence: A Biography of Martin Luther King, Jr.,* (New York: Harper, 1959), 147.

35. *National Guardian,* February 11, 1957; Du Bois Speech, "The New Negro Liberation Movements," circa 1956, Reel 81, #1033, *Du Bois Papers; San Diego Lighthouse,* March 30, 1956.
36. *Crisis* 6 (May 1913), 12; Robert Miller to Du Bois, February 14, 1949, Reel 64, #25, *Du Bois Papers;* Charles Levy to Du Bois, September 14, 1949, Reel 64, #29, *Du Bois Papers;* George Marks III to Du Bois, January 14, 1949, Reel 64, #24, *Du Bois Papers;* Brooklyn College NAACP to Du Bois, March 9, 1949, Reel 64, #23, *Du Bois Papers;* Edith Meyer to Du Bois, October 18, 1949, Reel 64, #31, *Du Bois Papers;* Charles Campbell to Du Bois, March 6, 1949, Reel 64, #141, *Du Bois Papers;* Esther Cooper Jackson to Du Bois, January 25, 1949, Reel 63, #818, *Du Bois Papers;* Du Bois to Helen Gordon, January 6, 1953, Reel 69, #829, *Du Bois Papers;* Du Bois to Robert Webb, November 18, 1953, Reel 70, #122, *Du Bois Papers.*
37. Du Bois Speech, "In Memory of Joel Elias Spingarn," December 11, 1953, Reel 81, #766, *Du Bois Papers;* Paul Witkovsky to Du Bois, March 30, 1956, Reel 72, #144, *Du Bois Papers;* Roy Wilkins to Du Bois, November 16, 1956, Reel 72, #143, *Du Bois Papers;* Muriel Symington, June 10, 1957, Reel 72, #1021, *Du Bois Papers;* Roy Wilkins to Muriel Symington, June 13, 1957, Reel 72, #1022, *Du Bois Papers;* James Ivy to Harry Ronis, March 27, 1957, Reel 72, #986, *Du Bois Papers;* T. J. Sellers to Du Bois, July 15, 1599, Reel 73, #893, *Du Bois Papers.*
38. Garfield Hinton to Roy Wilkins, August 10, 1959, Reel 73, #813, *Du Bois Papers;* Roy Wilkins to Du Bois, February 20, 1959, Reel 73, #823, *Du Bois Papers; National Guardian,* August 3, 1959.
39. Robert Hall to Du Bois, December 13, 1959, Reel 73, #721, *Du Bois Papers;* Du Bois to Robert Hall, December 5, 1959, Reel 73, #722, *Du Bois Papers;* Roy Wilkins to Du Bois, January 28, 1960, Reel 73, #611, *Du Bois Papers;* Arthur Spingarn to Du Bois, July 13, 1962, Reel 75, #48, *Du Bois Papers.*
40. Roger Keeran, *The Communist Party and Auto Workers Union* (Bloomington: Indiana University Press, 1981); Donald T. Chritchlow, "Communist Unions and Racism: A Comparative Study of the Responses of United Electrical Radio and Machine Workers and the National Maritime Union to the Black Question During World War II," *Labor History* 17 (Spring 1976), 230–44; H. L. Gage to Du Bois, August 4, 1944, Reel 56, #521, *Du Bois Papers;* John Miller to Du Bois, January 31, 1946, Reel 58, #1278, *Du Bois Papers;* Milton Walker to Du Bois, January 10, 1949, Reel 64, #320, *Du Bois Papers.*
41. Du Bois to M. E. Travis, September 20, 1950, Reel 65, #128, *Du Bois Papers; Crisis* 56 (August–September 1949), 250; Du Bois Transcript of Radio Broadcast, November 3, 1950, Reel 81, #37, *Du Bois Papers;* Du Bois Speech, "The American Negro 1901 to 1950,"

February 10, 1950, Reel 30, #1333, *Du Bois Papers;* Helen Mangold to Du Bois, November 10, 1950, Reel 65, #638, *Du Bois Papers;* Abraham Lederman to Du Bois, February 24, 1950, Reel 65, #697, *Du Bois Papers;* Edith Hurley to Du Bois, March 2, 1950, Reel 65, #699, *Du Bois Papers;* Belle Bailynson to Du Bois, May 16, 1950, Reel 65, #719, *Du Bois Papers;* James Durkin to Du Bois, March 30, 1950, Reel 65, #728, *Du Bois Papers.*

42. *The New York Times,* April 6, 1952; Abraham Lederman to Du Bois, January 28, 1952, Reel 68, #1025, *Du Bois Papers;* Mindy Thompson, *The National Negro Labor Council: A History* (New York: AIMS, 1978); *Crisis* 59 (August–September 1952), 451; R. L. Chambers, "The Negro in New Mexico," *Crisis* 59 (March 1952), 145–47.
43. Richard Stephenson, "Race in the Cactus State," *Crisis* 61 (April 1954), 197–204; Du Bois Speech, February 12, 1954, Reel 81, #792, *Du Bois Papers;* W.E.B. Du Bois "Trade Unions and Colored Workers," unpublished articles, January 1954, Reel 83, #596, *Du Bois Papers; Chicago Globe,* April 7, 1950, Reel 84, #7, *Du Bois Papers;* Lula Stone to Du Bois, February 8, 1954, Reel 70, #399, *Du Bois Papers;* Russel Lasley to Du Bois, April 19, 1953, Reel 70, #100, *Du Bois Papers;* Du Bois to Cedric Belfrage, April 22, 1955, Reel 71, #610, *Du Bois Papers;* The Emeriti Census, circular, May 22, 1957, Reel 72, #543, *Du Bois Papers; Crisis* 68 (October 1961), 507; James B. Carey, "Race-Hate Wins a First Round," *Crisis* 64 (November 1957), 589–94, 645.
44. Percival Roberts Bailey, "Progressive Lawyers: A History of the National Lawyers Guild" (Ph.D. diss., Rutgers University 1979), iii, 18, 107, 127, 280; Kluger, *Simple Justice,* p. 221.
45. Bailey, "Progressive Lawyers," 353, 354, 338, 339.
46. Ibid., 370, 396, 420, 428, 452; Robert Silberstein to Du Bois, January 29, 1949, Reel 64, #122, *Du Bois Papers;* Du Bois to Rachel Ellis, January 31, 1950, Reel 65, #357, *Du Bois Papers.*
47. Frank Adams, *Unearthing Seeds of Fire: The Idea of Highlander,* 169; Howard Zinn, *SNCC: The New Abolitionists,* 270–73; James Forman, *The Making of Black Revolutionaries;* August Meier and Elliot Rudwick, *CORE: A Study in the Civil Rights Movement, 1942–1968,* 270–71; Nathaniel Patrick Tillman, Jr., *Walter Francis White: Study in Interest Group Leadership* (Ph.D. diss., University of Wisconsin, 1961).
48. Charles G. Gomillion to E. Franklin Frazier, February 15, 1951, Reel 66, #698, *Du Bois Papers;* Du Bois to Charles Gomillion, June 23, 1944, July 12, 1944, Reel 55, #123, *Du Bois Papers;* Bernard Taper, *Gomillion Versus Lightfoot: The Tuskeegee Gerrymander Protest* (New York: McGraw-Hill, 1962); Woodrow H. Hall, *A Bibliography of the Tuskeegee Gerrymander Protest: Pamphlets, Magazines and Newspaper Articles Chronologically Arranged* (Tuskeegee, Alabama: Tuskeegee Institute, 1960).

49. Du Bois Speech, August 18, 1956, Reel 81, #1022, *Du Bois Papers;* Du Bois article, "Segregation in Higher Education," June 19, 1950, Reel 84, #39, *Du Bois Papers; National Guardian,* May 31, 1954; *National Guardian,* July 8, 1957; "Petition of Rights to the President, the Congress and the Supreme Court of the United States," circa 1957, Reel 86, #1556, *Du Bois Papers.*
50. Du Bois Speech, "The American Negro and the Darker World," May 1957, Reel 81, #1059, *Du Bois Papers; Afro-American,* April 12, 1958; S. J. Wright to Du Bois, May 26, 1958, Reel 79, #998, *Du Bois Papers;* S. J. Wright to Du Bois, November 10, 1959, Reel 79, #991, *Du Bois Papers.*
51. Sidney Poitier, et. al., to Du Bois, August 26, 1959, Reel 73, #535, *Du Bois Papers;* Du Bois to George Murphy, December 1, 1959, Reel 73, #816, *Du Bois Papers;* Martin D. Jenkins to Du Bois, March 25, 1960, Reel 74, #573, *Du Bois Papers.*
52. *National Guardian,* May 23, 1960; Du Bois to Ishmael Flory, April 6, 1960, Reel 74, #20, *Du Bois Papers;* W.E.B. Du Bois, "Whither Now and Why," *Quarterly Review of Higher Education Among Negroes* 28 (July 1960), 135–41.
53. Dr. C. O. Simpkins to Du Bois, March 9, 1960, Reel 74, #843, *Du Bois Papers;* Du Bois to Dr. C. O. Simpkins, February 3, 1960, Reel 74, #845, *Du Bois Papers;* Circular appeal, circa 1960, Reel 74, #413, *Du Bois Papers;* Invitation to Southern Conference Educational Fund Reception, March 22, 1960, Reel 74, #801, *Du Bois Papers;* Invitation to Reception for Reverend Fred Shuttlesworth, October 18, 1960, Reel 74, #801, *Du Bois Papers.*
54. L. R. Perkins to Du Bois, June 29, 1960, Reel 74, #846, *Du Bois Papers;* S. J. Wright to Du Bois, August 20, 1960, Reel 74, #227, *Du Bois Papers;* S. J. Wright to Du Bois, Novembeer 28, 1960, Reel 74, #228, *Du Bois Papers;* W. C. McCreary to Du Bois, August 10, 1961, Reel 75, #667, *Du Bois Papers;* Jerome McIver to Du Bois, March 1, 1960, Reel 74, #37, *Du Bois Papers;* Henry Yost to Du Bois, July 9, 1960, Reel 74, #53, *Du Bois Papers;* Dennis Phombeah to Du Bois, September 7, 1960, Reel 74, #36, *Du Bois Papers.*
55. John Procope to Du Bois, February 15, 1961, Reel 75, #801, *Du Bois Papers;* L. H. Stanton to Du Bois, September 25, 1961, Reel 74, #1017, *Du Bois Papers;* A. C. Gilbert Speech, November 9, 1961, Reel 74, #1019, *Du Bois Papers;* Clarence B. Jones and Arthur Kinoy to Du Bois, November 30, 1961, Reel 75, #340, *Du Bois Papers.*
56. Du Bois to Barbara Lindsay, April 27, 1961, Reel 73, #392, *Du Bois Papers;* Janet Stevenson to Du Bois, August 2, 1960, Reel 74, #813, *Du Bois Papers; Crisis* 66 (June–July 1959), 325–29; Graham, *His Day is Marching On,* 327.

57. "A Petition to the President of the United States, the Honorable John F. Kennedy," February 1961, Reel 86, #1562, *Du Bois Papers.*
58. Jake C. Miller, *The Black Presence in American Foreign Affairs* (Washington, D.C.: University Press, 1978), 182.
59. Anne Braden. "The Civil Rights Movement and McCarthyism," *Guild Practitioner* 37 (Fall 1980), 109–116; Numan V. Bartley, *The Rise of Massive Resistance: Race and Politics in the South During the 1950's* (Baton Rouge: Louisiana State University Press, 1969); Chandler Davidson, "Negro Politics and the Rise of the Civil Rights Movement in Houston, Texas" (Ph.D. diss., Princeton University, 1968); Delany Sanford, "Congressional Investigation of Black Communists, 1919–1967" (Ph.D. diss., State University of New York at Stony Brook, 1973).
60. *The New York Times Magazine,* April 29, 1962; Theodore White, "Texas: Land of Wealth and Fear, Part I," *The Reporter* 9 (March 25, 1954), 10–15; Charles J. V. Murphey, "Texas Businessmen and McCarthy," *Fortune* (May 1954), 100–101, 208–16; Charles Alexander, *Holding the Line: The Eisenhower Era* (Bloomington; Indiana University Press, 1975), 115, 200; Allan Wolk, *The Presidency and Black Civil Rights: Eisenhower to Nixon* (Rutherford, N.J.: Fairleigh Dickinson University Press, 1971), 17, 54, 62; Poppy Cannon, *A Gentle Knight: My Husband, Walter White* (New York: Rinehart, 1956).

CHAPTER 18. DU BOIS AS AN INTELLECTUAL FORCE

1. Elitot Rudwick, *W.E.B. Du Bois: Propagandist of the Negro Protest* (New York: Atheneum, 1968); *The Progressive,* February 1958, p. 20; Harold Isaacs, "Pan-Africanism as Romantic Racism," in Rayford Logan, p. 245; *Du Bois: A Profile.*
2. *National Guardian,* July 27, 1959; *National Guardian,* July 3, 1961.
3. Du Bois to Francis Broderick, May 3, 1951, Reel 66, #257, *Du Bois Papers,* Du Bois to W. M. Brewer, August 6, 1959, Reel 73, #761, *Du Bois Papers; Crisis* 69 (February 1962), 125–27.
4. Lenneal Henderson, Jr., "W.E.B. Du Bois," *Black Scholar* 1 (January–February 1970)), 48–57; *Journal of Black Studies* 5 (June 1975), 436–43.
5. Daniel W. Wynn, *The NAACP Versus the Negro Revolutionary Protest: A Comparative Study of the Effectiveness of Each Movement* (New York: Exposition Press, 1955); George Murphy to Du Bois, August 31, 1956, Reel 72, #92, *Du Bois Papers.*
6. Paul Robeson to Du Bois, January 1953, Reel 79, #1123, *Du Bois Papers;* Philip Foner (ed.), *Paul Robeson Speaks: Writings, Speeches,*

Interviews, 1918–1974, 4, 474–78; *Crisis* 65 (March 1958), 187; *Freedom,* June 1952.

7. Lorraine Hansberry to Du Bois, June 15, 1954, Reel 70, #494, *Du Bois Papers;* Muriel Symington to Du Bois, June 2, 1958, Reel 73, #418, *Du Bois Papers;* Du Bois to Alice Childress, November 19, 1954, Reel 70, #505, *Du Bois Papers;* Alice Childress to Du Bois, April 16, 1953, Reel 69, #1149, *Du Bois Papers.*
8. Dorothy Parker to Du Bois, October 10, 1949, in *Du Bois III,* 269; Sylvia Golden to Du Bois, May 12, 1949, Reel 64, #1107, *Du Bois Papers;* Harold Cruse, *The Crisis of the Negro Intellectual* (New York: Morrow, 1967).
9. J. Fred MacDonald, "Radio's Black Heritage: Destination Freedom, 1948–1950," *Phylon* 39 (First Quarter 1978), 66–72; Langston Hughes, *Fight for Freedom: The Story of the NAACP* (New York: Norton, 1952); Du Bois to Lorenzo Greene, February 5, 1954, Reel 70, #828, *Du Bois Papers;* Du Bois to First International Congress of Colored Writers and Artists, October 6, 1956, Reel 72, #318, *Du Bois Papers;* Richard Wright, *White Man, Listen* (Garden City, N.Y.: Doubleday, 1957); *New York Herald Tribune,* March 4, 1945; *Crisis* 60 (June–July 1953), 38; Du Bois to George Padmore, December 10, 1954, in *Du Bois III,* 375.
10. *Crisis* 60 (October 1952), 504; Paul Murray to Du Bois, May 2, 1952, Reel 68, #585, *Du Bois Papers;* Du Bois to Albert Kahn, June 17, 1954, Reel 70, #493, *Du Bois Papers.*
11. Horace Mann Bond to Ernest Alexander, February 12, 1948, Reel 60, #467, *Du Bois Papers;* Arthur Huff Fauset to Du Bois, July 7, 1954, in *Du Bois III,* 363.
12. John Hope Franklin to Du Bois, February 13, 1956, Reel 71, #1148, *Du Bois Papers;* John Hope Franklin, "The New Negro History," *Crisis* 64 (February 1957), 69–75; Elliott Skinner to Du Bois, May 1, 1957, in *Du Bois III,* 407; Hollis Lynch to Du Bois, July 15, 1959, Reel 73, #796, *Du Bois Papers;* Hollis Lynch to Du Bois, August 25, 1960, Reel 74, #503, *Du Bois Papers;* Gwendolen Carter to Du Bois, February 3, 1961, Reel 75, #62, *Du Bois Papers.*
13. Mervyn Dymally to Du Bois, January 14, 1947, Reel 59, #1369, *Du Bois Papers;* Kenneth Kennedy and George Murphy to Du Bois, February 21, 1947, Reel 60, #987, *Du Bois Papers.*
14. Roland Wolseley, *The Black Press, USA* (Ames, Ia: Iowa State University Press, 1971), 40–44; Mel Tapley to Du Bois, August 121, 1954, Reel 70, #668, *Du Bois Papers;* John Davis to Du Bois, February 11, 1954, Reel 70, #568, *Du Bois Papers;* Graham, *His Day is Marching On,* 210–11.

15. Martin Luther King, Jr., to Du Bois, March 19, 1956, in *Du Bois III,* 399; George Edmund Haynes to Du Bois, March 14, 1957, Reel 79, #1023, *Du Bois Papers.*
16. *National Guardian,* May 20, 1957; W. Alphaeus Hunton, *Decision in Africa: Sources of Current Conflict* (New York: International Publishers, 1957).
17. Du Bois Circle circular, circa 1957, Reel 72, #530, *Du Bois Papers; Crisis* 64 (June 1957), 371; Howard Zinn to Du Bois, April 5, 1960, Reel 74, #805, *Du Bois Papers;* Du Bois to Howard Zinn, April 13, 1960, Reel 74, #805, *Du Bois Papers;* L. D. Reddick to Du Bois, August 6, 1969, Reel 73, #871, *Du Bois Papers.*
18. Marshall Field to Du Bois, March 25, 1947, Reel 60, #6, *Du Bois Papers;* Carl Gebuhr to Du Bois, February 9, 1948, Reel 60, #380, *Du Bois Papers;* Senator Arthur Capper to Ernest Alexander, February 5, 1948, Reel 61, #547, *Du Bois Papers;* Van Wyck Brooks to Du Bois, February 18, 1948, Reel 61, #496, *Du Bois Papers.*
19. Eric Goldman to Du Bois, December 11, 1948, Reel 60, #767, *Du Bois Papers;* Du Bois to E. A. Ross, April 30, 1952, Reel 68, #692, *Du Bois Papers;* Sandra Parrini to Du Bois, July 18, 1960, Reel 74, #819, *Du Bois Papers;* Richard Evans, "In Quest of a Useable Past: Young Leftist Historians in the 1960's" (Ph.D. diss., Case Western Reserve University, 1979); Bettina Aptheker to Du Bois, September 15, 1962, in *Du Bois III,* 436.
20. Orlando Ward to Du Bois, August 15, 1950, Reel 65, #756, *Du Bois Papers;* John Russell to Du Bois, August 25, 1950, Reel 65, #770, *Du Bois Papers;* Du Bois to August Meier, April 21, 1953, Reel 69, #1007, *Du Bois Papers;* Eleanor Flexner to Du Bois, September 20, 1954, Reel 70, #622, *Du Bois Papers.*
21. Lawrence Howard to Du Bois, June 17, 1955, Reel 71, #441, *Du Bois Papers;* Kathleen Long to Du Bois, October 28, 1955, Reel 71, #525, *Du Bois Papers;* Du Bois to Harvey Wachtel, December 4, 1956, Reel 72, #255, *Du Bois Papers;* Nathanial Tillman, Jr., to Du Bois, January 27, 1956, Reel 72, #237, *Du Bois Papers;* W. Brem Mayer to Du Bois, January 23, 1956, Reel 72, #77, *Du Bois Papers;* Eugene Genovese to Du Bois, April 11, 1955, #71, #389, *Du Bois Papers;* Du Bois to Eugene Genovese, April 21, 1955, Reel 71, #390, *Du Bois Papers;* Eugene Genovese to Du Bois, March 30, 1956, Reel 72, #224, *Du Bois Papers;* Harvey O'Connor to Du Bois, march 30, 1956, Reel 72, #170, *Du Bois Papers.*
22. Henry Miller to Carey McWilliams, October 20, 1956, in *Du Bois III,* 401, n.1.; Milton Gould to Du Bois, March 9, 1950, Reel 65, #640, *Du Bois Papers;* Du Bois to James Proctor, November 23, 1949, Reel 64, #248, *Du Bois Papers;* Du Bois to Howard Fast, March 10, 1952, Reel 68, #255, *Du Bois Papers;* Beverly Daniels to Du Bois, April 21,

1951, Reel 67, #236, *Du Bois Papers;* Truman Capote to Du Bois, October 20, 1959, Reel 73, #604, *Du Bois Papers.*

23. Robert Giroux to Du Bois, July 13, 1950, Reel 65, #79, *Du Bois Papers;* Du Bois to Jessica Smith, July 21, 1950, Reel 65, #659, *Du Bois Papers.*
24. Herbert Aptheker to Du Bois, September 26, 1950, Reel 65, #247, *Du Bois Papers.*
25. P. S. Joshi to Du Bois, December 22, 1956, Reel 72, #30, *Du Bois Papers;* Stephen Frichtman to Du Bois, February 10, 1955, Reel 71, #356, *Du Bois Papers;* Du Bois to Stephen Frichtman, February 14, 1955, Reel 71, #367, *Du Bois Papers.*
26. Du Bois to T. C. Johnson, May 19, 1953, Reel 69, #928, *Du Bois Papers;* Du Bois to A. M. Townsend, April 8, 1953, Reel 69, #1039, *Du Bois Papers;* Jean-Jacques Fol to Du Bois, April 16, 1957, Reel 72, #552, *Du Bois Papers;* Giangiacomo Feltrinelli to Du Bois, April 26, 1955, Reel 71, #350, *Du Bois Papers;* Du Bois to S. K. Narayanan, November 24, 1953, Reel 69, #1026, *Du Bois Papers;* Jessica Smith to Du Bois, July 9, 1958, Reel 73, #327, *Du Bois Papers.*
27. Lawrence Lader, *Power on the Left: American Radical Movements Since 1946* (New York: Norton, 1979), 111; Roy Wilkins, "Editing the *Crisis,*" *Crisis* 58 (March 1951), 147–51, 213; *Crisis* 58 (June–July 1951), 364; Wilson Record, "Role of the Negro Intellectual," *Crisis* 60 (June–July 1953), 329–332; *Crisis* 62 (February 1954), 84.
28. *Crisis 64 (December 1957), 641; Crisis* 65 (May 1958) 314; *Crisis* 65 (April 1958), 220–21; *Crisis* 66 (February 1959), 75; August Meier, "From Conservative to Radical: the Ideological Development of W. E. B. Du Bois, 1885–1905," *Crisis* 66 (November 1959), 527–36.
29. *Crisis* 66 (November 1959) 578–79; *Crisis* 67 (January 1960), 34; *Crisis* 68 (December 1961), 643; G. W. Sherman, "John Brown—He Gave His Life for Black Folk," *Crisis* 66 (May 1959), 273–79, 314; *Crisis* 69 (May 1962), 281; Du Bois to NAACP Board, November 11, 1956, in *Du Bois III,* 405.
30. Du Bois to Leslie Hill, December 6, 1954, Reel 70, #676, *Du Bois Papers;* Shirley Graham to Carl Murphy, February 8, 1957, Reel 72, #344, *Du Bois Papers;* Du Bois to Prof. R. B. Garrett, July 20,1954, Reel 70, #636, *Du Bois Papers;* W.E.B. Du Bois, *Mansart Builds a School* (New York: Mainstream, 1959), 43.
31. Du Bois to Samuel Sillen, January 5, 1953, Reel 69, #988, *Du Bois Papers;* "List of Organizations," undated, Reel 70, #308, *Du Bois Papers;* George Murphy to Du Bois, October 11, 1955, Reel 71, #577, *Du Bois Papers;* George Murphy to Charles Wesley, December 14, 1955, Reel 71, #583, *Du Bois Papers;* Du Bois to Joseph Felshin, March 1, 1956, Reel 72, #75, *Du Bois Papers;* George Murphy to Du Bois, March 1, 1956, Reel 71, #90, *Du Bois Papers.*

32. W. E. Heuston to Du Bois, March 4, 1957, Reel 72, #758, *Du Bois Papers;* Herbert Aptheker to Du Bois, April 17, 1957, Reel 72, #759, *Du Bois Papers;* Joseph Felshin to Du Bois, July 23, 1957, Reel 72, #762, *Du Bois Papers; Pittsburgh Courier,* May 25, 1957; *Afro-American,* May 18, 1957; Du Bois to Leo Huberman, July 14, 1958, Reel 73, #270, *Du Bois Papers;* Joseph Felshin to Du Bois, January 13, 1960, Reel 74, #536, *Du Bois Papers;* Herbert Aptheker to Du Bois, August 5, 1958, Reel 73, #481, *Du Bois Papers;* Du Bois to Herbert Aptheker, February 8, 1960, Reel 74, *Du Bois Papers.*
33. *National Guardian,* July 17, 1961; *Crisis* 68(June–July 1961), 378; Alice Childress to Du Bois, March 21, 1955, Reel 71, #279, *Du Bois Papers;* Van Wyck Brooks to Du Bois, April 24, 1957, Reel 72, #449, *Du Bois Papers; National Guardian,* July 22, 1957; *Afro-American,* June 1, 1957; *Crisis* 64 (August–September 1957), 454.
34. Keith Eldon Byerman, "Two Warring Ideals: The Dialectical Thought of W.E.B. Du Bois" (Ph.D. diss., Purdue University, 1978), 20, 279–98, 304, 309, 331; Arnold Rampersad, *The Art and Imagination of W. E. B. Du Bois* (Cambridge, Ma.: Harvard University Press, 1976).
35. Arnold Perl to Du Bois, July 8, 1957, Reel 79, #49, *Du Bois Papers;* V. S. Bogatyrev to Du Bois, December 27, 1949, Reel 64, #377, *Du Bois Papers.*
36. *People's Voice,* September 6, 1947; *People's Voice,* June 14, 1947; *People's Voice,* December 27, 1947.
37. *Freedom,* February 1951; *Freedom,* October 1952; *Freedom,* April 1954; *Freedom,* April 1953; *Freedom,* May 1952; *Freedom,* September 1951.
38. Shirley Graham, "Return After Ten Years," *Freedomways* 11 (Second Quarter 1971), 158–69; Du Bois Speech, circa 1961, Reel 81, #1419, *Du Bois Papers.*
39. Cedric Belfrage and James Aronson, *Something to Guard: The Stormy Life of the National Guardian, 1948–1967* (New York: Columbia University Press, 1978), 137–40, 145, 250; Elmer Benson to Du Bois, May 29, 1950, Reel 64, #984, *Du Bois Papers;* Du Bois to Cedric Belfrage, April 24, 1950, Reel 65, #339, *Du Bois Papers; National Guardian,* October 12, 1959.
40. Richard Moore to Du Bois, May 19, 1958, Reel 73, #65, *Du Bois Papers;* James A. Boyer to Du Bois, June 10, 1958,m Reel 73, #66, *Du Bois Papers;* Richard Daley to Du Bois, May 5, 1958, Reel 73, #80, *Du Bois Papers;* M. Lafayette Smith to Du Bois, May 20, 1958, Reel 73, #168, *Du Bois Papers;* J. H. Brockett to Du Bois, May 20, 1958, Reel 73, #247, *Du Bois Papers;* Hollis F. Price to Du Bois, May 19, 1958, Reel 73, #347, *Du Bois Papers;* William R. Strassner to Du Bois, May 20, 1958, Reel 73, #379, *Du Bois Papers;* Albert Manley to Du Bois, May 16, 1958, Reel 73, #415, *Du Bois Papers;* W. J. Davis to Du Bois, May 16, 1958, Reel 73, #422, *Du Bois Papers;* L. H.

Foster to Du Bois, May 15, 1958, Reel 73, #464, *Du Bois Papers;* George Murphy to Du Bois, June 3, 1958, Reel 73, #283, *Du Bois Papers; National Guardian,* March 10, 1958.

41. *Afro-American,* March 16, 1958; *The New York Times,* March 3, 1958; *Pittsburgh Courier,* April 12, 1958; *Pittsburgh Courier,* August 8, 1959; *Afro-American,* September 29, 1959, Du Bois to Virginia Perry Banks, June 4, 1958, Reel 73, #58, *Du Bois Papers.*

CHAPTER 19. DU BOIS AND FOREIGN AFFAIRS

1. Willard B. Gatewood, "A Black Editor on American Imperialism: Edward E. Cooper and the Colored American, 1898–1901, "*Mid-America* 57 (January 1975), 3–19; Arnold Shankman, "Brothers Across the Sea: Afro-Americans on the Persecution of Russian Jews, 1881–1917," *Jewish Social Studies* 37 (Spring 1975), 14–21; William A. Scott, "A Study of Afro-American and Ethiopian Relations, 1896–1941" (Ph.D. diss., Princeton University, 1971).
2. Du Bois, *The Autobiography of W. E. B. Du Bois,* 333; *Crisis* 62 (May 1955), 262; *Crisis* 58 (April 1951), 269; *Crisis* 60 (December 1953), 615–16; Gloster Current, "Fiftieth Annual Convention—A Jubilee for Civil Rights," *Crisis* 66 (August–September 1959), 400–410.
3. Mary Frances Berry, *Black Resistance/White Law: A History of Constitutional Racism in America* (New York: Appleton Century Crofts, 1971), 175–76; Carl Solberg, *Riding High: America in the Cold War* (New York: Mason & Lipscomb, 1973); William E. Leuchtenberg, "The White House and Black America: From Eisenhower to Carter," edited by M. V. Namorato in *Have We Overcome? Race Relations Since Brown,* (Jackson: University Press of Mississippi, 1979), 121–46; Carl M. Brauer, *John F. Kennedy and the Second Reconstruction* (New York: Columbia University Press, 1977), 240; *Crisis* 54 (May 1947), 137; *Crisis* 60 (January 1953), 39.
4. *Crisis* 60 (November 1953), 548–49; *Crisis* 64 (February 1957), 89–90; *Crisis* 59 (May 1952), 311–12; Walter White to Herbert Lehman, February 5, 1951, Special File, #931a, *Lehman Papers.*
5. Alan Harper, *The Politics of Loyalty: The White House and the Communist Issue, 1946–1952* (Westport, Ct.: Greenwood Press, 1969), 49; David Caute, *The Great Fear: The Anti-Communist Purge Under Truman and Eisenhower* (New York: Simon and Schuster, 1978), 276; Richard M. Freeland, *The Truman Doctrine and the Origins of McCarthyism: Foreign Policy, Domestic Policies and Internal Security, 1946–1948* (New York: Schocken Press, 1974), 218; Alfred Baker Lewis, "Step Up NAACP Propaganda Work," *Crisis* 67 (November 1951).

6. W.E.B. Du Bois, "Africa and the American Negro Intelligentsia," *Presence Africaine* 4 (November 1955–January 1956), 34–51.
7. J. Saunders Redding, *An American in India: A Personal Report of the India Dilemma and the Nature of Her Conflicts* (Indianapolis: Bobbs Merrill, 1954); Carl T. Rowan, *The Pitiful and the Proud* (New York: Random House, 1956); *Freedom,* July 1951; *Pittsburgh Courier,* September 2, 1950; *New York Herald Tribune,* September 3, 1950; *The New York Times,* October 16, 1950; *The New York Times,* May 12, 1951.
8. M. Mandelenakis to Du Bois, April 5, 1948, Reel 60, #346, *Du Bois Papers;* Senator Claude Pepper to Du Bois, April 7, 1947, Reel 60, #1071, *Du Bois Papers; People's Voice,* April 12, 1947; *Los Angeles Sentinel,* March 20, 1947; *California Eagle,* March 20, 1947; *St. Louis American,* March 22, 1947; *Afro-American,* April 5, 1947; *Philadelphia Independent,* April 5, 1947; *Pittsburgh Courier,* April 5, 1947.
9. Du Bois Testimony, August 8, 1949, Reel 63, #916, *Du Bois Papers; New York Compass,* August 11–12, 1949; Alfred Werner, "Germany's New Pariahs," *Crisis* 59 (May 1952), 291–96; *Crisis* 65 (May 1958), 378; Gabriel Gersh, "Color Bar in Liverpool," *Crisis* 65 (November 1958), 547–49; L. W. Malone, "A Negro Reports From Denmark," *Crisis* 68 (August–September 1961), 541; *Crisis* 62 (February 1954), 92; Otto Leichter, "The Negro Probelem—Interpreted for Europeans," *Crisis* 62 (April 1955), 215–20; James Ivy, "American Negro Problem in the European Press," *Crisis* 57 (July 1950), 413–18, 472.
10. J. A. Kingsbury to Du Bois, March 11, 1949, Reel 64, #470, *Du Bois Papers;* Du Bois to M. A. Chamberlain, April 24, 1953, Reel 69, #1177, *Du Bois Papers; Crisis* 60 (April 1953), 228–29.
11. Du Bois to Morris Fine, March 1, 1948, Reel 60, #366, *Du Bois Papers;* Du Bois to Joseph M. Proskauer, November 14, 1944, Reel 55, #877, *Du Bois Papers;* Du Bois to Edith of PM, July 8, 1947, Reel 60, #751, *Du Bois Papers.*
12. *Chicago Star,* Mary 8, 1948; *Chicago Defender,* May 15, 1948; Julius Schatz to Du Bois, May 5, 1948, Reel 60, #347, *Du Bois Papers;* Du Bois Speech, "Civil Rights and Democracy," Reel 80, #1068, *Du Bois Papers;* Joseph Keller to Du Bois, March 26, 1948, Reel 62, #225, *Du Bois Papers;* Du Bois Speech, November 30, 1948, Reel 80 #1159, *Du Bois Papers;* Du Bois Speech, "Ralph Bunche," March 2, 1949, Reel 80, #1196, *Du Bois Papers..*
13. William Leuner to Du Bois, February 15, 1951, Reel 66, #52, *Du Bois Papers;* Du Bois Speech, circa 1950, Reel 81, #61, *Du Bois Papers;* Herbert Aptheker, "The Souls of Black Folk: A Comparison of the 1903 and 1952 editions," *Negro History Bulletin* 34 (January1971), 15–17; Simon Federman to Du Bois, Mach 16, 1953, Reel 70, #88 *Du Bois Papers.*

14. Hubert Delany, "Hubert Delany Reports on Israel," *Crisis* 63 (November 1956), 517–26, 574; *Crisis* 69 (January 1962), 23; W.E.B. Du Bois, "Suez," *Mainstream* (February 1956); *National Guardian,* August 4, 1958; Du Bois Speech, July 19, 1958, Reel 73, #479 *Du Bois Papers.*
15. C. E. Edwards to Du Bois, October 26, 1947, Reel 59, #1338, *Du Bois Papers;* Norman Manley to Cedric Dover, February 19, 1948, Reel 62, #339, *Du Bois Papers.*
16. Du Bois to Ben Davis, April 18, 1955, *in Du Bois III,* 381–82; Graham, *His Day is Marching on,* 216–17; T. A. Marryshow to Du Bois, May 4, 1955, #71 #553, *Du Bois Papers;* Gordon Mancici to Du Bois, June 6, 1958, Reel 73, #438, *Du Bois Papers.*
17. Janet Jagan to Du Bois, February 13, 1956, Reel 72, #178, *Du Bois Papers;* Cheddi Jagan to Du Bois, June 7, 1961, Reel 75, #324, *Du Bois Papers;* Cheddi Jagan to Du Bois, November 11, 1961, Reel 75, #327, *Du Bois Papers;* Leon Ouat to Du Bois, August 10, 1961, Reel 75, #253, *Du Bois Papers.*
18. *Crisis* 63 (November 1955), 571; *Crisis* 69 (October 1962), 472; *Crisis* 69 (January 1962), 53, 55; Petition, April 11, 1950, Reel 64, #1112, *Du Bois Papers;* Von Leers to Du Bois, May 31, 1955, Reel 71, #755, *Du Bois Papers;* Barbara Lindsay to Du Bois, May 16, 1961, Reel 75, #392, *Du Bois Papers.*
19. *Crisis* 68 (January 1961), 29; Thomas Richardson to Du Bois, August 31, 1948, Reel 63, #320, *Du Bois Papers;* "Committee to End the Jim Crow 'Silver-Gold' System in the Panama Canal Zone," August 31, 1948, Reel 61, #674, *Du Bois Papers;* Paul Robeson to Du Bois, September 15, 1948, in *Du Bois III,* 212; *New York Star,* October 21, 1948.
20. Eleanor Lebsky to Du Bois, November 17, 1947, Reel 59, #959, *Du Bois Papers;* Du Bois to J. B. Siauw Hian Bio, February 20, 1961, Reel 75, #630, *Du Bois Papers; Chicago Globe,* August 4, 1950; *Chicago Globe,* August 9, 1950; *Chicago Globe,* August 23, 1950.
21. Circular on "National Conference on American Policy in China and the Far East," January 23, 1948, Reel 62, #433, *Du Bois Papers;* Du Bois to Talitha Gerlach, January 14, 1949, Reel 63, #789, *Du Bois Papers;* Agenda of China Welfare Fund Board Meeting, November 29, 1949, Reel 63, #809, *Du Bois Papers.*
22. William Worthy, "Our Disgrace in Indo-China," *Crisis* 61 (February 1954), 77–83; William Worthy, "Of Global Bondage," *Crisis* 61 (October 1954), 467–472, 512; *Crisis* 62 (January 1955), 23–26; Jake Miller, *The Black Presence in American Foreign Affairs* (Washington, D.C.: University Press of America, 1978), 174–76.
23. Du Bois Message to the Bandung Conference, April 6, 1955, Reel 71, #936, *Du Bois Papers;* "Memorandum on the Bandung Confer-

ence," April 1955, Reel 71, #935, *Du Bois Papers; Crisis* 62 (May 1955), 291; George Padmore to Du Bois, June 21, 1955, Reel 79, #1079, *Du Bois Papers;* Ajoy Ghosh , "The Bandung Conference," *Political Affairs* 34 (June 1955), 13–19; *National Guardian,* May 9, 1955.

24. "Manifesto of the Afro-Asian Students' Conference of the UK," May 15, 1955, Reel 71, #171, *Du Bois Papers;* W.E.B. Du Bois, "The Freeing of India," *Crisis* 54 (October 1947), 301–302; Jawaharlal Nehru to Du Bois, February 21, 1948, Reel 62, #574, *Du Bois Papers;* Du Bois article, "Gandhi and the American Negroes," July 1957, Reel 82, #653, *Du Bois Papers;* Du Bois to Marie Nosek, undated, Reel 74, #689, *Du Bois Papers;* "An Open Letter to Pandit Jawaharlal Nehru," October 10, 1949, Reel 63, #1152, *Du Bois Papers.*
25. Du Bois to Jawaharlal Nehru, December 26, 1956, Reel 72, #1, *Du Bois Papers.*

Chapter 20. Du Bois and the Communists

1. Du Bois to Herbert Aptheker, December 21, 1954, in *Du Bois III,* 378; Herbert Aptheker to Du Bois, December 24, 1954, in *Du Bois III,* 378.
2. Loren Baritz (ed.), *The American Left: Radical Political Thought in the Twentieth Century* (New York: Basic Books, 1971), 336; Nathan Glazer, *The Social Basis of American Communism* (New York: Harcourt Brace, 1961), 180.
3. *Amsterdam News,* September 28, 1935; Jabari Onaje Simama, "Black Writers Experience Communism: An Interdisciplinary Study of Imaginative Writers, Their Critics and the C.P.U.S.A." (Ph.D. diss., Emory University, 1978), 270; Phillip Abbot Luce, *Road to Revolution: Communist Guerilla Warfare in the U.S.A.* (San Diego: Viewpoint Books, 1967), 45; Ibid., *The Social Basis of American Communism,* 169; William D. Andrew, "Factional (Spring 1979), 227–55; Roger Keeran, *The Communist Party and the Auto Workers Unions* (Bloomington: Indian University Press, 1980), 235; Mark D. Naison, "The Communist Party in Harlem: 1928–1936," (Ph.D. diss., Columbia University, 1975), 269; Harvard Sitkoff, "The Emergence of Civil Rights as a National Issue: The New Deal Era" (Ph.D. diss., Columbia University, 1975), 164, 184.
4. Joseph Rockman, "Tasks in Broadening the Fight for Peace," *Political Affairs* 31 (June 1952), 15–29; John Graves, "Reaction of Some Negroes to Communism" (Ph.D. diss., Columbia University Teachers College, 1955), 96; Harvey Klehr, *Communist Cadre: The Social Back-*

ground of the American Communist Party Elite (Stanford: Stanford University Press, 1978), 60, 62, 67; John B. Kirby, "Ralph J. Bunche and Black Radical Thought in the 1930's," *Phylon* 35 (Summer 1974), 129–41; Pat Lee Greech Schotten, 'Militant Women for Economic Justice: The Persuasion of Mary Harris Jones, Ella Reeve Bloor, Rose Pastor Stokes, Rose Schneiderman and Elizabeth Gurley Flynn" (Ph.D. diss., University of Indiana, 1979), 57.

5. Bernard Sternsher, *Consensus, Conflict and American Historians* (Bloomington: Indiana University Press, 1975); William D. Andrew, "Factionalism," 236; Roger Keeran, *The Communist Party,* 11; David Oshinsky, *Senator Joseph McCarthy and the American Labor Movement* (Columbia: University of Missouri Press, 1976); Robert Griffin and Athan Theoharis (eds.), *The Specter: Original Essays on the Cold War and the Origins of McCarthyism* (New York): New Viewpoints, 1974); James Prickett, "Communism and Factionalism in the UAW, 1939–1947," *Science and Society* 32 (Summer–Fall 1968), 257–77; James Prickett, "Some Aspects of the Communist Controversy in the CIO," *Science and Society* 33 (Summer–Fall 1969), 299, 332.
6. David Jacob Group, "The Legal Repression of the American Communist Party, 1946–1961: A Study in the Legitimation of Coercion" (Ph.D. diss., University of Massachusetts, Amherst, 1979), 97, 105, 107, 109, 112–20, 152, 162; Eleanor Bontecou, *The Federal Loyalty-Security Program* (Ithaca: Cornell University Press, 1952); Marie Jahoda and Stuart Cook, "Security Measures and Freedom of Thought: An Exploratory Study of the Impact of the Loyalty and Security Program," *Yale Law Journal* 61 (March 1952), 296–333; Walter Gellhorn, *The States and Subversion* (Ithaca, N.Y.: Cornell University Press, 1952); Thomas J. Emerson, David Haber, and Norman Dorsen, *Political and Civil Rights in the United States,* vol. 1 (Boston; Little, Brown, 1967); Leo K. Adler and Thomas G. Paterson, "Red Fascism: The Merger of Nazi Germany and Soviet Russia in the American Image of Totalitarianism," *American Historical Review* 75 (April 1970), 1046–4; *National Guardian,* April 15, 1957; *National Guardian,* January 13, 1958; Robert K. McKay, "The Repression of Civil Rights As An Aftermath of School Desegregation Cases," *Harvard Law Journal* 4 (January 1958), 9–34.
7. Peter Lincoln Steinberg, "The Great Red Menace: U.S. Prosecution of American Communist," (Ph.D. diss., New York University, 1979); *We Speak for Freedom: Conference of the Communist Parties of the British Empire,* London, 1947; *Crisis* 57 (May 1950), 297; G. W. Westerman, "Canal Zone Discrimination," *Crisis* 58 (April 1951), 235–37.
8. I. F. Stone, *The Truman Era* (New York: Monthly Review Press, 1953), 160; Henry Winston, "The Meaning of Industrial Concentration," *Political Affairs,* 31 (July 1952): 27–36.

9. Thomas R. Brooks, *Walls Come Tumbling Down: A History of the Civil Rights Movement, 1940–1970* (Englewood Cliffs, N.J.: Prentice Hall, 1974), 67; *Phylon* 35 (Third Quarter 19640, 307–8; *Crisis* 58 (November 1951), 623–24; Wilson Record, "American Racial Ideologies and Organizations in Transition," *Phylon* 26 (Fourth Quarter 1965), 315–29.
10. "1948 Election Platform of the Communist Party," *Political Affairs* 27 (September 1948), 937–944; "Resolution on the Question of Negro Rights and Self-Determination," *Political Affairs* 26 (February 1947), 155–58; George Phillips, "American Imperialism and the Colored World," *Political Affairs* 26 (July 1947), 596–611.
11. Frederick Hastings and Charles P. Mann, "For A Mass Policy in Negro Freedom's Cause," *Political Affairs* 34 (March 1955), 7–29; James Jackson, "The South's New Challenge," *Political Affairs* 36 (December 1957), 1–18; Walter White, "The Negro and the Communists," *Political Affairs* 57 (August–September 1950), 502–6, 537–38; *Crisis* 55 (November 1948), 346.
12. Elizabeth Healy to Du Bois, January 2, 1947, Reel 60, #214, *Du Bois Papers;* W.E.B. Du Bois, "Negro Voters Face 1956," *American Socialist* 3 (February 1956), 10–11; *National Guardian,* March 26, 1956; *National Guardian,* April 16, 1956. *National Guardian,* June 25, 1956; Conference for Legislation in the National Interest, April 17, 1956, Reel 71, #1101, *Du Bois Papers.*
13. Carnegie Hall Debate, May 27, 1956, Reel 71, #1140, *Du Bois Papers; National Guardian,* June 4, 1956; *Daily Worker,* May 13, 1957; Senator James Eastland to A. J. Muste, May 17, 1957, Reel 72, #378, *Du Bois Papers.*
14. Harry Braverman to Du Bois, October 11, 1955, Reel 71, #311, *Du Bois Papers;* W.E.B. Du Bois, "I Won't Vote," *Nation* 183 (October 20, 1956), 324–25; *Crisis* 63 (August–September 1956), 419.
15. Circular, February 4, 1958, Reel 73, #443, *Du Bois Papers; National Guardian,* June 21, 1958; *Daily Worker,* June 1, 1958; *National Guardian,* July 6, 1958; Circular, October 15, 1958, Reel 73, #193, *Du Bois Papers.*
16. Du Bois to Editor of *National Guardian,* September 23, 1960, Reel 74, #626, *Du Bois Papers; Worker,* March 16, 1960; *Crisis* 67 (June–July 1960), 372; Gloster Current, "Why Nixon Lost the Negro Vote," *Crisis* 68 (January 1961), 5–14; Jim Peck, "Not So Deep Are the Roots—14 Years Later," *Crisis* 68 (June–July 1961), 325–31; Gloster Current, "The 53rd—A Hard Working Convention," *Crisis* 69 (August–September 1962), 377–92.
17. *Chicago Defender,* February 8, 1947; Du Bois to Charles Dixon, June 21, 1945, Reel 57, #48, *Du Bois Papers;* W.E.B. Du Bois, "The San Liberal," *Soviet Russia Today* 17 (September 1949), 7–26; Du Bois to

Dr. Vada Sommerville, February 17, 1950, Reel 65, #648, *Du Bois Papers.*

18. W.E.B. Du Bois, "Abolitionism and Communism," unpublished article, circa 1952, Reel 83, #533, *Du Bois Papers;* Du Bois to Douglas Stuart Moore, June 23, 1952, in *Du Bois III,* 335; *Crisis* 60 (April 1953), 279; *National Guardian,* May 4, 1953; Du Bois to Hershel Meyer, June 4, 1958, Reel 73, #266, *Du Bois Papers;* Manning Johnson, *Color, Communism and Color Sense* (New York: Stuyvesant Press, 1958), 63.
19. Leonard Bernstein to Du Bois, November 13, 1946, Reel 58, #507, *Du Bois Papers;* Harry Haywood to Du Bois, March 31, 1947, Reel 60, #102, *Du Bois Papers;* Doxey Wilkerson to Du Bois, November 3, 1947, Reel 60, #376, *Du Bois Papers;* Du Bois to Harry Ward, April 19, 1948, Reel 61, #606, *Du Bois Papers;* Lyman R. Bradley to Du Bois, April 15, 1948, Reel 60, #478, *Du Bois Papers.*
20. Paul Robeson, et. al. to Du Bois, July 28, 1948, *NAACP Papers; Amsterdam News,* August 28, 1948, Du Bois, Dashiell Hammett to Thurgood Marshall, October 18, 1949, *NAACP Papers.*
21. Paul Kern to Du Bois, February 8, 1949, Reel 63, #856, *Du Bois Papers;* Du Bois to Herbert Aptheker, April 11, 1949, in *Du Bois III,* 261; Nathan Witt to Du Bois, December 7, 1949, Reel 64, #282, *Du Bois Papers.*
22. National Non-Partisan Committee to Defend the Rights of 12 Communist Leaders, May 18, 1950, Reel 65, #360, *Du Bois Papers;* Doxey Wilkerson to Du Bois, September 14, 1950, Reel 65, #662, *Du Bois Papers;* "Application for Leave to File Amicus Brief," U.S.A. v. John Gates, circa 1950, Reel 64, #90, *Du Bois Papers;* Edward Barsky to Du Bois, March 23, 1950, Reel 65, #166, *Du Bois Papers;* Du Bois to George Marshall, September 15, 1950, Reel 64, #1059, *Du Bois Papers.*
23. "Joint Telegram Greets Eugene Dennis on Birthday," circa 1951, Reel 67, #204, *Du Bois Papers;* Du Bois to Philip Foner, September 27, 1951, Reel 66, #643, *Du Bois Papers;* Dashiell Hammett to Du Bois, March 18, 1952, Reel 68, #144, *Du Bois Papers;* "National Conference to Win Amnesty for Smith Act Victims," June 14, 1952, Reel 68, #628, *Du Bois Papers;* National Committee to Defend Negro Leadership to "Dear Editor," November 1, 1952, Reel 68, #614, *Du Bois Papers;* Du Bois to James Ford, October 20, 1953, Reel 69, #1049, *Du Bois Papers;* National Committee to Defend Negro Leadership, January 11, 1953, Reel 69, #1042, *Du Bois Papers.*
24. *Political Affairs* 31 (December 1952), 57–62; Edward Barsky to Du Bois, February 18, 1954, Reel 70, #866, *Du Bois Papers;* Du Bois to Pierce Cot, et. al., March 4, 1954, Reel 70, #526, #557, #563, #570, #581, #590, #638, #661, #686, #736, #743, #745, #746, #747, #829, #830, #847, #859, #955, #963, #1070, #1139, *Du Bois Papers;* Du

Bois to Celia Zitron, June 17, 1954, Reel 70, #871, *Du Bois Papers;* Hewlett Johnson to Du Bois, April 12, 1954, Reel 70, #435, *Du Bois Papers.*

25. Louis Harap to Du Bois, April 21, 1954, Reel 70, #731, *Du Bois Papers;* Du Bois, "Testifying at Ben Gold's Trial," Reel 82, #640, *Du Bois Papers;* Louise Patterson to Du Bois, July 21, 1954, Reel 70, #971, *Du Bois Papers;* Du Bois Statement on William Patterson, July 2, 1954, Reel 70, #517, *Du Bois Papers;* Alice Meyers to Du Bois, Februry 22, 1954, Reel 70, #825, *Du Bois Papers;* Lillian Lowenfels to Du Bois, August 26, 1954, Reel 70, #788, #789, *Du Bois Papers;* Du Bois to Lillian Lowenfels, September 10, 1954, Reel 70, #790, *Du Bois Papers.*
26. Circular Eleventh District Un-American Activities Committee of the American Legion, May 24, 1952, Reel 79, #9, *Du Bois Papers; The New York Times,* April 1, 1956; Eva Bittelman to Du Bois, November 26, 1955, Reel 71, #247, *Du Bois Papers;* Eugene Dennis to Du Bois, May 16, 1955, Reel 71, #315, *Du Bois Papers; National Guardian,* May 9, 1955; Circular, Hugo Gellert Testimonial, January 16, 1955, Reel 71, #378, *Du Bois Papers;* Du Bois to William Albertson, March 25, 1955, Reel 71, #290, *Du Bois Papers.*
27. *United States of America* vs. *Alexander Trachtenberg, James Jackson, et. al.,* before Hon. Alexander Bicks, D. J. and jury, July 29, 1956, U.S. District Court, Southern District of New York (Stenographer's minutes); George Charney, *A Long Journey* (Chicago: Quadrangle, 1968), 242; Charles Duncan to Du Bois, August 10, 1956, Reel 71, #1127, *Du Bois Papers.*
28. "Committee to Defend Grady and Judy Jenkins," undated, Reel 72, #498, *Du Bois Papers;* "On the 90th Birthday of Dr. W.E.B. Du Bois," *Political Affairs* 37 (February 1958); Herbert Aptheker, "Five Who Made History," *Political Affairs* 38 (February 1959), 22–35; Claude Lightfoot, "The Negro Liberation Movement Today," *Political Affairs* 61 (February 1961), 62–76; Leadership of People's Republic of China to Du Bois and Shirley Graham, January 8, 1962, Reel 75, #900, *Du Bois Papers.*
29. Du Bois, "James Ford," eulogy, June 25, 1957, Reel 31, #1083, *Du Bois Papers;* James Ford to Du Bois, January 6, 1945, Reel 57, #185, *Du Bois Papers; Daily Worker,* June 10, 1945; March 15, 1947, 100–99729–11, Federal Bureau of Investigation (in possession of author); L. D. Reddick to Du Bois, December 10, 1957, Reel 59, #451, *Du Bois Papers.*
30. James Ford to Du Bois, October 21, 1953, Reel 69, #811, *Du Bois Papers;* James Ford to Du Bois, November 12, 1955, Reel 71, #375, *Du Bois Papers; Daily Worker,* June 21, 1957; Rena Ford to Du Bois, July 1, 1957, Reel 72, #564, *Du Bois Papers.*

31. Du Bois, Message on William Z. Foster's Birthday, March 1, 1956, Reel 72, #242, *Du Bois Papers;* Du Bois to William Z. Foster, April 17, 1951, Reel 66, #646, *Du Bois Papers;* Benjamin Davis to Ernest Alexander, February 14, 1948, Reel 61, #335, *Du Bois Papers;* Du Bois to Benjamin Davis, July 29, 1949, Reel 63, #976, *Du Bois Papers;* Du Bois to "Dear Friend," October 7, 1949, Reel 63, #1150, *Du Bois Papers;* Du Bois, "Vito Marcantonio—Benjamin Davis Election Speech," October 27, 1949, Reel 80, #1256, *Du Bois Papers;* Du Bois, "Government and Freedom," November 6, 1949, Reel 80, #1276, *Du Bois Papers.*
32. *Freedom,* December 1953; Lloyd Brown, *Stand Up for Freedom: the Negro People* vs. *the Smith Act,* Benjamin David to Du Bois, undated, Reel 71, #308, *Du Bois Papers;* Du Bois to Benjamin Davis, April 18, 1955, Reel 71, #309, *Du Bois Papers.*
33. John Gates, *The Story of an American Communist* (New York: Nelson, 1958), 106; Benjamin Davis to Du Bois, May 14, 1956, Reel 71, #1115, *Du Bois Papers;* William Z. Foster, "Notes on the Struggle for Negro Rights," *Political Affairs* 34 (May 1955), 20–42.
34. Benjamin Davis, "The Challenge of the New Era," *Political Affairs* 35 (December 1956), 14–54; Eugene Dennis, "For a Mass Party of Socialism," *Political Affairs* 35 (June 1956), 1–7; Cyril Briggs, "On the Negro Question (A Discussion)," *Political Affairs* 39 (March 1959), 58–65; William Z. Foster and Benjamin Davis, "Notes on the Negro Question," *Political Affairs* 38 (April 1959), 33–45; Benjamin Davis to Du Bois, August 7, 1959, Reel 73, #641, *Du Bois Papers.*
35. *The New York Times,* October 21, 1946; *Daily Worker,* February 3, 1947; #100–99729–A, Federal Bureau of Investigation (in possession of author); *The New York Times,* October 23, 1946, Central Intelligence Agency (in possession of author); Du Bois to Esther Cooper, October 23, 1946, Reel 59, #549, *Du Bois Papers;* James Jackson to Du Bois, circa 1945, Reel 57, #445, *Du Bois Papers;* Du Bois to Freda Diamond, October 3, 1946, Reel 58, #814, *Du Bois Papers.*
36. Howard Selsam to Du Bois, April 27, 1945, Reel 57, #451, *Du Bois Papers;* Du Bois to Harold Collins, October 28, 1946, Reel 58, #1092, *Du Bois Papers;* Howard Selsam to Du Bois, December 16, 1947, Reel 60, #167, *Du Bois Papers;* Howard Selsam to Du Bois, February 17, 1948, Reel 61, #162, *Du Bois Papers;* Du Bois to Doxey Wilkerson, January 18, 1949, Reel 63, #1161, *Du Bois Papers;* Du Bois to Doxey Wilkerson, November 6, 1951, Reel 66, #939, *Du Bois Papers;* Howard Selsam to Du Bois, May 27, 1953, Reel 69, #889, *Du Bois Papers; The New York Times,* December 31, 1954; Howard Selsam to Du Bois, May 25, 1954, Reel 70, #720, *Du Bois Papers;* "Statement of the

Board of Trustees of the Jefferson School of Social Science," circa 1954, Reel 72, #12, *Du Bois Papers.*

37. Iris Merrick to Du Bois, March 9, 1945, Reel 57, #698, *Du Bois Papers;* Du Bois to Herbert Aptheker, February 25, 1948, Reel 62, #352, *Du Bois Papers;* Du Bois to Doxey Wilkerson, November 11, 1952, Reel 68, #432, *Du Bois Papers.*
38. Richard Morford to Du Bois, May 25, 1946, Reel 59, #22, *Du Bois Papers;* Jessica Smith to Du Bois, June 5, 1946, Reel 59, #558, *Du Bois Papers;* Jessica Smith to Du Bois, December 3, 1946, Reel 59, #561, *Du Bois Papers;* Du Bois to Reverend William Howard Melish, November 16, 1946, Reel 59, #25, *Du Bois Papers;* Du Bois to Richard Morford, November 16, 1947, Reel 60, #337, *Du Bois Papers;* Jessica Smith to Du Bois, January 29, 1947, Reel 60, #865, *Du Bois Papers;* Du Boisto Richard Morford, September 21, 1949, Reel 64, #55, *Du Bois Papers;* Reverend William Howard Melish, April 3, 1958, Reel 62, #444, *Du Bois Papers;* John Kingsbury to Du Bois, February 28, 1950, Reel 65, #307, *Du Bois Papers;* "Annual Report by the Director to the Members of the National Council of American-Soviet Friendship Annual Meeting," March 30, 1950, Reel 65, #308, *Du Bois Papers;* Du Bois to Jessica Smith, January 15, 1953, Reel 69, #1128, *Du Bois Papers.*
39. Atlanta Bureau of Federal Bureau of Investigation to Federal Bureau of Investigation Director, August 26, 1948, 100–99129–12; Washington Bureau of FBI to FBI Director, circa August 1948, 100–99129–12 (both in possession of author); *Daily Worker,* January 31, 1954, Du Bois to Alan Max, January 14, 1954, Reel 70, #559, *Du Bois Papers;* James Jackson to Du Bois, February 2, 1960, Reel 74, #895, *Du Bois Papers.*
40. W.E.B. Du Bois, 'On This First Day of October" (New York; New Outlook, 1961); *The New York Times,* November 23, 1961; Herbert Aptheker, "W.E.B. Du Bois and Africa," *Political Affairs* 60 (March 1961), 19–29; Herbert Aptheker, "Dr. Du Bois and Communism," *Political Affairs* 40 (December 1961), 13–20.
41. Ellis Bowles to Du Bois, October 15, 1962, Reel 75, #859, *Du Bois Papers; National Guardian,* February 21, 1963; Lawrence Lader, *Power on the Left,* 174, 210, Du Bois to Vivian Hallinan, March 22, 1963, Reel 76, #277, *Du Bois Papers; People's World,* November 25, 1961, Central Intelligence Agency (in possession of author); Report of Founding of Du Bois Club, circa 1963, Air Force Office of Special Investigations (in possession of author).

CHAPTER 21. DU BOIS AND THE SOCIALIST COUNTRIES

1. Du Bois to Shirley Graham, June 24, 1949, in *Du Bois III,* 264; *National Guardian,* February 5, 1957; *National Guardian,* April 29, 1957.
2. *Crisis* 61 (December 1954), 584; *Crisis* 70 (May 1963), 286–87; Graham, *His Day is Marching On,* 213; Du Bois to Dr. W. M. Brewer, August 6, 1959, Reel 73, #761, *Du Bois Papers.*
3. Jonathan Evers Boe, "American Business: The Response to the Soviet Union, 1933–1947" (Ph.D. diss., Stanford University, 1979).
4. *Chicago Defender,* June 12, 1946; *Chicago Defender,* March 2, 1946; Du Bois, "Broadcast," October 15, 1948, Reel 80, #1127, *Du Bois Papers;* Du Bois to New Writing Foundation, July 9, 1947, Reel 60, #456, *Du Bois Papers.*
5. *Daily Worker,* April 17, 1949.
6. Robert Giroux to Du Bois, October 17, 1949, Reel 63, #1117, *Du Bois Papers;* Du Bois to Du Bois Williams, July 17, 1950, in *Du Bois III,* 284.
7. Joseph Hansen to Du Bois, October 20, 1950, Reel 65, #78, *Du Bois Papers;* Du Bois to Yugoslav Information Center, September 18, 1950, Reel 65, #1050, *Du Bois Papers.*
8. Lorraine Cousens to Du Bois, January 26, 1953, Reel 69, #737, *Du Bois Papers;* Du Bois to Lorraine Cousens, February 19, 1953, Reel 69, #738, *Du Bois Papers;* Du Bois to A. A. Roback, December 8, 1959, Reel 73, #880, *Du Bois Papers;* W.E.B. Du Bois, "America and World Peace," *Soviet Russia Today* 20 (November 1952), 49–52.
9. *National Guardian,* March 16, 1953; John Kingsbury to Richard Morford, June 24, 1956, Reel 72, #37, *Du Bois Papers;* John Kingsbury to Shirley Graham, June 23, 1945, Reel 72, #36, *Du Bois Papers;* Du Bois to John Biddle, April 24, 1956, Reel 71, #1047, *Du Bois Papers;* Du Bois to Anna Graves, July 8, 1956, Reel 71, #1177, *Du Bois Papers.*
10. W.E.B. Du Bois, "Colonialism and the Russian Revolution," *New World Review* 24 (November 1956), 18–22, W.E.B. Du Bois, "World Changer," *Masses and Mainstream* 19 (January 1957), 1–5.
11. Du Bois to Holland Roberts, December 14, 1956, Reel 72, #206, *Du Bois Papers;* Du Bois Speech, "Marcantonio, Two Years After," December 10, 1956, Reel 81, #1026, *Du Bois Papers.*
12. *Crisis* 63 (January 1956), 35; Roy Wilkins, "Barriers Broken, Pathway Cleared," *Crisis* 66 (August–September 1959), 394–99, 450; *National Guardian,* December 31, 1956; *Amsterdam News,* December 15, 1956; *Pittsburgh Courier,* November 24, 1956; *Amsterdam News,* December 15, 1956; *Afro-American,* December 18, 1956; S. Dziengielswki to Du Bois, undated, Reel 72, #533, *Du Bois Papers.*

13. Du Bois Speech, "A History of the Last Forty Years," March 31, 1958, Reel 81, #1147, *Du Bois Papers;* Du Bois Speech, "Pan-Africa, 1919–1958," December 1958, Reel 81, #1213, *Du Bois Papers;* Du Bois Speech, "Socialism and the American Negro," Reel 81, #1313, *Du Bois Papers.*
14. *Accra Evening News,* March 13, 1957; Graham, *His Day is Marching On,* 227, 236.
15. Graham, *His Day is Marching On,* 241, 243, 247, 250; Du Bois to Yolanda Williams, December 10, 1958, Reel 73, #472, *Du Bois Papers;* Du Bois to George Murphy, December 26, 1958, in *Du Bois III,* 432; *National Guardian,* November 10, 1958.
16. Graham, *His Day is Marching on,* 270; *National Guardian,* October 27, 1958.
17. Du Bois to Yolanda Williams, December 10, 1958, Reel 73, #472, *Du Bois Papers;* Du Bois, "A Proposal to the Soviet Union to Undertake a Scientific Study of Africa," January 1959, Reel 73, #942, *Du Bois Papers;* I. Potekhin to Du Bois, May 10, 1960, Reel 74, #12, *Du Bois Papers; National Guardian,* March 2, 1959; M. F. Nesturkh to Du Bois, November 24, 1959, Reel 73, #095, *Du Bois Papers; Ogorek Magazine,* January 1959, Central Intelligence Agency (in possession of author) 201–7123.
18. *National Guardian,* December 14, 1959; *National Guardian,* September 17, 1959, Du Bois to S. A. Dangoulov, April 20, 1960, Reel 74, #167, *Du Bois Papers.*
19. *National Guardian,* November 14, 1957; *The New York Times,* February 14, 1959.
20. W.E.B. Du Bois, "Normal U.S.-China Relations," *New World Review* (August 1954), 13–15; *Freedom,* February 1955.
21. Kenneth Ray Young and Dan S. Green, "Harbinger to Nixon: W.E.B. Du Bois in China," *Negro History Bulletin* 35 (October 1972), 125–28; W.E.B. Du Bois, "China and Africa," *Peking Review* 2 (March 3, 1959), 11–13; *National Guardian,* June 8, 1959; *National Guardian.* May 11, 1959.
22. *National Guardian,* June 1, 1959; Shirley Graham, "Hail the People's Republic of China," *Political Affairs* 38 (October 1959), 25–34.
23. Du Bois to E. Franklin Frazier, July 17, 1959, Reel 73, #665, *Du Bois Papers;* Du Bois to Virginia Banks, December 2, 1959, Reel 73, #586, *Du Bois Papers; National Guardian,* October 12, 1959.
24. Joan Wallerstein to Du Bois, February 22, 1960, Reel 74, #866, *V. Ivanov to Du Bois, April 29, 1960, Reel 74, #104, Du Bois Papers;* Du Bois Statement on Radio Prague, November 2, 1959, Reel 73, #637, *Du Bois Papers.*
25. Z. J. Radak to Du Bois, August 7, 1955, Reel 71, #302, *Du Bois Papers;* V. Strand to Du Bois, October 21, 1955, in *Du Bois III,* 388;

Du Bois to Miloslav Ruzek, June 17, 1960, Reel 74, #155, *Du Bois Papers;* Du Bois to Grace Goens, October 3, 1960, Reel 74, #295, *Du Bois Papers;* Du Bois to George Murphy, August 21, 1961, Reel 75, #453, *Du Bois Papers.*

26. Du Bois to Richard Gibson, September 28, 1960, Reel 74, #221, *Du Bois Papers; Afro-American,* April 22, 1961; Du Bois, "The United States, May-1961," unpublished article, Reel 83, #737, *Du Bois Papers;* Juan Rene Detancourt, "Castro and the Cuban Negro," *Crisis* 68 (May 1961), 270–74.
27. I. Potekhin to Du Bois, October 6, 1961, Reel 74, #1008, *Du Bois Papers;* M. F. Nesturkh to Du Bois, September 7, 1960, Reel 74, #590, *Du Bois Papers;* Du Bois to O. D. Kalug, December 16, 1960, Reel 74, #742, *Du Bois Papers; National Guardian,* October 15, 1962; U. S. Embassy-Bucharest to U.S. State Department, March 9, 1962, 201–7123, Department of State (in possession of author); Deputy Director Plans to FBI Director, December 7, 1962, Central Intelligence Agency (in possession of author) 201–7123.
28. Shirley Graham to Marie Nosek, September 4, 1960, Reel 74, #690, *Du Bois Papers;* Du Bois draft of letter to USSR and People's Republic of China leaders, circa 1963, Reel 79, #1139, *Du Bois Papers.*

CHAPTER 22. DU BOIS AND AFRICA

1. Graham, *His Day is Marching On,* 301; John Hennings, *The Attitudes of African Nationalism Toward Communism* (Pittsburgh; Duquesne University Press, 1962), 57.
2. Du Bois to Jawaharlal Nehru, November 7, 1946, in *Du Bois III,* Du Bois to Anna Graves, November 17, 1934, in *Du BoisIII,* 27; Zbigniew Brezezinski, "Conclusion: The African Challenge," in *Africa and the Communist World* edited by Zbigniew Brezezinski (Stanford: Stanford University Press, 1963), 204–29; Office of Strategic Services State Department Intelligence and Research Reports, Part VI: *The Soviet Union,* "The USSR and the Colonial Problem: Africa," Washington, D.C., 1946.
3. *National Guardian,* December 13, 1948; Petition to President Harry S. Truman, April 29, 1952, Reel 68, #394, *Du Bois Papers.*
4. Walter Sisulu to Du Bois, March 23, 1953, Reel 69, #438, *Du Bois Papers;* W. Alphaeus Hunton to Du Bois, April 3, 1953, Reel 69, #690, *Du Bois Papers;* Du Bois Speech, "Africa and Afro-America," April 24, 1954, Reel 81, #833, *Du Bois Papers.*
5. Herbert Wright, "World Assembly of Youth," *Crisis* 58 (October 1951), 509–13; *Crisis* 60 (January 1953), 38; Gloster Current, "Fifty

First Annual NAACP Convention—Accent on Youth," *Crisis* 67 (August–September 1960), 405–20; *Crisis* 66 (January 1959), 38; *Crisis* 66 (December 1959), 622–23.

6. *Crisis* 66 (January 1959), 30; *Crisis* 67 (November 1960), 595; *Crisis* 68 (February 1961), 99; *Crisis* 68 (February 1961), 100; *Crisis* 68 (October 1961), 492, 499; John E. Own, "U.S. Race Relations—A World Issue," *Crisis* 61 (January 1961), 19–21.
7. *Crisis* 59 (November 1952), 579; Thurgood Marshall, "The Cry for Freedom," *Crisis* 67 (May 1960), 287–90; *Crisis* 68 (March 1961), 164.
8. Shirley Graham, Tashkent Asian-African Writers' Conference, October 14, 1958, Reel 89, #913, *Du Bois Papers;* Du Bois Speech, "The Early Beginnings of the Pan-African Movement," Conference of All African Students Union of the Americas, University of Chicago, Chicago, Ill., June 20, 1958, Reel 81, #1192, *Du Bois Papers;* J. Kwame Adaderoh to Du Bois, March 30, 1960, Reel 74, #893, *Du Bois Papers.*
9. *National Guardian,* February 13, 1961.
10. Du Bois to Immanuel Wallerstein, May 3, 1961, Reel 75, #722, *Du Bois Papers;* Du Bois to Ishmael Flory, April 18, 1960, Reel 74, #21, *Du Bois Papers.*
11. W. Alphaeus Hunton to Du Bois, January 5, 1962, Reel 75, #1005, *Du Bois Papers;* Dorothy and W. Alpheaus Hunton to Du Bois, August 7, 1960, Reel 74, #366, *Du Bois Papers;* Ray Alexander to Du Bois, February 5, 1960, Reel 74, #31, *Du Bois Papers;* Alice Citron to Du Bois, November 8, 1961, Reel 75, #69, *Du Bois Papers.*
12. Du Bois to Grace Goens, November 7, 1960, Reel 74, #298, *Du Bois Papers;* Du Bois to A. M. Graves, November 7, 1960, Reel 74, #308, *Du Bois Papers;* Secretary of Nigerian Prime Minister to Du Bois, October 27, 1960, Reel 74, #298, *Du Bois Papers;* W. D. Goodluck to Du Bois, August 1, 1960, Reel 74, #685, *Du Bois Papers.*
13. Du Bois to Eleanor Hakim, March 22, 1961, Reel 75, #646, *Du Bois Papers;* Du Bois to Carl Marzani, February 20, 1961, Reel 75, #389, *Du Bois Papers;* Du Bois to Nnamdi Azikiwe, March 6, 1961, Reel 75, #492, *Du Bois Papers.*
14. Du Bois to Jomo Kenyatta, April 28, 1961, Reel 75, #348, *Du Bois Papers;* Du Bois to Tom Mboya, April 27, 1961, Reel 75, #438, *Du Bois Papers;* Tom Mboya to Du Bois, May 23, 1961, Reel 75, #438, *Du Bois Papers;* Oginga Odinga to Du Bois, June 16, 1961, Reel 75, #501, *Du Bois Papers;* Du Bois to Oginga Odinga, August 21, 1961, Reel 75, #502, *Du Bois Papers;* Charles Cobb, "Atlanta to Zimbabwe," *Southern Exposure* 9 (Spring 1981), 85–88.
15. Du Bois to Julius Nyerere, April 28, 1961, Reel 75, #655, *Du Bois Papers;* Du Bois to Dr. H. K. Banda, April 28, 1961, Reel 75, #3, *Du Bois Papers; Muhammad Speaks,* November 11, 1963; Prof. V.

Chkhivazada to Du Bois, May 12, 1961, Reel 75, #306, *Du Bois Papers;* Shirley Graham to V. Chkhivazade, May 20, 1961, Reel 75, #306, *Du Bois Papers;* Du Bois to Paul Kaye, March 7, 1961, Reel 75, #345, *Du Bois Papers.*

16. Dan Kurzman, *Subversion of the Innocents: Patterns of Communist Penetration in Africa, the Middle East and Asia* (New York: Random House, 1963), 94–112; George Padmore, *Pan-Africanism or Communism;* P. Kiven Tunteng, "George Padmore's Impact on Africa: A Critical Appraisal," *Phylon* 35 (First Quarter 1974), 33–44.
17. Du Bois to George Padmore, October 27, 1951, Reel 67, #311, *Du Bois Papers.*
18. R. E. G. Armattoe to Du Bois, April 22, 1952, Reel 67, #1177, *Du Bois Papers;* George Padmore to Du Bois, January 8, 1952, Reel 68, #764, *Du Bois Papers;* George Padmore, "Bloodless Revolution in the Cold Coast," *Crisis* 59 (March 1952), 172–77, 197–98.
17. Albert Kofi to Du Bois, July 29, 1952, Reel 68, #314, *Du Bois Papers; Spotlight on Africa* 12 (March 19, 1952), 4; *Accra Evening News,* January 15, 1953; George Padmore to Du Bois, December 3, 1954, Reel 70, #, *Du Bois Papers.*
20. Du Bois to George Padmore, December 10, 1954, Reel 70, #959, *Du Bois Papers;* George Padmore to Du Bois, November 2, 1955, Reel 71, #640, *Du Bois Papers;* Du Bois to George Padmore, January 27, 1956, Reel 71, #643, *Du Bois Papers;* Du Bois to George Padmore, March 25, 1955, Reel 71, #649, *Du Bois Papers;* George Padmore to Du Bois, March 10, 1955, Reel 71, #645, *Du Bois Papers; National Guardian,* October 12, 1959.
21. *National Guardian,* March 11, 1957, Du Bois to Kwame Nkrumah, February 7, 1957, Reel 79, #996, *Du Bois Papers;* Du Bois to Kwame Nkrumah, April 17, 1957, Reel 79, #1004, *Du Bois Papers;* Du Bois to George Padmore, March 26, 1957, Reel 79, #1084, *Du Bois Papers.*
22. *Crisis* 64 (April 1957), 208; Circular, National Committee to Defend Negro Leadership, April 30, 1957, Reel 72, #866, *Du Bois Papers;* Kwame Nkrumah to Du Bois, February 5, 1958, Reel 79, #1012, *Du Bois Papers; National Guardian,* December 22, 1958; *National Guardian,* December 29, 1958.
23. *National Guardian,* April 21, 1958; Shirley Graham, "Africa Lifts Its Voice," *Political Affairs* 38 (February 1959), 1–8; Charlotte Pomerantz to Du Bois, April 16, 1961, Reel 75, #561, *Du Bois Papers.*
24. Kwame Nkrumah to Du Bois, June 18, 1960, Reel 74, #252, *Du Bois Papers;* Du Bois to Nkrumah, July 4, 1960, Reel 74, #255, *Du Bois Papers; National Guardian,* September 19, 1960, Du Bois Speech, "A History of Africa," Ghana Academy of Learning, Ambassador Hotel, Accra, Ghana, July 5, 1960, Reel 81, #1374, *Du Bois Papers;* Rockwell Kent to Du Bois, August 19, 1960, Reel 74, #411, *Du Bois Papers.*

25. Graham, *His Day is Marching On,* 327, 363; Shirley Graham Du Bois, *Du Bois: A Pictorial Biography,* 146, 155, Du Bois to I. Potekhin, circa January 1962, Reel 75, #857, *Du Bois Papers;* Herbert Aptheker, "W.E.B. Du Bois and Africa," *Political Affairs* 60 (March 1981), 19–29.
26. Du Bois to Helen Boardman, September 22, 1947, Reel 59, #1061, *Du Bois Papers;* Du Bois, "Proposed Plans for an Encyclopedia Africana," Reel 75, #955, *Du Bois Papers;* W. Alphaeus Hunton, "Concerning the Encyclopedia Africana," *Freedomways* 7 (Spring 1967), 139–49; Form 867, June 17, 1965, Central Intelligence Agency 201–7123.
27. John Blassingame, "Black Studies and the Role of the Historian," in *New Perspectives on Black Studies,* edited by, John Blassingame (Urbana, Ill.: University of Illinois press, 1971), 207–26, Du Bois to Kwame Nkrumah, October 10, 1960, Reel 74, #276, *Du Bois Papers;* A. A. Kwapong to Du Bois, February 10, 1961, Reel 75, #208, *Du Bois Papers;* A. A. Kwapong to Du Bois, May 16, 1961, Reel 75, #212, *Du Bois Papers;* Du Bois to Ghana Academy of Learning, May 23, 1961, Reel 75, #214, *Du Bois Papers;* Du Bois to E. A. Boateng, September 21, 1961, Reel 75, #221, *Du Bois Papers.*
28. Du Bois, "Estimated Expenses of the Proposed Encyclopedia of the Negro," circa 1961, Reel 75, #226, *Du Bois Papers;* Committee of African Organizations," March 20, 1961, Reel 74, #81, *Du Bois Papers;* Richard B. Morris to Du Bois, April 17, 1961, Reel 75, #78, *Du Bois Papers;* Du Bois to Kenneth Dike, March 9, 1961, Reel 75, #116, *Du Bois Papers;* David Apter to Du Bois, July 10, 1962 Reel 75, #867, *Du Bois Papers;* Claude A. Barnett, June 16, 1962, Reel 75, #878, *Du Bois Papers.*
29. Robert Byrnes to Du Bois, April 25, 1961, Reel 75, #295, *Du Bois Papers;* Chester G. Starr to Du Bois, April 14, 1961, Reel 75, #291, *Du Bois Papers;* R. I. Rotberg to Du Bois, April 21, 1961, Reel 75, #272, *Du Bois Papers;* Du Bois to Paul Stallworth, May 5, 1961, Reel 75, #419, *Du Bois Papers.*
30. Du Bois to Thomas Hodgkin, April 5, 1961, Reel 75, #281, *Du Bois Papers;* Du Bois to Sekou Toure, April 27, 1961, Reel 75, #259, *Du Bois Papers;* A. K. Mayanja to Du Bois, October 3, 1961, Reel 75, #681, *Du Bois Papers;* Jamal Mohammed Ahmed to Du Bois, undated, Reel 74, #1011, *Du Bois Papers;* Secretariat for an Encyclopedia Africana, Information Report, No. 3 (Accra: December 1962); Participants to International Congress, December 11–18, 1962, Reel 75, #1020, *Du Bois Papers.*
31. Du Bois to Prof. E. A. Boateng, May 10, 1962, Reel 75, #936, *Du Bois Papers;* Du Bois to Prof. E. A. Boateng, May 12, 1962, Reel 75, #936, *Du Bois Papers;* Minutes of the Meeting of the Standing Committee on the Ghana Academy of Sciences, May 14, 1962, Reel 75,

#938, *Du Bois Papers;* Du Bois to G. M. Johnson, April 7, 1961, Reel 75, #334, *Du Bois Papers;* Du Bois to President, University of Ghana, April 7, 1961, Reel 75, #228, *Du Bois Papers;* Du Bois to George Murphy, March 22, 1963, Reel 76, #321, , *Du Bois Papers.*

32. *Crisis* 69 (March 1962), 193; Du Bois: "America—the View from Africa," unpublished article, 1962, Reel 83, #757, *Du Bois Papers; National Guardian,* August 6, 1962.
33. Harold A. Drayton to Du Bois, January 13, 1962, Reel 75, #918, *Du Bois Papers;* Mrs. Huang Hue to Du Bois, August 31, 1962, Reel 75, #900, *Du Bois Papers;* M. W. Kanyama to Du Bois, June 11, 1962, Reel 75, #875, *Du Bois Papers.*
34. Du Bois to Harold Drayton, February 20, 1962, Reel 75, #919, *Du Bois Papers;* Du Bois to Anna Asian, May 21, 1962, Reel 75, #870, *Du Bois Papers;* Shirley Graham to International Institute of Peace, February 6, 1962, Reel 76, #66, *Du Bois Papers;* Report of Dr. Himsworth, August 7, 1962, Reel 76, #66, *Du Bois Papers;* Shirley Graham to Friend, February 12, 1962, Reel 75, #62, *Du Bois Papers;* Du Bois to W. Alphaeus Hunton, September 14, 1962, Reel 75, #1015, *Du Bois Papers.*
35. *National Guardian,* May 30, 1963; William B. Edmondson, American Embassy Accra "to Department of State, Confidential," October 30, 1961, 761.00/10–3061, U.S. Department of State (in possession of author).
36. Deputy Directors, Plans, to FBI Director, January 9, 1962, Central Intelligence Agency, Dispatch to Central Intelligence Agency, November 16, 1961, Central Intelligence Agency; Report to CIA, January 20, 1962, Central Intelligence Agency; Memorandum, "Subject: American Communist in Tanganvike," December 3, 1962, Central Intelligence Agency (in possession of author) 201–7123.

CONCLUSION; THE DEATH OF DU BOIS

1. Du Bois to Shirley Graham, June 26, 1961, Reel 79, #605, *Du Bois Papers;* Du Bois to Shirley Graham, April 5, 1961, Reel 75, #318, *Du Bois Papers;* Shirley Graham to "Cousin Laura," August 3, 1963, Reel 76, #304, *Du Bois Papers;* Shirley Graham to Laura McIlvain, May 4, 1964, Reel 76, #525, *Du Bois Papers.*
2. "Arrangements for the burial of Dr. W.E.B. Du Bois," circa 1963, Reel 78, #229, *Du Bois Papers; Accra Evening News,* August 30, 1963; *Amsterdam News,* September 7, 1963, *National Guardian,* September 5, 1963; W.E.B. Du Bois, *An ABC of Color,* intro. by John Oliver Killens (New York: International Publishers, 1969), 9.

3. *Philadelphia Tribune,* August 31, 1963; *The New York Times,* August 28, 1963; *The Wall Street Journal,* November 4, 1963; Herbert Aptheker, "To Dr. Du Bois—With love," *Political Affairs* 42 (February 1963), 35–42; *Crisis* 70 (October 1963), 469; Du Bois Memorial, February 23, 1964, Reel 76, #421, *Du Bois Papers.*
4. *Washington Star,* September 28, 1963; *Washington Post,* August 29, 1963, Central Intelligence Agency (in possession of author); *Accra Evening News,* August 30, 1963 201–7123.

Bibliographic Note

The sources for this work are imbedded in the notes. This bibliographic note is added only as a concise guide to sources. The study of W.E.B. Du Bois perforce must begin with an examination of his papers, which are now microfilmed and readily available. Du Bois was not a pack rat but he did have a habit of saving and retaining quite a bit, hence his papers are quite full and scholars writing on any aspect of United States history of the last century would do well to consult these papers. The NAACP Papers at the Library of Congress are a similar treasure trove and are well indexed. Other relevant manuscript sources, for example, National Negro Congress Papers, Civil Rights Congress Papers, (Schomburg Library) Southern Negro Youth Congress Papers, (in possession of Dorothy Burnham) American Civil Liberties Union Papers (Princeton University), National Lawyers Guild Papers, and so on (Martin Luther King Center) are likewise worthwhile though many of their nuggets are to be found in the Du Bois Papers. Special mention should be accorded to Abbott Simon, whose papers on the peace movement were opened to me and were quite helpful.

As already noted, certain fields on which this study touches, have become veritable cottage industries. This holds true particularly for the Cold War. However, a number stand out. The study by Percival Roberts Bailey ("Progressive Lawyers: A History of the National Lawyers Guild," Ph.D. diss., Rutgers University, 1979) is essential for an understanding of this period, though it would have been well if it had extended to the 1960s. Jonathan Boe's dissertation ("American Business: The Response to the Soviet Union, 1933–1947," Ph.D. diss., Stanford University, 1979) helps in understanding the economic underpinnings of the Cold War. Don Edward Carleton's dissertation ("A Crisis of Rapid Change: The Red Scare in Houston," University of Houston, 1978) is useful in comprehending the abject terror wrought by Cold War repression. The insights provided by Wayne Addison Clark ("An Analysis of the Relationship Between Anti-Communism and Segregationist Thought in the Deep South, 1948–1964," Ph.D. diss., University of North Carolina, 1976) are so varied that all thinking persons should be obligated to read it. David Jacob Group ("The Legal Repression of the American Communist Party, 1946–1961: A Study in the Legitimation of Coercion," Ph.D. diss., University of Massachusetts-Amherst, 1979) has given us a well-documented study of repression. M. E. Mantell ("Opposition to the Korean War: A Study in American Dissent," Ph.D. diss., New York University, 1973) cogently reminds us that objection to Asian adventures did not commence with Vietnam. Aldon Douglas Morris ("The Rise of the Civil Rights Movement and Its Movement: Black Power Structure, 1953–1963," Ph.D. diss., State University of New York at Stony Brook, 1980) here pioneered in setting the record straight on the civil rights movement. Kenneth Waltzer's dissertation at Harvard on the American Labor Party should be noted. All this tells us that the graduate schools continue to produce a number of works that are worthy of publication.

The United States government, a principal player in this story, also provides us with bountiful sources. House Un-American Committee reports have been mined by many writers and a principal reason is that they are well indexed, which facilitates research. Their content provides more than a glimpse of the hysteria that gripped the era. Other congressional committees, such as the Senate Judiciary Committee, are similarly endowed. These congressional reports have the virtue of not only having questioned just about every progressive of the era, hence providing remarkable primary documentation, but also having taken their road show to virtually every major United States city. I received a number of documents from the FBI, CIA, and other such agencies but researchers should know that there is quite a bit left to be obtained from these tightfisted bureaucrats.

Special mention should be made of the work of Herbert Aptheker, particularly his *Annotated Bibliography of the Published Works of W.E.B. Du Bois* (Millwood, N.Y.: Kraus-Thomson, 1973); all references to Du Bois' published writings can be located here. As Du Bois' literary executor, Aptheker performed yeoman service in insuring that Du Bois' papers are in such estimable shape; also he has moved to have published anew some of Du Bois' books, collections of his book reviews, correspondence, and so on.

As with dissertations, one could go on indefinitely discussing noted books and articles that helped to shape and inform this work. The *Crisis,* journal of the NAACP, has to be mentioned; the articles and information it contains could keep a new generation of graduate students busy. The seminal article by Leo K. Adler and Thomas G. Paterson ("Red Fascism: The Merger of Nazi Germany and Soviet Russia in the American Image of Totalitarianism," *American Historical Review* 75 [April 1970], 1046–64) continues to aid in understanding how and why the image of the Soviet Union in the United States changed so quickly after the war. The papers assembled by James Allen and Doxey Wilkerson (*The Economic Crisis and the Cold War.* New York: New Century, 1949) are as helpful as Jonathan Boe's dissertation in understanding the economic basis for the Cold War. Along that same line, the Communist party journal *Political Affairs*—especially articles by such writers as Benjamin Davis, Pettis Perry, and William Z. Foster—is similarly indispensable in not only understanding left and Communist policy but in comprehending the era as a whole.

Memoirs by such writers as Charlotta Bass (*Forty Years: Memoirs from the Pages of a Newspaper.* Los Angeles: Bass Publishers, 1960), Cedric Belfrage and James Aronson (*Something to Guard: The Stormy Life of the National Guardian, 1948–1967.* New York: Columbia University Press, 1978), and Shirley Graham (*His Day is Marching On: A Memoir* of W.E.B. Du Bois. Philadelphia: Lippincott, 1971) are rich with detail and insight. Graham's writings in particular, as reflected in the notes, need to be underscored as a source for this work.

The discernment of Alfred O. Hero ("American Negroes and U.S. Foreign Policy: 1937–1967," *Journal of Conflict Resolution* 8 [June 1969], 220–51) aided my own understanding of this critical field. Ralph Levering (*American Opinion and the Russian Alliance, 1939–1945,* Chapel Hill: University of North Carolina Press, 1976) has demonstrated conclusively that anti-Sovietism is no more inevitable than racism and it is ratcheted up or down depending on the needs of prevailing elites. Though others have tried, Curtis MacDougall (*Gideon's Army*, New York: Marzani and Munsell, 1965) continues to provide the most arresting study of the Progressive Party and the campaign of 1948. The collection edited by Thomas Paterson (*Cold War Critics*, Chicago: Quadrangle, 1971) was one of my early inspirations in deciding to tackle this subject. J. Saunders Redding (*An American in India: A Personal Report on the India Dilemma and the Nature of Her Conflicts*, Indianapolis: Bobbs-Merris, 1954) has penned a striking memoir of the deleterious impact of United States racism on United States foreign policy and how this hit an Afro-American who wanted to support his government.

Index